INDIA:
THE NEXT DECADE

PUBLISHED BY

ACADEMIC FOUNDATION

IN ASSOCIATION WITH

THE INDIRA GANDHI MEMORIAL TRUST

India

THE NEXT DECADE

Edited by Manmohan Malhoutra

ACADEMIC FOUNDATION
NEW DELHI

Published in 2006

by : ACADEMIC FOUNDATION

4772-73 / 23 Bharat Ram Road, (23 Ansari Road)
Darya Ganj, New Delhi - 110 002 (India)

Tel : 23245001 / 02 / 03 / 04
Fax : +91-11-23245005
E-mail : academic@vsnl.com
www.academicfoundation.com

Published in association with the
INDIRA GANDHI MEMORIAL TRUST
New Delhi

Cataloging in Publication Data–DK
    Courtesy: D.K. Agencies (P) Ltd. <docinfo@dkagencies.com>

    India : the next decade / edited by Manmohan Malhoutra.
       p.   cm.
    Includes bibliographical references.
    Includes index.
    ISBN-13: 978-81-7188-564-0
    ISBN-10: 81-7188-564-0

    1. Democracy--India-Forecasting. 2. India--Politics
    and government--21st century. 3. Economic
    forecasting--India. 4. India--Economic conditions--21st
    century. 5. Social prediction--India. 6. India--Foreign
    relations--1984- . 7. India--Forecasting.   I. Malhoutra,
    Manmohan.

    DDC 303.495 4   22

Designed and typeset by Italics India, New Delhi.
Printed and bound in India.

10 9 8 7 6 5 4 3 2 1

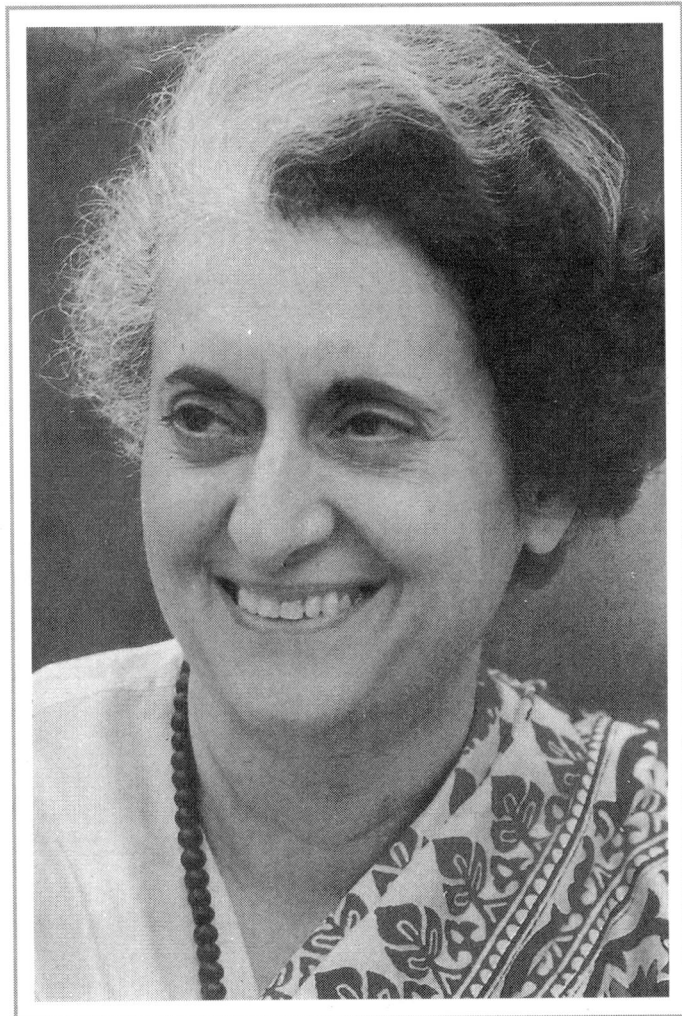

INDIRA GANDHI
(1917-1984)

Contents

Section I
Democracy: Challenges and Prospects

—— *Background Papers* ——

Section II
Economy: Growth and Equity

—— *Background Papers* ————

Section III
Society: Changing Values

—— *Background Paper* ——————

—— *Presentations and Discussion* ————

Section IV
India and the World

—— *Background Papers* ——————

Contributors / Discussants

Ahluwalia, Montek S.

A distinguished economist Montek S. Ahluwalia is presently Deputy Chairman, Planning Commission, Government of India. Earlier, he was Director, Independent Evaluation Office at the International Monetary Fund, Washington. His previously held positions include Member, Prime Minister's Economic Advisory Council, and Finance Secretary, Government of India. Mr. Ahluwalia has published several articles in reputed journals and has numerous contributions in major reports and edited volumes.

Ahmad, Aijaz

Aijaz Ahmad currently holds the Khan Abdul Ghaffar Khan Chair at Jamia Millia Islamia, New Delhi. Professor Ahmad has authored several books and is Senior Editorial Consultant for *Frontline*, Chennai.

Bajpai, K. Shankar

K. Shankar Bajpai is Chairman of the Delhi Policy Group. He was formerly Secretary to the Government of India, Ministry of External Affairs. From 1970 to 1974 he was the Government of India's Representative in Sikkim, and subsequently Ambassador to the Netherlands, Pakistan, China and the United States. After his retirement, he was Visiting Professor at the University of California, Berkeley, and Professor at Brandeis University.

Banga, Manvinder Singh (Vindi)

Manvinder Singh (Vindi) Banga, has held a variety of positions in Unilever since he joined in 1977. In April 2005, Vindi joined the newly formed Unilever Executive (UEx) and was appointed President (Foods). He is also non-executive Chairman of Hindustan Lever Ltd. and is actively involved on the Boards and Managing Committee of many trade and non-trade bodies.

Benegal, Shyam

Legendary film-maker, Shyam Benegal is one of the pioneers of the new cinema in India. The Government of India has conferred on him two of its most prestigious awards, Padma Shri (1976) and Padma Bhushan (1991).

Bery, Suman K.

Suman K. Bery is Director General of the National Council of Applied Economic Research (NCAER), New Delhi. Earlier he served at The World Bank, Washington. Beside his expertise in Latin American economies, he has written extensively in the press and elsewhere on current issues in the Indian economy.

Bhaskar, C. Uday

Commodore Uday Bhaskar is one of India's leading defence analysts at the Institute for Defence Studies and Analyses, New Delhi. He has contributed over 50 research articles/papers to professional journals and books published in India and abroad.

Bhatt, Mahesh

Renowned film-maker Mahesh Bhatt gained acclaim for his bold films *Arth* ('82), *Saaransh* ('84), *Janam* ('90), *Daddy* ('91), *Tamanna* ('97) and finally *Zakhm* ('99)... all of them born from his own experiences. Today, he has moved on to writing books and films. He is Chairman of Vishesh Entertainment and is the creative backbone for Fisheye Network.

Chandhoke, Neera

Neera Chandhoke is Professor, Department of Political Science, University of Delhi and Director, Developing Countries Research Centre, University of Delhi. She has authored and edited several publications.

Chellaney, Brahma

Brahma Chellaney is Research Professor of Strategic Studies at the Centre for Policy Research, Delhi. A specialist on international security and arms control issues, Professor Chellaney has held appointments at Harvard University, the Brookings Institution, the Johns Hopkins University's School of Advanced International Studies and the Australian National University. Until January 2000 he served as convenor of the External Security Group of India's National Security Advisory Board.

Chowdhary, Rekha

Rekha Chowdhary is Professor of Political Science, University of Jammu. She has been working in the areas of Indian and state politics, specialising in the politics of Jammu and Kashmir. She is currently the coordinator, UGC Special Assistance Programme on Jammu and Kashmir.

Dev, S. Mahendra

Professor S. Mahendra Dev currently Director, Centre for Economic and Social Studies, Hyderabad, has written extensively on agricultural development, poverty and public policy. He has been a member of several government committees and has also been associated with international bodies like the UNDP, IFPRI, ESCAP and The World Bank.

Gandhi, Sonia

Sonia Gandhi is the President of the Indian National Congress Party which made a remarkable comeback under her leadership in the 2004 General Elections for the 14th Lok Sabha. She is also the Chairperson of the Coordinating Committee of the ruling United Progressive Alliance (UPA) and the Chairperson, Indira Gandhi Memorial Trust.

Ganguly, Ashok S.

Ashok Ganguly is currently the Chairman of ICICI OneSource Limited and ABP Pvt. Ltd. and has been a Director on the Central Board of the Reserve Bank of India, since November 2000. In addition, Dr. Ganguly heads his own company, Technology Network India Pvt. Ltd. He is a recipient of the Padma Bhushan, one of India's highest honours.

Gupta, Dipankar

Dipankar Gupta is currently a professor in the Centre for the Study of Social Systems, Jawaharlal Nehru University. He has authored and edited several books. He is also co-editor of *Contributions to Indian Sociology.*

Hasan, Zoya

Zoya Hasan is Professor of Political Science at the Jawaharlal Nehru University. She has been recently appointed as a Fellow of the Human Development and Capability Association of the Global Equity Initiative of the Asia Centre of Harvard University. She has authored and edited several books.

Hazarika, Sanjoy

Sanjoy Hazarika is Managing Trustee, Centre for North East Studies and Policy Research (C-NES); Consulting Editor, *The Statesman* and Visiting Professor at the Centre for Policy Research. He has written extensively on the Northeast and made documentary films about the region and countries in its neighbourhood. He is an award winning former correspondent of *The New York Times.*

Hoskote, Ranjit

Ranjit Hoskote is a poet, art theorist and independent curator of contemporary Asian art. He is the author of seven books, among which three are collections of poetry. Hoskote has received the Sahitya Akademi Golden Jubilee Award for Literature (2004) and Sanskriti Award for Literature (1996). He is currently Assistant Editor with *The Hindu*, Bombay.

Jha, Prem Shankar

Prem Shankar has been editor of *The Economic Times, The Financial Express,* economic editor of *The Times of India* and editor of the *Hindustan Times.* Currently he is a columnist for the *Outlook* magazine, *Hindustan Times, Dainik Bhaskar* and several other newspapers. He is the the author of many widely acclaimed books.

Kakar, Sudhir

Psychoanalyst and writer, Sudhir Kakar has been Professor of Organisational Behaviour at the Indian Institute of Management (IIM), Ahmedabad and Head of Department of Humanities and Social Sciences at the Indian Institute of Technology (IIT), Delhi. Dr. Kakar's many honours include the Kardiner Award of Columbia University, Boyer Prize for Psychological Anthropology of the American Anthropological Association, Germany's Goethe Medal, and being elected to the Académie Universelle des Cultures in Paris. Several of his books have been translated into 20 languages around the world.

Kanwar, Amar

Amar Kanwar is an independent film-maker working from New Delhi. His films were exhibited at DOCUMENTA 11 and in several international film festivals. His films have been essentially on issues of ecology, human rights, sexuality, art and politics. He has received several awards at the International Film Festivals.

Karnad, Bharat

Bharat Karnad is Research Professor in National Security Studies at the Centre for Policy Research, New Delhi, and has authored books on nuclear weapons and India's security. He regularly lectures at various military forums.

Khilnani, Sunil

Sunil Khilnani is currently Professor of Politics and Director, South Asia Studies at the Paul H. Nitze School of Advanced International Studies, Johns Hopkins University, in Washington DC. He has authored several well known books, including *The Idea of India.*

Kidwai, Naina Lal

Naina Lal Kidwai is the Chief Executive Officer of HSBC in India. Besides being the first woman to head a foreign bank in India, Ms. Kidwai was also the first Indian woman to graduate from the Harvard Business

School. Ranked 3rd in Asia by Fortune magazine in their first ever listing of 'the world's top women in business in Asia' in 2000 and subsequently ranked in the 'top 50 women in Business', internationally, by Fortune magazine in the first such listing in 2001 and subsequently in 2002 and 2003. Also listed by Time magazine as one of their '15 Global Influentials' 2002.

Kumar, Radha

Radha Kumar is Visiting Professor at Jamia Millia Islamia, New Delhi, and trustee of the Delhi Policy Group, where she is directing a programme on "Durable Peace Processes and Partners" jointly sponsored by the India International Centre. She is currently writing a book on the India-Pakistan peace process. Her articles have been widely published in reputed national and international journals.

Malhoutra, Manmohan

Secretary-General of the Rajiv Gandhi Foundation since 2001, 'Moni' Malhoutra was formerly Assistant Secretary-General of the Commonwealth and later, a member of the Board of Directors of International IDEA – the Institute for Democracy and Electoral Assistance, Stockholm. Educated in Delhi and Oxford, he was a member of the Indian Administrative Service (1961-1978) and served in the Secretariat of Prime Minister Indira Gandhi from 1966 to 1973. He then moved to London to the Commonwealth Secretariat, where he played a leading role in Commonwealth efforts to end apartheid in South Africa.

Mehta, Pratap Bhanu

Pratap Bhanu Mehta is the President and Chief Executive of the Centre for Policy Research, New Delhi. He has published widely in reputed national and international journals. He has been a prolific contributor to public debates and his columns have regularly appeared in *The New Republic, Foreign Policy, The Hindu, The Indian Express, The Telegraph, Yale Global* and numerous other papers.

Menon, Asha (Revathy)

Revathy was introduced into films by the veteran director Bharathi Rajaa in the year 1933. Since then she has done more than 95 films in five Indian languages. She has received several national and international awards. Revathy is an exponent in classical Bharathanatyam. She is now involved in many social activities involving people with disabilities and children.

Monteiro, Vivek

Vivek Monteiro is currently the Secretary CITU, Maharashtra State Committee; Convenor CITU Maharashtra State Coordination Committee for Unorganised Sector Workers. He is also a member of the Maharashtra State Committee of CPI(M). Dr. Monteiro joined the trade union movement in 1977. He has worked primarily on issues pertaining to the unorganised sector. He is also an active member of the Group for

Nuclear Disarmament and has written extensively on labour, science and technology and nuclear weapons.

Mukherjee, Mridula

Mridula Mukherjee is Chairperson and Professor of Modern Indian History at the Centre for Historical Studies, Jawaharlal Nehru University, New Delhi. She is member, executive committee of the National Council of Education Research and Training (NCERT) and the Indian History Congress. She is closely associated with Shantha Sinha's movement for abolition of child labour and for universal school education. She has authored and co-authored some best-selling books.

Munjal, Sunil Kant

Sunil Kant Munjal is the Managing Director and CEO of Hero Cycles Ltd. He is the past president of the Confederation of Indian Industry (CII), India's premier business association. Mr. Munjal has been a member of several national level Government committees, is currently a member of the Prime Minister's Council on Trade and Industry, and the Consultative Group on Industry, Planning Commission, among others.

Munjee, Nasser

Nasser Munjee, a monetary economist, is presently the Chairman of Development Credit Bank. Earlier, he was the Managing Director and CEO of Infrastructure Development Finance Company Limited, India (IDFC) and introduced the concept of private financing of public infrastructure to India. Mr. Munjee is on the Board of many corporates and is deeply interested in development issues. An ardent lover of jazz, Mr. Munjee is the Chairman of Jazz India.

Narain, Sunita

Sunita Narain is the Director of the Centre for Science and Environment (CSE), and the editor/publisher of *Down To Earth*, India's first science and environment fortnightly magazine. She has received many national awards and honours for her contributions to the environmental cause.

Narayan, Jayaprakash

Jayaprakash Narayan describes himself as a physician by training, a public servant by choice, and a democrat by conviction. He resigned from the IAS in 1996 and in the same year started the Foundation for Democratic Reforms, a non-partisan think tank, to promote political and governance reforms. Dr. Narayan also started Lok Satta, a grassroots movement to exert positive pressure to institutionalise good governance. Lok Satta is now India's largest non-partisan movement for governance reforms, with popular support and credibility.

Nayyar, Deepak

Deepak Nayyar, formerly Vice Chancellor of the University of Delhi is an eminent economist; has taught at the University of Oxford, the University of Sussex, the Indian Institute of Management, Calcutta and

Jawaharlal Nehru University, New Delhi. Professor Nayyar is Chairman of the Board of Governors of the UNU World Institute for Development Economics Research, Helsinki, and Chairman of the Advisory Council for the Queen Elizabeth House at the University of Oxford. He is also a Member of the World Commission on the Social Dimension of Globalization.

Ninan, T.N.

T.N. Ninan is the editor and publisher of *Business Standard*. He is also a familiar figure on national television as a commentator on economic issues. He has won the B.D. Goenka Award for excellence in journalism (1992), and the Sachin Chaudhuri Award for excellence in financial journalism.

Parthasarathy, Ravi

Ravi Parthasarathy is the Vice Chairman and Managing Director of Infrastructure Leasing & Financial Services Limited (IL&FS). He is on the Board of several companies, including The National Stock Exchange of India Limited. He is also a Member of the Expert Committee on Infrastructure, constituted by the Government of India.

Prahalad, C.K.

C.K. Prahalad is Paul and Ruth McCracken Distinguished University Professor at University of Michigan. Professor Prahalad is a globally known figure and has consulted with the top management of many of the world's foremost companies. His research specialises in corporate strategy and the role and value added of top management in large, diversified, multinational corporations.

Prasad, Chandra Bhan

Chandra Bhan Prasad is the first and only Dalit writer to run columns in mainstream newspapers. Author of the famous *Bhopal Document* (2002) for the Government of Madhya Pradesh, Mr. Prasad is a diversity advocate for Dalits in India. He has written *Vishwasghat* (in Hindi), detailing landholding patterns in India's 16 major states.

Raina, Vinod

Vinod Raina worked as a software consultant at Delhi University. He resigned in 1982 to work full-time at the grassroots level for the qualitative improvement of rural school education, and co-founded the Eklavya Group which has done pioneering work in this area since then. He was also associated, from its inception, with the mass literacy campaign model. For this purpose he co-founded the Bharat Gyan Vigyan Samiti (BGVS), a movement of half a million volunteers working on elementary education, health, women, livelihoods in 250 districts of 20 states. He is currently the General Secretary of BGVS.

Rampal, Anita

Anita Rampal is working with the Central Institute of Education, University of Delhi. She is a member of the Executive Committee of NCERT and has been closely associated with the development of new textbooks. She was earlier the Director, National Literacy Resource Centre, Lal Bahadur Shastri Academy of Administration, Mussoorie and has been involved in major educational initiatives like the National Literacy Campaign. She has authored several books and academic papers.

Ramphal, Shridath

Sir Shridath ('Sonny') Ramphal was the Foreign Minister of Guyana before being elected as Secretary-General of the Commonwealth, a post he held for three terms (1975-1990). He was a prominent member of all the independent international commissions of the 1980s. In the 1990s he was Co-Chairman (along with Ingvar Carlsson, the then Prime Minister of Sweden) of the International Commission on Global Governance.

Sanghvi, Vir

Vir Sanghvi is Editorial Director, of the *Hindustan Times*. He is an accomplished writer and columnist, and anchors influential and popular programmes on television. He has won innumerable awards for his writings and journalism and was named a Global Leader of Tomorrow by the World Economic Forum in Davos in 1983.

Sen, Mrinal

"I'm a film-maker by accident and occasionally an author by compulsion," claims Mrinal Sen. He started writing on the aesthetics of cinema, its philosophy, its socio-political relevance, and dreamt of a genre, called New Cinema. He has received numerous awards, national and international. He has served on the juries of many film festivals. For nine continuous years, he remained the Chairman of the International Federation of Film Societies.

Setalvad, Teesta

Teesta Setalvad has been a journalist since 1983, when she was the editor of *Communalism Combat*. She is a trustee of the Women's Centre, D.D. Kosambi Trust, Bombay. She has written and directed various documentary films and has received many awards including the Rajiv Gandhi Sadbhavna Award 2002.

Singh, Manmohan

Dr. Manmohan Singh is the Prime Minister of India. A distinguished economist, Dr. Singh is widely regarded as the principal architect of India's economic reforms, a process initiated in 1991 when he was the Union Finance Minister.

Varadarajan, Siddharth

Siddharth Varadarajan is Deputy Editor of *The Hindu*, with primary responsibility for writing on strategic affairs and internal security. In addition to his academic writings in edited books, he himself edited a volume on the Gujarat violence, *Gujarat: The Making of a Tragedy* (2002).

Vasudev, Aruna

Aruna Vasudev is the Founder-Editor of *Osian's-Cinemaya*, the Asian Film Quarterly, founded in 1988; Founder-Director of Osian's-Cinefan, the annual Festival of Asian Cinema in Delhi, and President of NETPAC (Network for the Promotion of Asian Cinema) International. She is a member on the Board of the Public Service Broadcasting Trust in Delhi. She is a regular writer on film for various newspapers and periodicals. She has been a member or President of the international juries of several international film festivals.

Vatsyayan, Kapila

Kapila Vatsyayan is Chairperson of the IIC-Asia Project, India International Centre and represents India on the UNESCO Executive Board. She is also Vice-Chairperson of the Central Advisory Board on Culture of the Government of India. Dr. Vatsyayan's work in education and culture has received recognition nationally and internationally, including eight Honoris Causa degrees; the Rajiv Gandhi National Sadbhavana Award 2000, and most recently, the Lalit Kala Ratna Award on the occasion of the golden jubilee of the Lalit Kala Academi.

Yadav, Yogendra

Prof. Yogendra Yadav is Senior Fellow at the Centre for the Study of Developing Societies (CSDS), Delhi. He is the Founder Convenor of the Lokniti network. Prof. Yadav has designed and coordinated the National Election Studies from 1996 to 2004—the largest ever series of academic surveys of the Indian electorate. He has contributed about 200 articles in various newspapers and magazines. He is currently the Executive Editor of *Samayik Varta*, a monthly Hindi magazine.

Yechury, Sitaram

Sitaram Yechury is a Member of Parliament (Rajya Sabha) from the Communist Party of India (Marxist). He is a member of the party's Central Committee and Politburo and has authored various publications on communalism, economic policy and social and cultural issues.

Organising Committee

K. Natwar Singh

Vice-Chairman of the Indira Gandhi Memorial Trust.

Sheila Dikshit

Secretary of the Indira Gandhi Memorial Trust and Chief Minister, Government of National Capital Territory of Delhi.

A. K. Damodaran

Former Ambassador for India to Sweden and Italy.

H. Y. Sharada Prasad

Vice-President of the Indian Council for Cultural Relations, New Delhi.

Kapila Vatsyayan

Chairperson of the IIC-Asia Project, India International Centre and Vice-Chairperson, Central Advisory Board on Culture, Government of India.

Mushirul Hasan

Vice Chancellor of Jamia Millia Islamia, New Delhi.

Manmohan Malhoutra

Secretary-General of the Rajiv Gandhi Foundation since 2001.

Poonam Sahi

Assistant Secretary of the Indira Gandhi Memorial Trust.

Introduction

MANMOHAN MALHOUTRA

THE story of a rising India has surprised the world but also captured its imagination. It is said that no other democracy has ever achieved levels of sustained economic growth comparable to India's over the last two decades. Unsung until recently, partly on account of China's much more dramatic progress, India's 'stealth-economy', as it has been dubbed, has lifted hundreds of millions out of poverty and put the country on the path of transformation. The world wants to know how this has happened and, even more, what is likely to happen in the future. Is India's rise inexorable or could India once again disappoint? Are its ambitions to accelerate its trend rate of growth to at least 8 per cent on a long-term basis achievable? Is the agenda of economic reform an electoral asset or liability? What are the cross currents in India's political economy through which decision makers will have to navigate? Can India really get its act together in the face of its fractured polity and poor governance? Are its great power ambitions credible?

These are questions of interest not only to the world, but to all Indians. The next 10 years will clearly be crucial in determining which way India goes. It was for this reason that the 2004 Indira Gandhi Conference chose the coming decade as its theme. It sought to do so through four interrelated prisms—political, economic, cultural and external—each of which would interact on the others. Thus the challenges and prospects for Indian democracy could not be viewed in isolation from the trajectory of the Indian economy and the overriding imperative of combining high growth with greater equity. Both would, in turn, be coloured by the changing *mores* of Indian society and its increasingly youthful demographics. Overarching them all were issues of how the outside world and India would impinge on each other, not just in obvious political and economic ways, but also at the deeper level of culture, values and aspirations.

To do justice to this challenging agenda, the conference brought together different streams of thought, experience and perspective. There were well-known figures from public life, economists and social scientists, educationists and trade unionists, diplomats and journalists, business people and industrialists, academicians and strategic thinkers, social activists and film-makers. This was no monochromatic gathering, but a coming together of an unusual and diverse mix of individuals. The resulting richness will, I hope, be evident from their contributions, both written and oral. Mrs. Sonia Gandhi, who was present throughout the proceedings, described the conference as one of the best sabbaticals she had ever had. This feeling of having been a participant in a valuable learning experience was shared by all. It is hoped that by publishing the background papers and the debate which they generated, a wider audience will be able to share this experience, both in India and abroad.

Did the conference serve its purpose? It was not meant to be a scenario planning exercise, systematically developing possible futures. Nor were the participants oracles or seers. In the space of two days of discussion, they could obviously not have sought to develop specific scenarios, which by their very nature require extensive and detailed study. Quite rightly, therefore, the conference eschewed pop futurism. Instead, it tried to explore trends, the big forces that would be at work over the next 10 years, along with some of the significant variables that were likely to influence the course of events. If there was an excessive focus on the negatives, it was in the context of urging that they be put right in order to ensure that the India story did not get derailed.

The unexpected but salutary outcome of the 2004 general elections was seen as a source of hope and a landmark in India's democratic evolution. All were agreed on the need to deepen Indian democracy and give it more substance. If this was not done fast enough, there was a real danger that the next 10 years would see a weakening of the sense of a national civic identity in favour of many debilitating sub-identities. We were still far from giving full meaning to the triad of concepts and values of a liberal constitutional democracy. Indeed, in important respects, we were regressing. The growing tension between the constraints of a liberal constitutional democracy and the rule of law on the one hand, and on the other, the strident demands and practices of the political marketplace and the tendency to convert citizens' social and economic rights into discretionary allocations by the state, needed to be addressed. Institutional reform for more effective governance was the crying need of the hour. However, institutional reform would only succeed if the incentives to comply with institutional norms were self-reinforcing, without constant punitive supervision by the state.

It was pointed out that beyond the 'formal' sector of constitutional procedures, institutions and political parties lay a host of informal democratic practices that had given substance and strength to the functioning of Indian democracy. Social class was a factor in political loyalties in all countries. There was therefore no reason to feel embarrassed or apologetic about the organic links which competitive politics in India had developed with caste: far from caste taking over politics, it was politics which was transforming caste in fundamental ways. The issue for concern was that this informal sector, with all its energy and transformative possibilities, was in danger of drying up. The real crisis of Indian democracy was that there were now many more parties without more choices being available to ordinary citizens. Improving the quality of the game was more important than rewriting the rulebook or reforming formal institutions. Political formations must learn to reconnect with, and draw strength from, the informal.

Nevertheless, despite its many failings, Indian democracy remained a success story. Notwithstanding middle class disenchantment with politics and the political class, the balance between hope and despair would continue to tilt towards hope. Reform would come slowly, but in the usual messy democratic way. Democratising and decentralising the party system, curbing money power in elections, refashioning the judiciary, decentralising power and making imaginative use of IT to instill transparency and accountability, not least among elected representatives, were singled out as key priorities. The electoral system, based on first past the post, also perhaps warranted a fresh look.

In contrast to the muted pessimism about India's capacity to bridge its democratic deficit in the near future, there was a more optimistic, almost sanguine, belief in India's economic prospects. The trend rate of growth was above 6 per cent and accelerating. Entrepreneurial energy had been unleashed (though more could and should be done in this regard), new and sophisticated manufacturing capabilities were being established and the services sector was booming, with a huge multiplier effect on urban development. Yet, despite this elan, there was a significant economic deficit—a failure to create adequate employment. Jobless growth, however high, was inequitable and unsustainable and would prove socially destabilising and politically disastrous. The jury was still out on whether the conventional nostrums of economic reform were appropriate to India's situation or whether they would impose too high a political cost. Since liberalisation began, India had become an even more unequal society, with the rich gaining disproportionately. While all development created asymmetric benefits, corrective action was necessary.

Many ideas were offered as a way forward. The neglect of agriculture and the rural economy over the last decade was not only a source of widespread farmer distress but a major brake on economic growth. Liberalisation had yet to be extended to rural industry. India needed to grow not just the top-end knowledge economy, but agriculture and manufacturing as well in order to cope with its bulging demographic profile. The pitiful value-add of 6 per cent in the agricultural sector, compared with 82 per cent in Thailand, showed how much potential existed to make agriculture the biggest catalyst for higher growth with high employment during the next decade. This would require huge public investment in rural infrastructure, marketing innovations and tenurial and legislative reforms, along with the provision of capital to assist small and big entrepreneurs. Policy frameworks to sustain and enhance the livelihoods of hundreds of millions dependent on 'green capital'—common property resources—also needed to be put in place.

On the issue of infrastructure, India had not yet learned to think strategically about public-private partnerships or to promote cluster development in favourable locations that would attract foreign investment. Resources should be targeted incrementally at particular districts to obtain high returns. Integrated area development was the lesson we needed to learn from China which had concentrated on modernising its coastal regions, rather than spreading resources all over the country in a diffused way. The debate about private sector, state sector and civil society was an outdated one. What India would need during the next decade was the convergence of all three, in ways not yet imagined. Poverty should be seen not as an intractable problem but the result of a system which denied the poor access to markets and their opportunities, as well as dignity and choice as consumers. If this could be cracked and the necessary innovations put in place, development with equity was achievable.

Ironically, however, the opening up of the Indian economy was being paralleled by a closing of the Indian mind and the hollowing out of older value systems. The physical manifestations of a modernising economy now contrasted with an increasingly illiberal society in which cultural freedoms were being infringed. The public sphere of freedom of thought and expression envisioned by the Constitution had shrunk in recent decades at the hands of the state, political parties, vigilante outfits and self-styled moralists. A curious new right had emerged on the political and social landscape—the right to take offence, and to express offence violently. Young people in particular seemed to be directionless, devoid of ideas and ideals.

Out in the countryside, there was growing anger and despair. The processes of capitalism and industrialisation were fuelling naxalism, communalism and a growing cult of violence among those who saw themselves as victims of a heartless, uncaring development.

The 'unchanging' Indian village was in fact in the throes of change. Landholdings were generally small and offered poor economic rewards. With the near collapse of the closed village economy, patron-client relationships were breaking down: there was no longer a dominant caste. To migrate to a town was a new status symbol. The extent of rural non-farm employment was much higher than was commonly imagined. Paradoxically, as the economic grip of the caste system loosened, an exaggerated sense of caste identity had emerged both as a form of defiance and of social and political assertion.

Films were a good mirror of society. The idealised Indian village, so beloved by earlier Indian film-makers, was now a thing of the past. Films about rural India and the village as an embodiment of traditional and noble Indian values no longer commanded a market, not even among rural folk. They wanted out from the harsh realities of village life, on the screen as much as in life.

There were, however, some glimmers of hope. A young generation of documentary and fiction film-makers was creating a cinema that was thoughtful, artistic and critical of society. They needed encouragement and the removal of the heavy hand of the censor. Films of this nature could implant and shape values among the young in a way that nothing else could. Much greater emphasis should also be given to science teaching in schools throughout the country to inculcate a spirit of rationality, of scepticism and of questioning. Only in this way could religiosity and fundamentalism be combated.

On the issue of India's relations with the rest of the world, there was much less agreement. Although India commanded a new level of respect abroad, there was as yet no consensus within the country on what India's role in the world should be. Did India aspire to be a great power or would it be preferable to be a great and successful nation? There was no clarity about what India wanted to become. Unlike China, India lacked a long-range vision and a well considered mix of economic and military approaches to power. The romantics who thought that India could become a great power on the cheap, on the strength of its size and moral capital, needed to be disabused of their illusions. That was not the way the world functioned. There was a lamentable and continuing ignorance in the country about strategic matters, resulting in *ad hocism*, risk aversion and levels of weakness in various arms of the state, including intelligence and planning, that were incompatible with India's pretensions.

It was also not clear what India stood for. Bangalore presented one image to the rest of the world, Gujarat another. Economic progress by itself could not ensure national coherence or a consistent image.

How should India seek to position itself in the emerging world system, in which the US was the most decisive actor? As the world's largest open society, India enjoyed a unique legitimacy which could be an asset in defining its role. The centrality of India-US relations in the achievement of critical national goals hardly required underscoring. For this, India would need to cultivate important constituencies within the US—business, academia and the diaspora—and secure their ongoing support. Building relations on deep interdependencies should be the goal. Equally critical would be the skill with which India handled its relations with its immediate neighbours on the subcontinent and with the other regions of Asia. India was an important element in the rise of Asia, but there was no question of it acting as a foil against China. Over the next decade, if it played its hand well, India would have a unique opportunity to create a distinctive space for itself in the emerging international order, combining its growing economic and military strength with a projection of distinctively Indian values. A hard-headed, intelligent pursuit of self-interest would need to be its watchword.

Some of the major concerns of the Conference have been much in evidence over the last 18 months, and will continue to be in play in the years ahead. The enactment of the Right to Information Act, perhaps the most progressive anywhere in the world, has been an important step towards accountability and improved governance. India's democracy should be the stronger, but the recent decision to limit access to file notings is yet another instance of the Indian predilection to take two steps forward and one step back. The National Rural Employment Guarantee Act, another landmark, is part of the continuing search for greater equity in development. However, the controversy over reservations and quotas in higher educational institutions for other backward castes shows how difficult the pursuit of equity can prove in practice. Overall, the state's increasing inability to deliver on development and provide quality public services to the poor will remain an issue of overriding concern for a long time. In particular, education and healthcare must be recognised as the true entitlements for enhancing human capacities, not just on paper, but in redefining the very role of the Indian state and the way in which it allocates resources.

This briefest of overviews is offered in the manner of an *amuse bouche*, to whet the reader's appetite. It can hardly do justice to the quality and range of the background papers and the ensuing discussion. By tapping the insights of some of India's most talented individuals from diverse disciplines, this volume offers a unique insight into the interplay of forces in the coming decade.

1 | Shaping Our Future

SONIA GANDHI

IT is 20 years since Indiraji was cruelly taken away from us.

Magnanimous in victory, gracious in defeat, defiant in the face of might and danger, unwavering in her commitment to India's progress and integrity, she has passed into legend. Indira Gandhi is remembered by millions in our country for her charismatic leadership and her deep concern for the poor. Her love for nature, her sensitivity to the arts and, quite simply, her pride in being Indian, enhanced her allure and added lustre to her leadership.

Politics may have been her calling, but she never allowed politics to shut out the other things which make life worth living. She delighted in books. The world of ideas held a special appeal for her. In her travels within India and abroad she sought out writers, thinkers, scientists and artists. She greatly valued her conversations

with them because they enabled her to keep in touch with new trends and intellectual currents. She also shared a deeper bond with them. She understood that it is not politics alone which changes the world. Novelists, philosophers and artists do so too through their ideas, their passionate social critique. Always in search of new perspectives and insights which might enrich politics itself, bold and adventurous in her approach to all that life offers, she admired others in different fields whose creativity and sagacity took them to new frontiers.

It is in that spirit that the Indira Gandhi Conferences are held. They honour the memory of a human being who tried to connect the world of politics to the world of thought.

Most of the earlier conferences were international ones on broader issues of concern to humanity. We have deliberately shifted our focus this year to India to explore what the next decade might hold for us. We

---

Speech delivered at the inaugural function of the Ninth Indira Gandhi Conference, "India: The Next Decade", New Delhi, November 19, 2004.

cannot predict the future but we can try and shape it. This is a moment of opportunity for our country, to build a society that offers justice, dignity and development to all our people. We need to reflect on how we can grasp it. Do we just carry on or can we possibly find agreement on some fresh key goals for the next decade—as well as the means of achieving them? Inevitably, the external environment will impact on us in many ways because the world will not stand still during the next 10 years. We have, as you will all agree, a lot of catching up to do.

Our social and economic achievements in the last half-century have changed India profoundly. The talent and creativity of our people and their enterprise are beginning to impress the world. There is a current of energy, a stronger sense of self-confidence, a readiness to take risks, and a greater openness to new ideas. This is a society in the throes of ferment and questioning, impatient with the shackles of the past, witness the struggles for empowerment by the marginalised and the numerous social movements all over the country. Witness, too, the expansion and diversity of our media, the extent of experimentation in the arts, the varied social concerns of our film-makers. Globalisation is bringing in new values and aspirations, especially among the urban young. These changes will accelerate in the coming decade. India will become more urbanised and more youthful. As a result, society, economy and political system, will face new and testing pressures. There will be a need to adapt, to reform and to innovate—but also to preserve and to uphold those time-tested values which make us what we are and give us our unique

identity as Indians, anchored in our secular, pluralistic heritage.

In the medley of disparate voices of our parliamentary system, the larger vision which should guide us tends at times to get blurred. The challenges of the next 10 years are clear.

We cannot take our democracy for granted—it is a process which requires constant care and nurturing. The gradual but continuing erosion of standards in key institutions must be checked in order to sustain our people's faith in the democratic system. The fuller empowerment of women remains crucial.

We have to preserve our national integrity and coherence if we are to realise our potential. The politics of religion or of identity must not be allowed to weaken our secular pan-Indian consciousness or to create internal conflict.

We must achieve higher economic growth but strike a better balance between urban and rural, between economy and ecology, and between rich and poor. The quality and reach of public services must improve.

We must find a new equilibrium between tradition and the cultural values fostered by a more open economy and technological change.

We must build productive partnerships with our neighbours.

We must strive for excellence in education for all our children and create world class institutions of learning at all levels.

No government has a monopoly on wisdom. If we are to meet these challenges, we will need the help of our best minds to identify obstacles and opportunities and to articulate a truly national agenda to take India forward. I hope this Conference will be part of that larger process.

Countries fall into two broad categories—those that are more than the sum of their parts and those that are less. With our enormous ethical, intellectual, cultural and material assets, we must ensure that India reclaims its place firmly in the first category. During the next decade, the old taunt that "India is a country of the future and will always remain so" must finally be laid to rest.

2 | India: The Next Decade

Imperatives and Reflections

MANMOHAN SINGH

THE Indira Gandhi conferences celebrate the life of a woman whose breadth of vision and depth of knowledge surpassed that of most political leaders of the 20th century. She thought big, she thought far. Indira Gandhi's concerns were of course Indian, but her perspective was invariably global. She was passionately committed to India's development, to our well-being and welfare and to restoring to our country our rightful place in the comity of nations. Indiraji was intensely nationalistic and a true patriot. Yet, she had a global perspective and was a citizen of the world. The lessons she learnt in world history from her father created a solid foundation of knowledge on which she constructed the framework of her world view.

The themes we have discussed in the past at these conferences, therefore, quite correctly reflect the mind and personality of Indiraji. The subject of this year's conference also fits into this mould. For there cannot be

a more challenging and a more enduring concern, not just for us in India but for all thinking intellectuals of our time, than the course India will take over the next decade.

A decade is not a long time in the history of an ancient land like ours. Yet, for people who for centuries have seen very little change, the past few decades have been epochal. Place yourself at the beginning of any of our post-independence decades and ask the question whether the point at which one was standing gave any idea at all where the nation and the economy would be after a decade, and the answer clearly is no. A decade ago, for instance, few would have forecast the embarrassment of riches on the foreign exchange front. Gone are the days I would spend sleepless nights worrying about debt rescheduling! Today, we can proudly claim that foreign exchange is no longer a binding constraint. If we choose to be more welcoming the world is willing to invest in India. The next decade can open up even more opportunities for us if we draw the correct

Speech delivered at the inaugural function of the Ninth Indira Gandhi Conference, "India: The Next Decade", New Delhi, November 19, 2004.

lessons from the past and gather the courage to think boldly about the future.

India was conceived as a political laboratory in which the boldest social experiment of the 20th century was to be conducted. Among the first of the colonies to ignite the fire of freedom from colonial rule, this land was also the first to commit itself wholeheartedly to development in a democratic framework based on universal adult franchise. The principles that define our constitution, written by the founding fathers of our republic who were steeled in the national struggle for freedom, have since come to be accepted as universal principles of civilised existence—pluralism, secularism, republicanism, social justice and equality of all under the rule of law. We have much to be proud of in this inheritance.

Yet, we have some way to go before we can demand of the world the respect our experiment in pluralist democracy deserves. This is because we have not yet demonstrated to the world, and indeed to our own people, that this political framework we have willed for ourselves can also liberate us all from the scourge of poverty, illiteracy and backwardness and build a strong, open, equitable, competitive and prosperous economy. Of what use is political freedom, it is often asked, if it only grants us the freedom to speak but not the right to be fed. Can hungry mouths speak for the future? Can sullen minds think for our posterity? If India does not make the grade on the economic front, can it continue to do so on the political? I am sure some of these questions will engage your attention in this conference.

Looking into the future is always a hazardous enterprise. This has, however, not deterred soothsayers and forecasters from doing so and my tribe of economists have followed suit with their sophisticated models and statistical tools. I am, however, chastened by the dire warning of Dante who believed a special place was reserved in hell for those who dare to forecast the future! But having accepted your invitation I must soldier on.

Before we consider the next decade, let us pause and reflect on our inheritance. The historian Angus Maddison has painstakingly constructed the structure of world income over the past three centuries and has shown us that in 1700, before the dawn of the industrial era, India, China and Europe accounted for similar shares of world income. Each had a near 23 per cent share of world income. By the middle of the 20th century India's share was down to a paltry 3 per cent and China's down to 5 per cent. Europe and the United States together accounted for more than 50 per cent of world income. On this foundation of two lost centuries we have tried to rebuild our home. Compared to a near zero rate of growth of national income per year in the period 1900 to 1950, the Indian economy registered a 3.5 per cent rate of growth between 1950 and 1980 and over 5.5 per cent growth per annum between 1980 and now. Given this track record, I do not see why the next decade cannot record 7.5 per cent growth if we manage our resources well. This is do-able.

Clearly the question for us is what must we do now to secure the required acceleration of growth in the near term? The answer is easy to comprehend. India needs a renewed bout of economic dynamism. A new wave of investment based on the entrepreneurship and creativity of all those who believe in the 'idea' of India. There is now before us a new generation of Indians with a new commitment and a renewed stake in the future of our country. There are many more across the world who also want India to succeed, to prosper. We must enable their creativity, their enterprise, and their faith in India to find expression in as many ways as possible. We have to put in place a policy framework which rewards entrepreneurship, innovation and creativity.

For our part, in government, we have to address immediately the inadequately addressed agenda of human development. This we must do to convert our large population from being a liability into becoming an asset. Illiterate, unhealthy, unskilled and disempowered people are an economic and social liability. Literate, healthy, skilled and empowered people are an asset. The foundation of sustainable growth. We must very rapidly improve upon our record in education and health.

Second, we must ignite a new revolution of creativity and enterprise in the rural areas. Agrarian India must be transformed into a modern, viable economy, generating incomes and employment, attracting new investment in infrastructure, education and health care. India needs a Second Green Revolution aimed at increasing the returns on investment and the productivity of both land and labour in agriculture. India's villages must thrive. The farm economy must become robust and competitive. This is a priority for us. One of Indiraji's early and long-lasting contributions to India was the Green Revolution. Her courage and foresight and her faith in professionals and in scientific solutions to human problems enabled us to win the war against hunger. From a 'ship-to-mouth' existence we are today in a position to claim that we are not only self-sufficient, but also surplus in food.

But food security is not the only aim of the modernisation of the agrarian economy. We must create new employment in rural areas, new infrastructure, better connectivity and improve human capabilities. The education of our farmers, the induction of modern science and technology and management and marketing practices into agriculture. The transformation of our agrarian economy and of rural life is an imperative of the next decade. Furthermore, we must broaden our vision of food security to mount a frontal attack on malnutrition which affects the well being of a large mass of our population, particularly women and children as well as elderly people.

Third, the country as a whole deserves world class infrastructure and greater engagement with the global economy. This is an agenda we have set ourselves. By the end of my term in office, I would like to see world class power generation, world class highways, world class ports and airports and world class banking and communications infrastructure. We must raise our standards, our benchmarks of performance and expectations. We must replace our 'make-do' attitude with a 'can-do' spirit. This is particularly important to the acceleration of growth of our manufacturing sector. The past two decades have witnessed a relative decline in India's manufacturing competitiveness, especially *vis-à-vis* China. We cannot afford to lag behind developing Asia in the manufacturing sphere.

Over the past decade we have gradually managed to come out of our inward-looking shell to become more engaged with the world. This process must gather momentum. India must emerge as a major trading nation. Our share of world merchandise and services trade must reflect our capabilities and potential. India has been an important part of the world economy since millennia. We must rediscover this spirit of adventure and be actively engaged with the world economically, politically and culturally. However, while taking full advantage of the opportunities offered by the evolving global economy to increase our productivity, we ought to resist the temptation to copy the consumption habits of the post-industrial economies of the West. These consumption habits constitute a grave threat to the life-support systems of our planet and do irreparable damage to the environment. Copying these lifestyles will hurt our environment and will also lead to the accentuation of disparities in income and wealth. The challenge ahead is to abolish mass poverty and unemployment even at a relatively low level of per capita income.

Fourth, we must keep up the tempo of building a knowledge economy and making sure that it envelops the entire nation. The experience of some of our more enterprising centres of excellence must be replicated elsewhere. The 'knowledge economy' cannot be an island in an ocean of mediocrity, nor can it be delinked from the rest of the economy. We must make sure that it strikes deep roots in all walks of life, creating a more efficient, transparent, accountable and responsive system. It must improve the efficiency of both government and of the industrial and agricultural sectors. Experiments like *e-choupal* show the way forward in the application of modern science to the betterment of the life of the people. We need more such examples of entrepreneurial creativity.

I would like to submit for your consideration the idea that building a knowledge-based economy is more than just creating information technology capabilities. It is not just about producing more professionals and technically qualified people, ensuring better power supply and creating broadband connectivity. A truly knowledge-based society must impart a scientific and rational outlook. Our efforts to refashion social and economic processes and our political programmes and policies must be shaped by a scientific temper. This was the great intellectual contribution of Panditji and Indiraji to the intellectual discourse in our sub-continent. Their passionate commitment to the inculcation of a scientific temper in all of us. The India of the 21st century must be a forward-looking, modern and rational India, where religious fanaticism, casteism and superstition have no place.

It must also be a compassionate India. Caring for its under-priviliged. For scheduled caste and scheduled tribes, for religious and linguistic minorities, for women, children and senior citizens. Even as we empower the weak, we must create social safety nets that protect the marginalised from the adverse consequences of change. The challenge ahead is to combine this abiding concern for social equity with the quest for excellence and to sustain the processes of wealth creation.

I am convinced that in each of these areas we can reach new heights of creativity and enterprise. The next decade must be a decade of the unleashing of Indian creativity based on individual enterprise and collective effort. Crony capitalism and the politics of populism cannot take us very far. We owe it to our people and to the future to recognise the fact that ours has been a land of creativity and enterprise and that we must unleash these elements so that the boundary of possibilities is widened and pushed forward.

The government, our political leadership and civil society, have the obligation of ensuring that this process is politically stable, and socially and environmentally sustainable. Our democratic institutions have so far served us well in ensuring that we do not tilt too much in one direction and lose our balance. Our political and social systems have in-built correctives that have stabilised the process of change. We must remain mindful of this need. Imbalances between regions, between communities, between linguistic and ethnic groups, between man and nature, between us and our neighbours, must always be corrected.

These are the basic requirements of a growth process that will enable us to realise our true potential. But there is something more to a nation than its economic capability. By the end of the next decade we will be the world's largest nation. We already are the world's largest multi-cultural, multi-religious, multi-ethnic, multi-linguistic democracy. The success of the Indian experiment in nation building and in the social and economic empowerment of a billion people is vital for the very future of mankind in the 21st century. But we have some housekeeping to do even in this area and I do believe that in the next decade this is a challenge our youth will take up.

Our political life needs more professionals and leaders with a social conscience and personal integrity. Our civil society organisations need to be continually energised and empowered. Our democracy must be constantly rejuvenated by the infusion of fresh blood. Over the next decade our electoral cycle must cease to be defined by what has come to be dubbed as "anti-incumbency", and the negativities it entails. It must come to be defined by the positive politics of change, empowerment and modernisation. Ways and means must be found to prevent the use of religion and caste for manipulating political processes. Politics must rediscover its role as a purposeful instrument for the management of social change and not merely as a ticket for power. In this context, great importance attaches to the reform of the functioning of political parties. The financing of political parties must be as transparent as possible. The hold of unaccounted income and wealth on our political processes must be greatly reduced.

If this is the India we build at home, it will find itself in a new world. The world will look anew at us. Our neighbours will find us more welcoming and will welcome us more warmly. Over the next decade I would like to see India living in a neighbourhood of shared prosperity and peace. I would like to see India more actively engaged with all of Asia and all of the Indian Ocean region. I would like India to be actively engaged with the world's major powers in all international forums, participating willingly in the preservation of peace, the protection of the environment and the creation of prosperity.

India 2015 will be a nation of capable and empowered men and women, well-fed and gainfully employed, modern and rational, and actively engaged with the world. That is my dream for India at the end of the next decade. A decade is not a long time, indeed. I do hope you share my sense of urgency in doing what we have to. I welcome you to work with us in making the India of our dreams.

Democracy:
Challenges and Prospects

BACKGROUND PAPERS,
PRESENTATIONS AND DISCUSSION

INCREASED electoral participation, especially of the poor and previously excluded, has given greater depth and vitality to Indian democracy. However, in a number of other respects, there is a growing democratic deficit. Fostering the deeper values of a democracy in a caste-based and unequal society remains an abiding challenge. Looking to the decade ahead, what are the most critical areas where new normative standards need to be developed? Will India's democratic institutions be able to subordinate political interests to public rules? Can Parliament reclaim its role as an arena of public deliberation? What reforms are needed in the institutional architecture of representation? What are the implications for representative democracy of identity-based politics or religion-based mobilisation? Can there be incentives for political parties to become more institutionalised, with greater internal democracy and transparency? What should be done to control the influence of money in politics and yet give parties a chance to acquire the finances they need to contest elections? How can the functions of government be made more responsive and accountable? Can democracy be made to work better for the poor?

3 | Aspects of Democratic Accountability in India

PRATAP BHANU MEHTA

Introduction

India had for the past 50 years been a complex experiment in institutionalising democratic accountability. It has sustained, against great odds, a lively, stable, multi-cultural and functioning democracy with regular elections, a free press, independent judiciary and an extraordinarily vibrant civil society. Yet the institutions of democratic accountability have worked, at best, only imperfectly. One measure of their imperfection is that India has performed relatively less well on most human development indicators, such as health and education, and the effective policy outcomes of this process have left much to be desired. It is beyond the scope of this paper to explain the successes and failures of India's economic performance. This paper, rather, seeks to highlight facets of India's experiment with democratic accountability. A good deal of stress is placed on this issue because this is the single most important challenge to India's security. The challenge of producing institutions that can facilitate collective action, solve

practical problems ought to be the single most pressing issue. As we have seen the break down of institutions, whether under the pressure of the kind of communalised politics carried out by groups such as the (Vishwa Hindu Parishad), or by the state's own neglect, can bring all our achievements to nought. I would like to stress that at this stage, this paper is more a survey of the different facets of democratic accountability in India; it does not contain a sustained argument; nor does it answer the question of what kinds of political coalitions will sustain institutional reform. It attempts to suggest a set of questions that would bear further investigation.

To begin with we operate with a basic and simple concept of accountability—for a person or institution X to be accountable to an agent Y is for X to act on behalf of Y, and for Y to be empowered by some formal or informal mechanism to reward or sanction X for their activities.

While the basic concept is simple, the institutional expression that makes accountability effective is far from simple. For one thing, the range of principals and the agents to who they are accountable is vast. Second, the mechanisms for eliciting accountability are complex. For example, removing a whole range of regulatory tasks from the direct control of elected representatives is often thought to reduce accountability. Regulatory agencies like the Securities and Exchange Board of India (SEBI), or the Reserve Bank of India (RBI), or the Telecommunications Regulatory (TRAI) Authority are delegated specialised tasks over which elected representatives exercise only very indirect control. But ceding direct control can enhance accountability rather than diminish it. Independent agencies such as these increase the ability to commit to desirable policies and increase transparency in the sense that specialisation makes the agent responsible more easily identifiable. In this sense accountability is potentially enhanced rather than diminished.

There are few simple formulas for designing accountable institutions. This is because there is a series of tensions internal to the concept of accountability. The autonomy required for an agency to act properly on our behalf may be impaired by the structure of sanctions we impose upon them. In elections for example, it is notorious that there is a trade-off between seeing elections as a device to sanction the behaviour of incumbents and seeing them as a screening device for selecting the best candidates. Transparency is sometimes in tension with responsiveness and representation in tension with both. The crucial point is that harmonising

the different components of accountability cannot be done by conceptual fiat. *It is an empirical matter addressed by institutional design and the concrete work of politics.* A proper discussion of accountability requires that, at a minimum, attention be paid, both to the formal institutional mechanisms by which sanctions can be effected and the collective actions required to ensure that these sanctions are effected. The notion of accountability mentioned above raises two sorts of questions—how does the design of institutions provide the opportunity to hold policy makers accountable? What are the incentives and mechanisms of accountability? The second sort refer to actions of the principals involved—What are the forms of collective action that are required to take effective advantage of the opportunities that institutions offer? These questions are analytically distinct but related at the same time. Often citizens will not engage in public action if institutions are designed in ways that makes their prospects of responding remote. On the other hand public action outside the formal confines of institutions is, in democracies at any rate, a significant incentive that shapes institutional behaviour. Our suggestion is that any study of accountability tackles both aspects simultaneously. In this paper, we can do no more than suggest some of the questions that such a study ought to address. We divide this paper into two parts. In Part One we focus effecting accountability through public action. This part of the paper has three steps. In step one we examine how the electoral process manages or fails to produce accountability in India. We focus on the strengths and limitations of the electoral process in having an impact on policy formulation. We acknowledge that election and participation in regular forms of politics is only one form of public action. Accountability can also be generated by numerous others kinds of public activity—NGO's civic associations, the media and so on. But our focus here is on political mechanisms. In step two we examine the relationship between collective action and economic accountability and conclude that public pressure has been largely ineffective in forcing the state to make provision for public goods. In this section we illustrate the ambiguous and contradictory nature of the political process in India by looking at its impact on recent debates over economic policy. Step three makes an argument about strengthening political accountability through decentralisation of formal political institutions.

In Part Two we provide a framework for looking at the micro dynamics of accountability in India's leading institutions. We stress that this is, as yet a framework an not an argument. It can be used to generate research questions and is more in the nature of research proposal. But we feel that this is amongst the most neglected aspects of the study of policymaking in India.

The Importance of Institutional Design

Although it is a commonplace observation that societies are well governed and well organised to the extent that their public institutions can adequately manage the demands imposed upon them. The Indian state, like all states, secures legitimacy and is held accountable through a diverse range of institutions—executives, legislatures, courts, police, regulatory authorities, bureaucracies, commissions of inquiry, independent statutory bodies, development agencies, etc. Sometimes a broad based ideological vision may impart to this myriad of interlocking institutions, laws and agencies a degree of coherence and semblance. But even under the most homogeneous of ideological constellations these institutions often compete with each other, set bounds on what other institutions can do, interpret directives in their own peculiar way and provide the structures of accountability. Numerous studies of political and economic development in India have long recognised the important role the state plays as an autonomous actor—i.e. its capacities to often act free from societal constraints and manipulate them and its capacities to set the agenda for society. In comparative politics, drawing from the insights of 'new' institutional economics and historical institutionalism a considerable body of work exists that emphasises that institutions matter and how. Combing the two perspectives allows an integration of micro incentive questions with larger structural questions (Weaver and Rockman, 1993). Nonetheless, with the exception of the literature on central banks and more recently on the judiciary, there is little systematic analytical work on India that examines the myriad of institutions, both formal and informal, the commitments to procedures, the formal and informal incentives within state institutions, through which the state is both constituted and enabled to act on the one hand and constrained in its powers and capacities on the other.

Much of this neglect of the diversity of the institutions within the Indian state, the mechanisms by which they are held accountable, and the problems that arise from adverse incentives within institutions, has stemmed from certain methodological proclivities. In Marxist or structuralist inspired paradigms which dominated the political economy of the Indian state, the state was simply considered epiphenomenal to social forces. As such its own internal constitution, rules, incentives and procedures had at best marginal bearing on outcomes. While there is a substantial body of literature that has recognised the state as an important autonomous actor, it treats the 'state' in aggregative and diffuse terms. Although this literature pays considerable attention to the policy choices that states make and demonstrating that the state can act autonomously from societal forces, comparatively little attention is paid to the constituent institutions of the state itself. Economic approaches to the 'state' have paid more attention to the broad incentive structures that result from overextended and excessively dirigiste states but for the most part its focus has been to demonstrate how the state has been captured by interest groups. The constitutive institutions of the state particularly in poorer countries, remain for the most part a 'black box'. There has been relatively little attention paid to the relationship between institutional design and accountability.

In the Indian case, take for example the institutions that enforce *legal* accountability. Agents that enforce legal accountability include not only agencies of law enforcement like the police, or the judiciary like the courts, but also the investigative arms internal to bureaucracies and governments. In India, these institutions comprise financial oversight bodies like the Comptroller and Auditor General, investigative agencies like Central Vigilance Commission.

There is a general consensus in India that these institutions of accountability, taken singly and collectively, have underperformed. The Indian Judiciary is a case in point. On the one hand the judiciary has been extraordinarily active in calling the executive branch to account. The explosion of public interest litigation has meant that the judiciary is a conduit through which citizens make the executive accountable on a whole range of issues like health, sanitation, environment and social justice. But the overall effectiveness of the judiciary is very much open to question. For one thing, as the limitations of public interest litigation has demonstrated, the judiciary can at most provide immediate redress in a specific set of cases, but its power to generate enduring legislation that is widely enforced is extremely limited. But the main weakness of the judiciary has been its own judicial shortcomings rather than its ability to sanction the executive branch. As the Malimath committee noted, using data from India's Courts, there were a staggering 28 million cases pending in 1996. A survey of 1,849 companies that had pending cases in the High Court reported that 59 per cent of these cases had been pending for more than a decade. The causes of insufficient judicial performance are complex. Much of the litigation arguably stems from poorly drafted legislation. The Courts inability to dispose cases is, in part related to insufficient resources: "Insufficient financial outlays of State Governments, lack of proper manpower planning in response to workload increases, unduly cumbersome procedures of appointment contribute to inefficient courts." But most of the weaknesses are internal to the working of courts and a product of adverse incentive structures. There is wide variation in the management of case loads amongst different Chief Justices. Other factors influence the disposal rates of cases considerably—the extraordinary laxity in code of conduct of lawyers, the length of workday, norms of classification and allocation of cases amongst judges, the reliance on long oral arguments and procedures for taking witness depositions, provisions for appeals, the schedule of court fees, the structure of payments to lawyers can all have vast impact on the performance of courts. All these measures, that were ostensibly designed to render the courts more transparent have, by their cumulative effects, rendered them less responsive.

The effects of judicial delays are momentous. Delays mean that the use of 'extrajudicial methods' to alter the stakes in a judicial dispute become more attractive, especially since these methods themselves are unlikely to be punished swiftly. The more extrajudicial institutions like system of patronage are resorted to as a means of resolving disputes, the more fairness, transparency and certainty are likely to be sacrificed. Uncertainty and delay in judicial decisions on economic matters heightens uncertainty and raises the cost of investment. Politically, these delays undermine the credibility of the judiciary as a whole, because they give the pervasive impression that legal accountability can be avoided. By and large the judicial system has, because of its own internal micro-dynamics, been unable to hold politicians accountable in an effective way. And politicians used to a system that protects them from punishment are more likely to weaken the judicial system. Indeed, it is arguable that judicial reform will be the linchpin of any effective accountability. It is beyond the scope of this paper to give a detailed account of judicial accountability. The example here is meant to illustrate a simple point—the micro-dynamics of individual institutions can have system wide effects on accountability. A similar argument can be made for a whole range of institutions of regulation in India like the Comptroller and Auditor General, the Enforcement Directorate, the Revenue Service and so on. An interesting question to explore is the way in which institutional design has enabled or impeded accountability. In Part Two we provide a series of questions that need further exploration.

I

Elections and Accountability

India is a robust and contentious parliamentary democracy. Elections are one of the principal mechanisms of sanctioning the conduct of politicians in a parliamentary democracy such as India and holding them accountable. But elections can often be a blunt instrument of accountability and the nature of institutional design can impact this process in different ways.

In order to hold governments accountable, voters must be able to assign clear responsibility for government performance. But the ability to assign clear responsibility can be limited in several ways. In the first instance, voters need full information about how their representatives voted in Parliament on a full range of issues. It is arguable that in India voters do not have or do not seek much of this information about representatives. The press and the public debate almost never carry detailed information about how members of Parliament voted on particular bills or what legislation they introduced as private bills. In some respect, this lack of information is not as serious as might first appear, because in a parliamentary system each individual legislator's record is less important than the positions taken by the party. But even party manifestoes avoid cataloguing legislative accomplishment in any significant detail.

One particular aspect of the lack of information is particularly important in the Indian case. This has to do with the time horizons of the electorate by which they judge government performance. Ideally voters ought to be concerned about their welfare not only during the present term of the government but also the impact

government decisions have on prospects of their future welfare. This requires that they make inferences about the impact policy is going to have on their future welfare. These inferences are notoriously difficult to make and theories of voting behavior have tried to wrestle with it. Theories of 'retrospective voting' argue that voters basically make inferences about the likely consequences of what government did based on whether these policies had beneficial impacts in the current term of government. The comparative evidence on this is mixed. In most economies undergoing transition, it has been argued that voters treat inflation and wage levels inter-temporally (they try and anticipate future gains in these areas) but are risk averse about employment figures (Przewroski, 1996; Stokes, 1996) There are however other studies that claim the opposite (Frankel and Rose, 1996).

The question of the temporal dimension of accountability requires more study. But in the Indian case two things are very clear. First, the impact of policies on well being is judged less by aggregate future expectations of the impact of policies. Notoriously, aggregate measures like growth have seldom been political issues in India. Governments have routinely lost elections with high growth rates. Because of the dominance of the agrarian sector, aggregate measures of employment have not played a part. The one measure of well being to which the Indian electorate is extremely sensitive is inflation, especially of essential commodities. This measure affects a large number of people, in a direct and transparent way, but it also indicates a preoccupation with present welfare rather than inter-temporal gains.

This has a profound effect on the incentives this sets up for politicians. The time horizons under which politicians operate crucially determines policy outcomes. Most interviews with politicians confirm that this is how they understand their incentives. Politicians have less of an incentive to enact policies whose benefits are distant and uncertain. Arguably, this argument can be turned on its head: if the effects of policies are distant and uncertain why don't politicians enact them? There are two responses to this. One, politicians are more likely to be worried about the particular interests these policies hurt in the present than possible future beneficiaries. Second, even when present constituencies are not directly hurt by these measures politicians have less incentive to pay attention to them. Most Indian politicians operate with short time horizons; this makes them risk averse in that they are not willing to sacrifice present constituencies for possible future gains, unless those accrue within the time horizon of the next election.

Secondly, for reasons that Hamilton pointed out in *Federalist* 70 that accountability is very difficult to assign in cabinet executives: "But one of the weightiest objections to a plurality in the executive is that it tends to conceal faults and destroy responsibility. The circumstances which may have led to any national miscarriage or misfortunes are sometimes so complicated that there are a number of actors who have different degrees and kind of agency, though we may clearly see upon the whole than there has been mismanagement, yet it may be impracticable to pronounce whose account the evil which may have occurred is truly chargeable." In circumstances where the lines of decision making are obscured, the questions of who is to be held accountable becomes notoriously difficult.

The problem of assigning responsibility plagues not only cabinet government but the civil service as well. A large class of decisions are 'collective' decisions within the civil service in the sense that there are more than one signatories before a file can be approved. Often decisions are made through 'committees' which makes accountability difficult. Ostensibly committees serve to prevent individual officers from acting arbitrarily. In practice the large numbers of committees make civil servants dependent upon each other in that they know they will require the cooperation of their colleagues on some future occasion. This leads them to sign on to decisions with which they might not individually agree. In doing so, the decision is granted collective legitimacy which makes accountability difficult. The institutional mechanisms by which the line between one civil servant and another is blurred makes accountability difficult. The management procedures and the incentive structures of the Indian Civil Service are such that individual responsibility is very difficult to establish.

Third, in principle voters must be able to vote out of office parties responsible for bad government. But the nature of the electoral system makes the connection between voter preference and government formation more indirect. For one thing, in a first past the post system, the number of seats that a party gets in Parliament is not in direct proportion to the number of votes they receive; second which parties form government is not a function of aggregate voter preference but of the way in which votes are distributed geographically; third, under conditions where no party is in the majority, the making and unmaking of governments is even less a direct consequence of voter choice. Pasquino's statement with regard to Italy where the fact of coalition governments led to a situation where "governing parties seemed to expropriate the voters of political influence by the making and unmaking governments at all levels with very little respect for electoral results", has become more true of India in an era of coalition governments. In many instances, voters do not know what coalition a party is going to be part off, once elected. Coalition governments will blur the lines of responsibility even further. In instances where small parties are held responsible for arbitrarily breaking governments (as the AIADMK was in 1998) their conduct is cashiered. But whether praise or blame can be assigned for policies is less clear.

Fourth, elections as a mechanism require that the opposition both closely monitor the government and inform the citizens. In principle the opposition has incentives to monitor government and to inform voters about the performance of incumbents. Yet the existence of an opposition that can effectively articulate a critique of government cannot be taken for granted. In some instance smaller opposition parties can collude with government; in others the opposition may be too deeply divided and preoccupied with internal fights to monitor incumbents. Such is now arguably the case with India's parliament. There is compelling evidence that both the quantity and quality of deliberation in India's Parliament has declined substantially in the last decade or so. As one commentator pointed out, opposition parties monitor only a very small range of issues and bills closely; legislation related to most departments passes virtually without debate or notice. One telling statistic about India's upper house of Parliament, The Rajya Sabha, is very revealing in this respect. In 1985, this chamber of Parliament spent a total of 791 hours discussing government bill; in 1996-97 this number was down to a mere 7 hours. Similarly the time spent on short notice questions declined from 275 to a mere 35 hours. We are in the process of compiling statistics for the lower house of Parliament, but the preliminary trends suggest a similar picture. Most parliamentary committees have been weak or moribund during much of the 80s and 90s. The most crucial parliamentary oversight committee, the Public Accounts Committee scrutinizes only a negligible number of government audit reports and most standing committees have been seriously hampered by lack of information provided by the government. Under one party dominance, it was virtually impossible for opposition members to get Parliament to censure the government for lack of information; fragmentation of Parliament has made it difficult for parties to take collective action to rectify the weakness of parliamentary committees. (Rubinoff, 1999). There is virtual unanimity that Parliament has become very ineffective in its monitoring functions.

Oppositions parties face another dilemma. They cannot always oppose the government for they may be blamed for obstructing business; nor can they let the government get away with credit for enacting legislation. Opposition is effective when it neither colludes with, not always obstructs the government. Arguably this dilemma is keenly pronounced in recent Indian parliaments. There are numerous examples of legislation that are held up in Parliament because—a) either some small party that is part of the coalition government is exercising veto power, or b) many parties do not want legislation passed not because they disagree with the contents of the legislation but because they do not want the government to be able to garner credit for passing it. Given the fragmented character of parliamentary composition in India, the pace of legislation is extremely slow, even when there is substantive disagreement amongst the parties. For instance, a bill to liberalise insurance markets in India was first introduced in 1993 and took a full six years to pass (for details see Kapur, 2000).

The lack of effective intra-party democracy in most Indian political parties has impeded accountability considerably. It is a familiar point that voters choose their candidates from a menu of options. How this menu of candidates on offer comes to be determined is itself a complex matter—the motivations of those who enter, the probability of winning, the barriers to entry in terms of costs all have an effect. In some sense working through existing political parties can lower the costs of entry into politics and increase the probability of winning. The mechanisms by which parties select their candidates become important determinants of the menu of options. In most Indian political parties the selection of candidates has been extremely centralised and there is little inter-party democracy. This has momentous consequences for accountability.

First, political parties in general are not transparent and deliberative forums. They do not educate their members in the issues and do not act as conduits of information for political activists. Whatever their other disadvantages, intra-party primaries have a profound educative function on the rank and file of voters. Election campaigns in India are relatively short and the lack of intra-party democracy implies that groundwork preparation is not done. Second, parties do not allow for the genuine preferences of voters to manifest themselves clearly. The criteria for candidate selection is untransparent and uninstitutionlised. This often prevents key information about voter preferences from flowing up party conduits and prevents them from selecting candidates that are the most appropriate for particular locations. It is the case that in the long run most political parties pay the price for this lack of information and transparency. The most persuasive account for the decline of the Congress Party in North India stresses the degree to which lack of intra-party democracy prevented it from incorporating newly mobilised social groups like the backward castes and the rising peasantry. Arguably the lack of intra-party democracy has contributed much to a fragmented party system. Newly mobilised groups usually find it more difficult to capture significant power within existing parties, because there is no clear procedure for doing so. Hence, they set up their own parties. But the long-term interests of the party and the short-term interests of the leadership are at odds with one another. Party leaders like to pick candidates who are beholden to them and can be used to shore up their power; they dread independent voices. Hence they, unless in exceptional circumstances it suits them, are resistant to genuine inter-party elections. The net result is that parties can impede rather than enhance representation. Given the high cost of entry, parties have the power to restrict voter choices rather than expand them. Rather than being "institutions that knit the state and society together" (Kohli, 1998) the lack of intra-party democracy can help keep them apart. More subtle forms of accountability therefore require a pluralisation of the sites of accountability and a greater expansion of the forums for deliberation. Genuine intra-party democracy is an essential component of this process.

The electoral process in India has produced two outcomes in the last few years that merit attention. On the one hand incumbents find it very difficult to regain office. Aggregate incumbency rates for all legislative bodies have been around 25 per cent (Chhibber, 1999) during the last decade or so, whereas the incumbency rates for Parliament have hovered around 50 per cent. On the other hand the margins by which incumbents are overturned have not been very substantial. In other words, most candidates lose either because in the first past the post system the number of opposition candidates can have an impact on their chances, or because candidates, while managing to hold onto their core constituencies, lose the support of a small but critical segment. Cumulatively, these have had two effects. The incumbency rates of governments are extremely low; second, the party system has become more 'ethnicised'. This is taken to mean that at the local level there is a great correlation between social cleavages and party identification. Political parties thus find it very difficult to transcend social cleavages and do so only incrementally. This feature of Indian elections can be taken as a sign of the relatively non-deliberative character of the process. This politics structured around social cleavages aims more at advancing the cause of particular groups by obtaining access to state power rather than at formulating sound policy. The effects of these two trends on government performance have not yet been fully understood. One hypothesis in the literature is that high turnover in government is a sign that the electorate is cashiering policy makers for their misconduct. But how are politicians responding to these signals. There is some good evidence that paradoxically, the high rate of turnover has increased, or at least not diminished the rent seeking behaviour of politicians. If anything it has increased the *need* to seek rents. The paradox here may be that too little security about one's position in power can be as corrupting as too much security.

The impact of high turnover in governments seems to again have had a paradoxical effect on the formulation of economic policy. At one level, political instability (India has had five Prime Ministers and seven coalition governments in the last decade) has been helpful in promoting economic reforms. An experience of power has forced most parties to confront the economic realities, albeit with varying degrees of enthusiasm. Frequent changes in government and the imperatives of coalition government have helped produce a convergence of economic ideologies across much of the political spectrum. This however makes it difficult for voters to assign accountability since in terms of economic ideology the voters are faced with Hobson's choice.

But while instability has produced greater economic convergence, it also poses a serious impediment to inter-temporal accountability. A government may give free water and electricity to current consumers at the expense of future ones. Ecological issues pose the most obvious challenge for inter-temporal accountability; but so do issues of public investment in capital projects. Policy inaction on two issues discussed below pose a serious long-term challenge for India. These issues are examples of the consequences of lack of inter-temporal accountability mechanisms that have only been exacerbated by India's political structure.

First, with markets rather than the central government emerging as the principal allocative mechanism for investment, states which have been progressive, administratively transparent, and pro-reform have been attracting more investments. In contrast with the past when the potential for some states to grow faster than others was circumscribed by federal policies, thus reducing overall growth, India seems to be moving in the opposite direction with the variance in growth rates across states increasing. This has its own implications, some positive, some less so, as faster growing states become resentful of the handicaps posed by slower moving states. As a result, regional inequalities are widening, whose long-term political consequences on the Indian Union are troubling. The states that are falling behind are also among India's largest and poorest states (principally in the North and East) which are locked into a state-level political equilibrium that is unlikely to change soon in the absence of shocks to the system. A looming fiscal crisis and state bifurcation may, however, break this equilibrium.

Second, the reforms have largely bypassed the rural sector, where the two-thirds of India's population and poor live. One of the puzzling trends of the post-reform era is the lack of a significant trend in the levels of poverty and inequality. Robust growth does not seem to have translated into a commensurate decline in poverty, but neither does it seem to have led to a marked increase in inequality. The most recent analysis of poverty trends seems to indicate that the mid-1980s were a significant watershed in the evolution of living standards in India. Both rural and urban poverty rates declined markedly between 1973–74 and 1986–87, but nothing comparable has occurred since then. The stagnation in rural poverty seems largely attributable to the lack of growth in agriculture, while the moderate growth in urban living standards appears to account for the decline in urban poverty measures. The post-reform record on inequality seems marked by an equal absence of a significant trend in inequality in either sector, although inequality at the national level is likely to have increased as a result of greater urban-rural disparity.

Low growth in the rural sector has been hampered by declining public investment, which itself is a victim of India's inability to limit government consumption that has spilled over to stubbornly high revenue and budgetary deficits. Aggregate states' gross fiscal deficit has increased from 2.8 per cent of GDP in 1991–92 to 4.3 per cent of GDP in 1998–99. These figures underestimate the magnitude of the problem due to the rising contingent liabilities by way of sovereign guarantees. These off-balance sheet liabilities, nearly 10 per cent of GDP, exceed the fiscal deficit and are equivalent to about one-eighth of the total debt (domestic and external) of the federal and state governments taken together. Article 293 of the Constitution of India makes it mandatory for state governments to seek permission from the federal government to borrow. As a result, the states appear to

have been subject to a hard budget constraint. Article 293, however, merely advises state governments to exercise self-restraint in extending repayment guarantees for loans mobilised by enterprises owned by it. Faced with mounting revenue deficits that have crowded out budgetary capital expenditure, state governments have increasingly used this constitutional loophole to extend guarantees and move to off-balance sheet financing. The cumulative effect has been a slowing down of public investment. The states' contingent liabilities now exceed those of the federal government. However, the latter's liabilities are also understated if the contingent pension liabilities resulting from the Pension Act of 1995 (which moved the pension provision from defined contribution to defined benefit, contrary to the worldwide tendency in the reverse direction) are factored in. In the absence of new institutional mechanisms, such as a statutory cap on the fiscal deficit through a Fiscal Responsibility Act (which has been mooted) or a massive crisis, the structure of Indian politics is likely to prevent any sharp improvement in India's fiscal health. At the moment the imperatives of coalition formation seem to be weakening rather than strengthening inter-temporal accountability mechanisms.

The closer link between social cleavages and party identification has created a fragmented party system which has in some ways enhanced representation. At one level it has allowed hitherto marginalised groups like the backward castes and scheduled castes more effective voice through their own parties. The fact that no single national party is dominant and that the formation of government depends crucially upon alliances with the smaller regional parties has effectively given regional parties more influence. This has had two beneficial consequences. On the one hand power in the Indian Union has become more effectively decentralised. Second, some small regional parties can, because of their pivotal position in coalition governments, wield inordinate influence over economic policy. In the previous government for instance, the Chief Minister of Andhra Pradesh, whose Telegu Desam Party was a member of the ruling coalition at the Centre, exercised just such influence in the formulation of India's policies in the technology sector. Moreover, smaller parties in the coalition government have effectively vetoed many of the policy ideas of the single largest party in the coalition— the BJP. For instance, largely under the pressure of its coalition partners, the BJP has had to drop not only its fundamentalist agendas but also its protectionist economic policy. On the other hand many smaller parties have been able to block rolling back subsidies and other discretionary grants to the states. The point is this. Policy formulation and the character of accountability is crucially determined by the electoral system, the character of the party system and the contingencies of coalition formation.

All this is not to minimise the importance of elections but emphasise that elections are an inherently blunt instrument of control. Their effectiveness as mechanisms of accountability are contingent, fraught with unintended consequences and the incentives they impose upon policy makers need to be understood in more precise ways.

II

The Unresolved Question

The reform and regulation of the ways in which elections are financed remains the single most difficult challenge for Indian democracy. Arguably, all attempts at reform will come to naught unless the question of political finance is tackled head on. The imperative to raise money for elections, combined with unrealistic, unworkable and unenforceable existing laws on campaign finance produce profound distortions in the working of Indian democracy. The need to raise funds for elections is one of the primary motivations for collecting an estimated 70,000 crores over a five-year cycle of all elections. With politicians almost required to use their office to raise such funds the entirety of government becomes one giant edifice to collect rents. At least some of the roots of corruption lie in the imperatives to raise finance in a context where the cost of elections is high, the legitimate rewards of office low, the chances of re-election uncertain, and the organisational effort required to mobilise voters is massive. The repercussions of the existing ways of collecting campaign finance are felt across all areas of public life.

Most democracies attempt to regulate election finance in four ways. Democracies can limit political expenditures of parties, they can place limits on private donations and contributions, they can offer public funds for contesting elections, or they can introduce measures that bring about transparency in the process of generating funds. The idea behind the last measure is not so much to restrict fund raising activities, as it is to provide information to the voters on who is raising money from whom.

The Indian effort to regulate election finance has largely concentrated on limiting election expenditures. But this measure has proved to be self-defeating for a number of reasons. Given the complicated logistics of most constituencies a ceiling of 15 lakh rupees for parliamentary constituencies and 6 lakh for assembly constituencies are arguably unrealistically low. The state also, as the recent report of the National Commission to Review the Workings of the Indian Constitution reiterates, continues to try and micro-manage campaigns by fixing the length of the campaign and so forth. Most of these measures are ineffective in regulating campaign finance.

The attempts to place limits on private donations, by for example allowing companies to contribute up to five per cent of their profit to political parties has proved ineffective for a number of reasons. Most importantly, under the present legal dispensation both the donors and parties have very little incentive to reveal the extent of their donations. Monitoring and enforcing limits on individual contributions is impossible in the absence of any kind of transparency. But the challenge for the Indian state is that the widespread opaqueness of our financial system all across the board makes it difficult to monitor such financial flows. Arguably we cannot get realistic campaign finance reform unless whole sectors of our economy like real estate markets that generate 'black money' and the system of taxation that more effectively scrutinizes the flow of money that makes elections possible is reformed. But we are in a vicious circle where we will not get reform of the state in part because of the need to generate rents to finance elections, and an unreformed state will continue to be ineffective in regulating election money.

The third means of regulation, state financing of elections has not been much tried in India. In almost all democracies except the US and UK, the proportion of public financing of elections has been consistently rising in relation to private funding. The costs of public financing are not as high as might seem. Lok Satta, the only organisation that is doing imaginative work in this area, has circulated a proposal that evolves a complex formula for public supplement of private funding, that would cost less than 250 crores per election based on an assumption that the total ceiling for each constituency will be somewhere in the region of 50 lakhs. The good news is that as percentage of GNP, the costs of elections is probably going down substantially and public funding, properly instituted, is not entirely unaffordable. Public funding can take not only the form of direct grants but also indirect subsidies like free radio and television time. The challenge for public funding however is this. It appears from comparative experience that public funding, ironically, works better in systems that are already effective and transparent to some degree. For public funding formulas to be effective certain conditions have to be met. First, public funding must encourage rather than supplant private funding, because if seen as a substitute for private funding it becomes prohibitively expensive. Second, public funding should be fair and transparent. It should not be a means for already existing party oligarchies, which usually derive their power from their ability to raise funds, to strengthen their hold on parties. In short, to be fair, public funding presumes that political parties are transparent, well run and considerably democratic in their internal workings. Most Indian political parties have no effective intra-party democracy, and in the absence of serious reform in party structures, public funding is unlikely to yield good results. Third, one should not overestimate the degree to which public funding can be a panacea. Every single European country with public funding of elections, from Germany to Italy and Belgium has continued to experience financial scandals relating to politics.

The fourth prong of regulation, transparency, has been very weak in India as well. Although party accounts are supposed to be audited regularly, these have proved to be an ineffectual check on party finances. Much of the recent effort of bodies like the Supreme Court and the Election Commission has been to try and strengthen the disclosure requirements for political parties and candidates. Declaration of a candidate's assets, regular scrutiny of part accounts that require the disclosure of all donors who contribute more than 10,000 rupees, and the filing of party tax returns are all steps in the right direction. A tax return is hardly the most reliable register of the true well being of most Indians. Inducing transparency in election finance is parasitic upon the state being able to better regulate other non-electoral institutions that impinge upon election finance.

Any sensible strategy for regulating campaign finance will have to work on all these four dimensions simultaneously and bring them together in sustainable, realistic and imaginative ways. Unfortunately, comparative experience suggests that there are no quick legislative remedies. Indeed campaign finance reform all around the world is replete with an ever expanding universe of dead letter rules that cannot be enforced, though effective disclosure and transparency norms certainly help. The real issue is—can the costs of getting elected be held down? A substantial amount of spending on the logistics of elections is inevitable and we ought to be realistic about these expenses. But evidence from India suggests that a substantial amount of campaign resources go into placating various constituencies, a polite way of describing 'vote buying'. Ironically the costs of elections increases as the distinguishing characteristics of individual candidates matter less and less to elections. What increasingly distinguishes one candidate from another, is mobilisational and fund-raising capacity, not ideology or personal competence. So long as elections remain largely about the former, campaign costs will continue to soar. But unless a genuinely creative solution to the problem of campaign financing is found, money will continue to usurp politics, or in Gibbon's words, "corruption will remain the one infallible sign of our liberty".

Towards a Post-democratic Age?

One of the more profound paradoxes of democracy in our times is this. On the one hand democracy as a practice has gained unprecedented legitimacy. The assertiveness of civil society, the pressure to devolve power in different ways directly to the people, the greater politicisation of social existence, demands for representation in the structures of power all suggest a great clamour for democratisation. On the other hand, there have been far reaching changes in the structures of governance, all across the world that are effectively transferring greater power and legitimacy to non-elected institutions. The prestige, authority, power and faith in the efficacy of institutions that are not subject to popular authorisation, like courts, independent central banks, utilities commissions, market regulators, independent human rights commissions and transnational institutions is almost unprecedented. We are living through what might be called a post-democratic delegation revolution. If delegation is understood as an authoritative decision that transfers policymaking authority and powers away from established representative institutions like legislatures and executives to non-elected institutions, then we are indeed in the midst of a subtle constitutional transformation.

During the last decade or so India has also created an unprecedented number of statutory bodies that are designed, in theory at least, to have greater immunity from legislative influence and control. The Courts are playing an unprecedented governing role in Indian politics. The number of transnational treaties and agreements that bind Indian legislature are multiplying rapidly and there is great clamour to free even more agencies like the CBI from government control all together.

The increasingly widespread practice of constitutional democracies to remove certain types of policy choices from the direct control of electorally accountable office holders is motivated by a variety of concerns. Delegation represents widespread disenchantment with the mechanisms of electoral accountability. Electoral accountability is, on this view, too blunt an instrument with which to secure the public good. Accountability itself has different components—transparency, representatives, responsiveness and the power to sanction misdeeds. Electoral accountability may not always secure all dimensions of accountability effectively. For example, the fact that an institution is representative does not automatically make it responsive; transparency is not the same thing as effectiveness. In some instances, delegation of powers away from ministries can apportion the lines of responsibility more clearly and secure more effective accountability.

Second, policy choices involved in modern economies often require high level of technical complexity; good decisions depend on expertise and non-elected bodies empower experts. Third, independent agencies and delegation by treaty also allow governments and legislatures to make credible commitments by shielding decision making from short-term pressures and lobbies. These agencies provide political cover for taking decisions that politicians have no incentive to take, but which are nevertheless in the public good. Fourth, a greater number of independent agencies provide more effective checks and balances. If the executive fails for instance, the human rights commission or the courts can intervene; if politicians are economically imprudent, a host of regulatory agencies can ensure that the economy is not brought to ruin entirely. The separation of powers that the proliferation of non-elected institutions represents can be seen as a kind of insurance policy, where we bind ourselves to protect us from the worst possibilities of electoral politics.

Many of the considerations that lie behind delegation to non-elected institutions are compelling, and in many instances they help ensure that government by the people is indeed government for the people. But it would be stretching logic to pretend that the proliferation of delegation is synonymous with democracy itself. Indeed, the constitutional revolution of delegation raises profound questions about democracy itself.

Delegation often has serious disadvantages from a democratic point of view. One of the virtues of democracy is that we can sanction those who act in our name. The more independent an agency, the more difficult it is to subject it to any kind of sanction, as the case of the Courts has demonstrated. Democracy, to simplify somewhat, is a means of authorising officials to exercise power over us. By what means do non-elected institutions derive their authority? There are two possible answers to this question neither of which is wholly satisfactory. The first response is to say that these institutions become authoritative by the quality of their decisions, by the output they produce. So long as the Courts do a good job of protecting rights, regulators of taking economic decisions, they are legitimate. But this response often begs the question of whether there are independent criteria of what counts as good decisions.

A second response says that since these agencies and statutory bodies are themselves creations either of the Constitution or Parliament, there is no problem about their authority. But the difficulty is that often these institutions are designed in ways that they are not directly accountable to Parliament. And the ministry in whose jurisdiction the relevant agency comes simply denies that it has any responsibility, since after all the relevant agency is independent. So on the one hand Parliament cannot easily hold RBI or SEBI directly accountable; yet the Finance Ministry is not responsible for their decisions either. We have yet to settle on a clear doctrine of how the democratic accountability of these agencies is to be secured. In the case of international treaties, most of the treaties India has been signing do not have prior parliamentary approval and become almost a *fait accompli* for the legislature.

In some cases delegation has impeded the ability of legislatures to make the relevant trade-offs. If everything from the price of utilities to the technology to be used in broadcasting, from interest rate management to telecom regulation falls outside the ambit of legislative power, can legislatures make the relevant trade-offs that they have been authorised to do so? The virtue of independent delegation is also its vice—it increases the number of veto points. In a curious kind of way we now have the possibility of politicians being penalised for decisions that they did not take and were powerless to control. If tomorrow the electorate decides that it is unhappy with utility pricing or something, it is very likely that politicians might be blamed simply because of the fact that they are the only ones subject to popular sanction.

None of these concerns should be taken to imply that all forms of delegation to non-elected institutions are unjustified. But delegation to non-elected institutions is increasingly posing a challenge to the central tenets of democracy. Representation is the central axis of a modern democracy. Decisions have to be linked to the citizens by a chain of authorisation. In a democracy we organise collective power through our representatives, and these representatives are also subject to sanctions we impose upon them. The difficulty is that non-elected institutions are often not representative, the link between their authority and citizens is so remote that it is often meaningless, and their independence from the legislature and executive alike makes it difficult to sanction them. The proliferation of non-elected institutions could lead to a situation where government have very little incentive to mobilise consent, since decision making power has been delegated. The proliferation of such delegation might mean that there is no representative body entrusted with integrating different spheres of social and economic life and making the relevant tradeoffs. To each agency its own power becomes a new principle. And there might be competing sources of law as we are already witnessing in the contest between legislatures, courts and transnational bodies, all of which are becoming sources of law in their own right.

Many countries undergoing the delegation revolution have taken steps to ensure a greater modicum of democracy in delegation. For instance, parliaments of New Zealand, Australia and Great Britain have democratised treaty negotiations in a manner that ensures that treaties do not bypass Parliament. Or they have, in some instances, made independent agencies directly accountable to Parliament. The future of representative government requires that we think imaginatively and constructively about these issues, acknowledging both the necessity of delegation, but also the challenges it poses for democracy. It does not help to have a Parliament that is sleepwalking its way through these profound changes in the structure of governance. But representative government is too precious to be sacrificed to either of the unsubstantiated claims of experts.

Economic Policy, Public Action and Accountability

The manner in which economic policy functions in India's electoral process is complex. Probably the single most important puzzle at the heart of any study of accountability in India is the following. Why has India's record at poverty alleviation not been better? Why is there less pressure on the government to deliver a whole range of crucial services like health and education? These two questions are analytically distinct—the first can more readily be explained by poor policy choice; the second demands closer scrutiny. These puzzles are compounded by the fact that an old explanation for India's lack of failure in this respect does not hold. This explanation suggested that either the poor do not vote, or some form of coercive or clientalist relationship prevents them from voting on their true preferences. In the Indian case where there is now reasonably disaggregated data available on voter turn outs, the picture is exactly the opposite of what this explanation hypothesises. First, the incidence of coercion exercised by local elites in voting matters has gone done significantly and social relations have been politicised to the extent that old fashion clientalist relations are very difficult to sustain. Second, the poor in India have tended to vote more than the middle classes and the rich, rural turnouts are better than urban turnouts and in recent years lower and backward castes have voted more than upper castes (Yadav, 1997). Yet they have not been able to extend concerted public pressure in areas of health and education. One measure of this is captured in government spending statistics on health and education. In education, the central and state governments spent 4 per cent of GDP for all levels of education in 1996-97 or 13.4 per cent of total government expenditures, which is below the developing country average of 17.5 per cent for all developing countries. India's public spending on health is very low—1.2 per cent of GDP which places India amongst the lowest quintile of countries. There is wide variation amongst Indian states on these matters. State expenditures on education for example range from 3-7 per cent of GSDP and from 16 to 29 per cent as a share of total state expenditure. The reach of public criticism has been much less effective in Indian democracy when the deprivations people face fall short of the extreme hardships that say famines signify. The state's failures in these areas are well known. What is less well understood is the demand side of the equation. Why is political mobilisation on *these* issues less effective? Can one just assume that this is simply a product of the state's failure or is there something about the structure and ideologies in civil society that impedes the formation of effective demand for health and education?

There are complex reasons for this phenomenon that will bear serious scrutiny. First of all, as with any claim with respect to India, there is wide regional variation in the mobilisation for collective action on these issues. We would submit that empirically this is the least well understood area in Indian politics and our understanding of the ways in which governments can be held more effectively accountable hinges on an answer to this question. The range of factors that influence the extent of collective action for the provision of public goods is complex. It has been shown for instance that the Indian states whose land distribution arrangements have historically displayed the greatest inequality also have the lowest collective action for public goods (Drèze and Sen, 1995; Kohli, 1988). Two large North Indian states of UP and Bihar both have the most inegalitarian land distributions and the greatest political apathy compared to the southern states of Kerala, Karnataka, Tamil Nadu, etc. The latter states historically had more egalitarian land tenure systems and were also the beneficiaries of more effective land distribution after independence. It appears that some degree of redistribution of assets is necessary before demands for public provision become more effective. The second key factor facilitating collective action for public goods seems to be the existence of a cadre based party of the Left that can facilitate mobilisation on class lines as Kerala and West Bengal have had. These parties have been instrumental in not only producing land reform but also increasing public provision (Sen and Drèze, 1998; Kohli, 1988). Third, Indian states which have had a longer history of social mobilisation, such as resistance to caste discrimination are also more successful in collective action for the provision of public goods. Again, South India, which has had a much longer history of anti-upper caste movements compared to the North provides good evidence for this point. It seems that anti-upper caste movements in the South were a precursor to more effective mobilisation for tenancy rights, land reform and education (Menon, 1994). It has been very

clearly demonstrated that India's poor record in the provision of education and the abolition of child labour owes something to the ritual stratification that caste produced (Weiner, 1985) and a history of anti-caste movements seems to lead to better public provision in general. North India has only recently begun to experience such anti-caste movements and their outcomes are still indeterminate.

Perhaps this is an appropriate point to raise, a question that needs more study in the Indian context. There is some evidence in the literature that in terms of the relationship between class and ethnicity the best results are obtained for the poor when mobilisation along class and ethnicity coincide rather than clash. The former, termed "ranked ethnic systems" (Horowitz, 1985) seem in democratic settings to produce the most effective forms of collective action for the poor. The distinction between ethnicity and class does not mark the politics of all societies but in India these have been seen as rival locus of mobilisation. Ethnicity in general has been seen to be an easier locus of collective mobilisation. Mobilisation along class lines alone has on the whole been much less effective than instances where class and ethnicity have co-mingled. The Communist Party of Kerala was more successful because it was both an anti-upper caste movement and could draw upon a *repertoire* of caste symbols, as well as a class movement.

It is not the case that the exercise of franchise has not had a significant impact on economic policy and poverty alleviation programmes. But the nature of this sort of accountability has to be studied more carefully. The three ways in which that impact is visible are the following. As Sen has very effectively argued, India's ability to avoid significant famines in post-independence era has largely been a function of democratic pressures being brought to bear upon government. Second, in comparative terms India's aversion to inflation has been attributed to the workings of electoral politics. Inflation has been the simplest measure of people's current well being; its impact is direct and widespread. Third, politicians have preferred what are known as 'direct' methods of poverty alleviation. It has been shown that in the case of food and agricultural subsidies there is a very direct link between increases in subsidies and electoral cycles (Chhibber, 1999). Of course direct methods of poverty alleviation are preferred for many other reasons. Direct monetary transfers are administratively easier to enact than long term structural changes; they can be more easily targeted at the discretion of politicians. But cumulatively the kinds of pressures that have been brought to bear through the franchise suggest that immediate benefits are electorally more salient than long time horizon changes.

Surveys done on the electorate's knowledge of economic liberalisation point to one crucial fact. While the electorate seemed to have detailed knowledge of pivotal *political* events like religious mobilisations and ethnic conflict, they gave less evidence of being aware of economic liberalisation. In 1996, half a decade after the initiation of economic reforms about 32 per cent of the urban electorate claimed to have heard of them, while only 12 per cent of the rural electorate knew of the reforms (Yadav, 1997). In some ways this is understandable—industrial policy regimes, tariff rate reductions, exchange rate policies have only very indirect impact on the bulk of the electorate. These electoral pressures explain why by and large the first generation of economic reforms undertaken in India have stayed away from critical areas that could have engaged mass politics—agriculture, labour market reforms, privatisation and restructuring of state bureaucracies (Varshney, 1999).

Accountability and the Politics of Reform

What about dominant interest groups' ability to impede accountability. There are, after all powerful groups who hold governments accountable *to* them, in the sense that these social groups have policy preferences and the power to sanction politicians. It is commonplace that politicians, even when not self-serving, need to raise resources. In order to win they have to raise resources. It is precisely because voters do not care about policies that do not have a direct or only a marginal impact on their welfare that politicians can sell to interest groups policies that, taken individually, inflict only a small cost on most voters but which allow politicians to raise resources. A traditional explanation of India's poor economic performance was precisely this—a tripartite collusion of rich farmers, public sector professionals and industrial capitalists exercised an effective lock over governments policy. None of these classes was powerful enough to singly dominate the state, while their combined fears about the consequences of altering state policy meant that change was structurally inhibited (Bardhan, 1985; 1988; 1993).

This powerful and influential explanation accounted for much stagnation in Indian economic policy. But this explanation has been less useful in thinking about the process through which India has, during the last decade undertaken a serious economic liberalisation programme. Bardhan's explanation suffered from two weaknesses. First, it was too deterministic and underestimated the political room for manoeuvre possessed by political elites. Second, Bardhan failed to follow through on the implications of his own argument. Bardhan posed the following question, "Why the dominant classes, who have so much to gain from long term economic growth, do not pull together in their long run collective interests and cooperate in dredging the silted channels' of surplus mobilisation and investment which were in the danger of being overrun by patronage and subsidies?" His answer was that it was difficult to mount collective action in large and heterogenous coalitions and hence elites took on action in changing the system in a way that would lead to their long-term interests. But the logic of this argument can also be turned on its head. This argument would also suggest that when government does take action it would be difficult to mount collective resistance against its policies. In other words, the very phenomenon that explained stagnation might also

explain how government could, with artful manoeuvre, initiate change. Governments can initiate change and it is often difficult to mount resistance against it. Governments can exploit divisions between interests and take advantages on the ambiguities that surround the effects of policy to seize the initiative (Jenkins, 2000).

But these changes can be taken only under certain conditions that underlie the character of policymaking in India. First, the reform programme has succeeded to the extent it has largely because it has been gradual and has noticeably involved a major public debate. Observers of parliamentary debates over reforms have noticed that most governments have not acknowledged that they were undertaking radical action. A broad vision that underlies the reforms has seldom been argumentatively justified or explained to the public. In fact the rhetoric of continuity is more pronounced than the acknowledgement of disjuncture. On the one hand, this makes the government's intentions less transparent to the public and in that sense renders it less directly accountable. On the other hand, by avoiding debates on ideological fundamentals, the government also avoids a potentially damaging polarisation. This allows it to oddly enough, be more responsive. Second, gradualism has allowed governments to avoid shocks. The one sense in which economic reforms can become an issue in mass politics is if they lead to a major shock to the economy. Indian politicians and policy makers have by and large been risk averse, in part because electoral compulsions force them to avoid policies that might potentially be experienced as a shock. It would be a fair conclusion to say that in the Indian case electoral accountability renders policy makers risk averse.

Third, policy makers are risk averse in another sense. Politicians are concerned less with the aggregate consequences of economic policy and more with the impact these have on their distributional coalitions. They like in other words to manage the distributional consequences of their policies. This does not mean that they are averse to change. What it has implied in the Indian context is that politicians will use policy to solidify new constituencies and raise resources from new sources before they go against the interests of old ones. The decisive determinant of reform in the Indian context is not, a) whether the state is granted autonomy from social forces or as Haggard and Webb put it the "key parts of the bureaucracy can be insulated from public pressure", or b) whether the elites can be incorporated within the structure of the state to facilitate systematic negotiations on economic policy and produce a consensus as was the case in Japan, or c) whether an economic ideology can be politically sold to the electorate at large. The key question is whether policy makers can use policies to generate new groups that can sustain reform and devise creative compensatory schemes that can allow for divide and rule tactics to flourish. The critical hypothesis is that neither structural constraints, nor open accountability, nor electoral pressures, but political creativity determines the nature of policy reforms in India.

Decentralisation and Accountability

To the extent that democracy is a system of popular control over decision making, an inverse relationship between size and direct participation, means that popular control over decision making is likely to decline with expanding size. This does not mean that citizens do not exercise control on their agents, but rather that the process is more indirect. Small size allows for more direct participation and greater representation of individual (as opposed to group interests). Moreover, the smaller the unit, the greater the likelihood of homogenous preferences which in turn allows for greater collection action driven accountability. Moreover, since informational asymmetries are often at the heart of accountability problems, the smaller the size the less such informational asymmetries. Small democracies allow for both more local observation of problems on the people solving the problems are actually there, watching and experiencing them—and better communication among citizens and their representatives, since there are less of them.

On the other side of the ledger for size are economies of scale and scope. Another advantage, the greater specialisation of skills that comes with size, has become less important with international trade. And while diversity may hamper collective action, it could enhance creativity—the homogeneity of Tokyo cannot match the creativity of the Tower of Babel that is Silicon Valley. Moreover, size diversifies risk. Small democracies are more prone to single-party dominance, which carries with it the risks of any monopoly.

To the extent that the evidence on the benefits of centralisation *versus* decentralisation favours the latter, an important question remains. What is the optimal size and number of subnational units that would balance efficiency, representation and accountability? Consider for instance that India with four times the population of the US, has half as many states. Would India's economy and democracy be enhanced if the number of states were to increase? If decentralisation is good, transferring greater power from the federal government to more rather than less states seems preferable to the present situation of a small number of states over whose jurisdiction runs over a vast number of people. What then is the limit to this scenario? If India were to have the same ratio of subnational units to population as in the US, the number of subnational units would have to increase eight-fold. Not only would this make coordination at the federal level much more problematic, but there also appears to be little correlation between the size of subnational units and economic dynamism.

While externalities and scale economies come with large size, the advantages of small size are organisational and informational. Large organisations face three problems—limited human ability to gather and process information, incomplete transmission of information, and the inevitable possibility of human fallibility. Human ability to gather and process information is limited, thus the greater bulk of it involved, the less accurate the decisions based on the gathering and processing will be. Second, transmission of information is inevitably incomplete, so that the more levels between decision makers and information makers, the more 'noise' in the information. Furthermore, there may also be additional advantages that accrue from the inverse relationship between size and the number of subnational units. More subnational units would allow for greater amount of experimentation with different tactics for solving problems, leading to innovation. It would also induce greater competition (on the likes of Weingast's 'market-preserving federalism') among states, with the supposed benefits that accrue from competition. These theoretical questions can be addressed only by more concrete study of the mechanisms of accountability.

The 73rd and 74th amendments to the Indian Constitution have sought to strengthen accountability by decentralising power to the locality more than had been the case in the past. The devolution of power towards local government has been implemented very unevenly and it is too early to say what the results are. But the experience of decentralised governments in states like Karnataka is promising. Local governments ought to be the locus of discussions of accountability. It has been clearly demonstrated that there is a high degree of correlation between the participatory character of local government and the more efficient delivery of public goods like health and education. (For latest on this issue, see Jayal, 2005). The Indian experiment in devolution is striking for one other reason as well. One-third of all seats for these councils will be reserved for women, which makes it the largest reservation scheme for the representation of women anywhere in the world. Again, it is too early too tell what the precise implication of these reservations will be; much will depend upon what other changes are introduced to complement this enhanced representation. But despite the slow nature of the process, the reservation of seats for women in local government is showing palpably that enlisting women's agency in the political process directly will have a substantial impact on politics and accountability in India. This topic will bear further exploration in the near future.

What were the key features of the change brought about by the 73rd and 74th amendments? The bills retained uniformity in the number of tiers across different states. Only the smaller states with population below two million were exempted from this structure. There is now a three-tier structure (village, intermediate block/*taluk*, and district) in large states, including those such as Kerala, which, after much experimentation and debate, had chosen to have two-tiers of local government prior to the amendment. The crucial change in the new Acts is the reduction of state government discretion in the holding of elections to local government bodies. Under the new laws, elections to *panchayats* must be held every five years. Elections to constitute new bodies must be completed before the term expires. If a *panchayat* is dissolved prematurely, elections must be compulsorily held within six months, the new body to serve out the remainder of the five-year term. These provisions will prevent situations such as

that in Tamil Nadu, where at one stage *panchayat* elections were not held for 15 years, being repeatedly announced and then postponed by successive state governments. With regard to urban local governments, there is a similar strengthening of the electoral requirements, preventing lengthy supersession of local powers by the state government, and replacing appointed posts with elected ones. Cumulatively, these provisions will make local governments more regular in their functioning.

The 73rd amendment gives considerable attention to the nature of elections for the three levels of *panchayats*. Direct elections are specified for seats at all levels. Seats are reserved for scheduled castes and scheduled tribes in proportion to their population, and offices of chairpersons at all three levels are also reserved in proportion to their population in the state. One-third of the seats and of offices of chairpersons are reserved for women. Chairpersons at the intermediate and district levels are to be elected by the *panchayat* membership, while either direct or indirect elections of chairpersons are permitted at the village level. State level election commissions are to be created to supervise and manage the electoral processes. At the intermediate and district levels, chairpersons of *panchayats* one level below can be made members, as can MPs, MLAs and MLCs (Members of Legislative Councils).

The Act provides for one additional potential avenue of representation and accountability of local government. Each village or group of villages will have a *gram sabha*, comprising all registered voters in the area. The functions of the *gram sabha* are left up to the states, and are not further specified, but the Karnataka Panchayat Act of 1983 provides some indication of how these may function. This Act (now, of course, superseded) provided for periodic meetings of *gram sabhas*, to consider the report of the *panchayat*, proposals for new programmes for village development, implementation of sanitation and drainage schemes through voluntary labour, programmes of adult education, etc.

Another vital feature of the reform is its attention to the financial resources of local government. State governments are expected to provide adequate funds for local governments, through grants, the assignment of tax revenues, and authority to collect taxes, tolls and fees. This will not be entirely discretionary, since in each state a finance commission must be established (with five-year terms, as is the case with the Central Finance Commission) which will determine the principles for providing local governments with adequate resources. This creation of state level finance commissions is particularly significant, since it has the potential to enhance the independence of local governments. The envisaged structure parallels that of the Central Finance Commission, as well as being similar to the provisions of the Karnataka Panchayat Act of 1983. States will retain considerable discretion and control, but the experience at the centre-state level suggests that state finance commissions, though advisory in nature, will have an important role. States will also be responsible for making provisions with respect to the maintenance and auditing of lower level government accounts. The way this scheme is implemented will turn out to have crucial implications. Traditionally the problem with local government has been that it received a significant proportion of its funds by way of discretionary grants. Discretionary grants are not only unpredictable, they effectively relocate power at higher levels of authority. Studies have shown that the more well defined the assignment and sharing of revenues between levels of government the more successful the local governments have been. Kerala is a significant example.

Other aspects of the reform include the creation of a new (11th) schedule in the Constitution, of 29 subjects (including agriculture, animal husbandry, land and water management, irrigation, roads, education, electricity, and welfare programmes) as *panchayat* responsibilities; specific responsibilities for preparing development plans; the creation of district planning committees to consolidate the plans prepared by *panchayats* and municipalities; and additional provisions concerning eligibility for and composition of rural local governments. All of these provisions have been debated, and often criticised, in some detail.

The 74th Amendment, known as the Nagarpalika Act, provides a parallel set of reforms for urban and transitional areas. For areas in transition from rural to urban, *nagar panchayats* are to be constituted, and, for most purposes, are combined with municipalities. The composition of municipalities remains under the guidelines of the states, subject to the population categories outlined in the amendment (5,000 to 10,000 for a *nagar panchayat*, 10,000 to 20,000 for a municipal council, etc.). A noteworthy feature is the legislative creation of tiers within larger municipalities, in the form of wards and zones, with their own committees. As noted above, a key feature of the legislation is the strengthening of local election procedures, with members at the ward and municipal level being chosen by direct elections. The zonal committees are more of an intermediate level, their composition being the chairpersons of the ward committees in the zone.

Many of the provisions of the Panchayat Act, including composition, reservations, duration, and the role of state finance commissions, are directly applied to municipalities in the Nagarpalika Act. Paralleling the creation of the 11th schedule in the Constitution, the legislation also creates a 12th schedule for municipalities, including public health and sanitation, communications, and various welfare services. Law and order are not on this list. Finally, the Act requires the constitution of planning committees at the level of districts and metropolitan areas.

It seems that the strengthening of local government can do two things in the direction of greater decentralisation, greater responsiveness to local preferences, and, hence, greater efficiency, despite an argument that it strengthens the centre by weakening state government control. First, it provides an easier route for channelling central funds directly to the local level. While this may not seem to get away from 'topdownism', it can have two positive effects. It reduces the possibility of 'skimming' of funds as they pass through multiple levels of politicians and bureaucrats; and, furthermore, the political influence equation is different between the centre and a locality, *versus* the centre and a medium sized or large state—no single locality or district matters politically in the way a large entity such as a state can. Thus, two types of influence costs might be reduced. It may also be noted that the more general economic reforms have increased the power of the states, for example, by freeing them to attract private investment, and reducing central control over the location of industrial activity. Obviously this claim needs to be tested more empirically. At one level, the more the layers of government the more potential points there are for corruption. Indeed classically, concern over corruption was used as an argument for centralisation. Manor (1999) argues that though this was his *ex ante* hypothesis, his investigation yielded paradoxical results. But decentralisation 'made the political process much more transparent and the theft of funds and the sale of influence far more visible'. One of the mechanisms by which decentralisation achieves this is that the more the parties that have information about budgets, etc. the more difficult it is to conceal how funds are managed.

There is also arguably still enough monitoring by higher levels of government which retain considerable power over local government—for example, MLAs can simultaneously be members of *panchayats*, and states will set the terms of reference for their finance commissions. Thus, the perception of the 73rd and 74th amendments as weakening the states *vis-à-vis* the Centre is implausible.

The second positive consequence of stronger local government, one that may be more important from the perspective of accountability and responsiveness, is that such governments may be able to raise funds more effectively. While there are always potential economies of scale in raising revenue, the Indian fiscal system has been marked by a greater degree of centralisation of revenue relative to expenditure than in other federations. At the centre-state level, this has meant that states rely heavily on transfers from the central government. This is less true at the state-local level, with 10-25 per cent of urban local governments' funding coming from grants and other transfers. However, while local governments do not rely heavily on external funding, it has often been noted that the level of services that they provide is quite low on average. Expanding the authority of local governments, by giving them a firmer legal status and more certain terms of office, may help in opening up avenues of raising revenue. This will complement the potentially firmer position of fiscal transfers to local government bodies through the working of state finance commissions. In the long run, and if financial markets continue to develop as one would expect, based on the ongoing and proposed reforms in the financial sector, local authorities may also be able to borrow from the market for capital expenditures. One of the chief defects of revenue sharing schemes has been that there have been few incentives

for local cooperation in revenue collection. Distribution of revenues by origin, while it runs some risk of regional imbalance, enhances the incentives to aid in collection.

Expanding fiscal capacity is by itself not sufficient. Fiscal effort also matters. For example, the issues of tax enforcement, of incentives to restructure taxes, and of user charges are critical. Will local governments be any better at this than they have been, and better than state governments in the past? Three things should help. First, the firmer political footing for local government should increase accountability to local constituencies. This will increase the pressure to deliver public goods and services more effectively, and to raise the resources to do so. Second, local governments may now have greater freedom to access and manage their funds—even a seemingly small change such as the ability to maintain funds in local banks instead of the state treasury can provide considerably more effective control, and increase the incentive to raise funds. Third, the small size of local constituencies, relative to the size of states, makes it easier to impose hard budget constraints on local governments, forcing them to look to internal sources of funds. In general the thought here is that the larger the unit, the more power of blackmail it has over higher levels of government. Decentralisation may make fiscal discipline less hostage to political expediency. Fourth and finally, incredible as it may sound, the problem in some of India's poorest states like Bihar and UP has been an underutilisation of funds especially in areas allocated for education and health. In part this may have been a consequence of the fact that information about these funds still does not trickle down to its intended target; hence, there is little effective pressure to spend them speedily. Decentralisation may potentially solve this problem.

None of this is going to be automatic. There are serious issues about the structure of governance than will still need to be thought through. In the case of rural areas, in many cases the *panchayats* will be starting from scratch in developing revenue sources. Again, this will not be easy, but there are successful examples of villages that sustain a high level of corporate organisation when there are net material benefits to be obtained from such organisation. To aid this kind of outcome, several complementary aspects of reform, in addition to political responsiveness and managerial efficiency, will need attention. There is now considerable evidence that the more distant the monitoring agency from the targeted location of particular programmes, the less accountable they are to the intended beneficiaries. One small example illustrates this well. One of the problems in rural schools has been teacher absenteeism. School teachers for government schools were recruited by the state governments and were judged, evaluated, transferred and fired by them. It has been noted that in the case of teacher absenteeism, local populations had not other redress but to approach the state government for disciplinary action. The procedures for doing so were cumbersome, the likelihood of punishment remote and the response time was too long. It has been shown that delegating accountability of government employees to the locality of their targeted beneficiaries (giving villagers the right to recruit and fire school teachers) has a dramatic impact on teacher absenteeism. Madhya Pradesh has made great strides in this area. Again, Crook and Manor's study of Karnataka found that absenteeism amongst government employees decreased considerably after the introduction of effective *panchayats* in Karnataka. Here local accountability enhanced effectiveness.

That the 73rd and 74th amendments have altered the nature of local politics and the incentives governing politicians is without doubt. As we had suggested earlier, the principal problem in the past has been the extraordinarily confused assignment functions between states and local government. Despite having the authority to do so on paper, in practice local governments required a vast array of approvals from the state. Arguably, local elected officials would have more incentives to make sure that projects (infrastructure for example) are carried out than a higher level state bureaucrat or elected official does. Obviously some projects require economies of scale and technical and financial assistance that only the states can muster. Nevertheless, it is true that the absence of regular local government has, on balance, diminished, the incentives that states have to respond to local needs and queries. Almost all studies of local government where these governments have been allowed to function stress that the speed, quality and quantity of responses to local needs increased considerably. Elected councillors were easier to contact at the local level; they had more incentive to pass requests for official action, and the flow of information between locality and the civil servants was greatly enhanced.

Another political benefit of decentralisation may be the following. We know that a credible opposition and the prospect of a viable alternative have an important role in determining the accountability of government. We also know that the larger the unit of governance, the configurations of social cleavages produces more uncertainty about what the alternatives are. James Manor (1998) has argued that, "Decentralisation made the political process much more transparent and the theft of funds and the sale of influence far more visible. A lively two part system ensured that it was not left to citizens to detect and protest against corrupt acts."

Much of the analysis of India's economic reforms and decentralisation has been conducted in separate forums. The latter always invariably focuses on administrative decentralisation—from the centre (the first-tier of government) to the states (the second-tier) and from subnational governments to local governments (the third-tier). This shift, discussed earlier has been pronounced, especially the latter. However, another significant consequence resulting from economic reforms is the decentralisation in economic decision making inherent in greater role of markets. Markets are a decentralised allocative mechanism. Accountability in this case, assuming competitive markets, is based on Hirschman's 'exit' and 'loyalty' principles. If a product or service is unsatisfactory, the consumer exits and shifts

his/her loyalty to another supplier. At least in the case of commercial services, allowing competition and a greater role of market forces, has increased accountability.

Unfortunately, for most of India's population, a host of services are not subject to market forces; indeed, incomes are so low, that even if markets are completely liberalised, a scenario of competitive markets in a wide range of social and public services would not materialise. Nonetheless, just as fears that decentralisation would result in a 'corruption irruption' have proven unfounded, fears that a greater role for market forces would inevitably be inimical for the poor are also exaggerated. For reasons documented earlier, the Indian state is much less accountable to its citizens than is either desirable, or expected, given the deep roots that electoral democracy has taken in India. Wealthier citizens seek out markets for the provision of public services, be it health, education and even security. The poor neither have the resources to 'buy' such services from the market, nor the institutional means to hold the state accountable for the provision of such services, despite the ostensible expenditures by the state on such services. In this bleak scenario, giving direct cash transfers to the poor in lieu of indirect government services, thereby allowing the poor the option of 'buying' public services, either from the state or from the market, might give the poor the critical weapon they lack to press for improved accountability—choice. Either way the prospects for accountability look less than sanguine in the near future.

References

Bardhan, Pranab (1985). "Poverty and Trickle-Down in Rural India", in J.W. Mellor and G.M. Desai (eds.), *Agricultural Change and Rural Poverty,* Johns Hopkins University Press, Washington, DC.

———. (1988). "The Dominant Proprietary Classes and India's Democracy", in Atul Kohli (ed.), *India's Democracy: An Analysis of Changing State Society Relations,* Princeton University Press, Princeton, NJ.

———. (1993). "Capitalist Development and Democracy", in David Copp, Jean Hampton and John E Roemer (eds.), *The Idea of Democracy,* Cambridge University Press, Cambridge.

Chhibber, Pradeep (1999). *Democracy without Associations: Transformation of Party Systems and Social Cleavages in India,* University of Michigan Press, Ann Arbor, MI.

Drèze, Jean and Amartya Sen (1995). *India: Economic Development and Social Opportunity,* Oxford University Presss, New Delhi.

Frankel, Jeffrey A. and Andrew K. Rose (1996). "Currency Crashes in Emerging Markets: Empirical Indicators", *CEPR Discussion Papers* 1349.

Horowitz, Donald (1985). *Ethnic Groups in Conflict,* University of California Press, Berkeley, CA.

Jayal, Niraja Gopal (2005). *Local Governance in India: Decentralisation and Beyond,* Oxford University Press, New Delhi.

Jenkins, Rob (2000). "Appearances and Reality in Indian Politics", *Government and Opposition* 35, (2).

Kapur, Devesh (2000). "India–1999 Review", *Asia Survey,* January-February.

Kohli, Atul (1988). "The NTR Phenomenon in Andhra Pradesh: Political Change in a South Indian State", *Asian Survey,* October.

———. (1998). "India Defies the Odds: Enduring Another Election", *Journal of Democracy,* July.

Manor, James (1998). *Democracy and Decentralization in South Asia and West Africa: Participation, Accountability and Performance,* (with R. Crook), Cambridge University Press, Cambridge.

———. (1999). *The Political Economy of Democratic Decentralization,* The World Bank, Washington DC.

Menon, Dilip (1994). *Caste, Nationalism and Communism in South India: Malabar 1900-1948,* Cambridge University Press, Cambridge.

Przeworski, Adam (1996). "A Better Democracy, A Better Economy", *Boston Review* 21, (2), (April/May).

Rubinoff, Arthur G. (1999). "Conflicting Ambitions in Goa's Parliamentary Elections", in Ramashray Roy and Paul Wallace (eds.), *Indian Politics and the 1998 Election: Regionalism, Hindutva and State Politics,* Sage Publications, New Delhi.

Sen, Amartya and Jean Drèze (1998). *The Amartya Sen and Jean Drèze Omnibus,* Oxford University Press, New Delhi.

Stokes, Susan C. (1996). "Public Opinion and Market Reforms: The Limits of Economic Voting", (Introduction to a special issue, *Public Opinion and Market Reforms in New Democracies*), *Comparative Political Studies* 29(5), October.

Varshney, Ashutosh (1999). "Mass Politics or Elite Politics? India's Economic Reforms in Comparative Perspective", in Jeffrey D. Sachs, Ashutosh Varshney and Nirupama Bajpai (eds.), *India in the Era of Economic Reforms,* Oxford University Press, New Delhi.

Weaver, R. Kent and Bert A. Rockman (1993). "Assessing the Effects of Institutions", in Weaver and Rockman (eds.), *Do Institutions Matter? Government Capabilities in the United States and Abroad,* The Brookings Institution, Washington, DC.

Weiner, Myron (1985). *The Child and the State in India: Child Labor and Education Policy in Comparative Perspective,* Princeton University Press, Princeton, NJ.

Yadav, Yogendra (1997). "India's Democratic Revolution", *India Briefing,* M.E. Sharpe, New York.

4 | Indian Democracy: An Audit

YOGENDRA YADAV

EVER since I received this invitation to reflect on the 'challenges and prospects' of democracy in India, I have been more nervous and tentative than I have known myself to be. Not because the theme is new to me or is something I have not spoken earlier about; I can recall that the title of more than one public talks I have given in recent years was 'Bharatiya Loktantra ki dasha aur disha'. I suspect the theme of this morning's session is not very different from that. Nor do I feel nervous for the other more common reason, of having exhausted whatever I had to say on this subject. The source of my unease lies elsewhere. Any judgement on the future prospects and the challenges before Indian democracy today not only makes strenuous demands on the empirical skills of packing millions of isolated bytes of information into a coherent story, it also presupposes a higher degree of assurance about answering some foundational questions than I have been able to muster.

These foundational questions have to do with the yardstick implicit in any attempt to measure the success or otherwise of the democratic enterprise, something inescapable for any attempt to address the prospects and challenges of democracy in any part of the world. In discussing this theme, I have had to pretend that I know what democracy is, that I can say what it means to advance or regress on the path of democracy (democratisation is the name for this presumably much traversed and well mapped path these days), that I can measure the deficits of the democracy of the day from a vantage point of an ideal that is within cognitive even if not practical reach, that I can spell out a 'roadmap' for democracy reform, just as my learned colleagues can spell out very confidently the roadmap for reforming everything else from electricity and economy to the country itself. I suspect it is necessary to go back to the drawing board and revisit some of the taken for granted assumptions about the coordinates, before we set out to sketch a roadmap. In other words, we need to get our theory right. It seems to me that the challenge of making sense of Indian democracy is as much a theoretical puzzle as it is an empirical task.

This paper does not seek to resolve this theoretical puzzle, except by way of referring to the paradox that informs contemporary thinking on democracy and how that might have influenced our understanding of Indian democracy. After hinting at the possibility of an alternative understanding, I turn to an assessment of the experience of the working of democracy in India for the last 57 years, while being acutely conscious of the fact that the audit report may be contaminated with the theoretical infirmities to which I have made a reference above.

Usually, talking about democracy in India involves application of a presumably global theory to the Indian case. This is as true of the academic exercises conscious of these theories as it is of journalistic and even some practitioners' accounts that do not consciously imbibe these theories. But such is the hold of the established common sense that it seeps through all forms of reflections. The trouble of course is that this theory is itself very narrow. Based on the historical experience of democracy in a very small though privileged part of the globe, this theory threatens to marginalise different experiences and conceptions of democracy in different parts of the world. In many ways this constitutes the central paradox of our times. On the one hand, democracy as a form of government is expanding throughout the globe, thanks to the 'fourth wave of democratisation' in the last decade. On the other hand, our conception of what it means to be a democracy has been shrinking in this period. Gradually a one-dimensional, institutional definition of democracy is taking over the democratic imagination. This imagination privileges form over substance and draws our attention selectively to only the formal or the organised sector of politics to the exclusion of the informal domain of politics that constitutes the substance of democratic political contestation in our society.

The dominant and narrow conception can be described as a 'checklist model' of democracy. According to this model there are some standard institutional requirements to qualify as democracy—if you have these you are democracy, if you don't you are not. This approach treats democracy as if it is a piece of hardware. You can pick it and install it anywhere you want. The dominance of this approach, has marginalised another possible way of looking at democracy, one that treats democracy like software. In its essence it is a language, which must make sense to the users if they have to do things with it. It must be adapted to suit the users' requirements, their taste, and their level of training. In this sense culture is not external to democracy, not one of the 'factors' which aid or inhibit democracy—it constitutes the heart of the democratic enterprise. A more flexible and pluralist notion of democracy alone can enable us to do justice to the rich historical experience of democracy in different parts of the globe.

The dominant perspective on democracy invites us to see the practice of democracy in India as a series of absences or 'lacks'—lack of 'properly' functioning and autonomous democratic institutions (a parliament that hardly transacts its 'normal' business, a civil service that is anything but autonomous, judicial institutions that only intermittently perform the function of checks and balances, and so on); lack of an institutionalised party system characterised by a stable and enduring alignment of voters with political parties (we have, instead, low level of party identification, high rates of aggregate and individual volatility, resulting in high prevalence of party fractionalisation and proliferation); lack of issue orientation and ideology in democratic politics (we demonstrate 'clientalistic' as opposed to programmatic political orientation, parties are pragmatic rather than ideological, electoral competition is nothing but auction of competitive populist promises, citizens are swayed by charismatic personalities); lack of pure interest based political identification and organisations (role of ascriptive identities, ethnicities, politics of caste-community based vote banks, group identification of interest and political preferences rather than individual voting); lack of informed citizenry (low level of popular knowledge and awareness); and lack of popular control over political power (routine anti-incumbency that does not yield much by way of policy outcomes).

Such a reading, that typically invokes the assumptions of the modernisation theories of the 1960s, appears plausible for the game of competitive politics appears similar all over the world and lends itself to easy surface comparison. The familiar format or register distracts our attention from a more fundamental disjunction. The historical conditions in which the game of competitive politics is played are radically different in India. What goes into the making of this game and what comes out of this are therefore so radically different that it is more appropriate to see this as a different game altogether. This difference is not the result of any essential cultural difference or Indian exceptionalism—it is simply the outcome of the historically unique circumstances in which democratic set-up was instituted in India. The sudden opening of the flood gates of universal adult franchise, institution of political equality alongwith entrenched socioeconomic inequality, organisation of political interest by the national movement, existence of the Congress party and the beginning of nationwide political competition in a society that had not experienced such a scale of operation of political power created a unique situation for the unfolding of the logic of political competition. At a still deeper level, it is a function of the structure of public sphere in modern India. The challenge therefore is to capture the specificity of this encounter between the modern structure of formal political choice (instituted through a system of 'free and fair' elections through a given set of rules) and the historically constituted public sphere with its own definition of politics and its patterns of organisation of political interest. This encounter produces some of the apparently unique features of Indian democracy that need to be understood in their specific context and not merely as absence of something.

In order to capture something of the specificity of this encounter, we need to distinguish between the formal and the informal domain of Indian democracy. The formal sector is the one privileged in the dominant reading of democracy. It includes the legal-constitutional design of democratic governance from the President right down to *Panchayat*, but is not confined to these. It also includes the formal instruments of organised politics like political parties and organised interest groups including 'civil society' organisations that seek to guard formal freedom and procedural norms. At the ideational plane it includes the domain of officially articulated ideologies and manifestoes. This formal sector of democratic politics can be contrasted with the 'informal' or the unorganised sector that fill in the void left by the functioning of the formal institutions. This utterly messy aspect of politics is well known among lay and professional students of Indian politics, but is not considered worthy of theoretical attention. The informal domain of politics is noted as an embarrassment rather than a structural attribute of Indian democracy. This 'informal' sector is present at every stage of the game of democratic politics—from the presence of subaltern beliefs in public opinion that do not conform to high ideologies, to the role of caste and other factors in elections and the exercise of state power by political families. An understanding and assessment of Indian democracy must therefore attend to the interaction of the formal and the informal sector of politics.

Establishment of democracy was an invitation by the Indian elite to the ordinary Indians to join them in playing a new game. It is true that the invitation must

not have come as a surprise to keen observers of nationalist politics in the decades prior to independence. In opposing the British rule, the nationalist leaders drew upon the most progressive strands of modern European thinking. No wonder, democracy was an article of faith for them. Besides, the last two decades before independence were marked by intensification of popular movements that gave rise to expectations of self-rule among the lower orders of society. All this left a very narrow range of options for the Indian elite when it came to choosing the form of government. Yet those options were more than is realised now. Pakistan's choice of what in effect was a Viceregal system illustrates the options open then. The establishment of democracy in India was undoubtedly a bold invitation, for the rules and the possible consequences of this game were not entirely clear to the elite, and more importantly, they did not know their guests very well.

The history of Indian politics since independence is the story of how the Indians accepted the invitation and discovered this new game, at first with hesitation and amusement and then with an obsessive fierceness. It is a history of what this encounter did to them and to the game itself. What happened afterwards is not difficult to anticipate. After the initial unease, the guests felt at home in this new setting and then changed the rules to suit their taste. For the first few years everyone felt guilty about demanding language to be the basis of political reorganisation of the federal map of India, but very soon it became an indisputable principle. The invitees now turned their back to the hosts and started enjoying themselves. It was a different game now. It took a life of its own and was played for purposes substantially at variance with the textbook versions or the intentions of the original hosts. The consequences of the game of democracy turned out to be radically different from what anyone had intended or anticipated, throwing up a new set of opportunities and constraints for which there were no well known precedents in the history of democracy in the West.

Half a century ago the decision to establish democracy in a poor, unequal, post-colonial society did not look as courageous as it does now in retrospect. The spirit of the time helped everyone overlook the fact that no other society had successfully taken this path before. Nor has anyone done so since then. India failed to remove poverty or inequality or shake off the cultural burden of colonialism, yet it succeeded in remaining a democracy. In 1947, hardly anyone had thought about this possibility, of democracy being the lone survivor in the family of ideals we set out with. Neither the historians nor the political theorists of democracy had prepared us for this possibility, nor have they done so ever since.

The founding fathers of our democracy, the original hosts to this game, entertained the illusion that the democratic idea will remain intact as it travels downwards. They assumed that the grafted institutions and ideas of western democracy would percolate down in their pure form to the masses. Their understanding was unspoilt by the suspicion that the recipients of these ideas were themselves thinking minds, that they could transform the received ideas just as the elite had done to the doctrines of liberalism. What this understanding did not have, to use the recent vocabulary of social science, was a theory of reception. This was a crucial lacuna, for the success of democracy depended in large measure on recreating the democratic dream in popular imagination, in anchoring the universal ideal in the specifically Indian context. Some of the founding fathers may have entertained a different kind of illusion—that the idea of democracy will be automatically transformed by the people when it travels downwards. In this romantic version the people make democracy speak their language and devise the system best suited to their needs.

The experience of the last five decades confirms neither of these versions. The journey of the idea of democracy in India not only changed the lives of the millions it touched, it also changed the idea of democracy itself in ways more than one. Call it creolization or vernacularisation of democracy, this transformation is at the heart of whatever success democracy has achieved in India. Serious attempt to marry the democratic idea to the popular beliefs, to develop shared protocols with the pre-existing language of the people, is what has distinguished India from other countries where the democratic enterprise never took off.

It is a comment on the imaginative charms of the understanding of the founding fathers of our democracy that Indian politics is still understood as a series of deviations from it, that every deviation is seen as a sign of decline and disorder. This tendency contributes to the predominant way of telling the story of Indian politics. The storyline is simple and powerful. Like all stories of its kind, it has the power to give meaning to any event, big or small, and to supply the yardstick for distinguishing normal from deviation. Like all stories, it looks at things from one vantage point and whispers a moral in our ears. Thanks to its charms and the English speaking elite pedigree of those who publicly articulate ideas about Indian democracy, this narrative continues to dominate the imagination of all the political analysts, academic or otherwise. Implicit in this dominant story of Indian democracy, or for that matter in the contemporary democratic theory, is what may be called a hardware approach to democracy—democracy is above all an institutional mechanism that can be made to work properly in any setting, given the right conditions of installation.

The story of Indian democracy can be told differently. The challenge of understanding India today requires that we tell this story differently. It requires that we treat democracy like a language or a software that cannot even begin to work without establishing a firm protocol of shared symbols with its users. If it has to have a life, democracy must exist in and through the minds of ordinary people, it must learn to work its way through the beliefs and values they happen to have. It is necessary to change our approach, for the palace-eye

view of politics has hidden from us for far too long the story of popular contestation of designs imposed from above, of the participatory upsurge of the lower orders of society, of the less known attempts to weave dreams of social emancipation in the language of modern democracy. It is also crucial to contest the dominant story, for its moral is deeply, if subtly, anti-political.

In evaluating the experience of the last 57 years, one needs to distinguish between two different questions—Has India succeeded in establishing a democracy? And, has the Indian democracy succeeded in achieving its goals? While the first is a question about what democracy is, the second is about what democracy does, or can be expected to do. Both these are inescapably political questions. If democracy is one of the essentially contested concepts of modern social theory, the cognitive entreprise of making sense of democracy, of thinking, writing or doing research on democracy cannot but be inescapably political. The questions we ask, the kind of answers we aim at and the manner in which we go about answering those questions—all these involve choices, choices that are never free of subtle play of power, of various kinds of domination and subordination.

The first question allows a more cheerful answer, if only because of the sad record of most other post-colonial polities which this question reminds us of. If one goes by the baseline definitions of procedural democracy, India is and is likely to remain in the foreseeable future a democracy. In order words, democracy has come to be the 'only game in the town'. And that, as the students of comparative democratisation never forget to remind us, is no mean achievement. This is recognised across the political spectrum in India, including by the harshest critics of the system. A few years ago, when the Communist Party of India (Marxist-Leninist) came overground after years of underground violent anti-system politics and decided to contest elections, they were unwittingly paying a big compliment to Indian democracy.

This is not to say that there are no exceptions to this norm—the experience of Emergency was and must be remembered as the most notable, though not the only exception to this norm. This period showed how fragile the institutional edifice of Indian democracy was. It needs to be remembered that political opposition was silenced very easily, civil services and the judiciary did more or less cave in and that the record of the press and the intelligentsia was far from heroic, notwithstanding later reconstructions. There were of course honourable exceptions in each of these categories. Yet, what brought India out of that phase was not the heroism but something that must be described as the spirit of democracy. Something of that spirit continued to give Mrs. Gandhi a bad conscience and ultimately forced her to call general elections in 1977. It was the same spirit that translated into the loss of popular legitimacy of her regime at least in the north, the epicentre of Emergency's authoritarian excesses.

To say that India is a democracy is not merely to make a statement about the formal constitutional structures of democratic governance that India has retained, and not just in name. More importantly, it is a statement about the presence of the language of democracy in India. India has, to use Shiv Vishwanathan's memorable phrase, "by-hearted" democracy—this characteristically Indian English expression captures so well how Indians have creolized the idea of democracy. They have accepted the western idea of democracy as their own and then proceeded to take liberties with it as one does with one's own things. As a result the idea of democracy has been localised and routinised. Note, for example, the frequency with which the virtually unlimited franchise election is used in settings that do not require it—from academic council of the universities to managing committees of colleges to the chairmanship of the cooperative banks to sports selection committee. Election has come to be the principal mode of settling competing claims to power in the entire public arena. Or witness the ubiquity of protest culture, from matters significant to trivial—collective public protest is an ever present reminder of the belief in democratic rights. In its Indian version the idea has come to shape ordinary Indians' beliefs about citizenship, their political rights and virtues of political participation. It has, above all, come to supply the only valid criterion for claims to legitimate rule and correspondingly the moral basis of political obligation.

The idea is embodied in the political processes which have on balance retained a certain dynamism up to this point. Barring some pockets, the fundamental trend towards greater participation and more intense politicisation has continued to spread the idea of democracy both vertically and horizontally. Competitive politics has retained its dynamic capacity to draw hitherto non-political segments, articulate cleavages and build bridges. Thanks to its capacity to connect itself to the pre-existing social cleavages and to transform them, democracy has taken roots in Indian society.

The idea of democracy also has by now, powerful and reliable carriers. India has a wider catchment area for recruitment of political elite than most of the post-colonial polities. A rough estimate suggests that the number of elected political representatives at one or the other level, from national to the village level, is no less than 3 million. Consequently, there is a large contingent of political actors (at least 10 million including representatives, rivals, hopefuls and also-rans) whose instinct of self-preservation can be relied upon in defence of democracy. The logic of competitive politics has ensured that these active participants do not come only from within the traditional social elite, though they continue to enjoy a larger than proportionate share. There are a large number of parties, though their dynamic capacity and legitimacy has sapped somewhat over the last two decades. Party is no longer a western import; it has merged into the landscape of every village and found its way into practically every Indian language.

Last but not the least, there are the movement groups, non-party political formations and various other organisations of the civil society including many NGOs that have done a lot to deepen the idea of democracy in India. They have taken up causes which do not lend themselves to easy aggregation, demands of groups which are electorally non-viable and issues which are yet to make their mark on the national political agenda. They have kept the spirit of democracy alive as and when the machinery of competitive politics has failed to nourish it.

Lest this description makes democracy look more secure a possession than it actually is, let us also recall the aspects which cause concern for the future of democracy in the procedural sense, even if there is no immediate or imminent danger of its collapse. The formal institutional apparatus of Indian democracy has never been quite strong; the institutions of liberal democracy did not quite undergo the kind of by-hearting the idea of democracy did. It is true that these are still stronger than their counterparts in other post-colonial polities; but they are not the strongest links in the democratic chain, and the very process of democratisation is weakening these further. Claims which cannot be processed in the electoral arena have not found anything like adequate attention. The judicial apparatus never appeared like taking on the load of litigation thrust upon it. Over the years its effectiveness has gone down sharply, especially at the lower rungs where it matters to the people, notwithstanding the recent activism of the upper levels of judiciary. The civil service was always politicised, right from the colonial times. Democratisation has made it more politicised without the corresponding benefits of accountability, for the bureaucracy has still to outgrow its colonial legacy. The combined effect of both these maladies is the denial of an effective rule of law to ordinary citizens.

Intermediary political institutions which were to act as the link between the people and the centres of power have declined considerably. The near collapse of democratic procedures within political parties has left a major void which of late has been filled by managerial style politics and criminalisation. The very autonomy of the political process, which lies at the heart of India's path to democratisation, faces encroachment as a result of the instrumental linkage of political power with the dominant economic interests as also the structural limits created by the integration of Indian economy in the world market. To be sure, all these are not signs of the impending demise of democracy, as many radical democrats would have us believe. But if these trends continue to grow without adequate counter from within the political process, we could be moving slowly towards a 'low intensity democracy'.

As we proceed from a procedural to a more substantive definition of democracy, from a definition focused on a set of institutional inputs to one that demands a desired set of outcomes, the distinction between the two questions suggested above, between what democracy is and what democracy does, disappears.

At this level it also becomes difficult to sustain a universal checklist definition—democracy cannot be defined without reference to the historically specific dreams and ideals which got articulated through this label. This brings us to the four goals pursued by the Indian elite with reference to which the achievements and failures of democratic polity can be discussed. These four goals were—political democracy, national integration, economic development and social transformation.

Achievement and sustenance of procedural democracy itself partly realises the first goal of political democracy. A democracy provides dignity and liberty by simply being there. Given the Indian model, democracy was also the key instrument, the necessary condition, for the realisation of all other goals. In that sense, taking into account the growing limitations mentioned above, Indian polity has achieved something worth defending. It has also met, at least until now in most parts of the territories which fall within its boundaries, the minimal substantive expectation from any regime, democratic or otherwise—protecting its own form and protecting its citizen from complete anarchy. The fact that India has kept at bay even a remote possibility of a military takeover, has successfully defended (at times through severe repressive measures as in Kashmir, Nagaland and Mizoram) the territorial borders it inherited and that most of its citizens do not ordinarily experience complete anarchy is unlikely to enthuse a radical democrat. But it is useful to remember that democratic regimes usually collapse not because they fail to realise the higher ideals associated with democracy but because they cannot be relied upon to meet the bare minimum expectations.

The achievements of democracy as a set of institutions or as a regime does not, of course, satisfy the deeper ethical impulse associated with the idea of democracy. As a political ideal, democracy gives rise to the promise of a community of equals, where the ordinary citizens enjoy true liberty and are governed by none except themselves. The nationalist movement in India had translated this ideal as the goal of *swaraj*, of self-rule in a deeper sense. It would indeed make impossible demands on one's credulity to suggest that Indian democracy has come anywhere close to meeting this ideal. Perhaps no democracy has, but this constitutes a poor consolation to those who accepted the ideal for its ethical appeal. Ever since the famous 'tryst with destiny' speech on the midnight of the 14-15 August 1947, the promise of a community of equals has been an unfulfilled promise. What has come about as a result of the working of democracy is neither a community nor equality. The political community, or rather politicised social communities, it brings into existence are no communities, for their shared life is shallow, if not perverse. The liberty it offers, at least formally, is distributed in extremely unequal measure. The power it brings to the people as an abstraction is rarely, if at all, exercised by the real people. And there are still many people—full citizens of the republic of India—who feel as powerless under this democracy as they did under the British rule.

The performance of Indian democracy in achieving national integration has left a lot to be desired (one can look at the current situation in Manipur to realise this), but as the examples from India's neighbours show, we could have done worse. There are areas (once again, Jammu and Kashmir, Nagaland and Mizoram spring to mind) and periods which constitute an exception, but on balance the Indian elite has stuck to the 'salad bowl' rather than the 'melting pot' model of integration of diversities. That is to say, various communities and aspiring nationalities have not been forced to give up their identity as a pre-condition of joining the Indian entreprise. They have been accepted as distinct and different ingredient in the Indian mix of multi-culturalism. And, again on balance, it has worked—legitimate political articulation of social and regional diversities and the mediation of competing claims through mechanisms of political accommodation has achieved what consociational arrangements for power sharing among different social groups do in other societies.

There have been more than one instances of majoritarian excess. The massacre of Muslims in Gujarat in 2002 with the connivance of state government and the abdication of its constitutional role by the central government is the worst but by no means the only example. The massacre of Sikhs in 1984 was not qualitatively different. But democratic politics seems to have evolved mechanisms of self-correction in this respect—the belated regrets offered by the Congress Party on 1984, the defeat of the BJP in UP after 1992 and the defeat of the NDA in the first national elections after the Gujarat massacre illustrate these mechanisms. In retrospect, effective political accommodation of visible diversities might look like one of the outstanding achievements of Indian democracy in the last 50 years.

But by its very nature, it is an inherently fragile achievement, ever contingent on the skills of the political actors in working out the power sharing arrangements or in allowing the mechanisms of self-correction to work themselves out. This is a lesson well worth remembering as politics of diversities has come under stress in recent years. The most serious challenge to the survival of diversities comes from forces which are less organised, less visible and may not even be considered political in the ordinary sense—forces of cultural homogenisation, the monoculture of modernity and the ideology of nation-state. While there is something to be said for the capacity of democratic politics to deal with the more obvious and political challenges to diversity, it has proved a very weak ally in the struggle against these deeper threats from within.

The promise of social revolution which the democratic invitation always contained has been realised only in parts and in fragments. It is not that democratic politics left the society unaffected. In fact, these 50 years may be recorded in the history of Indian society as years of fundamental transformation triggered above all by the mechanism of competitive politics. At least in one respect it did bring about something of a revolution—the role of ritual Hindu hierarchy as a predictor of secular power diminished dramatically over the last 50 years. While it is a fundamental change, it does not in itself guarantee equality. On balance, unsurprisingly, the functioning of democratic politics has contributed more to a vigorous circulation of elite and to expanding the circle itself than to the establishment of social equality. Its contribution to social equality is mainly by way of politicisation of castes and communities, which then struggle in the secular domain for equality of self-respect.

Since gender divide does not lend itself to easy aggregation on party political lines, competitive politics has failed to bring about the kind of change in this aspect that it has on caste inequality. The representation of women in the parliament and the state assemblies has stagnated at abysmally low level of 8 and 4 per cent respectively over the last 50 years. The national movement may not have had a greater proportion of women's participation but it did ensure that women had a stronger voice in public life. If women's question gets talked about much more in the political arena than their presence in legislatures or voice in political parties would warrant, the principal reason is the politics of ideas to which the growing women's movement has contributed a great deal. Consequently, India has had fairly 'progressive' legislation on gender justice including the provision for reservation of one-third seats in the election of local democratic bodies.

The single biggest failure of democratic politics lies in the non-fulfilment of the promise of material well being. Far from ensuring a life of equal and reasonable comfort for everyone, it has not succeeded even in providing the minimum needs of the people, or in removing the worst indignities or the ugliest disparities in the material conditions of life enjoyed by its citizens. It is true that the conditions of life for most of the people have not deteriorated substantially, that India did achieve some reduction in the proportion of the poor in its population, that the Indian economy is not caught in the impossible spiral of inflation or in a debt-trap. That is perhaps an achievement, at least in comparative perspective. It is also true that a majority of the population feels that its economic condition has improved in the recent past and an overwhelming majority thinks that their children have better opportunities in life than they did. But there is a significant minority—mainly artisan communities and scheduled tribes—that disagrees and has experienced an overall deterioration in the quality of their life. For others too, there has been a visible decline in some of the crucial resources like the availability of public health and the quality of public education.

Democratic politics only provided a formal mechanism for conversion of the potential majority of poor into a political majority which then take charge of the state power to redistribute the material resources and to augment them in such a way as to meet the needs of the most disadvantaged. The functioning of democracy by itself does nothing to ensure that the mechanism is actually used to this end. The other conditions, that of the availability of political agency which can transform the potential majority into political majority (class in itself to class for itself) by winning their political trust has proved to be highly contingent. The Indian model expected politics to provide three crucial elements to what was then called economic development—politics was to provide the blueprint for economic development; it was to give the political will to implement the design in the face of structures of economic interests and it was to create a popular support for egalitarian politics. In practice, it succeeded in providing only the third component and that too partially. The most recent phase of 'globalisation' and liberalisation threatens a retreat from politics of egalitarianism, notwithstanding much hype about *aam adami* during and after the latest general elections. A combination of political amnesia and cognitive paralysis on the question of poverty poses the most important challenge to the ethical impulse underlying the Indian enterprise today.

5 Seeing the State in India

NEERA CHANDHOKE

Introduction

With, 'the acceptance of market liberalism and globalisation', states India's Tenth Five Year Plan (2002-2007) document:

"It is expected that the State yields to the market and the civil society in many areas where it, so far, had a direct but distortionary and inefficient presence...It also includes the role of the State as a development catalyst where, perhaps, civil society has better institutional capacity. At the same time, with the growth of markets and the presence of an aware and sensitive civil society, many developmental functions as well as functions that provide stability to the social order have to be progressively performed by the market and the civil society organisations. It means extension of the market and civil society domain at the *expense of the State* in some areas."

The Tenth Plan accordingly suggests that the role of voluntary organisations, non-profit making companies, corporate bodies, cooperatives, and trusts be strengthened in social and economic development, making them thereby partners in development. The Tenth Plan in effect deepens the thrust, which had originally been initiated by the Seventh Five Year Plan (1985-1990) towards reliance on the voluntary sector as an agent of social development. The Seventh Plan had sanctioned a perceptible shift from government to civil society organisations and to the market in matters of service delivery. Thereupon, whereas the Central Government had earlier spent Rs. 500 million each year through non-governmental organisations (NGOs) on social sectors, the Seventh Five Year Plan increased the funds available to NGOs operating in this sector to Rs. 2,000 million. The ministries that subsequently came to rely heavily on NGOs for the execution of their mandate are the ministries of rural development, health and family welfare, social justice and empowerment, human resource development, and the ministry of environment and forests. In the 1990s, plan allocation for poverty alleviation and social development registered a sharp increase, and expectedly NGOs benefited from all this even as they shouldered more and more functions that hitherto fell within the provenance of the state.

In 1994, the Planning Commission, after a meeting with almost 100 NGOs, cabinet ministers, and high ranking government officers, issued a document titled *Action Plan to bring about a Collaborative Relationship between Voluntary Organisations and Government*. The document stated that the objective of NGOs should be "to mobilise and organise the poor with a view to empowering them, breaking the culture of silence and dependence and converting the lowest strata of society from passive recipients of doles to active participants in the process of planned development". NGOs were accordingly given the responsibility of looking after community forestry, education, health, and other kinds of service delivery. In Delhi the role that is accorded to NGOs by the state government in vital areas is indeed phenomenal. In both the Ninth Plan and the Tenth Plan the state government has stressed the need for the cooperation of, and partnership with NGOs in three crucial areas—public health and medical care, general education, and urbanisation and environmental hazards. It is not surprising that the NGO sector expanded dramatically in the wake of these developments. A recent study by PRIA has calculated that the total number of non-profit organisations in India is more than 1.2 million and that 20 million people work for these organisations either in a voluntary capacity or on salary.

These developments generate some interesting questions of and for India's democracy. Firstly, given that civil society organisations are now partnering the state in crucial areas of collective life, whatever happened to the much vaunted autonomy of civil society? Secondly, the wide preference for NGOs, which is mainly premised on their capacity to deliver services efficiently, is also premised on the assumption that they are apolitical. Have the welfarist dimensions of the democratic state, which historically have been a matter for and of political contestation, been subordinated to technocratic notions of efficiency? Has the messy but often creative world of politics been subordinated to considerations of administrative efficiency? Is the 'ngoisation' of the state and civil society a constitutive part of what John Harriss calls the "anti-politics machine" (2001)? Has the ordinary citizen, in the process been transformed from the *producer* of an activity called politics to being a *consumer* of services delivered by a plethora of agencies? Thirdly, is it possible that governments across the 'third world' have used their own inefficiency in matters of service delivery as an alibi to offload responsibility to the non-profit sector? Creveld suggests that since established sovereign states are often regarded with sullen indifference, even hostility, this "may be one reason why, far from attempting to guard their sovereignty, they are in the process of voluntarily relinquishing it to other entities supposedly more capable of serving the economic needs of their citizens" (1999: 335). Other scholars are more charitable— Simmons for instance is of the opinion that the downsizing of the state combined with the increase in new challenges to development make it inevitable that

NGOs step in to fill in the breach—"willy nilly, the UN and nation states are depending more on NGOs to get things done" (1998: 87). Whatever may be the specific reason for devolution of functions to the NGO sector, the question that confronts us is—has the democratic state instead of strengthening its own institutions for the delivery of vital services—health, primary education, housing, water, electricity, sanitation, and a clean environment—actually liberated itself from obligation to its citizens?

If that is so, then the fourth set of questions belongs to the realm of accountability. For much of the 20th century it has been assumed that the government is accountable to its citizens in vital areas of policymaking and policy implementation; in matters such as the creation of conditions that enable people to live a life of dignity. Now that governments are sharing responsibility with and delegating functions to NGOs, who are NGOs, we may ask, accountable to—their clients, the government, multilateral funding agencies, or northern NGOs who also fund them? As two scholars have pointed out the problems of accountability are particularly difficult when the actors work across great power differences with little shared organisation, when goals, values, ideologies and interests are diverse, ambiguous or conflicting; and when actors differ about who is in charge or responsible for different tasks (Brown and Fox, 1998: 440). When welfare functions become the business of organisations outside the state, which is the regime that is in a position to enforce

accountability? Or if the cluster of welfare functions is dispersed among a plurality of organisations some within the state and some without, resulting in the establishment of what Wood calls the "franchise state" (1997: 87), upon which agency does the mantle of responsibility fall? It is not difficult to imagine that all this leads to bewilderment, even as citizens wonder which organisation to hold responsible for acts of omission and commission.

Fifthly, whatever has happened to the state or at least the state as we have come to be familiar with it for much of the 20th century? For whatever be the discrete charms of the concept of civil society; whatever be the obvious seductions of the idea that one single centralised state should be ideally replaced by networks that enter into collaborative instead of conflictual exchange relationships, it is obvious that the emphasis on civil society belongs to a *post-statist* world of politics. This is simply because the concept gestures towards the decentring of what used to be a single locus of authority and legitimacy—the state. Has the state disappeared? Now obviously the state cannot disappear, but it certainly has been pluralised in as much as it now shares its functions with a number of non-governmental organisations (Chandhoke, 2003).

All these are admittedly important questions for the study of the practices of the contemporary state, however, a seventh question that significantly has *not* been asked in the scholarly outpourings on civil society is—has the state also been pluralised in the collective political imagination? Consider that today the citizen is presented with a number of agencies that are in the business of delivering services and solving problems, from water harvesting to training people for local self-government. Citizens, at least in theory, have been emancipated from the 'paternalistic state' for they can logically approach the non-governmental sector, they can approach private agencies, they can participate in market transactions, and they can engage in self-provisioning or self-help schemes through building associational life in the neighbourhood community. Has all this served to dislocate the state from the centre of political imaginations? Some observers certainly seem to think so. For instance, Kirit Parikh in his overview of the *India Development Report 1999-2000* suggests that there "has been a sea change in ideas about the role of the state and the role of markets in India's economy. Discussions and ideas about how the country should function, that we take for granted today would have been considered profoundly subversive in 1990".

What we need to know is—and this may be a question that is of considerable relevance to democratic theory—does our ordinary citizen also share the perception that a sea change in ideas about the centrality of the state has taken place in India? How does he or she view the pluralisation of the state? What does he or she think about the entry of new actors onto the scene of service delivery? Has the state been emancipated from the responsibilities of welfarism in popular and political imaginations? In sum, given that the entire theory of governance is supposed to be citizen-friendly, we should at some point turn to the

citizen and ask what he or she thinks about the entire process? The answer to this particular set of questions is perhaps best elucidated through reflection on some of the findings of a research project on 'Rights, Representation, and the Poor' that was conducted in Delhi in 2003.[1]

A Note on Methodology

The research team in the course of its fieldwork requested 1,401 inhabitants of the city to respond to a questionnaire.[2] The objective of administering the questionnaire was to allow the team to map out patterns of politics in civil society—to see the magnitude of the various problems people encounter in their existential capacity, to look at how people deal with problems, to explore the adequacy as well as the relevance of formal as well as informal modes of politics, to see whether traditional and familiar practices of representation that were characteristic of mass politics for most of the 20th

1. The survey that was conducted by research scholars affiliated to the Developing Countries Research Centre, University of Delhi, and directed by me, is part of a wider internationally comparative project on 'Rights, Representation, and the Poor: Comparing Large Developing Democracies—India, Mexico, and Brazil'. The project forms part of the programme of 'The Future State' Research Centre at the Institute of Development Studies, University of Sussex, and is funded by DFID. The project seeks to compare the impact of globalisation and liberalisation on the capacities of different poor social groups to obtain political representation and solve collective problems in five cities. The other project partners are John Harriss of the London School of Economics, Peter P. Houtzager of IDS Sussex, Adrian G. Lavalle of CEBRAP and the Pontificia Universidade Catolica de Sao Paulo, Sao Paulo, and K. Nagaraj of the Madras Institute of Development Studies. The five cities are Sao Paulo, Mexico City, Delhi, Coimbatore, and Bangalore.

2. In addition, we surveyed 229 civil society organisations to map out patterns of associational life in the city. The total number of surveys carried out in the city therefore amount to 1,630.

century have slackened, to inquire what is it that people do if older forms have slackened, to explore popular perception of diverse modes of representation such as political parties, religious and caste associations, and NGOs, to inquire whether politics in the world of work and that in residential neighbourhoods diverge, and to evaluate the implications of all this on political awareness as well as on the possibilities for collective action.

The project team distributed the survey across different and distinct categories of residential areas, taking the categories provided by the Municipal Corporation of Delhi (MCD) as a base.[3] The MCD categorises residential settlements on the basis of (a) infrastructure—sewerage, public and internal roads, and public spaces such as community halls, and parks, and (b) services—primary schools, dispensaries, electricity, and water supply, provided to the area. On the basis of the provision of infrastructure and services, the MCD categorises residential areas into (a) planned colonies, (b) unauthorised regularised colonies, (c) unauthorised unregularised colonies, and (d) *jhuggi jhopris* and slums.[4] Six hundred (600) of the 1,401

questionnaires were administered to the relatively poorer sections of society living in b, c, and d categories of residential settlements. Eight hundred and one (801) questionnaires were distributed between the 4 types of colonies on the basis of the ratio between them within each of Delhi's 70 legislative constituencies.

On the basis of some of the empirical data generated by the survey, I seek to foreground the opinions, the interests, and the political activities of those who are governed, rather than concentrate on those who do the governing. In the first part of the essay I detail the responses of the inhabitants to three sets of questions—identification of the magnitude of the problems that people face in their daily life; who do they think is responsible for resolving of these problems, and which agency do they look to for problem solving. In the second part of the essay I look at the historical context, which has arguably shaped people's political expectations. In sum, by focalising the answers given by the respondents to questions in part B, C, and D of the questionnaire, I try to interpret the data in the wider context of state-society relations in India. I also try to figure out what the state means to the ordinary citizen—has it disappeared, or reinvented, or has it been pluralised in the collective imagination? Let us see.

Fixing Responsibility

In much of the literature on NGOs and civil society, it is more or less assumed that whereas the state is marked by the search for power and the market by the

---

3. The MCD administers 94 per cent of the territory of Delhi.

4. Unauthorised colonies refer to the conditions of their origin, in the sale of land by private entrepreneurs without government permission. Some of these colonies have been regularised by the Delhi government; others continue to be unregularised. Whereas planned colonies are provided with the highest degree of infrastructure and services, *jhuggi jhopri* or squatter settlements and slums are provided with either low or no infrastructure and services at all. We carried out 600 of the 1,401 surveys in colonies marked by low or negligible infrastructure and services, on the considered assumption that these colonies are inhabited by the relatively or the absolutely poor sections of society.

search for profit, people turn to NGOs because they 'do good' and because they are un-encumbered and untainted by either power or by greed. In the process, NGOs tend to be seen as organisations that help others for reasons other than profit or power. The question that anyone who lays claim to democratic credentials should be asking is—do citizens hold the same view? Would they rather approach civil society agencies, which are less bureaucratic, which reek less of power and the pomposity that power brings in its wake, which are more responsive to the needs of the grassroots and which are more approachable than the representatives of a distant state? Our research shows otherwise as the responses to three sets of questions illustrate.

The research project began its mapping of the politics of Delhi's civil society by asking people to identify the magnitude of the various problems that confront them in their daily life. It is perhaps not surprising that the identification of the magnitude of a specific problem corresponds closely to the living conditions of the inhabitants. For instance, 41 per cent of the total respondents held that meeting basic needs is a big/one of the biggest problem for them, and 42 per cent said that it was not a problem for them. However, if we look at the distribution of the 41 per cent of responses across colonies, it is clear that the percentage ascends from the inhabitants of the planned colonies to those living in *jhuggi jhopris* and slums. Whereas 13 per cent of people in the former category answered that meeting basic needs is a big/one of the biggest problem for them the corresponding percentage

for the latter category is as much as 73 per cent. In between these extremes, 45 per cent of people living in the unauthorised unregularised colonies, and 30 per cent of those living in unauthorised regularised colonies, identified the meeting of basic needs as a big/one of the biggest problem. Significantly however, across the board, 89 per cent of the respondents were of the opinion that meeting people's basic need is a big/one of the biggest problem for the country, whereas only 1 per cent said that it was not a problem for the country, and only 9 per cent of the respondents felt that it is a moderate or a small problem for the country.

It is of some interest that in response to the question of who is responsible for meeting people's basic needs, the majority of our respondents answered that it is the government's responsibility to do so. And this even if meeting basic needs was not identified as a personal problem for the respondent. Therefore even though only 13 per cent of the people who live in planned colonies identified basic needs as a big/one of the biggest problem for them individually, 80 per cent of the same constituency was of the opinion that it was the government's responsibility to meet basic needs. Equally whereas 45 per cent of the residents living in unauthorised unregularised colonies opined that meeting basic needs was not a problem for them, 83 per cent believed that the government was responsible for meeting basic needs, the corresponding figures being 72 per cent of the population who live in unauthorised regularised colonies, and 83 per cent of the residents who live in the JJ colonies, and slums.

We need to note two issues as of some worth. Firstly, even if citizens feel that meeting basic needs is not a problem for them personally, they seem to be convinced that it is a problem for the country, a nice illustration of the fact that the political is not always the personal. Secondly, even though the citizen today comes face to face with a plurality of agencies, which are in the business of service delivery, it is the government that is held responsible for meeting basic needs. Across the settlement 80 per cent of the respondents opined that it is the responsibility of the government to meet the basic needs of people. Less than 1 per cent said that meeting basic needs is the responsibility of private companies, community association or NGOs. And only 17 per cent of our respondents felt that individuals are themselves responsible for meeting basic needs. Similarly 93 per cent of the respondents held the government responsible when it came to providing medical care to the people, while a negligible percentage that is 2 per cent felt that it is the job of the NGOs to do so, and only 2 per cent responded that it is the duty of community association and health insurance companies to provide health care.

In a similar vein, as many as 69 per cent of the respondents believe that it is the responsibility of the government to control air pollution in the city, compared to the 9.8 per cent who are of the opinion that it is the responsibility of factories and public transport to control air pollution, and 11.6 per cent of people who believe that individual car owners are responsible for controlling air pollution. Only 4.6 per cent of the respondents opined that community associations should do so. As many as 83 per cent of the respondents felt that it was the responsibility of the government to contain violence and crime, and 90.5 per cent of our respondents held the government responsible for ensuring quality services (electricity, gas, water, sewers, roads, street lighting, public transport and garbage collection).

When it came to problem solving, the respondents were asked who they usually approach for solving their problems—political parties, a 'big man' that is caste, religious, and regional leaders, whether they had approached the judiciary, whether they solved problems on their own, whether they had ever participated in demonstrations, public protest, or other forms of direct action, or whether they had approached the government to help them. Our findings show that whereas 28 per cent of our respondents had approached political parties to solve their problems, only 2 per cent had approached the judiciary, only 9 per cent had approached 'big men' for help, hardly 10 per cent of the people had resorted to direct action, and 17 per cent of the respondents had engaged in self-provisioning action. The largest percentage of our respondents that is 36 per cent had approached the government directly. The variation across colonies is not much in this respect, 40 per cent of the respondents in the *jhuggi jhopris* and slums, 35 per cent of the inhabitants of the unauthorised unregularised colonies, 32 per cent of the residents of the unauthorised regularised colonies, and 35 per cent of the residents of the planned colonies normally approach the government for resolving their problems. Out of this number less than 1 per cent had approached the government through their party representatives. About 75 per cent of the 36 per cent who had approached the government said that they had taken the help of their acquaintances and family to do so. Not a single person had asked the NGOs for help in approaching the government.

Figure 5.1

Approaching Agencies for Problem Solving (Value in %)

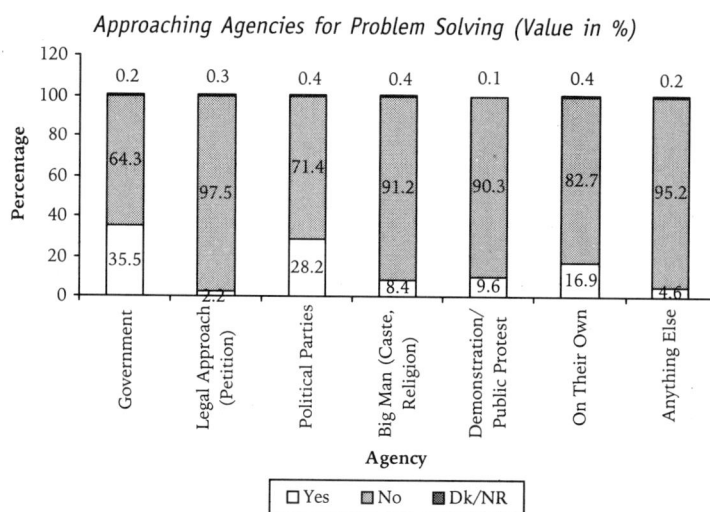

The state, it is evident from our findings continues to loom large in the collective imagination when it comes to providing the basic conditions that enable people to live a life of dignity. It is the state that is central to individual and collective life, despite all the changes that have been effected through the practices of governance. Why is this so? Why do people continue to repose hope in a state that has after all been found wanting when it comes to the delivery of the basic conditions of human well-being. It is true that the 1990s which heralded the

onset of economic reforms also brought a decline in poverty figures. In 1973-74, 55 per cent of India's population fell below the poverty line, this was reduced to 36 per cent in 1993-94, to further fall to 26 per cent in 1999-00. In absolute terms the number of poor declined from 323 million in 1983 to 260 million in 1999-00 (*India Human Development Report*, 2002: 38). The fall in poverty figures has been accompanied by a great deal of improvement in the basic parameters of human development. According to the 2003-04 Annual Report of the Ministry of Health and Family Welfare, infant mortality rate has reduced significantly from 110 per 1000 live births in 1981, to 66 per live births in 2001. The reduction of IMR is reflected in the increase of life expectancy from 54 years in 1981 to 64.6 years in 2000 (Annual Report, 2003-04: 13). According to the 2001 Census, literacy rates for the population above the age of 7 are now 65.38 per cent, compared to 52.21 per cent in 1991 (*www.censusindia.net.in*).

However, it is equally true that human development indicators vary widely both from state to state and from urban to rural areas. Kerala for instance has a literacy rate of 92 per cent which is comparable to that of Vietnam; on the other hand, Bihar continues to have a literacy rate of only 47.5 per cent. Also striking are urban-rural disparities, for instance whereas the literacy rate in urban areas is 80.30 per cent, the corresponding literacy rate for rural areas is only 59.40 per cent. Similarly, whereas the sex ratio according to the 2001 Census has improved slightly for the country in the decade of the 1990s, and is now 933 women per 1000 men compared to 927 women per 1000 men in the 1991 Census, the situation has worsened in Himachal Pradesh, Gujarat, Haryana, Punjab, and Delhi. Oddly enough at the very time Himachal Pradesh has witnessed a dramatic expansion of literacy level, the sex ratio in the state has declined from 976 females per 1000 males in 1991, to 970 per 1000 males in 2001. In effect, the mismatch between the sex ratio and literacy has deeply problematised the postulated link between literacy and women's status. More troublesome is the fact that country has high numbers of hungry people despite the existence of huge buffer stocks of food. And India's record in providing services—sanitation, clean drinking water, electricity, housing, and jobs is even bleaker. Too often, write Devarajan and Shah, "services fail poor people in India-in access, in quantity, in quality" (2004: 907). It is clear that the Indian state has not done too well on the front of social and economic democracy.[5]

The question that arises in this connection is—why do people not look to alternative organisations to help them access the basic conditions of life? After all the return of the concept of the civil society to political theory and to political practice in the late 1980s, had a great deal to do with creeping exhaustion with corrupt and power hungry bureaucrats and political leaders the

---

5. The normal exceptions to generalised ill-being in India are found in the Left governed states of West Bengal and Kerala. Madhya Pradesh has gained entry into the HDR in 2003 because of the advances that have been made in primary education and in *Panchayati Raj* in the state.

world over. In other words, the turn to civil society was born out of disaffection and disenchantment with the post-independence state in many parts of the world including India. The revival of interest in civil society in effect was, and is, a devastating comment on the malaise of the political order, in which ordinary human beings are condemned to live out their lives.

In India the disillusionment with the post-colonial state was more than pervasive and discontent continued to coalesce rapidly over the years. "The voices of anger, frustration, despair, and humiliation," wrote Rajni Kothari, "alongside assertions of those who are beginning to think of their separate identities and loyalties, add up to the discourse of alienation and occasionally of disengagement from the mainstream body politic" (1994: 56). By the beginning of the 1980s a number of social movements, particularly the civil liberties movement and the environmental movement had taken on the onus of negotiating troublesome political issues, and scholars had begun to hail what came to be called "the non-party process" in the country (Omvedt, 1993).

It is more than clear that in less than three decades after independence, the nationalist dream had simply petered out and democracy had been deeply compromised. The people, as the subaltern group of historians did not hesitate to state baldly, had failed to come into their own. Why is then the state still seen as the locus of popular expectations, as the repository of the public good, and as the institution that is responsible for welfare? Why, in short, do people continue to repose hope in the Indian state?

For it is clear from the responses to our survey that the political expectation that it is the responsibility of the government to provide for basic needs, is much stronger than the demand that the government institutionalise a system that would allow people to meet their needs, provide a legal framework for 'free' market transactions for instance. Across the board, citizens continue to have high expectations of the state despite the fact that the government has begun to delegate more and more of its responsibility to civil society organisations. Why?

Arguably political expectations have to do with popular imaginations about what the government is supposed to do for its people. But then expectations never arise in a vacuum; they are an outcome of historical and political histories, and of the role of the state as well as the citizens in these histories. In the section below, I shall argue that past histories shape current expectations of government responsibilities and action. The particular argument is made in the context of two questions that arise out of the responses to our research project:

- What accounts for the fact that a majority of our respondents prefer that the state be held responsible for their well being rather than other organisations that subcontracting for the state is more visible and perhaps more reachable?
- What is it that gives assurance to the citizens that their political expectations of the state are both legitimate and justified?

The Significance of Political Contexts

Let me begin the argument in this section of the essay by suggesting that political preferences—for the state in this specific case—are not given, and that they are the outcome of historical processes and institutions that should form the subject matter for analysis, or that preference formation takes place in a historical context; that of specific institutions or systems of rules. These shape interests, fix responsibility, and guide the formation of expectations. Scholars who subscribe to the school of historical institutionalism, suggest that preferences and decisions are artefacts of institutions, and that given different institutions political expectations could have been different. In other words, the shaping of political preferences takes place in the context of institutions that bear traces of their own history-constitutions, political organisations, state structures, and political movements, all of which mould state-society relations. Sven Steinmo for example shows how the constitutional structures left in place by different processes of democratisation in the US, Sweden, and France continue to exert strong effects on tax policy. "Institutions," writes Steinmo, "provide the context in which individuals interpret their self-interest and thereby define their policy preferences...And any rational actor will behave differently in different institutional contexts" (1993: 7). Viewed in this particular frame of reference, political expectations of the Indian state appear as a unique product of policies and political practices that historically took shape in the country for most part of the 20th century.

The legal philosopher Cass Sunstein has argued in another context that "preferences are not fixed or stable but are instead adaptive to a wide range of factors—including the context in which the preference is expressed, the existing legal rules, past consumption choices, and culture in general." He goes on to suggest that the reason "whether people have a preference for a commodity, a right, or anything else is in part a function of whether the government has allocated it to them in the first instance...The initial allocation serves to reflect, to legitimate, and to reinforce social understandings about presumptive rights of ownership." That allocation, he argues, has an important causal connection to individual perceptions about the good or right in question. Sunstein conceptualises the effect of an initial allocation of a commodity as the 'endowment effect' (1993: 197). The endowment effect in India, it is clear, has outlasted changed political contexts even as it has embedded the notion that the state should be responsible for the well-being of its people in popular expectations. In sum, claims upon the government or expectations of the government, are shaped by, and are the product of two historical processes that are intrinsically interrelated—the political rhetoric and the political practices of the state, and the practices of civil society that continue to fix responsibility on the state.

Consider that in the post-independence period, thinking about the kind of politics that is, the kind of politics that should *be*, political imaginations, political imageries, and political aspirations have been focused on the state, notably the kind of developmentalist and interventionist state that had been forged under the leadership of the first prime minister of India, Jawaharlal Nehru. And state-centred political imaginaries did not originate with the institutionalisation of the first post-independence government in the country. The historical possibilities for the emergence of the developmentalist state that would at one and the same time reverse economic underdevelopment, undertake social reform through legislation and through political activism, and look after the interests of its citizens through the creation of a network of social sectors of health and education, had been set in place by the third decade of the 20th century.

The belief that the state is central to the lives of people was the outcome of two sets of factors, the first being the global political environment. In England, the welfare state emerging at the turn of the century after a long and sustained struggle by the working classes had embarked on an ambitious programme of welfarism. In the US, the Keynesian state, largely the product of the economic depression of the 1930s had legitimised the recognition that even the free market needs to be supported and regulated by the state, or that the political regulates even orders the economic. In the Soviet Union, the state controlling the commanding heights of the economy had wrought a spectacular economic and industrial transformation, rolling back in the process centuries of underdevelopment. In Europe, it was only a powerful state that could bring order out of the disorder generated by the Second World War. This was the precise global context within which political expectations of the state in India were forged and consolidated.

The second set of factors had to do with the historical particularities of the Indian freedom movement, which while concentrating on the immediate need to put an end to British colonialism, was also to concentrate on the future; on the task of forging a society that would transit to development and to prosperity under the guidance of a state committed to the welfare of the people, a state that would be as unlike the colonial state much as the proverbial chalk is different to the equally proverbial cheese. In fact, much of the groundwork for the interventionist and developmentalist state had been laid down in the 1930s, at a time when the freedom movement had been successfully transformed into a mass movement under the inspired leadership of Mahatma Gandhi. In 1931, at the Karachi session of the Indian National Congress, a resolution that was adopted on social and economic rights of the people stated clearly that political freedom must mean economic freedom for "the millions of starving masses". The Karachi resolution laid the blueprint of a post-independence government by charting out both an elaborate code of fundamental rights and the corresponding obligation of the state. These rights included the rights of freedom of association, of speech and conscience, of religion, and of equal citizenship, regardless of gender and social status. But it also mapped the framework of government policy inasmuch as the government would ensure an egalitarian society through measures such as a reduction in land rent and revenue, progressive taxation on agricultural incomes, inheritance tax, the right to form unions, social protection of industrial workers, control of usury, state control of key industries and mineral resources, free primary education, abolition of salt duty, prohibition, and the exclusion of foreign cloth and yarn from India.

This particular development in the freedom struggle was expected as well as natural. After all, the leadership could hardly mobilise millions of people to enter the political process and participate in the unmaking of colonial history and the making of post-colonial history, and not meet the expectations of the ordinary individual who naturally looked forward to transiting from subject to citizen in and through the freedom struggle. The transition from subject to citizen required an agency which could fulfil the tasks that history had devolved upon it—this agency was the state, or at least the state as it would gain shape in the aftermath of independence.

The precise moment when this state-centred political imagination—at least in the realm of the economy—was concretised, was in 1944 in the shape of the Bombay Plan. An influential group of industrialists—J.R.D. Tata, Purushottamdas Thakurdas, Kasturbhai Lalbhai, G.D. Birla, and A.D. Shroff insisted that the state should take on the responsibility for the provision of infrastructure for development, as well as for projects that required large and heavy investment. Industrialists in other words actively supported the projected strategy of state sponsored and planned industrialisation even as they looked to the post-colonial state to protect their own endeavours in the field of the economy. Simultaneously, radical sections in the freedom struggle demanded that the government should play a central role in material redistribution particularly in the eradication of poverty, which relentlessly stalked the life of the ordinary individual in the country. The two goals that of planned development and that of material redistribution were not seen as contradictory, and that both these perspectives were deeply interrelated was the passionate belief of the architect of modern India—Jawaharlal Nehru. His speech on the eve of independence testified to this belief—"the service of India," he was to say, "means the service of millions who suffer...it means the ending of poverty, ignorance and disease and inequality of opportunity" (cited in Gopal, 1980: 76-77).

The first government of post-independence India was to initiate a massive process of the social, economic, and political transformation of society. Evoking the spirit of classical political economists that the key to all kinds of transformation was economic development, Nehru was to state in 1955, "I am fed up of politics. My entire life has been spent in politics and even now I have to give most of my time to it. But I do not want to waste my time in either politics or international affairs. My mind is full of our economic problems and the need to make economic progress, to make the people better-off, and so on...the

real problem before us is the economic progress of India" (cited in Brown, 2003: 236-37). "Increasing national wealth," writes the historian Judith Brown of Nehru's strategy, "particularly of encouraging industrialisation," was of primary importance to him for a number of reasons. In his view, "It would lift people out of poverty, and, by an ongoing process of 'trickle down', would ameliorate deep-rooted inequalities" (2003: 237).

It was in pursuit of material restructuring that the first post-independence government under Nehru enacted land reform legislation, built up a formidable public sector, assumed responsibility for economic growth, and took on the gigantic task of eradicating poverty through a variety of measures. Efforts to radicalise and restructure the economy were paralleled by efforts to socially reform and modernise a largely agricultural society, where millions of people were mired in want and misery and steeped in hierarchical and oppressive social structures. Central to this project was the notion of a planned economy, the inspiration for which was drawn from Prime Minister Nehru's commitment to Fabian socialism and its pledge to a gradual process of social and economic reform. Prime Minister Nehru simultaneously drew inspiration from the experience of the Soviet Union, which had tacked underdevelopment through the planning process. Consequently, the state by undertaking multifarious tasks—developing and diversifying industry, achieving food sufficiency, constructing infrastructure, embarking on social reform, and providing for the basic needs of the people, came to stand squarely in the middle of things. It simply came to occupy the centre stage of political imaginations. This is not surprising when we recollect that political rhetoric promised primary education and the subsidisation of higher education, guarantees of health, removal of poverty, generation of jobs and incomes, institutionalisation of inter-group equalities and removal of inequalities within the group, and protection of the needy, the vulnerable, and the poor. Control over vital sectors of heavy industry such as steel, energy, and mining, communications, transportation, and defence allowed the state to garner resources and regulate the economy as well as eradicate poverty (see Bagchi, 1995; also Corbridge and Harriss, 2001 on this).

The Planning Commission which was established in March 1950 had the task of drawing up and implementing the five-year plans in order to give body to policy pronouncements and to the developmental objectives of the leadership. If planning was to ensure development, it was also to ensure the creation of an equalitarian society. Prime Minister Nehru repeatedly insisted that his idea of a socialist pattern of society embodied the determination to provide to the people six basic necessities of life—food, housing, clothing, health care, education, and employment. This was to be ensured through rapid economic growth, expansion of employment, and a reduction in economic inequality. Subsequently, public spending was increased to emphasise capital goods production and import substitution based industrialisation. Public investment in industry doubled in the Second Five Year Plan. Meaningful institutional reforms in the countryside to achieve agricultural development and productivity were set in place. And all this was not exclusive of other goals such as a commitment to equality and freedom.

In retrospect, it is clear that the strategy to simultaneously reform and radicalise the economy, society, culture, and hence politics through major state intervention, was not only far too ambitious but also counter-productive. It was to result in a top-heavy state, to the concentration of power in the hands of bureaucrats and politicians, to corruption and to statism. By the late 1960s, multifarious problems had began to be identified with this model of the state, which had proved more interventionist than developmentalist, and which had led to the creation of a powerful alliance of bureaucrats and politicians wielding enormous power. Even as the alliance between bureaucrats and politicians increasingly arbitrated interests in civil society, it also subordinated society to its own logic of power gathering. India was to see little development and even less amelioration of poverty in this period. The inadequacies of the developmental model and financial mismanagement led to the reversal of economic policy from the 1980s onward, as the government withdrew from its own commitments and devolved more and more powers to the market. That the withdrawal of the state was in major part an effect of neo-liberal ideologies that swept the world in the 1980s has been extensively documented and does not bear repetition.

In 1991, as the government approached the World Bank for a loan it adopted a far reaching programme of economic reform. This drew back the government from an overtly interventionist into a directive role. The state's former role in controlling the commanding heights of the economy was ceded to the market, and its role as the mainspring of social development was increasingly ceded to non-governmental organisations. It was more or less admitted that NGOs with their knowledge of the cultural and socioeconomic circumstances of the people of the country, coupled with a high degree of organisational flexibility and great motivation, may be more effective than the government in promoting social changes. The state in the process has delegated more and more of its power and responsibility to the market and to civil society organisations.

But political practices and rhetoric tend to breed their own logic. For almost 40 years the 'Nehruvian' state symbolised not only an interventionist and developmentalist state, but also a state that was committed to the well being of its people. This was to consolidate not only the image of the state as the guardian of individual and collective interests, it was to result in a spiral of political expectations that the citizens could look to the state for the institutionalisation of the basic conditions of well being.

In sum, the role that the state had taken on at one point of India's political history had taken firm hold of popular imaginations even if the state has begun to redraft its own role.

Consequently, although the state has been pluralised to a large extent, although it now shares both power and responsibility with a host of civil society actors, and although large swathes of scholarly opinion would rather that the state withdraw in favour of the market, the ordinary citizen continues to fix responsibility on the state.

Conclusion

Across dominant streams of thought and policy prescriptions, the general consensus seems to be that the government is the problem. Instead of trying to make the state deliver what it has promised through constitutions, laws, and rhetorical flourishes, policy makers and advocates of civil society organisations would rather establish a parallel system, which can substitute for the state in areas of service delivery. And yet one significant factor inhibits the realisation of this plan, the fact that people as the responses to our questionnaire show, repose little hope in the ability of civil society agents to negotiate their problems. They would rather fix responsibility on the government, which has through most of India's post-colonial history presented itself as the guardian of the collective interest. But this in turn implies that the articulation of political expectations is not given, and that it is itself the product of historical political processes. Or that political expectations are the product of complex social and political transactions, which go into the construction of historical memory about what politics is and what it can be in a given society.

References

Bagchi, Amiya K. (1995). "Dialectics of Indian Planning: From Compromise to Democratic Decentralization and Threat of Disarray", in T.V Sathyamurthy (ed.), *Social Change and Political Discourse in India: Structures of Power, Movements of Resistance*, Vol. 4 on "Industry and Agriculture in India Since Independence", Oxford University Press, Delhi.

Brown, David L., and Jonathan A. Fox (1998). "Accountability within Transnational Coalitions", in Jonathan A. Fox and L. David Brown (eds.), *The Struggle for Accountability: The World Bank, NGOs and Grassroots Movements,* MIT Press, Cambridge, M.A.

Brown, Judith (2003). *Nehru: A Political Life,* Oxford University Press, Oxford.

Chandhoke, Neera (2003). "Governance and the Pluralisation of the State: Implications for Democratic Citizenship", *Economic and Political Weekly,* 12-14th July.

Corbridge, Stuart and John Harriss (2001). *Reinventing India; Liberalization, Hindu Nationalism and Popular Democracy,* Oxford University Press, Delhi.

Creveld, van Martin (1999). *The Rise and Decline of the State,* Cambridge University Press, Cambridge.

Devarajan, Shantayanan, and Shekhar Shah (2004). "Making Services Work for India's Poor", *Economic and Political Weekly,* Special issue on "Delivering Basic Services for the Poor", Vol. 39, No 9, February 28-March 5, pp. 907-919.

Gopal, S. (ed.) (1980). *Jawaharlal Nehru: An Anthology,* Oxford University Press, Delhi.

Harriss, John (2001). *Depoliticising Development,* Leftword, Delhi.

Kothari, Rajni (1994). "Fragments of a Discourse: Towards Conceptualization", in T.V Sathyamurthy (ed.), *Social Change and Political Discourse in India: Structures of Power, Movements of Resistance,* Vol. 1 on "State and Nation in the Context of Social Change", Chapter 1, Oxford University Press, Delhi.

Ministry of Health and Family Welfare (2004). *Annual Report 2003-2004,* Government of India, Delhi.

Omvedt, Gail (1993). *Reinventing Revolution,* M.E. Sharpe, New York.

Parikh, K. (1999). "Overview" in *India Development Report*, pp. 1-24, Oxford University Press, Delhi.

Planning Commission (2003). *Tenth Five Year Plan 2002-2007,* Vol. 1, "Governance and Implementation", Government of India, Delhi.

PRIA and John Hopkins University (2003). *Invisible Yet Widespread: The Non-Profit Sector in India*, PRIA (Participatory Research in Asia), Delhi.

Simmons, P.J. (1998). "Learning to Live with NGOs", *Foreign Policy*, 112, Fall.

Steinmo, Sven (1993). *Taxation and Democracy: Swedish, British and American Approaches to Financing the Modern State*, Yale University Press, New Haven.

Sunstein, Cass R. (1993). "Democracy and Shifting Preferences", in David Copp, Jean Hampton and John Roemer (eds.), *The Idea of Democracy,* Cambridge University Press, Cambridge.

Wood, Geoffrey (1997). "'States without Citizens: The Problem of the Franchise State", in David Hulme and Michael Edwards (eds.), *NGO's, States and Donors: Too Close for Comfort,* St Martins' Press, New York.

6 | Our Democracy—The Challenges that it Must Address

PREM SHANKAR JHA

EVERY mature, functioning democracy has evolved through a process of trial and error. Indian democracy has been doing the same for 50 years, by and large with remarkable success. From a highly centralised, 'quasi-federal' constitution in the early fifties, we have developed into a unique 'ethnic' federal state, like no other in the world. Our states today are not administrative or historical units but ethno-national entities with distinct cultures, histories, and identities, that coexist in a uniquely peaceful manner that has been never seen before in human history. Today, Indians feel that their core identity is safe in their home states or autonomous districts. From this secure base they look out at the whole of India as their 'field of opportunity'– that much vaster area in which they have the legal and constitutional right to make their lives and seek their fortune. This ideal balance between security and opportunity is reflected in the fact that today somewhere between 60 to 80 million people work outside their home states. Yet there is not a murmur of complaint from the host states or people. That is nation building at its best, described a hundred and fifty years ago by Mazzini, the father of the Italian Risorgimento, as a process designed to increase the economic, social and cultural opportunities of the citizens. We have thus given an extremely positive meaning to nationalism and national unity.

But 50 years of the functioning of federal democracy have also revealed, and in some cases created, problems that have begun, increasingly, to put a question mark over our future. These too are by-products of the evolution of Indian democracy. They could not be foreseen by our founding fathers because they had no precedent in the other democracies, notably those of the UK and the US, on whom our constitution, and our electoral system, were based. That is one reason why we have been slow to recognise them and half-hearted in tackling them. The other reason is that every political system builds coalitions of interest groups, both of those who are able to exploit it and those who lose from it. In India so far, the former have been quicker to mobilise themselves and insitutionalise their grip on power than the latter.

Three serious and unforeseen developments are making India increasingly difficult to govern. These are:

i)   The fragmentation of the political system at the Centre and the increasing difficulty of initiating national policies that impose short-term costs in order to secure long-term benefits for the people. This is particularly true in the realm of economic policy.

ii) The criminalisation of politics and the attendant mushrooming of corruption, fraud, and extortion. This has reached a stage where, as Rajiv Gandhi said two decades ago, "only 15 paise out of every rupee of development funds actually reaches the people".

iii) The progressive transformation of India from a developmental state into a predatory state. This has begun in the criminalisation described above, but has been magnified a hundredfold by the lack of accountability in the bureaucracy at every level from the block to the state and central secretariats.

Weakening of the Centre

This is clearly visible in a growing failure to develop policies that tackle structural problems that have developed incrementally over the years. These range from the collapse of the judiciary to the seemingly uncontrollable rise of the revenue deficit and the progressive dysfunctioning of the public distribution system which piles mountains of foodgrains in central warehouses while tribals starve in Orissa and Madhya Pradesh.

The change is not transitory. On the contrary, its cause is the disappearance, after 50 years, of dominant party democracy. Today every government is a coalition, and the need to form and maintain a consensus forces governments to compromise on their policies. This can and does seriously limit their capacity to undertake economic development, which by its nature involves imposing immediate austerity in order to garner accelerated growth over a longer period.

That capacity existed as long as there was a single national party in power at the centre, i.e. the Congress. The cohesiveness of the party enabled it to take the long-term view and to impose the short-term sacrifices that economic development entailed. However, it did not use this power well, and adopted policies that gave India a 3.6 per cent GDP growth rate for over two decades with next to no growth in exports or in private sector employment, and therefore used the creation of unwanted jobs in the public sector to absorb the pressure for jobs, thereby laying the foundations of future bankruptcy is another matter. The unalterable fact remains that it asked for sacrifices from the Indian people in the name of growth and the Indian people made them willingly. India therefore remained a developmental nation state.

Dominant party democracy however began, to weaken in 1974-75 and disappeared finally in 1996. This gradually tilted the balance between direction and accommodation in the Indian polity in favour of the latter. With the emergence of coalition governments as a permanent feature of Central rule, the capacity to impose short-term sacrifices on the people for long-term benefits disappeared altogether. The change has taken place perfectly in accordance to the law through the continuing interaction of the constitution with political development in the country. As a result the very same features of the Constitution which gave India strength stability and direction between 1947 and 1996 are inexorably making the country less governable today.

The change has come so unobtrusively and yet so swiftly that few have understood the havoc it has wreaked on governance. Its origins therefore need to be studied more closely. Like Britain, India has a simple majority voting system. As in Britain, by enlarging the ratio of seats to votes of the largest party and doing the opposite to smaller parties this system has exerted remorseless pressure on the latter to merge with their immediate political neighbours in order to stay alive. As in Britain, over time this has tended to create two major parties or coalitions.

But the similarities have ended there. Unlike Britain, India is a federal and not a unitary democracy. Over 11 or more elections, the simple majority voting system has created two stable parties or coalitions in most states. But in the very act of doing so it has ensured that there will be a multiplicity of small parties at the Centre. It has done this by allowing each party or coalition that is well entrenched in a state to translate its hold on the vote there into a small but stable number of seats in the Lok Sabha. Since each small party at the Centre has a secure political base in the state, it is under no compulsion to merge itself with a political neighbour in order to

survive, or better its chances of capturing power. This makes it largely immune to the pressure that the simple majority voting system exerts on small parties to merge themselves with their neighbours to create a two party system in the central legislature. Not surprisingly, in the 1999 Lok Sabha elections there were no fewer than 63 recognised political parties in the fray. As a result, unlike the British Parliament, in which coalition governments have been rare and transitory, in India, coalition governments are here to stay.

Separation of Central from State Elections

The effects of the disappearance of dominant party democracy have been compounded by the separation of Central from state elections, and then the separation of state elections from each other, that has taken place after 1971. Somewhat surprisingly, this was not foreseen by our founding fathers. This has put every central government in what has come to be called "Election mode" within months of coming to power. As all politicians know, election mode is a euphemism for avoiding potentially unpopular decisions. Worse still, it has greatly increased the tendency for political parties to attack necessary administrative changes, such as an increase in oil prices, electricity and water tariffs, bus and train fares and the like, even when they know that had they been in power, they would have faced exactly the same decisions.

The baneful effects of the separation of central and state elections remained subdued so long as the dominance of the Congress at the Centre remained unchallenged. But that ended, decisively, in 1994. It was widely believed within the Congress Party in 1993 that if the party had lost the November state assembly elections in the four states where BJP governments had been dismissed in the wake of the Babri Masjid demolition 11 months earlier, the Rao government would have no option but to resign. This was mercifully not put to the test, but the Central Government's capacity to govern remained unimpaired only for another year. Most people attribute the collapse of economic reform to the exit of the Congress. But in actual fact it occurred in December 1994 after two shock defeats the Congress suffered in the Andhra and Karnataka state elections in that month. One of the two subcommittees the Congress set up to analyse the causes of the defeat reported that it had been caused by high inflation. Five months later, when the industrial boom was at its peak and inflation touched 11.1 per cent, the party decided that this had gone too far. Inflation had to be curbed by any means whatever. There followed a tightening of money supply that pushed call money rates (overnight interest rates between banks) to 60 per cent. The rise in interest rates knocked the bottom out of the share market and overall raised the cost of investment. Investment fell by 40 per cent in 1995-96. Industrial growth fell from a peak of 16.2 per cent in January to March 1996 to 3 per cent in November 1997. The ensuing slump lasted six years.

With the disappearance of one party government in 1996, probably never to return, both the baneful influences described are now working in tandem with each other. This was apparent during the United Front Government. Things were not much better under Mr. Vajpayee. That is why his government did nothing to tackle the mounting fiscal deficit, to revive public investment or to restore high growth and restart the growth of jobs. It paid the price for its paralysis in May 2004.

From Developmental to Predator State

Another structural change in the Indian polity that has not so much gone unnoticed as has been passively accepted, is the transformation of India from what political scientists call a developmental state into a predator state. It has two causes. The first is the rise of coalition government, the weakening of the Centre, and the shortening and growing uncertainty of tenure of governments.

In the heyday of single party dominance, the purpose of capturing power was to make and implement policies that would strengthen the nation and enlarge the national cake. The State was an instrument for this purpose. India was a developmental nation state and what came to be known as the 'Nehruvian' model of growth was its embodiment. The successive Five Year Plans; the adoption of a heavy investment oriented growth strategy designed to make India economically 'self-reliant', the adoption of a socialist pattern of society, and the all-pervasive control of the Central Government over who would produce, what would be produced and where the factories and plants would be located were all products of this developmental state.

In the end the Nehruvian model admittedly failed to give India either the growth or the self-reliance that it had aimed at, but it did create the economic sinews of national unity, and fostered the growth of an Indian entrepreneurial class which is today getting ready to conquer the world. However, the need for another model became apparent as far back as the beginning of the eighties, if not earlier. What India needed was a change in the goals and instruments of the developmental state. But as impotent coalitions replaced stable single party government and the political time horizon has shortened, what it got instead was the Predator State.

Today the goals underlying the pursuit of power have changed almost beyond recognition. Unable to make any changes to the condition of the people, political leaders have increasingly sought power in order to parcel out the wealth of the state among themselves. This is the reason for the rampant corruption, and kickbacks of the kind exposed by the Tehelka team, and the uncontrolled burgeoning of subsidies in the last dozen years.

There is a vicious circle built into this process. The more the State forsakes developmentalism in favour of predation, the more rapidly does it lose whatever legitimacy it enjoys in the eyes of the people. The more rapidly it does so, the shorter becomes the life of each successive government. The shorter its life, the greater is the temptation to prey upon the State during its time in office. In the end this leads to what students of Africa's political economy have called "clientelism"—the construction of coalitions of interests that come together

with the express purpose of robbing the state. In states like Bihar and Assam, this process is already virtually complete and bandits have begun to run parallel governments, extorting 'taxes' from the people. The cancer is spreading.

The Rise of the Predator State

Predatory behaviour is not, however, confined to the terrorist margins of society. It now affects even the relations of state governments with the Centre. A revealing example is the perversion of the public distribution system for foodgrains that had gone virtually unnoticed till a few years ago. In the late summer of 2001, the Vajpayee government was severely criticised for allowing starvation deaths to take place in Orissa and elsewhere, when the Central Government was sitting on a 60 million tonne mountain of foodgrains. How did this happen?

The short answer is that in an era of coalition governments food surplus states force the Centre to buy their farmers' output at prices well above what the market can sustain, while cash strapped food deficit states refuse to pick up more than the minimum they can get away with because they do not want to meet even the transport and distribution costs from the railhead and the FCI's warehouses till the ration shops.

In 2000-01 the output of foodgrains *fell* by 6.3 per cent but the procurement of foodgrains *rose* from 30.8 million tonnes to 35.5 million tonnes. The governments of the surplus states thus literally crowded out the private sector from the foodgrains trade by offering a price that bore no relation to the market. The foodgrains then remained in the government's depots because the off-take from the ration shops fell from 17.1 million tonnes in 1999 to 12.1 million tonnes in 2000.

How has the Indian state become the perpetrator of this monstrous injustice? How has a public distribution system that was originally designed to protect the poor against extortionate pricing during times of drought been turned into an engine of death? A closer examination shows that it is the product of each state-centred party in the ruling coalition taking a me first and the devil take the hindmost policy. The bulk of the rice and up to 86 per cent of the wheat that the Centre procures, comes from just two states, Punjab and Haryana. These states jack up support prices at will and evade the responsibility of selling their grain by forcing the Centre to buy it from them.

The opposite happens in the food deficit states. Since the distribution of even freely supplied foodgrains involves some cost to them, they prefer to minimise their off-take from the Centre's allocation. When forced by the Centre to take up some at least of their quota, they set rules for its sale that are designed to discourage purchase from the ration shops. Some of the balance finds its way into the black market, but in a final contemptuous slap in the face of the Central Government, some is sold back to it as grain 'procured' by the state government.

This is the classic behaviour of the predator State. Every one gains—the government and farmers of the grain surplus states, the government of the deficit states and the corrupt employees of the public distribution system. Only the consumers lose and the poorest among them die.

Such predatory behaviour is ubiquitous. The subsidies, described earlier, that have mushroomed in the nineties and pushed up the fiscal deficit to its present unsustainable level are other manifestations of the predator state. As was pointed out earlier, on an average a fifth of the power generated in the country is stolen outright and another one-third is sold to supposed agriculturists at a tenth of its cost of production. At least two-thirds of this power goes to small industrialists, shopkeepers and air-conditioned farmhouses. Four-fifths of the fertiliser subsidy goes not to the farmers in whose name it is regularly renewed but to the manufacturers who have gold plated their capital costs in ways too numerous to relate. Three-quarters of the subsidy on kerosene goes not to the rural poor who supposedly use it as a cooking fuel, but to adulterators of gasoline and diesel and to smugglers who ship it from Bihar and Bengal to Nepal and Bangladesh.

The Predator State and Rural Stagnation

The predator state has reached its apotheosis in rural government. Funds intended for rural development, the Tenth Plan has allocated the colossal sum of Rs. 122,000 crores for rural development—Rs. 5 lakhs per village per year, if this was properly spent it would end rural destitution in a single decade. In fact at least four-fifths of this money is siphoned off by a power structure that consists of the *Zilla Parishad* chief, the Block Development Officers and the *Gram Pradhans*, allied to the MLA and occasionally to the MP. The rural development funds are the common trough at which they all feed, and except in a very few states the District Magistrate remains an onlooker.

A Predatory Bureaucracy

Finally, predatory extortion—mistakenly described as corruption—has become a way of life for all but a small minority of civil servants in the state and central bureaucracies. Kickbacks are mandatory in every sale to a government organisation, whether it is for a rural development project costing a few lakhs of rupees, a power plant or an aircraft carrier. Kickbacks are indeed the reason why state governments regularly start new infrastructure projects, but seldom complete them. For the lion's share of the kickback has to be paid 'up front'. After that the government loses interest in the project.

Electoral Funding—The Core of the Problem

What has given the Predator State easy legitimacy is the ever growing need of political parties for funds to fight elections. This too is an accidental by-product of grafting the UK model of democracy, as opposed to the Central European one. In the UK, the average constituency, even today, has only 60,000 voters. A candidate can live at home, get into his car each morning and visit each and every town and village in his constituency within a month, returning home every night to sleep. His entire expenses amount to posters and the

hire of halls for his meetings. This is easily met by voluntary contributions. As a result no special need was ever felt for enacting any special legislation to govern electoral funding.

By contrast the average Indian constituency is 60 km to 100 km in area, has two million inhabitants, one million voters and requires parties to man over a thousand polling booths. To make matters worse the separation of central and state assembly elections has made it necessary to raise the money to fight elections not once but twice every five years. This had delivered the political system bound hand and foot to the criminal classes. Today they are so deeply entrenched in politics that virtually anyone who challenges them is crushed.[1]

An Agenda for Reform

Strengthening the Centre and Restoring the Developmental State

The above analysis of the structural changes that underlie the decline of the developmental and the rise

---

1. Witness the insidious campaign to discredit Rajiv Gandhi as being 'inexperienced' that began within the Congress Party after he made his Congress Centennial Speech in Mumbai, in 1985, in which he asserted that 85 paise out of every rupee of developmental outlays in the countryside went into private pockets and that the electoral system was the fountainhead of corruption. Witness the onslaught on and expulsion of V.P. Singh from the Congress Party in 1987 after he sanctioned an enquiry into illegal accounts held by Indians in foreign banks. Witness also the sustained attack on Narasimha Rao that erupted when he sanctioned the interrogation and prosecution of political leaders named in the 'Jain diaries' and suspected of having had *hawala* dealings with the Jain brothers. Most recently witness the way in which the terms of reference of the Venkataswami Commission which is examining *Tehelka.com's* exposure of corruption in defence deals were subtly altered to focus not on the corruption but on the supposedly dubious methods that Tehelka's journalists used to obtain their information.

of the predator state in India makes it exceedingly unlikely that even with the best will in the world, any future government will be able to tackle the core issues of accelerating growth, reducing the fiscal deficit and expanding productive employment without first reversing the weakening of the Centre and restoring the developmental state. Political reform is therefore, a precondition to sustainable economic development.

Reunite Central and State Elections

Since coalition governments are here to stay, a return to dominant party democracy is not on the cards, the only alternative is to reunite central and state elections. This needs an amendment to the constitution which could run somewhat as follows:

> "If a state government falls in less than the five years of its normal life, it shall come under President's rule for the period that remains. If the central government falls in less than five years, all state governments will also hold fresh elections at the same time as the new election to parliament."

At first sight, these provisions seem draconian, even unfair. Is a long period of President's rule not a denial of the people's right to be ruled by their own representatives? And isn't it doubly unfair to force a new election on a stable state government simply because the Central government coalition has broken down? Isn't this, moreover, denying to the states that assured five year span that they need to implement developmental policies? And is it right to force state legislators to spend still more money on elections that they have played no part in bringing about? Will the resulting decrease in the stability of the state governments not strengthen the predatory behaviour in them even as it weakens it at the Centre?

A closer look at the effect that such a reform will have on the political system shows, however that, like Article 16 of the French Fifth Republic, its very enactment will make its invocation unnecessary for it will eliminate instability not only at the Centre but also in the states. State governments first became unstable only after the 1967 assembly and Parliamentary elections. The cause was the loss of power in six major states by the Congress, its replacement by shaky coalitions of political parties and groups that had no experience of either governing or of working together, and a determined bid by the Congress to bring these governments down by enticing groups within them to defect. In 9 cases out of 10 defections were secured either by offering the defector a large sum of money or a ministership in the next government. Prime Minister Rajiv Gandhi succeeded in controlling the epidemic of defections to a considerable extent by enacting the anti-defection bill with the unanimous support of all political parties, in 1985. But defections have continued at less frequent intervals both in the states and, in the past six years, at the Centre. In all cases the bait has remained the same.

Reuniting assembly and parliamentary elections will remove this lure. Once an MLA in a state assembly knows that defection will not bring him money or a ministership but a long period of President's rule, he will defect only on issues of conscience. Defections will then become exceedingly rare.

But what about the premature fall of a government at the Centre? Since under the Constitution another election will have to be held within six months, will forcing all state assemblies to dissolve at the same time not impose a completely unwarranted punishment upon all of them? Once again, a close examination shows that while this eventuality cannot be ruled out in theory, it is exceedingly unlikely to arise in practice. Four central governments have fallen in the nineties. Three were minority governments that fell because one or other large national party that was supporting them from the outside withdrew its support. These were the governments of Mr. V.P Singh in 1990, Mr. Chandrashekhar in 1991 and Mr. Gujral in 1998.

This form of government formation was characteristic of the very early stages of dissolution of the dominant party system. With the rise and stabilisation of the NDA over the past three years, and the growing stability of the Congress-Left understanding, its day may well be past.

The experience of the last eight years of coalition governments has shown that a coalition partner is most likely to withdraw when it faces an election in its home state and is afraid that some policy adapted at the centre will make it unpopular in its home state. But this threat too will recede when one or other member of the coalition is not facing an election every year.

Finally we should bear in mind that reuniting central and state elections will halve the cost of elections and therefore of running an honest democratic system.

Reform of Electoral Finance

The constitutional reform described in detail above will go a long way towards rooting out the predatory state and bringing back the developmental one in India. Greater stability at the Centre and the assurance that barring truly unusual developments a government will complete its five years in office will give coalitions time to jell to formulate policies in the expectation that they will be around to garner their electoral benefits. But to complete the return to the developmental state a second reform is absolutely essential. This is the reform of electoral finance. The damage that was done by the 1970 ban on corporate donations, and the doubling of electoral expenses that followed the separation of central from state elections a year later, has already been described above. Reuniting central and state elections will virtually halve electoral expenses and undo a great deal of it. But only the institution of a state fund for financing elections will start the process of breaking the nexus that has developed between black money, organised crime and politics, especially in the states.

The proposal to set up such a fund is far from new. It was made first by a group of Congress Members of Parliament to Mrs. Indira Gandhi as far back as 1976. She promised to consider it but lost the election in March 1977. Since then the demand has surfaced repeatedly, usually in the opposition. But the very same parties that raised the demand showed an inexplicable lack of enthusiasm for it once they came to power. As a result bills have been introduced in Parliament for a reform of electoral finance more than once but been allowed to lapse. The ones that have been passed have made only cosmetic changes to the existing, by and large criminal, process. At present virtually every political party is committed on paper to the reform of electoral finance. In 2002, a Bill based on the report of a committee headed by Mr. Indrajit Gupta of the Left Front, was waiting to be tabled. Apart from establishing modalities for state funding, it was also expected to make corporate donations to political parties tax deductible. It has not been passed.

What will State Funding Achieve

It has often been argued that state funding will not end corruption and will only throw good money after bad. This will certainly be true if the funding is not sufficient to meet the expense of running the political parties and financing elections. But if it is, the following benefits will flow from it. What is more, even a generous system of funding will only be a necessary, not a sufficient condition for rooting out criminals and rewarding meritorious party workers. But that having been said, state funding will have the following beneficial results immediately.

First, and most important, it will stop the fragmentation of power within political parties and return it to their elected leaders. The fragmentation occurs because those who collect money for the party almost never give the entire amount to the treasurer. No one knows how much they hold back. But there is a premium on doing so, because the more they retain the larger will be the number of candidates they will be able to finance on their own, and to command the loyalty of, in future struggles for leadership. Thus, the present system rewards those who are disloyal even to their own party and its leaders.

Second, it will return control of the selection of candidates back to the elected leaders of the party. Today moneybags demand the privilege (some would say right) to select candidates in a given number of constituencies, and the elected party bearers are unable to say no. On the rare occasions when they do, the moneybags use the funds they have collected and not given to finance rebel candidates. This weakens the party and often forces humiliating compromises upon the leaders who have to take them back in order to capture, or stay in, power.

Third, the restoration of control will allow the elected leaders to do away with criminals and people with shady records, altogether. They may not initially want to do so. But the fear that a rival party may steal the election by nominating a decent highly respected candidate will make the leaders look for better candidates and to shun those whom the voters fear. Political competition will therefore clean up politics over two or three elections. But for this, political parties must first be liberated from the clutches of the criminals. Only state funding can do this.

A Model of State Funding

1. A fund should be set up for financing elections. It should be financed from the Central Exchequer. It should consist of two equal parts, one for the parliamentary and the other for the state assembly elections. The latter should be allocated between states on the basis of the size of state assembly.

2. State funds should be distributed to recognised political parties on the basis of their share of the vote in the last parliamentary or state election. The criterion for recognition should be to have obtained an agreed upon proportion of votes polled (e.g. three or five per cent) in the previous election.

3. The fund should be large enough to cut off the need for criminal funding altogether. (Rs. 1000 crore would be a good figure. It is only 0.23 per cent of total Central government expenditure in 2003-04.)

4. Individual and corporate donations should be permitted up to stipulated ceilings. TV time and other non-cash contributions would be very welcome but are no substitutes for cash.

5. The utilisation of funds should be audited by the election commission through a newly established auditor's department.

7 | Political Reforms and Economic Prosperity

JAYAPRAKASH NARAYAN

REVIEWING the healthcare in the United States 25 years ago, the prestigious *Daedalus* magazine coined the expression, "doing better, and feeling worse". That description certainly fits our economic scene. While on the one hand, when compared with earlier decades, our economy has been doing much better in terms of growth rates, the socioeconomic indicators have not changed radically.

The economic reform process started in 1991 certainly yielded good dividends. Growth rate went up. In a country used to the Hindu rate of growth of about 3 per cent, 6-7 per cent growth rate now is widely regarded as unsatisfactory. Consumer goods are better and cheaper now, and there is greater choice on offer. Investment has gone up, and exports boomed for a decade. Contrary to fears, opening up of the economy did not lead to a deluge of foreign goods. The Indian consumer proved to be very discerning, seeking good value for money. Nor did neocolonialism or economic imperialism threaten India's freedom. The percentage of poor people is showing decline, and population is reaching replacement level in the South and the West. Removal of foreign exchange controls did not lead to flight of dollars; reserves actually went up significantly. Reduction of tax rates led to higher revenues, and not lower. Many new enterprises came up significantly, and the young people are more ready than ever before to find jobs outside government. India saw a revolution in telecom and information sectors. Organised workers, who had enjoyed immense protection for long, now realise that their future is linked to the health of their enterprises. The person-days lost on account of industrial strife fell dramatically. The *doomsdayers* who prophesied disaster with liberalisation proved to be wide off the mark. Most people are actually better-off today than they were a decade ago. By all standards, the reform process has yielded good results.

It is now axiomatic that the government which governs the least is the best government. Public opinion has also come to accept that government has no business to run businesses. Libertarians naturally oppose high taxation or huge public expenditure. As Milton Friedman so succinctly explained, a citizen knows best how to maximise his happiness by spending, as he deems fit, the Rs.100 in his pocket. The alternative of transferring to the State most of it and hoping that someone, somewhere will take sound decisions for him (an unsound assumption), and receiving only a small fraction of it in the form of public goods and services (after transaction costs, leakages, inefficiency and corruption) is clearly unattractive to most of us.

But closer examination of the OECD countries shows that in the real world, most states pursue economic policies that combine the libertarian principle of *laissez faire* with expenditure for promoting social good in the form of education, healthcare and welfare. Notwithstanding Ronald Reagan and Margaret Thatcher, the public expenditure in OECD countries is about 45 per cent of GDP on an average. India's public expenditure as a share of GDP is lower than every OECD country, except the two city-states of Hong Kong and Singapore. The social expenditure alone accounts for 25 per cent of GDP, adjusting for country-variations. The high-income countries spend 5.6 per cent of GDP on public education and 6.4 per cent of GDP on public health. Medium-income countries spend only 4.6 per cent and 3.2 per cent of GDP on education and health respectively, while poor countries spend a measly 2.5 per cent and 0.8 per cent on these two sectors.

What does this indicate? Limited government and political and economic freedom to citizens are vital for individual growth and national advancement. But liberty cannot be construed in a very narrow and negative sense of state not abridging individual freedoms. State is not merely a necessary evil to defend our frontiers, maintain public order, protect citizens and ensure justice. State can, and should, also be a positive institution to create basic infrastructure, develop natural resources, and most of all to provide quality school education and effective primary healthcare. Liberal think tanks and academics have been vehemently advocating rollback of the State from these areas. While State's role in business is now universally opposed, there are no realistic substitutes to State in school education, primary healthcare and the like.

It does not mean that State alone should pay for these services. Private and voluntary sectors have a significant role, and nowhere in market economies is that role more pronounced than in India. Nor does it mean that State should necessarily deliver these services. Stakeholders groups and voluntary organisations often do the job much better. But the financing has to come from the State. And, the State does not mean the centralised, remote, big-government, but localised, citizen-centred government starting with a community of stakeholders, and expanding in concentric circles to local, provincial and federal governments based on the principle of subsidiarity.

We have to recognise that social goods like school education and primary healthcare cannot be accessed by most citizens without State's intermediation or funding. And in our country, with vertical hierarchies, caste divisions and moral neutrality to social inequities, State's role is critical. With the State failing in these sectors, the bulk of our gene pool is wasted, and educational opportunities are effectively limited to a quarter of our population; poor people end up suffering and spending much more than the rich in market-driven private healthcare systems. Making education a profit-making enterprise has resulted in mushrooming of countless colleges that produce mostly literate, semi-educated, unemployable graduates. It is easy for the well-heeled and well-connected to ridicule the role of the State. But the fact remains that the future of the vast majority of our children is dictated by the circumstances of their birth. The potential of most children remains unfulfilled. Opportunities for vertical mobility are severely restricted for the bulk of the population. Paradoxically, in the 1950s and 60s, children had better opportunities. But the decline in public education and healthcare makes the situation increasingly unacceptable. Abdication of State is no solution.

State, Resources and Development

As pointed out, the GDP share of public expenditure in India is low compared to OECD countries. But it would be wrong to conclude that State's incapacity to deliver is a result of shortage of resources alone. Indian State was never short of resources to abstain from carrying out vital functions necessary for development. Excluding the local governments' expenditure and inter-governmental adjustments, the combined total expenditure of the Union and State governments, according to the budget estimates is a whopping Rs. 2000 crore per day or in terms of purchasing power it is equivalent to $2 billion a day!

What do we get in return and what do we have to show? Eighty crore children with no access to school education, 70 crore people without access to proper toilets, shortage of teachers and excess of peons and clerks, appalling public services and woefully inadequate infrastructure. Without having to increase public expenditure, without having to seek aid from international agencies, these 8 crore children could all have access to basic school education. It just requires some re-allocation of funds and commitment of the governing class. At 50 children per classroom we need to build 16 lakh classrooms. Each classroom can be built at Rs. 1 lakh or less. This will incur a one-time expenditure/investment of Rs. 16,000 crore. This is equivalent to only 8 days' government expenditure! Running the school—teachers and basic teaching aids— would incur a recurring expense of Rs. 8,000 crore; a mere four days' expenditure! A very paltry investment when you calculate the social and economic returns to the country. Similarly, all it takes to provide a safe, hygienic toilet for every household is about Rs. 12,000 crores public expenditure (half the needy households can pay from their own resources, if technology and material are accessible, and a campaign is launched to promote proper hygiene and sanitation). This is equivalent to a one-time investment equal to six days public expenditure. Studies have also shown that our public health system can be completely revamped, and healthcare improved and made accessible to the poor and needy, at an additional cost of about Rs. 10,000 crores per annum.

These examples demonstrate that while resources are scarce, even the available resources are not properly deployed. The Indian State has increasingly become a stumbling block to our economic growth prospects. The State guzzles vast resources and produces very little in return. We have, in all, about 2.7 crore workers in the organised sector, or about 8 per cent of the total workforce in the country. Of them, an astonishing 2 crore, or nearly three-quarters, are in government! About 1.3 crore are directly employed by the government at various levels, and about 70 lakh are in public sector undertakings. This number in the last decade has actually increased by nearly 10 lakhs. The problem is not the size of government employment in absolute terms. Many nations have a larger proportion of population employed by government. Therefore, the solution does not lie in mindless downsizing. What we need is redeployment and greater productivity. Take a large State like Andhra Pradesh with 900,000 employees in government. About 180,000 or 20 per cent are unproductive for the people, as they are engaged as

peons and drivers! Another 30 per cent (270,000) are support staff (clerks, etc.) whose only purpose is to allegedly help the decision-makers. There are about 40,000 officials with decision-making power at some level or other, and they could perform far more efficiently and economically with a well-trained support staff of a total of 60,000. But we have 450,000 of them employed as clerks, drivers and peons! We have about 310,000 teachers, but the State probably needs another 300,000 teachers of good quality to sustain a credible school education infrastructure. The healthcare system is inadequately staffed. We have a total of about 15,000 judges in India. Germany, with a population of 8 crore, has 30,000 judges! We have far fewer police personnel than needed in modern times. All this demonstrates that it is not merely the size of the government, what matters most is the productivity of the government. If government is productive, it creates conditions for economic growth, which in turn promotes employment in private sector. The ratio of government workers then comes down in time.

Fiscal Rigidities and Indian State

The other important aspect that is curtailing productivity of Indian State apparatus is the rigidities that characterise the fiscal planning in India. One of the recurring themes of Indian public expenditure and budget making in the last decade is the fiscal rigidities making it difficult for governments to change policies and priorities. In the Union Budget, interest payments, defence expenditure, transfer of resources to States and wages are more or less inflexible, and there is no room for manoeuvring. It is now axiomatic that subsidies cannot be removed without incurring high political and social costs. Similarly, in States too, repayment obligations, wages, administrative costs, expenditure on ongoing schemes and projects, State's share in centrally-sponsored schemes, etc. are inflexible, leaving little room for innovation. Again, subsidies are hard to cut. The result is less than adequate social expenditure and poor quality infrastructure.

As early as in 1992, Dr. Manmohan Singh as Finance Minister lamented the shackles imposed by these fiscal compulsions. The only two changes subsequently are, defence expenditure shot up significantly in recent years, and wage expenditure of both the Union and State increased greatly with the acceptance of Fifth Pay Commission recommendations. Economists, analysts and politicians owe it to the country to evolve mechanisms to break this logjam.

However, there are realistic and effective options still available. But we need courage and skill to exercise them and achieve tangible results. Let us take subsidies as an example. For fiscal 2002-03, major Union subsidies account for Rs. 37,392 crore. Food subsidy alone will cross Rs. 21,200 crore. Power subsidies and losses (which will eventually be subsidised) in States will probably account for Rs. 40,000 crore. And there are other subsidies in States too. Is there a way of reducing these subsidies, re-targeting them without inviting massive social unrest and political opposition?

But there are ways of reducing subsidies in a politically acceptable way. Let us suppose the administration of food subsidy (the consumer part of it) is transferred to local governments. We can actually quantify the amount of subsidy based on the foodgrain off-take and price differential at the local level. Then the Union or State can ask the local government to re-target the subsidies to reach the deserving poor and cut down on leakages. This will work if the subsidy amount so saved is made available to the local government for other desirable activities, say infrastructure building or social expenditure. Once local government is assured of additional resources based on performance (cut in subsidies), it will have an incentive to reduce subsidies and unlock these resources. The money saved can thus be used for schools, drains, water supply, roads, health centres and sanitation. Since there is a clear link between subsidy reduction and alternative public goods and services, a powerful local constituency will be built favouring reduction in subsidies. In centralised administration, there are only losers in subsidy reduction, and no corresponding gainers. But once it is decentralised, and savings are alternatively deployed, the same family which loses a subsidy will gain directly through better public goods and services. Or there will be as many or more gainers as losers. We will then have achieved two objectives. Subsidies would be reduced, and expenditure is directed towards more desirable goals. This principle can be applied to several subsidies—food, agricultural power, irrigation, etc.

Public Sector Management and Indian State

The third important question pertaining to the productivity of government is the role of government in running enterprises, and the plight of infrastructure sector. It is by now well-recognised that public sector is often a euphemism for political patronage and private aggrandisement. Politicians, in power or out of it, and career bureaucrats as a rule have no respect for economic logic or wealth creation. A few more jobs to cronies, promise of illusory gains to constituents, cushy rehabilitation for favoured sidekicks, luxurious jaunts, and kickbacks in contracts and purchases are the golden eggs which make PSUs so attractive. In this anxiety to make a killing while the going is good, if the golden goose itself perishes, well, it's too bad! In any case, that is the problem for successors.

This cynical approach has been the hallmark of management of public enterprises. For decades, State monopoly in telecom sector held back services and growth and caused misery to hapless consumers. All this in the name of protecting the revenues of inefficient state monopolies and private oligopolies. Airlines have been managed as private fiefdoms of the presiding ministers. Any attempt to inject competition and efficiency, and invite investment is resisted fiercely with predictable invocation of pride in national carriers. Oil sector has suffered decades of loot by meddlesome politicians, and even now monopolies continue despite the facade of opening up. Steel plants were once the favoured trophies. But again, decades of wasteful practices and sloth led to disastrous consequences. And when a competent manager makes valiant efforts to improve efficiency and profitability, he is often victimised.

The analysis so far has demonstrated that the resources are not a vital constraint and yet the State apparatus regularly fails to provide basic services. Centralised governance has made it increasingly difficult to control fiscal profligacy and the State apparatus has become a dispenser of patronage, resulting in institutionalisation of corruption. Most Indians share a sense of unease and disquiet. Our potential remains unfulfilled even today. Impressive as they are by global standards, our growth rates are insufficient to make a significant dent in poverty, or to absorb the millions of youngsters joining the workforce. Fiscal deficits stubbornly remain at the 10 per cent GDP level. Government continues to be wasteful, inefficient and corrupt. As a consequence, there are many who ask—how come our political class is not displaying courage and skill to achieve tangible results? But political skills of individual leaders alone is not sufficient. There are large numbers of politicians who have consistently displayed courage in taking decisions that are bold and imaginative. Yet the crisis of bad governance persists due to distortions in our political process. What are these distortions? Huge, illegitimate election expenditure has resulted in money power becoming dominant in elections. The social divisions and the electoral system have facilitated rise of fiefdoms and legislator to become a disguised executive. The centralised governance system and vast bureaucracy are having pernicious impact on fiscal health of States and the Union. With these distortions, the State apparatus can never function in a productive manner. And an inefficient State apparatus will act as an impediment to economic prosperity. Hence, an exploration into causes of distortions in political process and reasons for absence of good governance will provide us with the keys to economic prosperity and political transformation of India.

Vicious Cycles

The distortions of our political process have significantly eroded the State's capacity for good governance. First, the positive power to promote public good has been severely restricted; while the negative power of undermining public interest is largely unchecked. Authority is delinked from accountability at most levels, and in respect of most functions. As a result, most State functionaries have realistic and plausible alibis for non-performance. Second, while the electoral system has demonstrated great propensity to change governments and politicians in power, the rules of the game remain largely unchanged. Increasingly, honesty and survival in political office are incompatible. Third, all organs of State are affected by the malaise of governance. Political executive, legislators, bureaucracy and judiciary—no class of functionaries can escape blame. For instance, 2.5 crore cases are pending in courts, and justice is inaccessible, painfully slow and costly. Fourth, at the citizen's level, there are no sufficient incentives for better behaviour. Good behaviour is not rewarded sufficiently and consistently, and bad behaviour is not only not punished consistently, it is in fact rewarded extravagantly. As a result, deviant and socially debilitating behaviour has become prevalent, and short-term individual interest has gained precedence over public good.

Interlocking Vicious Cycles

In a well-functioning democracy, the political process ought to find answers to governance problems. Every election holds a promise for peaceful change. People in India have been voting for change time and again. But the political process is locked into a vicious cycle, and has become a part of the problem. There are several factors complicating the political process, perpetuating the *status quo*.

First, election expenditures are large, unaccounted and mostly illegitimate. For instance, expenditure limit for Assembly elections in most major states was Rs. 6 lakh until recently, when it has been revised to Rs. 10 lakh. In reality average expenditure in most states is several multiples of it, sometimes exceeding Rs. 1 crore. Most of this expenditure is incurred to buy votes, bribe officials and hire musclemen. Sadly, the Southern States, which are hailed for better governance, have the dubious distinction of being the worst offenders in this regard. The expenditure incurred in Andhra Pradesh in the current Assembly and Lok Sabha poll is estimated to be about Rs. 800-1000 crores. On an average, the leading candidates for Assembly spend Rs. 1 to 1.5 crores each, and those for Lok Sabha about Rs. 3-4 crores each. The expenditure in the Kanakapura by-election (in Karnataka) for Lok Sabha held in 2003 was estimated by knowledgeable people at about Rs. 20 crores! The eventual winner was reported to have been heavily outspent by his nearest rival. Curiously, the stakes in that by-election were limited—only a few months of Lok Sabha membership was at stake, and both the leading contenders would have to sit only in opposition! Saidapet by-election in Tamil Nadu Assembly too was said to have broken records, with expenses exceeding Rs. 10 crores!

There are three features of such skyrocketing election expenses. First, large expenditure does not guarantee victory; but inability to incur huge expenses almost certainly guarantees defeat! There are a few candidates who win without large expenditure, but such constituencies are limited. Also in great waves, expenditure is irrelevant. The Lok Sabha victory of Congress in 1971, Janata in 1977, NTR's victory in AP in 1983—these are among the many examples when money power had no role. But in the absence of ideology, and increasing cynicism, large expenditure has become necessary to win. Desperate to win at any cost, parties are compelled to nominate mostly those candidates who can spend big money. Such large, unaccounted expenditure can be sustained only if the system is abused to enable multiple returns on investment. The economic decision making power of the State is on the wane as part of the reform process. But as the demand for illegitimate political funds is not reduced, corruption is shifting to the core areas of State functioning, like crime investigation. Robert Wade studied this phenomenon of corruption, and described the dangerously stable equilibrium, which operates in Indian governance. This vicious chain of corruption has created a class of political and bureaucratic 'entrepreneurs' who treat public office as big business.

Second, as the vicious cycle of money power, polling irregularities, and corruption has taken hold of the system, electoral verdicts ceased to make a difference to people. Repeated disappointments made people come to the conclusion that no matter who wins the election, they always end up losing. As incentive for discerning behaviour in voting has disappeared, people started maximising their short-term returns. As a result, money and liquor are accepted habitually by many voters. This pattern of behaviour only converted politics and elections into big business. As illegitimate electoral expenditure skyrocketed, the vicious cycle of corruption is further strengthened. With public good delinked from voting, honesty and survival in public office are further separated.

Third, this situation bred a class of political 'entrepreneurs' who established fiefdoms. In most constituencies, money power, caste clout, bureaucratic links, and political contacts came together, perpetuating politics of fiefdoms. Entry into electoral politics is restricted in real terms, as people who cannot muster these forces have little chance of getting elected. While there is competition for political power, it is often restricted between two or three families over a long period of time; parties are compelled to choose one of these individuals or families to enhance their chances of electoral success. Parties thus are helpless, and political process is stymied. Absence of internal democratic norms in parties and the consequent oligarchic control has denied a possibility of rejuvenation of political process through establishment of a virtuous cycle.

Fourth, in a centralised governance system, even if the vote is wisely used by people, public good cannot be promoted. As the citizen is distanced from the decision making process, the administrative machinery has no capacity to deliver public services of high quality or low cost. Such a climate which cannot ensure better services or good governance breeds competitive populism to gain electoral advantage. Such populist politics have led to serious fiscal imbalances.

Fifth, fiscal health can be restored only by higher taxes, or reduced subsidies or wages. The total tax revenues of the Union and States are of the order of only 15 per cent of GDP. Higher taxation is resisted in the face of ubiquitous corruption and poor quality services. De-subsidisation is always painful for the poor who do not see alternative benefits accruing from the money saved by withdrawal of subsidies. A vast bureaucracy under centralised control can neither be held to account, nor is wage reduction a realistic option.

Sixth, elected governments are helpless to change this perilous situation. As the survival of the government depends on the support of legislators, their demands have to be met. The legislator has thus become the disguised, unaccountable executive controlling all facets of government functioning. The local legislator and the bureaucrats have a vested interest in denying local governments any say in real decision making. The vicious cycle of corruption and centralised, unaccountable governance is thus perpetuated.

Seventh, the first-past-the-post (FPTP) system exacerbates our social divisions as it tends to over-represent geographically concentrated social groups and under-represent the scattered minorities. This representational distortion leads to ghettoization and marginalisation of the excluded social groups, which then indulge in strategic voting. This gives rise to vote-bank politics in which obscurantists become interlocutors of the group drowning the voice of reason and modernity. For instance, religious symbolism and not education and job opportunities become dominant issues of public discourse. This pandering of fundamentalism leads to competitive mobilisation of various groups based on primordial loyalties, leading to communal polarisation and social strife.

Eighth, the need for money power and caste clout to win a plurality of votes in FPTP system precludes political participation of men and women of integrity and competence. With their exclusion, bad public policy and incompetent governance become endemic, deepening the crisis.

Ninth, under FPTP system, only a high threshold of voting ensures victory. Usually a party needs 35 per cent vote or more to get reasonable representation in legislature, or social groups with local dominance get elected. As a significant but scattered support pays no electoral dividends, reform groups and parties below the threshold tend to wither away. Voters prefer other 'winnable' parties and candidates. This tends to marginalise reform parties, and national parties in many states. It is no accident that the main national parties, Congress and BJP, are directly competing for power in only a few major states. In most states, one or two regional parties are dominant. FPTP thus tends to lead to oligopoly of parties.

Given this complex nature of our crisis, many of the reforms that have been enacted and those in the pipeline are necessary, but not sufficient. Apart from reforms in local governments, judiciary and bureaucracy and effective instruments to enforce accountability and check corruption, we need to pursue systemic reforms changing the nature of elections and process of power. In my considered judgement, there are three such reforms required.

1. Mixed Compensatory Proportional Representation

The FPTP system that India has adopted led to several distortions, given the passage of time and

ingenuity of legislators. Politics of fiefdom at constituency level has forced the parties to rely on local strongmen. As a result, the political parties and independent candidates have astronomical election expenditure for vote buying and other illegitimate purposes. This has led to a significant weakening of the party platform and ideology, reducing elections to private power games. In many states, national parties have been marginalised where their voting percentage falls below a threshold. Following this, regional parties have occupied centre stage in several pockets, holding larger interests at ransom.

All these failings find expression in serious and long-term predicaments. The inability of all political parties to attract and nurture best talent is the primary issue. Difficulties of minority representation leading to ghetto mentality, backlash, and communal tension form another facet of the problem. Lastly, leadership is undermined by permanent reservation of constituencies (or regular rotation) in order to provide fair representation to excluded groups. The solution to this flawed system is adoption of proportional representation.

Pure proportional representation (PR) in India would invite three legitimate objections. First, in a caste-ridden society PR will lead to further political fragmentation, mushrooming of parties, and greater social schism. The answer to this problem lies in having a reasonable threshold of voting requirement, of say 10 per cent of votes polled in major states, for representation in legislature. Second, party bosses will become even more autocratic in nomination of candidates in list system. This tendency can be curbed by political party reform, mandating choice of candidates for elective office by members of the party or their elected delegates through secret ballot at the local level. Third, people are used to a system of territorial representation, and PR snaps the link between the constituency and its elected legislator. This can be addressed by electing half the legislators from single-member constituencies as now, and electing the rest from party lists in a manner that the final composition of legislature is based on the principle of proportionality of votes. The key features of the suggested system are as follows:

1. The overall representation of parties in legislature will be based on the proportion of valid vote obtained by them.

2. A party will be entitled to such a quota based on vote share only when it crosses a threshold, say 10 per cent of vote in a major state, and more in minor states.

3. Fifty per cent of legislators will be elected from territorial constituencies based on FPTP system. This will ensure the link between the legislator and the constituents.

4. The balance 50 per cent will be allotted to parties to make up for their shortfall based on proportion of votes.

    e.g. 1): If the party is entitled to 50 seats in legislature based on vote share, but had 30 members elected in FPTP system, 20 more will be elected based on the party list.

e.g. 2): If the party is entitled to 50 seats based on vote share, but had only 10 members elected in FPTP system, it will have 40 members elected from the list.

5. The party lists will be selected democratically at the state or multi-party constituency level by the members of the party or their elected delegates through secret ballot.

6. There will be two votes cast by voters-one for a candidate for FPTP election, and the other for a party to determine the vote share of the parties.

It needs to be remembered that PR system can be effective only after internal functioning of political parties is regulated by law. Otherwise, PR system will give extraordinary power to party leaders and may prove counter-productive.

However, the PR system has one more advantage of ensuring better representation of women in legislatures.

2. Political Party Regulation by Law

Political recruitment has suffered a great deal, and bright young people are no longer attracted to politics. Centralised functioning of parties is imposing enormous burden on leadership to manage the party bureaucracy, leaving little time for evolving sensible policies or governance. Party leaders are helpless in candidate selection, and the choice is often between 'Tweedledum' and 'Tweedledee'. An important reform to improve the quality of politics and restore credibility would be a law to regulate political parties' functioning, without in any way restricting leadership choice and policy options. A law needs to be enacted to regulate political parties in the following five key aspects:

1. Free and open membership with no arbitrary expulsions.
2. Democratic, regular, free, secret ballot for leadership election; and opportunity to challenge and unseat leadership through formal procedures with no risk of being penalised.
3. Democratic choice of party candidates for elective office by members or their elected delegates through secret ballot.
4. Full transparency in funding and utilisation of resources.
5. Clear Separation of Powers at the State and Local Levels through Direct Election of Head of Government

The other systemic reform that is needed to isolate the executive from unwanted influences, as has been pointed out, is to ensure direct election of Head of Government in States and Local Governments.

As election costs have skyrocketed, candidates spend money in anticipation of rewards and opportunities for private gain after election. Legislators perceive themselves as disguised executive, and Chief Ministers are hard pressed to meet their constant demands. Postings, transfers, contracts, tenders, tollgates, parole, developmental schemes, and crime investigation—all these become sources of patronage and rent seeking. No government functioning honestly can survive under such circumstances. While the legislators never allow objective and balanced decision making by the executive in the actual functioning of legislation, their role has become nominal and largely inconsequential. This blurring of the lines of demarcation between the executive and legislature is one of the cardinal features of the crisis of our governance system.

Therefore, separation of powers, and direct election are necessary in states and local governments. At the national level, such a direct election is fraught with serious dangers. Our linguistic diversity demands a parliamentary executive. Any individual seen as the symbol of all authority can easily become despotic, given our political culture. But in states, separation of powers poses no such dangers. The Union government, Supreme Court, constitutional functionaries like the Election Commission, UPSC, and CAG, and the enormous powers and prestige of the Union will easily control authoritarianism in any state. This necessitates adoption of a system of direct election of the head of government in states and local governments. The fundamental changes suggested find mention as under:

The legislature will be elected separately and directly, while the ministers will be drawn from outside the legislature. The legislature will have a fixed term, and cannot be dissolved prematurely except in exceptional circumstances (sedition, secession, etc.) by the Union government. The head of government will have a fixed term, and cannot be voted out of office by the legislature. Any vacancy of office will be filled by a due process of succession. The elected head of government will have no more than two terms of office. Even though these changes may not be panacea to all evils in the present structure of legislature and executive, they will certainly encourage more healthy and vibrant democracy and democratic processes. Further, clear and periodic delineation of functions between Union and States, and among various tiers of local governments, is also a necessary condition for a vibrant democracy. It is only a true federal structure that can ensure unity in this multi-ethnic and multi-religious society.

Conclusion

The above mentioned reforms are not panacea for all the ills that are plaguing the society, but they would, if implemented—radically alter the political landscape and make good governance possible. These reforms will change the nature of incentives in our political life and will promote choice and political competition. Honesty will once again be compatible with political survival and advancement, and the finest public-spirited citizens can play a meaningful role in rejuvenation of our polity and accelerating our economic growth. Indian society will rediscover its potential, and the nation will have unshackled itself from a moribund structure to play its rightful role in today's world. These reform measures will specifically help us combat the distortions in our political process which are undermining the effectiveness of the State and thereby the economic prosperity. Economic reforms are necessary, but are not sufficient. We need to restructure our governance process to make it supportive of a productive, competitive market economy. Political and electoral reforms, decentralisation of power, measures to enforce rule of law, and instruments of accountability—these are the vital tasks ahead. We already lost precious time, and any further prevarication will be costly. It is high time we recognised that good politics, good economics and stable and peaceful society go together. One cannot exist without the others.

8 | Justice Delayed is Justice Denied

Mass Crimes in India: A Challenge to Our Democracy

TEESTA SETALVAD

INDIAN pluralism and diversity have thrived and survived despite the severe challenges of the past century. While these challenges have been of various kinds, economic, social and political, it is the response of our democratic system to these that will ultimately provide an accurate assessment of whether or not our institutions and wings of democracy are geared for the maximum good of the maximum number; of whether real democracy in any sense has evolved in India after we became independent; whether our Structures of Democracy and our Institutions have truly evolved structures and systems that address the needs of the Indian people. Electoral democracy we have but do we have democracy in the real sense? Have the structures and institutions of democracy been genuinely democratised?

The pathetic and low rate of justice delivery in our criminal justice system is one area that has suffered from systemic and value based failure. While at many times of larger crises like communal or caste pogroms the judiciary is perceived as the last resort or final saviour, the huge backlog of cases that clog our courts and the utter failure of the judiciary to effect time bound trials (criminal trials could drag on 10 years and a civil suit to 25 years) has made a mockery of the justice delivery systems.

Witness vulnerability and protection has become a live national issue once again with the unfortunate turnaround of Zahira Shaikh in the Best Bakery case. But if we rise above the personality and look at the issue, what does this once again tell us? The desire for justice and retribution, for a victim and eyewitness to a ghastly and horrendous mass crime—where near and dear ones have been snatched away because of their community or caste—is and can remain strong if we have an effective justice delivery system, if the system aids and supplements every human being's desire to right wrongs that have been committed. But if the system makes a mockery of the tragedy, drags cases on (what has happened to the 1984 prosecutions is a case in point) can ordinary eyewitnesses and victims actually be expected to have the same zeal for right and retribution 10, 20 years on? They need emotional closure and need to move on. The system needs to radically reform itself so that we can proudly say that justice delivery and the rule of law are maxims that Indian state and society lives and swears by.

The low conviction rate in India's criminal justice system for all crimes poses a fair but harsh question to all wings of the Indian state. If this is the state of affairs for stray individual crimes, what happens when there are mass crimes perpetuated against a particular tribe, caste or community? Where the state has often been complicit or directly involved? Is the Indian state interested in the deliverance of justice, in the punishment of the guilty?

Nearly 30 months after the genocidal violence that rocked the western Indian state of Gujarat, searing questions that the tragedies have raised related to justice and rehabilitation remain completely unanswered. Specifically, issues of state accountability after mass violence, independent policing, adequate reparation and the response of democratic institutions of the judiciary to such crimes hang suspended in mid-air, as the proverbial shortness of public memory betters the best efforts to keep some of these issues alive.

Post-Independence, India has had it's shocking share of mass violence driven not just by community but equally, brutally, by caste during which the archaic Code of Criminal Procedure, penned by colonial masters has

proved itself inadequate. Often official or other Commissions of Inquiry have sat, examined these lapses and made suggestions. One common feature of these has been is that the political class, whatever its ideological hue, have simply not bothered to publicly debate or implement these suggestions. The Indian judiciary, at all levels has restrained itself to minimal intervention in matters of social justice and violence. The delay by the highest echelons of the Indian judiciary to respond and respond squarely to challenges posed by mass violence itself raises serious questions on the ability of our institutions to punish the guilty.

The cynical delay in the commencement and conclusion of investigations and trials, the huge backlog of cases in all our courts and the resistance in all three wings of the Indian state—the legislature, executive and the judiciary to enact swift and harsh reforms have worsened the state of affairs.

What happened after Gujarat 2002? Something similar. Senior jurists and others, sat in a Concerned Citizens's Tribunal and actually recommended the establishment of a Statutory National Crimes Tribunal that must contain its own evolved jurisprudence drawn from the International Law on Genocide[1] and further urged urgent and quick reforms in the Indian Police Force. Drastic reforms in the Indian police system

---

1. *Crimes Against Humanity, Volume II,* "Long Term Recommendations-Concerned Citizens Tribunal Report"; Tribunal headed by Justice V.R. Krishna Iyer and with members like Justice P.B. Sawant, Justice Hosbet Suresh, K.G. Kannabiran, K.S. Subramaniam, Aruna Roy, Tanika Sarkar, and Ghanshyam Shah.

including guaranteeing it's independence and ensuring representation and diversity had been recommended as far back as 1981 by the official National Police Commission itself.[2] The work of the Concerned Citizens Tribunal that lasted several months with no assistance from any official machinery is available in a two-volume report published from Mumbai.[3]

Today, judicial matters related to the genocidal violence in Gujarat have been brought centre stage through two pivotal cases currently being heard in the Supreme Court. The fact that this has happened at all is due in large measure to the initiatives taken by the statutory National Human Rights Commission (NHRC) since the justice process in the state was systematically derailed[4] backed by a gritty citizens group, Citizens for Justice and Peace, that has mandated itself the responsibility to continue the struggle for justice and reparation for the victim survivors, however tough this may turn out to be.

Efforts are alive through these judicial interventions to move the criminal trials of the worst carnages outside the state of Gujarat.[5] This argument for turning over both the investigation and conduct of the criminal

inquiries to an area outside the control of the current chief minister, Narendra Modi and the state and administration under him has been made since the start of the carnage last year, both by the NHRC (April 2003) as also by public interest litigations filed in the Supreme Court in April 2003 itself.[6] If these had been heard judiciously and promptly by the Apex Court when it had been first approached last year, concerns related to the utterly subverted and paralysed local atmosphere in the state of Gujarat would have been met and more promptly answered.

Unfortunately, judicial record in dealing with such mass community-driven carnages remains pathetic. Sikh widow survivors of the 1984 pogrom against their community in the country's capital (that followed the assassination of former prime minister Indira Gandhi by her Sikh bodyguard)[7] battle in vain for justice that 19 years later cynically and brutally evades them. Similarly, Muslim women survivors of 53 young males shot dead in cold blood in Meerut-Hashumpura (a town in western Uttar Pradesh) in 1989[8] still struggle for justice. The recent conviction of Dara Singh and associates for the

---

2. *ibid.* section on Recommendations—Police.

3. *ibid.* published by Sabrang Communications for *Citizens for Justice and Peace,* Mumbai.

4. NHRC Report and Recommendations during and after last year's carnage in Gujarat proved particularly embarassing for the State.

5. Plea in the SLP filed by the NHRC, dated August 1, 2003 and the SLP (Criminal) filed by *CJP* and Zahira Shaikh dated August 8, 2003 in the Supreme Court of India.

6. Two petitions filed by D.N. Pathak and others and Mallika Sarabhai and others prayed for the transfer of key cases to the CBI and investigations in these through this Independent agency.

7. Darpan Kaur, a Sikh widow who lost 12 family members and even filed a First Information Report with the police against former Congress minister H.K.L. Bhagat was first offered a bribe of Rs. 25 lakhs and when she refused, was even beaten brutally. She has refused to give in.

8. The FIR in this crime was filed by a police officer of the rank of SP in his own name, Vibhuti Narain Rai who today is the IG of Uttar Pradesh.

burning alive of Christian pastor Graham Staines and his two sons in January 1999 is a rare case of a sessions court punishing those guilty of communally-driven crimes. Most pertinently, the examples of these and many more such survivors to see justice done decades after the crime are living testimonies to the fact that human beings need to believe and find justice for unspeakable crimes before peace and reconciliation can be effected. A failure to administer to this cry for justice renders a system vulnerable; torn from within by festering wounds and hurts that do not heal but in fact create their attendant aberrations. This is the unfortunate reality in India today.

Gujarat Documentation and Legal Action

There was extensive documentation of the genocide in Gujarat by civil liberties organisations and non-governmental agencies. Thirty months later, as the struggle for justice gets intensified due to the efforts made in the Supreme Court of India in the Best Bakery case and the Godhra victims case, the difference between documentation and legal intervention becomes sharp and clear.

Where Lies the Problem?

Cumbersome Procedure in Indian Courts

Except for a brief spell in the eighties and nineties when a few judges of the Supreme Court of India, especially Justice V.R. Krishna Iyer, a doyen to the human rights movement in India and Justice P.N. Bhagwati took *suo motu* steps to make the Apex Indian

Courts intervene in the field if rights' abuse, generally attitude of the authorities towards interventions by civil liberties groups is grudging and resentful.

Law Courts, Institutions and Human Rights Bodies

The establishment of the National Human Rights Commission (NHRC) in the early nineties and the State Human Rights Commissions (SHRCs) in some states—though others like Gujarat have adamantly refused to establish them and some like Maharashtra have tried to cuckold these bodies—has in a sense drawn Indian establishment's attention to both the human rights issue as also International Human Rights Law; but the inadequacy of personnel has also severely limited the functioning of the NHRC. This combined with the fact that no independent investigation power has been given amounts to a severe lacuna in effective intervention for rights' abuse.

Limitation of the Code of Criminal Procedure, Indian Penal Code and Indian Evidence Act in Dealing with Mass Crimes

1. Failure of Criminal Justice system.
2. Failure of intelligence.
3. Preventive Arrests.
4. Police participation in the riots.
5. Illegal registration of FIRs (Problems with FIRs):
   a) their failure to record First Information Reports (FIRs) and in fact file omnibus;
   b) police complicity in not naming the accused despite repeated insistence of the victim/survivors that all accused should be named;

c) worst of all, their insistence on recording omnibus FIRs for whole areas, regions and towns instead of separate detailed ones for every crime and offence committed.

Section 154 of the CrPC (Criminal Procedure Code) deals with the First Information Report of cognizable offences and is the first crucial step in prosecution of offenders.

A. Omnibus FIRs

It is a fundamental principle of criminal law that every offence needs to be separately registered, investigated and tried. Filing omnibus FIRs is one of the simplest ways of avoiding detailed investigations and effective trials. In many cases in Gujarat where 80 or 90 shops have been burnt or a large number of people have been killed, instead of filing separate FIRs in respect of each incident, the police has registered collective FIRs thus virtually scuttling the possibility of detailed investigation or conviction. Apart from this, many incidents separated over time (sometimes days) and place and concerning different victims and accused have been clubbed together. Moreover, when individuals came forward to lodge their FIRs, they were told the FIRs have already been recorded, and that no second FIR was possible.

B. FIRs without Names of Accused

Most of the FIRs which have been filed, especially where police is the informant, do not contain the names of the accused and only say that an unidentified mob attacked. There are significant number of cases where the victims actually named the accused but the Gujarat police

have refused to lodge their names in the FIRs. Instead, the police took on the role of a partisan intermediary in evidence recorded from Naroda, Chamanpura, Odh, Sardarpura, Bharuch, Ankleshwar, Varodara, Mehsana, Himmatnagar, Sabarkantha and Banaskantha. In these cases, the police told the complainants that the FIR would be lodged only if the name of the accused is deleted. For example, at village Por, 3 women and 3 children were killed. The victims have identified and named 95 attackers but the police refused to include their names in the FIRs. The detailed area-wise list of incidents is covered by the Tribunal in the section on 'Summary of Evidence'.

Box 8.1

Points to Be Noted in Deliberate Manipulation on Investigations

i. Minority community victimised

ii. Deliberate obfuscation of identity of accused

iii. Unprofessional investigations

iv. Real culprits not arrested

v. No identification parades

vi. Combing operations

vii. Rape victims

viii. No action against media

ix. No Action against Hate Speech and Hate Writing

x. No action against VHP/Bajrang Dal

xi. Non-implementation of NHRC recommendations

xii. Status of criminal investigations into major massacres

xiii. Partisan language in chargesheets filed by the police

Status of Prosecution in Major Carnages

The Criminal Prosecution into major mass carnages has been derailed by deliberate manipulation and destruction of investigation.

Including the Best Bakery case where 14 persons were slaughtered and burnt alive, three other major carnages where 87 persons were burnt alive (Limbadiya Chowky, Kidiad) and 70 persons similarly butchered (two incidents in Pandharwada village in Panchmahal district) resulted in acquittals in October 2002. The Gujarat government has compromised its investigations and commitment to the Indian Constitution by not providing adequate legal aid for victims of the carnage and actually appointing persons belonging to rabid outfits like the Vishwa Hindu Parishad and Bajrang Dal as public prosecutors.

Investigations into Godhra Mass Burning

After the Godhra tragedy the Gujarat police arrested 62 persons, including at least 7 boys, all said to be under the age of 16. They were booked under the Prevention of Terrorism Act (POTA) by the government railway police (GRP) for the February 27 attack on the Sabarmati Express in Godhra. Following public outrage, the application of POTA to these 7 boys was withdrawn. But all the accused, including the 7 boys, still face charges of murder, attempt to murder, criminal conspiracy, arson, rioting and damaging public property. All are in the GRP lock-up in Godhra since February 27. Family members of the arrested minors were not informed in direct contravention of the orders of the Supreme Court in the Joginder Singh case. The boys are: Haroon Iqbal, Farooq Kharadi, Firozkhan Pathan (residents of Signal Falia); Asif Kader, Altaf Diwan and Naseer Pathan (residents of Vejalpur Road); and Hasankhan Pathan of Dahod. The attitude of the police after arresting minors is telling. The inspector of Godhra town police station, K. Trivedi said it was not possible to check their age at the time of arrest. "They were seen near the site of the incident, so we arrested them. The rest will be taken care of by the judiciary," he said. Hasankhan Pathan, who is a Class IX student in Dahod in the Panchmahals district, 150 km away, had come to Godhra to meet his aunt and uncle on February 26. His date of birth according to school records is October 31, 1986. Evidence recorded by the Tribunal records his relative Hussain Khan Pathan saying, "In the morning, he was playing with some other local boys, including Firoz and Mustaq, when they heard of something going on near the railway track. They got scared and came inside their houses. After a few hours, the police came and picked up Hasan near Ali Masjid on charges of mass murder." Under the Juvenile Justice Act, minors below 16 have to be sent to a juvenile home, not to a police lock-up. "But they have been kept in police custody along with other accused in this case. We showed the age-proof documents of these minors to police, but they did not listen to us," said Soukat I. Samor, a senior advocate, who represents some of the accused. This is one more instance of police misconduct in the context of the Godhra tragedy and the genocide that followed.

The Godhra police failed in their first major case, when Additional Sessions Judge Viram Y. Desai acquitted all 73 accused of all charges against them on September 22, 2002. The judge accused the police of extracting the names of the accused from those who were arrested first, and the investigating officer (IO) of fabricating evidence. He expressed doubts over whether one of the incidents occurred at all. These findings by the Judge cast a major cloud on the conduct of the police in the Godhra investigations.

Following the Godhra incident these 73 who were arrested, were charged with conspiracy, rioting, arson, inciting communal passions, attacking the police, robbery, etc. All the Hindus got bail, whereas most of the Muslims (accused of burning property belonging to their own community, including a mosque and school), remained in custody till the trial was over. Some of them continue to be in custody on the charge of burning the train. The witnesses for the prosecution were all policemen. The prosecutor argued that since curfew was imposed, it was difficult to find independent witnesses. Hence, the testimony of the policemen should be believed, as also the *panchnamas* made on the spot by them.

The Judge found that none of the charges were proved because of the conduct of the investigating officer (IO) who first brought in a set of accused persons to the police station, who in turn named others as co-accused, who were later arrested in combing operations. The Judge held that this revealed that "there is no concrete evidence against the 73 accused who were picked up out of 2,000 people". This verdict of the Sessions Judge points out several serious lacunae in police investigations. Yet persons, allegedly innocent, continue to be detained ostensibly for the Godhra Mass Burning Case in Gujarat.

Selective Use of Anti-Terrorism Law against Minorities in Gujarat

The Prevention of Terrorism Act (POTA) was brought into existence as an ordinance just a few months before the Godhra and Gujarat tragedies but enacted within the state of Gujarat only on February 28, 2002. Since, this law which has provisions that militate against basic protection of human rights of the citizen has been used selectively against the Muslim minority in Gujarat.

Medico Legal Issues

During the post-Godhra carnage, government and municipal hospitals that gave post-mortem reports recorded a shocking lapse when detailing causes of injury in the case of police firings. The post-mortem reports in such cases mentions nothing about injury by bullet but states that death was due to injury and shock. This lapse, we hope, is not deliberate, as otherwise it would legitimately invite the criticism that hospitals in Gujarat are not different from other public institutions which have been communalised.

Role of the Judiciary

The ostrich-like attitude of the Indian judiciary when such mass crimes take place as never more evident as in

Gujarat. To quote again from *Crimes Against Humanity,* "While we are clear that as a rule the courts cannot play the role of government or executive and take charge of the maintenance of public order, there comes a time when the judiciary is looked upon as the last resort. At such times, and such moments of time were evident during the Gujarat carnage and remain important to date, the judiciary is expected to rise to the full capability of it's Constitutional Obligations and Duties, take swift and clear *suo motu* action if necessary to restore the belief of disillusioned, marginalised and alienated sections of our population who have been victims of state sponsored massacres. *In not doing so, the courts fail in their primary duty.* We state with regret that the casualness with which matters relating to the Gujarat carnage have been handled by the court(s), high and low, is a matter of serious concern for the rule of law and the survival of constitutional principles in any real sense in this country.

"Even open acts of threats against two High Court judges belonging to the minority community, did not stir the high judiciary into any action against the government. This is a sad reflection on the judiciary which in the past had considered the slapping of a magistrate a sufficient enough reason to invoke the contempt jurisdiction of the Apex Court!"

Limitations of the Struggle for Justice

The struggle for justice to the victim survivors of the Gujarat genocide has narrowed itself down today. The weight of the system that we are battling forces us to pick and choose cases even in our struggle for justice. The magnitude of what happened in Gujarat has died in public memory; worse, even our battles are today constrained to attempting to get justice for only those victim survivors of the worst incidents where over a dozen persons were butchered and slaughtered.

What of the innocent victims, many minors who were shot dead by an unaccountable police? What of the girls and women who were killed after brutal sexual violence? What of some of whom survived and have been forced back to live in the same villages where the crimes were committed?[9]

What of the 10,000-odd homes that were destroyed so thoroughly that the pathetic Rs. 5,000–Rs. 40,000 paid in compensation to only a few is barely enough to pick up the threads and start living again? What about the reparation for the businesses destroyed and the agricultural lands seized?

No less than 1,16,000 persons were internal refugees thrown out of home and hearth and living in relief camps for over seven months last year. During this period, the state of Gujarat refused to give them food, water and medicines despite their Constitutional Mandate that they bear the cost of this internal displacement. Again, it took legal interventions in the Gujarat High Court—two writ petitions supported by CJP which included flying down

9. *CCT, Volume II,* "Short-term Recommendations of Reparation, Relief and Rehabilitation".

a senior lawyer from Mumbai since the atmosphere was so communally surcharged in the state that few wanted to appear in defence of minority community victims![10] As a result of this legal intervention Rs. 10 crores had to be paid out from state government coffers to the relief camp organisers.

International aid that flowed easily into the state just a year before the carnage when a tragic earthquake struck Kutch in Gujarat close to the Indo-Pak border (on January 26, 2001) was sorely missing as an utterly callous central and state government simply did not allow international aid agencies to come to the aid of the victim survivors of the genocide. This raises serious questions of the ethics of the international aid, issues that have arisen before whether it is during the UN sanctions in Iraq and what this meant for children and women or in Afghanistan.

The violence in Gujarat in 2002 was preceded for some months by the systematic distribution of material, some anonymous, that systematically spewed hatred and venom against the Muslim minority in the state. Even during the outbreaks of violence thousands of these pamphlets could be found—some advocated systematic economic boycott of Muslims and even printed an address of the Vishwa Hindu Parishad's office at the bottom;[11] others that were even more graphic and vicious advocated mutilation and rape.[12]

The systematic use of hate speech and hate writing has been a crucial part of the politics of communalism within India especially since the mid-1980s when the movement of the construction of a Ram temple at Ayodhya began. This period saw the sharp rise of communal forces from both within the Hindu majority and the Muslim minority. The opening of the locks of the Babri Masjid in 1986 was preceded by Parliament's enactment of a law that excluded rightful maintenance rights to Muslim women, a demand made by the patriarchal and communal Muslim male leadership. The cleverly constructed movement to 'construct' a Ram temple at Ayodhya was in fact (and remains to date as again October 17, 2003 is a deadline set by Hindu fanatic groups to begin construction of the temple with utter disregard for the law) always to destroy a Mosque and thereby teach a much-deserved lesson to the Muslim minority. Brute violence and threat was an integral part of this movement led and inspired by none less than India's deputy prime minister, L.K. Advani when he began his *rath yatra* from Somnath, in Gujarat in 1990. His close aide and organiser of the procession was none less than Narendra Modi, today Gujarat's chief minister and 'chief architect of the state sponsored genocide'.[13]

---

10. Mr. Aspi Chinoy along with Mr. Suhel Tirmizi argued the matter for over five hours before the Judge actually appointed a committee and thereafter passed orders that made the state government liable to make good the damages to the organisers of relief camps.

---

11. Pamphlet Poison, *Gujarat Genocide 2002, Communalism Combat March-April 2002.*

12. *ibid.*

13. *CCT,* Volume II State Complicity.

No actions have been initiated on grave violations of Indian law on hate speech and writing that provoke and demonise sections of the Indian people, especially the minority.

Serious Questions for the Indian Police Force

The utter collapse of confidence in the police among the citizenry and the dismal deterioration in their collective conduct in the state is more than serious cause for a national debate and concern. It is linked seminally with the wider issue of drastic police autonomy and reform. Senior policemen who have dealt with communally volatile situations have recommended, repeated and at various fora, the urgent need for accountability and reform within the police. Three reports of the National Police Commission,[14] a professional body that studies, reflects and analyses the state of police functioning in the country have also noted with alarm, growing reported evidences of prejudicial conduct and made harsh and specific recommendations. The content of these have unfortunately never become the basis for national debate and concern.[15]

After some in the Los Angeles Police were found through videographic evidence to be kicking suspected criminals or innocents simply because they were black; attempts were made to inject institutional safeguards against racial discrimination within the police in America. Post-WTC, the numerous unrecorded and unaccounted arrests of innocent immigrants has been the focus of a studied campaign by the American Civil Liberties Union. The Stephen Lawrence case in the United Kingdom led to the Macphearson Commission that has attempted some reform within the British police, also on the issue of racial bias. The issue then is not whether we will have institutions and set-ups that are entirely bias-free but whether we have the moral and ethical preparedness to accept that the malaise exists and thereafter set about attempts to cure it.

For this to happen, institutions and those individuals that symbolise or man them need to purge themselves of the state of denial. Psychologists say this is the surest form of defensiveness. Defensiveness suggests that the emotion hides a truth. So it is with communal bias in the Indian Police Force. First, there needs to be strong and committed effort to get out of the constant state of denial. Simply because, since 1981 there are just too many concrete examples to show that communal bias not only exists but seriously affects, detrimentally, professional and neutral functioning, trampling on therefore the fundamental rights of a section of the to equal treatment by and protection from the law.

The radical measures then needed include a re-vamping of the structure of the police. As important are prompt and punitive measures against officers and men

---

14. Sixth Report of the National Police Commission, March 1981: "Several instances where police officers and policemen have shown an unmistakable bias against a particular community while dealing with communal situations," adding that the composition of the police is "heavily weighted in favour of the majority community."

15. "Who is to Blame?", *Communalism Combat,* March 1998.

guilty of crude and gross misdemeanours that include ethnically-driven criminal acts including murder, loot and arson. In Hashimpura, Meerut, 1987, the Provincial Armed Constabulary of the UP police shot dead, in cold blood, 40 Muslim youth.[16] Not a single man in uniform has been punished to date. In Bombay, 1992-93, the then Joint Commissioner of Police, R.D. Tyagi shot dead nine innocent men believing them to be Kashmiri terrorists.[17] Though chargesheeted, his trial for conviction is yet to begin. This author tapped police wireless messages during the second round of Bombay riots, in January 1993, the transcribed text of which reveal a deep and abiding anti-minority hatred operating and affecting actions among a section of the Indian police.[18] In Gujarat, too, in all the scenes of recent massacre significant sections of the police were party to the crimes committed. It is unlikely that the struggle for justice against the criminals in uniform will chart any new path this time, without an outcry following a relentless national debate for drastic and radical police reform.

Law on Mass Crimes

Targeted violence directed at particular sections of society, be it an ethnic tribe, caste or a religious community, has over the past decades posed a serious challenge to traditional criminal jurisprudence. The very nature of these mass/collective crimes contain within them elements of pre-planning and complicity often compounded by the fact that both state and non-state actors are the perpetrators. Hence they require, clearly defined and special legal and jurisprudential instruments.

Internationally, democratic societies have responded to this disturbing trend that had hitherto allowed criminals in authority and uniform to go scot-free by enacting special laws pertaining to the prevention of, and punishment for genocide and crimes against humanity, as also adequate reparation for the victims of mass crimes.

The enactment and adoption of the Rome Statute and the establishment of the International Criminal Court collectively by modern nation-states was meant to ensure that the punishment for genocidal acts or crimes against humanity is not prevented by countries protecting home-grown perpetrators and that internationally, their prosecution is possible. Interestingly, neither the US nor India are signatories to the Rome Statute.

Within India, the cumulative experience over the past 25 years or so, of both officially appointed judicial commissions of inquiry and people's tribunals set up by rights' groups, points to the crying need for special jurisprudence that addresses the issue of genocidal or mass crimes and incorporates within its ambit the issues

16. "No Riot can Continue for more than 24 Hours unless the State wants it to Continue", Cover Interview of then DIG, BSF, V.N.Rai by Teesta Setalvad for *Communalism Combat*, February 25.

17. "Damning Verdict", *Report of the Srikrishna Commission*, published by Sabrang Communications, p. 114.

18. See Annexure 2, from "Saffron in Uniform", *Communalism Combat*, p. 5.

of just reparation and victims' rights (victimology). It was after the Gujarat genocide of 2002 that the Concerned Citizens Tribunal (Crime against Humanity–Gujarat 2002) translated this collective experience for the first time into recommendations for appropriate legislation.

Given the fact that the recently elected United Progressive Alliance (UPA) government has declared its intention to enact a special legislation to contain communal violence, we felt that the time was right for a collective Citizens' Consultation for the purpose.

Between August 21-23, 2004, the Minorities Council (Delhi), the Centre for the Study of Indian Muslims (Jamia Hamdard, Delhi), Citizens for Justice and Peace (Mumbai) and Communalism Combat jointly convened a two-day consultation in Delhi to frame a draft bill. Apart from those named at the end of the draft reproduced below, senior serving and retired IPS officials also participated in the consultation. Already, over 250 groups and mass organisations are signatories to this draft. Before the draft's submission to the Union Government, aspects of this Draft law have been circulated and discussed.

The name of the proposed law is *The Prevention and Punishment of Genocide and Crimes against Humanity (Draft) Bill, 2004.*

The Statement of Objects and Reasons states that, "The Common Minimum Programme of the Government promises the enactment of a Comprehensive law on communal violence." At present we have no less than 15 different laws applicable in a riot situation; yet they were all found wanting in situations like the Gujarat carnage, 2002, mainly because the concerned state authorities lacked the political will to effectively enforce them.

However, to draft a comprehensive law on communal violence may take its own time, as that in turn depends on the complex process of building a civil society that is secular, humane and sensitive to human rights; yet it cannot be gainsaid that with a view to prevent any such recurrence of what happened in Gujarat and elsewhere, earlier, (including Delhi 1984 or Bombay 1992-1993), it is necessary to enact a law enabling the Union Government to effectively enforce its constitutional obligations through enforceable legislative measures.

What happened in Gujarat and in similar carnage elsewhere, earlier, were not merely a matter of law and order; each of these were all organised crimes against targeted groups, the State Governments either actively conniving with the majority group, or remaining as bystanders, resulting in a total collapse of the rule of law and the justice system altogether. In Gujarat, after more than two years, a process of making the State Government, the politicians and the police accountable has emerged entirely as a result of the tenacity of civil and human rights groups, NGOs, the National Human Right Commission, and most significantly, the Supreme Court of India. This, however, cannot be the permanent feature of India in all such situations. The State and the Union Government cannot be allowed to abdicate their function.

India has signed, accepted and ratified the Convention on the Prevention and Punishment of the

Crime of Genocide, 1948. It is under obligation to enact the necessary legislation to give effect to the provisions of the Convention. The Convention, apart from defining the crime, makes all persons committing genocide, punishable, whether they are "Constitutionally responsible rulers, public officials or private individuals". The Union Government has a fundamental duty under Article 51(c) of the Indian Constitution to foster respect for international humanitarian law and treaty obligations. Under Article 253, the Parliament has the power to make any law for implementing international conventions, and decisions made at an international conference, association or other body. Besides, the Union has the constitutional duty under Article 355 to protect every state, which must necessarily include all people within the state, against internal disturbance and to ensure governance in every state in accordance with the Constitution.

Keeping the above obligations and provisions in mind, and at the same time, without requiring to resort to a Proclamation as contemplated under Article 356, this law is being enacted to enable the Union Government to inquire into, investigate, prosecute and punish all those, irrespective of their office or status, who are responsible for the Commission of the Crime of Genocide and Crimes against Humanity, and to prevent the commission of all such crimes, and for the aforesaid purpose to declare any area as disturbed so as to effectively deal with such situations. The law also provides for all reliefs by way of compensation, restitution and rehabilitation.

Among the major breakthroughs in this piece of legislation is the definition of 'Genocide' and 'Crimes against Humanity'.

For the purposes of this Statute, 'Genocide' means any of the following acts committed with intent to destroy, in whole or in part, any group:

(a) killing members of the group;
(b) causing serious bodily or mental harm to members of the group;
(c) deliberately inflicting on the group conditions of life calculated to bring about its physical destruction in whole or in part;
(d) imposing measures intended to prevent births within the group;
(e) forcibly transferring children of the group to another group; and
(f) effecting long-lasting social and economic boycott of the group.

'Crimes against humanity', means any of the following acts when committed as part of a widespread or systematic attack directed against any civilian population, with knowledge of the attack:

(a) murder;
(b) attempted extermination;
(c) forcible evictions and enforced migration;
(d) imprisonment or other severe deprivation of physical liberty in violation of fundamental rules of international law;
(e) torture;
(f) rape, sexual slavery, enforced prostitution, forced pregnancy, enforced sterilisation, debasing,

forcible insertions of objects into the private parts or any other form of sexual violence of comparable gravity;

(g) persecution of a group as defined under this Act;

(h) enforced disappearance of persons; and

(i) other inhumane acts of a similar character intentionally causing great suffering, or serious injury to body or to mental or physical health.

For the purpose of 'Goenocide' (section 4.iii) and ' Crimes against Humanity' (section 4.iv), the Act further stipulates:

(a) "Attack directed against any civilian population" means a course of conduct involving the multiple commission of acts referred to in sections (iii) and (iv) against any civilian population, pursuant to or in furtherance of a state or organisational policy to commit such attack;

(b) "Extermination" includes the intentional infliction of conditions of life, *inter alia* the deprivation of access to food and medicine, calculated to bring about the destruction of part of a population;

(c) "Forced evictions and enforced migration means forced displacement of the persons concerned by expulsion or other coercive acts from the area in which they are lawfully present, without grounds permitted in accordance with national and international law;

(d) "Torture" means the intentional infliction of severe pain or suffering, whether physical or mental, upon a person in the custody or under the control of the accused;

(e) "Forced pregnancy" means the unlawful confinement, of a woman forcibly made pregnant, with the intent of affecting the ethnic composition of any population or carrying out other grave violations of international law. This definition shall not in any way be interpreted as affecting national laws relating to pregnancy;

(f) "Persecution" means the intentional and severe deprivation of fundamental rights contrary to national and international law by reason of the identity of the group or collectivity;

(g) "Enforced disappearance of persons" means the arrest, detention or abduction of persons by, or with the authorisation, support or acquiescence of, a state or a political organisation, followed by a refusal to acknowledge that deprivation of freedom or to give information on the fate or whereabouts of those persons, with the intention of removing them from the protection of the law for a prolonged period of time; and

(h) "Social and economic boycott" means the sustained and systematic attempt to socially disenfranchise and economically cripple a specific group, caste or community.

Apart from basic and important provisions that include the access to, a special and independent investigative machinery and special courts that have the

Box 8.2

The Prevention and Punishment of Genocide and Crimes against Humanity (Draft) Bill, 2004 Section 18 to Section 21

18. Responsibility of State Actors

(i) This Statute shall apply equally to all persons without any distinction based on official capacity. In particular, official capacity as a Head of State or Government, or as a member of a Government or Parliament, or as an elected representative or a government official shall in no case exempt such a person from criminal responsibility under this Statute, nor shall such capacity, constitute a ground for reduction of sentence.

(ii) Immunities or special procedural rules which may attach to the official capacity of a person, whether under national or international law, shall not bar the Court from exercising its jurisdiction over such a person.

(iii) No person shall be entitled to claim any sovereign immunity and privilege for offences committed under this Act.

19. Responsibility of commanders and other superiors

In addition to other grounds of criminal responsibility under this Act for crimes within the jurisdiction of the Court:

(i) A public servant including IAS/IPS officials and civil or public servants effectively following a line of command from state actors (Government or High Officers of the State or Central government) shall be criminally responsible for crimes committed by forces or officers under his or her effective command and control, or effective authority and control as the case may be, as a result of his or her failure to exercise control the crimes get committed with impunity; where:

  (a) that IAS/IPS official and civil or public servants or person either knew or, owing to the circumstances at the time, should have known that the forces were committing or about to commit such crimes; and

  (b) that IAS/IPS official and civil or public servants or person failed to take all necessary and reasonable measures within his or her power to prevent or repress their commission or to submit the matter to the competent authorities for investigation and prosecution.

(ii) With respect to superior and subordinate relationships not described in paragraph 1, a superior shall be criminally responsible for crimes under this Act, committed by subordinates under his or her effective authority and control, as a result of his or her failure to exercise control properly over such subordinates, where:

  (a) the superior either knew, or consciously disregarded information which clearly indicated that the subordinates were committing or about to commit such crimes;

  (b) the crimes concerned activities that were within the effective responsibility and control of the superior; and

  (c) the superior failed to take all necessary and reasonable measures within his or her power to prevent or repress their commission or to submit the matter to the competent authorities for investigation and prosecution.

20. Superior orders and prescription of law

The fact that a crime within the jurisdiction of the Court has been committed by a person pursuant to an order of a Government or of a superior, whether military or civilian, shall not relieve that person of criminal responsibility unless:

(a) The person was under a legal obligation to obey orders of the Government or the superior in question; and

(b) The order was not manifestly unlawful.

Explanation:

For the purposes of this article, orders to commit genocide or crimes against humanity are manifestly unlawful.

21. (a) Whoever knowingly holds property derived or obtained from the commission of genocide, or crimes against humanity, or conspiracy or abetment to these crimes as laid out in section 15, 16 and 17 of the Act shall be punished with imprisonment for a term not less than 10 years and shall also be liable for fine.

(b) In addition, the proceeds, properties and assets derived directly or indirectly from the commission of genocide, crimes against humanity, or conspiracy or abetment to these crimes be forfeited.

power to prosecute as well as grant reparation, the most significant aspect of the new proposed law is the section 18 on *Responsibility of State Actors.* Under this section, the draft law states there is no immunity under this new law to heads of states or governments from prosecution.

The enactment of such a radical piece of legislation will not by itself remedy the gaping flaws that have emerged in India's criminal justice system. But its enactment if accompanied by radical police reform will radically shake the immunity of class, caste and privilege that have guided our system and re-open the debate for an independent, confident, upright police force more than ever before.

It is about time that we take this bold step forward.

Presentations and Discussion

"DEMOCRACY: CHALLENGES AND PROSPECTS"

This section corresponds to the proceedings of the First Session of the Ninth Indira Gandhi Conference, November 19-21, 2004, New Delhi.

Chair:

- Zoya Hasan

Lead Speakers:

- Pratap Bhanu Mehta
- Yogendra Yadav

Discussants:

- Jayaprakash Narayan
- Anita Rampal
- Vinod Raina
- S. Mahendra Dev

- Neera Chandhoke
- Aijaz Ahmad
- Vir Sanghvi
- Sunil Khilnani
- Mridula Mukherjee
- Prem Shankar Jha
- Sanjoy Hazarika
- Bharat Karnad
- Teesta Setalvad
- Vivek Monteiro
- Suman K. Bery
- Sunita Narain

- Chandra Bhan Prasad
- Rekha Chowdhary
- Sunil Kant Munjal
- Ravi Parthasarathy
- Nasser Munjee
- C. Uday Bhaskar
- Amar Kanwar
- Radha Kumar
- Naina Lal Kidwai
- Sudhir Kakar
- Siddharth Varadarajan
- Manvinder Singh Banga

9 | Introductory Remarks

ZOYA HASAN

THIS discussion is on Indian democracy and we will focus mainly on the framework and structure of democracy, especially political institutions. Our two lead speakers who will introduce the topic are Pratap Bhanu Mehta and Yogendra Yadav. Before I request Prof. Pratap Mehta to set the ball rolling, I would like to make a few preliminary remarks that address some of the concerns delineated in the annotation. My rather broad-based remarks summarise the important challenges confronting Indian democracy in the next decade.

Going by the 2004 elections, the Indian democratic process is spectacularly alive and there are no signs of it slowing down as a fountainhead of change. Indeed there are signs of its quickening in the last decade. India's democracy is expanding and politics and elections are providing space for contestation and avenues for expression of rights and claims. In the past half century no trend has been more powerful and transformative than the growth and expansion of democracy. It is producing greater politicisation, agency and discourses of equality, especially amongst the poor, the vulnerable and the disadvantaged, which suggest that Indian democracy now has a wider social base. While the persistence and consolidation of a democratic, secular and federal polity is a major political and human achievement, formidable challenges remain in the realisation of substantive democracy. Elections are the lifeblood of democracy—generating public debate, shaping the political agenda and influencing the distribution of power in government. It is in the procedural and political senses of the term, regular, free and fair elections, high voter turnout, and the enormous fluidity in the political structure that India's democratic experiment has succeeded. However, competitive elections are not sufficient to ensure social substance to the system of representative government. The quality of democracy depends on its levels of pluralism, equality, and justice, including responsiveness and accountability, which will be one of our major concerns here. In India the problem is the gap between the theory and practice of democracy and the gulf between the real world of democratic processes and the meaningful exercise of equal rights and citizenship that are compromised and undermined by inequalities in the distribution of resources and the concentration of economic and social power. What are the possibilities for the vulnerable and disadvantaged groups of enjoying meaningful citizenship in a democratic polity and the constitutional rights of equal citizenship?

Indian politics today, is a clash between two rival world views, one inclusive and egalitarian and the other exclusive and elitist. The first view backed by a wide spectrum of political opinion has constantly underscored India's plural ethos and placed paramount emphasis on secularism, equality and justice. Inspired by Nehruvian ideas, this model has ensured some level of tolerance and distributive fairness and at the same time sought to achieve economic growth, albeit slowly. The second world view favoured by the middle classes, media and bureaucracy which began to dominate the political discourse under the BJP led National Democratic Alliance government focuses on formal democracy and tends to treat democracy and the market as synonymous and with little place for compassion, equity and social justice. The core values of the republic embodied in India's constitution provide an admirable foundation for a society based on mutual respect and basic rights for all. However, the rise of the BJP began to change this. And there was a sense that it was willing to use state power to marginalise the minorities. In this sense, the defeat of the NDA in the recent elections and the formation of the United Progressive Alliance government signals much

more than a change of regimes, there is now considerable space opening up for ending the politics of polarisation of the last decade and the rearticulation and reassertion of democratic values particularly secularism and pluralism that had made post-independence India an exemplar of democracy in the developing world. The biggest challenge therefore in the next decade is to preserve primarily a concept of national identity based on the citizen's commitment to secular and civic nationalism. That citizenship should be defined purely in its rootedness in residence and territory.

The most fundamental challenge facing Indian democracy in the next decade is in maintaining the conditions for deepening and consolidating the full panoply of rights and democratic institutions. For this we need to move from formal to substantive democracy that will in turn require government formation to embody the policies and programmes agreed to in the Common Minimum Programme. If we do not move fast enough to ensure substantive democracy by incorporating these goals in the national agenda, the sense of belonging to a civic identity stands assailed by a host of debilitating sub-identities. It is important to remember that these identities have an appeal because of the loss of faith in the larger civic identity and the inability of the state to deliver its promise of equity.

Democracy in India has time and again failed to ensure equality. The most fundamental concern remains the creation of a more equal society and a reduction in the vast economic disparities that exist between regions, classes, groups and individuals, further aggravated by economic reforms and globalisation. While democracy in the past two to three decades has seen a transfer of power from the upper caste classes to the middle ranks it has not resulted in power sharing with those at the bottom of India's social structure. Nor has it facilitated any significant distribution of wealth and income. Rather, regular elections can obscure a growing concentration of power among the political and economic elites, which often operate outside the frame of party politics. The key issue then is the feeble capacity of the democratic state to alleviate mass poverty and provide amelioration in the material conditions of the vast majority of people mired in economic misery. A related issue concerns the crises of representation caused by the disjunction between the electorate and the government, and the extraordinary gap between voter choices and substantial outcomes. A vibrant political party can act as a conduit between the government and the people by representing the interests of constituents and overseeing the working of policies to ensure that something is done about the pressing problems of the people. However, it is precisely here that Indian political parties have been found wanting, failing to prioritise the fulfilment of the basic needs, welfare and livelihood issues of the people.

Another significant challenge lies in the area of caste and democracy. The political assertion of the historically disadvantaged castes in the 1990s has been linked to the implementation of the Mandal Commission report guaranteeing reserve quotas for members of these castes. The larger strength signified by these developments is the growth of identity politics. All the major parties are increasingly conceiving their constituencies in terms of sociocultural identities that seek to represent rather than work towards reconciling interests across constituencies, which in fact overlap and are politically negotiable. Thanks to the politics of caste, previously marginalised groups are entering the political arena in larger numbers. This has contributed to a major change in the architecture of representation and a shift in the balance of political power in governments and legislatures. But the new pattern of representation has principally benefited the backward castes, whereas the minorities and women have failed to get adequate representation in legislatures and the higher echelons of decision making. The inclusiveness of our democracy draws sustenance from a representation of Indian society exclusively in terms of its caste based social stratification. But the point that I want to flag is that the project for deepening democracy must go beyond caste, taking into account the complexity of Indian society in which caste is not the only axis of vulnerability; inequalities of gender and class also count, as do the disadvantages of belonging to a particular religious minority. In the contemporary conception of social justice, however, class differences are disregarded as inequalities which happen to be incompatible with caste. Basically, we need to re-examine the official conception of disadvantage, which ought to be broadened beyond caste taking into account contemporary realities of oppression in terms of caste, as well as other criteria of social stratification and difference.

Overall there are deep discontents with the functioning of democracy. But we need to contextualise the discontents to deal with them. In some ways the conflicts and differences that democracy has provoked are part of the deeper process of democratisation. But some of these conflicts have been aggravated by neo-liberal policies, and by the belief that the market system of capitalism is not only the best but also the only socio-economic system. Neo-liberalism in this sense is the cause of our contemporary discontents and not the solution. Diminishing the hold of neo-liberalism on our political discourse and frontally attending to the issues of economic and social justice alone can solve the sense of discontent manifested in the regular turnover of incumbent governments in elections since 1984. It is imperative, now more than ever before, to recognise that democracy and distress cannot coexist indefinitely. We have to recover egalitarianism from the all consuming arguments over fiscal and resource impediments which threaten to undermine the Common Minimum Programme that could provide social substance to India's democracy. By questioning the immanent logic of neo-liberal economics and conservative politics as the guiding lights of Indian democracy, the Common Minimum Programme of the UPA government creates an opening for an alternative and more humane trajectory of politics and development.

In the past few months there has been considerable discussion on the Employment Guarantee Act (EGA). Assuring the basic needs of the vulnerable has come to the forefront after a decade of identity politics that pushed livelihood issues into the background. The 2004 Lok Sabha elections have provided popular endorsement for this paradigmatic shift from identity politics to livelihood issues as rights and entitlements. Although the elections did not have a single-issue focus, the verdict was a categorical rejection of both the anti-poor economic policies passing off as 'development' and majoritarian politics projected as 'nationalism'. In this context the single most important promise made by the Congress manifesto and the Common Minimum Programme was an EGA that would guarantee at least 100 days of casual manual work at minimum wage for anyone who applies for work within a specified time frame. But as the time to table a bill on employment guarantee drew near, the initial consensus which led to its inclusion in the CMP is being replaced by growing scepticism as powerful forces are arraigned against it and have worked to dilute the provisions. The paradox is that the same underlying factors that provide the compelling reasons to enact such legislation also fuel the opposition to it. But when Parliament approves the EGA, it would be one of the most important policy initiatives by any government anywhere in the world and a vital step towards recouping democracy. A bold and imaginative leadership would readily recognise the significance of these initiatives, which can go a long way in bridging the gap between political equality and economic inequality and the problems of legitimacy of political authority that this creates.

With all its problems, India is admired worldwide as a successful democracy, as a nation-state, which has overcome threats to a united national identity, acute caste deprivation and minority weakness. It is very important that citizens do not lose their faith in the nation and the political system, and the idea of the nation-state is not superseded by a market-state. For this it is important to restore the original moorings of the republic—secularism and social democracy—and for our identity to be rooted in an all-embracing nationhood to impart a more equitable meaning to the idea of citizenship.

10 | A Liberal Constitutional Democracy

PRATAP BHANU MEHTA

TO talk in 10 minutes about arguably an issue on which the hopes of humanity rest, is a tall order. So what I will do is just raise three kinds of general issues which I hope can work as a sort of template for discussion later on, rather than going into the specifics of institutional reforms for which there are many more competent people here to talk about.

When one thinks of democracy, especially in the Indian context, it is conjoined with two other terms. We are a liberal constitutional democracy. And I think one of the challenges that Indian democracy is going to face over the next decade is actually giving full meaning to all three terms in this democratic package. One set of questions that we discuss in the context of democracy has to do with democracy as a way of organising power. How do we deepen democracy? How do we empower the people? How can we prevent the operation of money and power from distorting the workings of democracy? I would like to suggest that this is only one part of the question, and we can endlessly debate how this question

is to be answered. The other two terms in the Indian package which are embodied in our Constitution, which is a liberal constitutional democracy, are equally important. It is worth beginning by reminding ourselves of what they actually mean. The term liberal is not frequently used in the Constituent Assembly debates and has been hijacked by the critics of liberalism as a pejorative word, as in neo-liberal. But what are some of the basic presumptions about liberalism that underlie our constitution?

First, individuals are free to develop their fullest potential in whatever way they deem appropriate, compatible with similar rights for others. Our Constitution is liberal in the sense that it is egalitarian, not in the sense that socialism is egalitarian but egalitarian in the sense that each individual ought to be given the minimum basis of social self-respect. They ought to have their self worth affirmed by the public institutions of society. The thinking was that if individuals don't have their sense of basic self worth affirmed then you will get a society characterised by debased forms of oppression and competition. Second, our constitution is morally individualistic. This moral individualism is not to be confused with moral selfishness. It is rather a claim about the value of individuals. It is morally individualistic in the sense that each individual counts; to violate the rights of any individual is to mutilate the identity of the community. Third, it is liberal in the sense that religion, caste, ethnicity all particular identities shall not be the basis of citizenship not only formally but aspirationally; they should not be part of the practice of citizenship. Fourth, it is liberal in the sense that although it empowers the State, enjoins the State to improve the well being of the dispossessed, the means employed for this purpose will be ameliorative not revolutionary. They will be subject to a kind of continuous political process and political compromise rather than revolutionary takeover. Fifth, it is liberal in the sense that there is a suspicion of concentrated power. Power is best preserved, and serves the interests of society best, when it is diffused. Sixth, it is liberal in the sense that there is a great underlying commitment to public reason. And I think what is astonishing about the Indian national movement and the Constitution on which it was based was this idea that politics should be about the exchange of public reason, and not as it presently is, as the trading of incentives. Lastly, and most importantly, the general presumption is in favour of the people. When we talk of reforms, whether political or economic, the strongest argument for them is not simply economic benefits. The stronger

argument is political in that it seeks to restore the balance of presumption in favour of people's initiative and enterprise. It says to the people, "The state will not hinder you in undertaking whatever enterprise you actually see fit." This set of values at once becomes the ethical norm that underlies a democracy. It also becomes a yardstick by which to measure our democracy as well as a challenge for democracy. The question we need to ask is—will the practices of popular authorisation as they are currently practised sustain these values?

The second term of this package was constitutionalism. Constitutionalism means a set of the formally enacted laws, taken as authoritative constraints on the behaviour of citizens. Those norms shall not be transgressed for the sake of expediency. Are we a constitutional society in this sense? We do have a Constitution, but are we a constitutional society in the deeper sense of the practice of constitutionalism? Do we have an arrangement of powers where different branches of government actually respect each others' boundaries as enjoined by the constitution? Do the practices of politics take the constraints prescribed by the constitution as authoritative constraints? And lastly, what do the citizens want from a state? The essential core of the idea is that entitlements to human beings, should not be made matters of discretionary power. The failure of a state can be measured by the extent to which it converts citizens' rights, whether they be the rights to freedom, free enterprise, free speech or a right to basic entitlements, into matters of discretionary powers and allocations by the state. Our social and economic rights have become products of the discretionary allocations of the state. The challenge to Indian democracy is that the conversion of rights into discretion is afflicting the sovereign functions of all our institutions. The question we have to ask is what is going to be the relationship between democracy which is understood as the practice of popular authorisation and the rule of law which encapsulates something quite profound.

Zoya Hasan began by rightly pointing out that the real challenge for democracy is how to deepen it. What are the institutions that will sustain the deepening of democracy? I want to make two or three remarks about how we might think of institutional reforms. First, liberal and constitutional aspirations give us an intellectual and moral framework to think about what the point of institutional reforms is. The second methodological lesson we have to learn in any debate over reforms is that democracy emerges out of complicated processes. Sometimes bad people do lots of good things for democracy while sometimes the road to hell is paved with good intentions. This is a view that might be described as sceptical whig. It believes in the possibility of change for the better, but insists that there are no simple formulas. I think what is not going to work in thinking about institutional reforms is simply the promulgation of good intentions. What you need is an approach to institutions where the incentives to comply by institutional norms are self-reinforcing, and do not require constant punitive supervision by the state. Such

a system is going to break down. We have no dearth of good laws; we have no dearth of institutions created. But if those institutions do not give incentives to the various participants to act in self-reinforcing ways, as the system of VAT taxation does as opposed to other taxation, you are not going to get successful reforms. The question of institutional design has to take this as one of the premises, whether we are talking about election funding or judicial reforms. What is the mechanism by which these reforms become self-sustaining? A further point we have to think about in institutional reforms, is that any set of institutions, and democracy is no exception, embodies tensions within it. When we talk of democratic accountability we mean many different things. We mean transparency, we mean representativeness, we mean responsiveness and we mean efficiency. The unfortunate fact of life is that not all good things go together. You can have a transparent system that is not responsive. You can have a representative system that is not efficient. It is worth thinking realistically about what trade-offs we want to actually take on board when thinking about institutional reform, rather than promising too much.

One of the difficulties with democracy is that we can actually expect too much from it. Democracy can be causally saddled with all our achievements and all our miseries. But the simple fact is that democracy has little to do with a lot of our miseries. Lots of other things do. We need to think very carefully as a society through the political process, what are the trade-offs that should be our priority rather than assuming there aren't any. For instance take accountability. Accountability can mean lots of different things. Finally, there is no route to political reform or democratic deepening that will come from outside the domain of politics itself. What we can't do is social engineering; there are lots of good *ex-ante* designs about institutions and so forth. The culture of debating reforms, especially in this city, largely rests on the promulgation of new laws, and punitive measures. But if these bypass or if they operate under the illusion that we can bypass the trade-offs of politics, the many negotiations that any democracy has to undertake, then I think we are in for a rude shock. Politics and democracy fundamentally are about, as Max Weber said, "the slow boring of hardboards". And if we are to care about Indian democracy we have to take on the challenge of the slow boring of hardboards rather than magically wishing the problems away.

11 Script *vs.* Performance

YOGENDRA YADAV

I want to say something which is in addition to what I have already written in my paper. The distance between the script and the performance is quite central to the democratic enterprise in India. The script and the performance never match. Sometimes we wish they would match. On balance I think it is good that they don't.

Some 40 years ago one of the founding essays on Indian politics was written by Prof. Rajani Kothari. The essay was called *Form and Substance in Indian Politics.* The first serious student of Indian politics saw a distance between what is said and what is practised, which is not a relationship of hypocrisy but a serious comment on the nature of politics in our society. Recently another student of Indian politics, Prof. Partho Chatterjee, has come up with a somewhat different distinction between what he calls a civil society and a political society. I think we need to build on this fundamental distinction that is central to understanding democracy, because there is a danger of reading our democracy in a purely formal way. There is a pre-given set of expectations from democracy and fortunately these days you don't have to write your own script. Washington writes it for you and you just have to take it. A friend of mine once said that there is a checklist model of democracy which has been approved and quantified by Freedom House and everybody is supposed to conform to it. We are doing quite well on that. I think it is highly unlikely that the IMF or the World Bank would stop our grants on account of non-compliance with democracy requirements. And that is where the danger really is.

If we go by the formal script of democracy, if we go by the formal requirements of what democracy is, we can pat ourselves and say that everything is all right. We are doing fine. The problem or this dilemma is not confined to India alone. In the last 10 or 12 years, ever since the so called fourth wave of democracy started, democracy has been expanding all over the world. More and more countries are holding elections. Even Afghanistan is holding one and if they have their way, they will force one on Iraq as well. So while you have more and more countries which are democratic in a certain formal register, and democracy in that sense is expanding, our notion of what it means to be a democracy is actually shrinking. We are being handed down a certain narrow, one-dimensional view of what it means to be a democracy. And like everyone else we seem to be accepting it. And that is where we need to move away. We need to look at our own democracy in ways that are somewhat different.

In the economy we talk about formal and informal sectors. We recognise that when we talk about the formal sector we are looking at only about 10 per cent of our economy and that 90 per cent lies outside it. I would suggest that in thinking about politics, too, we should draw a similar distinction. The formal sector of our politics includes our constitutional procedures, the political parties, and the drama that is played out on the front page of newspapers. But there is something else, there is what may be called the informal sector. It includes millions of democratic practices that take place in society in ways that are often deeply embarrassing to us and which our formal register doesn't allow us to see as democratic practices. The trouble in going by the formal register is that sometimes we can begin to see our weaknesses as strengths and our strengths as weaknesses. Over the last few years many commentators on India politics have begun to heave a sigh of relief that we are gradually moving towards the two party system, at least we have a two block system emerging in Indian politics. There is a sense of disappointment that we don't have a two party system like they have in the

US, with the Democrats and the Republicans, but there is some satisfaction that at least we have a proxy for that. A certain way of looking at democracy teaches us that this is the ideal towards which any good democrat must move, overlooking the reality of what historically have been the costs of moving towards such a two party system. In a country and society like ours nothing can be more disastrous than forcing a two party choice. Two parties which look similar would then have to have very similar policies. So what appears as a strength can actually be a sign of weakness.

If we have a functioning democracy in this country, a democracy which has some substance to it, a democracy which is not just a paper work of set constitutional proprieties being followed, it is because competitive politics developed organic links with social divisions that are represented by caste. We Indians have a sense of scandal about it, as if India is the only place in the world where voting takes place on the basis of accidents of births. I have looked at about 25 to 30 societies and I haven't found one where it doesn't happen, where voting is not determined by where you are born, who are your parents, or which religion they practice. I believe that competitive politics developed because of deep linkages with caste. And instead of caste taking over politics I would suggest that it is politics which has transformed the institution of caste in some fundamental ways.

That brings me to the contemporary challenge. Everyone will acknowledge that the last 10 or 15 years, especially after 1989, have been years of churning in Indian politics, years which have been seen as messy years where things got topsy-turvy. I would argue that this was really the second major democratic upsurge, the first being the movement of the founding of adult franchise, the founding of the Constitution and the beginning of the Indian Republic. The second democratic upsurge was when informal politics touched upon formal open possibilities. What appeared to us as a messy churning taking place was really the opening of democratic possibilities. What appeared to many as the regretful decline of the Congress Party, opened up democratic possibilities in a very big way. And while there is a deeper sense of satisfaction in certain circles about how things are today, I would state that what we are looking at, is a fundamental closure of possibilities. This is not readily evident to us simply because we have had another election a few months ago and because all of us are in the *bachao* mode these days, as there was a point when it looked as if the idea of India needed to be saved.

In the longer run, I think we are facing a deep historical closure of the democratic possibilities we saw in the early 90s. The democratic upsurge and the participatory upsurge that it brought, has reached a point of stagnation. The party system transformation that took place has almost come to an end without expanding the menu of choice. We have more parties without more choices available to ordinary citizens. That to my mind is the fundamental crisis that we face. The crisis is not a crisis of formal institutions alone. The crisis is that in the last 50 years Indian politics could breathe a certain life, a certain strength, it could develop a certain connection with real life beyond the formal institutional mechanisms of our democracy in the informal sector as I call it. The real danger is of that drying up. If Indian democracy could face some of the biggest crises, the Emergency for instance, I dread to think what would happen if we had another emergency today. I dread to think what would happen if we had the riots of 1984, or if we had a bigger play of a mix of both, like Gujarat, which was the biggest. There was an element of emergency in Gujarat and an element of the 1984 riots mixed into one. What would happen if we had a national play of that? I think the formal institutional apparatus is not strong enough to resist that. What brought us out of some of those was what I call the informal sector. And if this dries up we will face a very serious challenge, a challenge that cannot be recognised by the formal checklist of democracy. A challenge that can never be quantified by the Freedom House index of how democratic we are. But a certain decline will take place, and the way out of that as Pratap Bhanu Mehta said is not more legislation.

I really think that in certain ways the entire discourse on political reform is a certain middle class fantasy being played out. We can't sit in this room and reform politics by tomorrow morning. One of the things we must learn to do is to understand the logic of politics being played by millions of actors and it is by improving the quality of that game rather than by writing the rule book over and over again, that we might actually end up strengthening democracy. In certain respects and especially on the questions of monetary resources and the question of information, some legal changes would help. But in the last instance democracy cannot be reformed sitting in rooms like this. It can only be reformed by strengthening political practices out there. And thank God for that.

12

Discussion

(Section I — Democracy: Challenges and Prospects)

Jayaprakash Narayan

I will bring the discussion back to earth. What we have seen so far is a very erudite and a very scholarly and academic approach. There are many distinguished film-makers here. I am reminded of four films, I will briefly mention them. *Saaransh* which was produced by Mahesh Bhatt 25 years ago depicted what happens to the citizen in this country on account of 'the democratic' process, the political process, the governance process, on a day-to-day basis—corruption, criminalisation and insecurity.

The second film is *Sookha* which in Hindi means drought (the original was *Bara*, with the same meaning in Kannada). The film depicts two characters—the Chief Minister and the Home Minister—obviously fighting for supreme power in the state. There is also a poor Collector, whom I always call the JNU-ite, a very well meaning, nice guy, who does not know what to do. In the midst of a major drought, the Chief Minister tries to engineer communal riots in the district so that the Home Minister has to resign and the competition is warded off. The Home Minister tries to prevent relief from reaching famine victims, so that the Chief Minister has to resign, giving him the chance to be the top man.

The third film is *Thanneer, Thanneer, Thanneer,* by Balachander. In *Water, Water, Water,* as the name indicates, residents of a village struggle for years to get drinking water. One day they go to see a Minister *sahib* visiting the *Taluk* some 30 kilometres away. They wait for hours at the guest house and finally manage to give their petition. In a classic one minute exposé of the political and governance system, the Minister receives the petition and hands it over to the Collector standing next to him; the Collector to the RDO; the RDO to the *Tehsildar;* the *Tehsildar* to the Revenue Inspector; the Revenue Inspector to the *Dafedar*—the fellow with a badge—a very formidable Indian institution in our offices; and the *Dafedar* finally puts it in the dustbin. Normally such a process of relegating the request to the dustbin takes about four to five years, in the film it happens in one minute.

The fourth film is *Hindustani*, in which Kamal Hassan played the leading role. It is about corruption and the extortionary impact of corruption. In it a freedom fighter tries to play by the rules. He is a very proud man, who does not pay a bribe in a government hospital, even to save his daughter's life. Ultimately the daughter dies, and of course in *filmi* style, he becomes violent.

The point I am making is, we are doing well, and we are doing badly, and both statements are equally true. From a historical point of view, I think Indian democracy at the current phase of our evolution, relative to the US in the 1920s, and the UK in the 1860s, is not bad at all. But we happen to be in the 21st century when expectations are rising much faster, technology is growing more rapidly and the people deserve more. They have the right to seek and the right to get more faster. So what do we do?

Self-correcting mechanisms cannot be institutionalised by quick fixes, as Yogendra said. Both the lead speakers talked about the primacy of politics. This is particularly crucial because unfortunately some of us tend to believe that the Supreme Court is the last word on Indian democracy. There can't be anything more dangerous than such contempt for politics. And finally, the process of power which ought to be the solution—has become the very problem itself. This perhaps is the most tragic element of our crisis today.

In any sensible democracy, the process of power, the democratic process through which individuals ascend to public office, is the one that ought to provide the solution. Given that, we must understand the nature and the vicious cycles afflicting the Indian political system. Deployment of vast, unaccounted money power in elections is leading to corruption. Electoral verdicts do not change anything. Therefore, there is only a change of players but there is no change in the rules of the game. With a class of political entrepreneurs rising, with political fiefdoms in almost every constituency, our notions of democracy are increasingly unreal. The great mass of Indian people by voting in and voting out parties, are not able to really force change in the way things are done. We think here in Delhi, there is a great battle between the secular and communal forces. Out there, almost 90 per cent of the legislators could have been members of the secular combination or the communal combination depending on where their bread is buttered on that day. That is the reality of the situation at the ground level. It is all about political fiefdom; it is not about secularism; it is not about communalism; it is not about socialism; it is not about economic liberalisation or capitalism. It is about political entrepreneurship. Politics is big business.

And thanks to centralisation, the fiscal corrections become increasingly difficult because there is no link between taxes and services. The survival of the government is no longer compatible with honesty. Individually there are many honest people in political office but institutionally it is virtually impossible to be honest and survive for any length of time.

Given these realities of our governance crisis, I think we have to look at three broad areas—judicial reforms, political reforms and the decentralisation of power. We must look at specific institutional solutions, and there are plenty.

The other day I was counting the number of words in the 73rd and 74th Constitutional amendments. There are 7700 words. The whole American Constitution, with all its amendments, has 7400 words. And yet, the heart of decentralisation, Article 243G in the Indian Constitution, is as obscure as it can be. I think no Constitution in the world has such a provision, which is so delightfully obscure and completely vague. We are in a situation where honesty is incompatible with survival. So let us come to brass tacks in terms of our institutional reforms. Excessive scepticism and pessimism or eulogizing our democracy will not really serve us very well.

Anita Rampal

The questions that come to mind are how does our democracy actually function, and how do our institutions help develop a democratic culture? If we look at elections, we can ask, who are the people that really keep them going? How many of us go and vote, to sustain the democratic institutions? Each time I think of elections I am reminded of a woman in Begusarai—a district in Bihar where criminal violence is alarming. She passionately said, *"Main mar jaaoongi par main vote zaroor doongi."*

What motivates her in this way? We find women thronging polling booths and waiting in long queues to vote. What is it that takes them there, against all odds? Why do they vote? It seems to be the only right they have; they have no food or rations through their ration cards, they don't have schools for their children that can give an education that makes any sense to them or makes a difference to their lives, and yet they are ready to face even death when they go to cast their vote. Women, in that same district, have shaped the literacy programme, and value education which actually talks of empowerment and of what democratic institutions should be like. The women there have actively come forth in *panchayats*, and are struggling today to make them more meaningful. However, our educational system has become more undemocratic. In fact, for the first time our state has actually changed the Constitution to say that we cannot provide education to all our children in the way that the Constitution had originally promised. The new Act that was almost passed early this year says that we shall give them only what "the state deems fit", not a regular school but only what is called the Education Guarantee Centre, which is a low-cost, poor quality option for those already disadvantaged. The divisions in democracy are created and legitimated through our own education system, which socialises us in this way, more sharply now than ever before, to accept inequalities. It shapes us so that we do not speak the language of ordinary people, we cannot stand in an ordinary queue, and so we cannot go and vote with them. Our educational institutions are creating an undemocratic divide, which is sharply increasing now, as the state recedes from its responsibility. This is something which we urgently need to address.

Vinod Raina

I think Gandhi's disenchantment with the British parliamentary system that he outlined in *Hind Swaraj* has a correspondence with what Yogendra calls the disjunction between the informal and formal; the informal for Gandhi would be the community, something he had great faith in. Gandhi wanted decisions for immediate needs to be taken locally; for the rest, he recognised there would be railways or shipbuilding that couldn't be decided upon locally, decisions which would have to be taken 'up' somewhere. Assuming that such a formulation is desirable, the challenge is to work out the convergence between the local and the central, the informal and formal. Shouldn't we begin to think of that rather than merely talk about the defects of the democratic system as it prevails? Is there a way of making such a convergence possible? That I think is the great challenge. It seems to me that there is more than a hint of autarchy in Gandhi's notion of republics of villages in ascending circles, which he thought would be the best form of democracy and governance for India. It may be a bit too utopian, but does that imply instant dismissal of the idea, or adopting it more realistically? And to my mind nothing in the area of institutional reform that the Congress Party did was as significant and substantial as the 73rd and 74th amendments; which in a sense tried to get to this convergence. I have always

been curious as to what made Rajiv Gandhi push through these amendments.

It is the formal, which I partially interpret as the state legislatures and central parliament, that are defective. There are about 5000 representatives, if one takes the state assemblies and the parliament together representing a billion people! What kind of democracy is this? I don't think a person can represent more than a thousand people really if it is to be truly representative. With someone sitting in parliament who represents a million people—what kind of accountability systems will such a democratic system have? Therefore, if we were to incorporate those ascending circles in our electoral politics, I think what we need to do, and this to me is the essence of the 73rd and 74th amendments, is to have a representative for about a thousand people, with the right to call him/her back. That to me would be the beginning of the convergence between the community and formal democratic politics.

The trouble is that the Congress Party, which brought in these institutional changes, the 73rd and 74th amendments, doesn't have a great deal of faith in it themselves. Just one example—I have seen in the much maligned state of Bihar, in Begusarai, what it means to have competent women elected at the local level. What it meant in Kerala was nothing short of revolutionary, where all the *panchayats* made the Ninth Plan—1,250 of them—based on the 16 indicators list of the Planning Commission. Taken together, they constituted the bulk of the state's Ninth Plan. The state made 40 per cent of the developmental budget directly available to the *panchayats* instead of giving it to the bureaucracy. It created miracles. But the point is, that was allowed only for a short while, till the next elections, when the entire system of local planning was dismantled back to the usual. Such processes were not allowed to continue in Kerala, nor will they be allowed to take root in other states, because the formal central systems, the legislatures and the parliament do not have faith in them. They see the erosion of their own powers by such systems. It is not because the people don't want them.

S. Mahendra Dev

My questions are more clarificatory in nature. Yogendra Yadav's paper is interesting particularly in the distinction between the formal and informal sectors. My first comment is that in economics we have a clearer notion of convergence. What do we mean by convergence in political science? He mentioned that the informal or unorganised sector constitutes more than 90 per cent of employment. It may be noted that in terms of output, the unorganised sector constitutes only 40 to 50 per cent.

My second comment is on Prof. Mehta's paper. He says that it is not institutional reforms but incentives which are important. We know about incentives in economics. What are the incentives in political processes?

My third comment is on Supreme Court judgements. When the executive stops taking decisions, Supreme

Court judgements become important particularly in regard to the right to work, right to food, etc. A few years ago the Supreme Court gave a judgement that all state governments should start mid-day meal schemes in schools. It had an impact on some of the state governments. They started mid-day meal schemes because of pressure from the Supreme Court. I think Supreme Court interventions are important when the executive is not active. It is a good thing to achieve the right to food. On the other hand, it also reflects the failure of the executive.

Neera Chandhoke

Much as I would like to believe in the argument that since formal democratic institutions have failed, let us look to the informal sector to rescue democracy, two sets of scepticism assail me. First of all, the informal economy is very much a part of the formal economy and the entire distinction between the formal and the informal is completely arbitrary. The informal economy provides not only cheap labour but also cheap resources to the formal economy in highly exploitative conditions. Therefore, this is not a distinction that ought to be validated in politics. Secondly, much as I hesitate to accept formal conceptualisations of democracy, unless we have them, how do we know that practices in informal politics are democratic? I end with just one comment—it is true that we have seen this great democratic upsurge as a result of backward castes and Dalit mobilisations. But do remember that the same parties who represent the backwards castes and the Dalits saw the BJP as untouchable in 1998, but they joined the NDA in 1999. Further, many of these parties are completely authoritarian, single leader parties and do not practice democratic politics within the community. Communities are composed of exploiters and the exploited, so let us not romanticise caste communities. If we privilege community and caste-based mobilisations, we will end up with populism, and democracy will be completely emptied out of our political lives. We have to have some notion of what democracy is about. I like Yogendra's paper but I have these two reservations on the argument.

Aijaz Ahmad

The word liberal actually leads us in two directions. One is liberalism which we use in the realm of politics and the other towards liberalisation which we use in the realm of economics. So liberal can mean a liberal political order, it can also mean free market ideology. This identification goes back to a very powerful western discourse where there is the idea that a free market and a free society are identical. My reservation there is that I think Prof. Mehta does not give enough credence to the fact that there is an actual tension, and even to a certain extent a contradiction, between these two uses of the word liberal. There is a contradiction between a free market or a corporate dominated market and a free society.

This leads me to my next point that to isolate moral individualism seems to me rather one-sided, because the tension in Indian democracy I think is between morality which undertakes collective justice but not at the expense of private personal freedom. That is why the Indian constitution is compatible with the idea of historical redress when it comes to the question of caste or women. That is why the Indian constitution has been compatible with land reforms, as the Nehruvian idea of India conceived it. That is why the Indian constitution is compatible with nationalisation as implemented by Indira Gandhi. So there is in the Indian constitution a very productive tension between individual liberty and the common good, and that the common good properly pursued can free us all even though it might limit the rights of property in certain cases.

My closing and rather provocative point is that any conference on the next decade should keep coming back to the last decade. One of the things that happened in the last decade was the churning of Indian politics where the whole history of caste was thrown open. One of the reasons why we are reaching a point of closure there, is the corruption of middle class caste politics and the failure, at least in the north, of Dalit politics to come into their own, and that hijacked into models of caste mobilisation set in motion by leaders of the middle class. That is part of the closure that is happening and there will probably be other kinds of upsurge in the future. But the last decade also dealt with the issue of communalism and liberalisation, not liberal democracy but the liberalisation of the market. In that, I slightly disagree with Zoya Hasan. The distinction she draws between the elitist model I entirely agree with, but I think there was too much of an identification of that elite model only with the NDA government. That elite model has deeper roots than the NDA model. And that was the issue for the electorate in the previous elections although it was not the issue on which the Congress and its allies actually fought the elections. The electorate acted on that issue. The electorate elected the Congress, its allies and the Left to power on that issue of liberalisation. And that is what the UPA government has to face. The issues of the Common Minimum Programme (CMP) are not reducible to issues of resource allocation here and there. They will have to shift resources from somewhere to the CMP. I entirely agree with you that the whole issue of the Employment Guarantee Act is a fundamental issue. After the kind of decade that we have gone through, the formation of this government is a grand reprieve but if we don't use it right we will lose it. The opposition will come back to power and bring back something very different from the UPA. It is a moment of great historical significance.

Vir Sanghvi

I think we have actually seen two different churnings over the last decade, one that we have talked about and one that we haven't. We have talked about the political churning and the emergence of caste-based politics. What we haven't talked about is the growth of the middle class and the way in which it has grown in the post-liberalisation era.

Both of these have happened almost simultaneously. If you take 1990 and Mandal as the turning point for politics, I think you have got to take 1991 and the beginning of liberalisation as the emergence of a newly assertive, newly confident middle class. My fear for Indian democracy in the next decade is that there is a gulf between these two groups—and that gulf is growing and leading to many of the tensions. You could argue, as I think many people do, that when a political system is seen as failing to deliver, people return to the loyalties that preceded the emergence of that system. And that is caste, that is ethnicity, that is religion, that is region and, to some extent, that is happening in India.

As Neera Chandhoke said, the parties that have emerged that represent these things are autocratic parties, built around single individuals. In many cases, they are parties that are entirely bereft of ideology. But because they use the right kind of caste combinations, they are also pretty undefeatable. So, no matter what Mulayam Singh Yadav does, no matter whether there is crony capitalism in his state or not, the Samajwadi Party can still get 30 to 40 seats in parliament. Similarly, even if Laloo Prasad Yadav runs Bihar to the ground, he will still get a certain number of seats because of the caste configuration.

We have also seen a second development—the increasing criminalisation of politics. But the fact is that even as we complain about criminalisation and the middle class talks about bringing in laws to debar criminals from entering political life, nearly every time a criminal stands, he tends to get elected. When this happens, as it inevitably does, middle class disillusionment with the political process and the results that it throws up increases.

Since 1991, we've seen a much more aggressive middle class; a middle class that has seen prosperity with the growth of satellite television. The growth of the knowledge industry and the pride people take in companies like Infosys demonstrate that the middle class sees itself on par with the rest of the world. I went to Infosys, to anchor a discussion there and without exception the people who spoke said they had much more in common with a computer engineer in Seattle than, say, a farmer in rural Karnataka.

As you see this divide growing, you see the middle class contempt for politics and politicians growing. One of the successes of the BJP was that it was able to package itself not as a communal party but as a party of the educated middle class. We saw that in the sort of people the party chose to represent it on television channels. They ran everything at the level of sound bytes. The result was a huge middle class following— people who were willing to forget what the BJP was really all about. In the process many of us in the media—because we look to the cities, because we look to the middle class—got the last elections completely wrong. We thought that the middle class view was what really counted in India.

My fear for the next decade is that as politics continues in this way and as the middle class grows more and more assertive, we are going to go into the

future not as one India but as two Indias—and that worries me.

Sunil Khilnani

I think Yogendra Yadav made a very strong argument for why we have to focus on and start at the bottom— to see reform as a sort of inductive process. And I think that is right. But—and there I want to return to a central question that Pratap Mehta raised in his paper and to quote his own words, "Can the current practices of popular authorisation sustain the range of values that are embodied in our constitution, embodied in the description of our political system as a constitutional liberal democracy?" Do the practices of competitive politics, and the units that are mobilised to compete, can these social agencies and these procedures which make up our practices of popular authorisation actually sustain those values that he outlined and which are I think rightly embodied in our constitutional democracy? This raises the issue of the consequences of increased participation: and I think we need to have a more refined and nuanced picture of the participatory process. That happened through the 90s and Yogendra Yadav has talked about it. Certainly these processes released in their intentions some very powerful and positive developments. But we also need to look at them in terms of the range of consequences they have released—and while participation has been a great thing, we need to have a more nuanced view. We need to ask in what respect has it sustained the core values of our liberal constitutional democracy and in what respect might it actually pose a challenge to or even threaten some of them? There may be moments of consolidation in a political system after moments of great participatory upsurge. So that what Yogendra Yadav talks about as a drying up, may it not in fact be a kind of taking a breath perhaps—a moment when institutions and intellectuals and political elites have a chance to actually come forward and offer a range of different possibilities and solutions which can then become part of the political process?

Mridula Mukherjee

I think there are some basic problems with the distinction which some of you have made between formal and substantive democracy. I refer to Yogendra Yadav's point about our democracy having to fit in with a checklist prepared by Washington. As a historian and as a student of the freedom struggle, I want to say that our democracy has not come about because of any checklist made in Washington or London. It was made right here and it was made at all levels, it was made in villages, in towns, in town halls, in assemblies, everywhere. The leaders of the freedom struggle and the people who fought in the freedom struggle did not recognise these distinctions between formal and substantive. Gandhi is not only the Gandhi of the *Hind Swaraj* where he critiques Western democracy. He is also the Gandhi who leads the movement for democracy. Nehru is not only the Nehru who talks about the rights of workers and peasants, he is also the Nehru who struggles for a Constituent Assembly right from the 1930s. If anybody fought a consistent struggle for political institutional reform, it was Nehru. He was not just a man of the masses.

We do not have a tradition of this disjunction between formal and substantive. And I think the way to move forward is through democracy which has integrated both these levels. The world moves with these formal structures and at the same time there are people out there who live lives in all kinds of ways, including informal set-ups. Just as we talk in these conferences, we also go and do other things in our normal life. I think there need be no disjunction between these rooms and the outside, just as there is not in life.

In the characterisation of the last decade, which Yogendra Yadav made, communalism disappeared somewhere. I think that in this whole concern with the so-called churning which took place in the 1990s (which we might call the Mandalisation of politics, and which may have produced certain positive changes as well), we forgot that in fact what dominated the 90s was the ascendancy of communal politics. It is the destruction of the Babri Masjid, the Ram Janma Bhoomi Movement, the coming to power of the communal forces and state power for the first time coming into the hands of communal fascist forces that dominated the 90s. What worries me is Yogendra Yadav's linking this churning with the decline of a party. It is one thing to say that we have to go beyond a single party system, and quite another to argue that the decline of the Congress was a cause of the churning. In any case, I don't believe the Congress even in its heyday represented a single party system. The Congress was much more than a party, it was a platform on which multiple interests were represented.

I would like to conclude by saying that we need to focus on what institutional changes we need in the next decade if the peoples' aspirations are to be fulfilled. I think there are certain things on which a consensus has emerged in Indian society. The criminalisation of politics does need institutional intervention. Women's empowerment does need institutional intervention. The system of financing of political parties does need institutional intervention. These are not things that can happen through popular mobilisation. But we also need popular mobilisation on fundamental issues like ideological struggles against communalism. So I would just say that there is integration in life between the formal or institutional aspects and the substantive or popular aspects of democracy and I think we should not in academics refuse to see that integration.

Zoya Hasan

Before I call upon Mr. Prem Shankar Jha to make his intervention, I want to make one clarification regarding Mridula Mukherjee's comment. You just referred to formal and substantive democracy and to formal and informal politics and you were suggesting that the two are the same. I think the formal and substantive democracy and the formal and informal politics that Yogendra Yadav was talking about are very different things. In fact, Yogendra Yadav was privileging the informal sphere because he

thinks that in the informal sphere people have an effective voice, whereas I was making a distinction between formal and substantive democracy in the sense of formal being procedural, institutional arrangements while substantive democracy is one in which democracy has a social substance or a strong social dimension. These are two very different things and we should keep them separate.

Prem Shankar Jha

My concern is actually with something which is often considered old fashioned, that is the relationship of democracy with nation building. You have heard a great deal about formal and informal, about grassroots, about substantive democracy *versus* formal democracy, all of it implying that in reality our democracy does not stretch very far down below the elite. I agree with all that but the fact is that nation building is a function of the elite, and we have seen around us a proliferation of failed states which show you what happens when nation building fails. By nation building I refer to the promotion of cohesiveness among the people, the progressive strengthening of democracy and the democratisation of regulatory and administrative institutions, the progressive improvement in the quality of life through economic progress, and a progressive strengthening of the rule of law. These are my four criteria for nation building. While we are criticising democracy, let us not forget that our democracy has been spectacularly successful in giving us extraordinary stability with growth over the last 50 years. The structures of democracy that we created have given us our federalism which is a unique ethnic federalism in which everybody's core ethnic identity is safe, but the whole of India is their field of opportunity. It is an extraordinary combination. We are probably the only country in the world which created this. And we should not run ourselves down. But having said this, I would say that there are a number of developments that are taking place which are in fact endangering this and they are coming out of the working of that same democracy. What makes it so hard to understand where the challenge and threats are coming from, is that they are coming from the same places that are responsible for our success. The dangers that we are facing today are the fragmentation of the political system at the centre, and therefore the increasing difficulty of initiating national policies that impose short-term costs for long-term benefits. This is of course mostly true of economics.

The second point, is the criminalisation of politics and the attendant mushrooming of corruption, fraud and extortion. The third is the progressive transformation of India from a developmental state to a predatory state. It is a change we are not aware of. Don't forget how developmental we were, when we went in for the First, Second, Third and Fourth Plans under Pandit Nehru. We the people of India were prepared to accept infinite postponement of benefits for our children. We accepted a growth model with very small employment potential because we would get accelerated benefits in the future.

We didn't get them but the fact is that is the kind of developmental state we were. The Centre had the power to impose a developmental state upon the people. That is also gone. We have now become a predatory state where the purpose of coming to power is actually to carve the body of the state and to take parts of it and put them in one's private pocket. This is privatisation of the worst kind. There are other things like the collapse of the judiciary, which others are much better qualified to talk about.

May I simply end by saying that there are two factors that we need to look at. The first is that the simple majority voting system which has given us bipartisan politics in the states except for two or three in the north, and therefore considerable political stability in the states, has given us 63 parties at the centre. The simple majority voting system is supposed to create pressures to give you bipartisan politics. At the centre it will not and cannot do it. We took this model from Britain which is a unitary nation state. Ours is a federal state. In each element of the federation you have got bipartisan politics but they are entrenched votes. The entrenched votes are carried to the centre and you get 63 parties. So coalition politics are here to stay. This was hidden during the days of Congress dominance but it is now out in the open. It has resulted in a dramatic weakening of the centre, its capacity to take long-term decisions and impose short-term sacrifices. This has been worsened by the separation of central and state elections. This has put every single government at the centre into what is called election mode where every state election becomes a referendum on their policies. This has further weakened our democracy while the predatory nature has been strengthened by the criminalisation of politics which is a result of our electoral finance system. We took our democracy from a country where the average constituency size is 60,000 people and you can stay at home and cover the entire constituency in a month in your own car, that is England. But here the average constituency size is 6000 sq. km and two million people. The Americans who faced this problem, revised their election financing laws nine times between 1865 and 1961. We have never done it. The whole question of state funding has been talked about but nothing has been done about it.

Sanjoy Hazarika

We need to look at the Northeast of India, to understand what elections actually mean in a state like Assam. They are an opportunity for people to express not just anger at governments but are also an expression of belief in something that they cannot speak about openly. In two successive Lok Sabha elections, the ULFA called for a boycott. In each election, the people came out and voted in large numbers—the percentage of voting in Assam was far higher than in any other part of the country! So it was an expression of belief in something that they could express silently yet boldly in the face of intimidation and pressure. This time, ULFA, realised there was no point in calling for a boycott. My

second point is the enticing of entire legislature parties, which has become an expression of absolute amorality. The most recent example is Arunachal Pradesh where an entire group walked over from one party to an other just before elections. The third is what I call co-option, partly in the informal process that Yogendra Yadav spoke of. In the first election in the 1950s in Nagaland, there was a complete boycott. Today every underground party, banned or not, there and elsewhere in the Northeast, actually supports a party, or group in an election. So we are seeing an informal co-option. I don't know how powerful this is in terms of sending a message to the rest of the country. But I think that, in that region, it says a lot about the system and the process of informal dialogue.

Bharat Karnad

Zoya Hasan spoke about the state's interventionist imperatives because of various deficiencies in government and governance. In regard to the Employment Guarantee Act, I have a problem. Is employment something synthetic that a government can by *obiter dicta* generate? If it is then aren't we moving back to the regressive tendencies of looking for statist solutions to every social or other problem symbolised by the failed Soviet Union? We need to weigh the efficacy of means in the scale of performance. If the state is an efficient deliverer of services and benefits, India should have by now been a socialist paradise. Rajiv Gandhi, in his political infancy, rued in 1985 (at the Centenary celebrations of the Congress Party)—that only 15 per cent of the development rupee actually reached the grassroot level; and that 85 per cent of the funds were lost as 'wastage' and 'leakage' (read corruption!) and by way of wages and other perquisites for governmental *apparatchiks*. Government today, has become predatory to the extent that most social welfare-development related spending goes in the upkeep of the government. In other words, the Indian state exists to serve itself, and not to serve the masses of the citizenry. Which is why we have to consider the efficacy of the means employed. There is no point in going back to the constitutional intentions of full employment, as if it and other public goods can be secured by a miraculous wave of the wand. So, either we get realistic 57 years after independence, or we stick to our *hubris* of 'the state that can do everything'. This is a *hubris* that the beneficiaries of any statist system, like in the erstwhile Soviet Union, were the Communist Party bigwigs and hangers-on who lacked for nothing, while the people were deprived.

Teesta Setalvad

This is just a word of caution to state that conferences in rooms like this must reflect the rumblings and concerns of the world outside. To maximise the utility of such conferences, we need to constantly evaluate how much impact they have.

The faith of a person in a village or a small *kasbah* town in the rule of law is implicit. In the wake of disaster and tragedy why does a witness or victim feel that by simply filing an affidavit or filing a case he or she will get justice? Because somewhere, deep down, with all the delays and cynicisms, there is a belief in the formal system, even though it doesn't always work. I would just like to quickly put down two or three aspects related to judicial reform which I have laid down in my paper. We have a horrendous number of backlog of cases. These are supposed to total a staggering 23 crores if we look at the whole country! Criminal trials take 5 to 10 years to reach completion.

Due to the recent and dramatic developments related to the Best Bakery case, people are sadly talking about witness protection. For me the issue is not witness protection alone. If we introduce witness protection without talking about police reforms—that have been suggested time and again even by the National Police Commission (NPC) for over 20 years—we are once again going to talk about one more piece of legislation without looking at the consequences. Between 1981 and 1990 this country saw eight police commissions that looked closely at the issue of police reform. They deliberated and brought out eight police commission reports. Those reports are on the shelf. No political party, with due humility, has had the guts to initiate police reforms in this country. According to me police reform is critical because it means when you approach a police station and register an FIR, you have faith that there is an independent non-partisan police force that will register your complaint, then investigate, and thereafter the matter will come to the judiciary.

I believe that among the key issues that we are talking about for the next decade, we need to come back to some very pragmatic issues. One of the serious issues that senior policemen in this country have been urging— not only civil rights groups, activists and NGOs—is the issue of a non-partisan police force. Senior and responsible policemen, too, have felt that we need an independent non-partisan police force that is not dictated to by the executive. Which political party would have the moral courage to legislate on police reforms?

I think it is a very critical issue and it is fundamental to the issue of the reform of the criminal justice system. We also have a judiciary which is a much eulogised institution. Unfortunately it has very little respect for basic human rights. When I talk about basic human rights I am talking about the right to education and the right to health. I think we need to have a human rights oriented institutionalisation of democracy. I would like to bring to attention three points before the esteemed persons gathered here, especially those who have close associations with the political class.

We had a first draft of the Indian Constitution, which was prepared in February 1947 and then a second draft which was brought out in October 1948 and legislated in 1950. We lost substantive amounts between the two drafts. What happened in between? Partition. That made the leaders of the political class extremely defensive about key issues of minority representation, about the safeguards for minority rights and even the inclusion of religious minorities as socioeconomically backward classes.

I think these are some issues we need to go back to, to analyse and pin-point where we have floundered. I remember reading about the first general election under Pandit Nehru. It was the only election where tickets were distributed without looking at caste and community. Because that was the moral highpoint at that time in the national movement. Today unfortunately caste and community are a major calculation in ticket distribution. Some of these subtle barriers to real democratisation need to be broken.

Finally, I would like to bring attention to the whole issue of communalism. I don't believe communalism is only about the demolition of the Babri Masjid. We have to remember the backdrop of partition. We have to remember what happened to Kashmiri Pandits in the Valley. When we look at communalism let us broaden our look to South Asia. We had such wonderful sentiments expressed yesterday at the inauguration about how pivotal a peaceful and solidly secular India is to the whole region. I believe real genuine secularism can be fostered within and without if you are able to link the rights of religious minorities, not just within here but within different countries of the region. We need to forge a South Asian understanding of this, because what happens in Kashmir plays out in Gujarat. What happens in Bangladesh is played out in rhetoric in communal politics elsewhere and because of the backdrop of partition these memories find resonance.

And since we are dealing with large numbers of people and how feelings can be manipulated, we need to understand how such issues find resonance. For me today, Gujarat is the biggest challenge to the Indian constitution and democracy. We are forced in the struggle for Gujarat, to look at just five or six cases that were major carnages. But today, according to me, Gujarat functions as a non-functioning democracy. Today, journalists are not allowed to enter the Secretariat. Today, you have the complete ghettoization of the state. Today the disturbing trend is that entrance to schools is determined in Gujarat by community and that this has been the situation for the past 15-20 years. The situation in Gujarat is summed up by the fact that even the opposition in Gujarat has been completely curtailed by the discourse of a virulent communal party. The opposition has been stifled into silence. Therefore, I think that Gujarat really challenges us at the very root because agricultural lands have been taken away after the carnage, rural lands have been taken away from victims. We don't even debate this. Rehabilitation and reparation have not been granted to victims of sexual violence. If you have lost four years of your lives through burning and other acts, there has been no state redemption or compensation. For me, Gujarat really poses a huge, practical challenge to our notions of constitutionalism and real democracy.

Vivek Monteiro

The underlying theme and concern of all of us here has been about deepening Indian democracy and giving it more substance. The earlier NDA government, had its version of this which it called "an agenda for governance". My first question is—to what extent do you feel that the last Lok Sabha elections were a popular reaction to this conception of democracy or to this agenda for governance? The present government has put forward another conception called the Common Minimum Programme. Zoya Hasan and a number of other speakers here today have drawn attention to the democratic potential of this programme. The second question is— to what extent can the Common Minimum Programme be a vehicle for promoting and deepening democracy in the country today? All of us here agree that phenomena like communalism and ethnic conflict, are anti-democratic. My last question is—to what extent can the Common Minimum Programme and its concerns be a means for containing, constricting and isolating these anti-democratic forces?

Suman K. Bery

How do we insert the perspective of rights into the given sketch of the Indian Constitution? Does it fit there naturally or not? Several speakers (including our chairperson) have drawn a new link between the economic reform efforts (and outcomes) and the verdict of the electorate. From the economists' perspective, real wages, inequality, etc. have not deteriorated over the last 10 years. What are the data that political scientists look at to reach their causal judgements? Is the government's record on service delivery an important or an unimportant element in people's voting decisions? My rather naïve reading of the Indian political science literature is that voting decisions are not affected by service delivery. Has that changed in the last decade?

This relatively loose link between economic success and what is happening in politics seems a global phenomenon. I see identity-based politics emerging in other parts of the world as well, not necessarily linked with economic success or failure. You see this in the US which has been moderately successful, you are seeing it in Europe which has perhaps been less successful. So economic strategy and delivery may just be orthogonal to voting behaviour, to use economists' terminology.

Sunita Narain

How do we use democracy for development? To me that is the big challenge today. This is clear in the areas I work, particularly water. Over the last 20 years we have decimated the state. All of us know that in the 1980s if something had to be done it could be done within the governmental system. Now even if the Prime Minister wants it done it is difficult to move the system. In other words, the Indian state has become extremely weak in its ability to deliver. We can consider increased dependence on the private sector as a delivery mechanism. But the problem is that given the intense inequity that exists in India, the private sector can never deliver on basic services like water, health, or even public transport. These are areas which demand public services and need governments to work for the poor. The private sector also needs the right regulatory mechanism and this again needs a strong state.

What is happening is that as governments cannot deliver on development they find short cuts. Take the example of water. All governments at the beginning say that water is a critical issue. They say to deliver water services they will reform the drinking water missions. They do some reform—some good, some bad. But implementation remains indifferent. So by the end of their tenure (take the NDA as an example) they realise they have not been able to deliver. And therefore they move towards big slogans whether it is the interlinking of rivers, or about large road building projects. This is only because governments cannot deliver. And I think that is the biggest crisis today. It is not about programmes. It is not about money. It is about the ability of the state to deliver on development. And I think the issue to discuss is the institutional reforms which will allow for effective governance.

Chandra Bhan Prasad

I would like to just reproduce a quote from Dr. Ambedkar. According to him, "Democracy is not a form of government, it is a form of society." A political democracy presupposes a social democracy. So when we talk of democracy we must always go back to that great statement. Today we don't have social democracy and most of the problems which we have in the form of political democracy relate to that. Secondly, if you see the journey of a democratic state and society, in the beginning the state was a dictator. Society was regulated by the wishes of the state. The state was the moral and constitutional guardian of society. Over a period of time when society became civil, it slowly acquired civility, the state slowly withdrew and society became the moral guardian of the State and society as well. In the context of India if we consider India as a young democracy, the state began well in 1947-1950. The abolition of *Zamindari* and affirmative action for the Dalits were the most fundamental changes introduced. Slowly the state began weakening. The first time, in the known history of India, when the state actually asserted itself over society to regulate and discipline it was during 1975-77. Most public welfare policies were introduced in 1975-77. The mandate of the Constitution was carried out during that period and if you see a solid Dalit middle class today it is the product of 1975-1977. So we should not, in order to suit our sentiments, ideas or things in fashion, dismiss history and facts. Mandal did bring many changes to Indian politics. But it was not necessarily the assertion of democracy. To me Mandal unleashed a phenomenon of the de-democratisation of Indian politics. Today most states are turning into caste republics.

Rekha Chowdhary

Coming from Jammu and Kashmir I would like to say that the people in the periphery also have a context of democracy, which needs to be further extended. We cannot talk meaningfully about democracy unless we talk about nation building, federalism, secularism and multiculturalism. And in this context the concept of nation building has itself entailed many tensions for the democratic politics of India. This was mainly because it has been following the ideals of 'unity with uniformity' and the concept of 'the melting pot'. Based upon the western context of nations surviving on 'commonalities' and 'uniformities', this process, by problematising differences of any kind, has not only generated greater strains for Indian polity, but has also resulted in an undemocratic political ethos. In Jammu and Kashmir with its asymmetrical federal relations with India constitutionally guaranteed by Article 370, that acknowledged 'difference' was pressurised from the beginning to undergo an undemocratic process of constitutional 'assimilation' and 'uniformity'. Emphasis on 'integration' and the resultant erosion of constitutional autonomy has not only to be understood as a crisis of nation building but also the crisis of the inclusive context of democracy.

However, due to political forces unleashed in the last five decades, the concept of nation building has undergone a transformation and in the process we are now thinking of multiculturalism, plurality and differences. Though democratically this is a more inclusive context, one needs to recognise one tension that underlies it—the context of identity politics. Identity is a very important social and political fact. We cannot ignore identity politics. In Jammu and Kashmir, identity politics has its intensely visible manifestations. In the present context of the democratic politics of India, it is very important to acknowledge identity politics. But identity politics itself incorporates an inherent tension that needs to be resolved. While identities cannot be ignored and suppressed, politics based upon identities cannot be encouraged beyond a point. Hence the question arises—to what extent do identities need to be recognised and at what point are they to be transcended? If we do not recognise identities then there exists the danger of the suppression of all possible differences in the name of unification. The result would be a kind of homogenisation. To that extent, all kinds of differences and the politics asserting these differences need to be recognised. But the fact remains that identity politics creates a sense of exclusivity. And one exclusive politics of identity has the potential of generating a chain of exclusivities. Multiple identity politics therefore, rather than adding to the inclusivity of politics, may lead to fragmentation. Moreover, identity politics has the inbuilt danger of responding to an elite interest at the cost of the masses. Once the state starts responding to identity politics, it may conveniently ignore its basic responsibility of building the capacities of its people. What is happening today, is that rather than building a discourse on citizenship and rights, empowering the people at the margins and building the economic and political infrastructure necessary for generating equity and equality, the state is responding to identity politics. This tension underlying democratic politics needs to be recognised and resolved.

Sunil Kant Munjal

We are a country of 650 million voters. There are 542 constituencies, and most constituencies have 10 to 15 lakh people. In the UK, the average is 68,000 while the US has roughly 2 lakhs in each constituency. Clearly it is a different world in these countries.

Even though we have developed our own unique model of democracy over time, I don't think it is a bad idea to look around and see what works in other countries. It never hurts to bring in good ideas. The public funding of elections is a serious issue which needs to be debated. In fact the Confederation of Indian Industry has worked on this subject for some time, and has made a number of recommendations. We need to look at how companies make donations. Donations should be above board, accounted for in annual reports, and approved by shareholders. The process should be transparent so that there is no room for doubt and friction.

Perhaps there is even a need for a separate mechanism that the government can set up to monitor political funding by corporates. I do agree the process could be complex in a country like ours, since we have so many different parties. But it is a challenge that needs to be met.

Diversity is another challenge that needs to be understood properly, because it is both a strength and a source of weakness. There are 28 states with 16 officially spoken languages, 54 cuisines, and 5000 spoken dialects in India. So clearly there is no one size that fits all. Yet not much time is spent on debating the advantages that can be derived out of this diversity. We are an extremely diverse group of individuals across this nation, yet it is important for all of us to understand that there is an underlying Indianness that glues us all together.

Diversity and Indianness was the first point I wanted to raise. Governance is the second. There has been an increasing public debate on the need for more open corporate governance in industry. Is there a need for a similar debate about governance in government? I believe there is.

There are more criminals getting in and winning elections decade after decade. We need to work on cleansing the system. Finance and functioning need to be devolved all the way down. There is a need for us to find a process of how to spend public resources for a larger common good.

There is also obviously a debate required on who decides the common good. There is a need right now to look for reform not just in politics but the other arms as well, including the executive, the judiciary and even the Fourth Estate to create the right kind of balance.

India's democracy is, being appreciated worldwide. I was in the US a couple of weeks ago and met many republicans and democrats. They don't like our public posturing, they don't like what we are doing at WTO, but they appreciate the fact that we stand up for our own kind of democracy and make our own comments in public. This clearly, is a more mature form of democracy than we had earlier.

But we need to move to the next level. Can we build in our democracy a process where the states learn to work better with the centre itself? Today there is a constant conflict between the states and the centre, and this is happening even if the same party is in power at the centre and the state. This is an issue of development which I think should attract attention.

I'd like to make a final point about employment guarantees. Can we as a nation look at the art of the possible, instead of the art of the impossible? Employment guarantee to my mind is not possible in a country like ours. What is possible and what must be done is to find ways to educate our people. We need to train people so that they are more employable. We need to provide a safety net by retraining those who lose jobs through retrenchment or restructuring. There are enough successful models from across the world that we can look at.

I believe the UPA government's focus on the health and education sectors will open up new opportunities for the private sector, which in turn will create new employment avenues.

Zoya Hasan

We can have our own type of democracy which you said is much appreciated in the US, we could perhaps also have our own type of economy.

Ravi Parthasarathy

We have heard a lot of issues relating to the criminalisation of politics. While we should all be concerned about it, perhaps we should also realise that India does not have a monopoly on corruption in public life. Many of the issues that we are debating are equally the US, UK, and Japan, just to mention three countries. You have pork belly contracts in Japan, you have defence contractors influencing the government in the US, the list is endless. We can agonise about this for as long as we want, but we are talking about fundamental human nature.

But the difference between the US and India, at the level of the common individual, is that the US citizen's interface with public officials is generally a pleasant experience. And whatever be the services he expects from any public agency, the hand of government is generally invisible and is generally efficient. Models of democracy and economic business models for a country will necessarily be influenced by what happens in other countries around the world. So let us assume we have a market oriented economy. The missing agenda that we need to define when we are talking about India in the next decade, is the governance needed at the level of the common man to make his life easier.

We will not be able to eliminate corruption; we can only strive to decrease it. It is not only politicians who are corrupt but at times doctors are corrupt, lawyers are corrupt, a lot of people are corrupt. But we can focus on the agenda of how to make life simpler for people interacting with government. We must focus on the art of the feasible, and the provision of services is a simple matter. We waste much productivity with people going up and down, back and forth to get simple things done. This is a major productivity issue, so if we want to up

prominent in the GDP growth rate, we must release the productivity of the people.

Nasser Munjee

Democracy is a process for selecting and changing governments which also requires very powerful sets of rules and institutions to ensure its efficacy. But democracies also require similar processes for governance between elections. These are two separate processes. We can improve what happens between elections through a system of rules and processes which almost every country has evolved on its own. Those edifices are weak in India and we need to strengthen them. We have had coalition politics since '91, together with the highest rates of growth India has ever witnessed in the last 10 to 12 years. The overall paradigm of consensus and checks and balances has ensured that an overall ideology imposed by one political party or another can no longer hold complete sway. The diversity of views of complex communities is expressed through a coalition of interests and it is this that determines policies. But what happened in Gujarat, as Teesta Setalvad just mentioned, raises a key question facing us today—to what extent is India in danger of becoming an elective tyranny? Are we in fact one? If we do not reform the institutions of governance between elections, let alone at the time of elections, we are in danger of nurturing many tyrannies from which the hapless citizen will have little redress. Gujarat shows that even despite the appalling violence that occurred in the state, the incumbent government through the electoral process succeeded in holding on to power with a thumping majority. The excesses of a domineering majority over minorities is precisely the fine line that needs to be defined and protected by a truly democratic process of governance. The issue therefore is—how are we going to address these contradictions or are we condemned to repeat history over and over again?

C. Uday Bhaskar

I want to take off from Pratap Bhanu Mehta's formulation about how the state has perhaps accorded to itself a certain discretionary right in terms of the provision of certain other fundamental rights that may be in the constitution and relate this to security. If we look at this in terms of the challenges and prospects of the Indian democratic experience we need to consider the current status of what the jargon calls LIC-IS, that is low intensity conflict and internal security, which is being aggravated by the practice of democracy as we know it. Whatever be the discourse about security and however normative it is in terms of the responsibility that devolves upon the state and the provisions in our Constitution, there are two sets of elements here. This is related to points made by other colleagues that the way in which the Indian state relates to the common person, or to governance, has now become extremely venal. The common man associates the state with a certain venality at the institutional interface and that in turns plays out into the way in which we lower certain public thresholds, whether of legitimacy or rectitude. If this is left unchecked and we believe that this is 'the

Indian example', it could have a very adverse impact on the internal security dimension of the country. This will be the more likely prospect if this challenge is not recognised.

A related point is that in as much as we talk about various reforms, of the judiciary, police and political practices including the funding of elections, we need to look to education to address this challenge in its most holistic manner. Many of our current practices, like the criminalisation of politics and the politicisation of crime, have an impact on the internal security dimension. If left unchecked, the deviant will become the norm. This will have adverse consequences on every aspect of our national endeavour and aspirations.

Amar Kanwar

I am here as a film-maker, a story teller and a listener. In the context of democracy and the next decade we need to look at the state not delivering—whether on water or development. And if we are looking at future challenges we must see that hope is very difficult to kill entirely. To push that a little further, it seems that it is not just a question of the state not delivering water and so on, but what is probably critical is that very large sections of our population are actually beginning to accept that the state will not deliver and neither will industry. It is thus a very serious crisis. I am referring to a situation of being convinced that there is now no hope. This means that if before your eyes and before the eyes of your children you find that your land is taken, or your water is taken, or your forests are destroyed, or your means of livelihood disappear and this process continues, then the issues of your relationship with democracy, the state, industry, patriotism, and the nation get thrown open. An ordinary individual starts to find himself in a situation of war. It is actually a war to survive and when you are in that kind of a situation nothing is fair or unfair. Before we talk about solutions we need to understand and define the nature and extent of this crisis.

Radha Kumar

I am really glad that so many people have highlighted the governance issue. India is one of the least governed countries in the world. We have one policeman per 10,000 of our population, which is a very poor ratio. I don't know what the equivalent in administration is, I assume it will be even worse as a proportional statistic. With these kinds of figures we are always going to have a policing problem, we are going to have a justice delivery problem, and we are going to have an administration problem. These should be the key issues for reform over the next 10 years. We need to work out the possibilities for actually expanding governance, and the training that would require. My impression is that we have very few training institutes both for administrators and for the police. And I am not even sure whether we have thought about having an urban-rural balance when it comes to training. Is there anybody talking about small-scale and dispersed training programmes as against centralised training? The figure of 8,000 elected representatives mentioned above is the sum of central and legislative assemblies members. If we add in *panchayats* and *zilla parishads*, which are meant to be our key elements of representation, what would the figure rise to? It is one reason why they are not added, the fact that there still isn't enough devolution of power.

The other issue that has been highlighted is plugging the gap between the administration and the formal and informal sectors, that is civil society participation, which we have seen occur from time to time. We have had phases of government in which outside expertise has been called in. The 1980s under Rajiv Gandhi were a time when a lot of experts were called in to help and advise. But that was again at the central level, and did not devolve through to the states and lower to the districts and village levels. Can we not borrow from models such as the race relations boards of Britain? That was a very good example of getting civil society into the business of community relations, or what Ravi Parthasarathy calls the interface between public and private. And finally we should underline the point that Rekha Chowdhary and Sanjoy Hazarika made. What about extending democracy to the periphery and to conflict ridden areas? We really haven't thought seriously about that issue at all, and it is one of the biggest sources of conflict. Today, we have a peace process going on in both the Northeast and the Northwest (Kashmir). This would be the time to start extending the necessary democratic reforms.

Naina Lal Kidwai

Just a point to highlight what Radha Kumar had touched on and that is of improved governance, which I would define as a triangle of efficiency, effectiveness and equity. And in alluding to it also, maybe throw up a solution which we, as those who give IT to the world, should really be giving IT unto us. That is simply by organising information for ourselves in an effective and transparent way. Why does a villager have to travel repeatedly to a collector's office to get his land records sorted out? Why can't we have a Bhoomi project replicated across the nation? Why can't we have information available on a database that doesn't require us to recreate poverty alleviation programmes which need to again and again define who the recipients are and who the recipients have been? Democracy defines for us very simply what is required by all of us in this country.

We need education and employment. But even more so—we need empowerment. We need for every individual to feel that he/she belongs. To me it is typified in a very simple story which I will allude to. Mona *Ben*, who has been a member of SEWA for many years, explained it to me as "You know until not very long ago I was my husband's wife, I was my son's mother. Today, I am Mona *Ben*." This woman from the meagre earnings that she makes from her working at home, is going to vote with her head not with her feet. She isn't educated and she is barely employed but she has understood all the issues to do with health and earning from her skills in craft and embroidery. What we need is more empowerment.

Sudhir Kakar

The maintenance of a positive balance between hope and despair is our challenge for the next 10 years, but how do we ensure that the balance remains tilted in favour of hope? We have been talking of all the reasons for the prevalence of despair, the problems in governance and many other kinds of problems. I think that there is a growing middle class which is telling others who still have the balance of hope and despair tilted in favour of the former that you are hoping in vain, you are hoping too much. I hope that this frame of mind doesn't succeed because then the vital balance will certainly be disturbed. We also need to address the sources of hope in our society. Perhaps the sources of hope lie outside our democracy or outside our politics and we should talk of them.

Siddharth Varadarajan

I think power is getting more and more remote from ordinary people and you see this in a variety of ways. You see it in practice with the growing role of businessmen and carpetbaggers who are now so involved in politics. They enter, and get elected as Members of Parliament with the acceptance of all political parties. You see this remoteness of power in institutional terms, in the raising of deposits that a candidate pays to contest. This was done after a village in Andhra Pradesh, which hadn't received water for seven or eight years, decided to have the country's longest ballot paper with about 8000 candidates. The government said okay no more of this and the deposit rate was raised. So for many poor people it is simply not a practical proposition, quite apart from the money you have to spend to participate. You see this remoteness in legal terms. I am referring to what I consider is one of the most regressive judgements of the Supreme Court which is upholding the so called two child norm. The right of a citizen to put herself or himself forward as a candidate, is I consider as intrinsic a part of democracy as the right to vote. Yet the two child norm is being implemented in state after state. Just as ethnicity or gender or race or language should have nothing to do with your rights as a citizen, surely the number of kids you have should have nothing to do with your democratic rights. But you have the Supreme Court upholding this regressive law. You have this notion that education has to be disclosed even though the Constituent Assembly debates discussed that there should be no educational criterion.

You see this remoteness of power, as Teesta Setalvad said most markedly with respect to a complete absence of the rule of law and the total politicisation of law enforcement, especially when it comes to human rights violations. And here I want to say as a journalist that media exposés have produced and do produce results. For example, the case of the petrol pumps scam. My suspicion is that most of the cases in which we produce results pertain to those where you are really talking about a fight over the division of spoils. In these kinds of exposés the courts and the law enforcement machinery are willing to act, but are less willing to do so when an exposé points to flaws in the institutional structure of the state which have to do with human rights violations. *The Times of India* did an exposé on the tampering of DNA in the Panchaldan case in Kashmir. It has been two years and nothing has happened. That was an open and shut case of murder. Somewhere along the line we need to examine or ask the question whether there is a conceptual flaw in the manner in which the Constitution conceives of power. And I know this is a very difficult question because when the BJP was in power a lot of us felt that we needed to defend the constitution because the BJP wanted to reopen the whole discussion with a particular agenda in mind. It seems to me that the discourse of rights has been artificially grafted on to a constitutional framework that was perhaps not meant to grant due recognition to these rights. That is why the Court has to intervene. Ambedkar in the Constituent Assembly stated that, "If this constitution were to fail, if India were to have problems, it would not be because the Constitution was bad or that the Constitution had failed but that the people of India had failed." I think this idea that the basic law is perfectly fine and that everything else is problematic needs to be interrogated, like the institutional voting mechanisms such as first past the post which is the core of the western system that we have adopted. Is an alternative voting system going to solve the problem or do we need to think in terms of more fundamental reforms? I do feel we need to focus more on the institutional structures of the state and examine in a very realistic way how these are actually becoming obstacles in the ability of people to exercise political power.

Manvinder Singh (Vindi) Banga

I have been trying to see if there are any parallels between organisational or business effectiveness and the issues we are discussing today. And the first point that occurred to me is the time span we are talking about. Ten years at one level looks very long but in the life of a nation it is an extremely short period. It is like one year in business and therefore I believe that we ought to be focused totally on the here and now. Because it really is about the short term, in the context of a nation, and it is all about implementation. That is the key issue, especially in a democracy where you have multiple stakeholders, who often lead you to slow down implementation or even stall it. What can we do about a situation like this? First and foremost we need to take on and commit only to what is actually possible in the short term, in that brief period that you have before your next polling drive gets under way. And what I mean by that is to draw a distinction between the enablers such as creating health, or avenues of good health education, and the end product of all that and more which is employment. Therefore it is very important that we should commit to what we can do—what we can

achieve—in the short term. The second point is a principle which serves organisations extraordinarily well. That is accountability, a much used term, but actually not practiced at all in the Indian government.

We need to reform our whole electoral system, but that will not take place in the next one year—it would take place over the next 20 years—if at all. On the other hand there is one major recent development— information technology—that can be immensely useful here. It has revolutionised our ability to contact masses of people at one point in time, either directly in communication terms, or by providing information and transparency. And therefore, I think that we could use information technology extraordinarily powerfully to be effective in our constitutency. IT can be used to instill accountability in our elected leaders. Why not publicise their electoral promises and then do a quarterly update for the people at large? Similarly, IT can be used to hold bureaucrats accountable as well. I strongly believe that IT is one of the keys to helping us govern and implement in our large and complex country.

I have been gradually feeling gloomy as the morning moved on. Are things all that bad? And then I looked at the last 10 years and I feel "hey, you know it has not been great, but it has not been destructive either". And you know I don't read too many history and sociology books. Possibly I am in the zone of ignorance which makes me transitorily happy. But there you go. I think one of the problems that we have faced in India, in Indian democracy, is that we have not highlighted the continuity of the state. A state is a continuum while a government is transitory. And therefore the confusion between ownership and trusteeship has brought us where we are. Now as soon as we were pushed to a corner, what is now popularly called liberalisation released a lot of energy from this ownership business into empowerment. And therefore, if you look at the economic growth of the last 10 years particularly, it has been significantly different from when government, as an owner, imposed itself upon the body politic.

The second phenomenon that has taken place is the decentralisation of power as a consequence of liberalisation. It is not happening out of goodwill and wisdom. It is happening because the state legislators are saying that if you run the whole country from Delhi, how will you ensure I deliver locally. And if I do not deliver I will not get re-elected. And that decentralisation is a positive movement, but it is still in transition. So I don't know whether it will be reversed. It might, but I personally feel it will not. Now the point is, it is affecting various states differently. The southern states or western states are leveraging this well. On the other hand, the eastern states are not, except for West Bengal. You have extreme lawlessness in Bihar. But there was a suggestion made earlier, and I make the suggestion again. If the Planning Commission were to sit as a Commission for a month in Guwahati, for a month in one of the southern states and for a month in Srinagar, the psychological impact of inclusiveness and care would have a greater transformation. Now you know employment will not come through guarantees, employment will come through economic development. There has been more employment generated in the private sector in the last 10 years than in the previous 50 years. And therefore the point that was made on free enterprise initiative opportunities—just let the people's energy be released is important. In the end, I would just like to mention a news item I read this morning. Along with President Putin from Russia, there is a delegation coming to learn from us how we have released the energy of free enterprise in this country—in the private sector, in the IT sector, in the biotechnology sector and in the telecommunication sector. And they are hoping that we will not go back to learn from them about socialism.

13 | Concluding Remarks

(Section I — Democracy: Challenges and Prospects)

Pratap Bhanu Mehta

My first general point is that there is a thread in a sense running through the session. There was a lot of talk about the different divides between the formal and the informal sector, between formal democracy and substantive democracy, between the UPA and the NDA. The truth is that most of these divides are actually running within us as individuals and running within constituent groups. I just don't see these as easily mapping onto social groups. We are sociologically differently positioned and strategically the needs of one group are different from the needs of another group. It is not helpful sociologically or politically to see the ideological structuring of our political parties in such stark contrast. That is simply to ignore the history of the last 25 to 30 years. If you look at what the periods between 1970 and 1985 and 1990 and 2005 meant, it is not easy to say whether there has been institutional decline or institutional renewal. I think these dichotomies and polarities, of who is better or worse, simplify the picture too much and don't reflect all the cross currents and entanglements that our politics actually exhibit. If I were to make one suggestion about deepening democracy I would look to the political party. If you look at the way in which representation is organised and if you look at electoral reforms around the world, it is the democratisation of the party system that is the mechanism for actually mediating both questions of size, and information flows upwards. How many political parties will let every constituency decide who is going to stand from there? The decentralisation of political parties is the medium through which political parties organise a democracy. None of our political parties have these mechanisms in place.

On the issue of the relationship between economics and politics, I actually tend to view that whatever one can make of the data we have, I think it is a very orthogonal and complicated relationship. You can't get a sense of straight readings. Wage rates are rising, or in a sense inflation is rising and political parties are being thrown out. There is some relationship but we have to approach the subject with a lot of humility and caution, in terms of reading what the electoral mandates mean. If you look at the share or percentage of votes it is not easy to come to any sort of singular conclusion about what signals the electorates are sending in an aggregate sense. The final point I would like to make is about the two meanings of liberal. I agree with the basic point that concentrations of power are dangerous for society and sometimes the operation of markets can produce this concentration of power. But what is an even worse danger for democracy is that the state puts itself in the position of second guessing the decisions of most of its citizens, including decisions about economic arrangements. It is a balance. It is not always that a free market will guarantee a free society, but it is almost certain that unfree markets will guarantee both poverty and over the long run on a free society. One has to put this discussion in a historical perspective which is that we are now seeing India's first genuinely post-colonial generation. It is not encumbered with the weight of history, and that is a source of immense help. In historical perspective it is premature to see this as a story of decline. I think we are in a period of uncertainty. We are not sure where all the chips will fall, and we are negotiating with those uncertainties in a messy democratic way.

Yogendra Yadav

It has been a fascinating discussion. I will begin with Prof. Chandhoke's comment because I think she may have completely missed the point and I fear many others may also have missed the point. The one lesson that I draw is that I shouldn't use phrases which are otherwise deployed for so many other things. So in that sense the use of the words formal and informal was unfortunate, because everyone has their own notions of what is formal and what is informal. May be I should follow my teacher Rajiv Bhargava and just talk about model A and model B. But they don't lend themselves to substantive meanings. The point was not to say that formal democracy has failed and the informal is wonderful. The whole burden of my paper is actually to celebrate the achievements of formal democracy in India. One cannot argue that formal democracy is not necessary, but in Delhi in the last few years in places like this you can almost make yourself believe that it is also sufficient. And that is my source of unease. It is far from a valorization of the politics of caste and other ethnicities indulged in by many parties. In fact, the whole point of calling it a closure as Prof. Aijaz Ahmad helpfully pointed out was to say that it is precisely because formations like the RJD, Samajwadi Party, Bahujan Samaj Party have failed in a substantial way to articulate the democratic upsurge, which was theirs for the taking, that we have reached this moment of closure. We may be a crony capitalism but we are certainly not a crony democracy. Our democracy was not manufactured in Washington and exported to us in order to secure IMF loans. Precisely because our democracy was manufactured in municipal halls and in the streets, in auditing democracy today we cannot go back to a formal register dictated to us by the IMF and the World Bank.

There is a soul to democracy in this country and in assessing it we have to be true to that soul, even if it doesn't lend itself to a very easy interpretation from the classical textbooks coming from abroad. The whole point of the formal and informal, therefore, is to talk about the convergence between the two, that outside the formal political apparatus there is churning, there is dynamism and there is hope. The point is—how does the formal political establishment connect with that and draw upon it? Whenever Indian democracy has acquired certain strengths, the formal political apparatus has drawn strength from the informal because it was able to connect with it. And it is the inability sometimes to connect that makes me fear what is happening.

What are the mechanisms through which we develop that connect? As Jayaprakash Narayan has pointed out in his presentation and his writings over the last few years on electoral political reforms, we must not give in to legal fantasies of reforming the world by tomorrow morning. Politics is about entrepreneurs. I have not known any part of the world where politics draws in the most noble, the most saintly motivated people of the country. It is political entrepreneurs who come in and the whole point of constitutional legal design is to have a structure of incentives and disincentives. The only thing to resist is to try and make rules not only about incentives and disincentives but also require political actors to do certain things.

Decentralisation I think is really the key. We saw one major move during Rajiv Gandhi's regime. But in order to give it substance another major move has to be made otherwise the connect between what is happening on the ground and what we see in Delhi will not take place. Reformulating the resource base of the polity in terms of financial resources by way of an act is essential. In thinking about resources for politics we are obsessed about putting a ceiling and are not concerned about securing a floor which is really the serious question of finance in politics. In information resources, democratising the media is something we never talk about simply because we cannot pass a law about these things but we must also talk about things which we cannot rectify by law.

These are some of the things that we can do which would enable us to convert the energy of the last 15 years. The last 15 years may have been years of confusion, of mess, but there was energy in those 15 years. These were years of churning which were not caused by the decline of the Congress, but the decline of the Congress system was the trigger that opened enormous political possibilities. The trouble is that in last 15 years the children of that possibility have not lived up to expectations. I am not sure if communalism was the story of the last 15 years. I think it is a by-product, and sometimes by-products can outgrow the central tendency and look like overshadowing everything else. Communalism is the most unfortunate monster that has come out of it. However, it is not the story of the nineties as I would see it. The rise of the middle class is certainly a story. A very important story as long as we remember two things—one, the ambivalence of this class towards democracy. And second, its ambivalence towards communalism. Both these things exist, and they are part of the story.

Two quick things before I end, about how to interpret the recent elections. Are they in some ways a reflection on the governance agenda of the NDA? I am not so sure. It is easy to say that whoever lost did everything wrong and who won did everything right. As Pratap Bhanu Mehta has said, I think we should resist stories of that sort. We should take a more nuanced view. About economic reforms my own assessment is that the recent NDA defeat was principally not because of its economic reform policies. I have solid empirical evidence which shows that if there had been a referendum in the country on the questions of liberalisation, the opening up of markets, the retreat of the state, the entire liberalisation project would have collapsed completely in the year 2004. The reason why 2004 was not a verdict on economic reforms is because there was no political force that represented an alternative to economic reforms. And I do think in a subtle way the fact that the government acquired a reputation for being anti-poor shows that people don't understand liberalisation. But the reputation for being anti-poor can either be seen as a moment of closure or a moment of consolidation. We can't judge this today. May be 50 years from now it would look to us like a moment of beautiful consolidation or may be it would seem like a moment where we frittered away whatever energy we had gathered over 50 years.

I now come to the Common Minimum Programme (CMP) and what it can do. The CMP is a document. A document can be a symbol for huge historical transformations, or it can be just a piece of paper and nothing more. The CMP if attached to a political strategy can become the New Deal of India which is to say the CMP can become the symbol of creating a new political constituency. It is for the Congress to see whether it can harness the energy that has come from the informal sector. Historically it has happened. Parties can gain from things which they have done nothing to create. The Congress in all fairness has done nothing to create these energies, rather at a stage it was actually an obstacle to creating these energies. Historically, the moment it can actually harness and institutionalise them and create a New Deal for India, it would create a long-term enduring political coalition of forces, which represent interests that have not been recognised in the last 10 years or so. The question about the Employment Guarantee Scheme is not about whether we should have it, of course we should. The point is, is there a political strategy? Can the Employment Guarantee Scheme become a central idea in a political strategy to harness a certain section of Indian society? Can it create a coalition of the disprivileged? The Congress Party is in a unique position of having a constituency which it has not created and done very little to court. But it is there standing at the door. That is I think an historic opportunity. We tend to overestimate the capacities of what people sitting at the top of political structures can do. We tend to overestimate that in places like Delhi. It is a very large Congress Party and these political structures are huge structures which people sitting at the top can tinker with, but in the last instance it is work being done on the ground, the struggles in town halls and in the streets which would give that energy a real life and our democracy vibrance.

Zoya Hasan

I think we have had an extremely interesting, rich and stimulating discussion. Broadly speaking, we have been concerned with two sets of issues. One that concerns the problems of democracy while the other is a problem with democracy. Problems of democracy have to do with procedures, institutions, governance and institutional design, and some of these areas call for institutional reform. Much of the discussion today, as indeed more generally, the discussion on political and institutional design in the world of political science scholarship, and more broadly in civil society and in the public and political domain, has focused mainly on the electoral system, campaign finance, role of money in elections, etc. in short, ensuring free and fair elections. Reforms in campaign and party finance are clearly very important issues. Surely, it is important to decide on the recommendations of the reports on state funding of elections, which even though they did not go far enough, did move in the direction of recommending state funding of elections. Campaign finance is also a very central issue as is the criminalisation of politics.

But one issue which we have not discussed adequately, and which Mridula Mukherjee and a couple of other participants mentioned, is the whole issue of political representation. If we look at political representation in parliament and particularly state assemblies, there is a major change in the social composition of legislatures from the 1960s and 1970s resulting in a shift of power from upper castes to lower castes. There is a dramatic shift in the social composition of our representatives. Yet, this shift has mainly benefited particular caste groups, while other groups, such as women and minorities, Muslims in particular, are hugely under represented in decision making structures as well as in legislatures. There are three states where Muslims constitute over a quarter of the population and yet their representation in decision making structures and legislatures is miniscule. This is an issue that needs to be discussed and addressed when we talk about democracy and political reforms. But we have not really addressed these issues.

Then there are the problems with democracy. The discussion today on the problems with democracy spoke of three sets of issues. One is the issue of democracy and diversity and I would like to emphasise the point that several participants have drawn attention to—the need to strengthen the rights framework, especially minority rights.

The second issue is the democracy and development debate, which has been gaining urgency in the light of globalisation and economic reforms and the economic divide that this has created. The 2004 election verdict was a verdict against this divide and the inequities of neo-liberal economic reforms and the dismal and unequal consequences of economic reforms for different sections of society.

Third issue, is the problem of democracy and representation. This issue pertains not only to under-representation of particular groups, but equally importantly, to the problems of the mechanisms of representation, that is political parties. Any discussion of institutional design must address the question of party reform—an issue that is hardly ever seriously debated and discussed. This has become more important because we now have a large number of political parties and most of them are leader-driven and have no internal democracy. I believe it's time to think about the need for party elections and whether or not recognition of parties should be made contingent upon holding internal elections, not as a formality, but as an exercise in internal democracy. In the 1970s there was a great deal of criticism of the tendency of centralisation in the Congress Party and concentration of power in the hands of the central leadership. But if we look at political parties today, both the more established and the new ones, they function in the most undemocratic manner. So while we were rightly concerned in the past with centralisation in the Congress, I believe we have not expressed the same concern with the centralisation and concentration of power in political parties today. Most of them are internally undemocratic.

Finally a number of questions have been raised on the Employment Guarantee Scheme. The issue is simply this—the social benefits of a universal time-bound employment guarantee scheme greatly outweigh the potential difficulties. If the government has understood the lessons of the 2004 parliamentary election, it must bring in a much larger employment programme which can start processes that will ultimately work to the advantage of the rural poor and the regeneration of the rural economy. Indeed, a bold and imaginative political leadership will readily recognise the historic significance of a universal and time-bound EGA as the most effective means for providing livelihood to the poorest and most disadvantaged citizens. If properly implemented it will be one of the most significant pieces of legislation since independence which will go a long way in bridging the gap between political and economic equality and will be the site for deepening democracy, just as in the eighties and nineties caste politics was an important site of empowerment and social justice. The Common Minimum Programme and the Employment Guarantee Act could become important sites for empowerment and therefore I think the critical issue really is the role of the state. NGOs, civil society and the private sector are all very important. But let us honestly look at the history of Indian democracy. Can we ignore the fact that the state has been the key site of both struggle and empowerment? We have not reached a stage of development in our country where we can jettison state intervention. But the point that a number of people have rightly emphasised is that it is not really state intervention, but the implementation of state policies that matters.

I would like to conclude on an optimistic note, which has come through in the discussion today and that is the obvious success of Indian democracy, and we can be legitimately proud of this achievement. It is a story of success, because unlike liberal democracies, Indian democracy has demonstrated a radicalising potential. If we summon the political will, we can realise the radicalising potential of democracy in the next couple of decades.

Section **II**

Economy:
Growth and Equity

BACKGROUND PAPERS,
PRESENTATIONS AND DISCUSSION

THERE is now a consensus that a higher level of growth is required if India is to address the basic challenges of poverty and unequal distribution. But there is no consensus on how higher growth can be achieved and how the consequences of uneven growth, between regions as well as sections of society, should be dealt with. What are the intellectual and practical policy responses needed to prevent inequalities between regions/states, between social classes and between urban/rural areas from becoming sharp lines of conflict? How can the rural economy be revived? How can state governments' finances be restored to health? Can India really achieve high growth and employment without a vigorous manufacturing sector and what should be done to create this? How can India progress faster as a knowledge economy? What has been the impact of globalisation on Indian competitiveness in key sectors? What will be the roles of the private and public sectors in furthering this process? What are the key reforms to drive competitiveness and levels of innovation? What should be the role of public investment in science, R&D and education? How can India overcome the factors which deter foreign direct investment? How will environmental costs and effects impact our economic development? Should public policy consciously seek to limit consumerism in the context of ecology? How can we shape and encourage economic integration within India (across states), within the SAARC region and with other Asian regional groupings?

14 | Agriculture and Rural Development

Policy Issues for Growth and Equity

S. MAHENDRA DEV

Introduction

In the post-economic reform period, there have been improvements in some indicators such as balance of payments, higher growth in services, higher accumulation of foreign exchange reserves, IT revolution, improvement in telecommunications, recent stock market boom, higher growth of exports, etc. It is, however, important to assess the impact of economic reforms on rural areas of the country as more than 70 per cent of India's population live in these areas. Agriculture plays pivotal role in Indian economy. Although the share of agriculture in GDP is less than 25 per cent, the share of agriculture in employment is still very high at 60 per cent. According to official estimates, around 260 million of India's population lives below poverty line and 80 per cent of these poor live in rural areas. Agriculture is the most important sector in rural India. Apart from the direct benefit that farmers gain from working in agriculture, the indirect benefits and linkages of the sector with the rest of the economy are also important. Poverty reduction in India thus mainly depends on the performance of agriculture sector. Several studies have even suggested that agricultural growth is pro-poor and helps directly to reduce poverty (Ravallion, 2000). The National Common Minimum Programme (NCMP) of the UPA (United Progressive Alliance) government has given highest priority to agriculture and rural areas. The Government intends to frame right policies for achieving higher growth of around four per cent per annum and also achieve equity in agriculture.

This paper examines the trends in levels of living in agriculture and rural areas and discusses policy issues for higher growth and equity in agriculture and rural areas.

Assessment of Rural India in Pre-and Post-Reform Period

Agriculture Growth

Growth in agriculture GDP in India declined from 3.4 per cent in the 1980s to 3.0 per cent in the 1990s.

In the post-liberalisation period it declined from 4.7 per cent in the Eighth Five Year Plan (1992-1997) period to 1.8 per cent in the Ninth Plan (1997-2002) period. Agricultural growth in the year 2002-03 was negative at (–) 5.3 per cent due to severe drought. In 2003-04, it was 9.1 per cent and expected to be around 1.0 per cent in 2005-06. Thus, agricultural growth in the first three years of the Tenth Five Year Plan is expected to be less than 2.0 per cent. This is a matter of concern for rural areas and poor people. The newly elected Indian Government has recognised the importance of agriculture and is concerned about the low growth in agriculture.

There was a deceleration in growth of production and yields for foodgrains and all crops in 1990s as compared to those of 1980s. The growth rate in foodgrains production declined from 2.81 per cent in the 80s to 1.98 per cent in the 1990s. Yield growth also declined drastically for foodgrains and all crops. This could have implications for farmers' incomes and employment.

Poverty

We examine here whether decline in poverty was higher in the 1990s as compared to 1980s.

NSS provides consumer expenditure data for both annual surveys and quinquennial surveys. We concentrate on the estimates based on the latter as they are more reliable. It is known that the 1999-00 NSS based estimates on poverty are not comparable with earlier years because of changes in the reference period. The reference periods for 1999-00 (55th Round) were changed from the uniform 30 day recall to both 7 day and 30 day questions for food and intoxicants and only 365 day questions for items of clothing, footwear, education, institutional medical expenses and durable goods. Official estimates have not adjusted for the changes in reference periods. On the other hand, individual researchers have made several adjustments to make the 1999-00 data comparable with those of earlier rounds. The official estimates based on expert group method and approved by the Planning Commission and alternative estimates are presented in Table 14.1.

Official estimates show that rural poverty declined from 45.7 per cent in 1983 to 37.3 per cent in 1993-1994. It declined by 8.4 percentage points over 10 and half period implying 0.8 percentage points decline per annum. In the post-reform period, it declined from 37.3 per cent to 27.1 per cent. It declined 10.2 percentage points over 6 year period indicating 1.7 percentage points decline per annum. Similarly in urban areas, the average annual decline in pre-and post-reform periods were 0.80 and 1.47 percentage points respectively. Thus, if we go by official estimates, the rate of decline of poverty in rural and urban areas was higher in the 1990s as compared to 1980s. Alternative estimates are also given in Table 14.1. The official estimates show 10 percentage points decline for rural poverty during 1993-94 to 1999-00. Deaton and Dreze show a decline of 6.7 percentage points while Sundaram

Table 14.1

Poverty Ratios: Official and Alternative Estimates: 1983 to 1999-00

Sources	RURAL						
	Poverty Ratios				Change in Percentage Points		
	1983	1993-94 URP (Uniform 30 day reference period)	1993-94 MRP (Mixed 30/365 day reference period)	1999-00	1983-94	1993-2000-(URP)	1993-2000 (MRP for 93-94)
Official	45.7	37.3	—	27.1	-8.4 (-0.80)	-10.2 (-1.70)	—
Deaton & Dreze (2002)	—	33.0		26.3	—	-6.7 (-1.12)	—
Sundaram & Tendulkar (2003)	49.0	39.7	34.2	28.9	-9.3 (-0.89)	—	-5.3 (-0.88)
Sen & Himanshu (2003)	—	—	31.6	28.8*	—	—	-2.8 (-0.47)

Sources	URBAN						
	Poverty Ratios				Average Annual Change in Poverty		
	1983	1993-94 URP (Uniform reference period)	1993-94 MRP (Mixed reference period)	1999-00	1983-94	1993-2000 (URP)	1993-2000 (MRP for 93-94)
Official	40.8	32.4	—	23.6	8.4 (-0.80)	8.8 (-1.47)	—
Deaton & Dreze (2002)	—	17.8	—	12.0	—	5.8 (-0.97)	—
Sundaram & Tendulkar (2003)	38.3	30.9	26.4	23.1	7.4 (-0.71)	—	3.3 (-0.55)
Sen & Himanshu (2003)	—	—	28.0	25.1*	—	—	2.9 (-0.48)

Note: Figures in parentheses refer to annual average change.

*Adjusted for 7 day question.

and Tendulkar show 5.3 percentage points decline during the same period. On the other hand, Sen and Himanshu show a decline of only around 3 percentage points in the 1990s. Thus, the decline for rural poverty during 1993-2000 varies between 10 percentage points (unadjusted official estimates) and 3 percentage points by Sen and Himanshu. Changes in number of rural poor also varies from 50 million decline (official estimates) to increase of 1.5 million during 1993-2000.

Which Class Benefited from the Reforms?

Poverty among Scheduled Castes (SCs)

The rate of decline for SCs living below the poverty line was marginally higher than that of the total population between 1993-94 and 1999-00. The gap between the total population and the SCs also decreased during the same period in both rural and urban areas. However, the incidence of poverty amongs SCs still continues to be very high with 38.38 per cent in rural areas and 37.84 per cent in urban areas (Table 14.2). The gap between SCs and all households was nearly 10 percentage points

Table 14.2

Population Living Below Poverty Line: Scheduled Castes and Total

Category	Rural		Urban	
	1993-94	1999-00	1993-94	1999-00
Total	34.20	28.93	26.41	23.09
SCs	45.69	38.38	42.85	37.84
Gap	11.49	9.45	16.44	14.75

Source: Poverty ratios are taken from Sundaram and Tendulkar (2003a); Gaps calculated by author.

in rural areas and 15 percentage points in urban areas. This is primarily due to the fact that a large number of SCs who are living below the poverty line are landless with no productive assets and with no access to sustainable employment and minimum wages (GoI, 2003). The women belonging to these groups suffer even worse because of the added disadvantage of being denied of equal and minimum wages.

Poverty among Scheduled Tribes (ST)

The poverty among STs also declined along with general population (Table 14.3). However, it is disquieting to note that the rate of decline in respect of STs is much lower than that of the general population. As a result, the gap between poverty ratios of STs and general population increased during 1990s. In the rural areas, gap increased from 14.6 per cent in 1993-94 to 19 per cent in 1999-00. Similarly it increased from 7 per cent to 12 per cent during the same period. Further, the incidence of poverty among STs still continues to be very high with 45.86 and

Table 14.3

Population Living Below Poverty Line: Scheduled Tribes and Total

Category	Rural		Urban	
	1993-94	1999-00	1993-94	1999-00
Total	34.20	28.93	26.41	23.09
STs	48.81	48.02	33.63	35.15
Gap	14.61	19.09	7.22	12.1

Source: Poverty ratios are taken from Sundaram and Tendulkar (2003a); Gaps calculated by author.

34.75 per cent living below the poverty line in rural and urban areas respectively.

Poverty Profile

Above estimates that, rural poverty for general population declined from 34.2 per cent in 1993-94 to 29 per cent in 1999-00. However, within rural areas some groups gained in shares while some others lost. As shown in Table 14.4, the proportion of agricultural labourers increased from 42.6 per cent in 1993-94 to

Table 14.4

Percentage Distribution of Rural Poor in 1993-94 and 1999-00

	1993-94	1999-00
By Occupation		
Self employed in agriculture	32.33	28.25
Self employed in non-agriculture	11.16	11.53
Agricultural labour	42.62	48.01
Other labour	7.84	7.12
Others	6.04	5.09
Total	**100.0**	**100.0**
By Caste		
Scheduled castes	28.19	27.10
Scheduled tribes	15.46	17.41
Others	56.35	55.49
Total	**100.0**	**100.00**

Source: Taken from Sundaram and Tendulkar (2003a).

48.0 per cent in 1999-00.[1] On the other hand, self employed in agriculture gained in their share in total rural poor. Similarly, scheduled tribes lost while other castes benefited.

---

1. This increase was partly due to increase in their share in the rural population during the same period.

Regional Disparities in Poverty

Poverty is concentrated in some states. In six states (Bihar, UP, MP, West Bengal, Orissa and Assam), the share in all India rural poor increased between 1993-2000 and 1999-00 (Table 14.5). In 1993-94, their share

Table 14.5

Percentage Distribution of Rural Poor by States: 1993-94 and 1999-00

States	Share in All India Rural Poor 1993-94	Share in All India Rural Poor 1999-00
Bihar	20.4	20.6
Uttar Pradesh	21.3	21.9
Madhya Pradesh	8.5	11.3
West Bengal	8.8	8.9
Orissa	6.2	7.2
Assam	3.4	4.5
Total of above Six States	**68.8**	**74.4**
Andhra Pradesh	3.0	2.9
Gujarat	2.3	1.9
Haryana	1.4	0.6
Karnataka	3.4	3.2
Kerala	2.3	1.2
Maharashtra	7.5	6.5
Punjab	0.6	0.6
Rajasthan	3.4	2.9
Tamil Nadu	4.9	3.9
Other states and U.T.	2.4	1.9
Total of above Nine States and other States and U.T.	**31.2**	**25.6**
All India	**100.0**	**100.0**

Source: Estimated from the data on number of poor given in Sen & Himanshu (2003).

was 68.8 per cent but increased 74.4 per cent in 1999-00. In fact three 54 per cent of India's rural poor live in three states *viz*. Bihar, Uttar Pradesh and Madhya Pradesh. As shown in Table 14.4, total share of nine major states and

others declined from 31.2 per cent in 1993-94 to 25.6 per cent in 1999-00.

Per Capita Availability of Foograins: Another problem with the 1990s is that the per capita net availability of foodgrains has not increased. It was 494 grams per day in the triennium ending in 1991. It declined to 445 grams per day in the triennium ending in 2001. Around 60 million tonnes were with the FCI in 2002-03 but more than 300 million were below the poverty line.

Personal and Regional Inequalities

One consequence of economic reforms is that inequalities have increased over time. Deaton and Dreze (2002) reveal the following findings on inequalities:

(a) Regional disparities have increased.

(b) Rural-urban inequalities have increased. The salaries of public sector employees have grown at 5 per cent per annum while agricultural wages grew at the rate of 2.5 per cent per annum.

(c) Intra-rural inequalities have not increased while intra-urban inequalities have increased.

In the post-liberalisation period, growth rates of SDP in some states such as Karnataka, West Bengal, Maharashtra, Gujarat, Tamil Nadu increased faster than other states. How does one explain the fact that whereas some states did experience significant rise in their SDP growth rates in the 1990s by benefiting from economic reforms and thereby pushed up the all India average growth rate, some other states could not respond in a similar way? The answer lies partly in the initial or pre-reform level of social and economic infrastructure conducive to growth and partly in the rate of capital formation, physical as well as human, in the post-reform period.

Employment and Unemployment

Faster growth through economic reforms is not always accompanied by a faster rate of poverty reduction. Poverty can be reduced if growth increases employment potential (quantity and quality). Similarly, the extent to which the working poor are able to integrate into the economic process also determines the impact of growth on poverty. For example, if there is a mismatch between the opportunities available due to economic reforms and skills of the workers, the poor will not be able to take advantage of such opportunities and gain from the reforms.

Employment Growth

The growth rate of rural employment was around 0.5 per cent per annum between 1993-94 and 1999-00 as compared to 1.7 per cent per annum between 1983 and 1993-94. The daily status unemployment rate in rural areas has increased from 5.63 per cent in 1993-94 to 7.21 per cent in 1999-00. As shown in Table 14.6, the overall employment growth declined from 2.04 per cent during 1983-94 to 0.98 per cent during 1994-2000. Much of the decline in the growth was due to developments in two

sectors *viz.* agriculture and community social & personal services. These two sectors accounting for 70 per cent of the total employment have not shown any growth during the 1990s. Similar trends can be seen for growth rates of employment based on current daily status.

Table 14.6

Growth of Employment, Usual Status and Current Daily Status

Industry	Usual Status: Principal and Subsidiary (% per annum)		Current Daily Status (% per annum)	
	1983 to 1993-94	1993-94 to 99-00	1983 to 1993-94	1993-94 to 99-00
Agriculture	1.51	-0.34	2.23	0.02
Mining & Quarrying	4.16	-2.85	3.68	-1.91
Manufacturing	2.14	2.05	2.26	2.58
Electricity, Gas & Water Supply	4.50	-0.88	5.31	3.55
Construction	5.32	7.09	4.18	5.21
Trade	3.57	5.04	3.80	5.72
Transport, Storage & Commn.	3.24	6.04	3.35	5.53
Financial Services	7.18	6.20	4.60	5.40
Community Social & Per. Services	2.90	0.55	3.85	-2.08
Total Employment	**2.04**	**0.98**	**2.67**	**1.07**

Source: GoI (2001) for Usual Status estimates and GoI (2002) for Current Daily Status.

Employment at State Level

The employment growth at state level shows that states like Kerala, Andhra Pradesh, Tamil Nadu, Himachal Pradesh and West Bengal show low growth of employment while Gujarat, Haryana and Punjab show high growth rate of employment (Table 14.7). The unemployment levels are high in Kerala, West Bengal and Tamil Nadu. In these three states unemployment increased over time. There is no strong correlation between growth of GSDP and employment growth at state level. Kerala has comparatively low growth of GSDP but low employment elasticity. On the other hand, Tamil Nadu and West Bengal have higher growth rates of GSDP with low employment

elasticities. Only 3 out of 16 states (Gujarat, Haryana and Karnataka) could combine high growth and high employment elasticity and achieve significant decline in the unemployment rate.

Real Wages

Another indicator of purchasing power is agricultural wages. At the all India level, the growth of real agricultural wages declined from about 5 per cent per annum in the 1980s to 2.5 per cent per annum in the 1990s. Table 14.8 provides growth rates of real agricultural wages for different states. Deaton and Drèze (2002) say that a healthy growth of real agricultural wages appear to be a sufficient condition for significant reduction in poverty in rural areas. In all the states where real wages have grown more than 2.5 per cent (Gujarat, Karnataka, Kerala, Tamil Nadu) have experienced sharp reduction in rural poverty. On the other hand, entire region Assam, Orissa, West Bengal and Bihar, Andhra Pradesh and

Table 14.7

Employment Growth, Unemployment and Employment Elasticity at State Level (Current Daily Status)

States	Employment Growth (1993-94 to 1999-00)	Unemployment Rates		Employment Elasticity 1993-94 to 1999-00
		1993-94	1999-00	
Andhra Pradesh	0.35	6.69	8.03	0.067
Assam	1.99	8.03	8.03	0.737
Bihar	1.59	6.34	7.32	0.353
Gujarat	2.31	5.70	4.55	0.316
Haryana	2.43	6.51	4.77	0.420
Himachal Pradesh	0.37	1.80	2.96	0.052
Karnataka	1.43	4.94	4.57	0.188
Kerala	0.07	15.51	20.97	0.013
Madhya Pradesh	1.28	3.56	4.45	0.272
Maharashtra	1.25	5.09	7.16	0.216
Orissa	1.05	7.30	7.34	0.262
Punjab	1.96	3.10	4.03	0.426
Rajasthan	0.73	1.31	3.13	0.104
Tamil Nadu	0.37	11.41	11.78	0.052
Uttar Pradesh	1.02	3.45	4.08	0.185
West Bengal	0.41	10.06	14.99	0.056
All India	**1.07**	**5.99**	**7.32**	**0.160**

Source: GoI (2002).

Table 14.8

Growth Rates of Real Agricultural Wages across States: 1990-2000

States	Growth Rates Real Wages (%)	States	Growth Rates of Real Wages (%)
Andhra Pradesh	1.3	Maharashtra	1.6
Assam	-0.7	Orissa	0.7
Bihar	0.3	Punjab	-0.8
Gujarat	5.1	Rajasthan	2.8
Haryana	2.7	Tamil Nadu	6.7
Karnataka	3.2	Uttar Pradesh	2.5
Kerala	7.9	West Bengal	1.6
Madhya Pradesh	1.8	**All India**	**2.5**

Source: Dreze and Sen (2002).

Madhya Pradesh experienced low growth in agricultural wages and lower reduction in poverty.

Using data from Rural Labour Enquiries (RLEs), Chavan and Bedamatta (2003) reveal that real daily earnings of agricultural labourers recorded highest growth in almost all the states during 1983 to 1987-88. However, the growth rates of real daily wages of female and male agricultural labourers declined during 1987-88 to 1993-94 and during 1993-94 to 1999-00 in majority of the states. This study also shows that daily labour earnings were higher than minimum wages for males in majority of the states. In the case of females, the daily earnings were lower than minimum wages. There seems to be increase in male-female ratio over time. It shows significant gender disparities in wages.

Casualisation of Rural Workers

Here we look at changes in the status of workers. NSS provides two types of data on Usual Status i.e. principal status and all (ps+ss). In the case of ps+ss for rural males, the share of self employed declined from 60.5 per cent in 1983 to 55.0 per cent in 1999-00. The share of regular employees also declined during the same period. In the case of casual labourers, the share has increased from 29.2 per cent in 1983 to 36.2 per cent in 1999-2000. In other words, there was 7 percentage points increase in the share of casual employment during the last 17 years. In the case of rural females also, the share of self employed declined while the share of casual labourers increased.

Employment and Education

Education is important for workers in order to get qualitative employment. This is one of the key variables for rural diversification. Literacy alone is at best only one indicator. Literacy definition covers anyone who can write their name and this means many people may be classified as literate although they may not understand simple written instructions. Unless we have these abilities for workers, the efficiency of the labour force in many occupations is likely to remain low. Table 14.9 provides the educational standards of the workers in rural India. It shows that the percentage of illiterates among male workers declined from 55 per cent to 40.3 per cent during 1977-78 to 1999-00. For females, the corresponding numbers declined from 88.1 per cent to 74.9 per cent. However, even in 1999-00, 68 per cent of the rural males and 91 per cent of the rural females are either illiterate or have been educated only up to primary level.

Table 14.9

Distribution of Workers (age 5 years and above) by General Education Category: 1977-78 and 1999-00 (per cent)

Category	Rural Male		Rural Female	
	1977-78	1999-00	1977-78	1999-00
Not Literate	55.0	40.3	88.1	74.9
Literate & up to Primary	30.8	27.7	9.1	15.7
Middle School	8.5	15.9	1.6	5.6
Secondary & Higher Sec.	4.7	13.0	1.0	3.0
Graduate & above	1.0	3.1	0.2	0.7
Total	**100.0**	**100.0**	**100.0**	**100.0**

Source: NSS Rounds on Employment and Unemployment.

In other words, less than 10 per cent of the female workers have education of middle school or above.

Health and Education

Jawaharlal Nehru at the time of Independence reminded the country the task ahead, "ending of poverty and ignorance and disease and inequality of opportunity". That dream is largely unaccomplished. This is not to deny considerable progress in human development.

Rural Literacy and Education

India's overall literacy rate increased from around 17 per cent 1951 to 65 per cent in 2001. Literacy in rural areas increased from 36 per cent in 1981 to 59 per cent in 2001 (Table 14.10). During the same time, literacy in urban areas increased from 67 per cent to 80 per cent. The rural-urban gap has declined from 31 to 21 percentage points in the last two decades. Female literacy increased over time but still around 53 per cent of rural females were illiterates in 2001.

Also, 30 to 33 per cent of rural girls in the age group 6-14 were not attending school in 1999-00 (Table 14.11). Similarly, among SCs and STs 40 to 45 per cent girls were not attending in the same school (Table 14.12).

There are significant interstate disparities in literacy and education. For example, rural female literacy in Kerala was 87 per cent while in Bihar it was 30 per cent in 2001. Similarly, the school attendance ratios for Kerala girls (6-13 years) were 97 per cent but in Bihar it was 35 per cent in 1995-96. There are also significant inter-state variations regarding school facilities like access to school, teacher-pupil ratios, classrooms, etc.

Table 14.10

Literacy Rates in India: Rural and Urban

Year	Rural	Urban	Total
1951	12	35	17
1961	19	47	24
1971	24	52	29
1981	36	67	47
1991	45	73	52
2001	59	80	65

Note: Figures up to 1981 relate to population above 5 years.

Source: Census of India 2001; quoted in Kumar (2003).

Table 14.11

Percentage of Children, Age 6-10 and 11-13 Attending School: 1999-00

	6-10 years			11-13 years		
	Boys	Girls	Total	Boys	Girls	Total
Rural	79	69	75	79	67	73
Urban	89	85	87	87	83	85
Total	**81**	**73**	**77**	**81**	**71**	**76**

Source: NSS 55th Round; quoted in Srivastava (2003).

Table 14.12

Percentage of Children Attending School, Age-wise: 1999-00

		Boys			Girls			Children		
		6-10	11-14	6-14	6-10	11-14	6-14	6-10	11-14	6-14
ST	Rural	69.9	64.7	68.0	58.6	51.1	55.9	64.5	58.3	62.2
	Urban	83.6	87.1	85.1	77.9	74.9	76.6	80.8	81.4	81.0
SC	Rural	75.9	73.4	74.9	64.5	56.6	61.5	70.5	65.5	68.6
	Urban	84.2	82.7	83.6	79.8	73.2	77.0	82.1	78.1	80.4
OBC	Rural	80.0	78.5	79.4	68.0	61.8	65.6	74.4	70.8	73.0
	Urban	88.6	83.2	86.3	83.5	77.7	81.0	86.2	80.6	83.8
Others	Rural	84.9	83.3	84.2	79.6	74.8	77.5	82.4	79.1	81.0
	Urban	92.4	89.2	91.0	89.8	85.3	87.8	91.2	87.3	89.5

Note: ST Scheduled Tribes; SC Scheduled Castes; OBC Other Backward Castes.

Source: NSS 55th Round; quoted in Srivastava (2003).

Rural Health

The life expectancy in rural areas was 59 while in urban areas it was 66 in 1992-96 (Table 14.13). Although the gap is narrowing down between rural and urban areas, it is still around 7 years. The infant mortality declined in both rural and urban areas (Table 14.14). In 1999-2001 infant mortality was 74 in rural areas while it was 43 in urban areas. In post-liberalisation period, the decline in infant mortality has been much slower in rural areas as compared to urban areas.

The health indicators for various social groups show that they are much lower for Scheduled Tribes and Scheduled Castes (Table 14.15). For example, under five mortality was 127 for STs as compared to 83 for others. The percentage of under nutrition was also higher for STs and SCs. The health indicators for rural areas were much lower as compared to those of urban areas (Table 14.16). In rural areas, nearly 70 per cent of the births are not attended by professionals (Table 14.17). Problems in health and education are given in Boxes 14.1 and 14.2.

Sex Ratio among Children: Census data shows that sex ratio among children have worsened (0-6 years) from 945 in 1991 to 927 in 2001. It is worth noting that major decline in sex ratio occurred in developed states like Punjab (82 points), Haryana (59 points), Himachal Pradesh (54 points) and Gujarat (50 points) (Kumar, 2003). Sex ratio declined in all states except in 5 states and union territories *viz.*, Kerala, Lakshadweep, Mizoram, Sikkim and Tripura.

Table 14.13

Rural and Urban Differences in Life Expectancy

Years	Rural	Urban	Difference
1970-75	48.0	58.9	10.9
1981-85	53.7	62.8	9.1
1991-95	58.9	65.9	7.0
1993-97	59.9	66.6	6.7

Source: Sample Registration System; quoted in Kumar (2003).

Table 14.14

Infant Mortality Rates in Rural and Urban Areas: Infant Deaths per 1000 Live Births

Year	Rural	Urban	Rural-Urban Differences
1971-73	144	85	59
1981-83	116	64	52
1989-91	90	54	36
1994-96	79	49	30
1999-01	74	43	31

Source: Sample Registration System; quoted in Kumar (2003).

Table 14.15

Health Indicators of Various Social Groups

	Infant Mortality	Under 5 Mortality Rate	% Undernutrition Rate
SCs	83.0	119.3	53.5
STs	84.2	126.6	55.9
Other Disadvantaged Groups	76.0	103.1	47.3
Others	61.8	82.6	41.1
India	**70**	**94.9**	**47.0**

Source: GoI, 2003.

Table 14.16

Rural and Urban Health Indicators: 1998-99

	IMR	Under 5 Mortality Rate	% Children Undernourished
Rural	75	103.7	49.6
Urban	44	63.1	38.4
Total	**70**	**94.9**	**47.0**

Source: National Family Health Survey (NFHS-2), 1998-99.

Box 14.1

Problems in Health and Education and Funding

- Engineers, but no fund for construction or maintenance.

- Doctors, but no medicine.

- Teachers, but no school building.

- Many senior officers, but little funds for travel or telephones, and hence poor supervision or monitoring.

- Very little capital expenditure and asset creation.

- Little funds for maintenance or repairs of assets.

- Highly paid employees, but no complementary investment or working expenditure. Salaries have crowded out high priority non-wage expenditure.

Source: Saxena (2000).

Box 14.2

A Study on Health and Education Sector in UP and Bihar

- Reveals that treatment from government PHCs is generally not available to poor.

- Medical staff at PHCs usually absent; when present, they give only prescription due to non-availability of medicines.

- Expenditure on private doctors leads to indebtedness and even loss of assets of poor.

- In most schools teachers were absent, or teaching is conducted by proxy teachers engaged on very low wages.

Source: Saxena (2000).

Table 14.17

Births Attended by Health Professionals

	Rural	Urban
1992-93	25.0	65.3
1998-99	33.5	73.3

Source: NFHS-1 and NFHS-2.

Issues in Agriculture and Rural Development

Issues in Agriculture

Food Policy

A large public distribution system supplemented by arrangements for moderating prices in the open market and concerted efforts for achieving self sufficiency in foodgrains, coupled with measures for maximising procurement from surplus areas, have been the twin objectives of food policy in modern India ever since the Bengal famine of 1943. "These objectives have held sway over the last 55 years, though with changes in emphasis and varying degrees of rigidity, from total control to total decontrol, depending upon the prevailing situation and assessment at each point of time" (GoI, 2000). Currently, food security system and price policy basically consists of three instruments—procurement prices/minimum support prices, buffer stocks and public distribution system (PDS). The government announces the support prices at sowing time and agrees to buy all the grain offered for sale at this price particularly for rice and wheat. Procurement policy mainly benefited few states, such as Punjab, Haryana, Uttar Pradesh, Andhra Pradesh and Tamil Nadu.

The second important component of food policy is buffer stock. The importance of building up a buffer stock of foodgrains, normally rice and wheat is to provide food security to the country. The argument in favour of bufferstocking is that where variability of foodgrains output is large either due to weather conditions or due to man-made factors, it would be essential for the state to ensure that food security is secured for the large mass of the people by building adequate buffer stocks from out of the surpluses in the good production years and/or by arranging to import the requisite foodgrains in times of need. Various committees have suggested the optimal size of buffer stock which varies from 15 to 25 million tonnes depending on the season in a year. The Expenditure Reforms Commission recommended 17 million tonnes as the total average stocks to be maintained for distribution and bufferstock. The levels in the first few years of this decade were much higher than the recommended levels. The stocks have declined recently due to severe drought in the year 2002-2003. The food stocks declined from 58 million tonnes in January 2002 to 23.6 million tonnes in October 2003 and to 24.4 million tonnes in January 2004.

The third component of food policy is public distribution system (PDS). The PDS is one of the instruments for improving food security at the household level in India. PDS ensures availability of essential commodities like rice, wheat, edible oils and kerosene to the consumers through a network of outlets or fair price shops. They are supplied at below market prices to consumers. Under this the network of public distribution system (PDS) has expanded over the years, since its inception during World War II. Currently, the foodgrains from the Government stocks are being made available through PDS to about 18 crore[2] households through a country-wide network of about 4.6 lakh[3] fair price shops. Various alterations have been made over the years to the PDS to improve its performance, including expansion of PDS in backward areas, special subsidised rates, etc. Food for work programmes can also be considered as part of the provision of food security to the poor population. In addition we also have nutrition programmes for children such as noon meal schemes and Integrated Child Development Services (ICDS).

Procurement increased significantly in the later part of 1990s from about 20 million tonnes in 1996-97 to 37 million tonnes in 2001-02—almost 20 per cent of foodgrains production. Buffer stock increased 16 million tonnes to 60 million tonnes during the same period. As a result of the accumulation of foodgrains, the food subsidy increased significantly in the late 1990s. Food subsidy increased from Rs.24.1 billion in 1990-91 to Rs.242 billion in 2002-03. As per cent of GDP, the food subsidy increased from 0.43 in 1990-01 to 0.51 in 1999-00. It increased significantly to 0.84 per cent in 2001-02 and to 0.98 per cent in 2002-03. Similarly food

---

2.   1 crore is equal to 10 millions.

3.   10 lakh is 1 million.

subsidy as per cent of total public expenditure also increased significantly from 2.3 per cent in 1990-91 to 6.0 per cent in 2002-03.

The related issue under food subsidy is that the producer subsidy has increased while the consumer subsidy has declined. Higher procurement with the reduced off-take resulted in the generation of larger stocks, which in turn led to higher carrying costs (comprising freight, storage, interest charges, etc.). In 1997-98, the buffer component of the food subsidy bill was only 13 per cent. It increased to 42 per cent in 2000-01.

The above discussion shows that buffer stock is becoming expensive and the share of consumer subsidy has declined over time. Many studies have shown that the impact of PDS on poor is not effective in many states of India. The issues involved in PDS are—how to improve the targeting of the PDS through innovative methods? What are the measures needed to reduce the diversion of commodities from PDS? How to improve the delivery system under PDS? Should the states take over the responsibility of PDS? Does the involvement of *panchayats* improve the performance of PDS? Should we introduce food coupon/food credit card system to improve the performance of PDS? What are the international best practices in targeting food subsidies to the poor?

A major reform is needed to allow the private sector to operate in the market without any restrictions in terms of the movement of grain, stocking limits, levy to the government agencies, exports, etc. (Rao, 2003). It would be good to encourage vertical integration even in the foodgrain sector. The freedom to operate a warehouse receipt system, direct buying from the farmers by the private companies, rationalising purchase tax on grains, *mandi* tax, etc. would encourage private companies to invest in the development of the grain markets, storage and processing of grain.

Subsidies and Investments

There has been a secular decline in public investment and it has been a concern as it is important for improving infrastructure. As compared to the target of 3.4 million hectares per annum, the irrigation potential harnessed during the Ninth Plan was only 1.8 million hectares per annum. The investment on research and extension is still around 0.3 per cent to 0.5 per cent of GDP. The estimates show that in 2001-02 public investment was Rs. 4,123 crores from Rs. 3,919 crores in 2000-01. But it was still much lower than that in the middle of 1990s. It is true that private investment has increased in the 1990s. However, public and private investments cannot be treated as substitutes as the compositions are different. Public investment is mainly in medium and major irrigation works while private investment is mainly in minor irrigation, mechanisation and land levelling (Sawant *et al.*, 2002). More public investment is needed in rainfed and backward areas. Many of the ills of the agriculture sector, namely, low productivity, low employment opportunities and inadequate infrastructure are attributed to inadequate and progressive decline in the public investment in agriculture. The public investment in real terms in the agriculture sector has actually declined in the last two decades. In spite of increase in private investment, the share of total investment was around 6.5 per cent in the 1990s. This share was substantially lower than that for 1970s and 1980s. It may be noted that inadequacy of investments has slowed the pace of technological change in agriculture with adverse effects on productivity.

There seems to be some trade-off between input subsidies and public investment in agriculture. The problem of mounting subsidies and its effect in terms of crowding out public agricultural investment has been highlighted in the Tenth Plan document. Input subsidies (on power, fertilisers and irrigation) have been rising while public investment has been declining. Some estimates show that these input subsidies along with food subsidy, amount to roughly five to six times the public investments in agriculture (Gulati and Narayanan, 2003). Subsidies in 1993-94 constant prices have increased from Rs. 38 billion in 1980-81 to nearly Rs. 250 billion in 1999-00. During the same period, subsidies declined from Rs. 75 billion to Rs. 45 billion. Therefore, reduction in input subsidies is important for raising public investment.

Another problem with input subsidies is that they are having adverse effect on environment in agriculture. These policies are leading to degradation of land and water. These subsidies caused severe deterioration of the systems due to the neglect of their maintenance in addition to becoming fiscally unsustainable. Further, they have led to the highly wasteful use of canal water, ecological degradation from water logging, salinity, pollution, excessive consumption of electricity, and overdrawal of groundwater resulting in the shortage of drinking water in several parts of the country.

Research and Extension

The yield growth for many crops has declined in the 1990s. Technology plays an important role in improving the yields. A fresh look at the priorities of Indian agricultural research system is necessary in light of emerging prospects. There is only marginal increase in the funds for research in the recent budgets. Of course states have to take a lead in research and extension. It is known that India spends only 0.5 per cent of GDP on agricultural research as compared to more than 1 per cent by other developing countries. There is considerable potential for raising the effectiveness of these outlays by re-ordering the priorities in agricultural research and redefining the relative roles of public and private sectors in research and extension.

There is a need to shift away from individual crop-oriented research focused essentially on irrigated areas towards research on crops and cropping systems in the dry lands, hills, tribal and other marginal areas. Dry land technology has to be improved. In view of high variability in agro-climatic conditions in such unfavourable areas, research has to become increasingly location-specific with greater participation or interaction with farmers. Horticulture crops that are land-saving and water-saving should be encouraged in dry land areas. Research has to be improved on horticulture crops.

Progress in post-harvest technology is essential to promote value addition through the growth of agro-processing industry. Private sector participation in agricultural research, extension and marketing is becoming increasingly important especially with the advent of biotechnology and protection being given to intellectual property. However, private sector participation tends to be limited to profitable crops and enterprises undertaken by resource rich farmers in well endowed regions. Moreover, private sector is not invested in research for better techniques of soil and water management, rainfed agriculture, cropping systems, environmental impact and long-term sustainability (Vaidyanathan, 1996). Therefore, the public sector research has to increasingly address the problems facing the resource-poor farmers in the less endowed regions. The new agricultural technologies in the horizon are largely biotechnologies. Effective research is needed to have biotechnologies suitable to different locations in India.

Regarding extension, the existing Travel and Visit (T&V) system of extension is top-down in its approach and there is little participation by the farmers. There is a need to take corrective steps to deal with the near collapse of the extension system in most states. One of the main reasons for breakdown of the system is the financial stringency experienced by the states as well as the centre. As a result, farmers are becoming increasingly dependent on the private sector for extension services.

In the absence of public provision of such services, the resource poor and gullible farmers are becoming the victims of exploitation by the unscrupulous traders and moneylenders interested in selling inputs such as seeds, fertilisers and pesticides. There is, therefore, an immediate need for reforming and revitalising the existing agricultural extension system in the country. The main ingredient of reforms should be—(a) active involvement of farmers through user groups/ associations; (b) participation by the private sector and the NGOs; (c) increasing use of media and information technology including cyber kiosks to disseminate the knowledge on new agricultural practices and the information on output and input prices; and (d) building gender concerns into the system, for example, by manning the extension services predominantly by women (more on this, Rao, 2003).

The returns to investment on research and extension will be much higher on agricultural growth as compared to other investments.

Irrigation and Water Management

Development of irrigation and water management are to be crucial for raising levels of living in rural areas. Around 40 per cent of country's cultivated area is irrigated. In other words, 60 per cent of the area is dependent on rainfall for cultivation. The ultimate irrigation potential of the country has been assessed at around 140 million hectares—58.46 million hectare from major and medium irrigation and 81.42 million hectares from minor irrigation, of which 64.09 million hectare is from groundwater sources. Nearly 37 per cent of the available irrigation potential from major and medium irrigation projects in the country still remains to be exploited. Over 400 such projects were in the pipeline at various stages during the Ninth Plan period. When these ongoing projects are completed, bulk of the remaining irrigation potential would have been exploited. Decline in public investment and the thin spread of resources over a large number of projects are responsible for the delay in completion of these projects.

Around 70 per cent of the available potential from minor irrigation sources (81.4 million hectares) consisting predominantly groundwater sources has been utilised. Further progress towards the exploitation of the remaining potential depends on availability of electric power for pumping water in the Eastern and Northeastern states where as much as 75 per cent of groundwater potential still remains to be exploited. Apart from electricity, there is also a need for devising affordable schemes for financing groundwater in these states, since most of the farmers in the region are resource-poor.

Conservation of surface and groundwater has become imperative. This is best achieved when water and power are priced according to the volume of consumption. Some state governments are providing free power for farmers. This is not sustainable. Involvement of rural communities is essential in setting the user charges as well as for assessing the individual consumption. A subsidy, say, on power, for all the farmers for a fixed number of units, irrespective of the size of holding, combined with volumetric rate for extra consumption could be a feasible solution, as it would provide greater relief to the small users while providing incentives to conserve the resources.

Rainfed areas constitute about 60 per cent of the 142 million hectares net sown area in the country. Rainfed agriculture is characterised by low levels of productivity and low input usage. Bulk of the rural poor live in the rainfed regions. Therefore, it is important to accord high priority to sustainable development of these areas through watershed development approach. In fact, watershed development has been given high priority, at least on paper, for several years, but it does not appear to be making much headway except in isolated cases, primarily under the initiatives and close supervision of a few NGOs. A possible reason could be that there is insufficient expertise available for this purpose. In addition, there are too many agencies of the centre and state governments implementing watershed schemes. This makes a coordinated approach towards prioritised planning and implementation rather difficult. Watershed development can be sustained in the long-run only through social mobilisation and capacity building. Land use should be made more remunerative through the new dry land technologies and the development of infrastructure. Watershed programme addresses two different concerns in the matter of land management. One is to conserve water in drought prone areas. However, the programme is equally effective in areas with a surplus of water where drainage and waterlogging might be a problem. The programme also addresses the question of improvement in agriculture and everywhere that it has been taken up, because of better soil and water management, increase in agricultural yield and diversification of crop patterns. Another area of concern is fodder, fuel and secondary timber availability. Because wastelands are treated under this programme, the availability of such forest produce has shown a significant increase. The Common Minimum Programme (CMP) has envisaged that the Government will introduce a special programme for dry land farming in the arid and semi-arid regions of the country.

Traditional water harvesting structures like tanks have become virtually defunct. The Finance Minister in his 2004-05 budget speech has announced a scheme to repair, renovate and restore all the water bodies that are directly linked to agriculture. Their restoration involves not only the physical aspects of the task but a clear demarcation of water rights. It is important to assign water rights to the community at large as a part of watershed approach that may be adopted for the afore-mentioned special programme for dry land farming in the arid and semi-arid regions in the country.

Farmers' Suicides

In recent years, farmers' suicides have increased in some states. Particularly it is notable in Andhra Pradesh and Karnataka. This is one of the darker sides of Indian agriculture.[4] A study on liberalisation and suicides of farmers in India shows that "crop failure and indebtedness emerge as the main and causative factors while social and psychological factors also contribute to the problem" (Rao, 2003). According to the study, "Sharper decline in absolute productivity, price uncertainty due to trade liberalisation and rise in costs due to domestic liberalisation, decline in credit and non-farm work intensified the crisis." In Andhra Pradesh, they are occurring regularly for the past 10 years irrespective of the rainfall situation, though drought has aggravated the numbers. Most of these studies have, rightly, identified that household indebtedness as the main reason for the suicides. However, indebtedness is due to increase in input intensity of agriculture.

Many farmers are shifting to commercial crops. In commercial crops, input intensity is higher than subsistence crops. There is no breakthrough in dry land technology. Cultivation is also being done in marginal lands. Risk is high in commercial crops and marginal lands. Main problems of the farmers in the present context are: (a) spurious input supply *viz.* seeds, fertilisers and pesticides; (b) inadequate credit from institutional sources and dependence on moneylenders for credit; (c) lack of water and drying up of groundwater; (d) farmers spend lot of money in sinking borewells; (e) lack of extension services particularly for commercial crops; (f) exploitation in marketing; and (g) lack of non-farm activities in rural areas.

Central government and state governments are sensitive to farmers' suicides and the above problems faced by the farmers. They are taking several steps to reduce some of these problems.

---

4. On farmers' suicides see Sainath (2004).

Credit and Crop Insurance

Credit

Despite having a wide network of rural branches and implementation of many schemes and programmes for expansion of credit for agriculture and rural development, a large number of very poor people still continue to remain outside the fold of the formal banking system. About 60 per cent of the credit requirements of farmers are now met by the institutional sources, and the remaining 40 per cent by informal sources like moneylenders who charge very high interest rates. However, small and marginal farmers (less than 2 hectares), including tenants, who account for nearly 80 per cent of holdings and one-third of area operated, depend far more heavily on informal sources. Among the formal credit institutions, the commercial banks have emerged as a major player in agriculture credit accounting for about 50 per cent followed by cooperatives (about 43 per cent) and Regional Rural Banks (RRBs) to the extent of about 7 per cent.

The credit system should reach marginal and small farmers. In fact, the growth rate of agricultural credit for small and marginal farmers declined in the 1990s as compared with the 1980s (RBI, 2002). During the same period, there was no decline of growth in credit for large farmers. There is a deceleration in the commercial bank's disbursements of direct finance to marginal farmers from 15.0 per cent in the 1980s to 11.0 per cent in the 1990s. The growth rate of direct finance to marginal farmers

decelerated to 13.0 per cent from 18.1 per cent during the same period (RBI, 2003).

The credit-deposit ratios increased from 55.1 per cent in 1980 to 97.1 per cent in 1990 (Table 14.18). But declined significantly to 49.3 per cent by 2000. The incremental CD-ratios also declined from 106.1 per cent in the 1980s to 36 per cent in the 1990s. Against the target of 18 per cent for 'priority sector', the direct agricultural advances by the commercial banks are only around 11 per cent. The position is much worse in the eastern and northern states. The Rural Infrastructure Development Fund (RIDF), started a decade ago as a measure to provide infrastructural support to agriculture in lieu of its falling share in commercial bank credit, has remained grossly underutilised, basically for want of matching contributions from the state governments. In the process, individual needs of the farmers for investment and production credit are not being adequately met.

Table 14.18

Credit-Deposit Ratios by Population Groups: Credit Data based on Utilisation

Population Group	CD-Ratios			Incremental CD-Ratios	
	December 1980	March 1990	March 2000	December 1980 to 1990	March 1990 to March 2000
Rural	55.1	97.1	49.3	106.1	36.0
Semi-urban	47.9	48.3	40.0	48.5	37.6
Urban	56.5	52.9	42.1	51.9	39.0
Metro	81.1	58.0	73.2	51.6	76.8
Total	**64.0**	**60.7**	**56.0**	**59.8**	**54.8**

Source: Shetty (2003).

Kisan Credit Scheme, aimed at providing adequate and timely support to the farmers from the banking system in a flexible and cost effective manner, does not seem to be working well because of various stipulations and restrictions. A more farmer-friendly credit card system needs to be operated so as to realise the objectives of the scheme.

With rising income, there will be diversification of crops. Investment needs for the production of high income-elastic agricultural products, such as dairying and livestock, horticulture, agro-forests would rise much faster now. Due to these factors, rural credit has to expand at a rate faster than in the recent past. Facilitating credit through processors, input dealers, NGOs, etc. that are vertically integrated with the farmers, including through contract farming, for providing them critical inputs or processing their produce, could increase the credit flow to agriculture significantly.

Self-help groups of women for providing micro-credit have been a success story in the country. Such households being essentially landless, credit by SHGs has been confined mainly to activities falling outside agriculture. As capital assets of these farmers are limited, community/group collateral and the produce on farmers' land, including that of tenants, should be considered as collateral in granting credit.

Crop Insurance

We have two crop insurance schemes—National Agricultural Insurance Scheme (NAIS) and Farm Income Insurance Scheme (FIIS). Field surveys, however, show that both the insurance schemes are largely ineffective although some farmers got the benefits. Many farmers have criticised compulsory insurance for loans taken from banks and they never got compensation inspite of low yields. There are some proposals that insurance based on rainfall should be considered instead of yields.

Domestic Market and External Trade Reforms

Economic reforms started in 1991 has neglected agriculture sector. The domestic and external trade reforms in agricultural sector started only in the last few years.

Domestic Market Reforms

There have been moves to liberalise agricultural markets since 2002. The Government is gradually moving towards a more deregulated regime and encouraging investment. Budget 2002-03 recognised the importance of agricultural diversification and food processing. It also recognised that removal of the remaining regulatory and procedural rigidities that still exist and improved rural infrastructure is essential for the revolution in diversification. In the Budget 2002-03, the Finance Minister announced the following measures as part of decontrol and deregulation of agriculture.

(a) Amendment of the Milk and Milk Products Control Order (MMPO) to remove restrictions on new milk processing capacity, while continuing to regulate health and safety conditions.

(b) Removal of small scale industry reservations related to various agricultural equipment items.

(c) Expansion of futures and forward trading to cover all agricultural commodities.

(d) Modernising and converging of several regulations for food standards: A multiplicity of regulations for food standards under the Prevention of Food Adulteration Act, the Food Products Order, the Meat Products Order, the Bureau of Industrial Standards and the Milk and Milk Products Order affect the food and food processing sectors. They need to be modernised and converged.

(e) Amendment of Agricultural Produce Marketing Acts is one of the measures announced as part of deregulation of agriculture.

Many of these announcements in the budget have been implemented. Restrictions on movement and stocking of several commodities have been removed to ensure common market. In February, 2002, the Government of India issued the Removal of licensing requirements, stock limits and movement restrictions on specified Foodstuffs Order, 2002.[5] Restrictions on futures trading were removed on 54 commodities including wheat, rice, oilseeds and pulses that were prohibited from futures trading under the Forward Contract

(Regulation) Act, 1952.[6] The Milk and Milk Products Order no longer restricts investments in new processing capacity.[7]

But many of the reforms require action on part of states since agriculture is a state subject. On agricultural marketing, Inter-Ministerial Task Force outlined several reforms. It recommended amendment to the state APMC (Agriculture Produce Marketing Committees) Act for promotion of direct marketing and contract farming, development of agricultural markets in private and cooperative sectors, stepping up of pledge financing, expansion of futures trading to cover all agricultural commodities, introduction of negotiable warehousing receipt system and use of information technology to provide market-led extension services to farmers (GoI, 2003). The states are requested to implement agriculture market reforms by bringing out suitable amendments in the existing state legislations. Government of Karnataka has already taken initiatives to amend the APMC Act.

Basically, domestic market reforms involve removing all controls in domestic market. Prevailing restrictions on domestic trade and processing of agricultural commodities were inherited from the post-war, pre-green revolution era of shortages. With the achievements of self-sufficiency in foodgrains, increasing trend towards

---

5. The Order mandates that "Any dealer may freely buy, stock, sell, transport, distribute, dispose, acquire, use or consume any quantity of wheat, paddy/rice, coarse grains, sugar, edible oilseeds and edible oils and shall not require a permit or licence therefore under any order issued under the Essential Commodities Act, 1955" (Source: *http://fcamin.nic.in/noti_15feb.htm*).

6. It was announced on 20th February 2003. Futures trading in these commodities are subject to the regulations of the Forward Market Commission.

7. Union Budget, 2003-04 indicates that "The Milk and Milk Products Order, 1992 has been amended on 26th March 2002. There is no restriction on creation of new processing capacity and registration will only be required for maintaining quality standards and food safety measures."

diversification of agriculture, globalisation of trade and WTO commitments, such restrictions on movement, storage and processing have outlived their utility and have become counter-productive. The restrictions also deny fair prices to producers as well as to consumers and inhibits much needed investments in the technological upgradation and modernisation of storage, marketing and processing. While doing reforms, however, some regulations are necessary to check unscrupulous practices by certain sections of traders and middlemen.

External Trade Reforms

External trade liberalisation is important and benefits the farmers. Trade liberalisation in agriculture has been faster towards the end of 1990s in tune with WTO agreements. There has been considerable progress in liberalisation of export controls, liberalisation of quantitative controls on imports and on decontrol of domestic trade. Quantitative restrictions on imports have been lifted since April 2000. Almost all agricultural products are now allowed to be freely exported as per current EXIM (export and import) policy. Export restrictions were removed on groundnut oil, agricultural seeds, wheat and wheat products, butter, rice and pulses from April 2000. Formation of exclusive agri-export zones is an important step taken to focus on agri-diversification, value addition and exports. In the recent export and import policy (EXIM Policy, 2003), government announced free export of paddy for farmers. They can sell directly to foreign millers now if needed.

Lifting of quantitative restrictions on imports since April 2000 has resulted in a number of agricultural products, which includes fruits, ketchups, meat products, etc. But, monitoring of the imports for 300 sensitive products has so far indicated that such imports constitute only a small proportion of total agricultural imports in the country (GoI, 2003). Thus, the concern of significant imports due to trade liberalisation has not been proved. India has considerable flexibility to counter flooding of the Indian market by cheap agricultural imports through imposition of tariffs (bound rates) under WTO.

India should move towards rules-based multilateral trading system through WTO negotiations. India does not have to change her food policies relating to, minimum support price, buffer stock and public distribution system. The actual tariffs for most of the commodities in India are much lower than the Uruguay Round bound rates. As such, it can easily check edible oil imports by raising its tariff. There is, however, a need for extreme vigilance in taking timely measures within the existing tariff bindings to restrict imports, which affect producers' livelihoods. In the negotiations, India along with other countries should keep pressures on developed countries to reduce their subsidies.

As the international trade in agricultural commodities is likely to be liberalised further, a greater preparedness is required to face and prepare for competition in the international market. Standards are fast becoming an important factor in global trade particularly regarding sanitary and phyto-sanitary (SPS) measures. The challenges that the developing countries face is that the standards may sometimes not be set in transparent manner or that they do not provide sufficient time to meet these standards.

In order to compete in the world trade and exploit the full potential of trade liberalisation, India should streamline its domestic reforms, infrastructure and institutions.

Diversification of Agriculture

There has been diversification of Indian diets away from foodgrains to high value products like milk, meat products and vegetables and fruits. The increasing middle class due to rapid urbanisation, increasing per capita income, increased participation of women in urban jobs and impact of globalisation has been largely responsible for the diet diversification in India.[8] Hi-value products have caught the fancy of the expanding middle class and the result is visible in the growing demand for hi-value processed products. There is growing demand for non-foodgrain items in India. The expenditure elasticity for non-cereal food items is still quite high in India. It is thrice as high when compared to cereals in the rural areas and over 10 times as high in urban areas (Table 14.19).

Table 14.19

Expenditure Elasticities for Cereals and Non-cereal Food in India

Commodity Group	Rural	Urban
Cereals	0.31	0.09
Milk	1.45	0.66
Edible Oil	0.85	0.37
Meat	1.02	0.54
Sugar	1.06	0.29
Pulses	0.57	0.30
Fruits and Vegetables	1.04	0.76
Other Food (other than cereals)	0.91	0.97
Non-food Items	1.37	1.50

Source: Dev *et al.* (2004).

Per capita consumption of fruits and vegetables showed the highest growth followed by edible oils (Dev *et al.*, 2004). The opening up of the economy in the 1990s led to a big rise in export demand for such products. The combined value of exports of fish and meat and their preparations, fruits, vegetables and their processed foods, which rose by about 70 per cent in the pre-reform decade, from US$ 490 million to 852 million between 1980-81 and 1990-91, rose by 270 per cent over the post-reform decade to US$ 2308 million in 2000-01 (GoI, 2002).

In response to this growing domestic and export demand for non-cereal items of food, there has been a discernible shift in the allocation of resources in Indian agriculture in the recent period away from cereals, particularly coarse cereals, to the enterprises like dairying, poultry, edible oils, meat, fish, vegetables and fruits, etc. (Joshi and Gulati, 2003). These enterprises,

8. See Pingali and Khwaja (2004) for more on this.

being labour-intensive, are suited to small holders and lead to a rise in wage employment. Besides, they are environment friendly, as they are generally less land and water intensive and also the rise in incomes of farmers growing high value products e.g. vegetables and fruits results in reducing pressure for bringing more land under plough.

The bottlenecks to the realisation of these benefits, by responding to growing demand, lie on the supply side. Agricultural policy in respect of price, technology, infrastructure and institutions has so far been foodgrain centred and has been slow to respond to the new imperatives on the supply side. Major policy initiatives are called for to bring the relative prices of foodgrains in conformity with the emerging trends in demand. Public as well as private investment has to be stepped up in agricultural research, especially bio-technology, focusing on the new activities and the unfavourable areas. Many of the new products being highly perishable, there is a need for the development and upgradation of infrastructure for roads, markets, storage and processing.

The value addition of food fortification is only 7 per cent compared to as much as 23 per cent in China, 45 per cent in the Philippines and 188 per cent in the UK Only 2 per cent of the fruits and vegetables are processed in India. This is against a processing of 30 per cent in Thailand, 70 per cent in Brazil, 78 per cent in the Philippines and 80 per cent in Malaysia (Patnaik, 2004). The Government of India targets to bring it to 10 per cent by 2010 and 25 per cent by 2025. The 10 per cent target would call for an investment of Rs. 1,40,000 crores. This is supposed to create employment to 77 lakh persons directly and another 3 crores of people indirectly in the country (Padmanabhan, 2001). The post harvest losses in fruits and vegetables are estimated to be Rs. 50,000 crores at the national level (EPW, 2002). It forms about 30 per cent of the production in the country. Food processing industries have a crucial role to play in reduction of post-harvest losses. The most important point in the food industry is that a substantial portion being rural based, it has a very high employment potential with significantly lower investment. The fruits and vegetable farming for processing is not only employment-intensive, but also enhances the gross as well as net returns of the farmers (Rao, 1994; Acharya, 1997; Dileep *et al.*, 2002). Further, agro-industry generates new demand on the farm sector for more and different agricultural output, which is more suitable for processing (Srivastava, 1989). On the other hand, the development of these industries would relax wage goods constraint to economic growth by enhancing the supply of their products (Desai and Namboodiri, 1992).

Constraints identified for development of horticulture products by GoI (2002) are:

- poor quality of seeds and planting materials and their weak assessment mechanism;

- preponderance of old and senile orchards and their poor management practices;

- small and uneconomic average farm size of the orchards;

- high order of perishability of horticulture produce, leading to high degree of losses;

- lack of modern and efficient infrastructure facilities, poor technological support and poor post harvest management practices;

- underdeveloped and exploitative marketing structures;

- absence of adequate standards for quality produce; and

- inadequate research and extension support to address specific problems of horticulture crops and their linkages with farming community and industry.

For small and marginal farmers, marketing of their products is main problem apart from credit and extension. The contract farming arrangements are particularly useful in developing countries where small-scale agriculture is widespread. The small and marginal farmers have problems in getting inputs, credit, extension and marketing. The services provided by the contract farming companies would thus be useful for small-scale agriculture. In recent years , there has been some form of contract arrangements in several agricultural crops such as tomatoes, potatoes, chillies, gherkins, baby corns, rose onions, cotton, wheat, *basmati* rice, groundnut, flowers, and medicinal plants. The contract farming arrangements have to be strengthened

in order to help the small farmers. There is silent revolution in institutions regarding no-cereal foods. New production–market linkages in the food supply chain are—spot or open market transactions, agricultural cooperatives and contract farming (Joshi and Gulati, 2003). The contract farming is spreading throughout India for several crops in states like Andhra Pradesh,[9] Tamil Nadu, Karnataka, Punjab and Maharashtra. The contract farming arrangements are particularly useful in developing countries where small-scale agriculture is widespread. From the farmers' perspective, there are risks of market failure and production problems while growing new crops. The sponsoring companies may be unreliable, may exploit a monopoly position, and/or have inefficient management and marketing problems that could result in manipulation of quota and non-fulfilment of commitments. Contract farming in India is neither backed up by law nor by an efficient legal system. This is the single most constraint to widespread use of contract farming in India. The legal system can be improved with legislative measures like the model contract and code of practice, registration of contracts with marketing committees and tribunals for dispute resolutions.

Diversification is unlikely to be a feasible strategy all over the country if it is restricted only to agriculture related activities like shift from cereals to horticulture crops. The true benefit of diversification will come if more emphasis is given on allied activities like animal

---

9. On Andhra Pradesh, see Dev and Chandrasekhar (2004).

husbandry and fisheries. The livestock sector contributes to 5.4 per cent to GDP and 22.7 per cent to total output from agriculture sector. Value of milk group (Rs. 1,03,804 crore) is more compared to paddy (Rs. 73,965 crores) and wheat (Rs. 43,816 crores). Rural women play a significant role in animal husbandry and are directly involved in major operations like feeding, breeding, management and healthcare. As the ownership of livestock is more evenly distributed with landless labourers, and marginal farmers, the progress in this sector will result in a more balanced development of the rural economy, particularly in the reduction of poverty ratio.

Institutional and Sustainable Agriculture

Environmental concerns are among the policy priorities in India. Particularly degradation of land and water is alarming. It is estimated that the cost of soil degradation alone is about 1.2 per cent of its GDP. That is, by checking degradation of soil the level of GDP can be raised by 1.2 per cent. Watershed development under the new guidelines, in general, has an overall positive impact on environment. However, groundwater tables are depleting at an alarming rate. The *de facto* privatisation of groundwater and subsidised power supply are the main culprits. There has been a neglect of minor irrigation sources like tanks. Shortage of drinking water has accentuated and quality of water has declined over time.

An integrated approach is needed for water resources management in the country. An appropriate strategy should integrate institutional approaches with market principles. Since institutional innovation (Water User Associations) is already in place for canal irrigation, it is time now to implement volumetric pricing. There is a need to de-link water rights from land rights in order to ensure equity and sustainability.

Institutions like the water user associations and watershed committees are important for water management. It is worth looking at the experience of Andhra Pradesh regarding water user associations. Andhra Pradesh is the first state in the country to enact in 1997 the Andhra Pradesh Farmers Management of Irrigation Systems Act, 1997, (APFMIS Act) making the formation of Water Users' Associations (WUAs) mandatory for the management of irrigation. This is designed to bring greater accountability in irrigation department as well as a sense of ownership of the management systems among farmers. More than 10,000 Water Users' Associations (WUAs) have been formed, of which about 80 per cent are in minor irrigation sector. However, bulk of the area covered is under canal irrigation.

The impact of WUAs has been encouraging in these areas, especially in terms of providing irrigation to tail-end farmers. This has been made possible by cleaning of canals and water courses and monitoring of water losses by the WUAs. Area under paddy is reported to have increased significantly following reforms. However, much of the reported increase could be statistical because of underreporting of irrigated area before reform, as this meant lesser payment of water tax to revenue department. Paddy yields are reported to have increased by 40 per cent.

Irrigation charges were increased by more than three times from 1997 in Andhra Pradesh. Even so, the surface water rates will at best cover maintenance charges, whereas in the case of lift irrigation the farmer also bears the full capital cost of the well or bore. However, despite a significant rise in irrigation charges, the farmers' support for reforms in respect of surface irrigation is visible. This is because the launching of these reforms was preceded by widespread consultation and awareness building among farmers about the benefits from reforms. Consequently, increased water tax is seen by farmers as supplementing the resources of WUAs for maintenance of irrigation systems. Even so, the effective rate of collection remains low at around 64 per cent. The reason could be that WUAs have not yet been made fully responsible for collection of water charges, making the process fully democratic and accountable. Another notable development was that the works were executed by WUAs themselves at lesser cost instead of getting them done by contractors. But the vested interests lost no time in adjusting to the new situation by presidents of the WUAs acting as contractors. This and other malpractices invited the wrath of farmers who in several cases used the provision in the Act for recall of the presidents. The only long-term solution to this is awareness building and promoting participatory monitoring and evaluation. Unlike in the case of canal irrigation, WUAs are not found to be effective in respect of tank irrigation due to insufficient allocations.

In the case of land and forestry, watershed approach and Joint Forest Management are crucial for protecting the environment. The critical issue is sustainability of these programmes. Although watersheds have shown positive economic impact, the social issues are missing. More participatory approach and involvement of women would lead to sustainability of watershed development approach. In the case of JFM, the focus is more on high income areas like timber. Low value products constituting sources of livelihoods for the poor have low priority. Customary rights of the tribals on *podu* (shifting cultivation) have to be recognised.

Awareness and involvement of the civil society is a precondition for checking environmental degradation. Environmental movements would have a discerning impact in this regard.

Another concern is the land degradation due to excessive use of fertilisers and pesticides. Government has programmes such as Integrated Pest Management (IPM) and Integrated Nutrient Management (INM). Keeping in view the ill effects of pesticides and also National Policy on Agriculture, Integrated Pest Management Approach (IPM) approach has been adopted as a cardinal principle and main plank of plant protection in the country in the overall crop production programme. The objectives of IPM approach are to increase crop production with minimum input costs, minimise environmental pollution and maintain ecological equilibrium. During 2004-05, besides ongoing activities, the thrust area will be pertaining to Pest Risk Analysis (PRA) and post entry quarantine surveillance. This has become essential in the light of WTO agreement, which will facilitate more and speedier movement of plants, planting materials globally.

Integrated Nutrient Management (INM) advocates the integrated use of all sources of plant nutrients like chemical fertiliser, bio-fertiliser and locally organic manures like farmyard manure, compost, vermicompost, green manures, edible and non-edible oil cakes to maintain soil health and its productivity. Organic farming is also being encouraged in the country due to demand for these products all over the world.

Safey Nets

Social safety nets are important to protect the poor in agriculture sector and rural areas. Many studies have pointed out the disturbing feature of the inability of agriculture sector in generating new employment in the 1990s. Therefore, social safety nets should be restructured in order to create more employment.

India has many safety net programmes such as PDS (public distribution system) and employment programmes. The country is spending lot of funds on food subsidy and public distribution system. Government started targeted PDS (TPDS) in 1997. Studies have shown that PDS/TPDS is regressive in the sense that poor states have benefited much less than the non-poor states. Also,

the coverage was same for both poor and non-poor in 1999-00 (the percentage of households using PDS for BPL and APL[10] was 34 per cent). It is true that access to PDS increased in poor states with the introduction of targeting. There was also increase in income gains for the poor in rural areas. Orissa gained significantly with the introduction of TPDS. However, still four Southern states are benefiting much more than the poor states in North and Eastern India. Less than 15 per cent of the rural poor were using PDS in Bihar, UP and Rajasthan. This percentage was less than 30 per cent for MP and West Bengal (Dev *et al.*, 2004).

A comparison of some anti-poverty programmes in India show that employment programmes fare better than food transfer programmes in terms of cost effectiveness, though ICDS appears to transfer income to the poor at lower cost (Dev *et al.*, 2004). The public distribution system and Andhra's rice subsidy emerge as very expensive. Cost per Re.1 of income transferred under PDS and Andhra Pradesh rice scheme was about Rs.6 to Rs.7. In the case of employment programmes, the cost was less than Rs.2.

Several measures are needed to revamp PDS, which can improve food security of the poor. There are two options for making changes in PDS. The first option is revamp the existing PDS with decentralisation or introduction of food stamps. The second option is to phase out PDS and replace it with food-for-work

10. BPL is below poverty line and APL is above poverty line.

programme in the medium to long run. In the short run, decentralisation of PDS and better targeting with *panchayats* can be tried. Also, PDS should be linked with employment programmes and ICDS in order to improve targeting. In the medium-term, one should move towards other options of food stamps and employment programmes.

The UPA government in its NCMP (New Common Minimum Programme) has stated that the government would ensure 100 days employment for one able bodied person of every poor and lower-middle income households at minimum wage rate through an Act of Parliament. The NCMP promised the Act within 90 days of coming to power. This is modelled closely on the Employment Guarantee Scheme (EGS) of Maharashtra except the national one is to be vested with *panchayats*. A unique feature of EGS is that it provides employment on public works on demand. Many evaluations of EGS in Maharashtra have shown that the scheme has many direct and indirect effects—it reduced unemployment, increased incomes and seasonal benefits, acted as an insurance mechanism, made an impact on agricultural growth and wages, made rural poor a political force, and have considerable impact on women. The UPA government wants to spread such benefits to major parts of the country. China wants to learn from Indian experience on public works.

It is true that there are problems regarding implementation of these schemes in the past because of top down approach, lack of peoples' participation, involvement of contractors, machines, etc. Delivery systems can be improved with the new approach of participatory development, social mobilisation, involvement of civil society and *panchayati raj* institutions.

It is also important to strengthen human resource base of rural areas through nutrition, health, education and empowerment of women. Improvements in skills would lead to shift of workers from agriculture to non-agriculture.

Approach during Tenth Plan and Agriculture in Common Minimum Programme

The National Agricultural Policy (NAP) 2000 as well as Tenth Plan Document envisages a growth rate exceeding 4.0 per cent per annum in the agriculture sector during the Tenth Plan. The overall target of GDP growth of 8.0 per cent per annum set for the Tenth Plan is based on annual average growth rate of 4.0 per cent in agriculture, 8.9 per cent in industry and 9.4 per cent in services sector. The average growth rate for the first three years of the Tenth Plan is only 1.6 per cent per annum. Several measures are needed to improve agriculture growth in the country. The Tenth Plan strategy is to give importance to the following areas in agriculture:

- Increasing cropping intensity.

- Diversification to high value crops/activities.

- Development of minor irrigation and utilisation of created irrigation potential.

- Rainwater harvesting and conservation for the development of rainfed areas—watershed approach.

- Reclamation/development of problem soils/lands.

- Utilisation of unutilised/under-utilised wastelands and degraded lands by allocation/leasing.

- Timely and adequate availability of inputs like seeds, fertilisers, implements, etc.

- Thrust on seed production-breeder, foundation and certified—to achieve the desired seed replacement rate.

- Bridging the gap between research and farmers' yields.

- Encouragement to the private sector for effective extension and input support services.

- Promotion of a farming system approach.

- Cost effectiveness while increasing productivity.

- Promotion of organic farming, with the use of organic waste, Integrated Pest Management (IPM), Integrated Nutrient Management (INM).

- Strengthening of marketing, processing and value-addition infrastructure.

- Upgradation of indigenous cattle and buffalo using certified semen/high quality pedigreed bulls and providing services at farmer's door.

- Conservation of threatened breeds of livestock and improvement of breeds used for draught and pack.

- Creation of disease-free zones and a national immunisation programme against most prevalent animal diseases.

- Adequate availability of fodder seeds and improvement of pasture lands.

- Increase in fish production from both culture and capture resources.

- Emphasising the quality and safety aspects of produce in agriculture, animal husbandry, and the dairy and fisheries sector.

Promises under National Common Minimum Programme (NCMP)

In order to address the problems faced by the agriculture sector/farmers, Government in its National Common Minimum Programme (NCMP) has identified following action points for focused attention:

(1) Stepping up public investment in agricultural research and extension, rural infrastructure and irrigation.

(2) Doubling rural credit in three years and substantial expansion of institutional lending for small and marginal farmers. The delivery system for rural credit will be reviewed. Immediate steps will be taken to ease the burden of debt and high

interest rates on farm loans. Crop and livestock insurance schemes will be made more effective.

(3) Introduce a special programme for dry land farming in the arid and semi-arid regions of the country. Watershed and wasteland development programmes will be taken up on a massive scale. Water management in all its aspects, both for irrigation and drinking purposes, will receive urgent attention.

(4) Minimum wages laws will be fully implemented to help farm labour. Comprehensive protective legislation will be enacted for all agricultural workers. Revenue administration will be thoroughly modernised and clear land titles will be established.

(5) Constitution will be amended to ensure the democratic, autonomous and professional functioning of cooperatives.

(6) Controls that depress the incomes of farmers will be systematically removed. Farmers will be given greater say in the organisations that supply inputs to them.

(7) Adequate protection will be provided to all farmers from imports, particularly when international prices fall sharply.

(8) Government agencies entrusted with the responsibility for procurement and marketing will pay special attention to farmers in poor and backward states and districts. Farmers all over the country will receive fair and remunerative prices. The terms of trade will be maintained in favour of agriculture.

(9) Ensure that dues to all farmers including sugarcane farmers will be cleared at the earliest.

The Government has already announced some measures to implement NCMP promises. For example, a special package for enhancing credit for the farmers was announced in the Budget 2004-05. Total flow of agricultural credit which is estimated at Rs. 80,000 crores in 2003-04 will be enhanced to about Rs. 1,05,000 crores in 2004-05. This will represent 30 per cent increase over the flow of credit in the previous year. Over time, many public policies will be implemented in order to improve agricultural productivity and growth.

Policies for Increasing Rural Employment

Decline in growth of rural employment and increase in unemployment rate in the 1990s in spite of higher GDP growth rate is a matter of concern. Appropriate sectoral policies and improvements in direct employment programmes can raise employment in rural areas. The government policies stress both on growth promoting policies as well as direct interventions to improve employment opportunities. The Task Force on Employment Opportunities (GoI, 2001) identified the five broad areas of policy which together constitute a strategy for employment generation. These are as follows:

(a) "Accelerating the rate of growth of GDP, with a particular emphasis on sectors likely to ensure the spread of income to the low income segments of the labour force.

(b) Pursuing appropriate sectoral policies in individual sectors, which are particularly important for employment generation. These sectoral level policies must be broadly consistent with the overall objective of accelerating GDP growth.

(c) Implementing focused special programmes for creating additional employment of enhancing income generation from existing activities aimed at helping vulnerable groups that may not be sufficiently benefited by the general growth promoting policies.

(d) Pursuing suitable policies for education and skill development, which would upgrade the quality of the labour force and make it capable of supporting a growth process which generates high quality jobs.

(e) Ensuring that the policy and legal environment governing the labour market encourage labour absorption, especially in the organised sector."

The Special Group on employment opportunities (S.P. Gupta Committee, GoI, 2002) stressed the importance of unorganised sector for employment creation during Tenth Plan period. According the Special Group, "The employment strategy for future, to meet the Plan's employment goals is to encourage the use of labour-intensive and capital-saving technology, in general and to rejuvenate the growth of the unorganised sector in particular, which at present contributes 92 per cent to the country's employment and enjoys more than seven times labour intensity per unit of production, as compared to the organised sector. However, the unorganised sector needs to be made more productive to sustain itself against the domestic and international competition by proper choice of programmes and policies compatible with India's economic reforms and WTO rules" (GoI, 2002, p.7).

According to Tenth Five Year Plan document "While a higher rate of economic growth is a necessary condition for increasing the demand for labour, the pusuit of growth objective in isolation may not be sufficient, at least in an immediate foreseeable future, to gainfully absorb the annual additions to labour force. Therefore, in the short run perspective of a Five Year Plan, growth will have to be supplemented by increasing the employment content of growth in order to fulfill the employment objectives of Plan" (GoI, 2002a, p.146). The document also provides an indicative list of labour-intensive sectors for appropriate policies as given in Box 14.3.

Box 14.3

Some Labour Intensive Sectors which Require Policy Intervention

- Agricultural and Allied Activities.
  - There is a need to step up public investment in agriculture. Simultaneously bringing additional acreage under cultivation of oilseeds and pulses by switching from cereals holds substantial potential for employment generation. Horticulture, farm management programmes, agri-clinics and seed production are other potential areas for employment generation.
  - Regeneration of degraded forests, watershed development and highly labour intensive activities.
  - Wasteland development.
  - Development of medicinal plants and energy plantation which have high growth and employment potential.
  - Minor irrigation.
  - Cultivation of bamboo and manufacturing of bamboo based products.
- Food Processing.
- Rural non-farm activities/industries, including *khadi* and village industries.
- Small and medium enterprises.
- Service sectors.
  - Health.
  - Nutrition.
  - Education.
  - Information of technology and communication.

Source: *Tenth Five Year Plan* Vol.1 (GoI, 2002a).

Sectoral Policies

Agriculture

The unemployment and underemployment is concentrated more among the landless, small and marginal farmers. Agricultural development is an important source of increase in employment. We already examined above the policies needed for higher agricultural growth.

Apart from the above policies, development of wastelands will also increase lot of employment opportunities. Currently, there are about 24 million hectares of land that are categorised as culturable wasteland and permanent fallows, which is feasible to be developed and brought into cultivation. There can be two alternatives here. First, one can think of distributing these lands to *panchayats* and small and marginal farmers. Another alternative is to give it to corporate sector on long lease of say 20 years. *Panchayats* and corporate sector can develop the wasteland by raising resources in the market. However, one has to make sure that corporate sector does not occupy the fertile land.

Rural Non-farm Sector

Growth in rural non-farm employment (RNFE) can improve rural wages and also be an escape route for agricultural workers leading to an improvement in their purchasing power. The importance of the rural non-farm sector in poverty alleviation and promotion of livelihoods is being increasingly recognised. Increase in RNFE is one of the main factors responsible for the reduction in poverty in the 1980s. One of the challenges of the reforms now is to improve the quality of employment and incomes in the rural non-farm sector. A three-pronged strategy is needed for enhancement in the livelihoods of the rural poor. First, the Government should have policies to improve education and skills of the workers. Second, they should have several policies to increase employment for the unskilled workers. Third, the incomes of the women have to be improved by creating opportunities in the higher productivity sectors. Most of the women are confined to agriculture. There was only 0.7 per cent increase in the share of RNFE during the reform period. For the above three strategies, pro-poor growth engines have to be identified at sub-sectoral level rather than at the level of broad sectors. Public investment in agriculture and rural non-agriculture has to be improved significantly to improve the quality of RNFE. In order to improve rural non-farm sector, there is a need to look at issues such as, rural-urban linkages, sectoral and sub-sector potentials, markets, regulations and promotional policies, human capital, training, entrepreneurship, skills and finally infrastructure and technology. Rigidities in these factors have to be removed to promote rural non-farm sector. Allowing the poor to contribute to and benefit from increased growth rates will pose particular challenges as employment in India is largely in the unorganised sector.

Conclusion

In the post-liberalisation period, improvements in some indicators such as foreign exchange reserves, physical infrastructure (like telecommnications and roads), and stock market boom in recent period, IT revolution, and prospects of 8 per cent growth in GDP in 2003-04. Our assessment shows that although there were improvements in some indicators, situation in rural India is not satisfactory. In this context, this paper examines issues in several policies and suggests changes in policies for higher growth and equity. In agriculture, we examined policies relating to food management, subsidies and investments, research and extension, irrigation and water management, farmers' suicides, credit and insurance, domestic market and external trade reforms, diversification in agriculture, institutions and sustainable agriculture and safety nets. We also examined policies needed for higher employment in rural areas. To conclude, rural investment (both public and private), technology, rural institutions and employment schemes are important for rural development.

References

Acharya, S.S. (1997). "Agriculture-Industry Linkages, Public Policy and Some Areas of Concern", *Agricultural Economics Research Review*, Vol.10, No.2, pp.162-175.

Chavan, Pallavi and R. Bedamatta (2003). "Trends in Real Wages in India", Paper presented at All India Conference on Agriculture and Rural Society in Contemporary India, Bardhmam, December 17-20.

Deaton, A. and Jean Dreze (2002). "Poverty and Inequality in India: A Re-examination", *Economic and Political Weekly*, September.

Desai, B.M. and N.V. Namboodiri (1992). "Development of Food-Processing Industries", *Economic and Political Weekly*, Vol.26, March 28, pp.A38-42.

Dev, Mahendra S. *et al.* (2004). "Economic Liberalisation, Targeted Programmes and Household Food Security: A Case Study of India", *MTID Discussion Paper No.68*, IFPRI, Washington, D.C.

Dev, Mahendra S. and N. Chandrasekhar Rao (2004). *Food Processing in Andhra Pradesh: Opportunities and Challenges*, Centre for Economic and Social Studies, Hyderabad.

Dileep, B.K, R.K. Grover and K.N. Rai (2002)."Contract Farming in Tomato: An Economic Analysis", *Indian Journal of Agricultural Economics*, Vol.57, No.2, April-June, pp.197-210.

Dreze, Jean and Amartya Sen (2002). *India: Development and Participation*, Oxford University Press, New Delhi.

EPW Editorial (2002). "Food Processing: Long Haul", *Economic and Political Weekly*, Vol.37, June 29.

GoI (2000), "Approach Paper to the New Food Processing Policy", Ministry of Food Processing Industries, as quoted in article "Food Processing: Many Investment Opportunities", *Agriculture and Industry Survey*, Vol.10, No. 9 and 10, September-October.

————. (2001). *Report of Task Force on Employment Opportunities*, Planning Commission, New Delhi.

————. (2002). *Special Group on Targeting Ten Million Opportunities Per Year*, Planning Commission, New Delhi.

————. (2002a). *Tenth Five-Year Plan 2002-07*, Vol. I, Planning Commission, New Delhi.

————. (2003). *Economic Survey*, 2002-03, Ministry of Finance, New Delhi.

Gulati, A. and S. Narayanan (2003). *The Subsidy Syndrome in Indian Agriculture*, Oxford University Press, New Delhi.

IIPS and Ministry of Health and Family Welfare (1995). *National Family Health Survey-I, India, 1992-93*, International Institute for Population Sciences, Mumbai

————. (2000b). *National Family Health Survey-II*, India,1998-99, International Institute for Population Sciences, Mumbai

Joshi, P.K. and Ashok Gulati (2003). *Agricultural Diversification: From Plate to Plough*, IFPRI.

Kumar, Shiva (2003),"Rural Poverty Across Indian States: An Assessment", paper presented at All India Conference on *Agriculture and Rural Society in Contemporary India, Bardhmam*, December 17-20.

Padmanabhan, M. (2001). "Set for a Quantum Jump", *The Hindu Survey of Indian Industry*.

Patnaik, Utsa (2004). "Rural India in Ruins", *Frontline*, Vol.21, No.5, March 12, Chennai.

Pingali, P. and Y. Khwaja (2004). "Globalisation of Indian Diets and the Transformation of Food Supply Systems", Inaugural Keynote Address, 17th Annual Conference, Indian Society of Agricultural Marketing, Hyderabad, 5-7 February.

Rao, C.H.H. (2003). "Reform Agenda for Agriculture", *Economic and Political Weekly*, Vol.8, No.7.

Rao, V.M. (1994). "Farmers in Market Economy: Would Farmers Gain Through Liberalisation?", *Indian Journal of Agricultural Economics*, Vol.49, No.3, July-September, pp.393-402.

Ravallion, Martin (2000). "What is Needed for a More Pro-poor Growth Process in India", *Economic and Political Weekly*, Vol.35, No.25-32, March, pp.1089-93.

RBI (2002), *Report on Currency and Finance 2000-01*, Reserve Bank of India, Mumbai.

————. (2003). *Report on Currency and Finance 2001-02*, Reserve Bank of India, Mumbai.

Sainath, P. (2004). "The Feel Good Factor", *Frontline*, Vol.21, No.5, March 12, Chennai.

Sawant, S. D., V. Daptardar, and S. Mhatre (2002). "Capital Formation and Growth in Agriculture, Neglected Aspects and Dimensions", *Economic and Political Weekly*, March 16.

Saxena, N.C. (2000). "Poverty Alleviation through Innovation Policies and Better Governance', paper presented at *Indian States' Reform Forum* 2000, November 23-25, New Delhi.

Sen, A. and Himanshu (2003). *Poverty and Inequality in India: Getting Closer to the Truth*, Centre for Economic Studies and Planning, Jawaharlal Nehru University, New Delhi, (*mimeo*).

Shetty, S.L. (2003). *Credit Flows to Rural Poor*, (*mimeo*), EPW Research Foundation, Mumbai.

Srivastava, Ravi (2003). *Right to Education*, (*mimeo*).

Srivastava, U.K. (1989). "Agro-Processing Industries: Potential, Constraints and Task Ahead", *Indian Journal of Agricultural Economics*, Vol.44, No.3,July-September.

Sundaram, K. and S.D. Tendulkar (2003). "Poverty in India in the 1990s: Revised Estimates", *Economic and Political Weekly*, Vol.38, No.46, November 15.

————. (2003a). "Poverty Among Social and Economic Groups in India in 1990s", *Economic and Political Weekly*, Vol.38, No 50, December 13.

Vaidyanathan, A. (1996). "Agricultural Development: Imperatives of Institutional Reforms", *Economic and Political Weekly*, Vol.31, Nos. 35-37.

15 | India's Northeast: Looking within, Stretching Eastward

SANJOY HAZARIKA

THE Northeast of India is located at the confluence of East, Southeast and South Asia. Home to over 300 ethnic groups speaking almost as many languages (although there are only a handful of scripts), the region abuts not less than four nations—Bhutan and China (Tibet) to the north, Myanmar to its east and Bangladesh to its south and west. A narrow land corridor, popularly called the Chicken's Neck and also as the Siliguri Corridor, links this eastern most part of the country with the rest of India.

The author and scholar B.G. Verghese calls the Northeast the region's third "landlocked" country after Bhutan and Nepal.

Its land borders with the 'motherland' are less than 1 per cent of its land frontiers—over 99 per cent lie with the four countries that have stronger historic, geographic and ethnic ties with this odd-shaped region, thrusting out of India as it were. One has often called this area Asia in miniature, where the great races, faiths and traditions of the continent have met and merged. Not surprisingly, relations with the rest of India are not as strong as they could have been with Assam remaining a kingdom apart under the Tai-Ahoms whose forebears travelled a great distance from the Shan province to cross the Patkai ranges and eventually conquer the Brahmaputra Valley—and hold it for 600 years (1228 to 1826) until the advent of the Burmese and then the British within a few years of each other.

The mix of in-migrants and their ideas has meant that Tibetan Buddhism has a foothold in the 300-year-old monastery of Tawang as does Buddhism from southeast Myanmar in the shape of the Tai-Ahoms, There are followers of Welsh and Scottish Presbytarians in the hills of Meghalaya and Mizoram, more recent converts from the 19th century, as are those owing allegiance to the Southern Baptists of the United States in Nagaland and the hills of northern Manipur. A wandering Iraqi prince brought Islam to the edge of the Brahmaputra, near Guwahati, in the 11th century and was welcomed by Hindu mendicants and others.

This is India's frontiers—land, where communities and migrants have come over the centuries and spanned great distances and despite enormous odds have established businesses and cities, brought the written word and different faiths, built schools, lakes and missions and developed a system of governance and administration. Yet, it remained extremely detached from the hustle of 'national' politics and development, a place apart. One American scholar[1] asserted over 35 years ago that as with Southern China, the borders of the region also did not mark off a cultural or linguistic area.

The then Indian External Affairs Minister I. K. Gujral (and later Prime Minister) spoke to an audience in Jakarta proclaiming that India and ASEAN were no "awkward strangers" but had been neighbours and friends "for as long back as we can remember".

Gujral should have in truth spoken only of the Northeast for it is this area which has had a long, if not comfortable, relationship with Southeast Asia. There are communities here who speak Mon-Khmer and are related to the Austric groups of Southeast Asia; the Lisus of Arunachal Pradesh migrated from Myanmar in the early part of the 20th century; the Khamtis of Arunachal also came from northern Burma in the early part of the 18th century. There are accounts which would have us believe that some ancestors of tribes in the Northeast came from across the seas now separating the mainland of Asia with major island groups in Southeast Asia.

"Our habits, customs and social mores, our myths and legends, the clothes we drape, the cuisine we savour, the art, craft and design that is our shared legacy, even the languages we speak—all bear testimony to this good neighbourliness." Gujral could not have been speaking either of Bengal or the Punjab or of Madhya Pradesh. The only geographical area that fits this description in India is the Northeast, in manner of dress, cuisine, cultures and language as well as looks.

These days, however, an interesting new strand bonds the Northeast to mainland India—in recent years, tens of thousands of young people from the Northeast have fanned out to centres of excellence and study across the country, in search of work, research and scholarship. But this is a comparative new development in an age of rapid change. Although relatively new, it has the potential, in the medium and long-term, of changing the face of the Northeast more definitely than any government intervention or non-state movement. We will reflect later on this.

Yet, although a sense of seeming remoteness persists even today, it is worth briefly examining whether it is more notional than anything else.

The Globalisation of the Northeast

The Northeast was actually one of the earliest 'globalised' places in South Asia. It remains so.

---

1. Kunstadter, Peter (1967). *Southeast Asian Tribes, Minorities and Nations*, Princeton University Press.

It had connections to Tibet, Nepal, Myanmar and Southwest China through the Southern Silk Route, among the less celebrated of the Silk Routes (the most famous was that followed by the Italian explorer Marco Polo in his travels to the court of the Chinese Emperor and the Great Khan—Genghis Khan of Mongolia). Along this route which spanned some 3,000 kilometres, silks, herbs, precious stones, handicrafts, ivory and slaves were transported. Parts of this route are still active today, with giant Chinese trucks making the long journey from Kunming in China's Yunnan Province to Moreh in Manipur state on the India-Myanmar border, through tortuous roads which stagger over hill and valley, across rivers as great as the Mekong and the Salween, the Irrawaddy and the Chindwin before disgorging the new goods of the 21st century—cheap Chinese electronic goods and garments, leather, aluminum and plastic, buckets and liquor, gold and precious stones, tinned and packaged foods—the list goes on. Much of it is illegal. But that is not as important, in my view, as what the route renews every day and reasserts, between people long-separated, traditions still distanced but connected through the strength of daily business and the promise of profits, despite all the hardships *en route*. It is in recognition of this historicity and potential trade strength that the Prime Minister of India, Dr. Manmohan Singh, flags off on November 22 a trans-ASEAN, if not Asian, rally that will take travellers and rallyists from Guwahati through Kohima and Imphal across Tamu and Kalewa in Myanmar's Sagaing Division and then down through Mongwa and Mandalay to Yangon and then to other cities of Southeast Asia before closing in Indonesia. Last year, I had the privilege of doing part of this journey, from Guwahati to Yangon, and it was an eye opener in terms of resonances of living connections between the Northeast and Myanmar—cuisines, ethnic groups, phrases, ecology and trade, from selling sticky rice early in the morning at the Nampharlong-Moreh gate to the use of the rivers as well as herbs and music in the Irrawaddy plains.

The world came to the doors of the Northeast in other ways too. In the Second World War, the advancing Japanese tide was halted, pushed back and eventually defeated on the tennis courts of the Deputy Commissioner of Kohima, now capital of Nagaland, and on the Imphal road in Manipur. The power of international ideologies and conflicting world views were visible.

The other aspects of an earlier globalisation, fanned by the pressures of colonial rule, remain visible if not as strong as before. Today, Assam produces the largest amount of tea in India, a crop which was commercially grown in the 19th century by British companies after an enterprising Briton first confirmed from his contacts with a tribal chief that the crop was native to the area and had potential. At that time, Chinese workers were initially brought in but did not last long. Colonial commerce shanghaied and otherwise transported thousands of people from Central Indian tribes, the Santhals, Adivasis, Mundas and others, by boat to the new tea gardens at the cost of many lives. The tea auctions at Guwahati are among the largest in the country. Information is available at a macro-second—if the power is there and the server is working—that can connect auctioneers and buyers to clients in London and elsewhere and finalise a deal. Yet, away from the auctioneer's hammer, across the Brahmaputra from Guwahati, at a sleepy trade outpost or inland container centre at Amingaon, containers of tea are also shipped out by train to the docks and airports of Kolkata and Mumbai from where they are exported.

Tea is having a better year in 2004 after a series of disastrous seasons with poor crops, increased competition (the new 'globalisation') and a collapse of small growers which were once the toast of small businesses.

The gas and oil industry in Assam was among the oldest of industries in the region, beginning over a century ago with the first oil find in Digboi, Upper Assam.

The Hindi heartland was never far away with entrepreneurs and traders from Rajasthan especially but other parts of the country making a strong base for their operations and settling there in the process, bringing families, traditions, capital—both cash and social. Some of the most successful businessmen in the Northeast are now those who were once 'outsiders'.

These facts stress one aspect–that although the Northeast remains among the most economically backward of regions in the country, despite the large amounts of funds poured in regularly by the Centre— it has remained one of the most continuously exploited

areas for over 150 years, taking commerce and profits to the world but yet remaining marginalised and underdeveloped. The regional gaps which have emerged in India and between the Northeast and other parts of the country have enduring roots in this and cannot be wished away.

Capital Formation in the Region has been Low

The financial planning in Delhi, Dispur[2] and other capitals of the region has led to an awkward structuring of systems and sectors. Without understanding local concerns and issues, a planning model has been thrust upon the region that is completely at inconsonance with it. The results are visible—a highly inflated tertiary sector, a weak primary sector and a virtually non-existent secondary sector.[3] There is a basis to the concern in the region that the Government of India's recently discovered desire to develop the Northeast is driven as much by altruism as by its vision that its short-term and long-term economic interests, as much as security interests, are threatened by the alienation and armed reactions to the visible exploitation over earlier decades.

There is one factor here which also cannot be wished away and which disrupted the life and condition of the Northeast as much as, if not more than, anything else.

---

2. Assam's capital, located at the edge of Guwahati, the main commercial hub.

3. *Report of the Committee on Revitalisation of the North Eastern Council 2004*, Ministry of Development of the North Eastern Region, Government of India.

Partition

Apart from causing extreme isolation, the Radcliffe Award of 1947 was economically catastrophic on the region, destroying traditional markets for example between the Khasi hills on the Shillong Plateau and Sylhet and Mymensing in the East Bengal/East Pakistan/Bangladesh plains below—fruits, vegetables and meat from the hills, salt, oil and other commodities from the plains. New roads had to be built to connect the outposts of India's new frontiers to district and state capitals, new transport services put in place, new markets developed. These have not been particularly effective. Connectivity was and remains difficult and rural communities especially on the border remain marginalised and poor. Thus to some, it is easier to go for medical treatment to a hospital in Comilla in Bangladesh than to Agartala in Tripura. Just as it makes more sense for students from Comilla to study in Agartala and elsewhere in the Northeast where, to them, education opportunities are better. Homes are literally divided with the bedroom in Bangladesh and the kitchen in India, making residents inhabitants of both countries who travel to each other's lands hundreds of times during a single day.

Sanjib Baruah approvingly quotes the historian David Ludden on the impact of Partition which "cut old routes of communication and mobility across new national borders more dramatically than almost anywhere in the world. The Bengal-Assam railway tracks from Guwahati to Dhaka were torn up at the Cahcar-Sylhet border in 1965. Today, it is much easier to communicate by phone or mail between Dhaka and London than between Dhaka and Guwahati."[4] Actually, Ludden is not quite accurate—thanks to better communication links, anyone can pick up a phone with international accessibility in Guwahati or Dhubri or Dimapur in Nagaland and call out to Bangladesh or anywhere else in the world.

In addition, now there are a number of medium-sized airports in at least five major states of the region—Guwahati, Jorhat and Dibrugarh in Assam; Imphal in Manipur; Dimapur in Nagaland; Aizawl in Mizoram and Agartala in Tripura. International fights to the neighbours, especially Yangon, Sylhet and Dhaka as well as Thimpu, could be another way in bringing the region closer together. Private airlines in Thailand have expressed interest in coming to Guwahati if an attractive tourist package can be developed. Again opportunities march ahead of preparedness on the ground and are unlikely to keep coming time and again, unless practical changes which welcome 'outside influences' are visible on the ground. Service related industries would grow—residents would need to learn language skills to deal with foreign travellers; high quality restaurants, new cuisines, guest houses and hotels again would need to be developed.

---

4. Baruah, Sanjib (2004). *Between South and Southeast Asia: Northeast India and The Look East Policy*, Omeo Kumar Das Institute of Social Change and Development, Guwahati.

The Strength of Memory

Meanwhile, Memories Remain Strong

A senior district official in Kurigram district, on the Assam-Bangladesh border (it lies opposite Dhubri district) once remarked to me when I told him that I was driving to the border that I was going on 'the Imphal road'. This was a reference to the road which led through Assam to Imphal in Manipur and was used as a major route for troops and goods transportation during the Second World War.

If memories are strong, so are movements of people. The answer to Partition is seen in how people have voted with their feet, especially in the east of the subcontinent.

For decades, a seamless flow of people from across the borders have continued to mark the region as India's continuing frontier-land—from Bangladesh and Myanmar and, in far smaller numbers, from Tibet. And as far as the influx from Bangladesh is concerned, whether a party such as the Congress acknowledges it or not, whether a party like the Bharatiya Janata Party wishes to exploit it or not, the facts remain clear, despite Dhaka's manifest protestations to the contrary—there is an influx of landless peasants and others, including unskilled labour, from Bangladesh into the Northeast and West Bengal in particular. These movements have triggered anti-'foreigner' and anti-outsider feelings and movements in several states especially in Assam. There have been riots and clashes between old and new settlers, immigrants and tribal groups, between the indigenous and the outsider which have caused thousands of deaths in the past two decades and more. But in the process, not less than 1.5 million have moved into Assam alone in the past 30 years, a figure which comprises about five per cent of the state's total population.

There are other current and harsh realities. The Northeast remains a disturbed region, hurt by the conflicts which have emerged from various uprisings against the State as much as the intensively coercive measures taken by the State to protect its interests. These began in the 1950s with the Naga movement for independence in the Naga hills. Insurgencies for independence followed quickly in Mizoram, Manipur and Tripura as well as Assam, the mother state. A burst of militant violence also affected Meghalaya but appears to have abated while two districts of Arunachal Pradesh, with borders on Myanmar, China and Bhutan, are troubled by the presence of Naga armed groups.

While the severity of the conflict, sharpest between the 1950s and 1980s, appears to have abated with closure of militancy in Mizoram, peace negotiations between Delhi and the Nagas as well as the Bodo and other tribal groups in Assam and factions in Tripura and Meghalaya, have picked up and continue, despite hiccups and suspicions of the motives of the other. A clear positive signal comes from the proposed visit of the two major Naga leaders to Delhi later in November to press the peace processes. But here as well as in other political and ethnic upsurges against the Indian State, the questions of ethnic identity, nationality, sub-nationality, borders and territory are very sensitive and complex issues which defy easy solution. Thus, the prospect of peace with one group is swiftly tempered by the threat from a rival armed group which says that there cannot be compromise on issues such as 'sovereignty'.

Peace talks do not mean that all is well—strikes and killings, kidnappings, extortions and intimidation are routine in some parts of the Northeast. At the same time, there appears to be an extraordinary and contradictory repose especially in urban centres where new businesses, stores and restaurants are opening every day, the prices of property are going up and bars and clubs are flourishing. While discussions with Delhi are on, so are extortions by groups involved in these conversations. In addition, they mete out justice on their own terms to individuals and groups who are seen as either challenges to their control or in simple need of chastisement, sending a loud message to silence those who disagree.

These extremely diverse economic and political situations, often contradictory and always complex, distance the Northeast from the rest of India.

There is no other part of the country which shares over 99 per cent of its borders with other nations. There is no other part of India which faces the challenge of such and so many vibrant and different ethnic groupings, each with contesting historical, territorial and ethnic spaces. Despite the many disruptions of social life, self-governing traditional institutions remain strong both in the hills and plains. Not all of them are democratic, most of them give few powers in the decision making process

to women but despite these shortcomings, there are few other societies in India which accord as much respect and strength to women as those of Meghalaya and Manipur, to give two examples.

Thus, this paper asserts that it is far more important that in economic terms, the Northeast build stronger relations with its neighbours. It makes for economic common sense. It would deal with the problem of imbalances of regional growth because the Northeast would stop wasting its time trying to catch up with West Bengal or Maharashtra and instead turn as a first step to its natural trading, investment and transport partners—its neighbours of Bangladesh, Myanmar and, to a more limited degree, China and Bhutan to the North. Bhutan at the moment has virtually closed its southern border with Assam, citing security concerns about a possible backlash by Northeast insurgents that it flushed out of its territory last year, smashing militant camps and image. Until that threat perception recedes, and it may with opportunities growing of dialogue between Delhi and the more intransigent of such groups, trade with Bhutan would need to be at a low level, although this is especially hurting Bhutanese farmers and weavers.

In the next logical steps to trans-border growth, a Trans-Asia highway and Trans-Asian railroad which are actually being built would enable the Northeast to reach out across Myanmar to Southeast Asia. This is where initiatives such as the South Asia Growth Quadrangle, BIMSTEC and the Kunming Initiative make eminent economic sense. But a Southeast Asian miracle will not come to the Northeast easily. There are a number of hurdles to overcome.

The Government of India appears to have embraced the first two and is tentative to the third because it represents a quasi-Track II approach with which it is uncomfortable, particularly with regard to the opportunities it may give a resurgent southwest China (especially Yunnan province) in its access to the Northeast. Despite an improvement in Sino-India relations, the unresolved border dispute in the Northeast (China claims all of Arunachal Pradesh and shows that state as part of its territory in its maps), the earlier Chinese support (officially closed since 1976) to Naga and Mizo fighters, the swamping of local markets by Chinese goods and the surge of Chinese-made weapons in the hands of local militants, continue to make New Delhi uneasy.

At the moment, a truck load of goods takes over 48 hours to travel between Agartala to Kolkata in West Bengal. If Bangladesh gave access through Akhura, south of Agartala, it would reduce travel time to a major port (in this case Chittagong) to less then eight hours and save thousands of rupees in energy bills and transport costs not including the wear and tear on vehicles and roads. Bangladesh, on the other hand, would gain through the services sector and taxing goods and vehicles which come in.

At the moment those making the biggest profits on this route are those who have used it seamlessly for decades—the 'informal' trade i.e. smugglers from all countries bordering each other. Their networks are extensive and profit margins are enormous—their commodities ranging from the non-lethal and traditional such as kerosene, wood, bamboo to areca nuts and betel leaf to the lethal—drugs, guns and, more recently, human trafficking, especially women and girl children.

Systems in place on either side on all three borders with Myanmar, Bangladesh and Bhutan would reduce the role of smugglers, who in places are involved with security forces, officials and local businessmen. But it would be foolish to discount the role that the 'informal trade'—three times that of the official trade between Bangladesh and India—plays in meeting the needs of ordinary people. Formal barriers and attitudes strengthen the informal.

Questions and Possible Answers

But there are several questions and issues before the Northeast as it moves into this new space.

Does the system have the capacity to deliver? Does it have the infrastructure? If it is to become a major trading and staging centre, what will it export—does it have anything surplus to export—after all, as of now, it is a net importer for almost anything used in the region ranging from computers, phones, matchsticks and stationary to tyres and fish? Can traditional skills be upgraded and marketed to reach and compete with international markets? Do its leaders and those in New Delhi have the vision and the practicality to make governance work and move from dreaming and designing plans to actual delivery?

The answers to these questions, at the present moment, are anything but positive. In terms of good governance or mere governance, the Northeast scores poorly. Its infrastructure, especially in the hill states, is crumbling. There is talk of major hydroelectric dams to boost the region's energy potential and market it but some of these projects, in the face of local and environmental concerns, are decades behind schedule. Every year, its major rivers explode with such ferocity across the Assam Valley and the smaller valleys of Arunachal Pradesh and Manipur that not less than two-to-three million are displaced and face deprivation and ill-health for weeks, not to mention a threat to life and the destruction of their property and their meagre investments—livestock, homes, clothes, etc.

This is why without a series of steps which must impact the following areas, the Northeast will be mired in desperation and conflicts arising out of failed promises and alienation.

One, strengthen the systems of governance and clean up the administration.

Two, take initiatives which involve rural groups and tackle the marginalisation that has grown with continuing natural disasters—thus, develop fleets of boats that will take to the displaced and marooned at times of flood; improve the *ghats* (river ports), including sanitation, involve communities in flood proofing instead of giving the projects to government departments which will ensure that the work is not done or at best done incompetently through a network of contractors with political and official clout. Involving people in projects like high platforms for flood time will generate millions of mandays, generate incomes.

Three, involve reformed and democratised traditional institutions in self-governance issues at the village and district levels.

Four, review where the tens of millions of rupees which were to have been spent in the region gone. If the Government of India can set up a Ministry for the Northeast's development, then surely the very least it owes the people is a Committee that reviews the major projects and announcements by various Prime Ministers (three Prime Ministers announced a total of Rs. 23,000 crore for the region between 1996-to-2000!) and state governments and unearths where that money has gone. Without the sting of transparency, all governments in Delhi and the states are condemned to follow a path that will fail because the powerbrokers among politicians and officials, and their conduits in business and the underground, will make sure it does not work.

Five, develop a network of container ports at various border and inland points which can quickly transport incoming and outgoing goods, adding value through services and local employment generation.

Six, use the Brahmaputra to transport goods and people extensively and develop it as the region's USP, particularly for tourism and trade, especially after launching pro-people, flood-proofing strategies.

Seven, resolve the internal political differences which have led to the conflicts over the past 50 years. This last tangle promises to be among the toughest, but without it neither can the region grow or reach out of itself to its neighbours.

Eight, do not try and do too many things. Attempt to do a few really well.

Large investments may be required. But more than funds, clear innovative ideas and specific strategies allied to common sense, governance, local interventions and rural growth are important.

The Northeast need not fear the future. It has been dealing with the world for centuries. We need not just one highway to Southeast Asia but many roads connecting people to each other and to the world, despite what the security analysts and *pundits* say. We must act, plan and think regionally.

In this, the tens of thousands of students and young professionals who are streaming out of the region's top research, study and work do not represent a lost resource to the Northeast. They are the very persons who can transform its face, giving their capabilities and professionalism, their skills and competitiveness. Politics may be a substantial problem as are contesting identities. But the students and young professionals are breaking the mould and creating a new image of the region, outside it and with the passage of time will play in making the connectivity which will help the Northeast to grow and change.

Baruah outlined the price for shutting up the Northeast, "By denying itself the use of its natural gateway, India is in effect setting back its ambitions in Southeast Asia."[5]

A robust Look East policy through the Northeast is the key to change and prosperity for India's eastern margins and its neighbours, placed by a history they cannot change but facing policies and attitudes which they must.

5. Baruah, S. (2004). *Between South and Southeast Asia.*

16 | Our Economy—How Growth Can Be Combined with Equity

PREM SHANKAR JHA

MAXIMISING the growth of employment—the Employment Guarantee Scheme (EGS) is not the best way. The irreducible minimum requirement—indeed the litmus test of success—for any effort to ensure equity with growth is to make sure that everyone who looks for a job finds one.

The UPA has recognised this problem, but is relying on a combination of higher economic growth and targeted sectoral employment guarantee programmes, to tackle this problem. I do not believe that this is the best approach. The latter is like applying poultice to a wound. It can give short-term relief but provides no long-term solutions.

Employment guarantee schemes mostly fail to create either permanent assets or permanent employment because it is inherently impossible to tailor the time and the financial outlays required by the investment schemes to the budgetary constraints of the programme. In every district the money and food allocated for the EGS annually is calculated on the basis of the number of likely applicants multiplied by the daily wage for 100 days. But investment projects have their own compulsions both in regard to the time they take and the labour (and machines) they require. Even the most efficient district administration can seldom ensure that the projects it has selected will be completed within these time and money constraints. If they remain incomplete, they are swept away by the next monsoons.

Check dams, roads and incomplete buildings are the worst sufferers. The money spent on these projects thus becomes a plain and simple dole. It creates no permanent assets and therefore no permanent employment. EGS schemes are therefore a solution for local distress caused, for instance, by a drought. But they are not a solution to the employment programme.

The correct way of maximising employment growth is also the simplest. It is to maximise the rate of growth of GDP. More specifically it is to maximise the rate of growth of industry and agriculture. Employment then takes care of itself.

I am aware that this is a bold assertion. It flies in the face of a great deal of 'revisionist' thinking in the 'seventies' by great economists like Dudley Seers, Paul Streeten, Mahbub-ul-Haq, and E.F. Schumacher. All of them advocated a 'direct attack' on poverty and unemployment, whose basic premise was that it was worth sacrificing some growth of GDP and labour productivity in order to directly alleviate the misery of the poor. The social benefits from doing so far outweigh the cost in terms of slower per capita income growth.

The crucial weakness of this approach is that it has learned nothing from the actual economic history of the first generation of industrialised countries, which now belong in the OECD. The experience of all these countries, over a 150 years, has been surprisingly uniform.

Between 1820 and 1970 none of them suffered from chronic unemployment. On the contrary, except during recessions all of them were voracious consumers of labour. North America's industrialisation was only made possible by the immigration of 80 million workers from the old world between 1850 and 1914. Northern Europe's industrialisation was made possible by the shift of 15 million workers from Southern Europe and the Balkans between 1870 and 1914. Britain relied for decades upon an inflow of Irish labour to alleviate the shortage of labour. In all of these countries agriculture and the domestic prices industries were emptied of people by the voracious urban, non-agricultural sector even before the immigration began.

In the mid-20th century the 'Golden age of capitalism' was only made possible by high levels of immigration into Europe and America, and substantial surreptitious immigration into Japan from Korea and China. In the last 40 years South Korea, Malaysia, Hong Kong, and Singapore have all achieved full employment and are straining at the seams. Hong Kong, with a 7 to 8 per cent growth rate had absorbed 6 million refugees from China by 1990 and still raised its per capita income to $25,000, close to that of the USA. In Malaysia, 25 per cent of the labour force is imported. South Korea similarly has large immigrant labour force.

The cumulative experience from all over the world, of almost two centuries therefore points uniformly and unequivocally in one direction—the higher the rate of growth, especially in industry, the faster is the rate of growth of employment.

But, the growth of employment does not take place entirely, or even mainly, in industry. It takes place in the services sector. That is why industrialisation has throughout been accompanied by a sharp rise in the proportion of the labour force employed in the services sector.

Table 16.1

Structure of Employment in the G-7 Countries 1960, 1974 and 1986

Sector	1960	1974	1986
Agriculture	17.3	8.0	5.4
Manufacturing	27.2	27.6	22.3
Services	46.0	54.9	63.3

Source: OECD: *Historical Statistics*.

The reason for this can be deduced from the following data collected by one of the world's greatest statistician, Angus Maddison. Maddison showed that ever since 1820, labour productivity in the industrialised countries has grown on an average 2.5 to 3 times as fast in industry as in the services sector. Because industry has sucked labour out of agriculture, labour productivity in the latter has kept pace with industry. Maddison's data for six OECD countries from 1913 to the present day are reproduced below.

Table 16.2

Average Growth of Labour Productivity by Sectors for Six Countries UK, USA, France, Germany, Netherlands and Japan, 1913 to 1987 (Annual Average Compound Growth rate) and Level of Output per Person as Percentage of Average for the Whole Economy, in 1987

Sector	1913-50	1950-73	1973-87
Agriculture	1.1	5.9	3.5
Industry	1.2	5.6	2.5
Services	0.4	2.5	1.1

Source: Maddison, A. (1991). *Dynamic Forces in Capitalist Development: A Long Run Comparative View.* Tables 5.13 and 5.14. pp.150-151, Oxford University Press.

Four conclusions emerge from these data:

1. At no time can the existing workers in the service sector meet more than 40 per cent of the transport, storage, distribution, finance, insurance, and other needs created by an increase in agricultural and industrial production. The balance 60 per cent will have to be met by recruiting more workers in the service sector.

2. Employment will continue to rise so long as productivity in industry and agriculture rise faster than productivity in services.

3. The faster is the increase in labour productivity in the former two the faster will be the growth of employment in the third. Thus the faster will be the overall rate of growth of employment in the economy.

4. If both labour productivity and employment grow in industry, then so much the better. But the above data show that total employment will grow even if there is no growth of employment in industry so long as the productivity of those already employed continues to grow.

The recent experience of the Indian economy vindicates this relationship. Between 1993-94, thanks mainly to the tremendous spurt of growth between 1993 and 1997, industrial production rose by an average of almost 8 per cent per annum. Employment in industry grew by 2 per cent so labour productivity in industry grew by 6 per cent per annum. The growth of employment in construction, trade, transport and financial services exceed 6 per cent per annum![1]

The policy prescription that emerges from the above analysis and data is that to maximise the growth of employment all one needs to do is to maximise the

---

1. All the above data have been calculated from the tables in the *Economic Survey 2003-04,* and the Ahluwalia Committee Report on Employment.

growth of labour productivity in agriculture and industry. To cite just one piece of episodic evidence of the large multiplier effect on employment of growth in industrial output, every additional vehicle manufactured and sold in India generated 5.31 jobs.

The experience of the mid-nineties contains unambiguous evidence that it is entirely feasible to absorb all entrants into the labour force by raising the rate of industry and agriculture. 1992-93 to 1996-97 saw a 7.2 per cent GDP growth rate, and a 10 per cent growth in industry. Despite a huge slump in the following three years, when industrial growth fell from 13 per cent in 1995-96 to 3 per cent in 2000-01, non-agricultural employment rose between 1993-94 and 1999-00 by 28 million. The rate of growth was thus a whopping 2.7 per cent per annum. Growth during the four 'Congress' years must have been even more spectacular—probably of the order of 3.5 per cent per annum.[2] Against this, the growth of population in the seventies and eighties (and therefore the maximum possible growth of labour force in the nineties) was just over 2 per cent.

These figures show that if the country sustains a slightly more than 7 per cent rate of growth during the next decades, it will be able to provide all the non-agricultural jobs that the young people coming into the job market will need. In fact it will be able to absorb all the children who are being taken out of agriculture today and being sent to schools instead.[3]

This is the reason why, between 1993 and 1997 everyone who came into the urban job market found a job. This was reflected in the stationary figures of the number of people on the live register of job seekers at the employment exchanges. This remained at 36.8 million between 1992 and 1996. After that it has been rising by more than a million a year.

Growth and Equity

Maintaining a seven per cent plus rate of growth presupposes a liberal, market-driven economy. Nothing else can attain the levels of efficiency that are needed. But market-driven economies generate inequality. Competition creates both winners and losers and the gap between them inexorably widens. The last elections proved yet again, if proof was necessary, that especially in a democracy, no government that ignores the poor or sides unthinkingly with the 'winners' can hope to survive. The experience of Venezuela and Mexico, which carried out textbook IMF style reforms in the early nineties, reinforces this observation.

The Common Minimum Programme has laid this out as a directive to the present government, but if the

---

2. NSS data on which the Ahluwalia Committee Report on Employment is based do not permit separate estimation for the years 1992-93 to 1996-97.

3. There are signs that the number of jobs created by each per cent growth of output will fall. So this estimate could prove too optimistic. But I am wary of excessive dependence upon the elasticity of employment figures. In 1994-2000, it was only 0.15. This means that it required a 7 per cent increase in GDP to yield a 1 per cent increase in employment. Yet the actual figures, as shown in the text above, were totally different.

employment guarantee scheme is a patchy, expensive and unproductive way of looking after the losers, then what is a better way.

The answer lies once more in the history of the social democratic capitalist states. The way to protect the poor is not to give them handouts disguised as employment guarantee schemes, or to keep them in jobs when the enterprises they work for have become bankrupt, but to provide them with social insurance.

Social insurance consists of five components—health insurance, accident insurance, maternity insurance, unemployment insurance and old age insurance, i.e pensions.

Bismarck provided some of these for Germany in 1871. Lloyd George did it far more comprehensively for Britain in 1909. Yet today, 50 years after we became independent we have only rags and tatters of a social insurance scheme that protects not even 1 in 10 workers in the country. These 1 in 10 are the government servants—18.1 million of them who have everything, health, accident, maternity, old age pensions and of course total security of employment. As for the rest, organised sector workers have an inefficient health insurance scheme that does not always cover maternity benefits, and a provident fund scheme for their old age. Industrial workers in large firms usually have accident insurance in one form or another. That is about all. Organised sector workers account for 8 per cent of the total work force—28 million out of more than 400 million. And even among them, apart from government servants no one even in the private organised sector, has unemployment insurance.

Unorganised sector workers have absolutely no protection whatever. Apart from being inhuman, the gender bias this incorporates is unforgivable. Ninety-six per cent of all women workers in the Indian economy are in the unorganised sector. Except a few cared for by SEWA, none of them have even maternity benefits, let alone anything else.

Why has government after government shirked this humanitarian challenge. The reason most frequently advanced is that it is politically not feasible to do this for the organised sector alone, and extending insurance cover to the 375 million workers in the unorganised sector is simply beyond the means of the state.

This is nonsense. In its last days the Vajpayee government broached the task of providing some form of insurance cover for at least the non-agricultural part of the unorganised sector but the scheme was hastily prepared and would probably not have worked. However, a number of NGOs, notably SEWA, have been wrestling with this problem for several years and have come up with innovative insurance solutions that take advantage of the existing insurance companies and their existing schemes. SEWA's experience has shown that all of these schemes cost very little and have all proved profitable.

An appendix to this chapter shows that it is possible to finance a comprehensive social insurance scheme for the entire unorganised sector including agricultural workers in a manner that does not put a significant burden on the more fortunate sections of society. Its basic principles are:

1. It should be contributory. Benefits cannot be an entitlement. They will have to be earned.

2. The contribution should pay only a small part of the benefit. The bulk of the money should come from the rest of society as a social obligation to a sector of the economy without whose contribution the economy literally cannot survive. This can be taken in one or more of several ways such as a payroll cess or a surcharge on the income and corporate tax.

3. The bulk of the money should be levied from a sector of the economy that is extremely well off, whose income is automatically shielded against inflation, which is most heavily dependent upon the informal sector workers, and which pays almost no tax today to the exchequer. This is the retail trade sector–shops. The appendix shows how a fairly modest floor tax upon more than 2 million 'pucca' shops can generate over Rs. 20,000 crores a year for the social insurance fund. In all, it is possible to raise Rs.35,000 crores a year to fund such an insurance scheme.

4. NGOs like SEWA should have a crucial catalytic role in ensuring that all unorganised sector workers are made aware of their rights, pay their dues in time and collect their benefits with the minimum of inconvenience and delay.

To sum up, the ideal way to combine GDP growth with employment growth and with true caring for the poor is to combine an orthodox strategy for maximising industrial growth with a comprehensive programme for providing social insurance. Insurance and not handouts is what the poor need most today.

APPENDIXA - 16.1

Social Insurance for the Unorganised Sector

The Congress-UPA government has committed itself in the National Common Minimum Programme to reconciling more rapid growth with justice and equity for the poor. As proof of its intentions it has passed the National Employment Guarantee Act. But there is a far more potent, and far less expensive way of benefiting the poor of India, that has received only cursory attention so far. This is the provision of social insurance for the working class. The difference between the two is not small. By the most generous estimates, the NREGA will provide an income supplement through 100 days of employment to about 30 million persons. An unemployment insurance scheme for the organised sector alone will provide an income supplement to the same number, at a time when they need it most. But this figure is dwarfed by the number that would benefit, and benefit in ways that completely transform their lives, from a social insurance scheme for the unorganised sector.

Strangely enough although India has been industrialising for almost 140 years, and although we have been a free country for almost 60 of these years, no government has even broached the challenge of setting up a social insurance scheme even for the organised sector, let alone the unorganised. The callousness of Indian ruling class stands out in sharp contrast to the social conscience displayed by Germany, a country that has not distinguished itself by its humanity in the 20th century. The German states took their very first steps towards the creation of a unified and protected national market in 1848. From that point it took Bismarck only 23 years to introduce the first legislation to protect workers against sickness, accidents and unemployment.

The UPA government has set up a National Commission on the Unorganised Sector, and this commission has given it a preliminary report on social insurance for the unorganised sector. But little is known about the recommendations it has made. A government that has passed the Right to Information Act has preferred to continue working in the most untransparent manner possible even on a subject of no conceivable political sensitivity. What little has appeared in the press suggests that the report has suggested a scheme that is unoriginal in its suggestions for financing and inadequate in its suggestions for relief.

The following paper attempts to outline a scheme for providing essential minimum insurance coverage to workers in the organised sector, on a financially sustainable and administratively feasible basis.

The Existing Situation

In 2001 there were 368.89 million workers in the unorganised sector, who made up 92.5 per cent of the work force. Of them 236,17 million were in agriculture. The balance were distributed as follows:[1] Manufacturing: 41.26 million; Trade 36.83 m; Construction 16.44 m; Transport 11.54 m; Mines 1.26 m; Financial services 3.4 m; Electricity 0.28 m; Personal (domestic) service 21.71m. The total number of workers in the unorganised sector outside agriculture amounted to 116.28 million.

These workers enjoy virtually no protection against illness, accidents and old age. Women are particularly vulnerable as, by one estimate, 96 per cent of all female workers work in the unorganised sector. An idea of their vulnerability may be had from the fact that in the most pressing of their needs—health—sample surveys by SEWA and the NSS show that of the average of Rs. 319 per capita spent on it in the country 75 per cent comes from the patients themselves. But these average figures are deceptive—in Gujarat the bottom 10 per cent of families spend nearly 100 per cent of their average disposable incomes on health and go into heavy debt to do so.[2] There is no protection for maternity and none for old age.

There have been some patchwork attempts to provide social insurance but these have been so ineffective as to virtually be non-

---

1. Ahluwalia Committee Report, Table 2.13.

2. Subrahmanya, R.K.A. (2000). "Welfare Funds: An Indian Model for Workers in the Unorganised Sector", in Renana Jhabvala and R.K.A. Subrahmanya, *The Unorganised Sector: Worker Security and Social Protection*, Sage Publications, p.25.

existent. There are six central welfare funds created by central legislation funded by a cess levied on their products. These are:

1. The Mica Mines Labour Welfare Act, 1946;

2. Limestone and Dolomite Mines Labour Welfare Act, 1973;

3. Iron Ore, Manganese Ore and Chrome Ore Mines Labour Welfare Cess Act, 1976;

4. Beedi Workers Welfare Cess Act, 1976;

5. The Cine Workers Welfare Cess Act, 1981; and

6. The Building and Other Construction Workers Welfare Cess Act.

The Kerala government also set up a number of welfare funds over the years, but these were funded by contributions from the workers and employers. The experience of the two systems has shown that the tax (cess) based funds are more effective at raising money, and have generally worked better. The Kerala Funds coverage was poor, funds limited, administration (through separate boards for each fund) cumbersome and administrative costs exhausted most of the funds that were actually collected, leaving very little for actual welfare activities.[3]

The actual number of workers covered by the central welfare funds is pitiful. Figures for all six are not available but three of them, the iron ore mine workers, the limestone and dolomite workers and the *beedi* workers covered 77,735 ; 53,549 and 2,734, 295 workers respectively, i.e a total of 2.865 million workers. Add an equal number for the remaining three funds and the total still comes to 5.73millon out of the 58.96 million workers in manufacturing, construction and mines sectors.

Disbursement is a problem. The benefits they provide are not merely meagre but much less than the money they collect. The actual amounts disbursed in 1993-94 amounted to a mere Rs. 79.65, Rs. 96.15 and Rs. 24.92 per worker in the above three welfare funds. Although the funds have listed a host of purposes for which they intend to disburse money, including accidents, sickness, maternity, education and housing, in practice most of this money had been

spent on health. A little has gone towards education of children. In practice there were no mechanisms for disbursement on other grounds. The inclusion of other goals seems to be a wish list made up by well meaning draftsmen rather than a feasible objective.

While benefits are meagre even the money collected by the funds does not get spent. In 1992 the limestone workers fund had spent Rs. 21.6 m but had an unspent balance of Rs. 129.3 m. The *beedi* workers fund had spent Rs. 99.6 million but had an unspent balance of Rs. 319.4 million. It seems that most of the intended beneficiaries either do not know of, or are not able to access the funds. Some form of entitlement system needs to be put in place that gives workers the right to demand and obtain help.

The system of registration of potential beneficiaries under each scheme has been ineffective. The common method is to make the employers register their workers. The employers have not cooperated. As a result, in even the *beedi* workers, one of the oldest, most stable and easily identifiable industries, only 2.7 m out of 4.3 m workers are registered. One doubts if even a fraction of construction workers are registered, or receive any benefits. Their fund is supposed to be funded by a 2 per cent cess on cost of construction. I have never heard of this being actually billed or deducted, except perhaps in a few very large public sector projects.

A particularly problematic area is maternity benefits. Women make up a third to half of agricultural workers, but have no protection. The existing attempts at providing maternity benefits barely scratch the surface of the problem, and are all urban or semi urban. Existing legislation is confined to the organised sector, and even here, a 1996-97 study in Tamil Nadu showed that barely half of the statutory beneficiaries were aware of their rights. Only 10 per cent received even part compensation and less than 6 per cent received full compensation according to their entitlement. Bribes and red tape took care of the rest.[4]

Conclusion

The conclusion reached by Subrahmanya and Jhabvala was that while a centralised, government backed system was better for collection of money for unorganised sector insurance,

---

3. *ibid*, pp. 62-72.

4. Swaminathan, Mina (2000). "Worker, Mother or Both; Maternity and Child Care Services for Women in the Unorganised Sector, in Jhabvala and Subrahmanya: *op. cit.* p. 126.

its disbursement needed to be decentralised with the maximum use being made of local bodies and NGOs. While these are sound principles, coverage is not likely to improve until the workers are both *entitled* and *motivated* to demand the protection that is their due. The experience of SEWA and some other NGOs with group insurance schemes for women suggests that workers will only begin to insist upon their benefits when they also make a contribution to their insurance.[5] That contribution becomes their entitlement. Paying it empowers them.

The scheme outlined below is based upon the above experience.

Financing the Social Insurance Scheme

The basic principle behind the scheme of financing outlined below is that the sectors that use unorganised labour most intensively barring agriculture) should bear a part of the cost of insuring them. Funds can come from four sources:

a) A small cess (e.g. 1/2 per cent) on Mining, Manufacture, construction and major services such as hotels, restaurants, finance, transport and communication.

b) A small cess on shopkeepers. This could be based upon the floor space occupied by their shop.(Retail establishment are among the main users of unorganised sector workers, especially in local transport, storage, packaging and so on.)

c) A small additional market cess (e.g. 1/2 per cent) on sales of agricultural products in *mandis*.

d) A monthly premium from the insured.

These are elaborated below:

a) A half per cent cess on the gross revenues of mining and manufacturing enterprises would yield approximately Rs. 7,000 crores.[6]

b) If an average cess is imposed on all 'Pucca' shops of Rs. 5,000 a month (ranging from Rs. 1000 in small towns to Rs. 10,000 in metropoli), for up to 1000 sq. ft. and *pro rata* thereafter, it could yield Rs, 16,800 crores a year.[7] This may look like a lot, but remember that this is the most lightly taxed sector of the entire economy.

c) A half per cent cess on market arrivals of foodgrains and cash crops would yield about Rs. 2,000 crores.[8]

d) The yield of pension premia would depend upon the number of persons who enrolled themselves. If 270 million agricultural workers are enrolled and the premium is only Rs. 2.50 per day for 200 days of work, i.e Rs. 500 per year, it would be Rs.13,500 crores.

e) Non-Agricultural workers can afford to, and may want to pay much more. Some NGOs estimate that they would happily pay Rs. 10 per day. Their benefits would therefore be correspondingly higher.

Premium collected from 100 million workers paying an average of Rs. 10 per day for 200 days a year = Rs. 20,000 crores.

Total resources of the Social Insurance Scheme (100 per cent coverage) = Rs. 59,300 crores.

1. Utilisation

1. Health, accident and disability (including death): These are hazards against which life insurance is already available in the country. A number of NGOs have therefore taken the lead in organising group insurance schemes and persuading the LIC and other insurance companies to issue the necessary coverage. In 1995-96 SEWA organised group insurance schemes with LIC and GIC to cover

---

5. *ibid.* Mirai Chatterjee and Jaishree Vyas. "Organising Insurance for Women Workers", pp. 74-89.

6. By CMIE data in 2001-02 the estimated gross sales of industry and mines and selected service industries was Rs. 1,077,300 crores. By 2004-2005 it will have risen to at least 1,400,000 crores in current prices.

7. An approximate estimate based upon the 2001 Census shows that there are about 2.8 million shops in 'pucca' i.e concrete roofed buildings in the urban areas of the country. According to the Census there are 7.823 million shops and offices in the urban areas. It is assumed here that shops and restaurants account for 75 per cent of these. The Census also says that 44 per cent of all 'houses' in the urban areas have concrete roofs. This proportion is applied here to obtain *pucca* shops.

8. Based on estimate of value if agricultural production of Rs. 550,000 crores, estimated value of cash crops as half of total and a 40 per cent market arrival of foodgrains.

various kinds of hospitalisation for sickness, accidents and disability and life insurance for at as little as Rs. 15 per year.[9] Even if the nationwide cost of a comprehensive scheme is as high as Rs. 100 per year, the annual cost of insurance for 370 million workers would work out to be Rs. 3,700 crores.

Getting everyone enrolled would require the help of all NGOs in the field. They could render a signal service.

2. Maternity Benefits

At present commercial insurance companies are not prepared to provide maternity coverage because, they claim, that maternity is not accidental or unforeseen but is planned. Yet this is perhaps the most important form of insurance that women workers in the unorganised sector need. However, SEWA and a number of other NGOs have been running maternity insurance schemes of its own for several years, and their experience can be a valuable basis for framing a contributory maternity benefit scheme. One way to ensure maximum reach and effectiveness would be to make maternity benefit a part of the Integrated Child Development Scheme and modify it accordingly. The ICDS has the requisite high priority, and will soon have the national reach.

The annual cost of maternity benefits would be of the order of Rs. 10,600 crores. This is worked out as follows:

Total female labour force in 2002 = 170 million. Of which unorganised sector= 155 million.

Benefits: a) Medical expenses = Rs. 5,000 per child. b) Six months income support at Rs. 1,000 per month. Total = Rs. 11,000 per child. If benefits are limited to 2 children total expense per employee over her lifetime = Rs. 22,000.

Total lifetime cost of scheme = 22,000 times, 155 million = Rs. 341,000 crores. Spread over 30 years, the average working life of most female workers, the annual cost = Rs. 10,600 crores.

Thus summing up 1 and 2, the annual recurring cost of disability, materity and life insurance will amount to Rs. 14,300 crores a year.

---

9. 43,700 women were insured for a premium of Rs. 655,000. A total of 318 women availed themselves of the insurance. *ibid.* p.87.

3. Old Age Pensions

By far the most expensive and ambitious scheme would be the provision of an old age pension. This would have to be modest. But how modest? The pension suggested here is Rs. 500 per month for agricultural workers and Rs. 1500 per month for non agricultural/ urban workers. At present prices this is just sufficient to meet the basic food needs of the pensioner, but no more. However from the social point of view its importance should not be minimised. For agricultural workers it will make the difference between parents being a burden on their children—something that is becoming increasingly onerous with the gradual break up of the joint family, and their not being a burden. It could therefore spell the difference between the continuation of the protection afforded by the joint family and its withdrawal.

In the cities the pension would have to be geared to payments, but at current prices it would have to average Rs. 1500 per month.

Some idea of the cost of such a pension scheme may be had from the following calculation:

1. Agricultural

Pension to be paid: Rs. 500 per month = Rs. 6000 per year

No. of persons reaching 60 every day = 10,000

No. of persons per year = 3.65 million.

Insured work force (75 per cent of total) = 2.7 million

Average life expectancy = 15 years

Peak number of insured = 22.5 million.

Peak pension payment = Rs. 24,600 crores per year

2. Non-Agricultural

Pension to be paid: Rs. 1,500 per month

No. of persons reaching 60 per day = 3,000

No. of persons per year = 1.1 million

Insured work force (60 per cent) = 660,000

Average life expectancy = 18 years

Peak pension payment = 10,700 crores

Total annual peak pension payment = Rs. 24,600 cr. + Rs. 10,700 cr. = Rs. 35,300 crores per year

Gross Cost of Social Insurance = 14,300+35,300 = 49,600 crores

Net Annual Surplus = Rs. 9,700 crores

Surplus Grossly Underestimated

Even the above account looks healthy but understates the true surplus of the fund by a huge margin. First, to qualify for the old age pension people should be contributors for a lock in period of at least 8 years. In that case the first payments will start being made in year 9, and the peak figure of Rs. 35,300 crores will be attained in year 27 (18+9) of the scheme.

Assuming that the pension fund is totally autonomous and that its funds are cautiously invested to yield no more than 10 per cent per annum, the capital corpus of the fund in year 9, the first year of pension payments, will be the sum of the unspent portion of the resources for 8 years plus the interest, dividends and capital appreciation accrued upon it at 10 per cent p.a.

1. Pension fund corpus

1. Surplus from annual collections plus interest thereupon:

Rs. 45,000+49,500+54,450+59,900+65,885+72,170+79,690+ 87,660=Rs. 514,255 crores.

2. Pension Fund income

2a. Annual interest income accruing on this corpus = Rs. 51,425 crores.

2b. Annual gross income of pension fund = Rs. 51,425 + Rs. 59,300 crores = Rs.110,725 crores.

3. Withdrawals (from 1 year 9)

These will start at Rs. 4,200 crores in year 9 (3.65 m. multiplied by 6,000 workers in agriculture and 1.1 m. times 18,000 in non agr., work force) and will rise to Rs. 35,600 crores in year 27. So the average withdrawal for 18 years will be Rs.20,000 crores per year.

Average annual unspent balance from year 9 to year 27 = Rs.89,275 crores.

By year 27 increase in corpus will be 18 times Rs. 89,000 crores plus interest @ 10 per cent p.a on the accretion to corpus. Total corpus of the pension fund in year 27 when outgoings peak will therefore be more than Rs. 5,000,000 crores.

Conclusion

A fund on the above lines will not only be totally self-financing, but after an initial lock-up period, the benefits can be increased gradually to keep pace with inflation and population growth, and extended to more types of healthcare and to education.

17 | Another India is Possible

Basic Needs, the Unorganised Sector and Science in India

VIVEK MONTEIRO

"Science is the cognition of necessity."

— *D.D. Kosambi*

"Democracy might therefore almost in a sense be termed that practice of which science is the theory."

— *Joseph Needham,*
The Grand Titration

"The people of India have voted decisively in the 14th Lok Sabha elections for secular progressive forces, for parties wedded to the welfare of farmers, agricultural labour, weavers, workers and weaker sections of society, for parties irrevocably committed to the daily well being of the common man across the country."

— *Opening sentence of the Common*
Minimum Programme

For the daily well being of the common man or woman across the country, another India is necessary. This paper looks at the question—Is it possible?

Introduction

The year 2004 could go down as a turning point in the history of our country. It represents the point at which a 20 year ascendancy of the right wing communal forces was checked and reversed at the polls. It could represent the beginning of a further process of containment, constriction and isolation of right wing communal politics by the democratic choices of the majority of Indian citizenry. But it could also be the other way around. In a sober appraisal, we also must realise that there was nothing irrevocable about the last elections. Communalism did perform rather well electorally in several states. It may be down but not out. It is therefore important to correctly assess the recent elections and chart a proper course for the decade ahead to consolidate and transform the recent electoral gains made by secularism/pluralism into something stronger, something irrevocable.

Two observations are pertinent at this point. Firstly, that the communal combine achieved notable electoral success in several predominantly tribal districts and backward regions where its front organisations had been working systematically for several years. Secondly, that in democratic elections in India, it is the votes of the unorganised sector which largely determine electoral outcomes. In urban areas, the slum dwellers and urban poor, in rural areas, the small and marginal farmers, the landless, artisans and those working in traditional industries, small trades and services constitute the bulk of the voting electorate. In the tribal dominated areas, almost the entire population belongs to the unorganised sector.

The ascendancy of the communal right wing in the eighties and nineties was based on political mobilisation of, and increased support from, many of these sections through communal cultural activity, mass ideological intervention *via* a section of the mass media and the educational system, communal polarisation through competitive chauvinism and riot-engineering, and mobilisation of financial resources from both government and corporate sources, and the foreign funded/corporate funded NGO sector to patronise these sections.

It was also not coincidental that the communalism grew hand in hand with the growth of neo-liberal economics. The communal right wing was the favoured political choice of international governmental and corporate interests who have a vital stake in the current Liberalisation-Privatisation-Globalisation (LPG) programme.

As will be argued later in this paper, it was not only the organised sector which came under attack under the LPG programme—its impact on the unorganised sector was no less adverse. LPG made it more difficult for the unorganised to survive. It sharpened the scramble for scarce jobs and means of survival. The cultures of the unorganised are the cultures of survival. One version, based on narrow mindedness and competitiveness as a value system, also glorified by LPG, engenders ethnic strife and communalism, which is utilised for political advance by the communal right wing.

Another important if unsurprising lesson of the last election is that in a society which remains democratic, policies which consistently hurt the majority will be thrown out sooner or later. This time, communalism was laid low by economics. Without a proper review of economic policy it could be secularism's turn to be dismissed the next time around. And after that, who knows—could it be the turn of democracy or even India itself?

What Constitutes the Unorganised Sector?

What is this unorganised sector (henceforth UOS) which is so important when it comes to elections? What constitutes this sector?

In cities like Mumbai or Delhi, there are several lakhs who earn their livelihood working in occupations such as:

- Workers in small industries.

- Domestic workers.

- Auto rickshaw drivers.

- Shop workers.

- Loading and unloading workers.

- Construction workers.

- Sex workers.

- Hotel and restaurant workers.

- Ragpickers (waste reprocessing).

- *Papad* rollers.

- Hawkers.

- Small shop vendors.

- Security guards and so on...

In India's villages, the crores of small farmers and the agricultural labourers belong to the UOS. Traditional industries like *beedi* rolling, handloom weaving, basket-making and fishing, each provide livelihoods to millions of working people and their families. In occupations such as *beedi* rolling and *papad* making, the workers are for the large part, women and their children.

According to available statistics, there are more than 400 million working people (employed persons above the age of 15) in our country. Out of these only 28 million (7 per cent) belong to the organised sector. Putting it differently, about 9 out of 10 Indians belong to the sectors which are not organised—the self employed, small enterprises, small farmer, landless labour, artisan, traditional, informal, marginal sector. Only 1 out of 10 Indians occupies what is commonly termed the *mainstream*. Those outside the mainstream are termed as the marginalised.

A Question of Terminology

The margin is the narrow blank strip on the left side of the page. If 90 per cent of the page is in the margin, the page must be upside down. What we call the mainstream is in the demographic margin. What we call the marginalised constitutes the demographic mainstream of India today.

In a democracy each citizen is a single value. Democratically speaking, our discourse and its terminology are upside down. Scientific discourse demands that our concepts and our terminology be turned right side up to conform to our specific social reality. It is unscientific to place the majority in the margin. It would be more correct to refer to the affluent as India's marginal sector. But the conventional mindset is so pervasive and resilient to change, that rather than risk confusion it is better to abandon terms like 'marginalised' in this paper and use an alternative terminology.

The other currently popular term for our subject of discussion is the 'informal sector'. This term has much in common with the term 'informal education'—a term used for the largely second class education which is now offered to school dropouts to comply with a constitutional mandate. Implicit in this terminology is the acceptance and tolerance of substandard options, by otherwise well meaning people, for a large number of young Indians on the plea that it is an improvement on their present condition. In a democracy, with its 'one person one value' principle, again, this is not satisfactory. We cannot use this terminology either.

We could use the term 'the common man', but this has the defect of gender bias.

Finally, let us use the term 'unorganised sector' for this category, that is actually the national mainstream.

What is the Unorganised Sector?

What is the unorganised sector? Extremely diverse in composition, it has many common characteristics.

It is a largely undernourished sector. In 1999-00, 77 per cent of rural households in India were below the poverty line with daily consumption standard of 2,400 kilocalories (kcal) per person. Average rural consumption in 1999-00 was only 2,149 kcal, down from 2,183, 6 years earlier, and 2,266, 20 years before that. At the end of a decade of LPG 'reforms' and accelerated GDP growth rates, evidently, mainstream India had less to eat. Why and how did this happen?

It is a sector which includes the growing numbers of unemployed and the underemployed.

It is largely an unauthorised sector. More than 60 per cent of Mumbai lives in illegal, unauthorised structures—slums. To obtain the basic necessities like shelter, water and electricity, Mumbai's mainstream is routinely compelled to commit further illegalities. The hawkers and vendors, whose days begin before dawn, have to daily break the law to provide fresh vegetables, fruits and other necessary services to the city, because their trade is unauthorised.

The large unauthorised and therefore illegal economy of the city is regulated by the underworld. With so many livelihoods regulated by gangster networks, it is not surprising that the underworld is seen differently by the underclasses. When society's mainstream is relegated to the realm of illegality, it is not an aberration when criminals get elected in democratic elections conducted under the rules of the election commission where citizens can vote without fear or favour.

It is also a sector where a large number are unregistered. Born in village homes, without birth certificates, having dropped out of school without leaving certificates, forced to migrate to distant cities for work, living in unauthorised slum dwellings, very often without any identity card or ration card, for many their name on the voter list is the only record of their existence as Indian citizens. (This too is sought to be denied, by a writ petition filed by well-known intellectuals in Maharashtra.) For many, the work they perform, like garbage sorting and waste reprocessing, or domestic service, though essential, is not supported by any documentation. It remains undocumented, and unaccounted for.

It remains not properly accounted for, because the attention received by the sector is also 'informal'. Contradictory statistics abound because the sector is not seen as deserving serious organised study. For example, in the LPG era of the nineties, the percentage of the population below the poverty line is shown as declining at the same time that the percentage of the undernourished increased.

There are many other common characteristics. It is an unprotected sector. The UOS elect the law makers, but there are no laws which make their existence legitimate or easier. Insecurity is endemic. Survival is difficult, even when one is young and in good health. For the old and infirm the only prospect is often death by starvation.

It is undereducated. There are 400 million illiterates in India. All belong to this sector. Seventy-five per cent of all Indian children do not pass high school. Almost all end up in the UOS.

The major problems facing the country today, of poverty, unemployment, child labour, undernourishment, child and mother mortality, food insecurity, endemic disease, urban slums, school dropouts and out of school children, crime, displacement and so on... are all problems of the unorganised sector.

Not a New Problem

The unorganised sector has never received sufficient recognition as a problem requiring serious, sustained intellectual attention. It has never been the central concern of economic policy. The neglect of this sector in the dominant discourse is not new. From ancient times,

Indian society has tolerated the exclusion of the majority from what are today considered basic needs and rights and in fact enforced their deprivation through the system of caste and untouchability. This tradition of exploitation and subordination continued during the medieval and colonial eras. It was only during the Independence struggle that ideas of equality first enter the Indian political and social discourse, through different streams. The efforts of pioneers as diverse as Phule, Ambedkar, Gandhi, Nehru and Bhagat Singh all contributed to this agenda.

In post-Independence India, it was assumed that the problem of the unorganised sector would get resolved as a collateral of the development process, based on a modern capitalist mixed economy in the Nehruvian paradigm. The growth of the public sector did give some access to many basic services and needs to broad sections of society for the first time in our history. But this minimal access was much too insufficient to make a decent life possible for the vast majority of Indians. The unorganised sector, excluded from progress and economic security, continued to grow and expand. It was this basic failure of the Nehruvian paradigm which led to the re-emergence of right wing politics and economics culminating in the full-fledged adoption of the LPG paradigm at the beginning of the nineties.

The Modern Problem

One of the main arguments for the shift to the LPG paradigm was that only accelerated development through the trickle down effect would take care of unemployment and poverty. The LPG package of import liberalisation, liberalisation of financial markets, foreign investment, privatisation of public sector infrastructure, delicensing and deregulation, withdrawal of the government from economic intervention and its replacement by market forces, would accelerate growth which would in turn create employment and alleviate poverty.

This is not the place to make a comprehensive assessment of the consequences of the LPG policy for the nation, though, for a proper and thorough discussion of the prospect for India in the next decade, this is both necessary and possible. With the organised sector itself shrinking under LPG, the UOS continued to expand ever more rapidly. As a consequence of some systematic causes, LPG resulted in greater insecurity, loss of livelihood, and a general deterioration of their conditions of life for much of the UOS. For example, during the LPG period the five million *beedi* workers nationwide have seen their livelihood shrink by half with sufficient work for only three days a week. The suicides of handloom weavers in Andhra Pradesh and small farmers in Andhra Pradesh, Karnataka, Maharashtra and even Punjab are also part of the widespread LPG phenomenon of falling finished product prices and rising input costs.

Reform or Grand Apartheid?

For the majority in the UOS this period has not been one of reform of their living conditions. The word deform might better describe the impact of the New Economic Policy on their lives. It is increasingly evident that the neo-liberal economic model does not provide any solution to the problem of the unorganised sector. On the contrary, under neo-liberal capitalism, the position of many sections of the UOS becomes more and more untenable.

Nowhere is this more starkly evident than in the Republic of South Africa. At the same time that India was embarking on LPG, apartheid was ended in South Africa. Thereafter, 14 years of democratic rule (in a country in which 6 out of 7 of the population is black) has been unable to improve the lot of the majority of the black population. There are still two South Africas, one affluent and largely white, the other, almost exclusively black, living in third world slums, travelling daily in cattle truck mode, their communities devastated by violence, crime, HIV/AIDS and unemployment.

As two sympathetic observers (Phyllis and Philip Morrison, writing in *Scientific American*) put it, "We are overjoyed that the petty apartheid of public humiliation and overt disrespect has gone from public view. It is Grand Apartheid, the asymmetrical economic and social privation of a landless and unserved majority, that remains a primary challenge for this energetic country, blessed with resources and watched by the eyes of the world."

The continuing plight of South Africa is of utmost significance and bears careful study. It shows the inability of mere political power to effect significant improvement in the lives of the majority when it is not backed with the power of significant economic control and intervention by the state. Under the neo-liberal capitalist system which was left largely untouched by the political change in South Africa, the reins of economic power and the commanding heights of the economy continued in the hands of the private corporations.

Despite a lower per capita GNP, the urban poor in cities like Mumbai and Delhi are actually in some ways better placed than their South African counterparts, with better transportation, access to electricity, domestic fuel, drinking water and telecommunications. This is due to the availability of public sector services in India in these areas.

Unlike Nelson Mandela, Bhimrao Ambedkar clearly foresaw the importance of a dominant public sector for tackling the problem of endemic exclusion. The public sector was necessary not only for technological self-reliance. It was also needed for equity and equality. A re-reading of Ambedkar's *State and Minorities* is extremely relevant at this juncture.

Neo-rationality

A customary derogation of Nehruvian Socialism became one of the clichés of the LPG era. The prevailing intellectual consensus of the new economic policy was that notwithstanding the Indian Constitution, the ideological baggage of socialism had to be replaced by the more efficient, flexible and economically rational liberalisation of markets, be they financial markets, power markets or labour markets.

It was this mindset which has given us Enron. Enron is not just a failed power project with unaffordable power. (What it ultimately delivered was thousands of displaced villagers and bankrupt local small entrepreneurs, three billion dollars worth of rusting assets and an imminent claim on the Indian nation by GE and Bechtel of the unbelievable amount of Rs. 26,000 crores.) Enron is also an intellectual syndrome, an exemplar of the neo-rationality of neo-liberal economics.

The Enron project was scrutinised by both the central and the state finance and power ministries. It was appraised by Crisil and the IDBI. It got past the full spectrum scrutiny of the statutory institutions and even the courts of neo-liberal India. If in the USA, the top executives of the Enron Corporation stand indicted in criminal proceedings, under the neo-liberal dispensation not a single person in India has thus far been called to account, leave alone booked, for the Enron debacle. In the USA, Enron has drawn attention to the failure of the audit institutions like Arthur Andersen. All the institutions, policies and personnel who were responsible for Enron in India continue with business as usual, with many bureaucrats and politicians still at the helm unaffected by the developments and consequences for the nation. Enron is a symbol of a systemic failure which is far wider than many are willing to admit. Unless this systemic failure is properly analysed, Enron is likely to be only the precursor of more systemic failure in the power, financial and infrastructural sectors.

It is not difficult to see from the available documentary record where and how the figures were fudged. Also on record in these interesting documents is a mindset which postulated that India would progress only if multinational corporations became the driving force of the new economy. Enrons were needed not only for their high technology, but also to spearhead the desired regulatory 'reform'. In this fast track perspective, the root problem with the Indian economy was regulation, with a one point solution—deregulation. This mindset continues to be influential. It refuses to accept the experience across the globe which shows that there are areas like power, telecommunications, public utilities and labour, where better and sometimes stronger regulation is necessary for the common good.

The NDA Government

The previous NDA government with its characteristic hypocrisy spoke of promoting the interests of the unorganised sector, while de facto doing just the opposite. It appointed the Second National Labour Commission, stacked with members with RSS backgrounds who actually recommended further weakening and diluting the very meagre legal protection available to the unorganised sector by proposing amendments to the Contract Labour (Regulation and Abolition) Act. The Social Security Scheme for the UOS launched by the former Prime Minister and the former Union Minister for labour with much fanfare and TV publicity was an empty gimmick, lacking both legislative basis as well as budgetary provision. In fact the crux of tackling the problem of the UOS is not less, but better regulation of labour markets, requiring the strengthening of labour legislation and its extension to unprotected sections.

The Bottom of the Pyramid

The potential of making profits at the bottom of the pyramid is receiving much international attention today. While bringing lower slices of the pyramid into the capitalist market is certainly possible and important, the lowest and broadest parts of the pyramid will not yield to this approach, which has the fundamental weakness that it focuses on the poor primarily as consumers. The more basic problem of the UOS is the problem of the poor as producers. The root of the problem is the issue of productivity.

The Devaluation of Muscle Power

One of the important characteristics of the UOS, particularly its lower strata, is poor access to commercial energy. The headload workers, the beedi workers, the sugarcane cutters, the cycle rickshaw drivers, the small farmers, the hawkers, etc. all have one thing in common—their work is carried out with only their own muscle power, or at most with the aid of animal power. A strong, healthy human being can perform work at a steady rate of 40 watts. With an eight hour working day and a minimum wage of Rs. 50 per day, one kilowatt hour from the human machine costs approximately Rs. 150. By comparison, the price of commercial energy produced from fossil fuels is between approximately Rs. 2-6 per kilowatt hour. Many human producers working with only their muscle power have to compete with their products in the same market against the produce of machines powered by commercial energy. It is a highly unequal contest, which is becoming more and more unequal under the globalised competition of LPG. The underlying feature of open markets and unregulated competition is the devaluation of raw human labour.

The handloom weaver *versus* the power loom *versus* the airjet loom, the traditional farmer *versus* the tractor and combine harvester, the cycle rickshaw driver *versus* the bus are all manifestations of this devaluation. The wonder is that so many muscle power occupations still survive and so many crores of Indians still earn a livelihood from them. Of course this is at the cost of longer and longer hours at lower and lower wages. With liberalisation of agricultural imports, the largest section of the UOS—the traditional farmer and agricultural worker, is pushed into this no-win contest.

Is it Intractable? Science and the UOS

The most important problem of the next decade is the problem of India's unorganised sector. It is a problem which has proved intractable to both the Nehruvian as well as the LPG paradigms. But there are good reasons to believe that is not fundamentally an intractable problem.

"It is science alone that can solve the problems of hunger and poverty, insanitation and illiteracy, of superstition and deadening custom and tradition, of vast resources running to waste, of a rich country inhabited by starving people... who indeed could afford to ignore science today? At every turn we have to seek its aid... the future belongs to science and to those who make friends with science."

Jawaharlal Nehru, who wrote these words in 1961, believed that science could make a difference to the UOS. In the Nehruvian paradigm, the nation built technological capabilities across a broad spectrum of core infrastructural areas and basic industries mainly in the public sector. A network of science and technology institutes were set up in the government sector. With all this, the problem of the UOS was not resolved during the three decades of Nehruvian economic policy. Nehruvian science was necessary but not sufficient. It remained in research laboratories and modern industries but it never took off to the fields and threshing floors. It was assumed that modernisation would somehow take care of basic needs for the common people. But basic needs for all did not become the nation's first priority. The political and economic policies needed to make this possible did not become a problem for the nation's scientific scrutiny.

Under LPG, modern science became equated with the latest technology. Catchwords like cutting edge and state of the art became the contemporary catchwords. Self-reliance and import substitution became taboo concepts. In the minds of many, Enron was to bring cutting edge science and technology to India. Nobody in the Electrical Engineering department, or in the new School of Management at IIT Mumbai pointed out that the project was not viable and would surely collapse. Nobody there, probably, even looked at those figures—or if they did, they kept silent—a telling comment on the state of science in India. Others, who did their sums correctly, had repeatedly pointed out both what would happen and how it would happen many years before the project collapsed. The elephant was not difficult to see if one looked at it in the face.

Seeing the Elephant

Science is about doing sums correctly, it is not about fudging figures. It is all about seeing the elephant.

Nehru was not wrong in believing that science could tackle and solve the problems of poverty and unemployment. But the problem would not be solved merely by introducing modern technology or targeting the achievement of self reliance. It is not being solved as a trickle down byproduct of LPG development.

The problem of poverty must become the main concern of the development process and of contemporary economic policy. It will not be solved unless and until the problem of the unorganised sector is taken up as the first priority on the Indian agenda as, democratically speaking, it should be.

A Problem for Indian Science

The problem of basic needs for the UOS must also be seen as the most important scientific problem facing the nation today. As of now it does not even figure in the list of priority areas for Indian science. Is the scientific method not relevant in defining the priorities for a nation's scientific efforts? What does it mean to take up the UOS as a problem for science?

In the first place the 'informal' manner in which the problem has been addressed must be replaced by serious scientific study. The wholly inadequate, substandard, unreliable and conflicting statistical data on this sector has to be cleared up. An accurate, reliable and internally consistent picture of the UOS utilising the considerable tools that are available must be arrived at. Various national institutions like the NCAER, IAMR geared to study this problem must be given the mandate to do so as their prime focus for the next decade The Planning Commission must coordinate such in an efforts. Competent and committed personnel, of which there is no dearth in our country, must be put on the job and allowed to do their work honestly and without fetters.

The UOS will have to be put on the top of the academic agendas of all government funded institutions that are equipped to study issues of productivity and economic viability. The IIMs and the IITs, and various regional laboratories and technical institutes will also have to be reoriented appropriately. In fact all government funded research institutes should be given this priority and asked to define their contribution to its fulfillment in the coming decade.

Just as it is a mistake to believe that there is a technological fix for the problem, which will allow us to avoid the thorns of having to deal scientifically with matters of economic policy and political choices, it would also be a mistake to believe that modern technology is irrelevant to this basic problem.

The problem of accounting for all members working in this sector and registering each person is necessary to begin the scientific engagement with the problem. This will require and present a challenge to the most modern information technology and systems.

Just as physics is essentially the accounting of energy transfer, any area which can be accounted and audited is amenable to being addressed systemically. With reliable information, economic policy can also be addressed scientifically. The area of work and labour certainly comes in this category. There are several institutions in India, both in the government and the private sector who have all the necessary capabilities to study and prepare effective systems for labour market regulation.

Better labour regulation is a critical input to the resolution of the problem of the UOS. The systematic implementation of minimum wages legislation across the country should be one of the key measures to addressing the provision of basic needs. There is a huge potential economic demand for basic needs. This can and should become the driving force of the Indian economy. The alternative economic policies which this would necessitate must become the prime problem for Indian economic science.

Organisation

Organisation holds the key to the solution. Enlightened labour legislation is important to organising the various sections of the unorganised workers without which there can never be effective implementation of minimum wages. It must be reiterated here that minimum wages are fixed by tripartite bodies which include employer representation.

Labour standards are good for the economy, and there is reason to believe that there can be a national consensus on this crucial issue for which governmental initiative is necessary. The area of comprehensive and enlightened labour regulation is one of the significant lacuna in the Common Minimum Programme. If we view this issue negatively as one of inspector *raj*, we will not be able to move on it.

The organisation of the unorganised into unions and cooperatives for various functions like production, credit, marketing, housing and so on makes systematic intervention possible. Organisation makes possible cost reduction through bulk purchase of raw materials, standardisation of quality and its improvement through technology upgradation, better marketing and credit facilities.

Productivity, cost and viability being key issues, organisation makes possible the application of systematic methods of science for improving the terms of trade to make daily existence less formidable and threatening for people in the UOS.

Common Minimum Programme

The CMP contains much that is significant to the problem of the UOS. It provides considerable space within its framework for beginning the necessary shift in national priorities. However, its approach is piecemeal, and the first question it throws up is, "Can the approach of the CMP be integrated into a comprehensive long-term vision and engagement with the unorganised sector?"

The commitments in the CMP to enact a comprehensive legislation for agricultural labour and to strictly implement minimum wages for them, for an umbrella social security legislation for the UOS and for a law to guarantee minimum employment, are highly significant measures that have the potential to galvanise and reorient the entire nation.

There are several specific areas where it is possible to make a dent in a few years of self-reliant, concerted and focused efforts, which can build the credibility and momentum for bigger challenges subsequently. These areas are all within the purview of the Common Minimum Programme. Some examples:

Food security and nutrition is a core area for the UOS. Increasing average consumption by four kilos of foodgrains per month per capita will take the bulk of the poor across the consumption poverty line. The total amount of foodgrains required for this is less than the total amount that is unaccounted for each year in the public food stocks. Strengthening the public distribution system, revamping the public sector FCI, with the tools of scientific management and the cooperation of the employees unions and officers associations is an entirely feasible package of measures to achieve this end.

If the same attention that is given by the private sector to making soap and cosmetics available in Indian villages and urban slums is given to bringing available safe drinking water there, it will not take the decade to solve the problem of drinking water for every Indian.

In Solapur, in Maharashtra, a township of 10,000 decent dwellings which will house 50,000 *beedi* workers and their families is nearing completion. Built without a rupee of World Bank funding or any other form of international assistance, the project has been entirely funded from the provident fund savings of *beedi* workers and the funds in the welfare funds which have accumulated through the cess collections under specific legislations enacted for *beedi* workers. They were organised first into a union to obtain implementation of the minimum wage and other basic regulatory legislation and thereafter in a cooperative to plan, execute and manage a major housing project of this kind. If this is possible with *beedi* workers, whose minimum wage is the lowest of all classes of workers, why cannot it be possible for many crores of other unorganised sector workers including construction workers.

Enabling legislation can make available land for public housing. Minimum wages, social security contributions and accumulations, cooperative societies and access to credit can make possible a massive programme of housing construction which will not only provide employment and fulfil a basic need symbiotically, but also add points to the GNP growth rate. Basic needs can be good for the economy. The problem of basic needs can be tackled even if no FDI comes into the Indian economy in the next 10 years.

Education is another area where radical improvement is possible within existing resources. It is possible to provide first rate, in fact world class, mathematics and science education in all urban municipal and rural *zilla parishad* schools with some suitable curriculum and pedagogical improvements and some attention to system function. With 150 hours of instruction each year in each class assured, and appropriate training and pedagogical inputs, experiments have shown that universalisation of primary school maths is possible in backward district government schools. The natural environment of the village can provide a rich laboratory for a do-and-discover approach to learning first rate science, far superior to the CD-based multimedia learning aids that middle class children are increasingly compelled to learn from.

The commitments in the CMP in the areas of education, ICDS, cooperatives, traditional industries and occupations are also significant in this context. These commitments taken with coordination, coherence and convergence in their implementation can begin to make a difference to the common people.

However, economic policy in the months following the adoption of the CMP has not yet reflected these emphases and concerns. The recent budget, for example, reflected other priorities. Is the page still upside down? When do we get around to turning the book around?

Redefining the Priorities in the Agenda

The problem of basic needs for the UOS is tractable. The time frame of a decade is not too short. Can this be done without redefining the national agenda priorities? How can we change the national priorities? These are really the questions which have to be answered by all of us. Setting up a Commission on the UOS, as has been proposed in the CMP would not suffice to redefine the national agenda. A far stronger policy and political commitment would be necessary.

The national agenda will not lend itself easily to redefinition. Neo-liberal vested interests, both national and international, that have been trying to force an opposing agenda, will resist it. With their disproportionate influence in the electronic and print mass media, they will get heard and appear to be influential.

However, democracy cannot be timid. The people and democratic opinion will be on the side of redefinition. It will be up to the progressive sections of the political establishment, the academicians, governmental institutions and mass organisations to bring about this redefinition resolutely in the coming months. Since politics seldom changes from top down, a vigorous and sustained movement of the unorganised—taken up by the trade unions, other mass organisations and political parties will be essential to sustain the democratic pressure for the necessary changes. One can expect a large section of the media to be hostile to such change and to try to undermine and derail it. Mass organisations working in the area of culture, education and popular science such as the All India People's Science Network will have to take up the challenge of building public opinion in favour of this democratic redefinition of national policy.

In Summary

The logic of the preceding analysis points to several inescapable conclusions:

1. The problem of basic needs for the UOS is the most important problem facing India today. This must become the new national consensus for the coming decade.

2. Neo-liberal economic policies have proved incapable in addressing this problem. If anything these policies aggravate the problem.

3. The problem is not intractable. A solution of this problem requires it to be placed prominently, in fact, centrally, on the national agenda. It will effectively redefine the national agenda.

4. The problem must be tackled as a scientific problem with a comprehensive and rigorous scientific approach. The scientific and technical institutions of the country must be geared up for the effort in a mission mode lead by the Planning Commission. Mass pressure is essential for sustaining the mission against the expected opposition which will be considerable and sustained.

5. Economic policy changes, where found necessary, must not be shirked.

6. Viable and sustainable economic policies exist to address the problem. These entail facilitating the sustenance and upgradation of the various occupations which make up the UOS with government policy measures including regularisation of their existence with enabling legislation, labour market regulation, preferential market access, technology support, credit access, public sector-UOS partnership, access to quality education, organisation of the UOS through unions, social and cooperative enterprises.

7. The Common Minimum Programme has several seminal aspects which could initiate this necessary process. However, it also has internal contradictions which will have to be resolved in favour of the new consensus.

This will require us to put the issue of social equity back on the national agenda, to revisit the defining Preamble goals and Directive Principles of our Constitution.

The political benefits of such a redefinition will be considerable. It will redirect the attention of the masses of the working people who constitute the bulk of the

UOS, to a positive agenda of promoting equality through the provision of employment, basic needs and quality education for all.

This will effectively isolate the divisive communal and fundamentalist forces in the country and establish a new consensus which could be the intellectual bulwark of a 21st century India based on the ideals of Nehru, Gandhi, Ambedkar and Bhagat Singh, a modern India whose ideals coincide with the ideals of the freedom struggle and whose people continue to work on realising its unfinished tasks. Another India is not only possible. It is feasible.

18 | India: A Partnership Agenda for the Next Decade

NASSER MUNJEE

INDIA began to reform just over a decade ago in 1991. Much has changed during this period. Even an eternal optimist would have found it difficult, at that time, to foresee the changes that India has in fact been through over this period. India began dismantling an all pervasive ideology based on central planning and bureaucratically managed processes financed through institutions largely controlled by the state. Much of this impetus for change was driven largely by one unassailable fact—bankruptcy both financial and intellectual of the old order. The overthrow of the paradigm is not now in doubt; the pace of change is dictated largely by the extent of fiscal crisis and the urgency of keeping it at bay at the central, state and local levels of government. Crisis is a powerful motivator for change and in India it would seem to be the predominant motivator for change. The crisis deepens and the motivation for change becomes even more compelling with the passing of every successive year.

The characteristic of our reforms have been the unshackling of 'sovietism' from the economy; freeing up economic activity from a plethora of controls and guidelines. In all areas where the economy has been freed it has done remarkably well. Pinpoints of excellence have emerged across the board, and in certain areas India has discovered its profound wealth especially in knowledge based services. The banking sector, spurred by the entry of private banks has transformed itself and the insurance sector is poised to do the same. International trade has increased several times—especially in services—as has the attractiveness of Indian enterprises to foreign direct and portfolio investments. What are the nature of the problems that remain and how do we tackle them? This will be the main thrust of my argument in this paper.

Not surprisingly, problems remain in those areas of the economy and polity where 'sovietism' is alive and well. Much of this is still prevalent in the governance frameworks of the country at all levels which in turn determine outcomes for citizen from a policy point of view. Infrastructure development, unfortunately, continues to be in the realm influenced by the old guard and in this sense has seen the slowest and most problematic progress over the past decade. Even in telecommunications where we have witnessed staggering progress, we faced considerable policy induced problems in the course of its development. Most countries have addressed the problem of infrastructure over time and in more recent times, China and Malaysia have seen dramatic transformations over short periods of time. Why do we in India have such difficulty in tackling problems that have been mastered decades ago by others? This is the 'enigma' of infastructure in India. This, to my mind, will be the agenda for India over the next decade—to rebuild infrastructure to meet world standards.

The word 'enigma' is an interesting one. It conjures up images with respect to the cracking of secret codes by the British during World War II. Alan Turing, the inventor of computing and the computer, worked very much in this area during the war and his biographer, Andrew Hodges entitled his book *The Enigma of Intelligence*. I use the word 'enigma' to convey the essential characteristic of mystery that surrounds challenges and puzzles presented to us either through everyday experience or through cleverly crafted mind benders for us to struggle with. What is interesting is not that we are confronted with puzzles and challenges but our responses to them; and why we find it so difficult to find appropriate solutions while others have done so without grave difficulty.

The Enigma

The major part of all Indian infrastructure is owned, controlled and managed by the public sector on behalf of the citizen of India. It is the largest public monopoly in the country with the bulk of the energy sector, (till recently) telecommunications, transport (railroads, airlines, roads, bus systems, ports) municipal services, water supply all classified as above—not to speak of the social sector such as education and health. Governments at all levels have continued to invest in capital assets, much of it wastefully, employ grossly excessive staff to run these enterprises, permit huge leakages from service delivery with archaic systems for user charge collections. Citizens, for whom these services are purportedly being provided at the expense of the taxpayer, are condemned to receive erratic and low quality services some at low or zero prices cross-subsidised by others at exorbitantly high prices. Most of these consumers of services have to seek limited, expensive but effective service delivery from the private sector if they cannot invest in services themselves (water, power, health and education services are prime examples). Worse, the poorest citizen have to resort to the private sector more often at much higher cost than middle income households who receive a higher quality of service at subsidised costs. This is essentially the 'enigma'. How can one comprehend a state of affairs where utilities being controlled by the government for the specific objective of making available adequate and affordable services to citizen simply fails to do so in adequate quantity, quality and price?

The way forward for effective infrastructure development would seem to lie in extracting infrastructure ownership, control and management from the public sector to place it into classifications that involve either entirely private sector ownership or some mixture of public and private involvement. Essentially the framework for extraction would lie in three buckets:

1. *Privatisation:* Governments sell all assets and place that particular infrastructure service in commodity space dictated by market conditions perhaps with regulatory frameworks where competitive market conditions are difficult to apply initially. Governments are no longer directly accountable for the delivery of that service to citizens though over the transition they would be held responsible.

2. *Commercialisation:* Governments sweat their assets without selling them. Here the public sector commercialises a particular service by concessioning out a service to the private sector which in turn would invest in and improve existing capital assets to provide a particular service without actually buying those assets. Citizen simply pays for the services that are eventually provided.

3. *Private Financing of Public Infrastructure (PFPI):* In Britain this bucket has been termed the Private Financing Initiative (PFI). (See Annexure A-18.1.)

Much infrastructure falls in the category of public goods or services which the government would like to subsidise for citizen and hence neither privatisation nor commercialisation would be an appropriate solution. Governments in this case assume direct responsibility to see that services are provided to citizen. Can the private sector be expected to play a role where citizen cannot afford to pay for services? The answer happens to be in the affirmative. Under this option government hands over capital assets to the private sector to deliver a specified level of service to citizen and then pays the private sector for that service. Here the contract is output specified and payments are contingent on the satisfactory delivery of a service. These output based contracts are monitorable and ensure that citizen actually receive services before the government pays for them.

There is no fourth bucket apart from business as usual where governments continue to attempt to do everything themselves. Essentially the problem of infrastructure is specifying into which bucket particular areas of activity will fall and having a well constructed process paradigm for each of them. There are extraordinary opportunities under all three scenarios for both the public and private sectors to reap considerable benefits despite the fact that citizen will get better quality and cheaper services than ever before. In essence, if well constructed, the entire process will lead to a virtuous circle where everyone benefits and no one is worse-off.

Some examples illustrate the approach. Infrastructure Development Finance Corporation (IDFC) created the framework conditions for the commercialisation of Indian ports as well as creating the first PFPI in India with the concession framework for annuity financed roads. Nine such roads have been contracted out well below benchmark pricing resulting in real value for money for public investments. Both frameworks are in use and the process paradigm has also been created for ports and roads. Similar frameworks are also being created for the area of power distribution (in Karnataka and Maharashtra while New Delhi has already moved ahead), in agri-infrastructure (in Uttaranchal, Tripura and UP) and most importantly on driving the whole framework for the third bucket—PFPI.

What will the infrastructure sector require in the next 10 years? There are five principal building blocks on which investment will be based.

Strong policy frameworks which are clear and unambiguous on both generic issues for investment in infrastructure as well as for specific sectors:

1. A fiscal regime which avoids making distinctions between long-term and short-term incentives; which is also crystal clear as to what the tax benefit means to a lender or borrower (not being subject to ambiguity and interpretation); a regime that does not eschew certain types of financial products (leasing for example in the Indian context).

2. A legal process which creates an overarching environment that removes generic issues from contract negotiations.

3. A regulatory process that emerges out of a clear philosophical position of moving the system towards private sector participation, competitive frameworks and above all putting citizens first with respect to the ultimate delivery of infrastructure services. As a tribe, regulators should be well versed in the intricacies of complex frameworks and the number of regulators need to be limited to ensure consistent and impartial application of regulations. (One Energy Regulator, One Utility Regulator and One Transport Regulator should cover a vast span of infrastructure services rather than having regulators for each subsector at both the central and state levels.) The independence of the regulator is a crucial element in fostering healthy development of markets and ensuring a fair adjudication in disputes.

4. An institutional presence on the ground that can track developments, help structure project finance, ensure that sound projects do not lack for equity support, and provide frameworks through which both equity and debt financing becomes available expeditiously. In short, provide the knowledge base to link resource pools to investment opportunities within efficient financial structures. An investment bank for infrastructure related initiatives. (IDFC could well play this role—and should.)

5. Create a PPP (Public-Private Partnerships) Task Force at the Ministry of Finance and Planning Commission to design mechanisms for the overarching framework for PPPs; redesign public expenditure programmes in a way that public investments leverages private investment; create budgetary processes that facilitates PPP structures; redesign planning mechanisms that take into account short-run and long-term investment needs as well as regional and national needs. The Task Force will not only produce the overarching framework for PPPs but will create deal structures at the project level to ensure that sound processes are adopted in delivering PPP projects to the market.

These five conditions need to be further broken down into the three financial framework buckets referred to above.

Infrastructure financing will need sound specialised investment banking skills. The days of specialised institutions intermediating funds are over. The twin pillars of financial soundness in the financial sector area will be accessing capital with competitive advantage and earning a healthy rate of return on equity. Real value has to be created on the ground in creating value through innovative structuring of projects, accessing capital and applying capital efficiently over the life cycle of the project. Risk appetites differ; classes of investors differ; project life cycles offer different types of risks and returns. The future of structuring will be matching differing appetites on risk and return with project economics.

Prospects for Infrastructure

India is making gradual progress with respect to infrastructure development. The Telecommunications sector is now thriving as a result of a clear policy framework and is attracting private capital, is expanding exponentially, providing state of the art services to citizen and competition has resulted in more than halving of costs. It is an exemplar for the argument of competitive frameworks using both the public and private sector operators resulting in huge value creation to the system and to consumers.

Similar frameworks need to be created in other sectors. The road sector is being transformed with over 7000 km of roads now being commissioned. The Rakesh Mohan Report on Railways is now available and sets a comprehensive agenda for reform in the future. Four major airports are being commercialised (hopefully) next year with the first major greenfield airport—Bangalore (and Hyderabad)—though signed has yet to take off. The transport sector is clearly poised for major progress.

The laggard in the piece has been the power sector. Even here, with the passing of the Electricity Act and the closure of projects involving over 4000 MW this year, some acceleration is evident. Power trading has begun and a number of players are likely to enter the market soon. Major investments remain in the development of a national grid and the development of an appropriate power distribution system. The re-entry of private investment will be crucial for all three components of the power sector—distribution, grid connectivity and generation—with not many new entrants waiting in a queue to participate. The grip of the public sector remains formidable.

Public-Private Partnerships

The success of Indian infrastructure will depend on its ability to attract private investment to commercially viable infrastructure projects in India and the Government itself, as partner in this process, will need to answer for its own willingness to support and engender the speed with which it is willing to let go of the infrastructure services it owns and controls. It is no longer possible to blame others for the lethargy with which the process moves forward in the future. Increasingly governments will be judged not on what they possess or on how much they spend but on whether they deliver. The issue no longer remains public sector control or privatisation, not on who does what but rather on how effectively services get delivered to citizens. The focus of attention is on outcomes not inputs. This is a fundamental shift in approach and it calls for effective partnerships between public and private sectors. The problem cannot be solved unilaterally.

The UK Experience

In Britain, where the PPP model has matured over a decade of experimentation, the Government committed itself to the partnership process with respect to infrastructure and then created the institutional mechanics to carry it forward. In India, we have done the reverse. We have created the institutional form—IDFC, and have yet to adopt a philosophy of action. Left to itself IDFC can play at the edges. Fundamental reform needs fundamental commitment to reform. PPPs are a key element in the UK Government's strategy for delivering modern, high quality public services and promoting the UK's competitiveness. They cover a range of business structures and partnership arrangements, from the private finance initiative (PFI), to joint ventures and concessions, to outsourcing and to sale of equity stakes in state owned businesses. (Essentially the three buckets referred to above.) PPPs are also being used to help state owned businesses to compete and to provide improved services to their customers, while retaining responsibility for public interest issues in the public sector. With early success, the UK Government is now extending the partnership approach to an ever widening range of public sector activities, drawing on business skills to develop and implement policy and using the expertise of private sector partners to make better use of public sector assets.

In essence, the approach recognises that partnerships with the private sector help to deliver the quality of public services the country deserves. Partnerships enable the public sector to benefit from the commercial dynamism, innovation and management skills from private investors who contribute their capital, skills and experience. They provide better value for money, which means the government can in most cases deliver more essential services and to a higher standard within the resources available than would otherwise have been the case. In Britain, on an average, PPPs save 17 per cent compared to public sector alternatives which amount to £ 2 billion on a £ 12 billion programme, equivalent to 25 new hospitals or 130 new schools. In India, IDFC demonstrated this in the annuity financing of roads, where after a detailed public sector cost comparator exercise, private bids were received, which were significantly below public sector costs, for a much more timely and better quality delivery of service.

Britain's PFI began in 1979 and was extremely slow to progress in the early years. In June 1997, when IDFC was being formed in India, Sir Malcolm Bates, carried out a review of PFI and recommended that a Task Force be created within the Treasury consisting of individuals with project management and financial skills and experience, who would help treasury officials deliver good quality and practical transactions. The Task Force was headed by Mr. Adrian Montague, who IDFC invited to India in 2002 and who initiated IDFC's own PPP efforts. This provided a huge boost to PFI projects in Britain. Since the Task Force had a limited life of two years, a further review was undertaken by Sir Malcolm at the end of that period. What the review found was that partnerships with the private sector require a range of private sector skills, which it has proved difficult to nurture within the Civil Service, such as commercial negotiation skills, project

management and project structuring. He was also concerned that insufficient resources were being devoted by public sector bodies in the development phase of privately financed projects with consequent delays and a failure to secure the best value for money. He thus recommended that the British Government create a new public-private partnership managed on private sector principles to support public sector PFI procurement and PPPs, with a combination of project and financial management skills. The British Government announced in July 1999 that it would establish *Partnerships UK*. India had already created an IDFC essentially designed with the same principles in mind in 1997.

India's Agenda with PPPs for Infrastructure

The key priority for the Government of India is to increase investments in India's infrastructure services, which are largely owned and managed by the public sector. One way of focusing attention on public expenditures and how they are carried out is to undertake a Comprehensive Spending Review on infrastructure by the Government (this was the subject of the 3iNetwork's India Infrastructure Report two years ago and last year's report). Simultaneously, it may be useful to create a National Assets Register listing assets owned by the government. PPPs will be about using publicly owned assets more effectively and efficiently. The government's own objective to develop PPPs would essentially be the following:

1. To ensure that a significantly enhanced quality and quantity of infrastructure services is delivered to citizens.

2. To release the full potential of public sector assets, including state owned businesses and hence, provide value for the taxpayer and wider benefits for the economy.

3. To ensure that stakeholders receive a fair share of the benefits of PPP—as citizen, customers, taxpayers and employees.

Under a PPP, the government specifies an output required from the investment made and leaves it to the private sector to produce the results, failing which appropriate penalties are applied. The annuity financing of a road is a classic PPP transaction. The government pays nothing until the service is actually provided. The private sector finances and implements the project while the government pays for the services over a period of time. A failure to achieve specified levels of services is met with penalties. At the end of the day, the private sector can offer better services, delivered more efficiently and providing better value for money for the taxpayer than public sector investment, provided the outputs can be specified and the risks of the project are allocated appropriately to those most able to assume them.

Very often it is argued that we ought not to take PPPs seriously as the government itself can borrow much more cheaply than the private sector and therefore, bring economies to the cost of infrastructure provision. There are two rejoinders to this. The first is that in today's environment the differential spread of borrowing is in the 1.5 to 2 per cent range. Since capital expenditures form only about one-fifth of total expenditures for service provision, the savings are marginal. Second, and more importantly, the value extracted from the use of funds is much greater by far than the price paid for the funds. Better design, execution, timely delivery, maintenance and operation over the life of the facility, risk management all add up to real value.

There is a large amount of experience of PPPs worldwide which India can learn from and avoid in structuring its own approach. It is not true that the best solution to public sector problems is to transfer as much activity as possible, as quickly as is expedient to the private sector. At the same time, it is true to say that wherever PPPs have been used appropriately they have indeed been beneficial for citizens. The World Bank's PPIAF facility (Public Private Infrastructure Advisory Fund) provides technical assistance to governments and has created several 'tool kits' and infrastructure reform strategies to help government agencies think through this transformation. PPPs clearly needs to be done carefully, mindful of the initial prevailing environment that needs to be created for this to succeed. Some of these lessons are as follows:

- Asset sales can be done upfront and too quickly with no recourse to subsequent value improvements as commercialisation takes place.

The taxpayer needs to recoup some of the benefits from sale once these benefits are realised.

- Efficiency gains are underestimated! Better results are achieved than expected. In order to ensure fair pricing to citizen, competition needs to be nurtured lest a public monopoly be replaced by a private monopoly. Without competition, shareholders gain at the expense of consumers.

- Promoting a competitive environment (such as in telecom) is a key to success. The environment needs to be challenging for providers of services, with a large choice set for consumers.

- Employees of existing entities must be allowed to participate in the process and reap some of the rewards. The proceeds of PPP need to be ploughed back into infrastructure investments thus creatig a virtuous circle and an accelerating environment for infrastructure investments.

At the end of the day, the government must formulate a more strategic approach to the process. The government's object of delivering better quality of services more efficiently is clearly universal, whether it is done through public sector institutions or through PPPs by the private sector. We will need to turn away from micro issues of public sector management to macro issues of what creates long-term value. Focusing attention on a few strategic targets would be a start. Power, Education and Tourism could be a good place to start for PPPs. It must be recognised that PPPs are not simply small interventions that are being used to put some systems right. PPPs are about changing the way the government does business and the manner in which it interacts with the private sector to ensure that the ultimate consumer—citizens—get the quality of services they deserve.

Conclusions

Major transformations in infrastructure development will require major transformations in how we strategise them. Setting up one or two institutions in the same contextual environment with the same situational logic and expecting great change is simply not possible. What we need at the present time from government is a strategic position based on PPPs for the transformation of Indian infrastructure. Institutions such as IDFC can play a pivotal role of producing the governing conditions and then ensuring that the structures that are put in place attract the required investments from the private sector. It cannot do this in the absence of a willingness to see the problem from a different point of view.

Even today the government is less than keen to see private participation in infrastructure development. In the road sector, besides the nine 'pilot' projects of annuity financing, despite their success, no further projects were undertaken though some are planned in the future. Despite years of work, the commercialisation of airports—especially Mumbai and New Delhi—were transferred to the Airport Authority of India to create joint ventures if they should wish to do so. The flip-flop approach ensued with a decision finally to commercialise the airports. Despite a forward looking Electricity Act, much of the initiatives to get things done lies at the state level. Almost no progress has been made in using the private sector in the water sector, which desperately needs it. Private involvement in urban development is minuscule and the potential for reinvesting in our cities is enormous. In the logistics field, we are seeing some improvements with the port sector vigorously pursuing private sector involvement in container berths (with huge efficiency gains) and much more private involvement in support services to port infrastructure. Despite the efficiency gains at the JNPT and the P&O ports there are huge delays in managing containers on the offsite infrastructure around the port leading to delays. These are problems that were foreseen and nothing done about them.

Clearly, we need to have a clear universal strategy for PPPs in infrastructure. Whatever has been done so far has yielded excellent results. We should be pushing forward and widening the envelope as soon as we possibly can. Bertolt Brecht wrote, "It may be a mistake to mix different wines, but old and new wisdom mix admirably." We need to add much more new wisdom to a considerable amount of old that we seem so comfortable with at the present time. The second most important issue for India with regard to infrastructure is the appalling management of our urban settlements. We have simply lost the ability to strategically position them and then to manage the investment and planning needs of our human settlements. Before concluding I would like to address some of these issues.

The Nature of Human Settlements: Cities

India today cannot point to one city that has gone through a transformation that makes it resemble any major city in Asia. Why? Cities around India have been through major transformation in the past decade in order to remain magnets for business and growth in the future. Dubai, Kuala Lumpur, Shanghai, Beijing, Hong Kong, Taipei, Singapore have all been through major transformations. Future locational decisions by firms will increasingly depend on cities rather than countries. What do cities have to offer in terms of comparative advantages in their labour markets, logistics, location, connectivity and entertainment and pleasantness?

Cities in the region will compete for the business of regional players in different markets. Will we be able to survive this competition if we refuse to transform our physical spaces to respond the new realities and expectations that have become commonplace? Even if we choose to do so (which is still not clear) how will we do it? The simplest of problems are difficult to fix owing to the complexity that we have built into our governance mechanisms. Where do we start? Even the profession of town planners has disappeared as a serious profession precisely at a time when we need a new generation of urban planners to rethink strategically the purpose of our cities and to realign them with new visions. After all, infrastructure investments are a derived demand arising from this new purpose. If we have no vision what are we to invest in? Perhaps this explains the moribund state of our investment climate precisely at a time when the financial system is flushed with funds. Where are these investment opportunities? And why don't they arise when our cities are crying for reinvention and investment?

The reasons are not far to seek. At the macro level we have been too attuned to the plight of three quarters of our population which still reside in rural areas. The structure of our GDP has shifted very rapidly to our cities and especially so as the service industries have become vital to igniting growth. Perhaps 60 per cent of our GDP is now produced by our cities. Can we afford to neglect them? Who will take the first step? The way to proceed would be as follows. The Central Government needs to declare two national economic clusters around New Delhi and Mumbai and three regional clusters around Hyderabad, Bangalore and Chennai. All five cities have huge potential as business and economic centres, have developed substantial cluster economies and have huge potential to boost national economic growth. All five need to create 50 year visions for their future keeping an eye on global comparative advantage. Their transformation needs to be strategised with respect to plug and play infrastructure and world class logistics and connectivity. Public investments would be made with central help and state facilitation in a manner which leverages private investments. The latter will always follow the former and the former would depend on clear strategic intent based on long range visioning.

This exercise alone would create the expertise needed for city transformation; institutions would need to be created; expertise assembled; stakeholders consulted; detailed plans drawn up and city resources mobilised. The learning from such a massive exercise would be institutionalised which would help transform smaller human settlements in a similar manner. We must begin a process that has the potential to transform how we do things so far as cities are concerned. The task is gigantic. We need to make a very rapid beginning.

The Annexure A-18.2 illustrates a simple model of urban transformation. Cities need three components—a strategic vision, a database and a workable planning process. No Indian city has either a strategic vision or a database and has a 50 year old planning process which is all but defunct. There is no surprise that cities are in the plight they are at the present time. Not a single city in India has a sanitary engineered landfill site in 50 years of independence. We have a very long way to go. The database is crucial to understand the city and would be required to develop a strategic vision and reform the planning system. How is this model to be applied? We don't seem to care even to think about the problems we face in this realm. Any yet when investors visit countries their first stop is in its cities.

The Special Economic Zones are a special type of cluster with very specific advantages. Experiments with their development would also help to demonstrate the nature of privates sector management of common resources and may also lead to the notion of privately run municipalities as corporate entities serving their constituencies. India needs to experiment with several examples of different ways to ensure better service delivery to specific constituencies. The present form of service delivery is woefully short of desired standards.

We are fortunate in that we can learn from a number of international experiences. Cities in Europe and the USA have also been through dramatic transformations (Indianapolis, Barcelona, Manchester, Glasgow to name a few). What is clear is that a city's survival is not certain if it does not respond to the changing economies it faces. Gary Indiana, Sheffied are examples of cities that simply gave way once their dominant economy dried up leading to social misery. With globalisation, outsourcing of jobs, rapidly changing technologies, these economies can change in a matter of months and not even years. Cities need to be carefully tuned into changing conditions, how others are adapting and how one can stay on top despite these influences. It is no accident that London continues to be the financial centre of Europe—it was not for the absence of contenders but the solid work it did to keep itself ahead of the pack through developing and nurturing its comparative advantages.

Which city in India is currently researching its future? Which city has a database which even allows it to understand itself? In how many cities do we know GDP growth, its components and the trend line of its components. Without this data we are blind to our own disadvantages. Much work needs to be done, building and understanding of Indian cities and driving the institutional forms that will help them prevent the fate that has befallen so many worldwide.

Concluding Thoughts

The one part of the Indian economy that depends on public investment and management is letting India down—infrastructure. It is the key constraint to future growth and an inhibitor of optimal investments that India could attract. There are essentially two ingredients required to reform our current practices:

- Building India Together: A Partnership between the government, business and citizen.

- A strategic approach to problem solving. 'Living in the present' is a habit we have got used to. Success in this global age will depend on strategic positioning—knowing where we are going and putting in place the components needed to get us there.

This partnership is a crucial element for our future. It will spell the ultimate demise of what I have called "Sovietism"—the power of the state over its citizen.

Making partnerships work is not a simple matter. It will require frameworks of action with each partner assuming responsibility for an agreed course of action under well-understood frameworks. I have described such a PPP framework briefly for the problems posed by our present state of infrastructure. Many countries are now moving in this direction.

In the UK, over the past decade, there has been a paradigm shift with respect to the public private process. A large part of UK public services are now managed by the private sector leading to a quantum improvement in the quality and quantity of services with an equally large saving in the cost of their provision.The themes outlined in this conference will need strategic initiatives. The partnership model will be crucial in trying to address them. While Corporate India has thrived with the dismantling of 'sovietism', governance of the rest of India continues to deteriorate. Addressing this component is perhaps the most important single element for us to create a 'caring society'. A refrain often heard is "who cares?" We need to identify those who care and empower them to interface with those responsible for the quality of governance that the citizens of India deserve.

Two themes that deserve urgent attention are the promotion of 'economic clusters' around logistics hubs as a way of attracting investments and the governance and investment in our cities so critical to the development of hubs. Today our cities have become metaphors for the state of anarchy that prevails in the way we as Indians are increasingly choosing to live our lives. The deterioration of the physical form of our cities, the destruction of beauty, the building of ugliness has had its impact on the manner in which citizens interact with each other and the collapse of civic sense or virtue. These are symptoms too dangerous to ignore.

I want to conclude with a quotation from Seneca, "If you do not know to which port you are sailing, no wind is favourable." Progress will depend on our ensuring that we do not fall into this syndrome and that we tackle our problems together. Partnerships and lighthouses are the path to the future; the former cementing our ingenuity and the latter lighting up our objectives in sharp focus. Combined, we have the best chance of finding the solutions we seek.

Annexure A-18.1

Framework for Transforming Indian Infrastructure

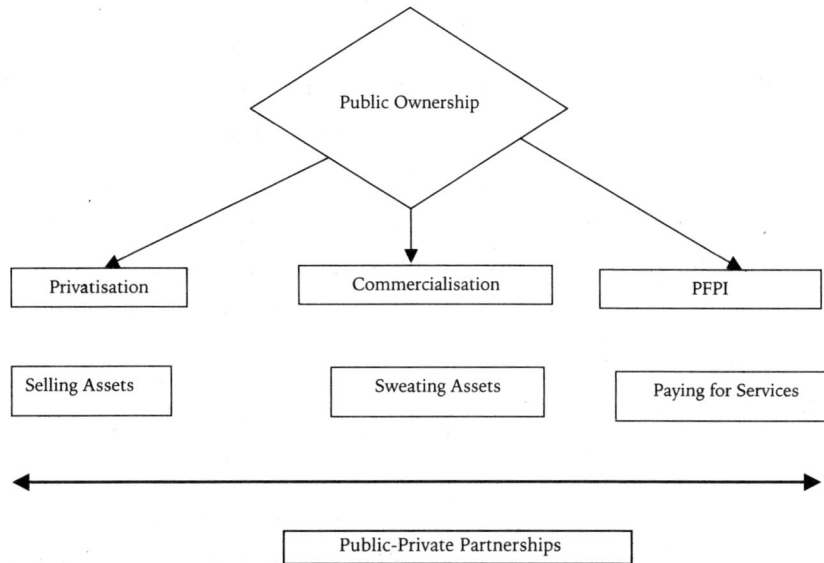

Annexure A-18.2

Cities: Defining and Urban Transformation

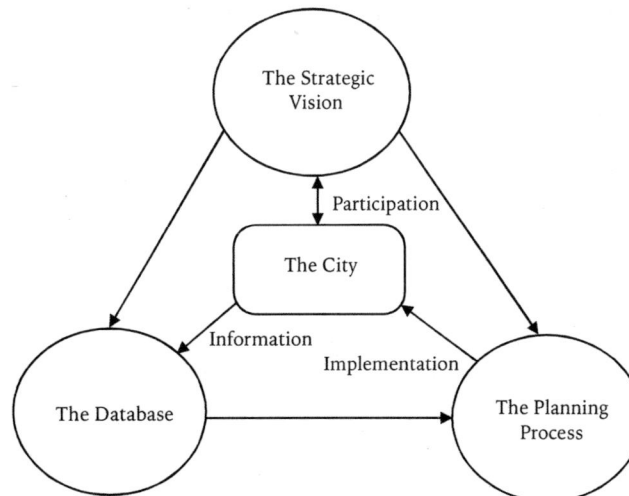

19 | Growth with Equity: Understanding Ecological Poverty

SUNITA NARAIN

The Environmental Challenge is about the Economy and Deepening Democracy

For people who live in an economy built on 'natural capital', *ecological poverty* is invariably the main cause of their impoverishment and leads to an inability to meet basic survival needs. In vast areas of the rural South, people survive within a biomass-based subsistence economy, that is, on products obtained from plants and animals. Food, fuel, animal feed, building materials like timber and thatch, medicinal herbs and other such needs are largely met through locally available biomass resources (Agarwal and Narain, 1989). The environment constitutes the survival base of millions of rural poor.

Ecological poverty can be defined as the lack of natural resources, both in quantity and quality, needed to sustain a productive and sustainable biomass-based economy. But environmental assets are fragile and their sustainability demands the creation of appropriate legal and institutional systems. In other words, environmental regeneration is not about planting trees but about the deepening of democracy in societies.

Environmental degradation, therefore, has a serious impact on the lives of rural people. A large portion of the world's rural poor today live in highly degraded lands in China, South Asia, Africa and Latin America. For such people, improvements in the Gross Nature Product are far more important than the Gross National Product (Agarwal, 1985). The poor do what is within their ability to conserve the environment and to make sustainable use of it. But they are caught in a daily struggle to survive and cannot invest in the rebuilding of the 'natural capital'. The 'economic globalisation' process is expected to leave a lot of these people untouched. The climate instability predicted for the 21st century will make life even more difficult for the world's rural poor living in degraded lands.

It is in this context that policy for poverty eradication needs a paradigm change. It needs to be built on the mobilisation of local, natural and human capital in which the poor are not the objects but the subjects of economic development.

It needs to be understood that 'ecological poverty' is a different concept from 'economic poverty'. While economic poverty is measured largely in terms of cash incomes and is almost irrelevant in a biomass-based subsistence economy. The approaches to deal with 'ecological poverty' and 'economic poverty' are also vastly different. While economists normally talk of welfare measures to deal with 'economic poverty', rural practitioners who have tried to deal with 'ecological poverty' talk in terms of 'institutional, legal and financial empowerment' with a strong emphasis on community-based property rights over ecological resources.

In this paradigm, the challenge lies in empowering and mobilising the labour of the marginalised billion to get out of their 'ecological poverty', create natural wealth, and develop a robust local economy based on that natural wealth. Villages in the developing world are usually highly integrated micro-ecosystems with numerous interactive components. Indian villages, for example, especially those situated in the semi-arid and sub-humid hill, mountain and plateau regions, are highly integrated agro-silvo-pastoral systems. In other words, each village has its own croplands, grasslands, and tree or forestlands, and each of these land-use systems interact with each other and with other components like water and livestock to yield a productive and sustainable rural economy. Changes in one component invariably impact other components (Agarwal and Narain, 1989).

The entire village ecosystem is often held in fine ecological balance. Trees or forestlands provide firewood. This helps villagers to avoid the burning of cowdung, which is used as manure to maintain the productivity of the croplands. The nutrients are gathered by the cows while grazing in the grasslands. Simultaneously, trees and crops help to complement the grasslands in the supply of animal feed. Grass is generally available from the grasslands during the monsoon period. As grass availability declines with the onset of the dry months, crop residues obtained from croplands and leaf fodder obtained from trees help animals to tide over the critical scarcity period. This finely tuned system can get easily split apart. As has happened in many parts of the developing world.

The natural assets that are restored are usually fragile and, therefore, need to be carefully managed in order to ensure sustainability. This sustainable management of the asset base is only possible if the local communities, who can also be called the local stakeholders, are involved in its management. There is clear evidence from micro-examples that ecological regeneration can lead to enormous economic wealth creation. On the other hand, there is also enough evidence to suggest that bureaucratic resource management systems have either failed or have proved to be cost-ineffective, which makes them irrelevant in a world where financial resources are limited. Therefore, policy interventions are essential to create an enabling environment for local action and resource management.

The challenge is to 'upscale' or replicate these extremely successful micro-experiences of community based natural resource management. It is often argued that these examples are not replicable. These micro-level changes have happened because of the efforts of outstanding and persevering individuals. This is precisely why it is essential for policy makers to understand the nature of the institutional and legal structures that need to be created so that change is enabled over large areas as well.

Economic Growth: A Challenge of Sustainable Resource Utilisation

As much as poverty needs to be redefined, the concept of environment also needs a revision. The concept of 'protectionist conservationism' is what prevails across the paradigms of environmental management in the Northern industrial world. But for Southern environmentalists, the concept is one of 'utilitarian conservationism'. In other words, the environmental challenge is not a conservation challenge, but one, which concerns the sustainable and equitable use and management of natural resources.

But unfortunately, in spite of this deep understanding of the nature of environmentalism in the South, public policy has lagged behind and aped the Northern conservation model. The history of natural resource use in most countries of the South, started with the state appropriating resources from local communities. It used it for extractive purposes—logging or mining—so that over the years there was rampant degradation. But as environmental consciousness grew, the state gradually moved from exploiting to protecting natural resources.

But even as nations legislated to protect the environment, they have not learnt to manage or regenerate the environment. Therefore, even if a state has policies to conserve its forests, it does not have adequate policies, which will lead to forest regeneration in the same measure. This is because unlike the industrial North, where forests can be protected as 'wilderness areas' in the South, forests are the habitats of local communities. People use the forestland for their survival. They are also worst affected by its degradation. Their involvement in its management is critical.

Instead state policy has imbued the principle of exclusion—people inhabiting protected areas are discounted, displaced, their livelihoods destroyed. It never accounts for the fact that in densely populated countries, biodiversity is not a pristine product of 'nature' but the result of millennia of human-nature interactions. In fact, it would be hard to find a piece of land where human interference has not existed for centuries. Therefore, the challenge is not to isolate but to incorporate the conflicting demands of 'endangered' species and subsequently 'endangered' humans.

Similarly, the Forest management policy has not learnt to differentiate between forests, which need to be protected at all costs—pristine forests, biological hotspots—and forests, which need to be cut and used and then regenerated. In other words, environment is still not a development challenge. Instead, environmental protection becomes an invariable conflict with development, a conflict between nature and jobs. This when what the South really needs is policies and practices to use the environment for the greatest enterprise of jobs and prosperity. It is for this reason that environmental planners must engage with development planners to evolve models of economic growth and environmental sustainability that can be replicated.

Water is the Starting Point for Change

Planners concerned with poverty eradication rarely realise that water management is their key to change. Water is not only vital for human survival but also for creating a sustainable biomass-based economy. Though substantial investments are being made in exploiting river and groundwater resources to support large-scale irrigation systems and supply of water to urban centres, these systems have rarely reached out to poor rural people.

One of the biggest environmental challenges that countries of the South face in the coming decades is to balance their increasing demand with the diminishing availability of water. Increases in population coupled with the ongoing processes of industrialisation, urbanisation and agricultural modernisation are, on one hand, leading to an increasing demand for water and, on the other, a decreased supply of freshwater, especially in the absence of effective mechanisms to regulate pollution. The future scenario is one characterised by overexploitation of water resources, decreased accessibility to clean water, and increased competition for and potential of conflict over water resources. Major institutional, policy and technological initiatives are, therefore, required to ensure an efficient, socially equitable and environmentally sustainable management of water resources.

India, for example, is one of the wettest countries in the world and yet a country that is facing a growing water shortage. It receives 400 million hectare-metres (mham) of precipitation, primarily as rain, which is supplemented by some 20 mham of river flows from neighbouring countries. But it uses only a small part of its water endowment. By 2025 AD, India is expected to use 105 mham (Nag and Kathpalia, 1975).

If all this water use was to be met from rivers and groundwater systems, these ecosystems will come under extreme stress, as is already being noticed across the country. River flows and groundwater add up to 247 mham, of which a substantial amount must flow out to neighbouring countries and to the sea (Nag and Kathpalia, 1975). But India still has an enormous amount—theoretically as much as 173 mham—that can be captured as rain or as run-off from small catchments in and near villages or towns. Capturing the floodwaters of major rivers can further increase water availability.

Two major discontinuities have emerged worldwide in water management since the 19th century. One, the state has emerged as the major provider of water replacing communities and households as the primary units for provision and management of water. Two, there has been growing reliance on the use of surface and groundwater, while the earlier reliance on rainwater and floodwater has declined, even though rainwater and floodwater are available in much greater abundance than river water or groundwater.

Theoretically, the potential of water harvesting in meeting household needs is enormous. Rain captured from 1-2 per cent of India's land can provide India's population of 950 million as much as 100 litres of water per person per day. There is no village in India, which cannot meet its drinking water needs through rainwater harvesting. Even in an arid area with an annual rainfall level of only 100 mm, one hectare of land can theoretically capture as much as one million litres of water. As there is a synergy between population density and rainfall levels, less land in required in more densely populated areas to capture the same amount of rainwater. And in such areas, there is usually more built-up area like rooftops, which have improved run off efficiency.

Water harvesting and integrated land-water management is not new to India or to many other parts of the Southern world. The art and science of 'collecting water where it falls' is ancient but this 'dying wisdom' needs to be revived to meet modern freshwater needs adequately, equitably and sustainably and modernised with inputs from science and technology (Agarwal and Narain, 1975). India's traditional water harvesting structures demonstrate the people's ingenuity at its best. Using unique modes and basic engineering skills, people living in ecosystems across the country have developed a wide array of techniques for satisfying their thirst.

Experience in India clearly shows that this local indigenous knowledge is the way to the future.

Over the 1980s, the ecological crisis in India has generated several successful community-based resource management experiences. These experiences are testimony to the potential of generating economic wealth from rainwater harvesting (Agarwal and Narain, 1999). It is important to learn from the micro-experiences to understand the policies needed for the transformation from ecological poverty to sustainable economic wealth. Many of these cases are now several years old and have reached an advanced high level of ecological succession and associated economic impacts.

'Up Scaling' Needs Institutional Change

It is important to realise that successful examples of resource management and poverty eradication remain scattered because the governance system needed to foster people's control over natural resources does not exist in the country. Therefore, the institutional framework for governance will have to be restructured keeping in mind the following principles:

Local Resource Management Demands Integrated Thinking

People living in villages know that their 'village ecosystem' consists of several integrated components—croplands, grazing lands, forest and tree lands, local water bodies, livestock and various energy sources. They know the interactions between these different systems are integral to its productive use. But bureaucracies do not understand integration. Current rural development efforts in most parts of the South are extremely fragmented—if they focus on agriculture, they discount livestock rearing, if they focus on ponds to hold water, they discount the catchment area which feeds the pond. Land is managed by one set of bureaucracies, water by another. The integration of these resources and agencies is best done through the strengthening of village-local institutions.

People's Participation in the Regeneration of Village Assets is Crucial

All new plantations and grasslands have to be protected. But since all common lands have intense users, any attempt to enclose a patch of degraded land will be strongly resented by the people, however underproductive it may be to begin with. If people's support does not exist, the survival rates of village assets like check dams, tanks will be extremely poor. It is important to note that ecologically resources like trees, grasses, ponds and tanks are fragile assets. They cannot be created and maintained by any bureaucracy.

People's Participation Will Not Be Possible Without the Strengthening of Village Institutions

Rational use and maintenance of village land and water resources needs discipline. Villagers have to ensure that animals do not graze in their protected commons, the catchments of their local water bodies are conserved and properly used, and the common produce from these lands is equitably distributed within the village. Villagers can do all this, and more, only if there is an effective village-level institution to energise and involve them in controlling and managing their environment. Deepening democracy at the grassroots is a critical determinant for ecological regeneration and local water management.

The settlement-level institution must work with a high order of democracy and transparency in decision making in order to engender cooperation and discipline within the group members. In India, village-level institutions have worked best when they are built on the Gandhian concept of a *gram sabha,* which is built on the concept of participatory democracy and not representative democracy. This is because open public forums, being more transparent by nature, work much better than small, elected village councils to bring about good natural resource management and sort out intra-community differences. Even in areas where inequality is intense, there will be greater chances of obtaining community decisions that are equitous in open village forums than in forums, which are closed and secretive. Resolution of intra-village conflicts and coordination are invariably easier in open village meetings because they introduce transparency, accountability and confidence in community decision making. Decisions taken in a non-transparent manner by a small *coterie* of village leaders rarely engender confidence within the less powerful members of the community that the benefits of their cooperation will accrue to them too, in an equitable manner.

No Village Institution Can Function within a Legal Framework that Prevents it from Taking Care of its Environment

Laws dealing with natural resources like land, water and forests will have to be changed to give people the right to improve and develop the village natural resource base. Currently, in India, the government owns a substantial portion of land and water resources in India. Natural resources are thus largely government property and not community property. The result is that village communities have lost all interest in their management or protection. This alienation has led to massive denudation of forests, overexploitation of grazing lands and neglect of local water systems. This will only change if the people get a stake in the improvement of the natural resource base by reforming the current legal structure of control over natural resources.

No Village Institution Can Function without Money

In most countries, various functionaries and agencies of the government control finances for village development. Ultimately, only a small proportion reaches the community and is spent on projects over which it has no control and for which it has not set any priority. One option is to channelise funds directly to village institutions. This approach has been successfully tried out in many parts of India and will be important to learn from.

Jobs and Growth: Using the Environment for Livelihood Security

Poverty eradication strategies will also demand ways of building economic futures of people. In large parts of the South, the answers to employment will lie in the better management of natural resources—land, forests, grazing lands and water. The formal industrial sector has never been the provider of employment in the country and in the years to come its contribution, with scale and mechanisation, will decline even further. The service economies—outsourcing including—will grow but cannot really absorb job seekers in a country the size of India. The key to employment lies in building productive and sustainable livelihoods based on natural resources. The potential is enormous—from planting trees for pulp to rearing animals for dairy farming to rearing worms for silk and growing medicinal plants for pharmaceutical industries.

In India, for instance, in spite of all efforts of the government, unemployment rates have increased over the past 20 years. The organised sector contributes only 8 per cent of total employment in the country, the rest comes from the unorganised sector dominated by agriculture and allied areas. Furthermore, the public sector—enterprises and government institutions—contribute 5.8 per cent of the total organised sector's employment creation. The trend is evident. Not only has the organised sector registered a negative employment growth during 1991-2003, but also the public sector is being heavily downsized. With capital-intensity increasing at the cost of labour-intensity in the organised sector, poverty is bound to increase. There is a similar crisis in the agriculture sector. In India, official statistics reveal that agriculture, which is the major employment-generating sector, has stopped absorbing new labour in recent years.

It is critical that employment and enterprise goes beyond the conventional economic opportunities. It is here that the challenge of sustainable resource utilisation becomes imperative. A study completed by the Centre for Science and Environment shows that trees planted for the pulp and paper sector in India can provide a fascinating model of growth with jobs in the country. Roughly 1.1 million hectares of land is required to supply the required 5 million tonnes of raw material to the industry currently. This in turn could provide employment to over 0.55 million farming families in growing wood and harvesting wood in a sustainable manner.

But this will mean that government policy will have to promote the use of wood grown by farmers on private land or by communities on degraded forestland. It also means that the Indian government cannot allow large-scale concessions over forestland by industry, as it would distort the market for farmer and community-grown wood. These are tough but strategic policy decisions, which will build the new economies in these countries.

Furthermore, governments will have to reorient their environmental policies from conservation to sustainable utilisation. In India, as in many other countries, there are many legal constraints that prohibit people from growing, transporting and marketing trees. These legal provisions are designed to protect forests, but they restrict people from regenerating forests. For instance, the Indian government has identified bamboo cultivation and its products as an important contributor to employment. But the law in most parts of the country does not allow people to grow and market bamboo. Poverty eradication will demand new innovation in managing the competing and complex needs of conservation and employment generation.

It will also mean that governments will have to take the fight to international trade forums. They will have to fight for the small producers and secure their place to compete in the international trade. They will have to argue that poor farmers compete in a world of overproduction, and cheap products because heavily subsidised. That as a result they over-work the land, over-fertilise it, over-use pesticide—all to increase production. They devalue the land and their labour to compete in unfair terms of trade. In other words, global markets do not allow them to capture the ecological costs of what they produce. Therefore, sustainable agriculture is not possible, without removing distorting subsidies in the North.

They will also have to explain that Southern governments are spending too little on domestic support—unlike rich governments—to create rural infrastructure for water security and biodiversity security, both critical to sustainable agriculture. In other words, they will have to spend more, not less, on agriculture and related activities.

Strengthening the Environmental Link in Poverty Programmes

A review of the anti-poverty programmes across the South will show that governments do not take this view of environment in their plans. Even where countries make poverty reduction a major objective in national planning, programmes do not address the linkages with resource-rights and resource utilisation. A further crisis confronts governments as they downsize and in this process end up deconstructing the public service infrastructure. The poor will become even more vulnerable in terms of accessing basic services like education and health and basic needs like water and food. In this circumstance, the only option the state has is to increase investment in the social security or welfare—just to provide some measure of safeguard against this institutional collapse.

Take the issue of healthcare. In 1990, India for instance, spent 1.3 per cent of gross domestic product on public health services; by 2002, this had reduced to 0.9 per cent. In this situation, private health services have blossomed and today, as much as 82 per cent of all outpatient visits take place in the private sector. The problem is compounded by the system, which promotes inefficiency in public institutions, leading to further decimation. The government then has no option but to support, in the name of social sector reform, the private sector healthcare providers. It gives away land at throwaway prices or directly subsidises the private sector, in the name of the poor. The hospitals are 'expected' to use their largesse to provide free or accessible services for the poor. But this rarely happens. But by now public health services are completely compromised. Worse, given the enormous disparities in income, the poor are denied access. This is increasingly the situation in countries of the South and not just for healthcare, but also for all essential public services that concern the poor.

As yet, in many countries, which have negotiated loans from multilateral agencies administrative reforms are geared towards downsizing the state. In this system, the decentralised local body for governance is viewed as a service related agency, which is more effective than the centralised state authority. But it is not viewed or strengthened as an autonomous institution capable of self- governance institution, which will deepen the state.

It is in this situation that anti-poverty policies will have to find all opportunities to build people's capacities to take charge of their resources and to secure their present. But these small and large innovations in governance need to be understood so that they can be replicated or amended. In other words, this learning ground for democracy demands careful and continuous scrutiny. This is a role that civil society organisations must play. They must be the promoter and critic in this laboratory of development.

The Decimation of the State

In Nagpur city, women gather outside a court. In broad daylight they lynch a local serial rapist. When four women are arrested, few hundred women own up to the crime. They say they killed Akku Yadav because the local police did little to stop his criminal reign of terror—they feared the court would release him and took matters in their hand.

To me, this incident is less about the women. It is more about their fear that they would not get justice. Their desperation shows just how disabled the state has become. The apparatus—of services, or law and order—is today thoroughly compromised. Broken in spirit, the state's capacities stand decimated, through deliberate abuse or apathy. For these women of Nagpur, there is no state.

Now switch to another scene—an evening lecture in Delhi. A middle-class audience is discussing the pollution of the river Yamuna, which flows through their city. This pollution is also about how the city's rich use water and the sewage system, but loathe to pay for it. The real pollution is the subsidy the rich enjoy, in the name of the poor, so that a public utility is unable to manage its business. But that is not the way this audience sees it.

They are categorical about their angst *vis-à-vis* the state. It should wither away, they believe. "We generate our own electricity with generators, we buy bottled water to drink, we have our own security agencies to guard us, we go to private hospitals to be treated." "Why should we pay for these services, why should we pay anything to the government?" So goes the rhetoric, of these rich vigilant citizens.

Was it then a coincidence, that in his Independence Day address to the nation, Prime Minister Manmohan Singh had to remind us "governments cannot be wished away". What does it mean when a nation's leader has to defend the right to the state to literally go about its business?

Whether it is a case of the state failing its citizens—Nagpur—or citizens failing the state—Delhi's rich—the fact is that, today, a system is being worked to death. We are working it to death. And helping us is the bureaucracy—the state's managers—by conveniently handing over its work to 'whosoever it may concern' without losing the perks that come with their non-jobs.

This is visible in every sphere of our lives—education, health, transport or water.

First, we deliberately disable our public institutions. We do this by not investing adequately in these services, and then in creating an interest in running inefficient and incompetent institutions for the sake of it. Most public institutions today run to pay salaries, not to deliver services to the people they are meant for. In public health service institutions, for instance, salaries gobble up 70-80 per cent of the total (meagre) funds allocated to this sector. How can such a system deliver? If its managers compromise the public system, its workers maul it; whatever is left becomes the playground of the very rich. And all of this happens in the name of the poor.

Second, we create vested interests, which then work against change. Transport is a perfect example of this. We have decimated the public transport infrastructure—railways and city buses—so that today, at best, it is a playground for petty trade unions politics, which survives on state largesse. In its place, there has come up a massive industry built on private transport—trucks, cars and scooters. The private sector has been given a free run, the argument being that it would be profitable and efficient. But few of us realise that all road infrastructure projects, being built by the 'efficient' private sector, are subsidised by the state—as much as 20-30 per cent of the land acquisition costs are borne by the exchequer in these projects.

Building a Public-Public Partnership

The deconstruction of the notion of public space and the practice of public service is evident and will cripple us enormously. But I am also clear that reconstruction will demand considerable innovation.

Let us be clear of the challenge. One, the state stands increasingly compromised, indeed decimated, in terms of its capacities. Two, the state is abdicating its role in favour of a growing and powerful private sector, which now is expected to provide everything from water to health security. Three, even as the state hands over its productive functions, it ensures its perpetuation, for its own sake or for the sake of the crumbs it doles out in the form of jobs to the poor. Four, the weakened system profits the rich, continuing to subsidise them in the name of the poor. And fifth, in all this state functionaries are ironically the single-largest beneficiaries of this dissipation as they gain by having more, even as they do less. Their perks and powers are intact. The state's stateliness is preserved with a pomp it does not deserve, all for the sake of appearance.

If we accept this, then it really means that the enemy is within. So any reform that seeks to strengthen its institutional fabric will have to be driven by its real political and public masters. In other words, the state will have to be driven to work.

How should this be done? First, I would argue we need to ascertain, quite literally, the role of government. This issue cannot be taken for granted anymore. We need to clarify what its role will be, so far as basic services, education and health and basic needs, water and food are concerned. We also must clarify government's role as the public interest regulator. This clarity of purpose is vital. For today, most government action is taken in a mindless and heartless manner. Government agencies have turned into paper pushers; they fiddle with procedures and budgets, without knowing why or what it is that they are doing. Government has become one-large bloated clerkdom.

Then, we need to plug its weaknesses. We need to critique its failures. Not so that we move to paralysis by analysis, but for the sake of catharsis by analysis. For instance, we must accept that public agencies today seriously lack expertise to manage change. We cannot continue to protect the inefficient and incompetent in the name of the public. Take water services. Everyone will agree that clean and safe water is a must for all. Yet, everyone will also agree that public institutions are not delivering this basic need. Therefore as the state falters, the private sector steps in. Today, large parts of rich urban India drinks bottled water. Remember, this is water the private entrepreneur does not pay for but simply rips off the aquifer, cleans (to some extent) and then bottles to deliver to homes. It's a rip off. But it services a need. The health costs of unsafe water are deadly for the poor. And in all this, the battered public services continue to provide subsidy to the water and sewage of the rich. Everyone will agree this is unacceptable.

But what everyone will not agree upon is the way ahead. Some will argue for public-private partnership, for them a euphemism for private take over of the publicly created facility. They believe in downsizing the state. Others will argue for control of the public institution—there should be no talk of private capital and certainly no talk of capitalist tools like pricing of water or fiscal regulations.

As I see it, both are right, to an extent. The public-proponents are right in saying that the public purpose of the water service must be maintained. But the private-proponents are also right when they say the public institution is weak in capacity and expertise. The Delhi Jal Board, for instance, has roughly 25,000 employees, far in excess of what it needs to discharge its functions as a public water utility. But what is even worse is that this is a workforce without expertise. Therefore, to do anything at all technical, innovative or specialised, it needs to call in external consultants. It needs external help because it cannot fix what it has within. Simply, it is easier to bypass than to reform.

Such a lack of expertise is a serious problem because it forces a silent takeover by parties that possess some knowledge but lots of vested interest. In all this, the role of the state as public regulator is grossly compromised because it just does not possess the ability to negotiate on behalf of public policy.

And so it happens that state institutions can work for private and sectoral interests in the guise of public interest. The system does not demand any performance or merit. It only demands complacency. Let the competing private interests slug it out.

In other words, the reform of public institutions will demand strengthening of its knowledge capacities. How will this be done? It is often mistakenly said, given the chimera of our software business, that we are a knowledge society. In fact, we must realise that we are increasingly a knowledge-proof society. Public institutions are immune to knowledge. In fact, I would say, they are insured against it. And it is precisely this insurance against change that must be dismantled. The chinks in the armour must become a hole. How? The mandate of the people, the very one our politicians love to boast about, must become our insurance for change.

References

Agarwal, Anil (1985). "Politics of the Environment", in *State of India's Environment 1984-85—The Second Citizens' Report*, Centre for Science and Environment, New Delhi.

Agarwal, Anil and Sunita Narain (1989). *Towards Green Villages: A Strategy for Environmentally Sound and Participatory Rural Development*, Centre for Science and Environment, New Delhi.

———. (eds.) (1997). *Dying Wisdom: Rise, Fall and Potential of India's Traditional Water Harvesting Systems, State of India's Environment: A Citizens' Report*, Centre for Science and Environment, New Delhi.

———. (1999). "Community and Household Water Management, the Key to Environmental Regeneration and Poverty Alleviation", *mimeo*.

Nag, B.N. and G.N. Kathpalia (1975). "Water Resources of India", in *Water and Human Needs*, Paper presented in the Proceedings of the Second World Congress on Water Resourcxes, Vol.2, CBIP, New Delhi, quoted in Anil Agarwal and Sunita Narain (eds.)(1985), *State of India's Environment 1984-85: Second Citizens' Report*, Centre for Science and Environment, New Delhi.

20 | Economy: Growth and Equity

ASHA MENON (REVATHY)

General Definition

Economics can be defined as a study of mankind in the ordinary business of life.

It examines that part of individual and social action, which is most closely connected with the attainment and with the use of material requisites of well-being. According to economist Lord Robbins, "Economics is the science which studies human behaviour as a relationship between ends and scarce means which have alternate uses." Economics includes the study of general principles of administration of resources, whether of an individual, a household, a business, or a State; including the examination of the ways in which waste arises in all such administrations. Economic activity optimises utilisation of available resources.

Resources or Factors of Production

The main resources which can also be termed as factors of production of a country are—Land, Capital and Labour.

(a) Land is a productive resource given by nature and existing in their natural state. Economist Ricardo defines land as "the original indestructible power of soil". However, land also covers minerals under the earth, the climate that maintains fertility, the fish in the sea, the mountains and rushing streams which are the source of hydroelectric power, the natural waterways along which goods can be transported.

(b) Capital is man-made resource and is accumulated out of income by saving. Capital is an income-earning asset, meaning it will produce income, either goods or services. To have more roads, houses, machines we need capital to create capital, we must consume less than we produce, i.e. we must save.

(c) Labour is human effort of any kind—manual, mental, skilled or unskilled, scientific or artistic. It includes the work of the office and salesman as well as the toil and sweat of the men on shop floor or agricultural fields. The productive capacity of a unit of labour would vary according to the quality of labour. Productivity of a work is a function of the amount of effort a man can put forth in a given period and of his skill.

Effective and efficient use of available resource is essential to ensure creation of wealth. Three factors to achieve this aim are, easy accessibility of resource, a desire for better living, and effective leadership—i.e. men of sufficient ability and initiative to recognise and exploit opportunities and take advantage of tides, which flow.

Capital is the most important of all the resources. Wealth depends on the willingness, the ability and opportunity to exploit resources. Only by the exploitation of resources we can raise the levels of income at which savings becomes possible. It is only by hard work, saving and enterprise, capital can be accumulated. Accumulated capital can then be employed for intensive development of resources, which in turn would generate and raise incomes further resulting in higher levels of saving and investment.

Economic Growth

Economic growth can be achieved only in a social climate, where the social and political institutions and the level of political capability favour growth. Capital equipment of several kinds, technical knowledge, transport and communications, efficient systems of finance and distribution—all are complementary, interlocking parts of the whole structure are all necessary. An undeveloped country cannot progress far by investing a little at a time, in one or two directions—it must eventually move forward on a broad front, and in fairly big steps.

Indian Perspective

We got our Independence on 15th August, 1947. After 57 years of Independence we are still a developing economy. Pandit Jawaharlal Nehru had this passage on his table.

"The woods are lovely dark and deep,
But I have promises to keep
And miles to go before I sleep,
And miles to go before I sleep."

— *Robert Frost*

True to these words, he kept his promises and laid the foundation for a strong India, to the extent he could during his lifetime. The nucleus of all heavy industries, chain of national research laboratories, Bhakra Nangal Dam, and so on were initiated at his instance. Calling them modern temples of worship, he exhorted public to contribute their might for building a strong India.

We had achieved self-sufficiency in food production within the first three decades of Independence, due to success of the Green Revolution, and the incentives provided to farmers by way of subsidised inputs and assured minimum support prices. Another achievement was the White Revolution, by which we became self sufficient in milk and milk products.

Growth in the GDP (gross domestic product) recorded a lower average during the first two years 2000 to 2002 of 4.7 per cent per annum weakening the base for the Tenth Five Year Plan 2002–2007, which commenced on April 1, 2002.

Factors that Slowed Down Economic Growth.

Some of the factors which have slowed down our economic growth are:

(a) The multiplying population.
(b) Non-continuity in government policies.
(c) Corruption at all levels.
(d) Lack of sincerity and discipline among government employees and public sector employees.
(e) Expansion of government departments without assessing the technical requirement and financial viability of the requirement.
(f) Complicated tax burden.
(g) Unbridled growth of government subsidies.
(h) Lack of appropriate leadership.
(i) Tension with neighbours, thus increasing the defence expenditure.

Poverty Alleviation

India is basically an agricultural/rural economy. Rural economy is the nerve centre of India. Hence it is important to stress on agriculture and agriculture-based industries. Poverty is more pronounced in rural areas as compared to urban localities. Hence there is a necessity

to generate more jobs for rural population, which should be labour intensive, thus enabling them to fetch standard wages. Agricultural productivity can be improved if fragmentation of small landholdings are consolidated for optimum utilisation of input. Small farms are not economically viable. Hence it would be beneficial for the farmers to form cooperative societies for cultivation, and the farmer should get his share basing on his landholdings. Thus he need not sacrifice ownership of his land. The cooperative society can also generate work in the fields of handicrafts, sculpture, etc., and agriculture based industries. These industries could be in the private sector.

Revival of Rural Economy

In order to fund the activities of the cooperative societies, a 'rural development cess' on foreign exchange earnings could be considered. 'Rural Development Bond' can be floated which could be given tax exemption in order to encourage public to contribute to the bond. More percentage of budgetary allocation could be utilised for development activities, if we could achieve a state of peaceful coexistence with neighbours. Some 50-100 villages could be adopted by a government machinery like village *panchayat* block development board. The village population, their skills and literacy, infrastructure available in the village, the potential available, etc. should be taken into consideration before deciding on the agriculture-based industry. For example the Aavin Dairy products in the state of Tamil Nadu, has captured worldwide market. Poultry farming, cottage industries inclusive of potters, weavers, skilled and semi-skilled labourers can be nourished and aided properly, so that every unit is not only self sufficient, but also aim to earn foreign exchange. The role of cooperative societies assumes greater significance in procuring seeds, manures, insecticides and pesticides and other agricultural inputs at very low prices. They should also have storage facilities and extend assistance in marketing the products at reasonable profit margin.

Prevent Inequalities between States and Restoring State Government Finances

A survey of potential of men, materials and natural resources in underdeveloped regions/states could be conducted by experts, in order to establish the core competence of each region/state. Then, development activity in that state/region could be concentrated on that core competence such as farm culture, cultivation—cultivation of land + rearing of cattle/pigs/poultry/aquaculture, etc. For example, Kerala has tremendous potential for tourism. Hence focusing development activity on that industry could boost our foreign exchange earnings. Andhra has a long seacoast. Promoting aquaculture using modern techniques could yield lot of valuable foreign exchange. Government can also consider encouraging large public undertakings to adopt few villages and develop them. As incentives they could be given certain tax incentives.

Manufacturing Sector and Foreign Direct Investment (FDI)

Manufacturing sector should be encouraged in order to attain high growth and employment. To achieve this stress is to be laid to improve infrastructure, and ensure availability of power, roads and water. Even though economy has grown over the decade, high fiscal deficits which are growing have to be addressed by major tax reforms, in order to make tariff reductions, as customs duty accounts for 30 per cent of the net government revenue. Only such positive actions can attract FDI. India's important role in WTO negotiations has been acknowledged, but major impediments to the growth of its international trade remains. In the case of large public sector projects, Comptroller & Auditor General (CAG) should be consulted and prior approval should be obtained in order to avoid/minimise objections on post mortem of the project.

Globalisation

A paradigm shift was effected in 1991, opening up India's economy through liberalisation of policies, in regard to trade, industry, exchange rate and balance of payments thus bringing to an end a long era of licensing and controls. Structural reforms were put in place through the decade. The hope was through higher growth of economy, there would be more employment and higher revenues would enable government to channel more resources to poverty alleviation and social development. The launch of liberalisation on the eve of the Eighth Five Year Plan, not only helped the economy to overcome the fiscal and balance of payments crisis but also set it on a higher growth path. For three years in a row India achieved GDP growth rates of over 7 per cent and an impressive rise in exports to around 20 per cent. Even though India entered the Ninth Plan (1997–2002) with a sense of optimism, the growth momentum began to falter after the first two years and the Plan ended with an average growth of 5.3 per cent against the Plan target of 6.5 per cent. The lower growth is attributed to adverse security environment, natural disaster—earthquake, cyclone and droughts, and to some extent to global economic slowdown. Recently our Prime Minister, Manmohan Singh has declared that his government's next budget would be on tax reforms.

He has averred, "India, in its totality, accepts liberalisation and the logic of greater competition from abroad." He has said that he recognised that investors both at home and abroad viewed as constraints, the lack of infrastructure, as well as the excess of bureaucracy and corruption. Strict labour laws and irksome procedures are deterrent to FDI. Labour laws should be made practicable in order to ensure a level playing field. Encouraging FDI in selective sectors would be advantageous for India. It would ensure high quality products, technically upgraded, at competitive prices to the consumer.

Stock Market

In India, primary market has performed the role of resource mobilisation through equity and debt issues, while the secondary market records the movements in share prices, which influence the day's buying and selling activity. Market sentiment in major emerging economies like India is considerably influenced by the movements in international stock markets, especially in those of USA, and, to some extent, in Europe and Japan, which wield power over the world economy. Securities and Exchange Board of India (SEBI) is the controlling authority, and has been doing a commendable job so far.

Other Factors to Improve Economy

(a) Interlinking of Rivers

The interlinking of rivers is pro-eco-friendly act. When agriculture is dependent on monsoon, monsoon failure and drought conditions can be effectively dealt with by interlinking of rivers so that irrigation is constant and never fails. It will also ensure flood and drought are well balanced across the country. The vast, uncultivated dry lands can receive water and dwelling area widened productively. The farm culture is not confined to selected pockets in the country, thereby taking the country to narrow down or even eliminate regional development and achieving overall progress.

(b) Herbal Products

There is worldwide demand for herbal and ayurvedic products. The demand is for both cosmetic and medicinal use. It would be an agriculture-based industry. Research and development could be concentrated on this area and demands of pharmaceutical companies could be catered for. It would be a good foreign exchange earner contributing to our exports.

(c) Solar Energy

Being a tropical country India gets maximum sunshine during major part of the year. Solar energy, which is a non-conventional energy, is undertapped in our country. It can be a useful alternative to petroleum products.

Research should be concentrated to tame solar energy and make it useful at affordable costs for domestic use.

(d) Gobar Gas Plants

As in the villages large number of cattle would be available, setting up of *gobar* gas plants could ensure an economically viable availability of fuel.

It would also reduce usage of firewood for cooking purposes.

(e) Aquatic Culture

India has a long sea stretch and economic aquatic culture could be beneficial. It is important to ensure environment is not adversely affected. For this purpose research should be concentrated to find an economically viable solution to protect ecology without limiting consumerism.

(f) Value Added Tax (VAT)

Value added tax comes into force with effect from April 1, 2005. This would ensure free movement of goods and services, by discontinuing interstate tax, entry tax, octroi, etc. It would also eliminate the high level of corruption prevailing in this area.

(g) Education

Education should eliminate illiteracy percentage. Enrolment at primary stage has gone up from 42.60 per cent in 1950–51 to 94.90 per cent in 1999–00.

The 83rd Constitution Amendment Bill, 1997 was introduced on 28 July 1997 in the Rajya Sabha to make right to free and compulsory education for children from 6–14 years of age a fundamental right. The target of universalising elementary education has been divided into 3 broad parameters—universal access, universal retention and universal achievement. As a result 94 per cent of the rural population has been provided primary schools within 1 km and 84 per cent have upper primary school within 3 km. Education does not necessarily mean to cater for white collared jobs. But skills should be developed to ensure employment capabilities. In this context the stream of education called "Nayi Talim" enunciated by Mahatma Gandhi could be considered. Description of the system is enclosed as Appendix A-20.1.

(h) Research and Development

Several national laboratories were established immediately after Independence. Some of them have excelled and produced results, which are appreciated. However the output from some of the institutions are not commensurate with the investment made. Time-bound target should be given and the progress achieved should be periodically evaluated. Good quality leadership is essential to ensure positive results.

(i) Human Resource Development

We have large number of management institutions catering to corporate sectors. The cream of these students look for opportunities in foreign countries, resulting in considerable brain drain. We need large number of leaders for our developmental activity. Hence it is vital to ensure appropriate employment opportunities are made available to attract such talents.

(j) Population Control

All our achievements in development are nullified by our unwieldy population growth. Hence there is an urgent requirement to enforce effective measures to control population growth. This has to be taken up on a war footing. Incentives for small families could be rewarding. Disincentives for big families should also be considered. A uniform code of law would give an impetus to such a policy.

(k) Government Subsidies

Government subsidies should be limited to such sectors, where the necessity demands such a concession. Reservation of jobs, education concessions, free power for farmers, etc., should be based on economic considerations and not on caste basis. The subsidies should be time-bound and can be extended from year to year, depending on the necessity after proper evaluation.

(l) Constitution

In our Constitution, 70th Schedule gives three lists. They are:

(i) Union List contains 97 subjects in which Union Government has exclusive authority.

(ii) State List containing 66 subjects, which are under exclusive authority of State Governments.

(iii) Concurrent List contains 47 subjects, where the Union and States have concurrent powers.

It would be beneficial for the country if the Union Government restricted themselves to the subjects enunciated in the Constitution. Important portfolios such as Defence, Finance, External Affairs and Home require top priority attention of the Union Government. Autonomous bodies like UGC could be considered for education, sports, social services, etc. Such a concrete action would reduce the government wages and expenditure to a great extent. In order to carry out a job evaluation, it would be profitable to invite an outside professional agency.

Conclusion

Mahatma Gandhi always reiterated the fact, "India lives in its villages."

President A.P.J. Abdul Kalam also adds to Gandhiji's philosophy. "The Village had its own economic philosophy—to produce as much as you can, consume as little as you can and waste nothing."

The present strategy of rural development mainly focuses on poverty alleviation, better livelihood opportunities, provision of basic amenities and infrastructure facilities through innovative programmes of wage and self employment. These goals will be achieved by various programmes of support being implemented creating partnership with communities, non-governmental organisations, community based organisations, PRIs and industrial establishments, while the Department of Rural Development will provide logistic support both on technical and administrative side for programme implementation.

A concerted, sincere, scientific, determined approach by all persons involved in the development programmes would ensure success in building an economically strong India—'An India for Indians'.

A P P E N D I X   A-20.1

'Nayi Talim'—A Method of Teaching Enunciated by Mahatma Gandhi

Mahatma Gandhi came up with a novel manner of imparting education. Even though the system of education in the country was too nervous to experiment with his ideas at the national level, in pockets his method, called *Nayi Talim* is being followed to yield impressive results.

Two introductions need to be made. The first one is easy. Meet Mohandas Karamchand Gandhi, the greatest leader of the 20th century. The second one is to the method of teaching as enunciated by him. He called it *Nayi Talim*, which literally translated means New Education. As you go through the ideas that form the basis of *Nayi Talim*, you realise, Gandhi had indeed loved and understood children and the learning process.

I will begin by relating my first encounter with *Nayi Talim*. I had gone to Kausani. This is a small quiet hill station in the state of Uttar Pradesh, northeast of Delhi. The majestic Himalayas as the backdrop and valleys hurling down as surprises were filled with stories of dynamic enterprising village women. They had protested against the opening of a liquor shop at one village. At another they had resisted deforestation. And the women were as conversant with the written as well as the spoken word.

The most revealing encounter was on one of our treks. We met two young women who had come in the traditional attire including the scarf on their heads. They also carried with them some bramble too. With the spirit of reformation high in city-bred me, I asked them if they were literate. They said they were not and that they did not see why they should study. For one hour I explained to them why. At the end of it, they casually revealed they were doing their Masters in Sociology. They were home on vacation! Imagine my shock and a feeling of utter foolishness. It took some time to reflect on the fact that all their education had not alienated them from their roots.

As I followed the source of such spirit in these women I was led to an uphill climb. No vehicle went up, you just had to trek it. It went up so many steps that I felt I would soon reach the heavens,

and in a sense I did. I was at Laxmi Ashram at Kasauni. It was set up in 1946 by Katherine Helliman, better known in India as Sarla *Behn*, an ardent follower of Gandhiji. Working with the people while building an awareness for the fight for independence, Sarla *Behn* noticed the amount of hardship a woman from that region underwent. She decided, under Gandhiji encouragement and insistence, that this was where an institution based on *Nayi Talim* should be set up. Beginning with three students, Lakshmi Ashram began imparting education to the people along Gandhian lines. Today the names of some of our major reformers and grassroot workers figure in the school's alumni.

When we entered the complex that is spread over many acres of open land, we saw some students and their teachers preparing a bed for vegetable sowing. One student, far out across the hill, was out grazing cows. A few others were in the kitchen making breakfast. Within half hour when we had gone around the neat but spartan complex, we came across yet another student. This time she was with a teacher trying to record the temperature from a barometer. The diverse activities were too distracting to the mind that went to see an ordinary school. So I sat down to hear and read about *Nayi Talim*, which was what the school was all about.

Gandhiji, on his return to India from South Africa, was struck by the failure of the modern system of education. He argued that beginning with the language in which children were and continue to be taught, the school syllabus based on Macaulay's system, was irrelevant to the country's context. After accessing that kind of education, it alienated the student from his or her motherland and culture. Yet it did not make him vocationally any worthier. The student community that dominated the thinking leader's mind comprised 80 per cent of India's rural folk. As he ruminated the problem in his mind, he decided the way to go about education, true education, was to give literary training through vocational training. Quoting Gandhi, "I hold that true education of the intellect can only come through a proper exercise and training of the bodily organs." In other words, the intelligent use of the bodily organs in a child provides the best and quickest way of developing his intellect. He went on to elaborate his idea with the example of a *takli*. The *takli* is the most primitive form of the spinning wheel. It is actually a tool that must have been fashioned before the discovery of the wheel. The use of the wheel for spinning came later in history. The initial *taklis* could have been fashioned out of clay or wet flour, dried and a bamboo splinter passed through it. In some parts of Bengal and Bihar, this kind of tool spin is still used. Most cloth in India was made of the *takli* yarn and the cottage industries still use it for finer counts of textiles.

There you are—that was just Gandhi's idea. Talk about the *takli* and you have per force to talk of the wheel, science, the coming of mill cloth, the dying out of *taklis*, the regional variations of *taklis*, the areas where cotton is grown and so on. History, geography, science and arithmetic are all taught through practical experience.

The education system should go to the people, should lure them for its value, both economic and intellectual. He argued that primary education should be spread across seven years and should contain the entire syllabus that children study till they leave school. In addition they will pick up one vocational skill. The *takli* was an example, it could be anything. Another quote from Gandhi's writings would be in order, "Then as to primary education, my confirmed opinion is that the commencement of training by teaching the alphabet and reading and writing, hampers their intellectual growth. I would not teach them the alphabet till they have had an elementary knowledge of history, geography, mental arithmetic and art. Through these three I should develop their intelligence. Question may be asked how intelligence can be developed through the *takli* or the spinning wheel. It can to a marvellous degree if it is not taught mechanically. When you tell a child the reason for each process, when you explain the mechanism of the *takli*, when you give him/her the history of cotton and its connection with civilisation itself and take him to the village field where it is grown and teach him to count the rounds he spins and the method of finding the evenness and strength of the yarn, you hold his interest and simultaneously train his eyes, hands and mind. I should give six months to this preliminary training. The child is now probably ready for learning how to read the alphabet and, when he is able to do so rapidly he is ready to learn simple drawing and when he has learnt to draw geometric figures and the figures of birds, etc. he will draw not scrawl the figures of the alphabet. I consider writing as a fine art. We kill it by imposing the alphabet on little children and making it the beginning of learning."

Gradually vocation should serve a dual process—it should pay for the students course and also develop his skill. Land, building and equipment are not to be covered by the student's labour. All crafts that are widely practiced in India can be taught with minimal investment. The self supporting aspect of Gandhi's New Education formula was in his opinion the only way to carry education to the crores of children in India awaiting education.

Higher education should be left to private enterprises and for meeting national requirements. The state universities should be purely examining bodies.

So when I looked up and saw the child returning from grazing the cows, I wondered what she would have associated with it—different types of greenery, love towards animals, the food cycle, milk, dairy farming... or the young women emerging from the kitchen, what would they have learnt about fire, cooking, nourishment, nutrition, agriculture and the growth of rice and pulses. A new desire seemed to sprout in me. I wished I could go back in time and sit amidst nature to learn.

21 | Social Equity: Can Market Reform the Society?

CHANDRA BHAN PRASAD

THE Indian State's public policy initiative of Affirmative Action or reservation in government jobs for untouchables/tribals (hereafter Dalits) has been a passionately-debated issue. Both the supporters as well as opponents of reservations muster all arguments and facts in defence of their respective case. An impassionate debate is yet to come.

To the supporters, job reservations for Dalits (forget Mandal, an ill-conceived concept) or preferential treatment in general, is needed to correct 'historical wrongs'—caste discrimination, untouchability, etc. To the opponents (the private sector to be precise), job reservations compromise efficiency/merit, and hence undesirable.

The politics, social activism, and intellectual theorisation in contemporary India revolve around the social question.

However, most of the parties—be they opposed to social equity or in favour of it—have never taken economic dimension into consideration.

Does job reservation contribute to economic growth? Even the proponents don't have an answer.

Does job reservation retard economic growth? The opponents don't have an answer, either.

Be it individuals, social groups, society, or a nation, what pre-destines their day-to-day thoughts, visions, programmes and actions, is all about money, in other words, the economic dimension.

The Economics of Equity

The Dalits account for one-fourth of India's population (over 250 million), much more than the combined population of Italy, France and the United Kingdom.

Due to the policy of affirmative action or reservations in government jobs, about 3.5 million (35 lakh) Dalits (my own estimates) have got into government jobs.

According to the Indian workforce census of 1999, there were 18 lakh Dalits in trade and commerce (small shopkeepers though). Another 15 lakh were in household industry (meaning that they had their own enterprise run from home, where family members comprised the workforce).

That means there were 33 lakh Dalits in manufacturing/trade/commerce. As per my own estimates, about a half of these businesspersons have been able to stand on their feet due to the support they receive from Dalit employees/officers who tend to lend a helping hand to their kith and kin.

That means, the Dalits in government jobs (3.35 million) and those in trade/industry (1.65 million), taken together, number more than 5 million.

The 5 million Dalits, multiplied by five (assuming that a family comprises five persons), becomes 25 million (or 2.50 crore), who are the direct products of affirmative action or reservations in government jobs.

In other words, the Indian State has added, through its emancipatory public policies, 25 million new members to the middle/lower middle class basket, who would otherwise have not come out of poverty and denial. Moreover, this segment has also moved over to urban and semi-urban areas where caste-based violence is totally absent.

How the Private Sector Gains through Reservation

If most middle/lower middle class households in India (often urban), subscribe to electricity connection, Dalits too must be doing so. In that case, every Dalit household must be buying on an average of 6 bulbs in a year. Or, the 5 million Dalit households buy about 30 million (3 crore) bulbs annually. If bulbs cost about Rs. 10 per unit, then, Dalits are contributing about 30 crore rupees annually to the electric bulb industry in India.

Most middle/lower middle class people also use toothbrush, and a person buys at least two toothbrushes a year, then, the 25 million Dalits must be buying 50 million toothbrushes annually. If a toothbrush costs Rs. 5, then Dalits are contributing Rs. 250 million annually to the Rs. 3 billion toothbrush industry. Well, toothbrush goes along with toothpaste. If a Dalit household spends an average of Rs. 10 on toothpaste/powder per month (Rs. 120 annually), then the 5 million Dalit households are contributing about Rs. 600 million annually to the Rs. 9.5 billion strong toothpaste/powder industry.

Or, if middle/lower middle class households buy at least 2 pencils a month, the 5 million Dalit households too must be doing the same. If pencils cost Re. 1 per unit, then Dalits are contributing Rs. 120 million annually to the pencil industry.

Maybe anecdotal, but the fact remains that Dalits are an integral part of the nation's economy. India's FMCG (fast moving consumer goods) industry is estimated to be worth Rs. 600 billion. Don't Dalit households contribute to this sector?

Assuming a government employee (an average derived from Groups A, B, C & D employees/officers) earns Rs. 10,000 a month and spends a half of it in the market, then Dalit employees/officers too must be following similar spending pattern.

In that case, the 5 million Dalits (each household spending about Rs. 5000 per month) must be spending about Rs. 25 billion a month, or Rs. 300 billion a year, an amount more than 4 times higher than the net income of the Reliance Industries, equivalent to the combined net income of Reliance, Tatas and Birlas for the current financial year!

Social Basis of the Consumption/Consumer Pattern

The opponents of the preceding argument can very well argue that—if there was no reservation, the positions now held by Dalits through reservation could have well gone to non-Dalits, and hence, the 5 million consumers would have been very much in place.

It may sound logical on the surface but nevertheless misleading. A little light on the social basis of consumers or consumption pattern can help us to arrive at a more accurate picture.

Dalits as Enterprising Consumers

Most Dalits who enter government jobs are first or, at best, second generation 'salaried' persons. Most Dalits in business are first generation businesspersons. Logically, then, most of this category of Dalits are the newest entrants into the consumer market.

Though there are no studies to substantiate the above statement, a common sense born out of lived experience would suffice to appreciate the point. A first generation Dalit employee—a school teacher, for instance—upon joining the job, becomes a ruthless customer of goods in the first decade of his/her service. He moves away from his/her family to join the job, and goes to a new place with virtually nothing. From good clothing, to household items, he buys all from the market.

A Dalit school teacher or a clerk, upon taking up the assignment, may buy two pressure cookers, two bicycles, and two wrist watches in the very first year of service. One set for himself, and the other for his family back home. He has to elevate living standards of his family, and his standing in the society. The cycle goes on till he has arranged minimum basic requirements of life, for himself and his extended family. Maybe, he continues buying two bicycles, and two wrist watches every year for his close relatives! Needless to add, he/she will buy a table/ceiling fan, and rest other necessities, including a colour TV, a phone, furniture, a fridge, and, may be a two-wheeler.

The first generation Dalit Civil Servant, like non-Dalits, need not buy a car, air conditioners, PCs, etc. as all these items are available at the State expense. But he needs to buy immediately, a high-end fridge, kitchen-wares, great clothing, etc. But, he will be immediately required to buy a two-wheeler for his family back home, plus a plenty of household items which his family never possessed. He keeps buying goods from the market for nearly a decade.

The Second Generation

The second generation has moved up in the economic hierarchy. A Dalit school teacher, or a clerk, whose father was in a similar position, has to buy for himself a two wheeler, and a silk *sari* for his wife. Within a few years in service, he must buy another two-wheeler for his family. He has to gift a colour TV, a better fridge, and a desert cooler for his extended family.

The second generation Dalit civil servants/doctors/ engineers, etc. remain perpetual customers, not for themselves alone, but for their extended family.

A non-Dalit who joins as a school teacher, or a clerk, often brings along half of the household items required from home itself. Often he/she need not buy two pressure cookers, two bicycles, and two wrist watches in the first year of service. He/she may have all that, and the family/relatives may not require any of those items. They have all that.

A non-Dalit *civil* servant/doctor/engineer/college-university teacher/IT professional, may have no family obligations. He invests his earnings in immovable properties. Most of his income is unused.

The Economic Saturation

The high rate of economic growth is relative to the growth in consumer base. In other words, often, the number of consumers can determine the rate of economic growth. It is axiomatic that more and more people need to be brought into the consumer society.

In India, the industry—manufacturing, trade, marketing, etc.—belong to the traditionally privileged castes. Traditionally, they have held wealth, flow of money is often confined to them. They form, in demographic sense, the backbone of India's upper/middle classes, the class with the potential to keep buying.

Therefore, when a member of this traditional social class takes up job or opens an enterprise, he/she already possesses most goods required in life. Unlike a person from historically disadvantaged group, he tends to be a less active consumer.

On the other hand, what is the size of the so-called Dalit consumers? A fraction of even the Dalits population, not to mention the whole population of India! A mass of millions who are not part of the economy, except as labourers at the low-end, will be a drain on the country. Can we continue to lead the life of contradictions where more than 200 million people are not even consumers? For how long? Poverty, discrimination and unchecked violence are forcing these masses into the lap of extremist outfits and leading to societal tensions. Is it not a concern for us?

Dalit economic emancipation is intrinsically linked to the country's future. The task before the nation is—How to integrate Dalits into the economy. To do that, we must address another more basic challenge—How to integrate them into the society. We cannot continue to present ideological arguments only to deny Dalits their place in the society.

If doing nothing is not an option, then, there are plenty of things we as a society and a nation can and must do.

Biggest Challenge before the Economy

India's biggest economic challenges are:

(1) The market is not acquiring a mass-character.

(2) Society with all its evils is masquerading as 'market'.

(3) How to make impersonal and secular market to determine values and standards for the country.

(4) Wealth is in the captivity of a few.

(5) Wealth, therefore, is not acquiring a social character.

Equity the Ultimate *Mantra*

Equity, therefore, in all our activity, is the ultimate *mantra* for a sustainable, accelerated economic growth. That can be achieved through a series of pro-poor measures aimed at broad-basing the market, be they affirmative action/diversity initiatives or workforce diversity/supplier/ dealership/contract diversity, etc. in order to expand the consumer base, giving a social character to wealth.

What about Merit?

White Americans till the '70s held views about African-Americans similar to the present stereotype of Dalits—inefficient, incompetent and unproductive. Today, the same African Americans are seen to be efficient, competent and productive. A majority of all economic activities are carried out by people mediocre in nature. Same holds true of the Whites, Blacks, Brahmins *and* Dalits.

22 | Achieving Economic Growth with Equity

RAVI PARTHASARATHY

I. Purpose

The purpose of this Memorandum is to outline two possible approaches that could be considered for accelerating infrastructure development and achieving economic growth with equity. This Memorandum is presented in two Sections as under:

(1) Creation of an Infrastructure Index to serve as a planning tool for allocation of resources and to prioritize infrastructure development.

(2) Use of the principal drivers of the local economy to monetise the latent economic potential at the level of the district.

II. Creation of an Infrastructure Index

(1) The Need for an Index

(a) It is commonly accepted that the availability of infrastructure spurs economic development. This principle is best illustrated by a comment widely attributed to President Roosevelt: "America does not have good roads because it is rich: America is rich because it has good roads."

(b) Unfortunately, the level of infrastructure created in India remains well below optimal requirements. Equally important, the development of infrastructure is quite skewed:

(i) The gap in infrastructure development between more progressive states and states that are economically disadvantaged is increasing perceptibly.

(ii) There is also a widening gap between the availability of infrastructure in rural areas and urban habitations.

(c) The foregoing would inevitably create a self-perpetuating cycle with lower levels of infrastructure development leading to impaired economic growth i.e., the gap would only increase with the passage of time.

(d) It is in this context that it is desirable to create an infrastructure index for each District and State in the Indian Union. The objective would be to utilise the index so created in order to direct incremental allocation of funds to the districts and states concerned.

(2) Available Indices

A number of indices have been created to reflect the level of economic development within a state:

(a) The India Today Index provides valuable statistics e.g., percentage of homes with electricity, per capita LPG connections, etc.

(b) The CMIE Index focuses on key infrastructure areas with a combination of weights relating to each sector. The indicators used for various sectors include surface roads per square kilometre of area, primary schools per lakh of population, telephone lines per hundred persons, etc.

(c) The Anant, Kishore, Chaudhry (AKC) Index developed by the Delhi School of Economics measures infrastructure facilities available in different states in terms of eight sectors and parameters, including administrative infrastructure.

(3) Limitations of Available Indices

(a) All the three indices have made important contributions to gaining a perspective relating to the level of development in a number of states.

(b) Nonetheless, the India Today Index and the CMIE Index may not have significant utility as far as the planning for growth is concerned. As an example, more homes may be connected with electricity in State A than in State B. However, the electricity actually consumed in State A might well be less than in State B.

(c) These indices provide a snapshot of the present as far as states are concerned, but provide no perspective in relation to their future potential.

(d) Most importantly, the parameters and weights used for different sectors remain the same for all states and districts, although the importance of a sector would necessarily vary from one region to another.

(e) The AKC Index appears to be mathematically more robust, and incorporates regional differences and also assigns weights to different sectors.

(f) The AKC Index nonetheless has limitations in that quality aspects are not considered, and no perspective is provided in relation to future potential. As the index is benchmarked with average values at the national level, increases and decreases in absolute value do not imply that the State has in fact evidenced an increase or decrease in the available level of infrastructure facilities.

(4) Optimal Level of Infrastructure

(a) The approach to the creation of an infrastructure index rests on the premise that the creation of infrastructure is the key driver to enabling a state realise its full economic potential and develop its local economies.

(b) Given the foregoing, and based on the demographic variables relevant to a specific state or district, it would be possible to conceive of the minimum level of base infrastructure needed in that state or district in order to realise the latent economic potential inherent in that location.

(c) The nature of infrastructure required would necessarily vary from state to state:

(i) As an example, ropeways and ski resorts would necessarily be of greater importance in Himachal Pradesh, as would be the creation of cold storage depots for preservation of horticulture products.

(ii) The foregoing would have little relevance in Rajasthan, where the focus would be on provision of water for all segments of the population with perhaps a secondary emphasis on tourism related infrastructure such as museums, temples, etc.

(d) Thus the initial exercise would require the conceptualisation of the base level of infrastructure needed in each state, and in each district within that state.

(e) The resultant list would be the Index 100. The actual level of infrastructure developed or available in that state could be assessed and would be determined at say 25 per cent or 50 per cent as the case may be.

(f) The task before the Planning Authorities is then to determine in what manner the index could be enhanced through the creation of relevant infrastructure in that state.

(5) Principal Drawback

The principal drawback to this approach is that it is subjective to a degree, and strays from conventional principles that stipulate the use of a uniform measure as the basis for comparative evaluation.

(6) Allocation of Funds

(a) By and large, the quantum of funds distributed to states under the aegis of the Finance Commission is based on constitutional principles i.e., it is the right of the state concerned to receive the funds allocated.

(b) The Government of India (GoI) could perhaps consider the use of an infrastructure index as the basis for direction of incremental funds allocation to the states.

(c) One of the parameters that hampers rapid economic development at the level of states and urban local bodies is the less than adequate institutional capacity to conceive and manage efficient project implementation.

(d) The allocation of incremental funds in the foregoing manner should ideally be tied to a mutually acceptable framework of implementation, ideally through a public-private partnership.

(e) Given such a framework, it may be possible to see discernible results on the ground as a result of such an initiative over a five year period.

III. Perspectives on Development

(1) The notion of backwardness in the conventional sense is often limited to comparison of select socioeconomic indicators across geographies: district, states, etc.

(2) While such measures provide a useful yardstick to compare and measure the relative standings of districts and/or states, they do not capture the intrinsic potential in socioeconomic developmental terms. As a corollary, existing indices do not provide a sufficiently rigorous basis to prioritize investments in regions.

(3) More importantly, the use of social indices, results in a real danger of perpetuating regional inequity. Indeed, a number of the regional inequities that have emerged are the result of emphasis on allocative efficiency rather than on the prioritization of investments to realise the socio-economic potential.

(4) In real terms, a district may be backward not just because it lacks in comparison to other districts but because it has not achieved its own rated potentiality.

(5) Results on the ground suggest that the delivery of co-generic projects in a specific region enhances the economic benefits of the region significantly more than economic benefits attendant to a singular initiative. There is thus a need to consider integrated area development as the optimal means for spurring economic growth.

(6) IL&FS has engaged in discussions on this subject with concerned officials of the Reserve Bank of India, the Finance Commission as well as the Planning Commission. Based on feedback received, IL&FS is presently suggesting an approach to integrated area development encompassing two broad initiatives:

(a) Creation of an infrastructure index which could serve as a planning tool for allocation of incremental resources to accelerate economic development.

(b) Using the principal potential drivers of the local economy to stimulate socioeconomic development at the district level.

(7) In order to more meaningfully present this notion, two specific projects/programmes are analysed below in more detail:

(a) The Tirupur Area Development Program (TADP).

(b) The Jalore Area Development Program (JADP).

Both programmes are distinct in their approach, aim to unleash different engines of growth, and target to build upon specific potentialities of that district. The TADP is currently at an advanced stage of implementation, whilst detailed planning is currently underway for the JADP.

A. The Tirupur Area Development Program

(1) Location

Tirupur, part of the Tirupur *taluk* of the Coimbatore district, is one of the most important industrial centres in Tamil Nadu.

(a) The town is located in the cotton rich Coimbatore-Erode belt, at a distance of 448 km to the south-west of Chennai, the state capital, and 50 km to the north of Coimbatore, the district headquarters.

(b) The river Noyyal, originating from the Velliangiri Hills, which flows through the centre of the town from west to east and the Western Ghats on the near west are the major geographical features of this region.

(c) Tirupur is well connected by road, rail and air. The National Highway (NH-47) connecting Salem and Kanyakumari passes through the town of Avinashi located at a distance of 12 km to the north of Tirupur. The nearest domestic airport is located at Peelamedu (Coimbatore), 48 km from the town. Tirupur railway station is part of the Chennai-Cochin-Trivandrum broad gauge railway line and is 56 km away from Erode.

(2) Regional Setting

(a) The district of Coimbatore comprises seven *taluks*. The district is one of the leading textile manufacturing centres of south India and also one of the most industrialised centres in the country.

(b) The industrial belt extending from Coimbatore to Tiruchirappalli and further on to Tanjore is the seventh largest industrial corridor in the country. In addition, the region holds the distinction of being one of the largest cotton and yarn production centres in the southern region of the country.

(c) Tirupur is the second largest town in the district of Coimbatore. The Tirupur Municipality (TM) covers an area of 27 sq. km and has a population of 2,35,661 as per the 1991 census. The Tirupur Local Planning Area (TLPA) had an overall population of 361,504 as per 1991 census. The industries are located within the TM as well as the entire TLPA area.

(d) The economy of the region revolves around the cotton knitwear industry, with the units spread both within TM as well as the entire TLPA.

(3) Demographic Characteristics

(a) Rapid Population Growth: The population of Tirupur town has witnessed rapid growth over the past two decades with an average decadal growth rate of 52.36 per cent (CAGR=4.3 per cent pa), principally due to the rapid industrialisation of the town.

(b) High Population Density: The rapid industrial growth has attracted population from nearby regions and as a result, Tirupur has a comparatively high population density compared to similar towns in Tamil Nadu. The high-density regions are generally concentrated in the central part of the district where the population density is over 15,000 persons/sq.km, while the low-density regions are distributed on the outskirts.

(c) Slums: As per the 1991 census, there are 99 notified slums in Tirupur with 32,353 slum dwellers distributed in various parts of the town. A majority of the settlements are concentrated in areas south of the city.

(d) Gradual Shift to Manufacturing: The shift in the occupational pattern from agriculture to manufacturing is also reflected in the land use pattern. According to statistics, while 78.52 per cent of the land in Tirupur town was used for agriculture in 1971, the figure dropped to 39.05 per cent in 1981 and further to 35.40 per cent in 1991.

(4) Tirupur's Economic Importance and Potential

(a) Over the years, Tirupur has earned international recognition as India's leading knitwear export centre. Currently, the town accounts for about 90 per cent of India's knitwear exports and contributes about USD 1 billion annually to the export earnings of the country.

(b) Exports from this area have been growing rapidly at over 15 per cent per annum in the last decade. The export centre has over 1,900 textile enterprises, which form part of the larger industrial cluster. The industries are spread over the entire TM and the adjoining TLPA.

(c) The extraordinary growth in exports in the region has been achieved despite severe infrastructure bottlenecks. Tirupur lacks adequate investment in basic infrastructure facilities in the areas of water supply, wastewater treatment, roads, transshipment facilities, power, telecommunication and other urban infrastructure.

(d) Singular amongst the infrastructure deficiencies is the shortage of water supply and inadequate infrastructure for collection, treatment and disposal of industrial/domestic wastewater. Significant improvements in the existing infrastructure stocks were considered imperative for the region to maintain its position as the centre of competence for cotton knitwear.

(e) While estimates vary, it is forecasted that on the basis of an adequate and efficient infrastructure platform, Tirupur could increase its exports to as much as USD 5 billion per annum.

(5) The Criticality of Water

(a) Water is an essential commodity in the cotton knitwear production process. The existing municipal water supply system does not provide water to most of the dyeing and bleaching industries. Consequently, the industries have largely relied on their own resources to access water required to meet the process requirements.

(b) Almost all the industries are currently tapping groundwater sources and transporting water over a long distance using tankers. Lack of reliable water supply has inhibited the growth of industries and has slowed down the flow of new investments into the area.

(c) Further, the exploitation of groundwater resources has severely depleted this natural resource. Water for industry is now trucked from a distance of up to 80 kms. Industries have also been discharging effluents without proper treatment.

(d) The TM does not have an integrated sewage collection, treatment and disposal facility. The lack of proper environmental management has resulted in contamination of water bodies and aquifers. The resultant poor quality of water could become a threat to households and industry.

(6) The Tirupur Area Development Program (TADP)

(a) The Government of Tamil Nadu (GoTN) evolved an integrated area development programme for Tirupur in 1993 with the assistance of Tirupur Exporters' Association (TEA) and IL&FS. The TADP recognises the need to improve local infrastructure and addresses the infrastructure bottlenecks in TM, local village *panchayats* and industries located in the TLPA.

(b) TADP envisages implementation of various infrastructure requirements of the TM/TLPA over a period of time. The scheme has the following broad components:

  (i)   A water supply scheme for 185 mld to serve the entire TLPA and the TM.

  (ii) A municipal sewage collection, treatment and disposal system.

  (iii) Industrial wasterwater collection, treatment and disposal system.

  (iv) Investments in roads, telecommunication and other urban infrastructure facilities.

(c) The implementation of the TADP is being done in phases, with the concerted help of various agencies. For example, part of improvements in telecommunications has been implemented by concerned government agencies. The TM has initiated a programme to improve the condition of roads, for undertaking development of new facilities and for upgradation of existing facilities. Many of the industries have implemented the installation of effluent treatment plants.

(d) However, the GoTN has been unable to allocate the significant sums required for implementing the balance TADP. Hence, the GoTN resolved to develop the TADP on a commercial basis with the involvement of private sector developers, under a public-private partnership (PPP) model.

(7) The Present Project

(a) The Project contemplates the construction of facilities to provide water to the TLPA comprising the TM, 14 villages *panchayats*, 2 town *panchayats* and to 5 wayside unions, which lie *en route* on the water transmission system corridor (collectively called the "Service Area").

(b) It is proposed to initially abstract 185 mld of water and increase the abstraction to 250 mld once the demand increases in the service area.

(c) Subsequently, it is proposed to set up a tertiary treatment facility for treating domestic sewage. These facilities would cater to the additional water demand for industries in the service area. The investments required for augmenting system capacity would be provided in phases.

(d) The scope of specific services include:

(i) Treated piped water supply to TM with a forecast population of 6,50,000 in the year 2030 where presently water is supplied for only two hours on alternate days.

(ii) Treated water supply to dyeing and bleaching industries within the TLPA. Presently, the municipal system does not provide water to these industries and they hence have to depend on water from private sources.

(iii) Sewerage system for TM, which neither has a sewerage system nor a planned organised open drainage system.

(iv) On-site sanitation facilities for slums within TM, which presently do not have access to such facilities.

(8) Special Purpose Vehicle

(a) Objective: New Tirupur Area Development Corporation Limited (NTADCL) was established under the Indian Companies Act of 1956, as a Joint Venture between IL&FS and the GoTN with the primary objective of implementing the Project, for which the GoTN and TM have granted it a concession. At a later stage, NTADCL will also establish additional infrastructure including fibre optic network, power cables, gas pipelines, wastewater recycling, etc. in the area either directly or through affiliates/subsidiaries.

(b) The Public-Private Partnership Model: NTADCL has entered into a Concession Agreement with the government to implement the project on a build, own operate and transfer (BOOT) basis. NTADCL has assumed complete responsibility for the design, construction, financing, operations and maintenance of the Project. This model provides an appropriate platform for risk participation by both the government and the private sector.

(9) Unleashing Tirupur Industry's Potential

(a) Structure, Products and Employment of the Tirupur Industry

(i) A Networked Cluster: Tirupur's growth has been achieved through a dense and complex network linking together its many knitting and manufacturing units, processing units, printing units and embroidery units into an industrial district. The structural interdependence of units has ensured that the closure of any single unit does not materially impact the industry as a whole and its growth.

(ii) Export Driven Market: The trend towards knitted garments in India is a recent phenomenon that is limited to urban centres. Limited domestic demand and better unit realisations from exports has been one of the primary reasons for the hosiery industry in Tirupur preferring the western markets for diversification. The industry has also upgraded its design capabilities to quickly adapt to changing fashion trends in the West. This export diversification has significantly benefited the industry over the last decade.

(iii) Employment Generation: The industry directly employs approx. 1,00,000 people and provides indirect employment to 3,00,000 people in services such as ginning, spinning, packaging and other related services.

(iv) Commitment of Labour: Tirupur thrives on the dedication and hardwork of labour. Workers are willing to work round the clock for extended periods of time to meet delivery commitments. The town has about six unions, but they have only limited memberships. There is a three-year agreement with the unions on the wage rate, bonus and other labour related issues.

(b) Industry Size and Cost Structure

(i) Industry Size: The water intensive units are limited to bleaching, dyeing and printing units which comprise 39.84 per cent of the total industries in the region.

(ii) Industry Cost Structure: The industry cost structure varies from unit to unit based on the type of technology used, the investment intensity and the market the unit serves. No formal data is available for the cost structure of an individual unit. However, based on discussions with various processing units, it is estimated that water costs constitute approximately 5 per cent of the total costs of the unit.

(iii) Current Cost of Water: The current cost of water for industry is dependant on the type of source from which water is being drawn, and ranges from Rs. 40 per kl to 50 per kl. Based on past trends, the cost of water is expected to increase at the rate of 12 per cent to 15 per cent per annum, in the absence of any alternate water supply sources. The current cost of water is an important factor used to determine the water pricing that NTADCL stipulates to industry.

(c) Comparison of Scenarios With and Without the Project

The benefits of the project are detailed below in Table 22.1.

The Project provides significant benefits to the region as illustrated above. The rapidly rising level of environment degradation and the significant hardship that the industry/community faces in the present situation could result in a severe industrial downturn and make the region difficult to live in. The local industry/community realises the foregoing, and the project hence has the support of the local community/industry.

Table 22.1

Comparison of Scenarios

System	Present Conditions	Without Project	With Project
Water Supply	Per capita supply of 46 lpcd	Reduced per capita supply with increase in population. Poor water supply leading to poor community hygiene, increased disease spread.	Increased supply to 100 lpcd for urban areas and 70 lpcd for rural areas will lead to improved health and hygiene and will significantly reduce health risk.
	Presently there is no system for supply to industries. As a result, currently industries depend on tanker supplies and local groundwater sources.	Increased groundwater abstraction leading to depletion in groundwater level.	Supply of 100 mld of water for industrial use will result in curtailing use of groundwater thereby improving groundwater situation in the region.
		Poor quality of groundwater and availability could result in loss of competitiveness.	Assured availability of water would enable the industries to move higher in the value chain.
	A fall of 8.85 m has been recorded in Tirupur Block between 1982 to 1993. Over-exploitation of groundwater recharge potential by 23 per cent has been observed.	Overexploitation of groundwater source will lead to enhanced depletion.	Control over abstraction from groundwater sources for industrial use and improved supply for domestic use will curtail abstraction and promote enhancement in the groundwater table over the long term.
	Abstracted water has a high TDS (1000-4000mg/L).	Deterioration of groundwater quality of sources will increase if industries continue using the high TDS containing water since this leads to a high TDS in the effluents.	Restoration of groundwater quality due to use of good quality water for processing and improved treatment at CETPs.
Domestic Wastewater Collection and Town Treatment	No sewage collection and treatment system in town.	Present environmental conditions will further deteriorate leading to unhealthy living conditions and land, surface and groundwater contamination.	Provision of sewerage system and sewage treatment and disposal facilities will arrest contamination and restore the quality of surface and groundwater sources. Due to reduced health risk, the project will also result in improvement in public health and hygiene.
	Overflows from septic tanks and untreated domestic discharges are disposed off directly into river Noyyal or open drains.		
On-site Sanitation at Slums	Present coverage of slum areas is only about 8 per cent.	Poor access to on-site sanitation facilities will cause serious public health risk and will lead to increased disease spread, poor aesthetics and unsanitary conditions.	Provision of sanitary facilities to all slums areas will improve the sanitary conditions, community health and hygiene and lead to an overall improvement in the aesthetic quality.

(10) Project Finance and Economics

(a) Project Cost: The total landed project cost of the TADP has been estimated at Rs. 10,230 million.

(b) Project Finance Plan: NTADCL successfully raised funding for the project as indicated in Table 22.2.

(c) Government Contribution: The total contribution of GoTN to the scheme in direct financial terms works out to around Rs. 800 million, with an additional contingent liability of Rs. 500 million.

Table 22.2

Means of Financing

	(Rs. Million)
Equity	3,430
Subordinate Debt	650
Long-term Debt	6,150
Total	**10,230**

(d) Recovery of Investment: The recovery of investment is predicated on the pricing of water supplied to industry, domestic municipal and villages. Internal cross-subsidy between classes of consumers has ensured that the price of the service is reasonable, acceptable and equitable.

(e) Financial Guarantees: All resources required for the project have been raised without the provision of financial guarantees from the GoTN.

(11) Setting NTADCL in the Regional Context

(a) The Institutional framework established for the Tirupur project has successfully demonstrated the feasibility of prioritizing investments in a region and in implementing the programme on the basis of a public-private partnership.

(b) NTADCL also provides a robust 'balance sheet' for the Tirupur district to undertake other infrastructure projects for implementation. Indeed, the Company has already been mandated to implement an Apparel Park to cater to the expanding local industry.

(c) At a second level, NTADCL is currently drawing up plans to expand its infrastructure mandate to cater to the infrastructure requirements of industry in terms of a common effluent treatment plant and energy efficiency programmes.

(d) Discussions are also underway to develop specific infrastructure programmes to support agriculture and agro-processing. In essence, the implementation of the TADP has served to unleash the socioeconomic potential of the region.

B. Jalore Area Development Program

(1) Overview

(a) Location: The district of Jalore is located in the Southwest region of the State of Rajasthan, close to the western border of India with Pakistan. Covering an area of approximately 2 million hectares and with a population of 1.4 million, the district is surrounded by desert in the west and marsh in the south.

(b) Backward District: The socioeconomic indicators for the district clearly indicate its economic and social backwardness. With subsistence agriculture the primary economic activity, the district has faced several constraints to development.

(c) Constraints to Development: Poor water availability, inadequate infrastructure, and low levels of investment in agriculture, education and health have undermined the significant developmental potential of the region.

(d) Migration of Population and Livestock: The severe droughts experienced in the district over the past decade resulted in significant migration of livestock and population thereby further eroding the developmental potential of the region. Excessive exploitation of groundwater sources has also resulted in large tracts of the district being unable to support even basic activities.

(e) Approach to Development: An approach is outlined herein to address the developmental challenge of the district on a comprehensive, integrated and self-sustaining basis. The targeted outcome of the proposed program is a significant increase in per capita income, drought proofing, and a demonstrable capability to sustain the economic and social development of the district.

(f) Caveat:

(i) Top-down Approach: The scheme detailed herein is multi-sectoral and capital intensive, and there is danger in following a top-down approach. Every effort is being made to ensure that the implementation of this program is undertaken within a framework of community development and participation. Detailed consultations with all stakeholder groups are being conducted prior to finalisation of the scope of the program, its design, priorities, implementation plan, etc.

(ii) Magic Wand: There is also the danger, given the overall objective of the program, that expectations are belied. It is to be understood that the JADP is a complex process and its successful outcomes will depend as much on social transformation as economic transformation.

(iii) Creating Markets: The end focus of the JADP is to link Jalore to markets. This objective would enable diverse economic agents to exploit Jalore's developmental potential. Accordingly, the JADP is structured to start simply and in a linear, progressive and integrated manner.

(2) Profiling the District of Jalore

(a) Water Availability

(i) Surface Water: The area lies 'outside the basin' and has no natural surface drainage. The average annual rainfall is barely 30 mm.

(ii) Rainfall: Rainfall in the area is not only scanty but also erratic. The average rainfall for the period 1901-2003, in the area is shown in Table 22.4. During the last 50 years, Jalore has witnessed drought conditions in almost every year due to non-availability of water, food and fodder.

Table 22.3

Rainfall Statistics

(Rainfall in cm)

Year	Normal Rainfall	Actual Rainfall	Variation from Normal Rainfall (%)
1997	42.16	67.89	61.03
1998	42.16	31.34	-25.66
1999	42.16	31.28	-25.81
2000	42.16	25.23	-40.16
2001	42.16	38.58	-8.49

Source: *District Statistical Profile 2002*, published by Directorate of Economics and Statistics, GoR.

(iii) Drinking Water: Due to the non-availability of surface water and the deteriorating quality of groundwater, drinking water in the area is largely scarce and contaminated:

- The only surface water source is the non-perennial River Luni and its tributary Sukri. River Luni's catchment area lies entirely in the arid zone and receives low rainfall.

- As of date, less than 25 per cent of habitations in the district have access to potable water. With demand of water mostly met from groundwater sources, the depth of groundwater in the area ranges up to 20 m as against 5 metres in the adjoining area of the Rann of Kutch. Jalore has recorded the maximum depletion of groundwater to the tune of 10.34 m in last two decades.

- The habitants, particularly women, are often required to devote a major part of the day in obtaining potable water from distances of up to 5 km.

- Excessive fluoride and chlorine levels in some of the villages has resulted in a high incidence of water related health problems. This has also resulted in increased morbidity leading to loss of productivity and disproportionately high expenditures on medical treatment.

(iv) Irrigation Water:

- The district of Jalore lies in the semi-arid zone, with agriculture almost wholly dependant on rains.

- Farmers grow crops that are largely salt tolerant; practice crop rotation; and leave large stretches of land fallow every alternate growing season. This has resulted in poor returns from agriculture, and a low total yield.

- The irrigated area as a proportion of gross cropped area in Jalore is significantly lower than the national and state averages as shown in Table 22.5.

Table 22.4

Average Rainfall Figures

	In mm
Jalore	393
Barmer	268
Rajasthan	575
All India	1,200

Source: *Economy of Rajasthan,* Nathuramka.

Table 22.5

Percentage of Irrigated Area

	Gross Irrigated Area (million hectare)	Gross Irrigated Area as % of GCA	Gross Cropped Area (million hectare)
India	76.33	40.23	189.74
Rajasthan	6.93	35.95	19.29
Jalore	0.25	38.8	0.6523

Source: *Monthly Review of Rajasthan Economy*-September 2004, CMIE.

(b) Economic Profile

(i) Overview: The district does not have any industrial base. Both agriculture and animal husbandry are at a subsistence level, largely providing sub optimal returns. As a result, the area has lagged behind as ranked across all developmental parameters.

(ii) Per Capita Income: The per capita income of the district has lagged behind the average figure for the state as depicted in Table 22.6.

(iii) Domestic Product Composition: Table 22.7 details the contribution to net domestic product by various economic sectors:

Table 22.6

Per Capita Income

(in Rs.)

Year	Jalore	% Change	Rajasthan	% Change
1991	4,044	-	4,502	-
1992	6,066	50	5,175	15
1993	6,224	3	6,182	19
1994	7,322	18	7,647	24
1995	6,955	-5	8,467	11
1996	8,221	18	10,102	19
1997	9,114	11	10,997	9
1998	10,215	12	12,348	12
1999	9,419	-8	12,752	3

Source: *Estimates of Net District Domestic Product of Rajasthan,* published by Directorate of Economics and Statistics GoR.

The principal contribution to the net domestic product is from the agriculture and animal husbandry sector. This sector contributes around 45 per cent to the NDP whereas the corresponding figure for the state is only 30 per cent.

Table 22.7

Net Domestic Product

(Per Cent)

	Agriculture and Livestock	Mining and Manufacture	Transport and Communication	Other Services
Rajasthan	29.39	28.64	22.17	
Jalore	43.52	17.37	16.63	21.97

Source: *Estimates of Net District Domestic Product of Rajasthan,* published by Directorate of Economics and Statistics, GoR.

(iv) Employment: There are practically no industries in the region and a majority of the workforce in the

rural areas of Jalore are engaged in agriculture as depicted in Table 22.8 below:

Table 22.8

Sector-wise Employment of Workforce in Jalore

(Per Cent)

Agriculture		Landless Labourers		Cottage/Family Business		Others	
Male	Female	Male	Female	Male	Female	Male	Female
62.39	70.88	8.02	14.72	3.47	2.84	26.12	11.56

Source: *District Statistical Profile 2002,* published by Directorate of Economics and Statistics, GoR.

(v) Per Capita Savings: Per capita savings rate in the region as provided in Table 22.9 below, are again low in comparison to the State average. This could be attributable to low income levels, higher cost of living, lower levels of literacy and poor banking infrastructure.

Table 22.9

Per Capita Savings

Bank Deposits Per Capita in Rs. (2001 to 2002)	
Rajasthan	5,594
Jalore	2,172

Source: *Monthly Review of Rajasthan Economy-*March 2004, CMIE.

(vi) Credit Offtake: The credit to deposit ratio is quite low in the district at around 35 per cent in comparison to the corresponding figures of the state which stands at around 55 per cent. This statistic indicates the absence of demand drivers either in agriculture or in industry.

(vii) Economic Backwardness Driving Social Indices: The economy of the region is predominantly agrarian. However, return on investment, in a clearly hostile terrain, is marginal and in many instances negative. This has also had a direct effect on the social characteristics and indices of the region.

(c) Social Profile

(i) Population: Jalore has a population of around 1.4 million, which is 3 per cent of the total population of the state. The rate of growth in population is higher than the national average, but is comparable to Rajasthan as provided in Table 22.10 below:

Table 22.10

Decadal Population Growth Rate: 1991-2001

	(Per Cent)
India	21.34
Rajasthan	28.44
Jalore	26.52
Barmer	28.27

Source: *2001 Census Report.*

(ii) Sex Ratio: The number of females per thousand males in Rajasthan is lower than the national average as detailed in Table 22.11. This comparative figure for Jalore is higher than Rajasthan and the national average largely on account of the extensive migration of male workers.

Table 22.11

Sex Ratio

	(Females per Thousand)
India	933
Rajasthan	922
Jalore	942

Source: *2001 Census Report.*

(iii) Education and Literacy: As detailed in Table 22.12 below, the literacy levels in the district is below the state average. The literacy rate amongst women at 27 per cent in Jalore is the worst in the state.

(iv) Health Indicators: The district records some of the highest incidences of flourosis and renal stones due to the poor quality of water in the area.

Table 22.12

Literacy Rates

	(Per Cent)		
	Literacy Levels (% of Population)		
	Total	Male	Female
India	65.38	75.85	54.16
Rajasthan	61.03	76.46	44.34
Jalore	46.51	65.10	27.53

Source: *2001 Census Report.*

(v) Migration: As there are no permanent and economically rewarding employment avenues in Jalore, the area reports extensive emigration of population and livestock. Results of a recently conducted socioeconomic survey revealed that 50 per cent of households had at least one person emigrating for work. Herds of cattle and small ruminants are also moved out before summer, in search of fodder and water. This scale of emigration has had a negative impact on the socioeconomic fabric of the family, especially the womenfolk.

(d) Agriculture Indicators

(i) Current Crop Yields: Due to inadequate availability of water and poor agricultural inputs, crop yields in the area are well below the corresponding figures for the state and the country as shown in Table 22.13 below:

(ii) Fertiliser Use Per Hectare: Due to lack of water and low returns on the agricultural inputs, farmers in the region are poorly mechanised and apply inadequate amount of fertilisers in the field. Table 22.14 below provides data on the use of fertilisers as per hectare basis.

Table 22.13

Crop Yields

	Per Hectare Crop Yield in Kg.			
	Foodgrain	Rapeseed and Mustard	Maize	Bajra
India	1740	1000	2020	880
Rajasthan	1099	1060	1450	740
Jalore	204	806	-	24

Source: *Monthly Review of Rajasthan Economy*-September 2004, CMIE.

Table 22.14

Fertiliser Use

	Per Ha. Fertiliser Application in Kg.
India	95.23
Rajasthan	42.37
Jalore	24.90

Source: *Monthly Review of Rajasthan Economy*-September 2004, CMIE.

(iii) Agriculture Marketing and Value Addition: The main agriculture *mandi* towns especially for the Sanchor region are either in Gujarat or in Raniwara about 50 km away. There are few agro-based industries in the area.

(e) Budgetary Spends in the District

(i) Elements of Budgetary Spend: Based on the State Annual Plan, Table 22.15 indicates the level of budgetary support available to the district under various heads.

Table 22.15

Break-up of Annual Budgetary Spend in the District

(Rs. Million)

Sectors	Jalore
Agriculture and Allied Sectors	10.00
Rural Development	95.00
Special Area Programmes	-
Irrigation	90.00
Power	290.00
Industries	1.10
Transport	31.50
Services	185.20
Total	**702.80**

Source: *State Five Year Plan Document.*

(ii) Focus on Subsidy: Approximately Rs. 700 million is spent annually across various activities. A majority of the investments are in the nature of subsidy or support for ongoing activities and not necessarily in the form of capital investments and/or investments in human capital development or institution building.

(iii) Spends on Drought Relief: The above estimate of budgetary expenditure does not take into account the expenditures in relation to drought relief and other emergency measures. At the current juncture, no disaggregated data on this item of expenditure is available at a district level.

(iv) Unutilised Plan and Non-Plan Expenditures: The above estimates also do not include unutilised portions of Plan and non-Plan expenditures available to the state under the various schemes of GoI across sectors.

(3) Need for a Broad-based Developmental Programme

(a) Present State of the Local Economy: In the absence of any external intervention, the local economy will collapse. Frequent droughts, absence of any effective safety net, and lack of alternate means of employment outside the farm sector are likely to have a catastrophic effect on the population of the area, most of whom are already living below the poverty line.

(b) Potentiality of the District: However, the project area has several advantages. These include hardworking people and good solid conditions that have the potential to support agriculture. Agriculture and animal husbandry have the potential to be the economic drivers of the region.

(c) Water as the Catalyst: The development of agriculture and animal husbandry in this region has hitherto been restricted due to the non-availability of water. If water is brought to this area, and distributed in an organised manner, it has the potential to act as a catalyst for development.

(d) Potentiality for Industrialisation: The region is also blessed with oil and lignite deposits. Recent oil discoveries in Barmer have also opened up avenues for industrialisation. Development of urban and social infrastructure would eventually open up the area for industrial development.

(e) Jalore Area Development Program (JADP): It is in the above context that a broad-based local area intervention programme has been formulated for the region. The objective of the programme is to provide the area with a range of supportive infrastructure programmes and projects, which would catalyse economic and social development in an integrated, self-sustaining, and time bound basis.

(4) The Jalore Area Development Program

(a) Programme Overview

(i) Need for a Broad-based Initiative: A single project or initiative, on its own, would not have the capacity to transform the Jalore area. Accordingly, it is proposed to formulate a scheme on an area development basis, which would have the potential to make a broad-based impact on the local economy.

(ii) Focus and Drive Agriculture: This broad-based intervention would need to take into account the predominantly agrarian nature of the local economy and create suitable interventions, which would maximise the agriculture and allied outputs from the region. The scheme would also need to address the requirement of enhancing the social infrastructure levels in the district.

(iii) Range of Interventions: In order to achieve the above objective, a range of interventions is proposed. These would cover the provision of physical infrastructure services like water supply, roads, electricity, etc; support infrastructure services like development of *mandis*, agro-processing, dairy development, etc; and a range of soft inputs relating to best farm practices, development of Water Users Association (WUA), education, training of all Government officials and the provision of health incentives.

(b) Programme Elements

(i) Irrigation

- The most important driver for development of the area would be the availability of water for irrigation.

- The JADP envisages a major intervention in the irrigation sector by developing the command area of the Narmada

Canal in around 1.62 lakh hectare of land in the Jalore district.

- Implementation of this irrigation project would be central to the overall area development strategy as water is the most critical input for an agrarian economy like that of Jalore. All other interventions would be made either to provide support mechanism for the agriculture or to enhance the value so created. The proposed scheme builds upon the learnings from the impact of the Rajasthan canal on Bikaner and Sri Ganganagar districts.

- The irrigation project would be developed on a community participation model so as to ensure delivery of maximum benefits to the farmers of the area. A detailed description of the water distribution project and its linkages are provided in Annexure A-22.1.

- The cost of developing the irrigation distribution system in the Jalore district is estimated to be approximately Rs. 3.50 billion.

(ii) Rural Roads

- Roads provide direct connection between the centers of production and centres of demands (markets). Improving mobility can reduce rural poverty by facilitating women, men, and children to more readily access services (education, health, finance, markets), employment, obtain goods and income, and participate in social, political and community activities.

- Proximity to markets in Gujarat also offer opportunities for export of commodities from the district. A well laid out network of roads will facilitate this exchange. Annexure A-22.4(B) provides a term sheet of the rural roads improvement programme.

- The proposed area development plan envisages the rehabilitation and creation of a network of rural roads aggregating to 440 km in the project area. The cost of this component is estimated at Rs. 1 billion.

(iii) Drinking Water

- There is presently no organised drinking water supply for the towns and rural population in the district. Most of the demand is met through regional water supply schemes, which are in the nature of a stopgap arrangement.

- The present water supply is completely dependant on groundwater. The continuous depletion of groundwater resources has resulted in severe over-drawal of up to 250 per cent. The availability of water is also intermittent with a reported supply level of 30 lpcd to 40 lpcd. The quality of water has been deteriorating rapidly with very high levels of salinity and fluoride, which make it unfit for human consumption.

- As part of the program, a drinking water scheme would be developed so as to provide, over time, potable water supply to villages and towns of Jalore district. Water for this scheme shall be drawn from the Narmada main canal. Annexure A-22.4(C) provides a term sheet of the proposed drinking water scheme.

- The cost of the project is estimated at Rs. 6 billion.

(iv) Electrification

- Provision of electricity supply to the project area is critical for the overall development of the region. Electricity is crucial for ensuring water supply to the agricultural areas, through the proposed irrigation and drinking water scheme. In addition electricity supply to rural households would enhance the quality of life in the district.

- Wherever feasible, the objective of electricity development and distribution under the program would be to develop model community based systems i.e., systems that generate and distribute electricity for a community in a self sufficient manner.

- Various sources of electricity generation exist. These include oil/gas as well non-conventional sources such as wind energy, biomass and solar. The power so generated shall be supplied in the project area for meeting the irrigation and residential demand in the project area. Any surplus availability could be sold to the grid.

- Annexure A-22.4(D) provides a term sheet for the project. The capital cost of the electricity generation and distribution scheme is estimated at Rs. 2 billion.

(v) Agriculture Support Services

- The agricultural value chain includes a diverse range of large and small agro producers, agro enterprises, farm input and service suppliers (seeds, fertiliser, and equipment), downstream processors, traders and retailers.

- These enterprises are interlinked in networks that together constitute a market system that match buyers and sellers, provide avenues for consolidating small lots and grading, facilitate physical exchange and price discovery, transmit information, and manage risk.

- The JADP envisages the establishment of linkages to well-developed markets as well as local *mandis*, in order to provide farmers with the incentive to invest in sustainable production systems, facilitate access to inputs, increase agricultural productivity and increase profitability. The local *mandis* will not only work as centres for commodity exchange but also provide a platform for exchange of information on crops, superior seeds and best practices for agriculture specific to the local area.

- This initiative will depend largely on decisions made by the community in relation to what to grow, where to sell, how to maintain soil fertility, how to manage common grazing areas, etc.

- As part of this project component, it is proposed to implement extension programmes that focus on non-farm employment, women's empowerment, enterprise development, governance, civic rights, etc. Such programmes are expected to help make the rural population more effective in the management of their day-to-day chores.

- Annexure A-22.4(E) provides a detailed term sheet of this component of the JADP. The capital investments required for this initiative are expected to be Rs. 100 million. Continuous monitoring of these initiatives would be an integral part of this program.

(vi) Animal Husbandry and Dairy Development

- The area presently has an estimated population of 18 lakh livestock. The total population of cows and buffaloes are 2,00,00 and 3,00,000 respectively. The total milk production is estimated at 45.5 lakh litre per day (lpd). At a yield per cow of 3 lpd and buffalo of 4 lpd, yields are significantly below desired levels of 8 lpd to 10 lpd.

- Based on a comprehensive package of interventions, including improved availability of fodder, the overall production of milk is expected to increase to 8 lpd.

- It is also proposed to facilitate the development of Co-operatives to provide a framework for collection and processing of milk and associated produce.

- Annexure A-22.4(F) provides a term sheet on this component of the program. The investment required in the dairy development and process is estimated at Rs. 100 million.

(vii) Credit and Insurance Facilities

- The current availability of credit through organised agencies for investment in agriculture, small-scale industries and other businesses is negligible. As part of the program, a consortium of banks could be established under the lead of NABARD or any other commercial bank to support the project finance and working capital requirements of the area.

- Existing banks and institutions, such as the RRB's, DCBs, PACs, etc. would form the core members of the consortium. The consortium would enter into common contractual documentation within the proposed institutional framework. This approach will significantly simplify procedures, provide better management of credit

in the district and ensure availability and support to prioritized initiatives in the district.

- Similarly, appropriate insurance products would be made available (including crop insurance) to support and mitigate a range of risks associated with agricultural and other activities in the area.

- The awareness of cost-benefits to farmers and other economic agents in the district would require continuous dissemination through awareness programmes, educational programmes, extension programmes, etc.

(viii) Formation of Water User Associations

- Water User Associations comprising around 20 to 25 farmers would need to be constituted in the project area. These associations would serve as the grassroot level forums for participatory management in the process for all stakeholders.

- The associations would actively participate in the management of the 'last mile' infrastructure and would be responsible for collection of user charges and remittance.

- The role of WUA would not be limited to management of irrigation water but would also encompass other sectors like animal husbandry, agriculture extension services, education, etc.

(ix) Marketing Arrangements

- Adequate arrangements are proposed to be made for off-take of farm produce from the area and its further selling at the appropriate price. A hierarchical structure of *mandis* could be created on a progressive basis to facilitate trading of the agriculture produce. The location and structure of *mandis* would be undertaken in consultation with the various stakeholders in the area.

- Additional arrangements would be made for sorting, packaging and storing of farm produce for better realisation of revenue for the farmer. An estimated amount of Rs. 100 million would be needed for creation of such facilities.

(x) Training Programmes for the Community and the Government

- The ultimate objective of the JADP is to put in place a sustainable development model. To achieve this objective, it would be essential to train local personnel and empower them across a range of topics including civic rights, women's employment, vocational training, enterprise development and management, health education and awareness, etc.

- The JADP would also seek to provide training on the best farm practices, water conservation, self-employment skills, etc.

- Concurrently, the JADP would impart training to all Government officials on a range of subjects which would enable them realise the changing role of Government in the new economy, the need for a shift in thinking from a process oriented role to a more result oriented one, etc.

(xi) School Improvement Programme

- The district of Jalore has 1,500 educational Institutions which are in various states of disrepair.

- An integral component of the JADP would be to improve the educational standards in the district by improving the physical facilities, providing IT infrastructure, teacher training and assisting in the introduction of ICT based education.

- In particular, the school improvement programme would establish a baseline of achievement in the current school/ educational institutions. The objective of the programme would be to achieve measurable improvement in pass percentages, student retention and in the motivation of teachers and students.

- In addition to the foregoing, vocational training, enterprise development, etc., would be introduced in all the educational institutions in the district.

(5) Programme Investment

(a) The break-up of investment in the various components of the JADP is provided in Table 22.16 below:

Table 22.16

Project Cost of the JADP

Component	Rs. Million
Irrigation Distribution	3,500
Drinking Water	6,000
Rural Roads	1,000
Electrification	2,000
Agriculture Support Services	100
Animal Husbandry/Dairy Development	100
Storage Processing and Packaging Facilities	100
School Improvement Programme	1,000
Training and Agricultural Extension Services	200
Project Management and Supervision	1,000
Total	**15,000**

(b) The above estimates will require to be finalised based on detailed engineering and on-the-ground surveys.

(6) Programme Benefits

(a) Outcomes of the JADP

(i) The JADP is expected to significantly enhance per capita income in the district. The direct and indirect economic benefits accruing from the availability of adequate water for drinking as well as for irrigation purposes will act as a catalyst for economic and social development.

(ii) The spin-off benefits from the project will also accelerate development in adjoining areas. The region has the potential to become the second granary of Rajasthan after the command area of IGMP.

(iii) The following Section discusses the likely benefits from the implementation of the JADP. Given the significant economic benefit it should ordinarily be possible to establish a framework for recovery of investments.

(b) Benefits to Agriculture

(i) Existing Cropping Pattern and Produce

  - At present the *kharif* crops of *Bajra*, *Moth* and *Guar* are the dominant crops, as they are drought resistant and thrive in saline soils.

  - These crops can usually survive on rain-fed irrigation and provide ample fodder even when there is a failure of the monsoon. Farmers are inclined to sow these crops as an insurance measure against crop failure, even though the average yield and the returns in terms of value realised from the market is low as compared to crops like wheat, mustard and other cash crops.

  - Emphasis on mixed cropping pattern (*Bajra*-pulse) is widely pursued as another measure to avoid-risk of crop failure. Thus, the present scarcity of water in the project area mandates sowing of economically low yielding crops.

  - Sanchore has a relatively larger irrigated area and hence has a winter crop of wheat, mustard and cumin. *Rabi* season crops are wheat, barley, mustard, etc., which are raised with irrigation by tube wells and dugwells.

Commercial crops like cumin and isabgol are also sown in areas where sweet water is available.

  - A little less then one-third of the total area is fallow land. The irrigated area as a per cent of cropped area is relatively small. Land use pattern and irrigated area (1999-00) is provided in Table 22.17 as under:

Table 22.17

Land Use Pattern

(Figures in Lac Ha.)

	Gudhamalani	Chauhtan	Sanchore
Total Geographical Area	3.98	4.69	3.01
Cultivated Area	2.32	2.23	1.39
Uncultivated Area	0.28	0.61	0.28
Fallow Land	1.15	1.62	1.09

Source: Tahal Consultancy *Report on Narmada Canal Project* 2004.

(ii) Post-project Cropping Pattern and Produce

  - Once water is available from Narmada Canal, the cropping pattern is likely to change resulting in a significant increase in the value of agriculture production. The benefits would result from the following:

    • Increase in the area under irrigation.

    • Increase in production yield per hectare.

    • Increase in production of economically rewarding crops.

  - As a result of the JADP, cropping intensity will increase, and more area will be covered under double cropping. Cropped area under irrigation in the Sanchore *tehsil* will increase from 39,000 hectare to 1.00 lakh ha. Annexure A-22.5 to this Memorandum gives the cropping pattern in the pre and post project scenario.

  - The cropping pattern will thus shift towards sowing of cash crops like groundnut, castor, tomato, fruits, cumin, *isabgol*, pea and oats (fodder) which would result in better realisation. The suggested cropping pattern takes into account various factors like soil texture, depth and topography.

- Yield for various crops would increase dramatically with availability of water and application of optimum fertilisers, as detailed in Table 22.18 below:

Table 22.18

Expected Crop Yields

(Production in Qtl/Ha)

Crops	Before Narmada Project	After Narmada Project
Castor	3.08	18
Cumin	2.72	10
Mustard	5.05	15
Wheat	5.37	35

Source: Tahal Consultancy *Report on Narmada Canal Project*.

Table 22.19 shows gross quantity of the major crops grown in the area both in the pre-project and post-project scenario.

Table 22.19

Quantities by Crop

Crop	Pre Project MT	Post Project MT
Bajra, *Moth* and *Gaur* fodder	883	3,68,823
Wheat	536	43,029
Mustard	319	49,435
Cumin	2,401	23,082
Isabgol	1,791	11,089
Vegetable	-	1,84,123
Fruits	-	41,402
Fodder Oats	-	1,10,647

Source: Tahal Consultancy *Report on Narmada Canal Project*.

The total crop production after the completion of the project is expected to be 9,00,000 MT in comparison to the pre-project levels of 66,000 MT.

- The gross value of the post project annual production is expected to be about Rs. 3.50 billion as against the pre project annual production of Rs. 10 million. This translates into a value creation of Rs. 22,500 per hectare or about Rs. 9,500 per capita per annum.

- In addition, the project would generate ample opportunities for employment, improvement in wage levels, and reduction in unemployment and under-employment.

(c) Benefits to Animal Husbandry

(i) Present Situation

- Animal husbandry is an important part of the economy of the region. Agriculture and animal husbandry form part of a mutually complementary mix within traditional farming systems.

- The Sanchore area is known for excellent varieties of cattle and other livestock. For instance, goats of the Marwari breed are a conventional source of additional nutrition and cash income.

- Table 22.20 gives livestock population of the Sanchore *tehsil* which is covered under the project:

- Income from animal husbandry is typically regarded to be more stable than income from agriculture, and provides a cushion against economic shocks. However, the district lacks adequate dairy infrastructure. The nearest milk collection, chilling/processing centre is 45 km from the irrigation project area at Sanchore.

Table 22.20

2001 Population of Livestock in Sanchore

Population (Lac)	3.68
Total Livestock (Lac)	3.96
Livestock per Person	1.10
Livestock per ha.	1.31
Land per Person	0.82

Source: *District Statistical Profile 2002*, published by Directorate of Economics and Statistics, GoR.

- The value of milk produced per household per annum varies between Rs. 5,500 and Rs. 32,800 in the district. This variation is largely dependant on the type of livestock, availability of fodder and water.

- Overall, the continual scarcity of fodder resulting from a lack of adequate water has also resulted in decline in the market price of cattle stock.

- The livestock industry in Jalore has been adversely impacted by encroachment on pasture lands, lack of processing and market infrastructure and non-remunerative prices for products like wool. The JADP seeks to address these lacunae.

(ii) Post JADP Impact

- Availability of water from the Narmada canal project and other supporting infrastructure would greatly improve the commercial aspects of animal husbandry in the district.

- Enhanced income earned from animal husbandry would be more pronounced in comparison to those from the agriculture as these improvements are less dependant on human intervention—availability of fodder can itself accelerate the well-being of cattle.

- A fast growing animal husbandry sector would fuel and necessitate development of ancillary industry like chilling plants and milk processing centres.

- Availability of water from the canal would also enable the introduction of better breeds of animals, which would further improve income realisations from livestock.

- As a result of the implementation of the JADP, around 8,00,000 litres of milk could be produced per day, which at the prevailing market rate for milk would generate additional income of Rs. 1 billion per annum.

(d) Income Multipliers

(i) Irrigated agriculture would result in diversification of not only the agriculture sector, but also of the local economy.

(ii) Growth of several non-agricultural activities due to the need for inputs and new requirements for servicing higher production volumes like transport, markets, processing and storage would transform the traditional economic structure.

(iii) The conventional output multiplier of investment in agriculture, particularly irrigation, is estimated to be 1.8 i.e., the income effect of an investment in irrigation would generate additional income that is almost twice the original investment. This additional income is derived from several non-agriculture activities due to input needs and the creation of new needs referred to earlier.

(iv) The project area can thus expect to generate additional income of around Rs. 7 billion.

(e) Environmental Benefits

(i) The crops chosen for the project are salt tolerant, require shorter duration for cultivation and require less water. The introduction of a sprinkler system of irrigation would entail increased frequency of irrigation, which would help in reducing the salt accumulation.

(ii) Irrigation with saline groundwater is restricted to about 30 per cent of the crop water requirement, which would be applied only during the growth stage of the crop.

The preceding and succeeding watering would be with canal water, which is of good quality, leading to a self-controlled leaching effect.

(iii) The soil will require application of gypsum or farm yield manure (FYM) or a combination of both for reclamation of soc soils and/or zinc sulfate to eliminate zinc deficiency, etc. Application of FYM would become an important and regular practice as it increases the water retention capacity of the soils and reduces environmental pollution. It also improves the physical, chemical and biological conditions of the soil.

(iv) The method of conjunctive use of water i.e., use of groundwater in conjunction with canal water and bio drainage as envisaged in the project proposals would ensure that the problems of waterlogging which have been experienced in some of the other large irrigation projects do not occur in the project area.

(f) Indirect Benefits

(i) Purchasing Power

- An increase in the per capita income resulting from agriculture, animal husbandry and other activities will place more purchasing power in the hands of the farmers, who may utilise it for health, education, farm mechanisation and other welfare activities of the family.

- Apart from the foregoing, it is envisaged that revenues accruing to the government would also increase.

- Implementation of the program would create opportunities for direct employment for skilled, semi-skilled and unskilled manpower of the area.

(iii) Capacity Building

- The project would operate on the basis of participatory management. It is estimated that around 1,000 WUAs would need to be formed in the irrigation project alone. The WUAs would also be actively involved in the implementation of the other components of the JADP.

- These committees would be responsible for O&M and for the equitable distribution of water. The WUAs would also be utilised for establishing cooperative structures for dairy farming and agriculture extension services. This would enhance the self-management capability of the local people.

- Membership to the WUA would comprise all traditional and non-traditional stakeholders in the area.

(iii) Health Benefits

- Increased rural road connectivity would improve access to better health services.

- Safe water supply would reduce risk of water borne diseases. Incidence of diseases like gastroenteritis, cholera which contribute significantly to infant mortality would decrease.

- A reduction in these diseases would also reduce the number of man-days lost due to ill-health, which in turn would have its concomitant impact on income levels and medical expenses.

(iv) Impact on Flora and Fauna

- Increase in per capita income would reduce pressure on natural forests and their produce and lead to protection of flora and fauna.

- Reserve forests have been included in the command area and would be provided the required water.

- Irrigation would be effected on an average in 40 per cent of the area during *rabi* season and about 20 per cent of the area in *kharif* season. The remaining area would be available for activities such as grazing of animals, operating wood lots, etc.

- Dependable availability of water would help the existing flora and fauna of the region.

- Availability of fuel wood for the rural population would also increase significantly, reducing the pressure on forests.

(vii) Drought Proofing the District

- As stated earlier, the economy of the region hinges upon the availability of water for agriculture. Perhaps the singular direct impact of the proposed scheme is that the district would no longer remain captive to the vagaries of monsoon.

- Development of alternate sources of employment, better mobility of labour and improved income from animal husbandry would immensely increase the resilience in the economy.

- As farm output increases, the demand for labourers would increase, leading to employment avenues for landless labourers.

(g) Summary of Impact: Table 22.21 below captures the net impact of the project in financial terms.

It is targeted that for an incremental investment of Rs. 15 billion, the project area would yield an annual output in the region of Rs. 8 billion, excluding any incremental benefits accruing through the income multiplier effect.

Table 22.21

Financial Benefits of the JADP

(Rs. Million)

Particulars	Value
Total Investments	15,000
Total Annual Benefits	
Incremental Agricultural Production	3,500
Incremental Milk Production	1,000

ANNEXURE A-22.1

Description of the Water Distribution Project

I. Project Components

(1) The principal conveyance system for carrying water from the Narmada reservoir to the three *tehsils* falling under the project coverage is being executed in three components as listed below:

  (a) Water Storage System and Main Canal in Gujarat

  (b) Main Canal in Rajasthan

  (c) Distribution network in Rajasthan

(2) Main Canal in Gujarat

  (a) The main water storage and conveyance system in Gujarat consists of Sardar Sarovar Dam and Narmada Main Canal. The capacity of the Sardar Sarovar dam has been fixed at 9.5 MAF.

  (b) Narmada main canal which runs for a length of 458 km in Gujarat before entering in Rajasthan at a village called Sillu in the district Jalore, has a design discharge capacity of 1133 cumec.

  (c) The losses in main canal system within Gujarat is expected to be of the order of 0.04216 MAF and thus a maximum of only 0.45784 MAF of water would be available to Rajasthan under this project.

  (d) Presently, Gujarat is in the process of implementing the Narmada Canal and it is estimated that water should be available at the Rajasthan border by June 2006.

(3) Main Canal in Rajasthan

  (a) Water carried to the Rajasthan border shall be further transferred to the project area through a main canal running for 74 km.

  (b) The canal would traverse the districts in question and would finally terminate at a place near Sinchava in Jalore.

  (c) Government of Rajasthan has been implementing the project through budgetary resources. Fifty-four kms of works has already been completed. It is expected that the balance works would be completed by 2006.

(4) Distribution Network in Rajasthan

  (a) The command area for the project as stated earlier, has been defined to include three *tehsils*, namely Gudhamalani, Chauhtan and Sanchore which happen to be the most backward areas of the region.

  (b) Cumulatively the project will affect the livelihood of a population of approximately 17 lakh covering an area of 2.46 hectares, falling in 129 villages of Jalore and 104 villages of Barmer districts.

  (c) A distribution system consisting of distributaries, minors and sub minors has been planned for the delivery of water to the agricultural farms.

II. Options for Water Delivery to the Fields

(1) There are traditionally two techniques for delivery of water to the field. One is based on the conventional technique of flow irrigation. The second is based on the concept of pressure irrigation using sprinklers and drips.

(2) Conventional irrigation has the following disadvantages:

  (a) Flow or surface irrigation though cheaper to build and maintain, creates problems in the long run.

  (b) The adverse impact of flow irrigation is more severe and immediate in areas with high soil and water salinity and in areas with high groundwater table.

  (c) As there is great amount of water loss under this system, owing to evaporation and leakages.

  (d) Field application of water through open channels has rendered thousands of irrigable land worthless in the command area of Indira Gandhi Canal due to water-logging.

(3) Pressure irrigation has the following advantages

   (a) This method employs application of water using either sprinkler sets or drip irrigation sets.

   (b) Water needs to be delivered under a certain minimum pressure to enable the adoption and functioning of this system.

   (c) This method results in a great saving of water and has been tried world over to achieve optimum application of irrigation water to the crops. Israel has used this technique to a great extent and has achieved superior farm yields even though the per capita water availability is lower in comparison to that of Rajasthan.

   (d) Sprinkler and drip irrigation methods are especially useful in areas where land is highly undulating, water is scarce and chances of waterlogging are high.

   (e) As water is applied in desired quantity only, using these techniques the problems like leaching of soil, soil erosion and waterlogging can be controlled.

(4) The option to be adopted for any project would have to be decided after considering a number of factors. These principally relate to soil conditions, environmental impact and cost of delivery.

(5) Soil Conditions in the Project Area

   The soils in the area, especially in the Sanchore. Gudhamalani and Chauhtan *tehsils* have been classified as moderately good irrigable to marginally irrigable. Soils in these *tehsils* are alluvial plain soils of rivers Luni, Sukri and their tributaries. The remaining tracts also can be brought under economic irrigation if suitable irrigation techniques are adopted.

(6) Adverse Environmental Impact (IGNP Experience): A recent example of conventional flow irrigation adopted by Rajasthan in similar soil conditions relates to the Indira Gandhi Nahar Project. Although the project has helped to transform the local economy, it has also resulted in severe degradation of environment. The following are the key lessons from the IGNP project:

   (a) The single most important problem of the IGNP project has been the problem of waterlogging known as "Sem" in local language. As the flooding method of irrigation is used in this project thousands of hectare of culturable land has become useless.

   (b) Flow irrigation has also created problems of leaching and large tracts of land have become infertile.

   (c) Waterlogging has also resulted in eruption of pests and diseases, never heard of in the area.

   (d) It has had adverse impact on the health of the local community too and incidences of diseases like malaria has dramatically gone up.

   (e) The unmindful use of water has also resulted in adverse effect to local flora and fauna.

(7) Considering the above experience and the advantage of the pressure irrigation system, Government of Rajasthan has decided to adopt the latter technology of pressure irrigation for water distribution in the project area.

III. Water Delivery System

(1) Water shall be applied to the fields using an innovative technology of Pressure Irrigation as opposed to the traditional methods of flow irrigation.

(2) Field irrigation system consisting of sprinkler sets shall also be provided to the farmers/WUAs. Cost estimates of the project also take into account provision for the same.

(3) Following schematic represents the water distribution system in the project area

(4) Water from the main canal shall be transferred to the distributaries network and then to minors under gravity or lift flow as per suitability. Water then, shall be delivered

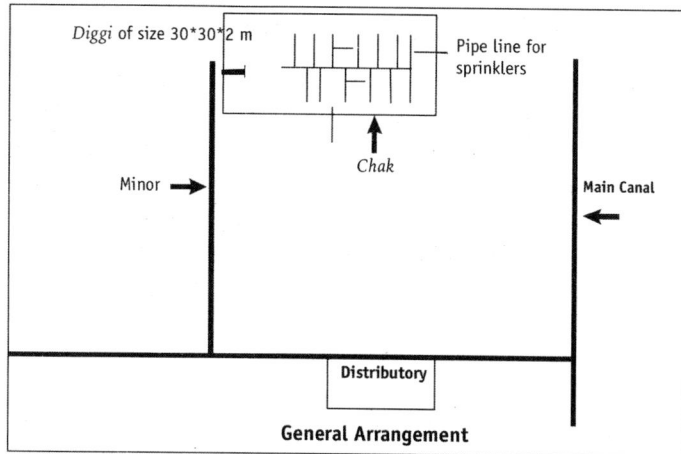

General Arrangement

to *diggies* (water collection ponds) which will cater to the needs of surrounding group of agriculture fields.

(5) A total number of 13 distributaries will off-take water from the main canal of which 3 will be lift distributaries. Total length of these distributaries shall be 390 km.

(6) The water shall be delivered to individual fields through a well laid out network of Canal Minors. The length of the network formed by these minors will be 1636 km.

(7) *Diggies* shall be constructed for a group of fields identified as one *chak* (approximate size 250 ha). A total no of approx. 1000 such *diggies* shall be constructed in the command area.

(8) Capacity of each *diggy*: Each of these *diggies* shall have a capacity sufficient to cater to the water demand of a particular *chak* for 2 days. Typical dimensions of a *diggy* would be 30x30x2 m (around 1800 m3).

IV. Key Features of System Design

The project has been designed for achieving optimum operational and financial efficiencies through innovative technical and implementation design. Due care has also been taken for minimising the damages to environment.

(1) It is based on new concept of conjunctive utilisation of available surface (canal) water and groundwater. For this purpose only 90 per cent of requirement will be supplied through canal water and the rest shall have to be met by dugwells or small bore wells.

(2) No flood irrigation has been proposed. There is complete switchover to pressure irrigation system (i.e. sprinkler and drip irrigation) with mandatory full atomisation.

(3) Farmers will be encouraged individually/collectively to construct shallow tube wells. They can pump limited quantities of groundwater to ensure supplementary irrigation. The same pumps can be used to lift water from the from the outlet point, in case secondary lifting is required to maintain requisite pressure at the sprinkler. The drainage problem in the entire command can be kept under control through this measure.

(4) Keeping in view the high cost of water, salinity in soils, geology of strata, quality of groundwater, etc. a low water allowance has been kept for the project area as under:

For Ned (Luni Delta) area	1.31 cusec per 1000 acres
Lift irrigation areas	2.40 cusec per 1000 acres
For flow irrigation	2.51 cusec per 1000 acres

(5) To ensure efficient utilisation, water will be delivered on a volumetric basis (at point of discharge) and charged accordingly unlike the prevalent practice of billing in which tariffs are levied on the basis of area.

(6) The project has been designed to include a number of water conservation measures for utilisation and extensive irrigation.

(7) Eco-friendly bio-drainage is being promoted to check any likely waterlogging.

V. Other Critical Components of the Project

(1) Electrical Works

(a) Dedicated power supply lines and power stations will be established for meeting the power requirements. The electrical works will thus consist of the following activities:

    (i) Erection of power lines and maintenance thereof, for lifting water to the lift distributaries.

    (ii) Erection of power lines for providing power to the sprinkler set systems, wherever required.

(b) It is estimated that around 5 MW power will be consumed in operating the pumping systems of the lift canals, and, on another 27 MW power shall be needed for running the sprinkler systems.

(c) The entity running and maintaining the irrigation system will bear the cost of power for operating pumps for the lift canals. Cost of power consumed in running the sprinkler sets shall be borne directly by the farmers.

(2) Service Roads

The scope of the proposed project also covers design and development of network of service roads along the water conveyance system for routine maintenance and inspection.

(3) Rehabilitation & Resettlement (R&R)

Since the project is focused on construction of canal system, no displacement of population or major land acquisition is envisaged. However, during the process of project implementation, a small strip of land along the canal alignment shall be acquired and temporary acquisition of land (for bypass works) would also be done. Issues pertaining to the land acquisition shall be addressed as per the provisions of R&R policy of the project, which is in accordance with the policy approved for the irrigation sector by the State government.

VI. Status with Respect to Project Implementation

A summary of the current status with respect to the various project components is provided below:

Component	Agency	Current Status	Likely Completion Date
Sardar Sarovar Dam	Gujarat Government	Completed	
Narmada Main Canal in Gujarat	Gujarat Government	Around 360 km out of 458 km completed	June 2006
Narmada Main Canal in Rajasthan	Rajasthan Government	54 km out of 74 km completed	June 2006
Distribution Network		Not started yet	

ANNEXURE A-22.2

List of Stakeholders and Possible Role Plays

Sl. No.	Possible Stakeholders	Role and Value Addition
1.	Government of Rajasthan	The participation of Government of Rajasthan would facilitate integration of the objectives of the company with state's objective. Further, Government of Rajasthan would act as an enabler for implementation of the various project components including enactment and creation of appropriate legal and regulatory frameworks.
2.	Financial Institutions/ Insurance	The participation in the project company of various development financial institutions, such as IL&FS, IDBI NABARD, etc. would facilitate development of the project as per acceptable commercial principles. This would ensure financial discipline in project implementation, thereby enabling the company to raise financial resources

contd. ...

... contd. ...

Sl. No.	Possible Stakeholders	Role and Value Addition
	Companies	from the market. Participation from insurance companies would also facilitate in introduction of various innouation methods in managing crop insurance.
3.	Beneficiary Community	The farming community who is likely to be direct beneficiaries of the project would represent the user group in the company. The participation of the user group would ensure that the projects taken up for development are priorities based on actual user requirements.
4.	Value Added Service Providers	This group consists of institutions/companies which would enable value addition to the agriculture community, e.g. participation of companies such as Mahindra & Mahindra, ITC, Pepsi, etc. would provide a mechanism to implement contract farming and modern agricultural support services. Participation of these companies would facilitate implementation of the necessary forward linkages, such as *mandis*, processing units, etc. which would ultimately create sustainable value for the local community.
5.	Other Service Providers	These could consist of investors interested in setting up and managing social infrastructure interventions, such as schools and hospitals.

ANNEXURE A-22.3

*Term Sheet for District Development Agreement between
Government of Rajasthan and JADCL*

Sl. No.	Term/Issue	Details
1.	Parties	Government of Rajasthan ("GoR") and Jalore Area Development Corporation Limited ("JADCL").
2.	Objective	To vest JADCL with the responsibility (and the corresponding rights and obligations) of implementing, and ensuring the due development, designing, financing, construction, operation and maintenance of certain types of infrastructure facilities, on a BOOT basis, within the district of Jalore.
3.	Infrastructure Facilities which would be covered by the DDA	JADCL would be given the responsibility (and the corresponding rights and obligations) of developing the following infrastructure facilities and provide related be services:

    i. Irrigation: Irrigation distribution channels across the entire district

    ii. Drinking Water: Drinking water schemes for the entire district

    iii. Rural Roads: Rural roads within the entire district.

    iv. Electricity Distribution: Electricity distribution facilities for the entire district. (Note: JADCL or the SPV created by JADCL will need a distribution licence from the RSERC under the Electricity Act, 2003 for undertaking electricity transmission or distribution activities.)

contd. ...

... contd. ...

Sl. No.	Term/Issue	Details
		v. Electricity Generation: Electricity generation facilities primarily using local resources.
		vi. Agriculture: Agriculture support facilities and services so as to enable farmers to access markets for their produce, efficiently manage of their produce, access working capital and crop insurance.
		vii. Animal Husbandry: Facilities for providing and improving animal husbandry.
		viii. Training Facilities and Services: Providing facilities and services for community training to selected people of the district and to government employees in the district with a view to restructuring and improving their skills and knowledge and enabling them to provide and deliver better administrative services for enabling the district administration to respond to the changing competitive environment and ensure the overall development of the district.
		ix. Schools: Providing new schools, improvement of the facilities of existing schools, improvement of the facilities of existing schools, providing training of teachers and undertaking such other tasks with the view to improve education in schools in the district.
		x. Additional Facilities and Services: Undertaking development of such other facilities and providing such other services as may be mutually agreed to between COR and JADCL from time to time.
4.	Tenure	The DDA would have an initial period of thirty (30) years and can be extended by mutual agreement for additional periods of five (5) years at a time The tenure of the DDA would be subject to extension in certain circumstances as provided in other provisions of the agreement (such as on occurrence of force major event, etc.).
5.	Development Board	The DDA will provide for the constitution of a Board Development that will comprise of representatives from GoR, District Administration and JADCL, which will essentially monitor the implementation by JADCL of the responsibilities vested in it under the DDA. JADCL will submit periodic reports to the Development Board specifying the specific infrastructure facilities that it has selected for development and the extent of the development of such facilities Development Board will comprise of a maximum number of persons to be agreed between JADCL and GoR.
6.	Overall Responsibilities of JADCL	JADCL will: i. Identify the specific facilities within the sectors identified above that it will undertake for development, construction, operation and maintenance from time to time. ii. Undertake the entire development (including designing), construction, operation and maintenance of such facilities identified by it. iii. Subject to GoR making its contribution to the Jalore District Development Fund and levy of user fee as and when recommended by JADCL, arrange and undertake the entire financing for the relevant facilities identified for development by it.

contd. ...

... contd. ...

Sl. No.	Term/Issue	Details
		iv. Will select and appoint such contractors as may be necessary in order to take the due development, construction operation and maintenance of the identified facilities.
7.	Grant of Rights to JADCL for Development of Infrastructure Facilities and Implementation through SPVs	The DDA shall grant JADCL all the rights required to enable it to develop, design, fiance, construct, operate and maintain infrastructure facilities that are selected on a BOOT basis. These rights shall *inter alia* include:
		i. Right to undertake due diligence, feasibility studies, land surveys, etc. in order to select an infrastructure facility for further development.
		ii. Right to design, construct, own, operate and maintain the infrastructure facility.
		iii. Right to appoint contractors/sub-contractors for undertaking any aspect of the development, design, construction, operation and maintenance of the relevant facility.
		iv. Right to undertake financing of the infrastructure facility at its sole discretion.
		v. Right to create security over the infrastructure facility in favour of the lenders that have participated in the financing of the relevant infrastructure facility.
		vi. Right to collect user fee (subject to the terms of the DDA) from the users of the relevant infrastructure facility GoR agrees that JADCL can establish SPVs for the development, construction operation and maintenance of specific infrastructure facilities. The rights granted to JADCL in relation to infrastructure facilities under the DDA shall be applicable and extend to any SPV created by JADCL for implementing a particular project.
8.	Jalore District Development Fund Account	JADCL shall constitute and maintain a separate trust and retention account with a scheduled bank agreed to by both parties to be known as 'Jalore District Development Fund Account' ("JDDF Account"). GoR shall contribute and deposit into the JDDF Account, as initial seed capital, an amount of Rs. 5 crore. This shall be a one time payment obligation only.
		JADCL shall deposit all monies that it collects as fees from the users of the various infrastructure facilities developed by it into the JDDF Account.
		The monies in the JDDF Account shall be used only for the purpose of implementation of projects under the DDA.
		JADCL shall have the obligation to ensure the due growth of the monies available in the JDDF Account after the GoR has made its initial construction.
		JDDF Account shall be operated by JADCL in accordance with the trust and retention account agreement that would be executed in relation to it.
9.	Levy of User Fee	GoR agrees that most of the infrastructure facilities developed by JADCL will have to provide services on commercial basis and a suitable user fee would be levied on the users of such facilities.
		JADCL will specify which of the facilities that it develops will require levy of a user fee.

contd. ...

... contd. ...

Sl. No.	Term/Issue	Details

The user fee will be based on the total expenditure incurred in the construction, operation and maintenance of the facility.

JADCL shall propose the methodology for determination of the user fee as well as the rates for user fee for a particular facility to the Development Board. Upon submission of the user rates to the Development Board, GoR shall notify the stated fee in respect of the relevant facility under the applicable law. (Note: the determination and levy of user fee will be subject to the applicable laws relating to the relevant facility.)

GoR will undertake any amendment to the applicable laws that are within its jurisdiction, as may be required in order to enable the levy of the user fee in relation to the relevant facility.

JADCL shall be vested with the right to collect the user fee for the relevant infrastructure facilities.

JADCL shall deposit the user fee collected into the JDDF Account, to be used for the implementation of the DDA.

If GoR does not want any user fee to be charged or wants any specific subsidy to be provided on the user fee in respect of a facility that has been identified as requiring the levy of a user fee, then GoR shall make regular contributions to the JDDF Account in order to compensate for the loss of revenue and ensure that there are due amounts available in the account for the implementation of the DDA. The amount of contribution to be so provided by GoR shall be determined by JADCL.

10. Annuity Payment

In consideration of JADCL undertaking to discharge its responsibilities under the DDA, GoR shall make an aggregate annual payment of Rs. 150 crore to JADCL which shall be paid in equal quarterly payments.

The quarterly payment shall be made before the 7th of the first month of the relevant quarter.
The annuity payment received by JADCL shall not be deposited in the JDDF Account and will not be subject to any obligation, trust or charge.

JADCL shall have the right to withdraw amounts from the JDDF Account in order to meet any shortfall in payment of annuity by GoR.

11. Support of GoR

GoR shall provide all reasonable support to JADCL for ensuring the due implementation of the DDA by JADCL. JADCL shall specify the nature of support that is required and GoR shall provide such support. The nature of support that may be required is expected to include, but not be limited to:

i. Providing land and undertaking land acquisition for specific facilities.

ii. Promulgation of such rules, regulations and notifications as may be required in order to enable the due development, construction, operation and maintenance of a facility by JADCL.

iii. Execution of such contracts/documents by GoR as may be required for enabling the due development, construction, operation and maintenance of a facility by JADCL.

contd. ...

... contd. ...

Sl. No.	Term/Issue	Details
		iv. Amendment of any particular state law that may be required in order to enable the due implementation of the DDA.
		v. Issue relevant instructions to authorities within its jurisdiction to support the due implementation of the DDA and to provide such support as may be reasonably requested by JADCL in obtaining relevant permits and clearances for the development, construction, operation and maintenance of infrastructure facilities pursuant to the DDA.
		vi. Execution of such contracts or promulgation of such notifications, rules or regulations as may be required in order to finance any particular infrastructure facility.
		vii. Assistance in obtaining the various clearances required for developing, constructing, operating and maintaining infrastructure facilities.
12.	Grant of Rights with Respect to a Particular Infrastructure Facility	The DDA provides the basic framework pursuant to which JADCL shall undertake the development, construction, operation and maintenance of infrastructure facilities of the nature specified in the DDA. However, GoR acknowledges and agrees that it may be necessary to vest JADCL or the SPV established by JADCL with rights to develop, construct, operate and maintain specifically for certain infrastructure facilities under applicable laws. GoR undertakes that when facility specific rights are required to be granted to JADCL or its SPV under applicable laws, GoR shall vest such specific rights are may be required with JADCL in such manner (by notification or execution of a specific agreement) as may be required by law or reasonably requested by JADCL in order to ensure the due financing of the relevant facility.
13.	Financing	JADCL shall have complete discretion in the manner of arranging for the financing required for the development of the various infrastructure facilities pursuant to the DDA.\n\nJADCL can create such security interests in favour of the lenders as may be required by them.\n\nGoR shall execute such documents, issue such notifications or rules or regulations as may be required by the lenders in order to finance a particular infrastructure facility.\n\nGoR shall provide for step-in rights and substitution rights in favour of lenders in relation to the specific infrastructure facilities as may be requested by the lenders and execute such documents as may be required in order to vest such rights with the lenders.
14.	Change in Law	If GoR initiates a change in law or policy or there occurs a change in law or policy that prevents JADCL from further implementing the DDA or restricts or removes any of the rights of JADCL, including but not limited to receiving annuity payments, then JADCL shall have the right to terminate the DDA and received adequate compensation in relation thereto.
15.	Dispute Resolution	Disputes will be resolved through arbitration under the Arbitration Act, 1996 by a three member panel. Venue of arbitration shall be New Delhi.

contd. ...

... contd. ...

Sl. No.	Term/Issue	Details
		Disputes relating to user fee or the extent of contribution to be made by GoR on account of waiver of subsidy of the user fee shall be determined by an Independent Expert who shall be a chartered accountant or a firm of chartered accountants of national repute.
16.	Termination and Transfer Period	GoR can terminate the DDA only if any of the following events occur ('JADCL Events of Default'): (i) JADCL fails to select any infrastructure project to develop within a period of 12 months from the date of execution of this Agreement, or (ii) JADCL becomes bankrupt for reasons other than a GoR Event of Default.
		JADCL can terminate the DDA if any of the following events occur ('GoR Events of Default'): (i) GoR fails to provide the initial contribution to the JDDF Account within a period of 6 months from the date of the DDA, (ii) there occurs a Change in Law that materially alters the rights of JADCL, (iii) GoR fails to provide support to the implementation of DDA as specified in the terms of the Agreement, (iv) GoR commits a material breach of the DDA that is not cured within a period of 30 days.
		Upon termination of the DDA a transfer period of 6 months shall commence ('Transfer Period'). No new project shall be implemented after termination notice has been issued.
		During the Transfer Period an Independent Expert shall be appointed to determine the total compensation payable by GoR to JADCL and JADCL's right to develop, construct, operate and maintain the facilities shall cease to be valid and the facilities will be transferred to GoR only after: (i) determination of the compensation payable, and (ii) payment of the compensation by GoR to JADCL.
		If the DDA is terminated for a JADCL Event of Default then the compensation payable by GoR shall be equal to the total outstanding financing relating to all projects implemented under the DDA, unless GoR and the lenders agree to transfer the debt from JADCL or JADCL's SPV to GoR or an entity selected by the lenders and GoR.
		If the DDA is terminated for a GoR Event of Default then the compensation payable by GoR shall be equal to the sum of: (i) the total amounts outstanding under the various financing arrangements, (ii) the total equity capital invested into JADCL including the SPVs established by JADCL, and (iii) all costs, expenses, claims that are to be incurred by JADCL (including the SPVs) due to the premature termination of the DDA (including but not limited to payments to contractors, consultants, etc.) and (iv) aggregate of (5) years of annuity payment and if the number of years remaining of the term at the time of termination are less than 5, then the aggregate of the annuity payments of the remaining term.
		The Independent Expert shall be a chartered accountant or a firm of chartered accounts of national repute.
		JADCL shall have the right to withdraw amounts equivalent to the compensation determined by the Independent Expert from the amounts in the JDDF Account.

ANNEXURE A-22.4(A)

Jalore Area Development Program

Term Sheet—Project for Water Distribution (Irrigation)

S.No.	Item	Description
1.	Project Area	The project area consists of approximately 3 lakh hectares in Jalore District. Project would cover approximately 3,60,000 inhabitants across 129 villages. The agriculture is mostly rain-fed in the region. Irrigation in some areas is done using groundwater but the quality of water is very poor resulting in low agriculture yields.
2.	Project Description	The Project would seek to distribute water from the Rajasthan canal to the project area. A distribution system consisting of distributaries, minors and sub minors has been planned for the delivery of water to the agricultural farms.
		Water shall be applied to the fields using an innovative technology of Pressure Irrigation as opposed to the traditional methods of flow irrigation.
		Water from the main canal shall be transferred to the distribution network and then to minors under gravity or left flow as per suitability. Water then, shall be delivered to *diggies* (water collection ponds) which will cater to the needs of surrounding group of agriculture fields.
		Field irrigation system consisting of sprinkler sets shall also be provided to the farmers/WUAs.
		The water shall be delivered to individual fields through a well laid out network of Canal Minors. A total no. of approx. 700 such *diggies* shall be constructed in the command area.
		Each of these *diggies* shall have a capacity sufficient to cater to the water demand of a particular *chak* for 2 days.
		To ensure efficient utilisation, water will be delivered on a volumetric basis (at point of discharge) and charged accordingly unlike the prevalent practice of billing ion which tariffs are levied on the basis of area.
3.	Cost of the Project Component	Approx. Rs. 350 crore.
4.	Project Implementation Time	Three years from start of construction.
5.	Project Benefits	The project will bring 1.62 lakh hectare of land under irrigation using water available from Narmada Canal. Key benefits include: - Improved productivity from farms. - Drought proofing of economy.

contd. ...

... contd. ...

S. No.	Term	Description
		- Improved income from animal husbandry.
		- Reduction in migration.
6.	Implementation Structure	The project would be awarded by the SPV to experienced contractors through an open bidding route. The contractor would be responsible for implementation and maintenance of the system for a period of at least 10 years. The contractor would ensure implementation and maintenance of the canal up to the *diggi*.
		The contractor would be also be entrusted with the responsibility of the maintenance of the main distribution canal within Rajasthan post construction by Government of Rajasthan.
		As part of the project each of the farmers in the project area would be provided the capital equipment required for implementing the pressure irrigation system. However, the Water Users Association/individual farmers would be responsible for maintenance of the water distribution system beyond the *diggi*.
		For more details see Annexure 22.1 and Annexure A-22.6.
7.	Cost of Operation and Maintenance	It is estimated that cost of maintenance of the system including electricity costs for pumping of water up to the *diggi* would be approximately Rs. 7-8 crore per annum.
8.	Role of Water Users Association	A water users association would be set up for each *diggi*. The WUA would be responsible for monitoring water use, collection of water charges and coordinating the farmer interests, communication of farm practices, etc.

ANNEXURE A-22.4(B)

Jalore Area Development Program

Term Sheet—Project for Rural Roads

S.No.	Item	Description
1.	Project Area	The project area which encompasses the whole of the Jalore district covers 10 lakh hectare.
2.	Project Description	The total length of rural road network in the Jalore district is estimated to be 2885 kms. Number of villages with a population of above 500 is 559 (no. of unconnected villages with population of more than 500 is 88). The project would seek to improve the quality of existing rural road network while improving the connectivity to all villages as per the PMGSY programme.

contd. ...

... contd. ...

S.No.	Item	Description
3.	Cost of the Project Component	The cost of improvement works is estimated to be Rs. 100 crore.
4.	Project Implementation Time	Three years from start of construction.
5.	Project Benefits	The proposed area development plan thus envisages creation of a network of rural roads in the project area, which will enable efficient flow of inputs and produce to and from the rural hinterland to markets both within Rajasthan and the neighboring state of Gujarat. Development of rural connectivity would increase mobility, provide better access to educational, health and market centres and generate increase income due to increase in flow of goods in and out of the area.
6.	Implementation Structure	The SPV will identity a list of critical linkage roads, which will require upgradation and maintenance and outlines standards for the same. It is possible to entrust the tasks for upgradation and maintenance of these roads to private sector for an annual fee. This mechanism ensures development and maintenance of quality infrastructure with the help of private sector finance and expertise.

ANNEXURE A-22.4(C)

Jalore Area Development Program

Term Sheet—Project for Drinking Water

S.No.	Item	Description
1.	Project Area	Presently there is no sustainable drinking water supply system for the towns and rural population in the project area. The present water supply is completely dependent on groundwater. The continuous depletion of groundwater resources has resulted in severe over drawal. The water in many parts is unfit for human consumption with high presence of fluorides and chlorides.
2.	Project Description	As part of the programme, drinking water would be provided to 665 villages of Jalore and also the town of Jalore. The estimated water consumption in the district would be in the region of *** 260 mld. The objective of the project would be to provide clean piped water supply on a 24-hour basis to the community.
3.	Cost of the Project Component	The cost of the project component is estimated to be in the region of Rs. 600 crore.

contd. ...

...contd. ...

S.No.	Item	Description
4.	Project Implementation Time	It is estimated that the project can be implemented within a period of four years.
5.	Project Benefits	The project is likely to have a positive impact on the overall development of the region through reduction in water related diseases, positive impact on women and children and on the overall socio-economic situation in the state.
6.	Implementation Structure	The project would be implemented by the SPV through a construction cum maintenance contract. The contractor would be responsible for design, project management, construction and operation and maintenance of the facility. Wherever feasible the SPV would install water meters for monitoring the consumption of drinking water. In addition, the SPV would levy nominal charges on the community for off setting the operation and maintenance costs of the water system.

ANNEXURE A-22.4(D)

Jalore Area Development Program

Term Sheet—Project for Electrification

S.No.	Item	Description
1.	Project Description	The project would seek to provide electricity to the district through a self sustainable model using as far as possible local sources.
2.	Cost of the Project Component	It is estimated that the total energy requirements in the villages covered by the project would be in the region of 50 MW. An estimated investment of Rs. 200 crore is provided to cater to the needs of future requirements, pressurised irrigation as well as distribution.
3.	Project Implementation Time	The project would be implemented coterminous with the development of the irrigation project.
4.	Project Benefits	The project is an essential ingredient of the area development programme. Without access to reliable power supply, the irrigation project component would not be able to function optimally. Further, the project would also set examples in development of self sufficient rural electrification clusters.
5.	Implementation Structure	The project would be implement by the SPV through specialised contractors who would be responsible for both construction and maintenance. Further, the SPV would charge users the cost of electricity at rates to be specified by the Government of Rajasthan for agriculture supply. It is proposed that Government of Rajasthan provides an annual revenue subsidy to compensate for the losses that would be incurred by the SPV in this operation.

ANNEXURE A-22.4(E)

Jalore Area Development Program

Term Sheet—Project for Agriculture Support Services

S.No.	Item	Description
1.	Project Description	The agriculture value chain includes, in addition to agricultural producers, a diverse range of large and small agribusiness enterprises, farm input and service suppliers (seeds, fertiliser, and equipment), downstream processors, traders and retailers. The project envisages establishment of well-developed markets to give farmers incentives to invest in sustainable production systems, facilitate access to inputs, and increase agricultural productivity. It is proposed to set up effective and sustainable extension systems in the project areas to help the rural population in management of their day to day chores by making intelligent and informed decisions.
2.	Cost of the Project Component	Rs. 10 crore.
3.	Project Implementation Time	This would be carried out coterminous with the development of the water distribution system. It is also envisaged that these services would need to be continued at the SPV level for an additional period of three years from the start of full commercial operations. Thereafter these can be internalised as part of the WUA responsibilities.
4.	Project Benefits	The support services proposed are an integral part of the area development programme. Activities such as farm extension services, value added services for insurance. WUA management, etc. are expected to contribute in the effective implementation of the Project.

ANNEXURE A-22.4(F)

Jalore Area Development Program

Term Sheet-Animal Husbandry and Dairy Development

S.No.	Item	Description
1.	Project Description	The area presently has an estimated population of 15 lakh livestock. The total milk production is estimated to 4.5 lakh litre per day. The yield per cow is 3 litre per day and buffalo is 4 litre per day, which is way below the ideal average yields of 8-10 litre per day. However, presently the yield is very low by domestic standards and, therefore, has significant scope for improvement. Further, there are presently inadequate facilities for processing of milk and production of value added produces. As part of the area development programme, it is proposed to facilitate development of cooperatives to provide a framework for collection and processing of milk and associated produce.

contd. ...

... contd. ...

S.No.	Item	Description
2.	Cost of the Project Component	The investment required in the dairy development and value added service is estimated to be Rs. 10 crore.
3.	Project Implementation Time	The project would be implemented over a five year time horizon.
4.	Project Benefits	Based on the interventions planned on the agriculture side and improved availability of fodder, the overall production from the region is estimated to increase to seven lakh litres per day.

ANNEXURE A-22.4(G)

Jalore Area Development Program

Term Sheet—School Improvement Programme

S.No.	Item	Description
1.	Project Description	The school improvement programme would cover in the first phase approximately 1,500 schools in the Jalore district. The objective of the programme would be three fold: (i) The SPV would initiate a physical infrastructure improvement programme for the schools in consultation with the local authorities. This programme would improve the general school environment including buildings, class rooms, toilet and first aid facilities, etc. in the school. (ii) The second part of the programme would address the issue of IT infrastructure including IT based learning techniques as well as teacher training programme. (iii) On a third level, other activities of overall child development including vocational training, entrepreneurial development, etc. would be covered.
2.	Cost of the Project Component	The school improvement programme is expected to cost Rs. 100 crore.
3.	Project Implementation Time	The first and second phase of the project would be implemented within a period of three years.
4.	Project Benefits	The project is expected to reduce the drop out rates, increase the overall literacy and education level of the younger generation and improve the overall enrollment rate in the district.

contd. ...

... contd. ...

S.No.	Item	Description
5.	Implementation Structure	The project would be implemented with the help of specialised educational service providers who have the prior knowledge and expertise in this area. For services rendered, it is proposed that a service fee be charged from each of the students or subsidised as part of the larger programme initiative.

ANNEXURE A-22.4(H)

Jalore Area Development Program

Term Sheet—Draft Shareholders Agreement

S.No.	Item	Description
1.	Promoter Shareholders	Government of Rajasthan and IL&FS.
2.	Initial share capital	Rs. 30 crore.
3.	Shareholding pattern	50:50.
4.	Board of Directors	Six with each party having the right to nominate three.
5.	Chairman	Shall be nominated by Government of Rajasthan.
6.	Managing Director/CEO	Shall be nominated by IL&FS.
7.	Objectives of the Company	- To develop, design, finance, construct, operate and maintain, through appropriate contractural and institutional mechanisms, all components of the physical infrastructure programme of the JADP, including irrigation, roads, electricity generation, transmission and distribution, water supply and distribution, etc. - To facilitate, through the introduction of appropriate schemes the development of markets for agriculture commodities; catalyse value added investments for agriculture produce, distribution and processing; facilitate the introduction and use of crop insurance; facilitate, if approved, development of private sector participation in contract farming, etc. - To assist in the establishment of Water Users Association (WUA), development of management practices with regard to WUA, establishment of tie-ups for the procurement of inputs, finance, insurance, etc.

contd. ..

... contd. ...

S.No.	Item	Description
8.	Specific Role of GoR	- Administrative support at the district level. - Land acquisition and programme management support. - State policy support. - Deputation of staff. - Capital for project development. - Capital Support in the form of annuity.
9.	Specific Role of IL&FS	- Programme Manager for the initiative. - Raising of financial resources for the programme. - Deputation of staff. - Project development support. - Financial support for specific schemes based on the viability.

ANNEXURE A-22.5

Area under Crops before and after JADP

Irrigated Area under Various Crops before and after Narmada Canal Project

S. No.	Before Project Crops	Area in ha	After Project Crops	Area in ha	Change Area in ha
Kharif					
Changed Area under the Same Crops					
1.	Bajra	984			(984)
2.	Bajra Fodder	44	Bajra/Guar Fodder	4821	4777
3.	Bajra/Moth	27			(27)
4.	Castor	1406	Castor	12144	10738
5.	Chillies	4			(4)
6.	Guwar	19			(19)
7.	Jowar	8			(8)
8.	Jowar Fodder	27			(27)
	Total	**2519**		**16965**	**14446**
			New Crops Introduced		
1.			Fruits (Pomegranate Date Palm, Gooseberry, etc.)	1804	1804
2.			Groundnut	9173	9173
3.			Vegetable (Tomato, etc.)	3214	3214
			Total	**14191**	**14191**

contd. ...

... contd. ...

S. No.	Before Project Crops	Area in ha	After Project Crops	Area in ha	Change Area in ha
Rabi					
Changed Area under the Same Crops					
1.	Barley	55			(55)
2.	Castor	304			(304)
3.	Cumin	12372	Cumin	15086	2714
4.	*Isabgol*	11441	*Isabgol*	7248	(4193)
5.	Wheat	3106	Wheat	8035	4929
6.	Mustard	9129	Mustard	21541	12412
7.	Lucuma	90			(90)
8.	*Methi*	1			(1)
9.	Onion	5			(5)
10.	Tarameera	8			(8)
11.	Tobacco	11			(11)
	Total	**36522**		**51910**	**15388**
			New Crops Introduced		
1.			Fruits (Pomegranate Date Palm, Gooseberry, etc.)	1804	1804
2.			Gram	9871	9871
3.			Vegetable-Pea, etc.	2392	2392
			Fodder-Oats	2459	2459
			Total	**16526**	**16525**
Grand Total		**39041**		**99592**	**60551**

ANNEXURE A-22.6

Economics of Water Costs vis-à-vis Farm Production

(a) To understand the sensitivity of the water charges on the overall costs matrix and on the individual farmers, an analysis has been carried out which seeks to outline the water costs as percentage of total costs of production. In order to carry out this analysis it is important to understand the economics related to farming.

(b) Assumptions relating to the farm economics have been lead out below:

  (i)   Average Farm Size: It is assumed that the average farm size is 10 hectare.

  (ii) Cropping pattern: For the analysis it is assumed that the cropping pattern for an average farm is exactly the same as prescribed for the project area under the project.

  (iii) Composition of crops in a 10 hectare farm is depicted below:

Crop	Area under Cropping
Kharif	
Groundnut	0.57
Castor	0.76
Vegetable Tomato	0.20
Fruits (Pomegranate, Date, Palm, Gooseberry, etc.)	0.11
Bajra Fodder	0.30
Rabi	
Wheat	0.50
Mustard	134
Cumin	0.94

contd. ...

... contd. ...

Crop	Area under Cropping
Gram	0.61
Isabgol	0.45
Vegetable - Pea	0.15
Fruits (Pomegranate, Date, Palm, Gooseberry, etc.)	0.11
Fodder Oats	0.10
Total	**6.14**

(c) Income:

For the purpose of estimation of annual income for the farmer the following production yields for various crops have been taken. Market value of the produce too has been worked out on the basis of prevailing market rates for the respective crops.

Crop	Produce in Quintal per ha	Total Produce in Quintal	Rates of Produce in Rs. per Quintal	Gross Value of Produce in Rs.
Kharif				
Groundnut	15	9	1447	12383
Castor	18	14	1275	17334
Vegetable Tomato	300	60	300	17992
Fruits (Pomegranate, Date, Palm, Gooseberry, etc.)	150	17	600	10100
Bajra Fodder	500	150	80	11995

contd. ...

...*contd.* ...

Crop	Produce in quintal per ha	Total Produce in quintal	Rates of Produce in Rs. per quintal	Gross Value of Produce in Rs.
Rabi				
Wheat	35	17	724	12665
Mustard	15	20	1379	27711
Cumins	10	9	7384	69284
Gram	17	9	1564	13442
Isabgol	10	5	2535	11427
Vegetable-Pea	100	15	500	7438
Fruits (Pomegranate, Date, Palm, Gooseberry, etc.)	0	0	0	
Fodder Oats	450	45	100	4499
Total				216270

	Amount in Rs.	As % of value of produce
Water Charges	36,000	15
Seed Cost	8,000	4
Manure and Fertiliser	7,200	3
Expenditure on Fodder	15,200	7
Expenditure on Tools	1,650	1
Expenditure on Hired Bullock/ Tractor and Labour	28,600	13
Misc. Expenses	10,800	5
Land Revenue	90	—
Electricity Charges and Sprinkler Maintenance	18,000	8
Margin	90,000	45
Gross Value of Produce in Rs. Lakh	2,16,000	

Thus the gross earnings from the annual produce for an average farmer holding a land of 10 hectare therefore, will be Rs. 2,16,000.

(d) Costs:

(i) Water requirements for various crops have been worked out and it is estimated that the for a 10 hectare field the total water consumption per year would be 18,000 kl per annum on an average.

(ii) At an estimated rate of Rs. 2 per kl the expenditure on water would amount to around Rs. 36,000 per year for an average farmer.

(iii) The overall cost structure is depicted in the following table below:

(iv) It is apparent from the above table that the water costs constitute only around 15 of the total value created. The cost of produce as well as the net profits for a farmer therefore is not very sensitive to the water cost.

(v) Presently the farmers in Rajasthan, in other irrigation schemes are charged on the basis of area irrigated (@ Rs. 151 per hectare of ICA) which has resulted in very poor collection of revenues and inefficient use of water on farm. The tariff being charged is too low in comparison to the actual economic cost of delivering water. For instance, if a cultivator does irrigation by pumping water from his own sources, the cost per hectare of ICA comes out to around Rs. 2,000 per hectare. The GoR has notified that the rates shall be increased to Rs. 550 per ha in the year 2007 to take care of the O&M costs which comes to around 30 paisa per kl.

(vi) As can be observed from the earlier section, for a full productive year, an average farmer is expected to realise total revenue of Rs. 2,16,000 whereas the total cost of production is Rs. 1,10,500. The water costs as a percentage of total value created is very less. This essentially means that the farmer would not have too much resistance in paying water charges as long as water is made available to him in the required quantities and at the appropriate time.

(vii) It should also be noted that the whole farm economic is based on the premise that an assured supply of adequate water will be available and the water costs therefore, are actually a form of investment for the farmer. The cost incurred on water will be more than offset by the handsome margins (around 50 per cent) that a farmer is expected to earn on the crops thus produced.

(viii) It is therefore suggested that the tariff for the water if fixed in the range of Rs. 2 and 2.50 for the project would contain the cost of water as a proportion of total cost of farm inputs at quite small levels and the farmers would not hesitate in paying the same looking at the overall value created. The collection risk will therefore, be considerably low.

(ix) Involvement of farmers through WUAs would also ensure timely collection of the water tariff and the collection risks associated would be mitigated to a large extent.

Section **II**

[...continued...]

Presentations and Discussion

"ECONOMY : GROWTH AND EQUITY"

This section corresponds to the proceedings of the Second Session of the Ninth Indira Gandhi Conference, November 19-21, 2004, New Delhi.

Chair:

- Suman K. Bery

Lead Speakers:

- C.K. Prahalad
- Deepak Nayyar

Discussants:

- T.N. Ninan
- Ashok S. Ganguly
- Sunil Kant Munjal
- Sitaram Yechury
- M.S. Banga
- Montek S. Ahluwalia
- Neera Chandhoke
- S. Mahendra Dev
- Prem Shankar Jha
- Bharat Karnad

- Naina Lal Kidwai
- Sanjoy Hazarika
- Vivek Monteiro
- Ravi Parthasarathy
- Sunita Narain
- Chandra Bhan Prasad
- Nasser Munjee
- Yogendra Yadav
- Jayaprakash Narayan
- Vinod Raina

23 | Introductory Remarks

SUMAN K. BERY

THIS session on the Economy: Growth and Equity has attracted the largest number of background papers. I would like to acknowledge the contributions of Mahendra Dev, Sanjoy Hazarika, Prem Shankar Jha, Vivek Monteiro, Nasser Munjee, Sunita Narain, Asha Menon Revathy, Chandra Bhan Prasad, and Ravi Parthasarathy as well as a report to the UN Secretary General on unleashing entrepreneurship where Dr. C.K. Prahalad was involved.

The agenda annotation invites us to address a rather large range of issues. I will read these out with some emphases of my own. "There is a consensus that a higher level of growth is required if India is to address the basic challenges of poverty and unequal distribution." We will test in the room whether there is indeed such a consensus in favour of faster growth. "But there is no consensus on how higher growth can be achieved and how the consequences of uneven growth between regions as well as sections of society should be dealt with." We need to judge whether or not there is a consensus on how higher growth can be achieved and the consequences of uneven growth. "What

intellectual and practical policy responses are needed to prevent inequalities between regions and states, between social classes, and between urban and rural areas becoming sharp lines of conflict? How can the rural economy be revived? How can state governments' finances be restored to health? Can India really achieve high growth and employment without a vigorous manufacturing sector? What should be done to create this?" These were many of the themes the Prime Minister addressed in his speech. "How can India progress faster as a knowledge economy, what has been the impact of globalisation on Indian competitiveness in key sectors and what will be the roles of the private and public sectors in furthering this process? What are the key reforms to drive competitiveness and levels of education? What should be the role of public investment in science R&D and education? How can India overcome the factors which deter foreign direct investment? How will environmental cause and effect impact our economic development? Should public policy consciously seek to limit consumerism in the context of ecology?" This issue was raised by the Prime Minister. "How can we shape and encourage economic integration within India across states, within the SAARC region and with the other Asian regional groupings?" Our lead speakers are Prof. C.K Prahalad of the University of Michigan and Prof. Deepak Nayyar, Vice-Chancellor Delhi University.

24 | Bottom of the Pyramid

C.K. PRAHALAD

THE recent crescendo in the global conversation about poverty reflects a consensus among development practitioners that dominant models of practice are not working. Most agree that these models must adapt to the changing roles of government, the private sector and civil society. But to develop a new practice, we have to first challenge the mental frames or the dominant logic of our thinking. Otherwise, we will simply re-package old solutions for our new realities.

Poverty and poverty alleviation are topics with a long history of research, public policy focus and practical experimentation. It is no surprise, therefore, that we have developed a dominant logic around poverty alleviation that restricts our ability to seek new and innovative solutions.

Let me start with making my assumptions on the relationship between development with equity explicit. I believe equity is about: (a) creating easy access to economic opportunities for all; (b) enabling everyone to participate in creating solutions; (c) ensuring market-based rewards for effort for all; and (d) protecting the wealth created by all individuals and families. In the long run, equity must rest on inclusion, co-creation of economic solutions, meritocracy, and property rights. The economic development paradigm for effective poverty alleviation must pass these tests of equity. The alternative of subsidising the poor to correct for failure of access to opportunities and markets will not do. Subsidies and aid can at best be only transitional arrangements.

I also want to make my assumptions about the 'poor' explicit. I do not see them as helpless victims but as resilient entrepreneurs. The poor are willing and able to make choices, if they are given access to information. In fact, they are telling us bluntly, household-by-household, what they consider a solution to their poverty. The costly process of rural-urban migration and global emigration is primarily an effort to gain access to functioning markets. Once we see poverty not as an intractable problem but the result of a system that denies access to markets and its related opportunities, and to dignity and choice as consumers, then a new approach to coping with poverty opens up.

We have to imagine a new approach before we can create it. The metaphor I would like to use is the well-known picture of elephants walking along the forest. That is one reality. Less obvious is that these elephants are carrying electronic polling booths to remote parts of India. India, for the first time in the world, conducted the entire general election using electronic polling booths and over 400 million Indians cast their ballots. The sheer scale and scope of the operation makes it unique. Dealing with poverty alleviation requires a similar view of reality—the reality of economic indicators of low income, disease, illiteracy and disenfranchisement coupled with a new possibility—'the electronic polling booths'. I believe that the poor of India represent the possibility of enabling India to leapfrog and innovate, solving simultaneously the problem of poverty in India and at the same time becoming a source of innovations for the rest of the world.

Imagining a future requires us to use a non-traditional research methodology. It requires us to amplify 'weak signals' and 'connect the dots.' So I have, in my work, consciously picked specific examples of success—entrepreneurial solutions in India that create economic development at the bottom of the pyramid—the so called 'weaker sections of society'—that illustrate the potential for creating a system that allows for growth with equity. The emerging practices, by definition cannot be subject to a large-scale statistical survey. The examples, I am going to share with you will, hopefully, allow you to imagine the future of India.

The Poor as Consumers

Irrespective of how poor a person is, she/he is a consumer. They have to eat, clothe themselves, find shelter and fight disease. I would like to identify five aspects of the bottom of the pyramid consumers in India that might inform our debate:

1. The Poor Live in a High Cost Economic System Embedded in the Larger Economic System

The paradox about poverty is that the poor pay more for everything they consume. For example, the poor in Dharavi, a slum in Mumbai, pay 50 times more than the rich in Mumbai for credit and about 37 times for drinking water. A poverty penalty is built into the lives of the poor. This is partly because the poor have no access to the organised sector (a bank) and the unorganised sector (moneylenders) is both local and operates local monopolies. This is the distortion brought about by denying access to competition. Should we not focus on eliminating the 'poverty penalty' by creating access to the regulated and organised sector?

2. The Poor Accept the Role of the Private Sector

The private sector is not just global corporations. The private sector ecosystem consists of large firms, small and medium enterprises, as well as cooperatives that work within the construct of a market system, and are bound by its rules. Indians as a whole, including the poor, accept the role of the private sector in their lives.

Consider education. The fastest growing segment is the private sector—schools, colleges, and tuition. The same is true in health, electricity (private power generators) and transportation. The poor are giving us a simple and a clear message. "We do not want free services. We want good services at acceptable prices." Whether the provider is the public sector or the private sector is not the issue. It is good quality at affordable prices.

3. The Poor Accept High-Tech Solutions

The growth of cell phone users is a clear indication of the willingness of the poor to accept high technology solutions if it helps them improve their lot. The desire for connectivity and access to information has propelled the widespread use of the cell phone. Because it was affordable, the diffusion has been remarkable. Similarly, the poor happily use PCs wherever access is easy, like in ITC's *e-Choupals*. We should not shy away from offering high-tech solutions to the bottom of the pyramid consumer. They can handle it if it is of value to them. Our task is to make it easily accessible.

4. The Poor are Responsible

Companies in the organised sector, especially large firms, usually avoid the bottom of the pyramid. They feel that the poor represent a 'risky business' as they cannot be trusted to pay back loans and the firm will not be able to enforce contracts. Nothing is farther from the truth. The poor, when properly organised, as in the Amul Dairy system in Gujarat or the sugarcane farmers in Parry's Corner in Tamil Nadu or soya farmers in Madhya Pradesh by ITC are very responsible and represent very low risk business partners. Choose the right organisation, build trust and establish reciprocity and you achieve a very different outcome. When organised, the bottom of the pyramid consumers, aware of their poor access to resources, are likely to be more credit-worthy than the rich.

5. The Poor are Natural Entrepreneurs

What is not obvious is that the poor have to be natural entrepreneurs to eke out a living. Every hut in Dharavi is also a business. So are day labourers in rural agriculture. Searching for work, being creative, being aggressive in seeking opportunities are all characteristics. Look at the poor children at traffic intersections in any city. They buy newspapers, flowers, trinkets, and washcloths and sell them. They are not organised and are beholden to local moneylenders. What if they could be organised by large firms, civil society organisations and cooperatives, such as Hindustan Lever Limited (e.g. Shakti Ammas or empowered rural women), SEWA (e.g. a wide variety of women's businesses) or ICICI (e.g. local self-help groups and federations)? Can they become not just consumers but producers of wealth? Can they improve their earnings and consumption potential simultaneously?

Even if we start with these parsimonious assumptions about the nature of the bottom of the pyramid consumers what logical conclusions can we draw? We can start with the following view of opportunities:

a. If we can provide access to affordable products and services and make it available, then the poor are likely to become very savvy consumers.

b. Affordability to the bottom of the pyramid consumer will force a new approach to business models all the way from product development to distribution and service. The price-performance improvement may have to be in the order of 50-100 times the current products sold at the top of the pyramid.

c. If we are committed to excellent quality at price-performance levels designed for the bottom of the pyramid, then we will have to focus on basic innovations. In this sense, the poor can be the catalyst for world-class innovations in business that can increase the global competitiveness of the involved firms.

Successfully Innovating for the Poor

Now, is there any evidence that this is possible? Are there examples, isolated as they may be, suggesting that this approach to innovation and service to the bottom of the pyramid is possible? Can markets create equitable forms of development in India? I suggest that it can, and offer several examples of innovations from India that combine commercial considerations with service to the poor.

Let me start with healthcare. The demand for every element of healthcare is immense in India—be it eye care (e.g. needless blindness due to cataract), the need for prosthetics (e.g. accidents, illness-based amputations), or cardiac care (e.g. due to genetic disposition, diabetes, and/or age). The same is true of AIDS, mental retardation (due to inadequate iodine intake among children) or deaths due to diarrhoea (poor quality water and bad hygiene) and respiratory disease (due to pollution). Can we bring a new approach to solving these problems?

The Jaipur Foot is an example of dealing with the problem of prosthetics in a novel fashion. The specification for the prosthetics in India is more onerous than in the USA. The poor have no use of a prosthetic if it does not allow them to walk bare foot (the prosthetic must look like natural foot—both in shape and colour), sit cross-legged, walk long distances and be able to work in paddy fields (stand in water). Further, the foot has to be customised in a very short time of less than eight hours. Given the paucity of doctors, well-trained technicians have to fit the prosthetics. The Jaipur foot does all the above and costs about $ 25 compared to a less functional prosthetic in the USA which can cost $ 10,000 and up. The Jaipur foot is given free to all and they only take donations based on the ability to pay. The group is profitable. They are also the largest prosthetic facility in the world fitting more than 16,000 in a year. The quality of the Jaipur Foot is as good as the American versions.

The Jaipur foot is not an isolated example. The Aravind Eye Care System headquartered in Madurai, Tamil Nadu performs more than 200,000 cataract surgeries/year and treats more than 1.4 million outpatients. Aravind is the world's largest eye care facility. The costs are affordable to the poorest. Sixty per cent of the patients get the treatment free and the others are charged about $ 45-300, including hospital stay. The cost of quality of private rooms increase the cost to those who can afford to pay. The equivalent costs are $ 3,000 in the USA. A comparison of the quality levels between the surveys of Royal Ophthalmic Society and the analysis of Aravind show that the quality is better at Aravind.

Narayana Hrudayalaya in Bangalore is another case of such innovations. Paediatric cardiac care in Narayana Hrudayalaya costs as little as $ 1,500 compared to over $ 100,000-200,000 in the USA. The quality is as good as the USA. The poor are increasingly offered an insurance scheme at Rs.10/month ($ 0.20) so that even the poorest, covered by the scheme, can afford cardiac care. Narayana Hrudayalaya is emerging as the world's largest cardiac care facility, performing more than 22 surgeries/day (compared with 3-5/day in any single facility in the USA).

Hindustan Lever (HLL) took on the problem of mental retardation in India where more than 70 million children are at risk. Only 15 per cent of salt in India is iodised. Moreover, the iodine in salt evaporates in storage and cooking. Therefore, to ensure adequate iodine intake, HLL had to learn to micro-encapsulate iodine so that it survives storage and processing.

What can we learn from these examples?

a. It is possible to get world scale and world class in India at affordable prices to the poor.

b. Each one of the examples involves basic innovations in the entire patient care process, including the surgery and post-operative care.

c. All these facilities operate on a commercial basis and are very profitable (have a surplus), even though the Jaipur Foot and Aravind are legally 'non-profit organisations'.

d. In every case, private sector and civil society organisations (in some cases government departments) need to cooperate. With the advent of market reforms, the distinction between the agendas and operating approaches between the private sector and the CSO are blurring. Contrary to the images of anti-globalisation protests, the emergence of market-based cooperation between CSOs and firms to address fundamental issues of poverty is undeniable—and this is a global phenomenon.

Let us look at access to finance. Micro-finance initiatives are well researched and understood. But access to credit is not the same thing as helping the poor understand and get the benefits of the entire range of financial services. Savings are as critical as gaining access to credit. Protecting the balance sheet of the farmer through rain insurance, life insurance or crop insurance is as important as providing access to credit. The example of the pioneering work done by The Bank of Madura, since acquired by ICICI Bank, is too well known to outline in depth here. The scope and variety of services offered to the poor at affordable cost is an indication of the innovations required. ICICI works closely with self-help groups, local NGOs and community banks to provide global standards and local responsiveness at the same time. What are the lessons?

a. It is possible to create a convergent system of SHGs, civil society, community banks and the national and global bank to create a wide range of services at the lowest cost and remain profitable.

b. The very low default rate of less than one per cent shows the poor are responsible borrowers.

Access to technology also plays a central role—and again market approaches can provide the solution. Let us consider agriculture. It is obvious that most of the farmers in India are subsistence farmers. How do we increase their ability to improve their incomes and at the same time regain some control over the disposal of their produce? The ITC *e-Choupal* provides one example of what can be done. By connecting villages through a PC to the Internet, ITC has enabled farmers to be sensitive to the price movements of soybean. Through this ITC can aggregate produce and get efficiencies in their logistics, and farmers get a better price. The farmers, in less than three months have become proficient enough to check the spot prices on the Chicago Board of Trade and decide at what price to sell. This scheme now covers about four million farmers. The network now allows the farmers to get access to other services—be it crop insurance, better seeds, fertilisers, or consumer goods.

A similar experiment on a smaller scale with similar results is going on among sugarcane farmers in Tamil Nadu, energised by EID Parry. The system allows farmers to get agronomic help, improve their yields, and become PC literate. The benefits of transparency in transactions provided by 'Parry's Corners' as the kiosks are called, has prompted the local administration to embrace new levels of transparency. The farmers are emerging as the most cashless subgroup in India. Over 67 per cent of the farmers do all their transactions using ATMs and PCs in the kiosks. What are the lessons from these examples?

a. The poor are willing to accept and use technologies.

b. They are willing to be co-creators of new services. In each of these cases, the farmers were as much involved in identifying new opportunities as the firms.

c. Technologies remove the asymmetry in information between the subsistence farmer (the poor) and the firm (the institutions). This makes it easier for the poor to enforce contracts, exercise choice and have a sense of freedom and dignity.

d. It can potentially connect the subsistence farmer to the global trading system.

Finally, for the bottom of the pyramid to be treated as consumers, they must have access to consumer products as well. Access and affordability is the key. We have to create a capacity to consume. India represents one of the boldest experiments in creating the capacity to consume in the consumer goods business. The availability of a wide variety of products—from shampoo to pickles to candy and tea—in single serve sachets represents a major change. Now everyone can get excellent products at low unit prices of Re. 1/sachet ($ 0.02). Further, the access to the rural markets through the creation of village level entrepreneurs is another innovation. The Shakti Ammas (HLL), Avon, Amway, and other direct distribution models penetrate deep into both rural and urban markets. The entrepreneurs here are earning more income, learning about working with the large corporation as an integral part of an emerging eco-system.

The Role of Entrepreneurs and the Private Sector

These examples (weak signals) of innovation in India suggest a new possibility for me. Poverty alleviation efforts in India must be built with the private sector and with the recognition of India's culture of entrepreneurship at its core. The above cases demonstrate that private sector development is possible with equity. In each of the above examples, firms are making breakthrough innovations to cater to the poor at affordable prices. This implies that there is an inbuilt accountability for efficiency and productivity (profits). In each case, the poor are involved in doing what is of value for them. They have a choice. They can decide, for example whether they will buy seeds through an ITC *e-Choupal* or not. They can decide when to sell. Freedom of choice and empowerment is part of the new system. Most importantly, there is a clear recognition that the entire resources of the country must be mobilised—the poor themselves as co-creators, the civil society organisations,

the small-scale sector and the large firms including the multinationals. We have to see them as an integrated ecosystem not as distinct elements in conflict.

What can the government do to make development with equity using the market-based model a reality? Of all the efforts that the government can put in, nothing is more critical than reducing corruption and improving transaction governance capacity in the country. Why is this so critical? Let us look at the data from around the world. Let us consider:

a. Data on GDP/capita (World Bank)

b. Human Development Index (from UNDP)

c. Corruption Index (Transparency International)

The correlations are striking. Not surprisingly, the GDP/capita is correlated with the human development index. India is low on the human development index (127 out of 175 countries). If we correlate corruption and GDP/capita, the same relationship holds. India has a score of 2.7 on a 10.0 scale. Corrupt countries are not rich!

We have to focus on removing the impediments to the development of an equitable society where access and transparency is the norm. This should be the role of government. Further, government needs to phase out subsidies as private firms demonstrate their ability to provide affordable solutions in different areas *via* market-based systems. Subsidies are often the primary impediments to private sector investment access and co-creation with the consumer.

I believe that the seeds of a solution to India's poverty problems are already visible in India. The innovations described here are weak signals and their successes pale to insignificant considering the enormity of the problems of poverty and disenfranchisement in India. But they provide a unique and new solution. We need to have the courage to follow the lead of these early experimenters. I believe that equity and market-based development are compatible goals for India to adopt. Without equity, development will certainly stall. But without market-based innovations we will not generate the solutions required to sustainably provide choice, access and dignity—the fundamentals of equity—to India's enterprising poor.

25 Growth with Equity: The Essence of Development

DEEPAK NAYYAR

THE well being of humankind is the essence of development. Therefore, development must bring about an improvement in the living conditions of ordinary people. It should ensure the provision of basic human needs for all, not just food and clothing but also shelter, healthcare and education. This simple but powerful proposition is often forgotten in the pursuit of material wealth and the conventional concerns of economics. Yet, people view the world through the optic of their living conditions and daily lives. The litmus test for the performance of an economy, hence government, is neither economic growth, nor economic efficiency, indeed not even equity in an abstract sense, but whether or not it meets the basic needs and the growing aspirations of people. Austerity now for prosperity later is neither credible nor acceptable. The essence of the tension between the economics of markets that work on the principle of one-rupee-one-vote, and the politics of democracy that works on the principle of one-person-one-vote, must be recognised. For those excluded by the economics of markets are included by the politics of democracy.

In reflecting on the times to come, I worry about the short-termism that characterises both our politics and our thinking. We need to think long. We should, of course, think of the next decade. But we should also think of the next 25 years. We must begin to change the reality of the two dichotomised worlds in which we live—the India in this room and the Bharat outside. For this purpose, it is essential that we create capabilities, provide opportunities and ensure rights for our citizens, about one-third of whom live in abject poverty with not enough nutrition let alone clothing, shelter, healthcare or education. And there are more poor people in India now than there were people at the time of independence. I believe that we cannot imagine India as a superpower in politics, which some do, or as a powerhouse in economics, which others do, unless it is built on the strong foundation of our most abundant resource and most valuable asset—people.

I have put my cards on the table. For I start with these priors. In this paper, I hope to set out some reflections on growth and equity in the wider context of polity and society. I intend to stress the importance of a redefined role for the state in a market economy. And I shall conclude with some essentials that most of us in such gatherings often forget.

Economic growth is clearly necessary but not sufficient to bring about a reduction in poverty. This may be attributable to the logic of markets which give to those who have and take away from those who have not, as the process of cumulative causation leads to market-driven virtuous circles and vicious circles. This may be the outcome of patterns of development where economic growth is uneven between regions and the distribution of its benefits is unequal among people, so that there is a growing affluence for some and persistent poverty for many. This may be the consequence of initial conditions and institutional frameworks, as similar economic performances in the aggregate could lead to egalitarian economic development in one situation and growth which bypasses the majority of people in another situation.

It cannot suffice to say that outcomes of economic policies should be moderated by social policies, in the form of safety nets. The dichotomy between economic and social policies is inadequate, just as the dichotomy between economic and social development is inappropriate. In fact, no such distinction is ever made in industrial societies. And the experience of the industrialised world suggests that there is a clear need for an integration, rather than a separation, of economic and social policies. Thus, I believe, it is important to create institutional mechanisms that mediate between economic and social development. We know from theory, history, and experience, that markets tend to widen disparities between regions and people through a process of cumulative causation. Better endowed regions experience rapid growth. Like magnets, they attract resources and people from elsewhere until congestion or pollution halts the process. In contrast, disadvantaged regions tend to lag behind. The same is true of poor people or excluded groups who are disadvantaged because they do not have sufficient income or assets, are not skilled or educated, and live in backward regions.

The extent of exclusion can be limited by providing public goods and services to such people, groups or regions, who are vulnerable, marginalised and excluded. For the people who remain excluded, it is essential to widen and strengthen the safety nets. But we must remember that safety nets represent transfer payments in perpetuity and cannot provide a sustainable solution to the problems of those who live in deprivation. There is a wonderful sentence from Joan Robinson that is most appropriate in this context, "There is only one thing that is worse than being exploited by capitalists, and that is not being exploited by capitalists." The same can be said about markets and globalisation. There are two essential correctives—foster inclusion where markets exist, and create markets where they do not. To foster inclusion, we need to invest in human resource development, particularly in education, just as we need to develop a social infrastructure which provides the poor with access to shelter, healthcare, clean water, sanitation and ensures a steady increase in social consumption. That depends almost entirely on the government, in a country such as India. The creation of markets, where they are missing, requires a substantial investment in physical infrastructure, particularly in rural areas. The government must therefore find resources for stepping up public investment in infrastructure. The premature withdrawal of the government from these sectors, in keeping with the ideology of marketisation and globalisation, is premature simply because sufficient private investment, whether domestic or foreign, is simply not forthcoming.

This leads into, and connects with, my second point about the importance of the economic role of the state. We have gone through a curious swing of the pendulum in thinking about the state. For a time we believed that the state could do nothing wrong. And now we believe that the state can do nothing right. These are caricatures of perceptions. The juxtaposition of government failure and market failure as either-or choices is a false debate. Both failures are a fact of life, for neither markets nor governments are, or can ever be, perfect. Indeed, markets are invariably imperfect and governments are without exception valuable. It is important to introduce correctives against both sets of failures. Interestingly enough, the state and the market provide mutual checks and balances, so that one can correct the failures of the other. We need to remember that efficient markets need effective states. For those who believe in the invisible hand of the market, may I simply say it is invisible because it is not there! Therefore, it is time for us to reflect on the role of the state *vis-á-vis* the market. My understanding is set out simply in the form of two basic propositions. First, the state and the market cannot be substitutes for one another but must complement each other. Second, the relationship between the state and the market cannot be specified once-and-for-all, as the two institutions must adapt to one another in a cooperative mode over time.

It has become necessary to redefine the economic role of the state in a changed national and international context. In the earlier stages of development, it is about creating the initial conditions. In the later stages of development, the state is neither a promoter nor a catalyst. It should provide functional intervention to correct for market failure, institutional intervention to govern the market, and strategic intervention to guide the market in the long term. The real question about the state is not 'how big' or 'how much' but 'what sort' and 'how good'. In this era of globalisation, surprisingly enough, the role of the state is more critical than ever before. This role extends beyond regulating domestic markets or correcting market failures. It is about creating the initial conditions to capture the benefits of globalisation, about managing the process of integration into the world economy in terms of pace and sequence, about providing social protection and safeguarding the vulnerable in the process of change, and about ensuring that economic growth also creates employment and livelihoods for the well being of people. In sum, governments need to regulate and complement markets so as to make them people-friendly. The reason is simple. Governments are accountable to people, whereas markets are not.

The object of any sensible strategy of development in a world of globalisation, over the next 10, or even 25 years, should be to create economic space for the pursuit of national interests and development objectives. In the pursuit of this objective, we need to think big and we need to think long. Such thinking must extend across several spheres—first, the creation of a world class infrastructure where any premature withdrawal of the state is a recipe for disaster; second, the development of human resources, through education, both as a means and as an end, because investing in human beings is important at every stage of development; and, third, the fostering of managerial and technological capabilities at a micro-level, without which no latecomer to industrialisation has ever succeeded.

It follows that the role of the state in the process of development will continue to be important for some time to come, even as the scope of the market increases through liberalisation in the wider context of globalisation. Most would find this argument persuasive. Yet, many would doubt whether such a role is feasible in terms of politics. The mood of the moment is not receptive to such ideas anywhere, for there is a disillusionment with the economic role of the state, which goes much beyond economists to political leaders, opinion makers, media persons, so that scepticism about the state runs deep. If we look at the world around us, it is obvious that states are not Plato's guardians. They are sectarian in terms of the interests, groups or classes they represent. Indeed, in extreme situations, the state is treated as family property or private property. Even so, I believe that there are some things that markets can and should do. There are other things that governments can and must do. If governments do those things badly, it does not mean that we can dispense with governments. There is perhaps reason for pessimism, if not despair, on the part of some. I must confess that I am an optimist. We must not give up hope as if we have entered Dante's hell. We need have neither an optimistic view nor a fatalistic view of the state. We need to have a realistic view of the state. For if politics is the art of the possible, change is in the domain of the feasible. And I am convinced that a better world is possible. We must recognise that our strength lies in our political democracy. We must also recognise that our weaknesses lie in the absence of transparency and accountability in that democracy. We do not have to be incurable romantics to believe that India can and must be changed.

In conclusion, I want to set out four propositions, which are essentials that are often forgotten in our debates, even when these do not border on a dialogue of the deaf.

First, the debate on economic reforms does not make a clear distinction between means and ends. For example, it does not recognise that markets, as much as states, are institutions evolved by humankind, that are means and it is development that is the end. What is more, there is a presumption that what is necessary is also sufficient. The management of incentives, motivated by the objective of minimising costs and maximising efficiency, or even unleashing creativity and innovation at a micro-level, is based on a set of policies that are intended to increase competition in the market place. Competition is obviously desirable, but there is nothing automatic about competition. Policy regimes can allow things to happen, but cannot cause things to happen. The creation of competitive markets that enforce efficiency may, in fact, require strategic intervention on the part of the government. The essential missing link is that this debate does not consider transition paths. It confuses comparison of one equilibrium position with another, with change from one equilibrium position to another. But it does not tell us anything about how we move from one position to the other.

Second, it is often forgotten that the well being of humankind is the essence of development. Thus, distributional outcomes are important. So are employment and livelihoods. Structural reforms associated with economic liberalisation have important implications for employment creation and income opportunities. For example, in so far as such reform increases the average productivity of labour, through the use of capital-intensive or labour-saving technologies, or through a restructuring of firms which increases efficiency, it reduces the contribution of any given rate of economic growth to employment growth. There is a contraction of employment in some sectors without a compensatory expansion of employment in other sectors. As employment elasticities of output decline, employment creation slows down. For any given level of employment, a globalisation of prices without a globalisation of incomes also threatens livelihoods. The poor at the margin are most vulnerable, but the non-rich are not immune. It is only natural that the people see the world through the optic of their livelihood. Hence, people do not judge economic liberalisation in terms of what it does for growth or efficiency. The real litmus test is whether it improves their living conditions. And, in so far as there are some winners and many losers, distributional outcomes in the sphere of economics shape electoral outcomes in the realm of politics.

The third essential we have almost forgotten is that there is a rural hinterland. Indeed, India lives in its villages. Yet, we discuss economic reforms as if the rural sector does not exist, or if it exists it does not matter. At the same time, we believe that there is a strong political consensus on reform. Those excluded from the benefits of this process do not have a voice that enables us to determine whether or not there is a consensus, but they question the apparent consensus at election time when they vote.

Fourth, the fundamental importance of good governance is not quite recognised. Governance is largely about rules and institutions that regulate the public realm in civil society. A democratic system seeks to provide for equal participation of the rich and the poor or of the strong and the weak as citizens in political processes. Good governance, where governments are accountable to citizens and people are centre-stage in development, is essential for creating capabilities, providing opportunities and ensuring rights for people. Governance capabilities matter in a much more concrete sense, whereas the role of the state is somewhat more abstract. Indeed, the quality of governance is an important determinant of success or failure with economic reforms. The most striking illustration of this proposition is provided by the wide diversity in economic performance across states in India despite common policies, similar institutions and an economic union. The moral of my story is not less governance but good governance.

26 Discussion

(Section II — Economy: Growth and Equity)

Suman K. Bery

Let me first remind everybody that we are really here to look at India in the next decade. Let me also say that the Prime Minister has talked of GDP growth of 7.5 per cent as something that should in principle be attainable. We have had a range of perspectives on what it might take to achieve this. The earlier discussion was firmly rejectionist—a warning to the political class to heed the message of the last election which was seen as a repudiation of the economic model of the 1990s. I think we have the take way from Prof. Prahalad that governance indeed is a crucial ingredient of growth. I would say that Deepak Nayyar was also urging us to use this opportunity to rethink the role of the state but in rather different ways from the discussion on democracy this morning. I had thought that economics was the dismal science but in comparison with the earlier performance by the political scientists, perhaps we have to change that judgement. On growth since the 1980s India's record is amongst the best in the world. It was in the top 10 both in terms of the magnitude of growth and its consistency. Per capita growth was accelerated from 3 per cent per capita to about 4.5 per cent. There is a huge divergence between the data that we use for growth and those that we use for measuring poverty and inequality. The expenditure and consumption data do not track GDP growth well. As a result a huge industry has developed around what has happened to poverty and what has happened to inequality. But there is concrete evidence that, even at the lowest levels of the society, wage growth has really been quite robust. Deepak talked about initial conditions and I agree those are terribly important. There is also the fact that our reform effort is relatively recent as compared to China. One of the important things about India is that the growth process has been relatively uninterrupted by major financial crises, we have not seen in India the kind of lurches downwards that we have seen in other parts of the world.

T. N. Ninan

I would like to highlight three or four basic facts. In the last 24 years, India has been among the top 10 fastest growing economies in the world. The point which is important here is that, however you slice that period of 24 years in any rational manner, the growth rates within that period don't change much. You can take the decade of the 80s up to 92, you can take the period since then, you can even take the five-year plan periods except for one which saw rapid growth—and you broadly get the same kind of picture, give or take a little bit. You get about 5.7 or 5.8 per cent growth. That is the first fact.

The second point that I would like to make is that in the international comparisons on the inequality that exists, and this is really looking at the income of the top 10 per cent *versus* that of the bottom 10 per cent, or top 20 per cent and bottom 20 per cent, and the ratio multiples—the inequality levels in India are not out of line with what other countries have. The inequality levels in India are less than what you would expect to see if you were to study many other countries. That is the second fact.

The third fact which I want to point out is that while the economic growth rate is rock steady, so is the rate of improvement in socioeconomic indicators. If you take the literacy rate, you get a literacy improvement of about 1 per cent of the population every year, give or take a bit—because there was some acceleration in the 1990s.

If you look at the rate of improvement in life expectancy since about 1980, you get an increase of about 0.8 per year as each year goes by. There are other indicators also which show a steady rate of change. If you look at human development indicators and the HDI index for India, and how it has changed over the different periods as measured by the UNDP, you again get a steady rate of change. If you look at China you get the same steady picture. In the last 30 years, India's index has improved by 0.32 (on a scale of 0 to 1), China's has improved by 0.35. You look at a series of other countries and the rate of improvement in the human development index is very steady.

So if you look at the broad macro picture, and you are talking about a billion people plus, what you see is a system that is extremely stable. It is set on a course and it is difficult to make it deviate by much, either up or down. And while we debate the pros and cons of a whole series of initiatives, at the macro-level it seems to make very little difference. And I want to suggest that we keep this in focus when discussing the next 10 years.

Frankly I was very relieved to read this morning that the Prime Minister in his speech said 7.5 per cent annual growth, because that is an improvement on the 8 per cent talked about so far. It brings us closer to reality.

Suman K. Bery

Yes, but that is per capita.

T. N. Ninan

Really, well that makes it worse. Dr. I. G. Patel is not here but he was in Delhi over the last couple of days and I had a chance to talk to him, and I think he was rightly sceptical about these numbers that are being thrown about, you know, 8 per cent and all the rest of it, because he said if you can get from 6 to 6.5 per cent, that is doing a lot for a system this size. And the magic of compounding those numbers is such that the end result is actually quite dramatically different. I do believe that we are at a cusp where, because of all the changes that have taken place since 1991, the rate of change that we can see in India looking forward is in fact going to be slightly better than what we have seen in the last 25 years. I don't think it can be dramatically better, given the facts on the ground, but it can be slightly better.

The most obvious examples are software and e-services. If software grows by a billion dollars a year and on average 20,000 dollars is the value created by an e-job, you are creating 50,000 jobs for every billion dollars of growth. And you are now getting 4 billion dollars of growth in a year in just software and e-services. Four billion dollars is 200,000 jobs. Again if you go by the industry yardstick, 200,000 jobs is 20 million square feet of office space. This goes back to Soviet-style planning. This also means a 140 million square feet of housing area. If you look at the implications of these numbers, you will see that the 4 billion growth this year will become 5 billion next year and 7 billion the year after. This then begins to have huge macroeconomic implications.

So I am an optimist. But even in my optimism I see the annual growth at just under 6 per cent so far, becoming a little over 6 per cent, and at some point by the end of the decade may be we will get to 7 per cent and at that stage it will become a tiger economy rate of growth.

As for what we have heard so far and Deepak Nayyar's point on where the state has come in India in its relationship with markets, I would go out on a limb to say that in most cases, other than when setting up regulatory mechanisms, in most cases when the state has interfered in markets, it has done so for the worse. This is our experience, whether it is food procurement, energy pricing, telephone pricing or almost any kind of pricing—sugarcane, water, electricity, you think of almost any kind of intervention in a market that the Indian state has done, and it is a change for the worse.

Ashok S. Ganguly

The reason why as an independent country we faced utter poverty and destitution was because the Industrial Revolution had passed India by as a colony, other than what was useful for the British and their economic needs. Whether it was the railways, or the postal service, it was to fulfil the needs of the British. However, the second revolution, after the Industrial Revolution, is the Knowledge Revolution, which emerged in the 1960s. The components of the Knowledge Revolution are information technology, biotechnology and wireless telephony. These are the three pillars of the Knowledge Revolution. As an independent nation, India has grabbed the Knowledge Revolution, especially through information technology, and which other countries are slowly starting to recognise. Therefore, the advances in information technology and some of the quantitative figures that Ninan has spoken about are not happening in a vacuum or due to government policy, but because of Indian entrepreneurship and market forces. Nobody had heard of Narayana Murthy or Azim Premji or Kiran Mazumdar, prior to 1990. After they had their ADR issues they got to be known more widely in the United States and in Europe. That is now also true for TCS. The best thing that happened is the release of entrepreneurial energy, and that has nothing to do with the five year plans or with government concessions. This does not in anyway downplay the role of the Planning Commission, but what I am trying to convey is that you cannot plan the process of releasing entrepreneurial energy by planning. The third issue is the ongoing debate about employment creation *via* manufacturing sector *versus* the services sector. The fact is that both these sectors will grow. Between 1991 and 2005, there has been a quantum jump in employment generation and, looking into the future, the rate of economic growth may well reach 8-10 per cent per annum. It is only by accelerating the economic growth rate that there will be surpluses to deal with India's core problem of poverty, employment, education and health.

A final word of caution before I close. The caution relates to our competitive advantage in costs *vis-à-vis* China and the rest of the world. This can be sustained as long as we do not pursue mindless consumption and erode savings. If our MBAs start commanding salaries that they do in New York, if IIT engineers start commanding international salaries, this would eventually imbalance the low cost of living in India. The salary levels and consumption expenditure could get completely out of hand. Such a state may take 5 or 10 years to develop, but if it were to take place, it will have a very debilitating effect on India's competitiveness.

In the age of the Knowledge Revolution, India will be amongst the leaders in information technology, biotechnology and wireless telephony. India will be able to sustain a much higher rate of economic growth provided we can sustain the advantage of low costs and high quality human resources.

Suman K. Bery

To capture the discussion at this point, I think Deepak Nayyar was really arguing that you cannot divorce the distributional aspects from the growth aspects. T. N. Ninan was arguing that, despite its weaknesses steady as she goes is not a bad model if you look at its achievements thus far. I hear T. N. Ninan saying and perhaps Dr. C. K. Prahalad as well that the future could be different from the past and that is what would provide the resources that would be needed, in this sense challenging what Deepak Nayyar is saying. Critics might argue that this is trickle down again, that you are focusing exclusively on growth and it is going to be the middle class elite that will gain with just crumbs for the people at the bottom.

Sunil Munjal

This is the problem with coming after speakers like these and most of the stuff I had written down got stolen in the last few minutes.

Suman K. Bery

Great minds think alike...(laughter...)

Sunil Munjal

One of the most important roles for the government should be to improve the standard of living of every single citizen of the country. This session focuses on growth and equity, improving livelihoods is all about that. But to improve livelihoods, we must be able to generate more wealth—so that we can distribute more of it. Otherwise we will end up distributing poverty—and that could be a problem.

Let's take demographics. Population growth has traditionally been identified as a disadvantage, but I believe that in some ways, it could become our biggest asset as we move forward. Fifty-four per cent Indians today are below the age of 25 and within the next 6 to 8 years we will be the youngest country in the world. It is a great threat and also a fantastic opportunity. If we handle it right and provide the right environment for the development of skills, we could have the best workforce in the world.

There have been many debates about outsourcing in the US and other western countries. Actually, there is no debate. These countries simply don't have the people to do these jobs. Some numbers have shown that between now and 2020 the entire developed world will fall short of 40 million people in the working age group (19-59 years). And India will have the exact number in surplus if we don't add any more jobs right now.

There are tremendous opportunities in the global basket—and people must be allowed to move and fulfil these opportunities. Therefore, the movement of people across Indian borders will be extremely critical for us. We will, therefore, have to find ways to make this work whether through the WTO—or any other global forum.

This will be crucial because of our poverty numbers. Two hundred and fifty million or so live at below 50 rupees a day, some significantly below 50 rupees a day. These poverty levels are spread across the country— many more in the eastern border of India, and less in the south, north and west. Eight per cent in Punjab are also below the poverty line, and this is supposedly one of the better-off states.

What then, is creating this difference? If you draw a line from Kanpur down to Hyderabad, the left and the right of that line is actually scary, they are like two different countries. On the right side, growth is at two, three or at best four per cent. Regions here face the largest problem of poverty, illiteracy and population growth. Of course, there are states in the right side that have also grown in recent years, but as a rule, the right side has prospered less than the left side.

Suman K. Bery

You are saying the left is growing faster. Is that what you are saying?

Sunil Munjal

Clearly, much much faster...(laughter...). Seventy-two per cent of the people in India as per the last census live in the rural areas depending largely on agriculture. But interestingly 40 per cent of them have incomes other than agricultural incomes. The overall 72 per cent contribute 22 per cent to the economy.

There is clearly a serious disconnect out here. There is a need for us to fix this, not for charitable reasons, but for our own personal and national interests. It is important for us to change that. I am aware that a new programme of direct intervention for the rural economy has been announced in the Common Minimum Programme. But along with intervention from the top, there must be intervention at the bottom as well.

At the same time, we must not forget the growth sectors. T. N. Ninan talked about growing the top end—the knowledge economy, and growing it aggressively. I believe that growth must come from all three domains, agriculture, manufacturing and services. Without this, a demographic structure like ours cannot be sustainable over a long period of time.

I am slightly more optimistic than T. N. Ninan. I think our past need not be necessarily the only model to project our future growth. Our future growth can be

higher and I believe significantly higher. We will go through cycles of ups and downs, which are always scary. But each time we face a downturn and think it will never end, it gets better. And if you look at our trend curve it is constantly rising. It is possible to take it up higher.

Let's take agriculture. We are the largest producer of milk in the world, and the second largest of vegetables and fruits. But our value add is only 6 per cent. In a small country like Thailand, the farm sector value add is 82 per cent. This is where I think direct intervention is required. We must force value in this sector, and make changes. Our agriculture sector today is the most neglected part of India, more than industry ever was and this has to change.

We have seen in the past that excessive government intervention does not create more efficiency; actually it reduces it. The agriculture sector is a typical case in point. We therefore need to value add in the farm sector. I believe we can add more value here than in any other segment of the economy. We also need to look at urban infrastructure because the current level of migration is unsustainable, and enough jobs are not being created in the rural areas.

For all this we need to create infrastructure, and this requires capital. There isn't enough of it in India so we must actively invite foreign capital to supplement the overall basket of resources available. We need to bring in more resources, instead of endlessly debating what should go where. We should, therefore, focus on infrastructure, reduce rules and regulations, keep them simple and implement them quickly and ruthlessly.

This should be the role of the state right now, because the rest of it will be taken care of by personal and private enterprises. And when I say private I don't mean only private industry. I mean private enterprise individuals, NGOs, companies and institutions. There is a tremendous amount of energy in India.

Sitaram Yechury

When we talk of growth with equity, having heard Deepak Nayyar, the equity aspect should not be seen as some sort of charity that we are doing for somebody in this country. The distributive element of growth with equity is not something that we are bestowing on or doing for the people who require it to be done. It is not mere philanthropy. I would like to stress the fact that growth without equity means that growth itself will suffer. There is an economist's point of view that I want to put across apart from the political point of view. Looking at the last 10 years of reform, there are three disquieting factors. I am surprised the economists have not referred to them. The first factor is that through these years of reform your share of manufacture to GDP has at best stagnated if not declined. Second, during the course of these reforms, your overall savings rate and therefore the investment rate has declined. Thirdly, during these years of reform, your tax-GDP ratio has declined. Now these three are very important parameters. These are disturbing features that happened during the course of these reforms. Why? You cannot talk in terms of equity if your tax-GDP ratio is declining, you cannot

talk in terms of being an industrial society when your share of manufacturing is declining, and you cannot talk in terms of the illusions of a post-industrial society that India has already become without first actually being an industrial society. Somewhere down the line, you will have to examine why and from where this mismatch has emerged. Seventy-two per cent of the people dependent on agriculture contribute to only 22 per cent of GDP. That is precisely where your poverty exists. And, this is an issue that needs correction. This can come about only through state intervention and not through state abdication.

State intervention does not mean fixing your telephone rates. We are not talking of state intervention to determine what should be the regulatory mechanism. This is a consequential element, but not the important element. We are talking of the state as the prime economic mover in society. All those who talk about the success of China, should remember one thing. During the years of reforms in China, and even today, the state is the most important economic player. By advocating the abdication of the state from such intervention, I think this entire issue of growth with equity is being looked at in a very distorted fashion. Growth is essentially determined by a very fundamental element of economics, i.e. the expansion of the domestic market. During the last decade of reforms, the domestic market in India has contracted. Now, there will be disputes on this depending on which area you are actually looking at. But this is testified by our political experience, when you find starvation deaths, when you find distress suicides happening in our rural areas today. The purchasing power of the vast majority of the Indian people has actually declined. Studies will be required to identify the magnitude of it.

This being the case, then there are certain distortions that need to be corrected. My understanding would be that equity is important in the sense that unless you increase or improve equity, you are not putting greater purchasing power in the hands of the people and unless they have a greater purchasing power, your aggregate domestic demand will not grow. This may sound very Keynesian. However, it is better to be a Keynesian fundamentalist than a fiscal fundamentalist. I believe the stage in which you are in, you have to target the growth of your domestic market. Here, the state's intervention becomes important as an economic player. The state will have to, as Deepak Nayyar said, increase its public investment and take up this task. However, where is it going to find the resources? Meanwhile, let us be clear on this particular aspect. In today's conditions in India, what is required is not the state abdicating its responsibility as an economic player and withdrawing from the economic scene, but greater state intervention in terms of increasing public investment. This is important, So, while I share your optimism, I am essentially a realist.

Suman K. Bery

Do you see an evolution in the role of the state as compared to say the '70s? In what direction would you see the role of the state in the next decade as being, perhaps in terms of nuance, different from the past?

Sitaram Yechury

It would be very different from the decades when the state was the main player building up your economic infrastructure. Right now, I see the role of the state as the catalyst in actually promoting public investment. The consequence would be the creation of an economic and social infrastructure. This sort of a public investment being the leading engine, so to speak, for expanding your domestic market is the role on which, I think, we ought to concentrate.

Sunil Munjal

Just to interfere for a moment, I wasn't quite through. So what I am going to do is leave a note here of action points that I think are necessary for us to move forward (see Appendix at the end of this Section).

Manvinder Singh (Vindi) Banga

According to T.N. Ninan, the current growth rate in our economy is six per cent. The bigger question is what is the trigger, what is going to make it change to eight per cent or a higher number? I agree with him that it is not going to change unless there is a structural change in something that we collectively do. I would like to suggest that this could come about through reform in the rural sector. In the last decade a fair amount of reform has taken place in the industrial sector, and the service and IT sectors have burgeoned. Both these sectors have got a momentum of their own and indeed have contributed to the strong structural pickup in the economy in the last decade.

In the next decade, I would recommend that we target the rural economy to provide that structural change. I was looking at a speech that I had made at our company's 2000 Annual General Body Meeting. All the points in it are still relevant today and will be four years from now. That signifies to me the urgency for us to look to this sector. Why? It is only 30 per cent of GDP, but it has a huge multiplier effect on consumer demand, as 60 per cent of our population is dependent on it. If you get a 3 per cent growth in agriculture, in itself it will give a less than 1 per cent GDP growth. But it doesn't, because a lot of money goes into rural India where 70 per cent of India lives and that will drive a demand increase on the industrial and service sectors. Our model shows that a 3 per cent growth in agriculture, gives up to a 2 per cent growth in GDP. I think that is a very big goal to go for.

However, here is the paradox. On the one hand, we have very high stocks of food, we can't export it at the procurement price, at which we have stored it. That means the cost of making food or producing food in this country is high. It is not economic. On the other hand, we also know that 40 per cent of the population eats below the balanced nutrition level. Why? Because they can't afford it. So we have a situation where a large chunk of our population can't afford food and the cost of

producing food is very high. I would liken this to industry. What has industry done in the last decade? We have become more competitive, we have become more productive, we have reduced our cost of production. That is exactly what we need to do in the rural sector. In doing so there needs to be a redirection of the role of the state from a regulatory one to a supportive one. It needs to support value addition, food processing, the farmer, and support the farmer manufacturer and marketeer coming together. I believe we need to remove restrictions on the movement and storage of food, and move towards a common Indian market.

We need to redefine the role of the Food Corporation of India. Instead of buying and storing grain, they can actually help market it overseas. There are many countries around the world that had made that change in their food bodies. The Australian Wheat Board is a classical example. For this, the legal framework needs to be altered, especially in the context of market—*mandi* legislation as well as in the food laws where there is a plethora of laws which are constrictive. A cross-ministerial body was formed by the previous government four or five years ago to achieve this, but actually it hasn't come to fruition yet. I believe that could be a huge catalyst.

These are some areas where the government could redirect its effort and create enablers. I think once these enablers come, the rest will happen because of the entrepreneurship of the farmer and the other players. I believe that the rest will come together to create a complementary partnership between credit suppliers, (banks are ready today—you have heard about ICICI Bank—they are ready to supply agricultural credit), agri-input companies who are willing to provide advice and recommendations on farming—and food processing companies like ours who are willing to buy directly from the farmer. So all these complementary capabilities could come together and change the food processing industry and thereby the rural economy. If we target a comprehensive reform of the agricultural sector, we could perhaps provide the biggest catalyst for a higher GDP growth for the next decade.

Montek Singh Ahluwalia

I would like to comment first on Deepak Nayyar's point on the relative roles of the market and the state. Deepak said that the state needs to ensure the provision of public services and to provide a safety net. I agree with this and I think there is a good case that we are not doing enough. On public services, if we look at the data, India's expenditure as a per cent of GDP on primary education and health, is lower than other countries, and must be increased over time. That doesn't, however, mean that if we simply provide more money we will achieve what we want. We also have to ask ourselves whether the way we spend money is actually providing public services. A lot of the public scepticism about government expenditure today is because of the complete lack of reform in addressing the question whether, when the state says it is going to do something for a particular purpose, it is actually going to do it in a way that achieves that purpose.

The first problem here relates to the facts. It is incredibly difficult, even if you are in government, to get facts about whether the state is actually achieving what it is meant to be achieving. I have been trying very hard, for example in looking at the effectiveness of public services in hospitals, to get data on outcomes rather than input. We have data on how many nurses, doctors and hospital beds there are per 1000 people, all of which are useful. But I cannot find out what the actual success rate is in terms of number of obstetric procedures performed, how many went well, how many didn't go well, how many of the people treated actually recovered within a certain period. The state produces information on what it spends but it just does not provide measures of what it actually 'produces'. Sometimes one can guess. If expenditure on primary education is high but drop out rates are not falling you know there is a problem. Similarly, if beds in community hospitals are unutilised, as is the case often, you know there is a problem.

A greater effort needs to be made to make transparent the effectiveness of the systems we have. If we had such information we would be better able to look at what works well and what doesn't and design policies appropriately. Without it, there is a danger of simply pouring money into whatever system exists in the belief that this will lead to output. It will to some extent, but when resources are scarce, it is very important to ensure that money is well spent.

This brings me to the point that Sitaram Yechury raised of low tax ratios of GDP. This is a fair point and it is a failure of the last 10 years, that we have not seen an increase in the ratio of taxes to GDP, though more recently there has been an uptrend. India is not an over taxed country because our tax ratio is low compared to others. We are a country which has relatively high rates of taxes, combined with a system in which it is easy to evade taxes. The answer clearly lies in major reforms in the tax system, focusing on removing exemptions and simplifying the system. One important recent development in this context is that the states have agreed to implement VAT. It is not really a comprehensive VAT—it is just introducing a VAT element into the sales tax component of states taxation—but still I regard this as a major step. It could lead to reduced evasion and higher realisation. Tax reforms that reduce the scope for corruption and evasion are extremely important.

We also have to address the issue of user charges. The national Common Minimum Programme says that we must have targeted subsidies, but the truth of the matter is that if we look at various subsidies that have become entrenched in the system, the degree of effective targeting is very low. Consider for example the low charges for power supplied to agriculture. The benefit which goes to small farmers compared to the larger farmers is very small and the landless don't benefit at all, as it is the larger farmers who own pumps who benefit. This means 80 to 90 per cent of the implicit subsidy is actually going to large farmers and not the target groups. In turn, they are depleting the groundwater, and lowering the water table, so that smaller farmers, who don't have pumps with strong motors, actually get less water from their shallow wells.

Cheap power for farmers also means that the utilities are broke and cannot expand electrification. This means UP, having electrified western UP which is the richer part, doesn't have money to electrify eastern UP which is poorer. The farmers in eastern UP therefore, have to use diesel powered pumps which means they pay more for groundwater extraction. This is clearly a highly dysfunctional system and we need reforms which focus on these problems. These reforms will be good for both growth and equity.

One can go through a list of such things but I won't actually do that. My main point is that we seem to have got locked into a system where dysfunctional subsidies have become the norm. Unfortunately, the public is not aware of the nature of the problem. When the present Chief Minister of Delhi took the bold decision to privatise distribution in Delhi, it was done at a time when the losses in the system, just electricity being stolen, was more than 50 per cent. In East Delhi, beyond the Yamuna, the losses were as high as 75 per cent, which by any standard is too much. Clearly many people were running small scale industries in their own residential premises. So when the Delhi authorities organised a 'raid', the MLAs complained about this high-handedness as the raid was conducted without warning. These are examples of how resources are wasted. We need to address a number of governance issues which limit the ability of the state to conserve resources to do what the state should be doing i.e. expanding public services.

Let me now turn to what is more conventionally called economic reforms. The general principle that Deepak Nayyar outlined was that we ought to create markets where they don't exist. I agree with that and many things follow from that principle. In fact 90 per cent of economic reforms is precisely about creating those markets, or removing distortions which prevent the market from functioning.

For example, we have completely locked up the urban land market. T. N. Ninan made the point that if we are to benefit from the software revolution to the extent which I hope we do, we will not be able to do it unless the Urban Land Ceiling Repeal is actually implemented. We will not be able to build the number of square feet, etc. of office space needed unless the land market is there. Two-thirds of the land in Delhi is locked up under the DDA. There is no market there. Here is a reform which is desperately needed. Similarly, some of the agricultural marketing laws today prevent the development of modern markets, which would help farmers. In the rural areas you have to go to the existing *mandis* which are actually run by the 'arthias'. It is very difficult to create a modern market—ask Amrita Patel of the National Dairy Development Board (NDDB) who has been trying to set up a first class modern agricultural horticultural market on the outskirts of Bangalore. The government actually gave them an exemption under the law, enabling them to set up a market with grading facilities and completely

transparent pricing based on electronic auctions, instead of the very shady sort of 'hands under the handkerchief or towel' method of exchanging signals to sell bags of produce which are not graded. In this traditional system, the farmer really doesn't know what price he has got for his product. And yet the NDDB had enormous difficulty in getting off the ground because the traders, who run the normal *mandis*, lobbied strongly against the new market. Unless we can deal with vested interests we will not be able to implement reforms which are good for both growth and equity.

One of the failures of the period since the mid-1990s is that the agricultural growth rate has been reduced to half of what it was between 1980 and 1996. In my view, a lot of the problems that we see in rural areas, the signs of distress, and unhappiness, etc. are not because we followed a growth strategy and ignored equity. It is because we didn't follow a growth strategy successfully. We allowed the growth impulses in agriculture to be eroded, and the post 1996 agricultural performance is really a failure of growth.

What is needed in agriculture is complex, and much of it involves public investment in rural infrastructure. But it also requires reforms. If you are going to go in for the diversification of agriculture, the marketing that is required for diversifying horticultural crops is completely different from the marketing for cereals. It is not just a question of taking something, putting it in a bag and selling it. You need to make sure that post-harvest technologies enable the quality of the vegetable or fruit to be really preserved, you need a cold chain, you need all kinds of grading and quality control. You probably need someone who knows what is saleable at the other end to a much greater extent than would be necessary, let us say, if you are buying wheat, which is going to be converted into *atta*. This brings in the role of the corporate sector but this often goes against the grain of what some people would normally think of as acceptable. There is resistance to the idea of bringing in the corporate sector. But consider the role of contract farming to encourage a group of farmers to actually grow the product that people want because they know what is needed back in the factory or at a particular market.

You may also find that in a particular area there are some farmers who take to this very naturally and want to get into this more 'risky' form of quality dependent agriculture. If they have limited land, they may want to lease land and expand their production. For that we need a major change in land laws in many states where in fact today the position is that the person who leases the land is protected. Normally, small farmers would be unwilling to lease land out to somebody else, because that person may be able to claim the benefit of tenurial rights and effectively they would lose their land. We don't have a rural land market where land can be leased out and resumed when needed. There is great reluctance to protect the rights of the landlord but what about a situation where a marginal landholder wants to lease out land? Perhaps we need a law that protects a landlord's rights for leasing out land.

Coming back to what Deepak Nayyar said, we must create markets where they don't exist, the principle is the right one and will point us in many directions towards reforms. Frankly 80 per cent of what is called economic reforms can be encompassed under that particular phrase. I agree with that view but I am not sure that everybody who accepts the general proposition recognises the implication of going from the general principle to what is needed at the micro-level. What we need is growth with a better spread of the benefits and our reforms should be tailored to that objective.

Deepak Nayyar

Just a one liner Montek. I think we need to make an analytical distinction between a situation where markets exist but are circumvented, distorted or regulated as the urban land market and a situation where markets do not exist. And I was referring to the latter essentially in rural India where there are missing markets.

Neera Chandhoke

As a political scientist, I have been trying to map out the social policies of the Indian state in research work. Therefore, I have become somewhat familiar with the domain of providing well-being for the poor. I happen to be an old fashioned political theorist who feels that the task of the state is to deliver well-being, which is its chief legitimacy claim as well. If a state gives up on that, it abdicates its claims to political obligation, for there is no reason to obey the laws of a state that does not secure well-being.

I want to address Prof. C. K. Prahalad's suggestions for turning the poor into an asset. This is a well known World Bank strategy and I have always had problems with it. The Tenth Plan document tells us that we have 260 million of the absolute poor, but a recent work by Dyson, Cassen and Visaria tells us that the figure is actually 300 million. These are people who are unable to access the basic consumption package needed for life itself, in other words, 300 million people live below the poverty line.

A majority of the poor live in rural areas, they are composed of either the landless or the marginal farmers whose landholdings are not viable, because of environmental degradation. They are, therefore, forced to seek work outside their land. It is this section that the Employment Guarantee Act seeks to target. But every single employment generation Act enacted by the Government of India since Independence, as well as all the poverty alleviation schemes and food for work schemes, have failed to work, because this section of the rural poor has neither land, nor assets, nor skills, though they have votes. They may have votes, but banks do not give them credit on these votes. The point is that it is not as if these strategies have not been tried out in India. India has great experience in enacting laws that remain on the statute book, either because of corruption, or because the rural poor are just not in a position to access employment generation schemes.

S. Mahendra Dev

My paper addresses the concerns of growth and equity. When you talk about the next decade one should also look at the performance of the past decade. There is a need for a higher growth rate of 8 per cent per annum for the expansion of wealth in the economy. But, during the recent elections, the electorate raised concerns about the performance of rural India. India was shining in terms of foreign exchange, exports, the IT sector, etc. but rural India was not shining. My paper addresses the issue of how to make rural India shine. One important concern is employment growth. Another concern is that if you consider the commodity sector (agriculture and industry) the growth rate of GDP was not higher in the 1990s as compared to that of the 1980s. As Montek Singh Ahluwalia mentioned, the growth rate of agriculture since the mid-1990s was 1.5 per cent per annum as compared to more than 3 per cent growth in the decade before the mid-1990s. There was also a perception that the BJP government neglected the rural sector.

Before going to action points I will give the problems in the agriculture sector. In recent years, farmers' suicides have increased in many states. The budget is silent on this problem. Many farmers are shifting to commercial crops for which the input intensity is higher than for subsistence crops. There has been no breakthrough in dry land technology. Cultivation is done in marginal lands. The risk is high in commercial crops and marginal lands. The main problems of the farmers in the present context are—spurious input supplies, *viz.* seeds, fertilisers and pesticides; inadequate credit from institutional sources and dependence on moneylenders for credit; lack of water and the drying up of groundwater; farmers spend a lot of money in sinking borewells; a lack of extension services particularly for commercial crops; exploitation in marketing; a lack of non-farm activities in rural areas; and higher health expenditures.

Suman K. Bery

Most of these issues are the domain of the states, so will central legislation help? Or, is it a question of policy failure or of implementation?

S. Mahendra Dev

I think both state and central government interventions are needed. The state will have to make investments in irrigation as state governments do not have the money. We interviewed one agricultural labourer in the Mahbubnagar district of Andhra Pradesh. She told us that she was a tenant cultivating 10 acres of land— 5 acres of cotton and 5 acres of maize. She had taken to commercial farming because she had to spend money on the health and education of her family. Her family spent 20 to 30 thousand on health problems. The privatisation of hospitals have had an impact on the health expenditures of the poor. She had already taken Rs. 2 lakhs from moneylenders for health, education and sinking borewells. Therefore, farmers including tenants have many problems in agriculture. As Montek S.

Ahluwalia mentioned, water and irrigation management are crucial for higher agricultural growth. If you do not have good water management practices, investment on irrigation projects will not help the cause of farmers.

I am hopeful that if you take the right policies, such as the diversification of agriculture, good water management practices and improvements in research and extension, agriculture will grow faster in the near future. There is a need to shift agricultural workers by promoting rural non-farm employment in the form of agro-processing and services.

Prem Shankar Jha

In my paper, I didn't say growth is all that matters. I said a particular kind of growth is all that matters and it has to be high. We can't have growth without equity, these elections prove that and in the Common Minimum Programme we have a powerful answer, a tool for trying to achieve both. The government is fully aware of the challenge and that makes this a very exciting moment in the development of policy in our country. It is not only exciting for us, it is exciting for the whole world which is facing this problem of liberalisation leading to increasing inequality between winners and losers. In our case equity involves two basic issues—one is growing inequality, and the second is growing insecurity— something that has not been talked about so far. The main cause of growing inequality, as indeed of insecurity, is the lack of employment. We are facing a major crisis here. The Montek Singh Ahluwalia Task Force on unemployment produced a wonderful report and I am using it liberally for what I have to say. Between 1992 and 2002, eight million people have been taken out of agriculture. All but a fraction of them are children who have been sent back to school by their parents. Their parents want them to obtain quality jobs. The job guarantee scheme is not an answer to this need. It may be necessary in order to stave off destitution, but it is not an answer to this problem. The answer to this problem is growth in the non-agricultural sector.

The question is how do you maximise employment growth, how do you get employment growth which is at least equal to the number of people coming into the work force every year? We had four years between 1992 and 1997 when we actually did it. One imperfect but nonetheless important indicator was the fact that the number of people on the live register for job seekers actually went down by 100,000 in this period whereas both before and after it the number has risen up by more than 1 million a year. We have to repeat that. For that we need not high overall growth, but high growth in industry and agriculture. The important thing about 1992 to 1997 was that you had a 10 per cent plus growth rate in industry in addition to a 4.7 per cent growth in agriculture. That is what generated the jobs.

The reasons are implicit in the work of an economist whom the Prime Minister mentioned, Angus Maddison. If you look at Maddison's data for the 6 major European countries between 1820 and 1970 and another 10 in the 20th century, you find that it is not the absolute rate of growth which is responsible for job creation. It is the ratio between the rise in productivity in agriculture and industry, mainly industry, and the rise in productivity in the services sector. Throughout this period in every industrialised country, labour productivity in industry and agriculture has been between two and a half and three times the growth of productivity in the services sector. So increases in productivity caused by the application of the most efficient modern technologies to industry and agriculture have led to increases in growth of employment in the services sector. And that is where most employment has actually taken place. So powerful is the demand for labour unleashed by the application of modern technology to production that every industrialising country in the OECD and today Malaysia, South Korea, Taiwan, Hong Kong and Singapore have all had to import large volumes of foreign labour. Even Japan has a large foreign labour force. The US imported 80 million people in the 19th century, Northern Europe imported 15 million people between 1870 and 1914. Twenty-five per cent of the working force of Malaysia today is foreign labour. Ten to fifteen per cent in South Korea's are foreign labour. It is only because our industry stagnated for more than 20 years between 1957 and 1980 that we did not have a similar employment growth. We therefore need high industrial growth.

Now let me come to insecurity. Very briefly, let me ask, why is no one talking about social insurance? Bismarck introduced social insurance in 1871 in Germany. Lloyd George did it in 1909 in Britain. But we have not yet done it till today. We simply haven't had the guts to do it. We are also a democracy, and we can do it. I have appended a paper on an outline for a social insurance scheme for the 400 million people of the unorganised sector to the background paper I sent for this conference. Please do read it. SEWA has done wonderful work to show how cheaply and profitably social insurance schemes of different types can be run. A number of studies have shown that today the poor spend more than 100 per cent of their income on health alone when they fall ill. They take loans and often bankrupt themselves to get the treatment they need. That is the reality of the situation in this country. And it can be tackled perfectly with social insurance.

Bharat Karnad

This is a non-economist's take on the discussions. On hearing Vice-Chancellor Deepak Nayyar, and Prof. C. K. Prahalad one gets the impression that Dr. Nayyar does not want to be bothered with facts and figures. He would rather stick with certain ideas he has. Now the problem here is with the experiences of other countries in poverty alleviation which is also the thrust of the Indian government. There is one interesting fact relating to how the US tackled poverty during the Great Depression of the 1930s. The bulk of the present highway system was built in the United States during this period owing to the work for food programme. People were given the proverbial 'chicken in the pot' and subsistence wages in return for their labour which was used to construct the highway system in America. Do we have a counterpart programme in India? And if not, why not? What we have instead is the enormous and regular waste of resources in make-work programmes, the kind of project work wherein near zero-quality roads, embankments, etc. are constructed which are then washed away with the first rains. The same roads are re-built only to be washed away again. The tax payer's money goes into such projects, but what is there to show for it even in terms of poverty eradication? We have the example of an American system that is purely capitalist in nature, going in for poverty alleviation schemes that have succeeded spectacularly. Why can't India, which has no dearth of poor, unemployed or under-employed people, do something similar?

Naina Lal Kidwai

I want to dwell for a bit on the issue of employment, which lies at the core of the growth and equity argument. If we look at IT enabled services, we see a very high people to capital ratio and high end employment. If you look at manufacturing this is preferable because it attracts lower end, lower skilled and maybe lesser-educated people, which may be better for poverty reduction. However, the dilemma here in terms of the manufacturing equation is if you look at Bajaj Auto today, which produces two and a half million two wheelers with about 10,000 people; six years ago it produced only half that number with double the number of people. What is happening in manufacturing is that it is becoming more labour saving than labour employing. In order to stay at the same level of manufacturing employment we need more capital and if you juxtapose this against a declining savings rate and a very anaemic FDI, where is this to come from? I am not sure how manufacturing or large-scale manufacturing is going to solve the employment situation. This leads us to the MME and SME sectors, the small/middle sized industry where there is scope to improve. In agri-business, though there are a lot of challenges, there is also a large scope for improvement. In industries like tourism and garments and textiles, which have traditionally been more labour-intensive than others, and which were natural strengths for us, why have we not succeeded?

If we can get to the bottom of this—where and how does the state get engaged or disengage itself in order to allow entrepreneurship to truly develop—we may find an answer for at least some of the employment generation we are seeking. For example, in agri-business, there are some six or seven Acts to do with food adulteration, essential food commodities, etc. all of which the government identified. There was a legal framework established through what was to become a Food Standards Supply Act 2003, which has disappeared into oblivion. Why have we not been able to resurrect this Act to bring it to a platform where industry—small industry—can benefit in the agri-business area? The average exporter faces—through the inspector *raj*, through approvals, through every piece of regulation that gets in the way—several nasty obstacles. And

therefore we kill entrepreneurship. In fact to start a company in India it takes 89 days, in Pakistan 24 days while in Australia it only takes 2 days. Why are we in a mode where there are so many hurdles to start an industry by the small entrepreneur? And then of course there is the financing side of the equation, which while it may be easier than coping with some of this regulatory mess, is still not easy. We do not have venture capital, and bank finance is not readily forthcoming. Infrastructure—you can't talk of rural development or small industry or the movement of agri-business without roads, without the cold chains. So the role of the state, if it truly believes in employment generation, must lie in addressing the impediments in the way of entrepreneurship, the issues of infrastructure, and the regulation and provision of capital to assist this.

And lastly, education. I was quite horrified to find out how little entrepreneurship is actually taught in an IIM or an IIT. In fact I sat on a Board, which tried to donate money to create chairs to do this, and we couldn't find champions in the leading institutions in this country. We do not have incubators, we do not teach entrepreneurship through management tools. Having a good idea is not good enough, if it is not bankable. The bankableness will come from the level of training and the credibility of the institution from which an individual comes particularly, if he/she doesn't have the experience. We need more IRMAs. We need to provide our people with more entrepreneurship related education tools. I don't believe we have addressed this part of our employment equation at all.

Sanjoy Hazarika

I am a little perturbed by what I have heard in this room, coming from where I am and where I work, much of the time in the Northeast. Where does the periphery stand in all these issues? Where do landlocked areas like the Northeast figure where 99 per cent of their borders are with other countries, and less than 1 per cent with India? How you are going to get growth there? I think the Deputy Chairman of the Planning Commission has just come back from there and I think the situation is far worse than what they have told you, which is probably a fairly rosy picture. Growth rates are the worst in the country. Governance is even worse. And it is not that largesse has not gone from Delhi; it has but it has come back here or gone into the pockets of people.

The last 57 years of planning have brought the Northeast to disaster. We are at a state where we have joined the Bimaru group, you might call it Bimaru Nee. Think of it—350 communities, almost as many languages and 99 per cent of its land border with 4 other countries. One can blame Delhi for pumping in money and the states for accepting it whole-heartedly and creating a situation of absolute dependency. We have not looked at our neighbours as economic partners. It is not going to happen soon but it is beginning to happen in a small way. The PM is going there, in a day or two, to flag off the Indo-ASEAN Rally which is a symbolic thing. But we have to look to our neighbours. The way out for the Northeast is to not turn its back on Delhi and the rest of the country but to embrace its neighbours economically. We need strong political connections with Delhi. But 50 years of this relationship have brought Assam from number four to fourth from the bottom. Good economics is also good common sense. If we at least strengthen those links, opportunities, trading possibilities, I think they would be important steps forward.

This session is also about regional imbalances. It is one of the reasons why people talk about money flows to the region and about non-accountability. But look at it this way—the Northeast was perhaps the first globalised region of South Asia, or among the first. For the last 150 years, it has been continuously exploited, not just in terms of its resources going out to India but across the world, benefiting other regions. Therefore, I wouldn't make a big fuss about the Rs. 10,000 crores or the Rs. 15,000 crores that go into the region every year. At the same time I would say that it is very important to recognise that the planning system that has evolved over the past years with regard to the Northeast has led to many of these problems, these disconnects. You have a Delhi centric or a capital centric planning process, which has no relevance to either the systems or the people of the region. For example, you can't have plantations in the hills. It just doesn't work. You don't look for alternatives to *jhum*, to slash and burn. For 120 years we have been looking for alternatives and there aren't any. These are the things that we need to understand if we are going to keep that region not just close to our hearts but also as a resonant economy.

I have four specific points on the region. One is that you can't look at it without the question of flood proofing. Every year, one-seventh of the population of Assam is displaced by flooding. And every year the states, districts and the centre respond in an absolutely ad hoc manner. So we need long-term planning and flood proofing. The second thing is connectivity to the region, and within the region. Three, we have to improve participatory planning which involves the people. Because ultimately it is the marginalised that we have to bring in. We all work in the field, we all have things that we try to do. And in this process finally, the political element cannot be discounted as in Kashmir—dialogue, processes of peace building, these are absolutely critical political initiatives. They are as critical as anything else in terms of bringing both governance and development to the region.

Vivek Monteiro

I will highlight a few points which are elaborated upon in the paper which I have written titled "Another India is Possible: Basic Needs, the Unorganised Sector and Science in India". I would like to speak as a trade unionist on this issue firstly to point out that when we talk about mainstream and marginal there is a serious problem of terminology. How many people are there in the mainstream? And what is the demography of the marginal? I think if you look at the numbers, then it is clear that the page is upside down. The second point on which we are all agreed is that the basic problem of the next decade is the problem of basic needs for this very large section of people who so far have been excluded, who are called the marginal sector, but who are in fact the mainstream sector of India. Now the question which has to be answered is—can this be done with business as usual? In other words, look at what has been happening over the last 10 years or 15 years and decide—is this going to happen with business as usual? Here there were some points of dispute—some of us felt that yes it is happening and it will happen if we step up the growth rate and the others were saying no, it is not happening, it is actually what has happened in the last 15 years that is creating the problem. The question is— why cannot this issue be decided? Is it such an ambiguous issue that it cannot be decided by examining the data? I would agree 100 per cent with Prof. Prahalad that we have to be data-driven and it is extremely important to decide this issue. We have to spend some time and resources to really examine and decide whether the problem of basic needs for the unorganised sector is being met by the kind of development that we have had so far. To take the analogy of the picture that was shown by Prof. Prahalad—when I looked at that picture what I saw was the elephant. Now there is the well known story about those six technical experts who examined the elephant and each of them gave a lot of data about different parts of its anatomy but mere technical expertise is not science. Science, the scientific approach is also about not missing the elephant. And the question is are we seeing the elephant when we are talking about the question of basic needs for the marginalised, which is really the mainstream and which I prefer to call the unorganised sector?

I would like to raise two more points. One is that Dr. Ambedkar, while writing his notes for the Indian Constitution was unambiguous and very emphatic that a strong public sector was essential for equity. In fact he wanted a much stronger commitment to this in the constitution. If you look at his writings such as State and Minorities, this is what he said. I think this is a basic issue which has to be examined. Can we have equity in this country without strong government intervention? The second is that the Common Minimum Programme is also something which is extremely important in the context of the unorganised sector. There is a proposal in it to have a commission on the unorganised sector. But I think the real question is can the problem of the unorganised sector in this country be tackled without making it the number one item on our agenda for the next decade? And if we are to make 'basic needs for the unorganised sector' the number one item on the national agenda for the next decade, then what kind of redefinition of the agenda is needed?

Ravi Parthasarathy

Dr. Vivek Monteiro started off by identifying that he was coming from the direction of the trade union. I am coming from a different direction i.e. how do you encourage economic development on the ground, and how do you actually stimulate economic development through the provision of infrastructure. We have got some past experience and I want to talk about three specific issues, and an idea that we are in the process of implementing. While these relate to the issue of having economic growth with equity, I would also focus upon some of the administrative difficulties we are facing in going through these kind of programmes.

The first issue is that it is universally acknowledged that infrastructure is the key to economic development. However, we don't have any approach within the country which encourages the use of infrastructure to realise the latent demographic potential of a particular district or of a particular state. We have all kinds of statistical indices, but it doesn't help us to know that one state or one district has 50 television sets per 1,000 of population or something equally meaningless. What is necessary is to look at the district level—I am taking a district because that is the administrative block of this country, it becomes very messy to go on any other basis—and to determine what are the 10, 20 or 30 things we have to do in order to unleash the monetary potential of that particular district. Call this index 100, take a stock of things on the ground and say okay we are only at 20. Then that becomes the basis of planning the use of incremental resources. This is relatively simple to do, and will not take much time. This approach will inevitably point out that Himachal Pradesh may need a ski resort or Rajasthan may need some museums to be upgraded and some other districts will need something completely different. This then becomes a powerful tool for directing incremental resources. This is the first point.

The second point is that when we do an actual programme around this idea, which we are in the process of doing, there is no point in doing anything other than integrated area development. And now this is going smack against the way the country is running and how public investment takes place. The simple proposition is that if you do a road plus electricity plus water supply and assist to take produce to market, you will get an exponentially higher return on your investment, as compared to doing one road in one district and something else somewhere else.

When you do an integrated area development programme and we are getting very good feedback on one of our existing programmes—you are really playing God because you cannot do this to all districts at the same time. You are moving away from a policy of having a hundred flowers bloom. Lets face it, after so many years of economic development and central planning, we don't have a hundred flowers anywhere in the country. And China—we keep hearing about China incessantly—but they didn't start by modernising the whole of China overnight, they started with their coastal regions. So you need to look at those districts which are key to economic growth and figure out how to put extra money on the table. There has to be some extra window which is given to undertake integrated area development in key pockets of the country.

Suman K. Bery

But Ravi, your inclination would then be to go for the low hanging fruit. Whereas I think a lot of the sense in the room would be to have no district left behind. And that is the issue.

Ravi Parthasarathy

No, it is about prioritisation, it is not about low hanging fruit. You can take different types of districts. You can take an industrial district, you can take a completely below the poverty line district, but the same approach will work, which brings me to my third issue relating to some of the very imaginative schemes in the Central Government. Ministry after ministry have really good schemes, there is nothing wrong with the schemes. But the way it works is that these Central Ministries give money to the states and then the states spread it out. There is no central mechanism to pool that money together and do rural roads along with rural electricity along with water supply and do it under one central command. Now we can spend a lifetime in all these ministries without getting anywhere unless there is a directive principle given by a body such as this that says let us look at integrated area development, let us see where it takes us. Let us take up half a dozen such areas.

Lastly, we have heard a number of suggestions around what is to be done, but if you want to address the issue of economic growth and equity, the sector I would suggest is water supply. The poor pay for water, the rich don't. And if you did water supply as a sectoral initiative or as a mission like we had 12 years ago, you would achieve higher economic growth, as the multiplier effect of water is the highest compared to any other sector. And you will have equity because you will be solving the problems of the poor who are paying through their nose for water, whether it is in Mumbai in the Dharavi slums, or in Rajasthan, or even in Guwahati which doesn't have enough water although it is located on the banks of the Brahmaputra.

Sunita Narain

I am glad to hear that growth with equity is not possible without a focus on rural India. But I think we don't even understand what we need to do in rural India to make it work. It is very clear that in rural India, unlike urban India, you are talking about the environment or the natural resources being your biggest asset. You are talking about land, forest and water, being the assets on which you have to build your economies. So it is the natural capital which has to be the basis of economic capital building. But what we do not know is how we will use that natural capital both with sustainability as well as with equity. And that is the biggest challenge. The laws are so repressive that people can't plant trees on government forest land. Only common land is available to plant trees but if you were a poor villager and you were to plant a tree on a government forest land you would go to jail. If it was revenue land you would be fined. If you build a check dam to hold water and then harvest it by tapping the stream that flows along your village, it is technically illegal by law. And therefore a lot will have to be done. We have talked about the role of the state. In this area we will have to restructure and deregulate the rural economy if we want it to work.

The other point is that there is a paradox here. The fiscal situation in your states today is desperate. If you are talking about letting people have a higher stake in the natural resources—which is what you would say would be the low hanging fruit or as I would put it is where the answers are going to come from—letting people plant trees, letting people use the watershed, letting them grow grass, letting them do organic farming, the problem is that the fiscal situation in the states is so poor that the states only source of revenue is natural resources. It is the same forest, it is the same water, it is the same minerals on which we are saying today that we want greater community ownership and greater community rights. And that is the big challenge that we will have to deal with if we want to move ahead. Along with the political challenge of deepening democracy (not just for effective delivery of services) we will have to consider power over natural resources. In other words power to the *panchayats*. Without rights to the land, to be able to use the land or rights over the water is not effective decentralisation. For effective transfer of funds we need systems. We have in the past experimented with the Jawahar Rozgar Yojana where funds went directly to the *panchayats*. Now we can go one step further and empower the *gram sabha*. This will bring in transparency and better fund management. The point is that there are answers but these will demand some hard decisions. I give you one clear decision that you will have to take in the area of the supply of raw material to the pulp and paper sector. Will you let the farmers grow the raw material? If you allow the farmers to grow the wood then you cannot distort the market by giving them wood from the forest department or by giving industry captive plantations because that will destroy the farmers market. So there are clear strategic directions to decide.

Take another example of the issue of urban water supply. On the one hand I am arguing for a reduction of the role of the so-called state, a deregulation of the state in the rural areas and greater powers to communities or greater decentralisation but at the same time I would argue that the role of the state in supplying essential services is critical. Take the issue of water services and sewage. In urban conglomerates where a large proportion of the population lives today, the political pressure is very high to bring water from all over the country—Delhi gets water from Tehri, Hyderabad is going to get its water from Manjira, Chennai doesn't even know where to get its water from—the role of the state will have to be defined differently. The economics of water supply and sewage is of a kind that the private sector, unless it is made of huge charitable intentions and has very deep pockets to spend, would never be able to substitute the role of the state. In rural areas communities should be given the power. They will find water through water harvesting, through watershed programmes and may be the Hindustan Lever approach of giving filters that you put at the household level will work. That is a decentralised water supply answer.

I totally disagree with the approach where you support the state even as an incompetent inefficient state which we know protects the rich in the name of the poor. This is the case with water supply, with transport and anything else. So I am saying reform the state in this new world, change the state but change it for this purpose of supplying public goods. You cannot run away from that. I think those two diverse approaches is what we need to follow.

Chandra Bhan Prasad

The Dalits or scheduled castes and scheduled tribes, are the first beneficiaries of job reservation in the government. Bizarre as it may appear, India's private sector is the second largest beneficiary of reservations for Dalits.

Due to reservations, about 3.5 million Dalits have got into government jobs (central/state governments/PSUs, etc.). This is my own estimate, based on the Fourth Report of the National Commission for SC/STs (1997-1998). Unfortunately, no central agency, including the Planning Commission, the Union Ministry of Social Justice and Empowerment, the Census Commissioner of India or the National Sample Survey, has any published report showing the number/percentages/position of Dalit employees/officers on an all India basis, including the state governments.

About another 3.30 million Dalits have got into trade/commerce/manufacturing (often small in terms of size and turn over), of which about half (1.65 million) may be due to reservations. Dalit employees/officers often finance their unemployed children to set up businesses.

That means, about 5 million Dalits have used reservations to join India's middle/lower middle class rank. In other words, reservation has produced 5 million Dalits, or 25 million Dalit people (assuming that an Indian household has 5 people) as consumers, who otherwise, through the natural process of development, may never have entered the market place. But, how does it help the private sector?

Most reservation-produced Dalits work and live in cities and towns, and follow the lifestyle and cultural behaviour of urban India. If it is a truth that most urban inhabitants with secured monthly income use toothbrushes, then the Dalits employees/officers/small business people too follow the same trend. Also assuming that most toothbrush users buy at least 2 toothbrushes a year, then the 25 million Dalits must be buying 50 million units of toothbrush annually. If on an average, a toothbrush costs Rs. 10, then Dalits are contributing Rs. 500 million annually to the Rs. 3,000 million toothbrush industry. Assuming that a Dalit household spends Rs. 120 per year on toothpaste/powder, then the 5 million Dalit households are contributing Rs. 600 million annually to the Rs. 9,500 million toothpaste/powder industry annually.

According to an estimate, about 61 million households in India use pressure cookers. The 5 million Dalit households too use on average a cooker per household. If the price of a pressure cooker averages at Rs. 300 a unit, then the 5 million Dalit households have contributed about Rs. 1500 million to the pressure cooker industry. If India's middle/lower middle class households buy at least 2 pencils a month, then the 5 million Dalit households are buying about 120 million pencils a year. If a pencil costs Re. 1, then Dalits are contributing about Rs. 120 million annually to the pencil industry.

India's fast moving consumer goods industry (soap/hair oil/shampoos/other cosmetics) is estimated at Rs. 6,000 million. If the urban middle/lower middle classes are the main consumer base, then 5 million Dalit households too must be buying these items. If Dalit households buy at an average of 2 soaps (a bath, and a wash soap) each month, then the 5 million Dalit households buy 120 million units of soaps every year. If soap costs an average of Rs. 5, then Dalits are contributing about Rs. 600 million annually to the soap industry.

The government employees/officers may be earning an average of Rs. 10,000 a month, and spending half of that in the market, then the reservation-produced Dalits contribute about Rs. 25 billion a month, or Rs. 300 billion annually to India's private sector, an amount more than the combined annual net income of Reliance, TATAs, Birlas and Dalmias. Dalits have used reservations to their advantage, and are grateful to Dr. Ambedkar who scripted this doctrine. Due to reservations, there is a Dalit middle class in the making, and this class of Dalits is ruthless customer of goods and services. Whatever the reservation-produced Dalits earn from the state, they return the same to India's private sector. Purely from a business angle, shouldn't the private sector confront the Rs. 300 billion question, and come forward to embrace reservations for Dalits?

Nasser Munjee

It is widely believed that in the next decade infrastructure is going to be a very important component of growth. Infrastructural problems have been mentioned right across the board. And if we do grow at more rapid rates than we can sustain, then we will creak at the seams reinforcing the problems posed by inadequate infrastructure. There are only two words that we need to keep in mind as we move forward with respect to infrastructure—the first is *partnerships*. We have heard a lot about the mistrust between the government and the private sector, public *versus* private, citizen and the state. But I think the future is going to be about partnerships and how we can bring these partnerships together around specific goals. Defining the mechanics of partnerships to solve common problems is the key. Neither the public nor the private sector can solve these problems on its own.

The second word is *strategy*. So often India lives in its present and in its past. The Lord Mayor of London, when he was in Bombay recently, said, "You know Bombay is a great city, I have been coming here for over 20 years but isn't it amazing that this city always lives in its present." We are so confounded with our present problems we have never projected, 5, 10 years into the

future. And that is true of almost all the infrastructure that we are currently implementing in India.

So what are the strategic options? Where are we trying to go? Two days ago I was in Colombo and visited Colombo port. Do you know that 70 per cent of India's transshipments of containers takes place through Colombo? That means Indian importers and exporters are paying extra to have their goods connected out of Colombo than through our own ports. Now this is a strategic option. Why does India, with its huge coastline and several excellent port locations, have to depend on Colombo? And when I asked them are you not afraid that your expansion plans will be affected by the expansion of Indian ports in the future, their response was that they were not overly worried as far as India was concerned as normally the left hand doesn't know what the right hand is doing. They seem quite sanguine that it will take a huge amount of time for India to wake up to strategic positioning. Even though international shipping lanes are close to Colombo, we have Cochin and Tuticorin and many other locations. So I think there are so many strategic options. Our plans are to build 50 ports of various sizes on our coastline but not necessarily develop two or three that would give us huge strategic advantages. This is what I mean by not thinking strategically. Bombay has a throughput of two million TEUs today. It was about 300,000 a few years ago. Despite the overwhelming increase in productivity it still takes six weeks to get a container into port. Why? Because the infrastructure around the port has not been upgraded to cope with the two million TEUs that the port is now handling. So the efficiency of the port is not being supported by its off site infrastructure.

There is only one institution called Concor which supplies the rakes. After protacted negotiations you might persuade them to increase accessibility. So where is the strategic thinking in terms of logistics and connectivity? Another example of the necessity for public-private partnerships to meet common goals.

If we are to attract new foreign (and domestic) investment in India we will need to strategise locational advantages in specific locations which have the ingredients for major development. Good governance, excellent connectivity, superb logistics, low cost of doing business, a vibrant labour market and a good social infrastructure are prerequisites for locational decisions. There are few situations that offer such potential. Mumbai's hinterland is one such location—Panvel as the logistics hub and the Pune-Nasik triangle. Strategic locations need to be exploited first as they have the best chance of success. A major success creates cluster economies which in turn encourages similar experiments elsewhere.

Partnerships in terms of infrastructure investment are a key component of any such enterprise. Partnership is not just a word, it is a paradigm that needs to be developed. Many different paradigms based on partnerships have been tested throughout the world. In infrastructure the options are limited—there are

essentially only three buckets into which you can drop publicly owned infrastructure. The public sector controlled 99 per cent of infrastructure investments in the country which has created the severe under investments that we witness today. It is said that governments are too big for the small things and far too small for the big things. Today, with this realisation things are changing. The private sector is being attracted into a space which was the preserve of the public sector, but the problem is that nobody quite understands under what framework this would be possible if the enterprise is to succeed on a scale needed in the country.

The three buckets are as follows—governments can fully privatise an activity by simply selling off assets and letting the private sector take over (power distribution in New Delhi, for instance, with a controlled transition period). Second, instead of selling assets, they can commercialise assets though long-term contracts (ports and airports would be examples). Both these techniques presume that user charges will work and the private sector would be able to charge for commercial services. For those activites where full user charges are not possible, the third alternative is to undertake private financing of public services (PFPI), for example the annuity financing of roads in India. This is where I disagree with Sunita when I say it is entirely possible for the private sector to deliver better healthcare, better education, better rural roads, better everything else. It may not be paid for by the beneficiaries, user charges may not be possible, but the government can pay through output-based contracts. There are many devices which we can use to ensure output. At the end of the day citizens should receive a level of service which you want them to receive and the government should obtain the best return for every rupee it spends. This again is a strategic move away from the traditional way of doing things—the government as a provider of services (for which it is particularly ill suited) to a government seeing to it that services are in fact provided in sufficient quantity and at a reasonable price and quality to the citizens.

All this does not mean that government has a smaller role to play—in fact quite the opposite. It does mean that it has a different role. The state must spend money wisely in a manner that leverages every rupee spent and ensures service delivery to specified standards. China did it surprisingly well. It developed special zones insulated from the laws of the rest of the country as action experiments, beginning with the proximity to Hong Kong and moving up its eastern seaboard. Now it is gradually moving inland, especially to its Northwest which was largely neglected. Which is the one cluster India is promoting? None. We don't have a strategy. Where is the cluster strategy? Where are the logistics? Where is the governance? It is pointless having an all encompassing 2020 vision with no strategic options available for the here and now. When investors come to India they want to know the opportunities now and are prepared to grow with strategic options as they unfold. We don't seem to have them on the ground leading to many investors continuing to wait and watch.

I want to emphasise our strategic options both in removing existing hurdles and striking new approaches. Partnerships are going to be very crucial. In Britain for example, in the last 12 years, traditional public sector services are being performed by the private sector and the market is growing rapidly, well beyond the 20 billion pounds at present. Debt markets have responded, as has the stimulation to private business to move into the new opportunities of performing public services. The entire paradigm of the provision of public services has been altered from public provision to private provision with government contracting and supervision. Many mistakes were no doubt made. But we can learn from them and move ahead and develop our own brand of public-private partnerships based on strategies that will deliver (at last!) quality public services to citizens, which they have lacked for so many years.

So I think if you look 10 years ahead you are really looking at what C. K. Prahalad said, it needs a radical approach, thinking out of the box with a clear purpose in mind. Small incremental tinkerings with present approaches are hardly likely to produce the results we desire. To end let me leave you with my favourite quotation from Seneca which is nearly 2,000 years old and is still as relevant as it was then, "if you do not know to which port you are sailing, no wind is favourable".

Yogendra Yadav

I have only one point to make, which is provoked by the public opinion data used by Prof. C. K. Prahalad. What surprises me is that I have normally known economists to make more rigorous demands on data they use, apart from the fact that it is a purely urban sample of 1,000 and we don't even know its class composition. There are serious public opinion data collected through social scientific theories, which have repeatedly asked these questions and I just want to share that information. On disinvestments, I quote a national election study which we carried out with a sample of 26,000, which reflected all the demographics of Indian society, in the 28 states of the Indian Union. So it is a reasonably reliable survey. To a very neutrally worded question whether PSUs or *sarkari companyan* should be given in private hands, the disapproval rating was 46 per cent, approval 24, and 30 per cent didn't know. And this disapproval rating was higher than when the same question was addressed to a national sample of a similar kind in 1996. In other words, in the eight years of some experience of disinvestments, ordinary Indians are now more strongly against disinvestments, than they were eight years ago.

Suman K. Bery

The question was the same?

Yogendra Yadav

Yes, identical question. We are serious survey researchers, who spend hours designing a question and keeping it identical across the years. On the entry of MNCs, the question asked was whether foreign companies should be allowed free trade in India. The approval rating was 30, and disapproval 39 in 2004. Over the years this has been somewhat stable but never has the approval rating won, in fact this was a slightly higher approval rating than ever before. On whether government employees should be reduced as their salaries are costly to the country, the disapproval rating was 42 per cent, and the approval 35 per cent. On another question of whether government hospitals should offer better services, even if it meant charging a higher fee, the people were in favour of reforms—48 per cent people said yes, and 39 per cent said no. On the standard classic egalitarian question—"should there be a legal ban on possessing land and property beyond a certain limit?"—the approval rate was 68 per cent, and disapproval 17 per cent. I am not saying that these are final verdicts by any means. I do not wish to say that people's opinion must be translated into policies because people can be completely deceived about what their own interests are. But I think it should be one of the inputs that we take into account. What worries me and what surprises me is the fact that India's economic establishment, the NCAER, the Planning Commission, Universities, etc. collect so much information about the economy—we are one of the most statistics rich country in the world—don't collect information about the people's opinion about the economy. Does it need political will to collect this information? It shouldn't be a very big thing.

Jayaprakash Narayan

Prof. C. K. Prahalad, Sitaram Yechury, Montek S. Ahluwalia, Vivek Monteiro—everybody has said that the state has a definite role. The point is what kind of a role? No one disputes the need for state intervention. I think we all recognise—even if we don't always state it explicitly—that the Indian state has done precisely what it ought not to do; and has failed to do what it ought to do. That is where the dilemma is. The issue is not state *versus* no state; it is 'what' the state ought to do. I think we have to emphatically recognise that and deal with that.

Twenty years ago, I was a special officer of the Vizag Steel Plant, then India's largest public sector investment company. That experience taught me that the public sector in India is nothing but the private sector of those in public office. Tragically, people don't know that. The perception is that the public sector is for the public, because that is what has been dinned into people's ears for 50 years, and these distorted notions have been reinforced. Therefore, even the perceptions of the people have to be accepted with a pinch of salt.

Now, for the four issues I want to flag. First, about UP, Bihar and the Northeast, according to Sanjoy Hazarika we need to look at economic linkages with Southeast Asia and China. There is no way out of this because politically the Union Government and the states have neither the capacity nor the will to change the situation. Only by integrating with the economies of Southeast Asia and China is there a realistic hope for UP,

Bihar, and the Northeast, i.e., for more than 300 million people.

The second issue is the Employment Guarantee Act. Even in the political part of our discussion today, we are dealing with a zero-sum game of limited resources and unlimited wants. If we have billion crores of rupees and can do a thousand things with it, then of course, we can have employment guarantee, education, healthcare and everything else, all at the same time. The fact is that we have limited resources in the kitty; the best way to utilise these limited resources is what we have to debate. For indigent people as a special measure, yes, some form of employment guarantee and social security is necessary. But we really need to look at education, healthcare and infrastructure, and not employment guarantee, as the true entitlements to enhance human capacities. Otherwise, our resources in most cases will simply go down the drain.

My third point is about healthcare, Prem Shankar Jha made an important point. On an average, an Indian spends 60 per cent of his annual income for one episode of hospitalisation. Forty per cent of the people sell their assets only to meet the cost of hospitalisation either in government or private hospitals. Twenty-five per cent of the people hospitalised fall below the poverty line, only because of hospitalisation. There is no greater antipoverty measure than better healthcare. It doesn't mean merely more of the same thing, for heaven's sake, but in a better way, with choice, with competition, by strengthening the public system and enforcing accountability. The NAC is looking seriously at the restructuring of our public health institutions and ensuring delivery. We hope the government will not do merely more of the same, but will change incentives to do things differently.

The last point is about higher education. Not a single additional rupee is required to improve the quality of university education. Higher education is in the doldrums. All of us are really atypical products of the Indian education system. And some of us are not even products of the Indian education system. Indian higher education is in a deep, deep crisis. We are hoodwinking ourselves into believing somehow that we have the third largest technical manpower in the world. But the reality is distressing. Specific non-monetary interventions are both necessary and feasible. We can improve things very fast because of the demand from society.

In conclusion my fear is that there is an ever-increasing market in India of criminals in our society. Criminals are not arising out of a vacuum. The criminal justice system, property rights enforcement, reparations for violated rights—all these have completely collapsed. The *goonda*, whom we revile, is actually the fellow who is somehow enforcing some kind of order and that is the reason why he is becoming indispensable and ending up as our legislator. And as a legislator, he is more effective than others because he simply orders: 'do it, or else!' and gets things done. Whereas Manmohan Singh or Natwar Singh will simply say, "*Kya kuch kar saktein hain*", and of course, the bureaucracy does not respond! Political reform is critical.

Vinod Raina

The question for me is the nature of state intervention. The reason for that is simple and is best illustrated by focusing our attention on employment and labour. Of the roughly 400 million labour force, over 370 million are what we call informal or unorganised. In the 57 years after independence and at an average growth rate of 3.5 per cent, the formal labour we have created is about 27 million. The question I would like to ask all the economists here is—if you have something like 7 per cent growth rate for the next 20 years, what kind of stable formal employment are you talking about? How many people will you be able to get into the formal sector from this 370 million strong informal sector? Does anyone have a clue? It is wonderful what the IT sector is doing. T. N. Ninan tells us that 50,000 jobs have been created at a billion investment, meaning at that rate an investment of 4 billion will lead to 200,000 jobs. But are these 200,000 people going to be from the sections which we call the unemployed or deprived or from other sections? The answer is unlikely to come from the economy or the market. It tends to become a political question, and that is where state intervention seems necessary. Are we entirely certain that we have increased these jobs? I think that the 27 million formal sector jobs have actually shrunk, because while we have created some new ones, we have also lost many from the traditional manufacturing sectors. The staggering requirement of employment is from this 370 million; out of which I reckon about 270 million require some sort of immediate support, the rest 100 million may have some unstable jobs in agriculture, handicrafts, artisan production, rural service sector and so on.

Two economists here seem to have answers, but have they segregated as to who will benefit from jobs from higher growth rates—will it be Adivasis and Dalits? The state therefore can not be kept out of it. What kind of job creation would ensure that the weaker sections benefit? I think M. S. Banga has made that point very clearly, it has to be job creation at the rural level. We keep on saying that we have liberalised the economy from '91, but which economy have we liberalised? Have we liberalised the rural industry since '91? A survey of five states reveals that the number of state regulations for rural industries has actually increased, whereas it has correspondingly decreased for big industries. Why do we then keep on saying that we have deregulated the economy since '91? The state has a larger role to play in another area, since over 400 million people survive through subsistence economies, the green capital that Sunita Narain talked about. They fulfil their water, domestic energy, housing and other needs from common property resources. Do we have policy frameworks that can help sustain these resources till they can find alternatives? Today when a person is displaced do we have the ability to provide viable alternatives? The Narmada debacle and similar examples provide ample evidence that the state cannot rehabilitate displaced people. Now if you cannot do that, what kind of policy frameworks must be put into place so that livelihoods are secured for millions?

Suman K. Bery

Do you have a quick answer to your own questions?

Vinod Raina

Yes, the answer is that the state has to transform and play a bigger role. The state is not playing that role, and if you say that we will take away the state you will throw millions to the wolves. There are instances of how sensible state interventions can ensure the well being of vast populations; the 20 year old Madhya Pradesh Minor Forest Produce Act is probably one of the most wonderful examples of liberalisation we have produced in this country, which has strengthened the livelihoods of millions. It has allowed people to use minor forest produce for direct trading and productive activities. If the government hadn't come out with this Act, who else could have? These are the kinds of state interventions we badly need at this point—the Employment Guarantee Act being just one of the kind.

27 | Concluding Remarks

(Section II — Economy: Growth and Equity)

C. K. Prahalad

My starting assumptions are simple. We should focus on income generation and wealth creation as much as distributive justice. Second, all the examples I showed are successful experiments, whether it is ITC or ICICI. The examples come from different states—the Jaipur Foot from Rajasthan, ITC from Madhya Pradesh, Aravind from Tamil Nadu, and ICICI from all over the South.

Thirdly, these examples encapsulate some fundamental principles. In every case where we have succeeded, we have walked away from the old debate about private sector, state sector and civil society. It is the convergence of the voices, skills, capabilities of civil society, private sector (large and small firms), and the government working together that created this wealth. We tend to constantly separate the role of the State and the role of private sector, rather than accept that the solution to India's problems lies in the convergence of these roles.

India needs role models of success. Imperfect as these examples may be, they can be motivators. There are no 'perfect stories'.

All development creates asymmetric benefits. That is the very essence of development in the short term. Therefore, the real question is whether we have the courage to scale these models and be sensitive to the corrections at the margin. All the cases I presented are inherently scalable.

While most of the interesting experiments are developed by civil society organisations, they do not often have the wherewithal to scale or in some cases the motivation to scale. That is why we need the private sector and civil society to work together. Leading civil society organisations are actively seeking partnerships with larger firms for this reason.

We have to imagine a future that does not yet exist and then move this country towards that future rather than just extrapolate the past. Let us celebrate success, let us see what is scalable. Let us create this extraordinary convergence of civil society, public sector and the private sector. Do not exclude any one of them because if you exclude it will be at our peril. We have tried that before.

Deepak Nayyar

First, economic growth is imperative. Second, even if growth is necessary, it cannot be sufficient. Third, it is neither feasible nor desirable to separate growth and distributional outcomes because they are inextricably linked with each other. Fourth, this link is provided by employment creation and employment opportunities. Jobless growth is not sustainable either in economics or in politics. Fifth, we must recognise that if we create employment in the process of growth it reinforces growth through virtuous circles. Sixth, there is a critical role for the state in the process of delivering growth with equity. Clearly, it cannot be more of the same, or business as usual, in terms of counter-productive or excessive state intervention. But the time has come to recognise the complementarities between the state and the market.

Our essential failure was that the two institutions did not adapt to each other as time and circumstances changed. Let me conclude with an observation about the natural complementarity between these two institutions which draws upon history. Our experience with reforms has been mixed—some successes and some failures. But, on balance, India has met more success with economic reform than most developing countries and transitional economies. To a significant extent, this success is attributable to institutional capacities and political democracy. Many institutional capacities existed at the time reforms were introduced, while the essential foundations were provided by the preceding four decades of economic development in India. Entrepreneurial abilities were created. A system of higher education was developed. The social institutions and the legal framework necessary for a market economy were in place. In this milieu, it was possible to create new institutional capacities with relative ease. Given the importance of initial conditions, economic reforms in India turned out to be a success in significant part because of the foundations laid by the preceding 40 years. The timing of our transition was wrong, but that foundation was important. And, despite differences, we can compare it directly with China, where economic reforms were introduced much earlier. In China too, these would not have been a success had it not been for the preceding 30 years which laid the foundations and created the initial conditions. In India, I believe, we also have the added advantage of political democracy. It provides early warnings, wake-up calls and alarm bells, which must be heard and recognised. This is the basis of my optimism about the future of India.

Suman K. Bery

A lot of the things I thought would come up did not—fiscal and monetary policy, FDI, trade. I am not sure quite how to read that silence, whether it is an indication of the composition of the participants or whether in fact many of those issues are now settled and what we are discussing are the things that are engaging people today, perhaps rightly. Second, that India clearly does not have a conservative tradition. I am reminded of a comment that I heard in Argentina soon after President Menem took office in 1989. Guido di Tella, who was then the Foreign Minister said, "Look, we tried 30 years of managing the public sector and we concluded we didn't know how to do it, so we just want to get out of it." That was on the basis of 2,000 per cent inflation and blood on the streets. India has not had a crisis which is perhaps necessary for a truly conservative tradition. There were some elements of that in what Jayaprakash Narayan was saying. But I think in that sense there is still a very complex set of attitudes towards the state. You have got Sunita Narain saying on the one hand it just is not capable of delivering—but I think she is not prepared to say that you have to make choices and we are probably better-off just having the state withdraw. That is the ambivalence that is probably reflected in the election as well as the reality that is reflected in the coalition. Third, is the focus on getting the rural economy working, and what that implies for state action at the local level. I think this is an enormous area and we have only just begun to scratch the surface of addressing where the impetus will come from at that level, how you actually articulate an agenda at that level and how you reconcile that with the very fluid politics at the state level.

Growth and Equity: The Way Forward

SUNIL KANT MUNJAL

THE result of the last election has made it clear that a government in power must improve the living standards of every Indian. Not only does India have to grow rapidly, it also has to create jobs quickly.

Thirteen years of economic reforms have certainly improved the growth and economy numbers. Today, India is among the lowest cost steel producers in the world. India has the largest numbers of CMM Level 5 engineers in the world; India is the world's largest producers of motorcycles and bicycles and the second largest manufacturer of storage media devices.

Both the manufacturing and services sector has started contributing to the growth process, but Confederation of Indian Industry (CII) believes that the agriculture sector can also be a significant contributor, if suitable legislative changes like the Mandi Act and the APMC are brought in.

It is also vital to be able to create more wealth in all sectors of the economy so that more wealth can be distributed.

Growth and equity are inextricably linked. Higher growth will ensure that livelihood of people at the bottom of the pyramid improve faster. At the same time, it is also important not to lose focus at the top end of the pyramid, since this is where the bulk the wealth is being created for distribution. For example, India must also never lose track of the competitive edge in the high-tech and knowledge industries acquired over the last decade—since this is a source of long competitive advantage.

Removing disparities: Drawing a line on the Indian map from Kanpur to Hyderabad, two Indias become visible. Towards the left, the districts are growing faster, there is better education, and there is less poverty. Towards the right, there is mostly poverty, accompanied by poor social indicators. Two hundred and fifty million people in India live on less than 50 rupees a day. The bulk of these people live on the right side of the line.

Of course, there are islands of growth even on the right side—West Bengal, for instance, has undertaken important rural reforms, and is now attracting private investment, and chief ministers of a number of states in this right half of India have become much more proactive. But the line still exists.

What are the ways of removing this line?

A rural emphasis: To begin with, there is a need to rejuvenate the rural economy; 72 per cent of population depends on the rural economy. However, 40 per cent of this population is not directly employed by the agriculture sector. As a result, this sector contributes only 22 per cent of India's GDP.

The value addition in the farm sector today is only six per cent, despite the fact that is India among the world's largest producers of milk, vegetables and fruits. Extracting value from this sector is difficult because it is one of the most regulated, and has the least infrastructure support. The supply chain is outmoded; free electricity is doled on to win votes, and the fertiliser pricing structure is distorted.

India needs a vibrant rural economy for two reasons: first, regular income streams in the rural sector will create a sense of security. It will also help rural consumers come into the economic mainstream. Eventually, this will make the country more competitive.

It is also essential to revitalise manufacturing. This sector contributes 17 per cent of India's GDP. China's manufacturing sector in comparison contributes 35 per cent.

Poor infrastructure and high taxes: A combination of poor infrastructure and high taxes (India's tax rates are among the highest in the world), has clearly stymied progress in the industrial sector. A leading US retaining chain was recently asked why it was not sourcing more from Indian suppliers. The chain said it would have liked to, but was constrained by India's infrastructure. The chain pointed out that if it sourced as much from India as it was from China, the country's ports and roads would get clogged and there would be a shortage of containers.

India needs to learn from China. On a recent visit of India, a senior functionary from the Central Bank of China commented, "We are condemned to growth." Before it started its reform programme, China looked at a number of development models and realised the only way to improve the living standards of its people was to embrace the world economy in the most practical manner possible.

China realised that if it did many things better than rest of the world, This would create not just growth but also individual: "We decided not to protect individual jobs or individual state-owned enterprises, but ensure that growth took place at such a pace that the employment market grows rapidly," the functionary said.

Since then, the Chinese model has delivered as per plan. Per capita incomes have gone up in multiples, and China has created infrastructure that is the envy of the rest of the world. There are important lessons to be learnt from this experience.

Internal reforms: Trade restrictions are another example of the restrictive business environment in India. Europe is a common market and ASEAN wants to become a common market. India has been talking about free trade agreements with other countries but is still not a common market. CII is not against FTAs (Free Trade Agreements); rather, we believe these controlled openings will help us prepare ourselves to compete with more and more countries.

Yet for all talk of free trade, our own internal reform is still incomplete—this has prevented many Indian companies from becoming globally competitive. VAT has been debated for a number of years—yet progress has been slow. Our attempt should be to ensure April 1, 2005 target is met at all costs, and one year later, India should have a single goods and service tax. This will give the government a single point for collecting duties; increase the tax base; improve tax compliance, lower transaction costs and benefit consumers.

Meanwhile, red tape continues to be a serious problem in India even 13 years after reforms. An exporter today has more than 200 forms to fill out before he can export. An investor wishing to set up a power plant has to take permission from 23 premises based in 17 locations. In most countries, this is not more than 10. Whether it is for conducting internal trade or for securing basic permissions, the interface between the government and the citizen must come down. E-governance initiatives are obviously an important solution and the governments of Andhra Pradesh, Karnataka and Kerala have shown how it can be done. E-governance is important for the simple reason is that it reduces interface. The higher the interface, the greater the corruption—and global studies show that the countries with high corruption are also those with poor social indicators and development track records.

Leveraging SMEs: It must be recognised that the small and medium enterprises have a vital role to play not just as employment generators (27 million) but also as exporters—with 50 per cent of India's SMEs contributing either directly or indirectly to the country's export effort. For example, the SMEs in Tirupur in south India account for 90 per cent of India's knitwear exports—and this has been achieved in 10 years. To keep this momentum going, CII is promoting 100 SME clusters next year and 1000 clusters the year after. This would be largest cluster initiative in the world.

Urban infrastructure: The rural poor are migrating to Indian cities in large number in search of jobs. This is putting immense pressure on India's cities. India's villages need access to better infrastructure in the form of drinking water and motorable roads. But there is also a need to restructure India's urban infrastructure—we need to explore various options to decongest cities. For example, India might want to experiment with the Exurbs concept as in the US—these exurbs are hubs of industrial activities with specialised parks and located away from urban areas, usually along highways.

Considering that India has an ambitious highway and rural road programme (the largest such programme undertaken anywhere in the world) this model might work. It could also help the economy take off in terms of improving market reach and access, in the same way as Eisenhower's highway programme kick-started the US economy in the 1950s.

President Abdul Kalam's PURA model (Provision of urban amenities in rural areas) is another viable option for decongesting India's cities and creating rural prosperity. It is imperative that all concerned stakeholders work together and make this vision workable.

The importance of training: There is a clear need to revamp the primary and secondary education system with an emphasis on vocational and industrial training. Recently, there has been talk about providing preferential treatment to certain sections of the population. While it is important to recognise social imperatives, CII believes that affirmative action is a more prudent option. The only sustainable way of tackling unemployment is to equip India's poor with requisite skills so that larger numbers of people can become self-employed and more employable. CII has made an important beginning by collaborating with 196 Jan Shikshan Sansthans for technical education. The seamless spread of technical skills will not only create more jobs; it will also make the Indian economy globally competitive.

While reforming and energising the education and training system, it is also important to understand 54 per cent of India is below 25 years of age. This makes India the youngest country in the world in terms of population. This is both a promise and a challenge, and needs to be factored in as part of the training initiatives.

Tourism and healthcare: Finally, no emphasis on growth and equity can be complete without focusing on tourism and healthcare. Tourism matters because it is the single largest creator of jobs, and healthcare matters because the welfare of the country depends on it. Since the government doesn't have adequate resources to provide comprehensive public healthcare, public private partnerships must be accepted, and we at CII have been stressing this at our health conferences year after year.

With its ecological, cultural and climatic diversity, India has much to offer the international tourist; yet India attracts fewer visitors compared to countries much smaller in size, scope and potential. There is a need to focus on the international visitor, but we should not miss out opportunities to tap into the domestic traveller who might be journeying to visit relatives, or visiting a pilgrimage spot. The objective should be to make travelling and holidaying in India an attractive proposition—for everybody.

The road ahead—focusing and working together: India faces significant challenges. But each one of these can be overcome. There will be those who'll point to historical data and say that India cannot grow beyond a certain rate.

But at CII, we've always believed that we're performing far below potential and can grow must faster, provided certain obstacles are removed. What we've done therefore is to group these challenges under six categories: rural economy, health, education, water, energy and tourism and set up task forces for each. Over the next few months, each task force will suggest workable development models in each area, and demonstrate their viability through pilot projects. These task forces could play an important role in taking the growth and equity challenge to the next level.

But, cracking the growth and equity puzzle isn't just in the domain of the government and corporate sector—NGOs, institutions and citizens can play an equally significant role. India, we must remember, belongs to all of us.

Section III

Society: Changing Values

BACKGROUND PAPER,
PRESENTATIONS AND DISCUSSION

INDIA is an increasingly youthful society. What has been the impact of the twin forces of globalisation and Hindu nationalism on the young in particular and society in general? What should be the content of Indian nationalism? How will technology and economic openness shape Indian society and ideas? How can liberal values be embedded more firmly in our society? How can we create space for greater cultural pluralism, as well as for individual talent and originality to flourish? How can artistic freedoms be protected with greater tolerance of individual views? Innovation, the capacity for original and counter intuitive thought, is at the core of the dynamic societies and economies in today's world: How can we encourage this in our own society? What kind of models might we learn from? Is the state best kept out of such matters?

28 The Enemy Within

MAHESH BHATT

INDIVIDUALS who enjoy lasting success have core values and a core principle that remains rock steady, while the world around them changes at a dizzying pace. The same is true of nations. These core values are a nations' essential and enduring principles—which it would hold even if they became a disadvantage; and this core purpose is the nation's fundamental reason for its existence. A truly great leader understands the difference between what should never change and what should be open for change, between what is genuinely sacred and what is not.

The day after the carnage in Gujarat had erupted, I found myself in the house of the then Minister of Human Resources, Mr. Murli Manohar Joshi. I was there at the behest of my producer friend, to request an extension of our weekly science-based show which was being pulled off Doordarshan. As I sat in his living room, which had an overwhelming amount of gods and goddesses in it, waiting for him to finish his meditation, I found myself wondering what place science had in this nation which had not been able to rise above tribalism.

When Mr. Joshi finally appeared, I could not resist telling him that India, which brags to itself that it is the mother of civilisation should hang its head in shame, as blood flowed in the streets of Gujarat. "If these are the kind of people your great heritage has produced," I said, "then its high time you flushed it down the toilet." Needless to say, we lost the science programme. But not before Mr. Joshi made one last ditch effort to convince me how the Indian Muslim needs to urgently embrace the attributes of his Hindu ancestors to bring about enduring peace in this country.

The core problem of conflict between communities and groups boils down to the abdication of individual identity and self expression in favour of identification with the group itself. By losing your humanity through a collective identification, you fail to recognise the humanity of others not in your particular group. Obviously most political parties understand this truth only too well. To be a member of good standing in one tribe it is necessary to be willing to dehumanise the members of the other tribe. And this is why tribalism can never be conducive to human progress, as it only serves to re-enforce irrational prejudices and ferments warfare. We have seen how the previous Government used the tribal instinct which is deeply ingrained in our nation to serve their own ends.

Tribalism had reached its pinnacle in Gujarat and has done irreparable damage to the core values of our country, as well as to Hinduism, which believes that even defence is offence, besides alienating the entire Muslim population of this country for generations to come.

India's core value is its pluralism. It defines us and what we stand for, for hundreds of years. It's the glue that holds us together, and if it disappears, we will disintegrate into a state of anarchy and chaos. What we as Indians cannot ever afford to let go of is this fundamental reality. This is the heartbeat of India.

Every nation requires a model to emulate. The shining example of true Indian thought came from one of our greatest leaders Mahatma Gandhi. Gandhiji was one of the finest examples of a man whose creed reflected in his deed. He did not succumb to this kind of tribalism and was finally killed by his own tribe, who thought he was trying to undermine the strength of his tribe by practicing love for the other tribe. The glue that holds a tribe together is hatred for the other tribe.

We must first understand what this model India is that we want to create, before we can even start to take the first step. As globalisation gets all pervasive and self-servicing cultures of each and every kind descend into our backyard in various forms and shapes, the younger generation is going to find it more and more difficult to retain their sense of Indianness, without resorting to a revival of the worst aspects of tribalism. Therefore it is imperative that we repeatedly whip up the pluralism that has been ingrained by icons like Gandhiji in our young people, while at the same time weaning them away from the outdated and outmoded beliefs. Kindling the scientific temperament will keep them ever curious about life, it will help them to question the age old beliefs and awaken in them the thirst for a better world.

However, before we speak about getting along with the rest of the world, we must first learn to get along with ourselves! All external conflicts between people are an extension of the conflicts that rage within our own hearts. The problems of nations are the problems of people. Whenever I witness man brutalise man, directly or in an underhand way, I have always noticed that the perpetrators of these acts are people who are not happy with themselves. People who make war with others have failed to conquer themselves. A famous comic strip has summed up the Indian situation in one phrase, which is "We have met the enemy, and he is us." The hardest person to get along with in the whole world is, in fact, yourself. Only by defining the face of this enemy to the young will we take the first step to neutralise it. And only then we may perhaps begin to make our presence felt in the world, because as of now, India is a nation enslaved by its own prejudices. We have neither economic power nor military might and therefore we have no say in world affairs. Only through relentless realism and confrontation with self will the youth of this country be able to shoulder the burden of taking this nation to a position of any significance in the next decade.

Section III

[...continued...]

Presentations and Discussion

"SOCIETY : CHANGING VALUES"

This section corresponds to the proceedings of the Third Session of the Ninth Indira Gandhi Conference, November 19-21, 2004, New Delhi.

Chair:
- Sudhir Kakar

Lead Speakers:
- Amar Kanwar
- Mridula Mukherjee

Discussants:
- Mahesh Bhatt
- Shyam Benegal
- Aruna Vasudev
- Mrinal Sen
- Dipankar Gupta
- Chandra Bhan Prasad
- Ranjit Hoskote
- Vinod Raina
- Jayaprakash Narayan
- Vivek Monteiro
- Siddharth Varadarajan
- Prem Shankar Jha
- Ravi Parthasarathy
- Rekha Chowdhary
- Aijaz Ahamad
- Anita Rampal

29 | Opening Remarks

SUDHIR KAKAR

THIS session asks us to address a number of important questions which are set out in the annotation. We have only one background paper by Mr. Mahesh Bhatt. But I think this session has attracted less papers than the sessions on polity and economy not because it is less important but because it is more complex, and perhaps even more diffuse.

Another dimension on which this session may differ from the ones on policy and economy is that the experience of other societies, relatively speaking, may be of less importance. I think we have to be more conscious of the particularities of Indian society and the necessity of Indian solutions. Let me give one example. We were talking about the youth. Youth is universally recognised as a period marked by the young person's search for identity. In Western discourse it is assumed that this identity of youth has to be in opposition to the parents' generation. This is not really the case with our society. The young person's search for identity is often in consonance, perhaps even in negotiation with the parents' generation. And we have been asking what does it mean to be the most youthful society in the world. We were talking yesterday of hope. Now hope is also one of the very important heritages of youth. And talking of hope, perhaps it has nothing to do with the state of our polity and economy. Perhaps it is just demography which makes us see contemporary Indian society as energetic and hopeful. Then, of course, youth is also a period of enhanced commitment to causes and ideas greater than oneself. This is also one of the great heritages of youth and ideologues of the extreme right and left have exploited this potential for devotion. They have of course a natural advantage because young people don't like to walk in the middle. But does this mean that centrist and liberal ideals are excluded from being nourished by this most vital of societal resources of youthful devotion and commitment? I don't think so. Gandhiji, Bose, Nehru did capture this particular youthful imagination at momentous periods of Indian history as did Rajiv Gandhi in the beginning of his term.

Can it not be done again even if not on the same scale? We know it cannot be done through slogans. I think we have experienced that slogans, whether they be of a strong India or a just India, are not enough. How do we transform slogans into visions? Because only visions can capture that devotion of the young.

I am of course not talking about closing windows to the winds blowing from the rest of the world, as Gandhiji said. We do have to consider the experiences of other societies. For instance, globalisation and nationalism. In our agenda for today, we have framed the question of globalisation and Hindu nationalism as twin forces. I wonder whether globalisation is not a father to Hindu nationalism, or at least an uncle. I would now ask Amar Kanwar and Prof. Mridula Mukherjee to start off the session. I am doing it in the reverse order just because we said at the start that India is a youthful society. Mridula may be the more youthful in thought than Amar but he looks more youthful. So I think we will start with Amar...(laughter...).

30 Learning to Deal with Our Contradictions

AMAR KANWAR

IT is probably true that all of us have within ourselves 'good and evil' and how this manifests has a lot to do with our own personal memories and histories and the circumstances that we find ourselves in. While India is an extremely complicated territory and it is difficult to make generalisations, it is important to learn how to deal with our contradictions. My presentation today is related to and traverses these contradictions between hope and despair. In this context we need to understand the lives of young people.

There have been many ways to analyse society, its present and possible future. Economists use statistical data to make conclusions and projections but there are other forms of 'data' available . A couple of years ago in an attempt to understand what was happening in my country I made a film called "A Night of Prophecy". I travelled along what I think are the fault lines of our subcontinent, through Maharashtra, Andhra Pradesh, Nagaland, Manipur and Kashmir, in search of the poetry found there. Poetry—written, sung and recited by ordinary people. Would I then understand time through poetry? Would the past and present unfold before us through poetry? And, if one could understand the passage of time, could one then see the future? In a very bizarre way, listening to the discussions here, several of those poems came back to me, as they too fundamentally addressed many of the issues raised in yesterday's sessions. I realise how important it is to search for and understand these other forms of data in order to understand ourselves and the future of this country and also how inadequate statistical data can often be.

A few weeks ago I was invited to screen this film at St. Stephen's College which is a premier institution. After the screening a young boy asked a question with considerable anguish. He asked, " I have a question that has been troubling me for quite some time and your film has forced me to ask you this. What I want to know is how do you decide what is right and what is wrong? I need to know how to decide, and I cannot figure it out."

An interesting discussion spiralled after that but at this moment I would like to shift from St. Stephen's to South Orissa, to the Kashipur Valley in Raigarha district and to another 18 year old, a tribal boy. He pointed to a low sloping hill and said, "Do you see this hill, it is about 22 kilometres long and 4 kilometres flat on top. It is filled with a 173 millions tonnes of bauxite." He then pointed to his head and asked me, "Do you see this. This is a skull. This is my skull, and it has a brain and this brain inside can think. Does that surprise you?" He added, "This hill has now been sold. The entire range has been sold as have several of these hills. This particular one, where I and the last three generations of my family and about 25 hamlets live, has also been sold." He then continued, "But I am not going to let it be sold. I am not going to let them take it away, I would rather die than let them take it away. I can see what is happening around me. I have seen what has happened in the next valley. I have talked, I have listened, I have analysed and I have come to my conclusions. It is because I have a brain which you do not think I have." I pushed this a little further essentially to see his reaction. I briefly spoke about the good of the nation and about the larger good *versus* the smaller good. Another tribal, a little older and sitting next to him, replied with an even stranger response. It was difficult to immediately understand but something worth remembering. I present it almost exactly as he said it. We were sitting outside, he pointed to a knife on the ground and said, "You see that knife, with it you can cut grass. Now how would you describe that action? You would describe it as the act of cutting. Now if you take the same knife and cut my throat how then would you describe that action. You could also describe it as cutting, a *kriya*, like a verb. The knife cut, the knife cut." Then he asked me, "Can you explain to me the difference between these two acts of cutting? Once you explain to me the difference between these two cuttings I will explain to you the difference between the nation's good and our good and the good of this little valley."

Both these young men were talking about values, of justice and of life. They were asking several very basic questions. They were asking—was the removal of bauxite or the purchase of entire hill ranges for mining only a question of economic growth or a question of ethics as well? They were asking—will we discuss why it should be sold, who will buy it, how much will be ours, to what extent will it be ours, what will be the nature of the mining, will it stop at some point, what will be produced from the mining? Will we benefit? Can we discuss benefits. Can we discuss the meaning of benefits and who would benefit and who wouldn't?

They were also talking about the Indian Constitution. The Indian Constitution is based on some very basic values of justice, life, liberty, dignity, and equal opportunity. A couple of years ago, there was a cabinet note prepared by the Attorney General with a reference to the Schedule V lands, which are constitutionally protected areas. I am sure you all know about Schedule V and Schedule VI lands and the rationale behind the creation of these protected areas, but the note submitted by the Attorney General to the Cabinet suggested the need and the methodology for removing the Schedule V protection for growth or rather for unregulated growth to become possible.

I know that these are difficult questions to answer and deal with and the more one addresses them, the more complicated they get. But I believe it is necessary to ask these questions. This leads me to another question. I am speaking essentially as somebody who has been travelling extensively over the last 15 years across this country but with time to hang about, to talk and to listen and watch. Obviously I speak from my own experience, I may be wrong, or may not give the full picture, but still I ask the question—how do you describe the state of mind of an animal that actually begins to eat its own flesh? What is this condition, when a body begins to harm itself? I can take you to a river which flows along a row of industries, both public and private enterprises with villages, farm lands and people living around it and if we take an empty Coca Cola or Pepsi bottle and fill it with the water of that river it will actually look like Coke or Pepsi because the water is extremely polluted and black in colour. There have been many studies done on this specific river by the World Bank, IIT, Greenpeace, etc. Many associations have analysed the water, the sources of pollution, the chemical compositions of the effluents, its impact on agriculture, health and so on. Yet the voices we hear from that region demand an opening up of space for investments for further economic growth, for reduced

regulations and restrictions. We are forced to ask the question that since we have all the information, we have all the analysis and the knowledge—why then does it not lead to wisdom? Why is it not leading to action, to rectification? Then there arises another question—are we incapable?

I know that success stories are important to inspire, to show us the way to go forward—emotionally, personally and socially. But I think it is important to keep analysing and redefining the crisis itself so that one can understand whether the success really is a success or not... at least to begin with. I would like to refer to a conversation I had with a Dalit boy, again about 18 years old. Grandson of a loader, a coal miner, his aspiration was to become a pianist. Obviously things have changed. He has a keyboard, he plays beautifully, he may become a professional pianist. Of course times may have changed but it has been a long and bitter journey and when I speak to him about life, he is very clear in his articulation. He still says that he has no faith in this nation. I am not saying that he is right or wrong. I am just repeating his words. He said, "I have no faith in this nation. I have no faith in the Congress, I have no faith in the BJP, I have no faith in the Left, I have no faith in anybody. I have seen it all." He is just 18 years old. He says I have seen it all. I don't want to discuss issues of justice or equity anymore." There is nothing left for me to discuss any more, it is very clear, I will take what I can get, however I can get it." It is difficult to argue and talk about larger values such as means and ends, of morality, of justice and the common good when faced with such a brief, bitter, clear response from such a young fellow. But it is necessary to try and understand the experiences of this boy's family that have brought him to this position.

It is this despair that I want to highlight. The illustrations above are very close to a certain bitterness and despair, a deep sense of loss, injustice and anger. Despair can express itself in a straightforward and simple manner. In spite of yesterday's rather optimistic discussions about the economic future of India my travels make me worried. What I actually see is increasing poverty and unhappiness. Of course we know that there is unemployment and so on, but what do you do when there is not enough food to eat and it is obvious that this impoverishment is closely connected to the taking away of the real wealth, the common properties of lands, forests, water. This is not something new, but the severity and speed of the appropriation has become shocking, especially in the last 10 to 15 years. How can this enormous process of appropriation be implemented and justified? How difficult is it to confront it? And what repression does one face in the process? Remember the three young men. The repression that they have been facing is awesome and despair can become quite natural. But what happens in this state of despair? If we do not have respect for life then we cannot expect others to have respect for life as well. If you destroy, all can begin to destroy. That is the zone of despair, that is the state of mind that is far more difficult to address than simple dissatisfaction. To confront despair you need an internal faith in the good of all, you must be able to emulate, you must be able to follow, be inspired. If you have no faith you have no inner strength to follow a value system, you cannot follow values of equity, of justice, of sharing, of compassion and so on. If we wipe out and devastate a community, a hamlet, a population we slowly sow the seeds of a spiralling devastation of values. Mining is not just about minerals and their economic potential.

Let me now shift to hope. We have all read, over the last couple of years, about the issue of censorship and the confrontation a few films had with the previous government and the Censor Board. This has all been reported in the newspapers, but let me quickly recap. The campaign arose in response to a clause in an advertisement released by the Ministry of Information and Broadcasting seeking entries for the Mumbai International Documentary and Animation Film Festival in 2004. The clause stated that in order to be eligible for the festival, all Indian films needed to submit censor certificates, while international films entered would not need such a certification. This actually meant that a British national could make and submit a film about Kashmir but an Indian couldn't send a film about Kashmir unless the Censor Board approved it. You may remember that there was a strong all-India campaign resisting this. After a year the censorship clause was withdrawn. Some films related to the Gujarat massacres were blocked and then subsequently approved and so on.

There are several other legal provisions existing that are equally ridiculous whether it is to do with theatre or film. For instance, in Gujarat, if you were to script and perform a play and then move to another district to perform the play again you would need to submit your written script and get police approval again. And the district administration would also have to see your script and give approval as you move from district to district.

However, what I want to highlight here is not just the success of the film-makers' anti-censorship campaign but the energy of thousands of young people who are actually coming out to talk. There are several who have seen through the grotesque justification of the United States attack on Afghanistan and Iraq and how the same justifications were presented for the attack on Muslims in Gujarat. These are mirror images of the same lie, the same justification was presented in Gujarat, electorally ratified and accepted. But in spite of this over the last two to three years what you see, not just in universities but in small towns and villages, in areas where there are no institutions as well, are young people coming out in hundreds wanting to talk, to ask what is happening in Manipur? What is happening in Gujarat? What is happening with this country? What is this whole question about Kashmir? Can we deal with it? Can we deal with Pakistan? The cross section of issues that they are wanting to engage with is enormous. Our films present issues of sexuality, history, ecology, religion, nationality, and land rights all in the same breath. The vocabulary of a new politics also must have the capability of

addressing all these isssues and many more with equal importance and understanding. We have experienced over the last few years, a situation where at times we turned back young audiences because we did not have the physical space and resources to engage with them. They are not coming to only see the films, they also want to argue and talk for hours. This is the zone of hope, of real growth and progress to which we need to respond. Do we have the capability?

I would like to end by saying that it is necessary for us to re-understand our relationship with dissent, it is necessary for us to accept that all of us can be questioned, all are accountable. Instead institutions of greed have become acceptable, profit multiplication has become a blind positive value. The only way institutions of greed can fundamentally be questioned continuously is if we have a culture of dissent. We cannot teach tolerance, we have to practice it. It was not long ago that there was an eerie silence in this country. I know people protested against the massacres in Gujarat and a communal campaign has been taking place over the last 10 years. But we cannot forget the silence, nor can we forget the smell of fear or the speed with which this politics was accepted and internalised. Rationality and science have failed the young folk. When you see senior scientists and religious leaders and their relationship with corrupt politicians and violent authoritarian communal movements, you realise quickly that we need the courage and faith of young people to question and challenge authority.

Many of the people in this gathering here are leaders in a sense. They control and impact opinions and institutions. It is essential to get rid of, for instance, the Cinematograph Act. I would love to invite you home for dinner, and show you my film about poetry, but it would be an illegal act. So we need to get rid of these laws, we need to look at classification of films and media. We need to categorise them, we need to inform people what they contain. We need to regulate but we don't need to strangulate. Apart from addressing these laws relating to theatre or cinema, it is also necessary for us to accept the fact that it is impossible for anybody to control in this digital age. There is no way you can do it. In five years people will be beaming and streaming films across the world through the internet if they haven't already started doing it. But more important than that is the need to create processes in different parts of this country that allow a free intermingling of politics, contemporary art, multiple opinions and diverse points of view. We need to hear the Manipuri or Oriya boys and girls face to face. It is only then that we will understand what is happening there and what tolerance really means. It is very clear to me, especially in the context of young people, that we have to talk about a new nation. It is not possible to relate positively to this nation or the concept of nation as it is now. It does not exist as a construct of hope any more in the way that it used to. We have to begin talking about a new relationship with this country, about a new understanding of what this country means and what its relationship with its own people is and should be. Economic policies with justice, compassion and interconnectedness as its soul can only come about by a radical re-understanding of what we want India to be. Any politics of greed, of hate and violence regardless of its political moorings can only be confronted by an open society alive with ideas and embedded with faith in a culture of questioning, of refusing to accept injustice.

31 Restoring Positive Values and Rejuvenating Mass Movements

MRIDULA MUKERJEE

WE are talking about society and changing values especially in the context of the dark times that we have been through in the recent decade and a half. I think Amar Kanwar brought that out very well—he talked of the fear, the trepidation, the silence and that is really true. I was shocked to find that in the heart of New Delhi in as prestigious an institution as the NCERT, with a faculty of about 500 members, people were afraid to get together for a cup of tea, lest they be accused of conspiring against the BJP government that was then in power. And this is not an exaggeration. We know what happened in Gujarat, we know of the attack on the democratic processes and values that have taken place across the country in various spheres of life. I will be talking about that in a specific context. But it is in a larger context that we have to look at the whole issue of changing values. In normal times we would have been talking about the normal processes of change and how the young and the youth of this generation are changing in response to changes to their environment, economic, social and political. But I think here the question has also become one of restoring certain positive values which were there and which have been seriously threatened and have come under attack.

I speak primarily as a historian but also as a citizen who is concerned about these matters. And I will try to bring to you initially, some of the wisdom of the freedom struggle because it was I think one of the most glorious periods in our history. It is close enough for us to still feel its warmth and learn lessons from the methods that were adopted by it. And I think especially in dark times, like the ones we have recently been through, it is necessary to recall the symbols of hope and glory, when ordinary people performed tasks which in normal times would be beyond them. That is one of the things that great movements do—they touch ordinary people in such a way that they become great. We need some of that inspiration. We also need a reminder that the times in which something as glorious as the freedom struggle flourished were darker than the ones that we have been through—with a foreign power that was actively promoting communalism. And yet if in those dark times such glorious things could happen, ours is not such an impossible task.

The freedom struggle imparted to the Indian people certain ideas, which took the form of values as they were internalised by the people. The most important among these were anti-imperialist nationalism, democracy, secularism and a pro-poor orientation. The freedom struggle was a prolonged mass movement lasting well over 70 years, a movement which reached down into the depths of Indian society and reached, to use Gandhiji's phrase, the "dumb millions of our society". It is this prolonged mass movement that helped ground these values deep into the minds of the Indian people. The movement could do it because it was one of the greatest mass movements of modern times, perhaps one of the greatest mass movements in world history. Hence, its reach was very extensive and deep. So we are not just talking about intellectual ideas that were thrown up in this period. We are talking about ideas that were internalised and became values in the minds of ordinary men and women.

The most important of these, which went hand in hand with anti-imperialism or nationalism, was the value of democracy and civil liberties. I will talk about nationalism later in a different context. But I want to emphasise that along with nationalism the value of democracy and civil liberties was a very critical one. The idea of democracy spread through various mechanisms among the people. It was spread through the work of nationalist workers who went deep into remote villages and into the *mohallas* and it spread through the written word. It spread through literature, it spread through pamphlets, through posters, through the press. It bears emphasis that the press then was privately owned. It was a nationalist press on its own. It was not a press owned by the Congress Party or by any other party but the press actually performed the role of an organ of the freedom struggle.

But most of all these ideas reached the people through actual political practices. I will give you three different kinds of examples to demonstrate what I mean. The political practice of the ordinary nationalist activist, when he went to a village, *mohalla*, slum, or to the street and talked about what the people had to do, when he tried to arouse nationalist consciousness, there were two basic things that he talked about. This is based on extensive evidence in files and oral evidence from people who participated in the freedom struggle. The first thing that he talked about, was the drain of wealth and economic exploitation, that is, the cause of our struggle for freedom was the economic exploitation by Britain. India was the *sone ke chidiya*, and there was a drain of wealth, and that we need to get the British out because they were exploiting us. After creating a justification for nationalism, he went on to ask, what do we want in its place? Do we want to restore the *Rajas* and *Maharajas* and be their *praja* or subjects? The notion of the citizen or the *nagrik* was then put in its place and it was said that we now want a government of the people. The concepts of *mazdoor kisan raj* was very much a part of the nationalist armoury as well. It was not something that was confined to the Left. The concept of the people in the sense of *aam aadmi*, *kisan*, and *mazdoor*, was used when talking about who would lead, and who would be the rulers. It was said that we, the people, would be the rulers, and not any king. As Nehru put it very evocatively in his presidential address, "You know I am not a supporter of the kings of old or of new, neither the modern princes of industry nor the old monarchs. I am a republican and a socialist." In essence that is the kind of flavour which went to the people.

Second, the value of democracy was internalised through the practice of the Congress Party and other political organisations. The Congress functioned as a proto-parliament and the name Congress was very consciously taken from the example of the US. The idea was to suggest that we are not a party but a parliament, a place where people come together to discuss, and take decisions for the nation. Elections in the Congress, after Gandhiji brought in reforms in the Congress Constitution in 1920, were always from the bottom up. You began at the village, then at the *taluk* or *tehsil* level, then the district and provincial level, and then the national. The AICC, the All India Congress Committee, which then emerged out of this elaborate election process, which took place every year was like the Parliament. And the Working Committee was the Cabinet. So at least from

1920, after the reforms had been put into place by Gandhiji, we can say that for almost 27 years the people actually saw democracy functioning. The Congress was like a shadow government. By this practice of democracy showed the people what democracy was going to be, what that future would be which they were to work towards. That is how democracy was internalised.

It is also important to point out that important decisions were taken through voting at annual Congress sessions. Even in the case of critical decisions like whether or not to launch the Non-cooperation movement, there was a division down the middle, there was a difference of only two or three hundred people. In 1942 as well, at the time of the launching of the Quit India movement, there was a sharp division of opinion. There were numerous occasions on which there were sharp splits and divisions but they were all in the open. This was accepted as part of the democratic process. It is important to remember that the *kisan sabhas,* trade unions and, students unions, all demonstrated the practice of democracy before the people by their actual functioning.

Third, and I think perhaps in some ways even more important are the political programmes and the methods of struggle that were adopted by the national movement, Gandhiji and the Congress, which required mass participation for their success. Once non-violence is an essential characteristic of a movement, there is no room for individual heroism, guerrilla struggles, or minority revolutions. Non-violence can only succeed if large masses, Gandhiji's dumb millions, actually participate in the movement. So this political practice of making mass participation an imperative and not a choice, was critical to the internalisation of democracy. There is nothing that internalises democracy more than people coming out onto the streets and demonstrating and participating in the process of democracy. So, it was not the British, but the Indian national movement, that internalised democratic practices in India.

The Indian leadership was always a decade or two ahead in terms of their constitutional thought and demands, compared to what the British were willing to offer. As early as 1895, Lokmanya Tilak came out with a Constitution of India Bill, which talked about universal adult franchise. We know that from 1919 onwards there were a series of constitutional reports that were issued. In 1928, the Motilal Nehru report talked about fundamental rights, and the Karachi Resolution of 1931 embodied those fundamental rights. From the mid-1930s, the demand was for a constituent assembly. By the time we actually wrote the Constitution there wasn't much left to write, it had all been worked out before. Just as the First Five-year Plan was only started in 1952, the preparation had begun when the National Planning Committee was set up by the Congress in 1937 and much of what was included in the plans had actually been worked out. What we saw around the time of independence was a distillation and crystallisation of this process rather than a nation beginning afresh. All these

things had been thought through, and practised for the last 60 to 70 years, which is why sometimes the transition looked so easy.

The leaders of the Indian national movement also had a very strong commitment to civil liberties. For examples, Lokmanya Tilak, in the *Kesari* of 16 June 1908, said, "Liberty of the press and liberty of speech give birth to a nation and nourish it." Tilak was known as a champion of the freedom of the press for which he suffered enormously. His press and money were confiscated because of the kind of freedom of the press he asserted. Gandhiji, for example, said, "Civil liberty, consistent with the observance of non-violence, is the first step towards *Swaraj*, it is the breath of social and political life, it is the foundation of freedom. There is no room here for dilution or compromise. It is the water of life. I have never heard of water being diluted" (*Harijan,* 24 June 1939, in *Collected Works of Mahatma Gandhi*, hereafter *CW,* Vol. 69, p.356). We all know of Jawaharlal Nehru's commitment to civil liberties and I quote, "If civil liberties are suppressed a nation loses all vitality and becomes impotent for anything substantial" (Nehru, *Selected Works,* hereafter *SW,* Vol. 7, p. 414). Jawaharlal Nehru was the founder of the Civil Liberties Union in India, and his commitment to civil liberties was total. The resolution on fundamental rights, passed by the Karachi Congress in 1931, guaranteed the rights of free expression of opinion through speech or the press and freedom of association.

I also want to emphasise that democracy was an absolute value. Not only for Gandhiji, but also for the socialist Nehru democracy became over time an absolute value. From the mid-1930s, Nehru increasingly talked about not sacrificing democracy at the altar of socialism and began to talk of the democratic path to socialism. In the post-independence days, in 1963 he said, "I would not give up the democratic system for anything" (R. K. Karanjia, 1963, *The Philosophy of Mr. Nehru*, p. 123). It was as absolute as that. Democracy for him was not a means to social, political or economic development. It was an end in itself. In the context of the discussion we had yesterday, while being aware that the terms formal and substantive are used in a certain way in political science discourse, I would like to say that when we say formal it almost begins to sound as if it is not substantive, that is, the substantive is outside the formal. What we call formal democracy is substantive in itself, it is an absolute value, it is a gain in itself, it creates other benefits, a whole system. That is something that Nehru was very conscious of from the mid-1930s. I believe that was his great contribution to and break with the Marxist Communist understanding of the 1930s, a contribution which is rarely recognised. He talked about a democratic path to socialism before anybody else in the world. He also believed that democracy was necessary for national unity, that there was no way you could hold this country together if you did not have democracy. The diversity of the country required that there be democracy because only in a democracy could all the different urges, including the clashes, come to the surface and not

be suppressed and then explode like they did, for example, in the Soviet Union. He said, "I have a revulsion against all that smacks of a dictatorship, regimentation and authoritarianism" (Bipan Chandra, 1994, *Ideology and Politics in Modern India,* p. 38). He believed in "socialism by democratic consent" (R.K. Karanjia, 1963, *The Philosophy of Mr. Nehru*, p. 44).

I shall now move on to secularism, which was also a very important value imparted by the Indian national movement. The first generation of Indian nationalists, whom we often call Moderates—Dadabhai Naoroji, Gokhale, Ranade, Pherozeshah Mehta, Surendranath Banerjea, G.Subramania Iyer, etc.—were completely secular and nobody has doubted their secularism. However, the Extremists, such as Tilak, Bipin Chandra Pal, and Sri Aurobindo, are in certain circles doubted as far as their secularism goes. I think this understanding of the Extremists is completely wrong. This is particularly important because the BJP is busy these days trying to claim the Extremists as their ancestors, as the fathers of cultural nationalism. This is in the history textbooks brought out by the NCERT during the tenure of the BJP-led NDA government, which students are still reading. In these, the national movement begins in 1893, with the publication of Aurobindo's articles, as Aurobindo is supposed to be one of the ancestors who founded Hindu nationalism. In this context it will be useful to look at what Aurobindo himself said at the height of the *Swadeshi* movement, of which he was a major leader:

"Nationalism depends for its success on the awakening and organising of the whole strength of a nation, it is therefore vitally important for nationalism that the politically backward classes should be awakened and brought into the current of political life; the great mass of orthodox Hinduism which was hardly ever touched by the old Congress movement, the great slumbering mass of Islam which has remained politically inert throughout the last century, the shopkeepers, the artisan class, the immense body of illiterate and ignorant peasantry, the submerged classes, even the wild tribes and races still outside the pale of Hindu civilisation, nationalism can afford to neglect and omit none. It rejoices to see any sign of life where there was not life before, even if its first manifestations should seem to be ill-regulated or misguided. It is not afraid of Pan-Islamism or any signs of the growth of a separate Mohammedan self-consciousness but rather welcomes them" (*Bande Mataram,* 22 December 1907, article on "The Awakening of Gujarat").

Another major extremist leader, Bipin Chandra Pal said, "The *Swaraj* of ours in not merely the Hindu, not merely the Mohammedan, not merely the Christian *Swaraj,* but the *Swaraj* of every child of India, Hindu or Christian or Mohammedan. The *Swaraj* will be the *Swaraj* of the Indian people, not of any section of it" (Bipin Chandra Pal, *Swadeshi and Swaraj: The Rise of New Patriotism,* Yugayatri Prakashak Limited, Calcutta, 1954, Introduction, p. iii).

Tilak is accused of making Shivaji into a hero by starting the Shivaji festival, and of promoting the Ganapati festival, thereby arousing Hindu religious consciousness. I would just like to read to you his own defence against the criticism of the Shivaji festival, "The Shivaji festival is not celebrated to alienate or even to irritate the Mohammedans. Times have changed, and, as observed above, the Mohammedans and the Hindus stand in the same boat or on the same platform so far as the political condition for the people is concerned. Can we not both of us derive some inspiration from the life of Shivaji under these circumstances?

"We are not against a festival being started in honour of Akbar or any other hero from old Indian history.... What makes Shivaji a national hero for the present is the spirit which actuated him throughout and not his deeds as such. His life clearly shows that Indian races do not so soon lose the vitality which gives them able leaders at critical times. It is a sheer misrepresentation to say that the worship of Shivaji includes invocations to fight either with the Mohammedans or with the Government. It was only in conformity with the political circumstances of the country at the time that Shivaji was born in Maharashtra. But a future leader may be born anywhere in India and who knows, may even be a Mohammedan. That is the right view of the question, and we do not think that the Anglo-Indian writers can succeed in diverting our attention from it" (*The Mahratta,* 24 June 1906, in *Bal Gangadhar Tilak, His Writings and Speeches,* enlarged edition, Ganesh and Co., Madras, 1919, pp. 49-51).

I could give many more examples, but let me just conclude this part with a quotation from Vivekananda because he is another figure sought to be appropriated by communal forces. Swami Vivekananda, writing on 10 June 1898 in a letter to Mohammed Sarfaraz Husain of Almora says,

"On the other hand, my experience is that if ever any religion approached to this equality in an appreciable manner, it is Islam and Islam alone.

"Therefore I am firmly persuaded that without the help of practical Islam, theories of Vedantism, however fine and wonderful they may be, are entirely valueless to the vast mass of mankind. We want to lead mankind to the place where there is neither the *Vedas*, nor the *Bible*, nor the *Koran*; yet this has to be done by harmonising the *Vedas*, the *Bible* and the *Koran*. Mankind ought to be taught that religions are but the varied expressions of The Religion, which is Oneness, so that each may choose that path that suits him best.

"For our own motherland a junction of the two great systems, Hinduism and Islam—Vedanta brain and Islam body—is the only hope.

"I see in my mind's eye the future perfect India rising out of this chaos and strife, glorious and invincible, with Vedanta brain and Islam body" (*The Complete Works of Swami Vivekananda*, Advaita Ashrama, Calcutta, 1989, Epistles, p. 415).

With this kind of perspective, it is hardly likely that he could become the apostle of a Hindu *Rashtra*.

As for Gandhiji, there is no doubt that he was secular, though attempts have been made to try and appropriate Gandhiji by saying that he was in favour of religion and politics being combined. This is a gross distortion of Gandhiji's views and a misinterpretation of his belief that politics must be based on morality, for which often the Sanskrit word *dharma* is used, which is also the word used for religion. Realising that his views were being misrepresented, Gandhiji clarified again and again that "Religion is a personal matter which should have no place in politics" (*Harijan*, 9 August 1942, in *CW,* Vol. 76, p. 402). He also made it clear that he was no votary of a Hindu *Rashtra*. On 9 August 1942, he asserted, "Free India will be no Hindu *Raj*, it will be Indian *Raj* based not on the majority of any religious sect or community but on the representatives of the whole people without distinction of religion" (*Harijan*, 9 August 1942, in *CW*, Vol. 76, p. 402). He said in 1947, "The state was bound to be wholly secular," and that, "the state of our conception must be a secular, democratic state" (*Harijan*, 31 August 1947, in *CW*, Vol. 89, p. 56 and M.K. Gandhi, *The Way to Communal Harmony*, edited by U.R. Rao, Ahmedabad, 1963, p. 396).

Gandhiji also opposed religious instruction as part of the school curriculum that was approved by the state. He told Zakir Husain in April 1947, "I do not agree that Government should provide religious education.... If you try to do so, the result can only be bad" (quoted in D.G. Tendulkar, *Mahatma—Life of Mohandas Karamchand Gandhi*, New Delhi, 1969 reprint, vol. 7, p. 383, note 11).

Gandhiji also rejected religious scriptures and doctrine if they came into conflict with reason. To quote, "The devil has always quoted scriptures. But scriptures cannot transcend reason and truth." And again, "I no more defend on the mere ground of authority a single text in the Hindu scriptures than I can defend one from *Koran*. Everything has to submit to the test of reason" (*Young India*, 19 January 1921, in *CW*, Vol. 19, p. 24, and *Young India*, 26 March 1925, in *CW*, Vol. 26, p. 415).

The one thing that I do wish to emphasise again is that the value of secularism was not imparted just through propaganda, just through ideas. Secularism was ingrained into the Indian people *via* the struggle against communalism. The failure to prevent Partition does not mean that there was lack of struggle or that there was an admission of defeat. The acceptance of Pakistan by the Congress did not mean the acceptance of the two-nation theory or of the demand for India to become a Hindu *Raj*. The acceptance of the two-nation theory would have meant if, at the time of Partition, when there was huge pressure from the Hindu communal forces to make India into a Hindu *Rashtra*, India had become a Hindu *Rashtra*. The two-nation theory was never accepted by the national movement and India did not become a Hindu *Rashtra* but evolved into a secular state after independence and partition. In Gandhiji's evocative words, "Do not accept Pakistan in your hearts," even though it is a reality physically. I would also like to recall Gandhiji's political practice—in Noakhali in Bengal, in Bihar, in Calcutta, in Delhi—in the 18 months or so before his death. I think

there are few moments in history more inspiring and humbling than those last months of Gandhiji's life. He went to Noakhali where Hindus were the victims of communal frenzy and, when people threw excreta in his path, he removed his sandals and walked barefoot. When they threw glass he did the same. He walked barefoot at the age of 78 through the village paths of Noakhali. He then went to Bihar where Muslims were the victims. People asked, "Why have you come, what can you do for us?" Gandhiji's reply was, "I have come like a family member. I have come to mourn. Can I not come and mourn with you even if I can't do anything else?" Through his practice he showed that there are many things that you can do even when you are in the depths of despair.

I found that very important when the recent developments in Gujarat threw many of us into the depths of despair. One did feel that at least one can mourn, that mourning itself is a political act, a statement of solidarity with victims. And what he could not do alive, Gandhiji did by his death. The assassination of 'the greatest living Hindu' (Nehru's words) by a member of the Hindu Mahasabha and the RSS, the unearthing of the conspiracy, delegitimised communal forces for a long time to come. Savarkar was named as one of the accused. He had been the President of the Hindu Mahasabha for many years, and there was no doubt about his involvement in the conspiracy. In fact Sardar Patel, the then Home Minister wrote to Nehru on 27 February 1948, "It was a fanatical wing of the Hindu Mahasabha directly under Savarkar that (hatched) the conspiracy and saw it through." Even though the initial trial did not return a verdict of guilty on technical grounds of law, Savarkar and the Hindu Mahasabha were politically finished. The final blow was delivered in 1969 by the Report of the Commission of Inquiry into the Conspiracy to Murder Mahatma Gandhi, which was headed by a judge of the Supreme Court of India, Justice Jivan Lal Kapur, which clearly pronounced him guilty. I am just reading out one sentence. "All these facts taken together were destructive of any theory other than the conspiracy to murder by Savarkar and his group" (*Kapur Report*, Part II, p. 303). And I think it is an index of the sad times that we live in that we have his portrait up in Parliament right across from that of the Mahatma's. I think one index of the change will be when we no longer have to live with this reality. Yet partition also showed that secularism had not been as deeply ingrained as a value in the minds of the Indian people as democracy. But Hindu communal forces did fail to gain legitimacy because they were increasingly loyalist and not anti-imperialist. It is worth noting that the extreme fascist phase of communalism, both Muslim and Hindu, which marked the last decade of colonial rule, was characterised by extreme loyalism. Both the Muslim League and the Hindu Mahasabha were more than happy to share power with the colonial rulers when the Congress was actually fighting them through the Quit India Movement and all its leaders and many workers were in jail. Offers of support and an actual sharing of power happily went on during this whole period. Because of the fact that Hindu communal forces and Muslim communal forces never participated in the struggle for freedom there was a delegitimisation. Gandhiji's death reinforced that. The Hindu Mahasabha was virtually dissolved, the Jan Sangh had to be started by the RSS in order to remove the taint of the association with the assassination, and for 40 years after Gandhiji's assassination Savarkar was not resurrected—the RSS/BJP waited for public memory to wane.

Discussion

(Section III — Society: Changing Values)

Mahesh Bhatt

I'm convinced that I learnt life's most enduring lessons even before I went to kindergarten. As Amar Kanwar spoke I was reminded of a story which my mother would tell me while feeding me. She would say "Son, there are two dogs in each one of us. One of them is a good dog and the other is a bad dog. These dogs keep fighting with one another all the time." When I asked her which one of them would finally win the fight, she would cleverly stuff a morsel of food in my mouth and simply say, "The dog you feed the most always wins." So if you want good to prevail over evil you will have to feed goodness.

Two years ago while I was shooting for a documentary in the jungles of Bastar, I came face to face with what I consider to be the core of India. There in the heart of a thick jungle right on the shore of a turbulent river, I met a young bronze-skinned boatman. This boatman made his living by carrying local tribes across the river for which he charged them hardly a rupee or two. As I was taking a shot of his beautiful ancient boat which belonged to his ancestors who also did the same business, I noticed that the local administration was constructing a bridge across this river. It was obvious that the day this bridge became functional the boatman would be out of business. "So what will you do in order to survive once this bridge is made," I asked the boatman pointing my digital camera towards him. He took a pause and then with heartbreaking integrity said, *"Ab hamara jo hoga so hoga, magar logon ka to accha hoga. Hum kuch aur kam kar lenge...."* I was stunned by his big-heartedness. Despite being face to face with the certainty of losing his only source of revenue this boatman was thinking of how the bridge would benefit the tribes of his jungle. That evening when I flew back to Bombay and reached home, I noticed my 10 year old daughter fiddling with her computer, talking to her friend on a cell phone, eating pizza and at the same time asking our driver to buy her tickets for the latest movie which was running in a posh multiplex around the corner. It was then that it struck me. Were we as a nation going to devote our energy to cater to these insatiable appetites of the affluent class, or were we going to do everything possible to retain the generous spirit of that boatman from Bastar which had mesmerised me?

There is no denying that globalisation is all-pervading these days. There is no way any one can turn that clock back. Recently I was reading a book in which it was mentioned that if you want to guarantee every person living on this planet the American way of life then it would take three of our planet earths to gratify that dream. I am told that in the United States of America these days they are marketing toilet paper with vitamin E in it. I agree with what our prime minister said in his keynote address. We cannot be driven by consumerism. These western nations first initiate this hedonistic culture of consumerism and they then give all the developing nations a speech on ecology. They are neurotic. They first rape the environment to fulfil their unreasonable wants and then launch a worldwide campaign to save it.

Amar Kanwar was also talking a lot about despair. I am not worried about despair. According to me despair is the lifeblood of all art. All great political movements are born in the dark womb of despair. In fact the bedrock of religion is despair. You know when a grain of sand gets into the craw of an oyster it causes the oyster great pain. The oyster in order to escape the pain caused by this grain of sand turns it around and eventually creates a marvellous pearl. Someone was

talking about a moving incident in the life of Gandhiji. During the riots some people threw pieces of glass and excreta in his path to humiliate him, but this did not deter Gandhiji. Instead of despairing and turning back he chose to walk on it. This 'pearl' of an incident from Gandhiji's life was born in the heart of despair. The India of today is going through tremendous despair. Today, we need great leaders who can give this despair direction. When I look back at my life I realise that it was fashioned by despair. My grandmother who was a Hindu fundamentalist devastated my childhood. She perpetually humiliated me and my mother because my mother was a Muslim. I subsequently made a feature film called *Zakhm* which depicted this part of my life. The film went on to win a national award but only after a long fight with the NDA government. The anguish that millions of people of our nation experience can be very effectively used to carve out a better future for themselves. All that our leadership needs to do is to provide these people with some tool to live with some dignity.

On censorship—I began my career in 1973. My very first film *Manzilein Aur Bhi Hain* was banned by the Censor Board. Twenty-five years later when I made *Zakhm* which dealt with the violence which erupted in Mumbai after the demolition of the Babri Masjid, I had major problems with the government of the day. In 25 years nothing had changed. I had to fight a solitary battle with the Censor Board to get my film cleared. This happened despite getting a clear verdict from the examining committee. The problem started when the chairperson of the Censor Board, fearing that the bosses in Delhi would be upset with her for clearing a film which depicted the Hindu fundamentalists as villains, submitted the film to the Home Ministry for clearance. The Home Ministry insisted that I digitally alter the saffron bands which were worn by the goons into some other colour or they would not release my film. I had to spend 40 lakhs of rupees to digitally transform the colour of these bands in order to get a certificate. It was a humiliating experience. But the joke is that the very same people later gave me a national award for making a film on national integration. I know that as long as there is a censor inside of me there will be a censor outside of me in some form or the other. Ever since man has stepped into the digital age, the state has lost all control. Today all that the state is holding on to is its illusion of control. My right to dissent is sacred for this democracy. It is important for India to emulate the model of Gandhiji. But along with this we must make sure that we whip up the scientific temperament of our people. We must make sure that we ignite in our people an unquenchable thirst for knowledge and free them from tribal emotions. Only when we do all this may we at last begin our journey towards greatness. As of now India doesn't have the military power or the economic might to make any difference in the affairs of the world. It is a tragedy that a nation of one billion people has no say in world matters. I sincerely hope that in the next decade we shall take drastic steps to free our young from the albatross of tribalism which has prevented this nation from being a force to reckon with.

Shyam Benegal

I think Amar Kanwar made an interesting presentation and came to some fascinating conclusions. I tend to agree with him on the subject of film censorship. Censorship of films has had its day and needs to be abolished altogether. What we need instead is a regulatory mechanism that is not subject to the prejudices and whims of three tiers of committees as are now constituted under the Central Board of Film Certification. Mahesh Bhatt gave an example of what the worst-case scenario is like. The best-case scenario is no better. When you present something on the screen—if it happens to be contentious—you are supposed to balance it with a contrary view. This is patently absurd and makes a mockery of the point of view you have presented. In other words, the Censor Board appears to have the power to impose change or neutralise the point of view of the film-maker.

The way it is constituted, the Censor Board has not worked well over the years and cannot possibly work well in the future. Although it has a semi-judicial status and a mandate that is meant to make its ruling accepted in all the states of the Indian Union, the states, the police and various other institutions and organisations can still prevent films from being shown even after they are given certificates.

Leaving that aside, there are a couple of things that Mridula Mukherjee mentioned that relate to changing values in the last few decades. Let me look at the culture of Indian cinema and the catalysts that have made for change. We have had several watersheds in this process of change over the years. The first landmark after independence was in the mid-1950s when Satyajit Ray came on the scene.

Without any kind of governmental support or intervention he created a mini-revolution in cinema with the films he made. This had a profound effect on film-makers who came after him. The Film and Television Institute of India set up by the Government of India at the beginning of 1960s became a catalyst for a second movement in the evolution of Indian cinema at the beginning of the 1970s. And later in the 1980s and the 1990s, Jamia Millia's Mass Communication Centre became a catalyst for the development of documentary films. Amar Kanwar is a product of that. However, no single catalyst can work forever, nor any single movement last forever. In the dynamics of change, you have to keep locating and finding change agents. I feel that the government has a role to play in this process. If you leave this entirely to market forces to shape, it is not likely to happen, since the market will support only that which makes a profit. And what makes a profit need not always be socially or culturally valuable.

Recently, an organisation called the Public Service Broadcast Trust with support from the Ford Foundation and Doordarshan initiated a programme of creating documentary films on social, political and economic subjects touching on all aspects of our lives and changes taking place in our country. A lot of our young people have got an opportunity to make documentaries, many of them finding their way to a telecast slot on Doordarshan on Sunday nights. The quality of these documentaries far exceeds anything that the Films Divisions has done in the last 25 years on which the government spends more than 20 odd crores of rupees every year in production funding alone. This is the kind of intervention that is needed—support from governmental agencies but not necessarily bureaucratic control. Unfortunately, it is very difficult for governments to do anything without exercising total control.

Besides this, what I really wanted to talk about was something more fundamental. It has to do with popular cinema and how it both reflects and shapes the cultural values of our urban society. The nationalist movement was a modernist enterprise since the concept of a nation, relatively new even in the west, did not exist before the movement began. And the freedom movement became nationalist under Gandhi since it aspired to represent everyone regardless of region, language, religion and ethnicity in the country. This totality was given a national identity. When cinema came to India and films began to be made, it coincided with the growth of the nationalist movement. This had a profound effect on cinema. Although the concept of nationalism was modern, the fact that it was anti-colonial and therefore anti-British by implication identified it in the popular mind with being pro-tradition and anti-western. This is how it got projected in Indian cinema until independence and after. Even today, popular Indian cinema invokes and places a premium on traditional values while it offers aspirational images of modern urban lifestyles that are totally contradictory to tradition. Popular Indian cinema has always opted for tradition against modernity even if it simply ends up being lip service. This idealisation of traditional values is *de rigueur* not only in cinema but also in urban Indian society where these values are fast disappearing alongwith traditional social hierarchies, extended and joint family systems and so on.

Quite a substantial number of popular Indian films are based on Hollywood films. Plagiarism would be a wrong word to use here since they are adapted and not simply copied. The process of adaptation is important for the success of the film. The Hollywood original does not have the same appeal to an Indian audience as the Indian adaptation. This is because the adaptation brings into narrative, traditional Indian values—necessary ingredients for its success. For the films to be successful, they have to be culturally Indian. Obviously these films are essentially parodies of Hollywood films. Recently, a Hollywood film, *Bride and Prejudice* tried to parody the style of popular Indian cinema. It did not succeed largely because you can't really parody a parody.

Over the years, popular Indian cinema has had a powerful influence on audiences, particularly the young. In the last 10 to 15 years, however, Indian cinema has become totally urban centric. Not only urban centric but high urban in the sense that these films are peopled by affluent upper middle classes whose lives and loves are portrayed for the edification of the audience. For the general public, narratives that deal with the lives of extremely well to do people have great aspirational

value. However, there is a downside to this development. Rural India has simply fallen off the map. Until, the 1980s subjects dealing with rural India still had an audience. Today, if one wants to make a film on rural subjects it would be almost impossible to get funding for it because nobody wants to see films with rural subjects, least of all rural people themselves. The last time I made a film with a rural subject was in 1998 and it needed the Ministry of Social Justice to finance it. It couldn't have been made otherwise. This is a problem that is very serious. We cannot allow rural India to become invisible. We need to recover it and put it back on the map. When Amar Kanwar talked about hope and despair, this is what he was referring to. The despair of people who have become invisible to the media and to us who have influence in our societies and those in the government and the peoples representatives who have a measure of power.

Sudhir Kakar

Where did you place *Lagaan*?

Shyam Benegal

Lagaan is an exception. Also don't forget it was not placed in contemporary times. It was in historical time and constructed like a fairy tale.

Sudhir Kakar

Thank you very much Shyam, as you can see he has raised a lot of questions. The interesting part is you are saying that rural India itself is invisible to itself. It doesn't want to see it. How do you recover that, which thinks that it is invisible?

Aruna Vasudev

I had prepared a paper for this conference where I had talked about the role of the arts in society and about the cinema as part of the arts. But I have discarded all that after listening to what people were talking about yesterday and this morning.

I have decided to talk only about cinema because it is the single most pervasive element in our lives today. In the lives of everybody, whether rural or urban, academic or political, everywhere you go, whatever you do, you cannot escape the cinema and, therefore, we cannot afford to ignore it. This is something I have been writing about for a long time. As well as how cinema could have been used by the government, by the powers that be, to promote India internationally the way Hollywood did, the way the Americans did. They very early recognised the enormous power of cinema and how the state could use it. It is through the cinema that the Americans were able to convert the world to the American way of life. Not only through the images and the ideas that they spread through their cinema, but also in terms of trade. How do you think hamburgers and jeans and Coca Cola became products that earned money for America? The craze for American goods, the craze to be a part of the American dream swept through the world *via* the cinema. Even our ideas of the world outside were shaped by the Hollywood films we saw. In our growing up years, that is all we saw. We rarely saw Hindi films at that time—Hindi films were very strongly rural-based in the '40s and '50s so one didn't feel as comfortable with them as one felt with Hollywood. I am talking of my generation, growing up under the British colonial hangover when we were more at ease with the English language and, therefore, Hollywood films. This was the era of vast Hollywood expansion, with Europe—and that includes Britain—still suffering from the after-effects of the war. Hollywood films spread through the world and converted generations of people to the American way of life.

As the Bombay film industry became more established it did imitate Hollywood, but here I just want to make a little point Shyam. Everyone points their finger at Bombay imitating Hollywood but at that time Hollywood itself was copying Europe; they had their scouts sitting in Europe to see what was doing well there so that they could come back and remake those films in Hollywood. They even enticed great actors and actresses from Europe to come and act in Hollywood. This very often finished their acting abilities but turned them into celebrities! It is a pattern that has been going on for many years, in many different ways.

I don't want to theorise about this situation—I have done it in books and papers and so on. Today, I just want to talk about what one can do, drawing upon what Amar Kanwar said. I have been watching this growing movement of young people, the documentary films they have been making and how through them, they express their enormous concern and passion for the country. This happened in Indian cinema for a while in the '70s when the National Film Development Corporation was ready to finance films that were in very easy simplistic terms 'non-commercial', and a movement emerged of cinema which was thoughtful, artistic and critical of society. In the usual Indian paradox these films that would sometimes be refused a censor certificate would win national awards. But in their criticism they were upholding the Constitution and pointing out the failures in implementing it.

This was happening in the '70s, and early '80s and I am really sorry that the movement just died because, as is typical of us, there is always money to do something but never enough to do it well. Money would be given to make the films, money was provided for training through film schools, the National Film Archives and what was then called the Films Finance Corporation which went on to become the National Films Development Corporation. Money was available but there was no corresponding interest in actually showing these films. So they naturally faded away because you couldn't continue to make films which were not shown in the theatres which just did not exist for such films. These were shown on television for a while when television for a few years devoted a slot on Sunday afternoons to show what they call regional films in different Indian languages which had been funded by the National Films Development Corporation and had won awards. They showed them with English subtitles on Sunday afternoon, they kept it up for a couple of years. But again, the

films would be shown without any introduction or discussion. They needed a discussion with the director, with those who had been involved in its making, to see why it was important, why it was worth looking at, thinking about. You must in a way, take on the role of an educator without being an educator, because people do want to know and they want to learn and understand. But this was never taken seriously enough.

At this moment what is really gaining ground is the documentary and the short fiction film which is a movement that has to be encouraged. I don't think government should step in and take part in it but I think it should not get in the way. Even if the government were to just hold back and let things happen without interfering, without placing obstacles in the way, a lot can happen. There have been individual initiatives, initiatives by groups, even by film festivals which make it possible for you not only to see other images, but to learn other kinds of cultural values than you do from popular films—the trouble, in fact, is that these are so seductive that you do enjoy seeing them! But no entertainment is value-free and through that entertainment you automatically imbibe values which even the film-makers are not always conscious of propagating. In film festivals you can see another kind of cinema which deals with issues and values film-makers have thought about, and which introduce you to cultures and countries you may not know otherwise. In that sense films and film festivals are a very important tool. Film festivals are coming up all over the country but they are obliged to seek government patronage because without it there are so many obstacles in your way that you cannot function. Now if government would only step back and say go ahead and do it, we will not prevent you, that alone would be enough. So I would make a plea to the government to step back, let things happen which are happening and which are positive forces. What does need rethinking by the government are areas like censorship, taxation, the Cinematograph Act itself which was established in 1918, rewritten in 1952, and has not been changed since then.

Mrinal Sen

Aruna got on with her speech in a delightful manner. Following two speeches made by two eminent film-makers, she has drawn examples from her film studies and has made her speech—short and cute. And now it is my turn. To talk on what? Obviously, not on anything other than my own subject—cinema. But having heard three speeches, one after another, on various aspects of cinema, the participants assembled here specialising in diverse disciplines may not like to hear the same any more and may find mine irritatingly repetitive. What then do I do?

The key issue this morning being The Changing Values in Our Society, I will talk about my interaction with my viewers—the viewers who form the bulk of the society we live in. Not long years ago, in 1979, I made a film called *Ekdin Pratidin*—a day like any other. It all happened in one night in an old mansion, ravaged by time, and let out to a dozen families living life at the bare edges of survival. It was all about a family of seven huddled in two small rooms and, more particularly, about the sole breadwinner in the family—a young woman in her 20s, remaining practically absent in the film until, an hour or so before dawn, she appeared on the scene, a bit tired. The story was about a night-long wait in the family because she did not return home after office hours. Something which she did not do, ever. A terrible night for the family of seven, and a whispering night for the other families. On the surface, a simple story, with plot and incident de-emphasised. The film gave me immense scope to probe, to capture every bit of movement of the arrow quivering into the flesh, and, indeed, to expose the people's connivance in a male-dominated conformist society. The point was to point my accusing finger at the enemy within, at my own community—all quietly, unobtrusively, furtively, as though the characters and the crowd in all the families appearing in the film were all at fault. Night deepened, and the huge decrepit mansion continued talking in whispers—some with genuine concern, some with mock sympathy. When, at last, a taxi roared loudly and stopped outside the gate, the entire mansion sprang to life. The girl appeared at last, unhurt. Just a bit tired, that was all. All safe and sound! A great relief to the family! No accident! But in an instant they were seized with terrible fear. One after another, they left the courtyard leaving the girl alone in the middle of the courtyard. They got frightened of the neighbours, as if the neighbours were pointing their accusing fingers at the breadwinning girl. The mother was desperately trying to fight back tears when in hiding inside the room. The film ended with the beginning of a day like any other. As the day began, the entire mansion broke into activities of all sorts, and the mother of the girl, after lighting her coal stove, kept sitting still, looking unafraid. And what remained unsaid was where had the girl been throughout the night.

The film ran for quite a long time. And for two weeks or so I was almost always there at the foyer, where I had my daily interaction with my viewers. I did not remember a single day when I was not mobbed, mobbed mostly by the young women, students and working girls. They loved the film, they said, but asked me one obvious question—"What happened to the girl? Where did she spend the night?"

The same question was asked everywhere and also at the special screenings in the metropolitan towns in Delhi, Bombay and Madras.

My answer used to be the same everywhere, "I do not know."

On repeated insistence I used to say—"I have no unhealthy curiosity of walking into somebody's privacy."

Even then they were insistent—women in particular—of diverse classes and of diverse ages.

I used to ask them—"Is it so important that you have to know what happened to her?" I even asked them if they liked the film at all? Perhaps not. No, they affirmed, they liked the film, they loved it. "Which means," I used to say, "you want me to issue a character certificate

testifying that the wage-earning girl did not do anything 'unhealthy' while spending the night outside."

And that was that, everywhere and everytime, in all parts of the country. Except once, when, in Paris, I had a session with an exclusive group of Scandinavian women who organised a screening of my film followed by an interactive dialogue with me. The film was well received as I could gather from the dialogue I had with them. At a point of time I asked them if it was true that theirs was one of the most permissive societies. And if so, didn't it ever occur to you that I built the film out of a trivial issue, that of a young woman, working in an office, coming home early next morning?

The answer that I got from one of them, and others agreed with her, was simply amazing. She said, "Yours is a film on issues related to your society. And, as a viewer, my job is to develop a kind of respect for the circumstances in which your characters and situations grow. Once the job is done, the rest of the film is as much mine as it is yours."

A remarkable answer to a question which had been worrying me for quite some time. Nowhere in Europe and in the USA and Canada did the viewers have any problem of the Indian kind.

Back to Calcutta. *Ekdin Pratidin* was still running to a moderately thin house at the city's big theatre, Metro. At the end of the screening one evening I was with a friend of mine at the foyer. Once again there was the same question from a couple of women, a mother and her daughter. My answer was the same. A respectable looking man, about my age, presumably a thoroughbred Bengali, asked me in English, assuming a tone that was distinctly superior, "Mr. Sen, it is important that we know what happened to the woman." He sounded a typical Bengali, sounding like me. Politely I said in Bengali that my answer would be the same. Then, sounding much less than superior I said, "My dear Sir, I made this film for you and your kind. For you to watch and suffer. You will suffer because you will not get the answer."

Much later, I was shocked and surprised when a Delhi-based national daily, *The Indian Express*, carried an excerpt of a letter from Satyajit Ray, written to his friend, reportedly, not for public consumption. It was possible that the mischief was done by a certain journalist who might have brought a personal and private letter to the press column. Anyway, the excerpt referred to the oft-repeated women's question and my answer about the girl of *Ekdin Pratidin*. Ray, then, made a strong comment. He said that never before had he heard of a film-maker showing such ignorance about characters authored by the maker himself.

A simple answer to a simple question made many years ago came to my mind. Someone in Samuel Beckett's time allegedly asked him how was it that Godot did not appear even once in his play, *Waiting for Godot*. To which the playwright's instant answer was, "Had I known it, I would have said it in my play."

Whether or not the Beckett-story is one of the funny anecdotes about famous people or just apocryphal is not my point. The point I want to make through interaction with my viewers is a big question—despite continuously changing times, do the values also keep changing? Highly debatable, indeed! *Ekdin Pratidin* is a case in point.

Let me take another example relevant to the question of changing values. In 1982 I made another film: *Kharij*—The Case is Closed. The principal characters were a husband and wife. They lived in a modest apartment with a five-year old son. Because the couple were busy in their offices and the son needed care and also because they needed someone to do the domestic chores, they engaged a whole-time boy, 12 or so, to live with them. The boy's father, coming from a nearby village, turned him, his youngest son, over to this urban family in exchange for a monthly salary, settled by the usual bargaining. Once, rare though, and that was how the film began, the city was in the grip of a cold wave for a few days. The boy was meant to be sleeping under the stairs on the ground floor. Because of the extreme cold, he went to the kitchen, tightly closed the door, and slept next to the coal oven, still burning. In the morning, the door was broken and the boy was found dead of asphyxia or carbon monoxide poisoning. The doctor came and left, the police were informed, the body was rushed to the morgue for post-mortem, and a curious crowd continued to collect outside the house. The father of the boy came to the city, the young employer took him to the police station, the whole-time boys of the locality joined them. No one was criminally to blame, but a different sort of blame, of guilt, was underscored by the death. Also, underscored was the treatment of the police with more of regulations and less of sympathy. Most importantly, following the cruel death, the focus was on the young couple. First came shock and pain, which, under the pressure of secret guilt, changed to self-protection and aggressive defence. So much so that one started hurling against the other, for reasons unclear to both of them. Unclear, because both of them were civilised, both were provided with exemplary sensitivity, both lived a happy marital life. The cremation took place on the third day. After the cremation, the father returned with the boys in the middle of the night, performed the rituals at the threshold of the house where the boy had lived and died. But a peaceful ending was yet to come. After the rituals were over at the threshold, all of them headed by the father crossed the threshold, they came inside, the father climbed a few steps, looked for the young employer and his wife and the lovely child whom his son had loved so much. Those were tense moments, those were the moments of breathless fear for the local boys who were present during the cremation. Without raising his voice—and the father had hardly any strength to raise his voice—he bade goodbye to everyone with folded hands and quietly left the house. That was how the film ended.

Soon after, having seen the film in Europe, my friend Lindsay Anderson, the stormy petrel of British cinema, wrote a one-liner to me—"I have been deeply impressed by the quiet dignity of the victim (the father of the boy)."

In my city, however, a section of viewers, and particularly those hard-core militant friends of mine who had by then retired from politics, felt utterly disappointed and hated such an incredibly tame ending. They, and they were quite a sizable number, felt disappointed that the father did not slap the young employer on his face. According to them, that would have been a powerful ending. And, indeed, a happy ending! A wish-fulfilling end!

Isn't it terrible? A section of the viewers, including my one-time hard-core militant comrades wanted to watch an all-embracing wish-fulfilling revolt on the screen and would have then come out of the theatre, satisfied, and in their everyday private life would have loved to see the *status quo* continuing merrily ever after.

If not the bulk of our society, at least a section of my viewers were not ready to get the slap right on their own faces which precisely was my intention.

Kharij, for what it is worth, is a slap on my face and on the face of my class. While making *Kharij*, I pulled myself by the hair, and forced myself to look in the mirror. By no means is it a film on child labour which, for sure, is rampant in our society.

Dipankar Gupta

Some six years ago I stopped teaching a course in my department at Jawaharlal Nehru University on peasant sociality because I figured that what we were discussing did not reflect reality on the ground. The books we were talking about in class dealt with tensions between landlords and tenants, between capitalist farmers and the landless proletariat, or about the urgent need for land reforms in order to curb the power of the rural rich and bring about greater equity in the countryside. But the truth is that in the Indian village today none of these things really matter that much any longer. In fact the village is changing so rapidly in front of our very eyes that we often don't have the right kind of concepts and tools to appreciate this transformation. Sometimes I think we make the big mistake of believing that the Indian village is unchanging and perhaps unchangeable.

What we must appreciate first of all is that there are very few people in villages who think of rural India in glowing terms. Whether rich or poor or middle class, they all want to leave the village as fast as they can. The village is no longer hallowed soil for the rural Indian, and has not been so for some time. True, India might have lived in its villages once, but if you look at the way in which people eke out their living in rural India today, one would hesitate to classify the rural economy as being agrarian in the same way as one would have a few decades ago. This should not be difficult to comprehend as about 80 per cent of landholdings are below five acres and 63 per cent are below three acres. I think this is a conservative estimate, but even so, the picture is quite clear.

There are very few big landlords in the villages today—in fact, one would be hard put to find one. So the idea of the big landlord swinging his cane and terrorising poor tenants and labourers does not quite fit in with reality. The big landlords in many of our books and in most of our films are now a near extinct species. This does not make the village a happy, harmonious and egalitarian place, far from it, but the nature of tensions is now different. It is this that we need to fully grasp and re-think some of our old categories. Instead of the big landlord I find a substantial number of owner-cultivators, who are a pretty scrappy lot, but cannot be likened to 'kulaks' as some of us tend to do.

I have often requested my colleagues to come and visit some of these places they talk about and realise how impoverished some of these so called *kulak* farmers really are. The point is that even the landed people are strapped for cash as they are far from being rich *kulaks*. So when a labourer works for a landed person there is an uncertainty regarding whether he will get paid once the job is over. Owner-cultivators often try to buy time by saying that they are not running away, or try to fob them off by giving them something, like cattle fodder, in kind. Such kinds of tension are, unfortunately, not reflected in any of the books I was teaching my students.

This brings me to the issue of changing values. In keeping with transformations in the agrarian class structure, the so-called traditional Indian values are also taking a beating. We no longer have a dominant caste whose decree is supreme in the village. This is because the parcellisation and sub-division of landholdings, coupled with the near collapse of the closed village economy, do not allow one to think in terms of patron-client relationships with calm certitude. Caste factions are not stable entities and vote banks cannot be depended upon either. Till very recently we used to talk about the patron-client relationships in the village and, related to that, of vote banks. But these things really don't matter as much as they used to, say, even 10 years back.

In the last decade or so huge changes have taken place and they are visible to the naked eye. Vote banks have gone and the dominant caste is not really a dominant caste any longer. West UP, which was known as a Jat stronghold can no longer be easily assumed to be one. If Jats were the most powerful caste in that region it was not because they were the most populous as their numbers never exceeded eight per cent of the population of that area. Their predominance came from their control over land, and that is what made others dependent upon them. They were also the most organised caste in west UP, and this allowed them to be politically the most visible and take a lead over other communities. But all that is changing now.

Cumulatively, these transformations have spelt the demise of the caste system where different *jatis* were integrated vertically with the dominant caste at the top. Instead of that system, what we have now is an exaggerated sense of caste identity. In fact, one might also argue that the emergence of caste identity in this strident form is a function of the collapse of the caste system. What subaltern castes could not dare do, or expect, they can now openly proclaim and advocate as the power of the dominant caste and the village patron has dwindled significantly.

This implies that there is greater scope for identity politics and that is why castes have become such important digits in contemporary calculations of power. Caste politics of this sort should not lead one to believe that the caste system is enjoying a surge of popularity, but rather, we are now witness to caste identities which were suppressed earlier in the regime of the closed village economy. Allegiance and subservience to old caste values have collapsed and the *Dharma Shastra* does not work any longer—yet caste identities do.

And why do caste identities work? Simply because the village economy has collapsed and that has brought about a great change in the values that people held and has also given the poorer castes confidence, even courage. Earlier these dominated castes may have wanted to assert their identities but they dared not extrovert them for fear of reprisals from dominant castes. Now that they do not fear the landed castes any more, they can talk about their identities freely. This is why we have a plethora of caste organisations all over the country pressing for the claims of their respective constituencies. In addition, these caste organisations now broadcast their origin tales with great gusto. All these tales, whether of Jats, Ahirs, Ad-dharmis, Jatavs, Holeyas, Baniyas, or Marawas, now claim exalted origins, sometimes even descent from the Gods.

Clearly, major changes are taking place at the structural level. Agrarian relations are no longer the same and the much vaunted caste system has broken down but caste identities remain. But these identities do not weigh upon the minds of villagers on an everyday basis. They periodically surface, but are not of critical importance. Considerations of caste do not determine their everyday lives, even though some anthropologists may not want to hear this. If I were to ask a villager to write about his or her village I can tell you that he or she would hardly spend 10 per cent of the time in talking about caste. We would, as professional anthropologists, perhaps begin with caste, and, in all likelihood, end with it. But the villager might see circumstances differently as there is little in terms of inter-caste relations to talk about. A person lives in his or her hamlet, goes and works somewhere and comes back home again. That is all there is to it.

Further, if one were to follow the trajectory of a migrant worker, one will again find significant shifts in values. I have asked young village boys who they look up to, and the answers again reflect a valorisation of a non-rural world. In many cases, if the father is in the village and is working primarily on the family farm, then his children tend to see him as a loser. The person the youth in the village look up to in that case would be the cousin, the relation, the friend, the neighbour who has left the village and found a job somewhere, often very far away. When I talk to migrant workers I find that many of them have only aged family members at home while the able bodied have all left the village or are on the verge of leaving it. When the migrant worker comes home it is usually during harvesting season when he can help on the tiny family farm, or earn a little money on other family farms that are short of labour at this critical time of the year.

Obviously, not all these migrant workers have a stable job outside the village. Even so, they do not want to return to live permanently in the countryside either. Also, those living in the village look for work outside the village, or even within it, as land cannot occupy them on a sustainable basis any more. In this regard it is necessary to mention the distinction that villagers make between *naukri* and *mazdoori*. When I asked villagers if they did *naukri* somewhere they often replied in the negative. That used to puzzle me as most of their weekly income was from non-agricultural sources. When I confronted them with this they replied that they did not have a *naukri,* and what they did was *mazdoori.*

Naukri is when you get a monthly income, *mazdoori* is when you are employed by the day or by the hour, and you do not know where your next job will come from and when. Every morning these aspiring job seekers in the village go to the bus stand, or to the tea shop on the main road looking for a job—on some days they are hired and on many occasions they return home empty handed. When they don't get a job they work in their little plot of land or do sundry things that they had postponed for some time.

We need to take into account these changes, both empirically and analytically. If we understand the profundity of these transformations then we should think in terms other than those that advocate the reinvigoration of the village. What scope is there for injecting fresh impetus in a system where landholdings are so fragmented? To insist on keeping the village alive in the way it is would be going against the grain, structurally as well as culturally. Villagers don't want to either stay in the village or work on the land. A villager might earn 10 or 20 rupees less plying a rickshaw but will not work in the field of the Jat landlord or the Gujjar landlord because in doing so their sense of self respect is violated and they feel humiliated. And if you don't believe me just go to any place about 50 miles outside Delhi and you will see abundant examples of this. Those who were once pejoratively called *chamars* are the most reluctant to work as agricultural labourers today, though till recently most of them toiled in others' fields.

Some may say that this freedom that the poor may be enjoying is double edged as it also invites despair and uncertainty. Yet, there are times when despair and crises are not always negative in their implications. In fact I remember Karl Mannheim once said that every society grows when faced with a crisis. No crisis, no development. Despair, in this case, can be helpful and progressive if tackled with empathy. For instance, the poor can no longer be herded to go along with the established cultural norms of society. Earlier they had to acquiesce on pain of being persecuted. In contemporary Punjab, for instance, the so called ex-*chamars* now call themselves Ad-dharmis and distance themselves from Jat run Sikh gurudwaras. As a symbol of the distance they now like to maintain from Jat Sikhs, they exhibit a

photograph or a bust of Sant Ravi Das in their place of worship which is otherwise not unlike any Sikh Gurudwara. No longer do they wear the turban or grow a beard, though their parents did so just a generation back. In their homes are photographs of their parents who don the Sikh visage, but they don't do so any longer.

This is a clear example of symbolic defiance. The *Ad-dharmis* are thumbing their nose at the dominant community. This story can be repeated with respect to other subjugated castes in other parts of India. This is true of the Jatavs of UP, the Parayas, the Chakliyas of Tamil Nadu, or the *Mahars* of Maharashtra. They are signalling in different ways their cultural alienation from established customs and practices by either turning Buddhists, or Ad-Dharmis, or in propitiating their own Gods in their own temples their own way without the mediation of Brahmins. The downtrodden of yore are now standing up and saying that we do not believe in the culture system that we had to be subservient to in the past. That they can do this is primarily because they are no longer tied down by the economic control of the earlier dominant castes. The Constitution and the law have helped, but a very significant factor in all of this is the gradual dismantling of the village economy hitherto controlled by rural patrons and patriarchs. It is not as if a revolution has occurred in rural India, but rather that the village has caved in from within on account of what might be termed as an agrarian involution.

There is, of course, the influence from the town, no doubt. But to believe that the village is becoming urban would be misleading. I still can't think of a term that can capture the current rural scenario appropriately. It is not an urban economy, nor is it rural. Perhaps it is a gap economy bidding its time before the pieces fall in place. The extent of rural non-farm employment is really quite staggering, even by conservative government standards. According to official figures, 45.5 per cent of rural net domestic product is non-agrarian. Over 50 per cent of rural households in Punjab, Haryana and Kerala are non-agrarian. Even in Bihar, 40 per cent of rural households are non-agrarian. In the course of my own investigations I have found that marginal farmers earn, on occasion, 60-70 per cent of their income from non-farm occupations. They live in the village, but they don't work in it. Some large statistical surveys have also shown that the number of people who live in the village and not work in it has doubled in the last decade or so.

The impact of all of this on changing values can be gauged from popular cinema. Why don't Hindi films eulogise rural India any longer? When was it last that there was a Bollywood blockbuster which talked about rural India? Mr. Shyam Benegal is quite right. Even the villagers don't want to talk about the village. They want to leave the village, as they think of it as a cesspool of degradation and worse. Unlike many urban intellectuals and developmentalists, villagers do not have any illusions about a rural arcadia. They know the village for what it is.

Chandra Bhan Prasad

Prof. Dipankar Gupta has vocalised at length about how the caste system has withered away in India. I would like to say a few things against this.

I would like to talk about Dalit dogs. A few months ago, India's premier news agency, PTI had flashed a story on 24 July 2004, from Madurai, the southern district of Tamil Nadu. According to the story, which was carried by many newspapers, Dalit dogs were not allowed to go into non-Dalit areas of a village in the neighbouring Tuticorin district. Non-Dalits feared that the Dalit dogs would mate with non-Dalit dogs, and that would be a violation of caste norms.

Only yesterday the Hyderabad-based Anveshi, a very prestigious women's research group, sent a desperate appeal to friends and well wishers all across the world, that a Dalit group in Guntur district had come up with a very radical demand and had asked the government to ensure separate bus stops for Dalits in the Guntur countryside.

Since December 2001, the village Chakuwara in Jaipur district has been in the news. Due to a drought, the village pond has been drying up. As per caste traditions, Dalits were allotted a separate *ghat* from where they take water, or bathe. The Dalit *ghat* dried up faster as it was located in the shallow area. A Dalit youth was caught bathing in the mainstream ghat. News spread like wildfire and a riot-like situation evolved. Only under huge police protection, were the Dalits allowed to draw water.

Incidentally, on 1 April 1936, this same village had been in the news. A Dalit had gone on a piligrimage and on his return, organised a dinner for his community. He had planned to provide the best food within his means, and arranged for *ghee* to be served to the guests. The news spread, and non-Dalits, armed with *lathis* and other traditional weapons, attacked the guests and hosts alike. The Dalits had to run for their lives. The food was later soiled. This shows that even after 65 years, Chakuwara remains the same, in terms of its value system.

Leave the countryside, and consider what is happening in urban India. Can any one of us provide a list of five Dalit journalists? Dalits number over 250 million, about the same as the combined population of Italy, France, UK, and Germany? From this population base, can any one name two Dalit columnists? Can any one name a Dalit company, which is listed on the country's stock exchanges? Can any one name one Dalit who is a member of the India International Centre?

A: There could be many, many.

How many? Two three? Please don't confuse between lower castes and upper castes, Dalits are outcastes. Many journalists and academicians commit the mistake of identifying Dalits in the 'lower caste' category. Lower castes are Shudras or OBCs, Dalits are outcastes. Mulayam Singh Yadav or Lalu Prasad belong to the lower castes, while Mayawati and Ram Vilas Paswan are Dalits. So, please keep this basic distinction in mind.

We all need to reinvent ourselves, and become genuinely modern and liberal. So far the caste system and untouchability have been problems for Dalits. But as the country opens, and the Western and Eastern world come closer, it will become a problem for all those who have enjoyed privileges out of the caste system. We must not shy away from what is happening inside India but rather should confront it.

Ranjit Hoskote

The Lok Sabha elections of 2004 swept the National Democratic Alliance from office and paved the way for the return of the Centrist and Left parties to power in India. The establishment of the United Progressive Alliance government ended a dark period during which majoritarian dogma had been imposed on the nation, the state apparatus misused to accomplish sectarian goals, the education system treated as an instrument of indoctrination, and the rights of minorities and dissidents trampled. As is only natural at such moments of joy after a long season of darkness, the proponents of the UPA have tended to treat this election result as a conclusive triumph for secular values and liberal thought. The truth is somewhat otherwise.

In the same spirit, I would like to suggest that, even as we look forward to the next decade in hope, we ought to look back over the last 10 years with heightened attention. The disquietudes and horrors of those 10 years, a record of criminal errors and cautionary tales, will not vanish instantly; and therefore it would be instructive to revisit and reflect on them. We must not forget that "The Murderers Are Among Us", to invoke the title of a celebrated German film made in 1945, after Hitler had fallen, and even as the Nazi apparatus had begun to melt seamlessly into the nascent civil society of post-war Germany.

I propose to look back briefly over the specific crises that have beset the reception of cultural production in the Indian public sphere, which has been manipulated and distorted by forces of repression acting in the name of a religious or ethnic identity said to be under threat. The Indian public sphere, has been vitiated almost beyond redemption by these forces of repression, which claim to represent identities that are above and beyond rational question.

By 'public sphere', I do not have in mind the angelic space of transparent expression envisioned by the early Habermas; instead, I would propose the more realistic vision of a reasonably open, if contested, space for multiple conversations—a space where opinions may be formed, tastes may be discussed, values allocated, consensus mobilised and dissensus articulated by citizens, operating in a free and intersubjective manner, beyond the reach of the state's claims to authority over all exchanges. This is a conceptual site worth preserving—it is a site where we may compare and contest versions of events, ideals, collective trajectories—where we may place different views of history beside each other and discuss their relative worth. It is a site where we can form ourselves, and also transform ourselves.

I would contend that such a public sphere, which was broadly available to the Indian citizenry from the early 1950s to the mid-1970s, has since 1975 suffered continuous attrition and devaluation, being encroached upon now by the state, now by political parties, now by self-styled social or cultural vigilante outfits with political affiliations. The Indian public sphere, envisioned by the Constitution of the Republic, has received numerous setbacks, in the form of official policy as well as street-level pressure, and from censorship, enunciated both by governmental fiat and by mob action. This gradual erosion of the public sphere—and what is expressively possible, what is performable within it—has had a very specific effect on artistic and scholarly production, on the freedoms of the creative and the inquiring mind. I will cite only two of the most recent cases here.

Not so long before the Lok Sabha elections that drove the National Democratic Alliance from power, on 5 January 2004, we bore witness to the destruction of the Bhandarkar Oriental Research Institute, Pune, by the Sambhaji Brigade, on the grounds that scholars affiliated to the Institute had helped the American historian James W. Laine in researching his study, *Shivaji: A Hindu King in Islamic India*, a book that had excited controversy in Maharashtra for its alleged denigration of the Maratha king. Regrettably, the book was promptly banned by the Congress-Nationalist Congress Party government of Maharashtra; and while some of the activists of the Sambhaji Brigade were arrested, the matter barely received the kind of official attention it deserved. The right to scholarly expression was crudely challenged in the name of an ethnic mystique and the cultic aura elaborated around a historical figure.

Tragically, in a manoeuvre that has become all too familiar in contemporary India, politicians of the Centre have been more eager to attack Laine and defend the ban than politicians on the Right; as though, by so doing, they could appease ethnic sentiment and garner support from a supposedly offended majority. Whereas, in fact, these politicians of the Centre have only diluted their original liberal charter; or perhaps many of them have never truly been persuaded of the virtues of liberalism. Whatever be the correct explanation, such opportunism has brought about an erosion of the binding guarantees made to its citizens by this liberal constitutional democracy. I shall return, presently, to this phenomenon of competitive populism.

Later that month, on 29 January 2005, militants belonging to the Vishwa Hindu Parishad and the Bajrang Dal attacked the Garden Art Gallery in Surat, in the Bharatiya Janata Party ruled state of Gujarat, in the belief that the allegedly blasphemous paintings of M.F. Hussain were being exhibited there. The attackers destroyed works by several other painters and marched off, proving the point that the most extreme form of destructive criticism—physical violence—is also the least informed, and indeed, has no stake in the production of art.

The trouble in this case was that, while artists such as Hussain have consistently employed and modified

Hindu iconography in their works from the 1950s to the 1990s, the national scenario has been irretrievably transformed after the demolition of the Babri Masjid in Ayodhya on 6 December 1992. After Ayodhya, the Hindu Right disputes the right of other discourses (such as art or open-ended faith) to constitute Hindu icons as their objects. On their narrow account, it would seem that only an aggressively politicised *Hindutva* religiosity can make the claim to constitute Hindu icons as its objects.

I have chosen these examples, not only because their proximity in time demonstrates to us the importance of not forgetting the excesses of the majoritarian ascendancy that India suffered during the rule of the National Democratic Alliance, but also because they dramatise several salient dimensions of our radically transformed—indeed, transmogrified—public sphere. These two episodes offer testimony to a growing tendency towards illiberal behaviour in a political and social space that was founded on the principle of a broad generosity towards plural expressions, alternative viewpoints, and competing versions.

In the decade between 1994 and 2004, we have borne alarmed witness to the manner in which groups, varying in scale from minuscule cells to mass mobilisations, can claim the right to take offence—and to demonstrate that sense of offence in the most violent and virulent manner possible. To provide only a few representative examples of this tendency, I would invite you to consider the campaign of vilification launched against M.F. Hussain in 1996 for his alleged depictions of a 'nude Saraswati'; the disruption by Shiv Sena activists, in 1998, of a concert by the Pakistani vocalist Ghulam Ali in Bombay; the force exerted on Deepa Mehta to stop work on her film, *Water*, in Varanasi, by auxiliaries of the Rashtriya Swayamsevak Sangh in 2000; the pressure exerted by Shiv Sena activists on the Sakshi Gallery in Bombay, in 2001, to withdraw an exhibition of paintings by Pakistani artists, in the belief that one of the works mocked the image of Sri Krishna.

This sequence of events forms part of the same curve that includes, at a tragic macro-level, the systematic violence against the Christian, tribal and Muslim minority populations in Gujarat; the subversion of the state apparatus to the ends of reactionary political formations; and the cultivation of an annihilationist attitude towards difference, dissent, or even the mere happenstance of otherness. This is why I have taken for my rubric here, not merely the infringement of cultural freedoms, but rather, the vitiated social, political and cultural contexts of which such infringements are symptomatic.

And such is the insidious manner in which this vitiation has been carried out that we have shared social space with the bearers of annihilationist illiberalism for a decade, and continue to remain on almost amicable terms with them, as they conduct their business in Parliament, in the State Legislatures, in the streets, at rallies, and in the realms of entertainment and business. I hope, briefly, to tease out some of the features of these vitiated contexts, these semantic landscapes within which

cultural freedoms are sought to be circumscribed or even negated.

I would regard such manifestations as those in Pune and Surat as occasions of performance for group identities that are not primordial—in the sense that they do not predate colonial or national modernity, do not reach back into some anterior tradition—but rather, are transactive identities. Such transactive identities, in my reading, are produced by political formations eager to mobilise groups *en bloc* for electoral gains—these formations would typically instrumentalise existing ethnic, religious or regional materials by appeal to ressentiment in communally febrile moments.

Typically, as we know, these instrumentalisations and mobilisations appeal to a sense of historical wrong—real or imagined, often inflated and generalised beyond a local setting—which, they argue, must be redressed by violent self-assertion. Such appeals speak to the experience of material asymmetries, to dislocation and uprootedness; they address and inspire those who have been left homeless in the grand *vistas* of capital, adrift on the sea of modernity. And so, from a combustible combination of cultural materials and psychic discontents, a tremendously violent self-assertion comes into play.

Thus, the Pune and Surat episodes are symptomatic of a society that has become increasingly illiberal to the point of schizophrenia. On the one hand, we have ridden the dramatic social and cultural transformations engendered by the globalisation process—this has brought us an illusion of advanced-economy status, complete with glass skyscrapers, credit cards, high-speed internet connections, and a consumerist anti-ethic. On the other hand, the loss of sovereignty and the renewed anxieties of self-definition have unleashed in our society the interrelated reactions of neo-tribalism, aggressive religiosity, and masculinist ego-assertion.

These collective reactions are combustible, as we have noted—they draw on a mixture of syndromes, including hyper-patriotism, maniacal economic aspiration, a sense of historic grievance, and the compensatory fantasy of blood-lust. Any resistance to these reactions, any criticism of the validity of these syndromes, any refusal to be co-opted into their workings, is perceived as evidence of disloyalty, to be crushed. We see this process unfolding, in varying degrees of brutality, in the Pune and Surat episodes.

The truth is that we are not as contemporary a society as we would like to believe—if a contemporary society is one that cherishes liberality of public discourse and guarantees the right to dissent. In present-day India, individuals tend to assemble under the rubric of collective selves constructed from the materials of ethnicity, religion, region or gender. Fragile as they are, these collective selves become ferocious in self-defence—lacking the positive dimensions of creativity or compassion, they can assert themselves only through negative, antagonistic gestures. They find their natural targets among those who insist on the right to individuation—those who unmask power disguised as natural condition, turn their x-ray vision on cultural dogmas, and posit open-terrain elsewheres against the regimented utopias advertised by the control elites.

The struggle to be heard in the public sphere pitches writers, artists and film-makers against the bizarre counter-modernity of yobbos who combine ignorance with adroitness, coordinating their revanchist manoeuvres over the cell-phone and posting their barbarous triumphs on self-congratulatory websites. While both sides speak in the name of the people, there is little agreement on who exactly the people are; or which sections of the people are represented, with or without their consent, by the rival claimants to the mantle of the popular. In such a polarised situation, there is, seemingly, little space for conversation between the creative imagination and the destructive one; and little hope, apparently, for that republic, constituted from exchanges among responsible, receptive and enlightened individual selves, which once animated a liberal idea of India.

The sociology of transactive identities that supports annihilationist illiberalism is an intimate feature of our vexed process of post-colonial modernity. Once we have taken it into account, we are obliged to introduce several complications into the deceptively simple model of 'Cultural Freedoms *versus* Regressive Politics'. Thus, we must recognise the paradox that, while one can bargain with the state—even force state action (or secure state inaction) in the name of the cultural freedoms of a group, one cannot make the same effective claim on behalf of an individual's cultural freedoms. Thus, for example, Laine's study of Shivaji was banned instantly when Maratha organisations protested against it; but Anand Patwardhan must fight legal battles for years before Doordarshan agrees to screen one of his critical documentary films. All things can be accomplished, it appears, if you unleash a display of violence in the name of the people.

Evidently, what achieves articulation in the Indian public sphere today is a meso-realm of segmented group goods, if such a characterisation can be offered for what is really a farrago of sectarian interests that vocalises the most regressive instincts if in ethnic or religious constituencies. This meso-realm lies intermediate between the Republic's declared pursuits of individual liberty and the greater common good, and crucially, it negates both.

Once we accept this rather more intricate picture of the contemporary Indian public sphere, we cannot admit the facile dichotomies of aesthetes *versus* philistines, radicals *versus* reactionaries or scholars *versus* demagogues, which are often—and justifiably, from a tactical viewpoint—invoked at the level of popular rhetoric by speakers and writers representing the resistance to annihilationist illiberalism. But since we are not discussing this phenomenon at the level of tactics here, we may take the liberty of espousing a deeper view.

What we see in contestation here are two accounts of the self and its sociality, two forms of imagination that claim India as their subject, two rival takes on the role of subjectivity in a group or even national-collective context. Thus, the militants or goons of the Hindu Right are rendered more dangerous by the fact that they do not represent a revivalism or a medievalism—rather, they embody, in their own eyes, an alternative wager on modernity. It is, undoubtedly, a counter-modernity, a para-modernity, an ersatz modernity—I have already alluded to its combination of brutalised feudal social mandates with advanced technologies of communication, transport and distribution—but it is nonetheless an insistent claim on the nation's present and future.

The instances of illiberalism that I have cited also reveal the extent to which the deplorable phenomenon of competitive populism has become an integral and almost legitimate feature of Indian political practice. It appears that virtually every political formation—whether ostensibly of the Centre, the Left, or the Right—must court transactive group identities and the material interests that they embody, irrespective of the merits of individual situations, the legal recourses available, and the rule of law that India's political parties are duty-bound to uphold.

I would suggest that competitive populism has serious implications for the logic of electoral democracy, as it is deployed in a society that can be mobilised so effectively on the basis of aggressive self-images and transactive group identities. In such a predicament, the electoral mechanism degenerates into a mechanism by which contending groups can divide the electorate along jagged lines of competition, each group leveraging its power of destabilisation to effect small gains. Thus, both the rights of the individual and the greater good of the nation formation as a whole are sacrificed at the altars of wedge groups and the megalomaniac well-frogs who lead them.

I would also speculate on the relationship between the ascendancy of politicised religiosity in political life, as a major element informing the spectrum of transactive identities. Perhaps more provocatively, I would ask whether this may be—not an aberration visited upon us by the Hindu Right—but, in fact, the dark, unacknowledged side of our cherished, if misnamed, secularism.

Classical secularism would dictate the separation of religion and polity—translated into our context, it could have meant the equidistance of the state from all religions. Instead, it has come to signify the hospitable treatment of all religious interests by the state, as encapsulated in the formula, *sarva dharma samabhaava*, the 'extension of the same feeling towards all systems of belief'. While this is a laudable ideal in a multi-religious society, ideally speaking, it has in practice allowed for the entry of religious interests as a source of pressure in political life. Our secularism began benignly as an *ecumenicism*—to give it its correct name—but it has perhaps carried within it the seeds of its own negation.

This stems from the fact that a fundamental contradiction separates the bearers of religious interests from the custodians of a public sphere, as we have defined it here. The bearers of religious interests—typically, orthodoxies that articulate both the power of belief and a belief in power—tend to constitute religion as a *magisterium*. The claims of a *magisterium* (from the Latin *magister*, master) tend to become monopolistic and singular in their perceived primacy, totalitarian across all aspects of the lifeworld, and absolute in their application. A *magisterium* has little use for dialogue, except to enshrine its own eventual triumph over all contenders; a *magisterium* can only permit the existence of an opposite or parallel perspective at the risk of dissolving itself.

Politicised religiosity is an unfinished project—it must have messiahs and enemies; periods of advance and the oppositions of conspiracy; bloodbath triumphs and elegiac retreats. It does not stop until it has converted the entire world, or its chosen territorial domain, to its cause. To gain its end, politicised religiosity can and does resort to the most unedifying violence. Politicised religiosity is also a spectrum-narrowing force—it suspects and resents the polychromy of the imagination, and rigidly monitors the human possibilities of expression, creativity, art, thought and love. In a word, all those freedoms that permit the human being to unfold in a plenitude of being; and which it is the duty of a Republic to sustain and nurture.

If the public sphere of the Republic opens itself to the claims and counter-claims of various *magisteria*, we would rapidly depart from the common ground of citizenship and deliver ourselves to fissured sources of wisdom, fragmented sources of judgement, each attempting to erase or diminish the others instead of flowering in a field of potentialities. Such a future would constitute a basic challenge to the Republic, and to its charter of plurality, its commitment to a public sphere that hosts many exchanges without permitting any monologue to drown out the multiplicity of voices.

Perhaps there is a serious need, at this distance from independence and the foundation of the Republic, to examine some of the core values of our national modernity, and to reassess them—to examine whether they have sometimes been counterproductive; whether they have sometimes been defeated by historical change, social upheavals, semantic manipulation, or simply by the seismic shifts of context.

I will close my remarks with a few questions, which seem to me to bear a particular urgency as we move forward into a century whose contours are only deceptively clear.

Can we recover the Republic as a community of conversations, rather than as a space segmented and partitioned by communitarian claims? Can we recover the Republic as an *ecumene*?

Can we allow for the interplay of diverse imaginations, where none exerts a monopolistic claim on experience? Can we protect the right to artistic truth and the right to critique?

Can we productively reconstitute the same objects in different discourses, whether faith, art, scholarship or humour, without inviting assault and the diminution of our civic and cultural freedoms?

Can we preserve nuance, detail, polychromy in our accounts of ourselves—as selves in society—without being coerced into subscription towards one group identity or another?

In conclusion, I return to the word conversation because it is resonant with the core values of the democratic experience—it is derived, etymologically, from *con-versare*, to be able to turn and see both sides, marking the ability of the self to recognise, acknowledge, consider the other, to work with it. Similarly, too, the Sanskrit word for conversation, *sama-vaad*, reminds us that such an activity expresses a relationship of equals.

To converse is to be made equal on the ground of discourse, where pasts are laid to rest and futures are proposed. Such words can never be blunted by excessive use; their edges remain bright and sharp; they remind us of the key values of mutuality and participative equality on which the Republic is founded. They remind us, also, as words denoting activity, that the Republic will never be embalmed in completion; it will always be, and this underscores our responsibilities towards it, a work in progress.

Vinod Raina

I will start with a couple of personal details. We have lost the village even in films, but some of us decided to give up the city to work in the village. I was a physicist, but I walked out—resigned—from a university job and decided to work for the quality improvement of education of rural government schools in Madhya Pradesh, in the beginning through the Hoshangabad Science Teaching Program.

Mridula Mukherjee's presentation tried to bring alive the motivations of people involved in the freedom struggle. The essence of what she said is that we can still try to capture that spirit in the present times. To my mind what stands out in the history of the freedom struggle is that otherwise well-endowed people went out to work with ordinary people. They did not try to reach out to them only through the media, newspapers, research papers and books, but they interacted with them. I think behind the greatness of Gandhi was a simple fact, that he interacted with people; that was his magic.

By and large, most of India still responds to personal interactions, rather than television appearances. It is empathy that moves people, and empathy requires person to person eye contact. And that was a decision many of us made—that we didn't wish only to only analyse and suggest, but to practice in partnership with ordinary people.

While Amar Kanwar talks of despair, I am prompted to counter that in most of rural India, the defining word is perhaps not despair, it is anger, which can be very positive. I do, however, find a great degree of despair and cynicism, in urban metropolitan India. Mindless consumerism is the resort of a despairing mind. You want to buy more, you want to eat more, and you want to

wallow in what is the ultimate end product of a despairing mind. In that sense American society is fairly sick, because its irrational consumerism signifies utter despair. I come to Delhi and feel engulfed by despair. I am not trying to romanticise the village. The village has got violence—an Indian village is by and large a violent place, it is not the romantic unified village we talk about. There is caste, there is patriarchy, there are brutal battles around land, there is murder, there is rape; it has got many fracture lines. But yet, I still find generosity there—something that is hard to encounter in urban metropolitan India.

I refer to what Dipankar Gupta said about rural India. I substantially agree with the data he presented, but contest some of his conclusions. Allow me to present an example, as evidence of what can still be achieved in rural India. In 1988, when Rajiv Gandhi set up the five technology missions with Sam Pitroda in charge, one of the missions was called the literacy mission. It was actually called the technology mission for literacy, which sounded funny, since people were unclear about the relationship between technology and literacy. The relationship was, however, specified in the founding document of the National Literacy Mission, which said that literacy would be done in a distance mode using satellites and televisions, and hence the term 'technology mission for literacy'.

Around that time many of us from the All India People's Science Network were also debating on what to do. There are many scientists like me who have come out to work in the villages directly with people—in education, health, water, livelihoods and a variety of areas. Sometime in 1988 we met in Karaikal in Pondicherry wondering how to intervene in a country that was then being torn apart by mainly two divisive issues, the *Mandal* and *Kamandal*. We were racking our minds for an inclusive issue—an issue such that if someone went on a public platform in its favour, no one could oppose it. Can there be such an issue, we asked ourselves? And in a couple of days we thought of literacy. Could there be any person, from any party, including the most fundamentalist, who could from a public platform oppose literacy? No, we felt certain. So we decided to work for literacy, but in a manner different from the way the National Literacy Mission had thought at that time. We selected the Ernakulam district in Kerala and through a campaign mode, raised volunteers who for 18 months worked throughout the district to make that district nearly literate. Before we began, people called us mad. This happened in Nicaragua, China, and Vietnam, as part of the social revolution. This cannot happen in a place where you have a parliamentary democracy. Ernakulam district produced 30,000 volunteers—housewives, electricians, bus drivers, policemen, most of those who had had an education, became literacy volunteers.

Sam Pitroda came to the concluding rally in Ernakulam and said, "I cannot believe this." If you guys are ready to support the Government of India, we will change the policy of the National Literacy Mission from satellite television and extend the campaign mode to the entire country. We obviously didn't have the strength to say yes, but how could we say no. If we had taken a rational decision the answer to him should have been a no. If you are seeking big changes, you have to be a bit mad. Your rationality is likely to make you sceptical about the possibilities of change. This is the thing I learnt in spite of being a physicist, that in order to work for any social change, particularly on a large scale, you must have a degree of madness. It was such madness that made us say yes, if the Government of India is willing to change its policy, we will collaborate to mobilise people for literacy all over the country. That was the beginning of the very long story from 1990 to 2000.

Twelve million volunteers worked in this country, most of them young women, in over 500 districts, to take the literacy percentage of 52 per cent of the 1991 census to 66 per cent in the 2001 census. This is the highest decadal increase of literacy in the country since independence. The best part was that the increase in the Hindi heartland was on an average higher than the 14 per cent for the country, with Chhattisgarh topping at 22 per cent increase. Most of the people who participated, both as learners and volunteers came from the villages. In fact literacy programmes in cities like Calcutta, Delhi and Mumbai floundered. What I am trying to say is that this couldn't have happened if there wasn't some kind of a reservoir of idealism in the village people that made them come forward and volunteer, in spite of all the violence and deprivation in rural areas.

There is indirect evidence from a different source pointing to such idealism that I wish to share with you. After the Babri Masjid demolition in 1992, elements of the *Sangh Parivar* physically attacked Eklavya, the organisation I co-founded in Madhya Pradesh to work in primary education. They broke our offices, manhandled our staff and burnt our published materials. At that point of time we decided to talk to the RSS boys who come to the *shakhas,* to find out what inspired them. We decided not to treat these boys as untouchables so as not even to talk to them, though it was clear we wouldn't talk to their organisers. And we talked to a couple of thousand of these young people. In answer to the question as to what made them join the RSS, nearly all of them said they wanted to do something for the country; since the RSS was there in the locality and reached out to them, they joined its activities. Since there was no other such organisation around and no one else reached out to them, this was their only option; and they would say—"now that you have come, we will talk to you".

We are all seeking solutions, and the solutions are staring at us. The question is, are we capable of taking up these solutions? Do we have the capability or the will to do that? When a literacy programme, government sponsored but implemented in a non-governmental manner and based on community mobilisation, reached out to the rural youth, they volunteered in millions for it. The movement I am involved in is large, about half a million volunteers form this movement, work on all kinds of issues. That is indicative of the fact that people can be motivated and they are prepared to work for the country. The question, however is, who should really be doing this task? Going back to what Mridula Mukherjee was saying, it is the political parties who have given up the task of grassroots mobilisation, except for the *Sangh Parivar*. They are expanding because they are doing exactly what political parties ought to be doing, but aren't. This is exactly what the Congress Party was all about during the freedom movement. It was reaching out to people and people were joining it. Therefore, when Gandhi said at the time of independence that the task of the Congress Party was over, its task was to give independence, and having accomplished that, it should not take power and disband, I think he was saying something very prophetic, as if he knew how these things were going to turn out.

But having taken power, it is not incompatible for the Congress Party to organise people at the grassroots, in the manner of the freedom movement. There is nothing that stops it. And my plea to the Congress Party and other similar parties is please do so, because the CPM in West Bengal is a living example which demonstrates that in spite of many distortions, the party has kept its presence in the villages of West Bengal, which has enabled it to remain in power for more than 25 years. It is such a political outcome that we need in this country rather than isolated successes of this or that NGO. Why hasn't the Congress Party built on the mobilisation of the literacy campaigns, given that it was its government under Rajiv Gandhi that launched the campaigns?

I would like to end by saying that of the 200 million children in the 6-14 age group that we have, 100 million are out of school. The new government that has been elected by the ordinary masses must quickly ensure that all these 200 million children are not merely taught, but also learn. We have the potential to make our future generations of a different kind. Now what that will lead to, what kind of village and town that will lead to, I have no way of knowing. But it has to be more positive than what it is today, this is something that I know clearly. Because while we seek to extol the values of tolerance, of democracy, of cooperation, the way we deal with our children and youth, whether in schools or outside schools are devoid of these values. The pedagogies we are using are authoritarian; even in the so-called secular states and secular schools our pedagogies are authoritarian. It is a short step for the *Sangh Parivar* to come to power and use these authoritarian pedagogies for their own ends.

To change would take time, but it is not as if change is impossible. People have done this. We created a model district of how to do so, beginning with the Hoshangabad Science Teaching Program. In the entire Hoshangabad district between 1972 and 2000, in 28 years, a model of how to educate in government schools, not nice public schools, with the same government teachers was developed. Not only in pedagogy, training and examinations, but in terms of management, administration and finances too. I am reminded of the comment the BJP Education Minister, Mr. Vikram Varma made in 1992, when they were on the verge of disbanding our programmes and asking us to quit.

Mr. Verma told an intermediary who had gone to meet him—"Tell these people to quit. *Inko kahdo ki apna bistara band kardein. Yeh gaon mei kaam nahi karsaktein hain."* They cannot work in villages, they can go and write articles in EPW and other English publications, they can work in towns but they will not work in villages. Now please understand that here is a *Sangh Parivar* politician telling you the value of the village which he wants to preserve as his domain. Have the other parties, the Congress, greatly threatened this domain of his? I think not—the Congress Party needs to organise from below.

It is quite difficult not to mention that it was the Government of the 'liberal' Mr. Digvijay Singh, who finally closed down the Hoshangabad Science Teaching Program running in about 1500 rural schools of 14 districts of Madhya Pradesh in the year 2000, in a move that was sparked by a protest letter signed by all the *Sangh Parivar* constituents—ignoring protests from nearly everyone of worth in science and education in this country and abroad.

Sudhir Kakar

Thank you. I think you have given us a new slogan because people have been talking about think globally, act locally whereas you are saying think realistically, act optimistically which is a very nice word.

Jayaprakash Narayan

This discussion once again reminds me that almost anything that you say about India is both true and untrue at the same time. I have four questions to ask, to understand where we go from here.

Prof. Mridula Mukherjee gave us a very exalted view of the nationalist movement and the values that formed it. But perhaps it was a less exalted notion of nationalism that underlined the anti-colonial struggle. It was a nationalism that was founded on racial bigotry, cultural atavism and idolatrous patriotism. These less exalting notions coexisted with the noble values she mentioned. Unfortunately, a redefinition of nationalism has not really been attempted subsequent to the attainment of political freedom. A corollary of that, has been the death of the reform movement. The Jyotiba Phules, the Narayan Gurus and even the Ramaswamy Naickers—all did enormous work during the era of the freedom struggle to mobilise the community and fight orthodoxy. I think such reform efforts died after Independence, because we thought that freedom was the end. How do we rekindle that spirit of reform? The only example I can find in recent years, of a social movement for positive change, is the Swadhyaya Movement of Panduranga Sastri Athavale. But even that, I am told, is not likely to outlast the founder.

The second question is that while there is much to celebrate in our own culture, legacy and family with all its strengths, there are some weaknesses, as we discussed earlier in the day. There are some serious problems within our society. All societies have problems, though they may not be the same in every society. While there is trust within a community—whether it is a caste group or a family or a professional group of teachers, doctors,

lawyers, journalists—across the groups, there is almost always mistrust, which guides our responses, leading to a zero-sum game in all interactions across groups.

And there is no sense of common fate across the society as one people. How do we get out of this tradition of mistrust across groups—both vertically and horizontally? And this is one of the key reasons why decentralisation has not taken roots. Delhi does not trust the states, and the states do not trust the local governments. It is not an accident. Even when you talk to a bureaucrat privately, he immediately says, "You can't trust a *panchayat*." I know a number of NGOs who say, "*Panchayat* leadership is not good." This is due to the absence of trust, both vertical and horizontal. How do we address it?

The third question is that there is a lot of anger and violence, the manifestations of which are communalism and naxalism. How do we create a mechanism by which people believe that there are democratic and peaceful answers in a society? We don't have to resort to the gun and the knife. Is there a way of doing something about that? Communalism and naxalism are both part of the same cult of violence arising from the belief that the gun can be the answer and not mediation.

The last question is about the media. A lot has been discussed in terms of films, but I think the power of the media is something we all recognise. It often seems to me that Mark Twain's euphemism holds good for the Indian media. He said, "Often a hen that only laid an egg cackles as if she has laid an asteroid." For instance, we had a glorious opening ceremony of this conference where high quality speeches were given by the Prime Minister, who tried to lay before us a sense of vision of the future, and Mrs. Gandhi's very elegant expression of the dreams and aspirations of the founding fathers and the past leaders of this country. But all we found in the newspapers was a photograph of Sharmila Tagore. Nothing was said about the conference themes. Some years ago, we celebrated the birth centenary of my namesake, Lok Nayak JP. On the same day, Amitabh Bachchan celebrated his birthday. There was a live television coverage of Amitabh's birthday party, but not a word about Lok Nayak Jai Prakash Narayan. We can go on and on. How do we make the media—this vibrant, independent, fierce, jealous in guarding its own freedom media—realise its vital role in creative dialogue and in the search for solutions? Because if that does not happen, and the media does not generate healthy, creative, constructive debate, then whatever we do in formal institutions is of very little consequence.

Vivek Monteiro

I want to focus on something that Amar Kanwar said and disagree with it, which was about the role of science and rationality. Amar spoke about it in a negative manner, contrasting what George Bush was doing in Iraq as one of the consequences of that science and technology. I want to begin by pointing out that George Bush was elected and re-elected essentially because of the growth of the religious right wing in the United States. Like we have our Islamic and *Hindutva*

counterparts here, there is a counterpart in the US which is the Christian religious right wing which was largely responsible for his re-election. And interestingly enough they were talking about values also, which is something we really have to chew over. Now how do we choose between values? How do we choose between feelings? Savarkar has been described by many as a *deshbhakt*, and I have no doubt that in his heart, he felt for the nation. But is that enough? How do you decide what is good for the nation, what is bad for the nation. When we speak about Savarkar, criticising him in Maharashtra, we say that yes, he may have been a *deshbhakt*, but much of what he stood for, some of his ideas, were bad for the nation. And why they were bad for the nation is something that we need to discuss.

I think the role of rationality and in particular the role of science is very important and we really have to think very seriously about how to inculcate what Mahesh Bhatt mentioned—it is a very serious problem before us—how do we inculcate this spirit of science, this spirit of questioning at a mass level right from a very young age? Now by science, I am speaking of science not as technology but in the sense in which Richard Feynman talked about it when he said "science is a long history of learning how not to fool yourself". I think that was a very good definition of science which means that science is not something which only talks about nature. Science also talks about values, science also talks about society, about history, about what we have to do in politics. And I think that this is an area where in fact we really can do something in the next decade without many additional resources. I know some people will not be happy with this statement. We do require more funds into education. We do require that two per cent cess, etc. But it is possible to have universalisation of elementary school mathematics. It is possible to have high quality elementary science in schools even with the existing resources. There are many examples. Eklavya is one example. There are many others. All of us who are working in this area feel this very strongly and I make the statement without exaggeration that with existing resources it is possible to have universalisation of primary school mathematics, in the municipal schools, in the *zilla parishad* schools, in the tribal *ashram shalas*. Why do we make this statement, why is it that we don't require very much more resources to achieve this? Because to learn science, at least elementary science, the world of the village, the natural surroundings of the village and a do and discover approach using these natural resources is the best way of learning science, far better than sitting on a computer with a CD and trying to learn science by using a mouse. For example, the sun has been described as a laboratory which no nation could afford to build, but in fact this resource is available everywhere, in every place where the sun shines. And there is so much science that can be learnt just by working with and studying the sun, all kinds of very interesting stuff—mathematics, energy, agriculture. Another example is water, drinking water. Just by studying why and how to analyse the quality of water and what you can do to water to make it better for drinking, is an excellent way of learning science in schools.

I would like to emphasise here that science, the scientific approach, is very important because at the root of it science is fundamentally opposed to fundamentalism. Fundamentalism is based on the unquestioning belief in some scriptures, whether it is the *Bible* or the *Quran* or the *Vedas* or whatever. Whereas science is fundamentally based on disbelief, on scepticism, on questioning, on learning from facts, respect for facts, not on respect for documents or authority or books. And it is this which I think we can try to build on, not only in pedagogy but also in systems because it is very important to have systems in order to have good pedagogy reach every child. I think that this is something which we can take up as an agenda item for the next 10 years and it is something which will cut fundamentalism, which will cut communalism at its very root because every child will learn science. This is one of those universals—all parents want their children to be good at science and these are some things where we can really achieve something at the grassroots. At this very fundamental level we can make a difference.

Siddharth Varadarajan

This is just to echo something that Ranjit Hoskote said which is part of a broader phenomenon and that is the closing of the Indian mind. We are increasingly coming to a situation where we cannot criticise or evaluate. In Maharashtra, Shivaji and Savarkar are no go areas and in Bengal you can't honestly talk about Subash Chandra Bose or Tagore. Books are banned at the drop of a hat if somebody makes a demand. There has been a lot of discussion on detox in terms of particular individuals. But I think two aspects of detox we need to look at, are the constitutional constraints that the NDA government imposed on academia, and the restrictions on the free movement of academics. If a university department wants to have a seminar on flood control and you want to invite scholars from China and Pakistan, you require political clearance from the Home Ministry. And the Home Ministry is not the most academically inclined ministry. For example, in Guwahati, the Dr. Sanjiv Baruah Centre wanted to have a seminar on the Nelli massacre of 1983, and a Japanese scholar was to present a paper, but the Assam government disallowed it and banned the seminar. However, if someone from the World Bank wants to come and lecture India about flood control or politics, there is no problem for him in getting a visa. Or if an Indian company wants to have a tie-up, there is no problem in a multinational employee coming here. But if a scholar wants to come and do research there are a hundred and one obstacles. A friend of mine who was at the NSD two years ago went to a seminar in Singapore on puppetry and was actually told by her boss to drop in at the Indian High Commission in Singapore and tell them what was discussed in that seminar. We really need to scrap these things.

Prem Shankar Jha

We have been discussing two sets of changes of values and the origins of these changes. One is the growth of despair and possibly out of that anger mainly in the rural areas, and the other is the growth of intolerance. Both are a product of the transformation that the country is going through today, both are a product of industrialisation and, more generally, of capitalism. Capitalism is inherently a brutal process. It feeds on markets, and as capitalism expands markets expand. They don't only expand geographically; they expand in terms of all the things in our lives that they take over and commercialise. Till the advent of industrial capitalism, land—that means nature—and human beings were outside the market. Markets existed to serve human needs. With industrial capitalism, as Karl Polanyi pointed out in his extraordinary book, *The Great Transformation*, both land and human brings became commodities, that could be bought and sold. Human beings were turned into 'labour'. After gaining its independence India embarked on rapid industrialisation. We tried to do it as humanely as possible, reconciling growth and equity through the Nehruvian policies. But we failed because of the sheer power of capitalism. We were not the only ones. Every country that sought an alternative to raw, market-driven, industrialisation also failed. We are absolutely in the grip of capitalism, so the question we need to ask ourselves is, "how do you moderate its rigour?" The boys in Orissa and Bastar that you have talked about are the victims of a double failure—the failure to get growth and the failure to get equity. They have no niche to fill in the capitalist world but they have been deprived of all the free goods of nature that they had in their traditional world. I think this is the source of the naxalism that now affects 157 districts. And the characteristic of naxalism today as distinct from Marxist communism and all kinds of other 'isms' in the past is that it has no political agenda. Everyone has a different reason for doing what they are doing. The absence of a political agenda, at least a credible, attainable one, is the manifestation of pure despair.

Where do we look for a solution? We have to have development; we have to create jobs; but both can be done without creating mindless alienation among the poor. In a nutshell, we have to adopt development policies that make the poor partners in development, and not its victims. Here is just one example of how this can be done. Development requires infrastructure, and infrastructure (as also mining and to a lesser extent industry) needs land. Land is in acutely short supply in India. It has a price but the price does not reflect its value because a family's caste, its status in a village, its self-esteem and its sense of security is bound up with the possession of land. That is why they fight tooth and nail to prevent their land from being alienated and hold up projects for years. Now, instead of taking away people's land for infrastructure projects, why don't we make them shareholders in those infrastructure products? They remain its owners and receive an annual 'royalty' or 'dividend', but no longer determine or manage its actual use. The continued possession of land safeguards their status, while the royalty safeguards their livelihood and provides them with security. This is not a perfect solution but it will be an acceptable solution. Best of all, it is so easy to implement! Why, in a country that called itself socialist, did no one think of this for more than half a century? Why is no one—not even the Left—implementing such policies in even the states they govern and have governed for 30 years?

Turning to intolerance, of the kind that leads to the persecution of minorities, this too is to a considerable extent a product of capitalism. It arises out of the shift of people from the villages to the towns. It loosens traditional bonds that knit society together, and gives birth in the new migrants to a new kind of fear—that of losing their identity. Much of what we call saffronisation today is therefore a counterpart of fascism in Europe in the first-third of the 20th century. Fascism came to the European countries when they were in the same middle stages of the industrial capitalism that we are in today. And therefore the birth of this particular form of intolerance cannot be avoided. It has to be fought and tamed. The taming has to be done through education. It has to be done not just through formal education but through films, television, and other media.

I want to say two more points here. First, just look at our educational system. In order to make our educational system 'secular' we have not only banned the teaching but also the study of religion. We are home to all the great religions of the world. Professors of comparative history never tire of repeating that all great religions teach essentially the same things. But this crucially important bit of knowledge is carefully hidden from our young people throughout their school years. Therefore when a Hindu thinks of Islam he has the strangest ideas in his head, and if you talk to Muslims boys, and ask them what they think of Hinduism, the ideas they harbour are even stranger. But the lack of knowledge does not stem curiosity. Its absence only vacates space for prejudice. From prejudice to animosity is but a short step. This transition can be largely avoided if children are given carefully constructed and monitored courses in comparative religion at the secondary level. I concede that there is a real danger of such courses becoming politicised, but that danger can be minimised by building an all-party consensus. It is a risk that we have to run because the alternative—of leaving children with no knowledge of the essential similarity of all religions—is worse.

Lastly, we have cut ourselves off from our own past by not having a classical language in our educational system. There is no Sanskrit. There is no Persian. Why have we done this? Where is the equivalent of Latin in our system, why have we become people of the never-ending present? And a society shorn of identity forced to live in a never-ending present, is precisely what you said it is—a society that consumes and consumes because it doesn't know what else to do.

Ravi Parthasarathy

I want to touch briefly on value systems attendant to the environment. And there is a linkage here between value systems, which we are discussing today and the economy that we discussed yesterday. This may be a little controversial, but simply stated, we have an environmental framework in this country where I feel we are over-regulated, and under-supervised. The law is fine, but it is completely lacking in its implementation. All of us see the dirt as a primary level of pollution around us. It also always amazes me when I see Indians over-running Singapore, but Singapore remains clean. So it is also an attitude problem. We have problems dealing with the subject because somewhere along the line, we missed out that our environmental awareness and the response you can make is also related to the level of development of society. As you know, the World Bank led by the Americans, strongly opposed the Narmada project and we went into a tailspin when we went to the World Bank for financial assistance. But the Tennessee Valley Dam systems were at least 10 times more damaging than the Narmada project. Similarly when we talk about ethnic cleansing, America has done it in the past, but they have now progressed to a stage of evolution where they can afford to be environmentally clean. Unfortunately we are not, and we are now forced to abide by a set of rules which is not commensurate with our present level of development

Suman Bery used the words low hanging fruit in previous session. Unfortunately, chunky projects are low hanging fruits for environmental activists. But the degradation of Juhu beach in Bombay is not and will not make the papers. So I think we need to look at this entire framework and perhaps segment it into five areas, rather than have the normative approach that we have today. If I am dirtying my own backyard, and I want to live in filth, okay, so be it. But if I am dirtying our beach, which is a public place, there has to be some constraint on my behaviour. Polluting a region by releasing sulphur dioxide into the atmosphere should trigger a separate set of causal factors and remedies. And rivers which are inter-state in nature obviously need to be dealt with at a higher level. The Kyoto Protocol operates at the fifth level—where global concerns are involved. But unless we take this approach, we are going to be agonising about one butterfly or a toad which stopped the Bombay, Pune Expressway construction for two years. Now I don't know of anybody who has missed that toad or butterfly after the government went ahead with the project. Now we have got a turtle which is going to be extinct holding up a port project in Andhra Pradesh. Don't get me wrong, I like turtles. But there has to be a sense of balance whether the odd turtle or mangrove matters. This country's maritime border is absolutely full of mangroves but when you try to clear one mangrove patch to build a port, a number of activists jump down your throat. So there has to be some balance, and I would request this to be an area to look at. At the same time, we have not undertaken a single initiative to instil respect for the environment as part of our value system that is completely missing in everybody's behaviour.

Rekha Chowdhary

I want to focus on the young in urban areas with reference to the campus culture. In the presentation of Amar Kanwar, there was a reference to the question that a young boy asked—what is the difference between what is right and what is wrong? I think that is a question, which haunts the minds of students in colleges and universities, and there is nobody to answer it. There is a sort of directionlessness in terms of basic values and the youth are just drifting without a link to society and community. What is lacking is a perspective towards a broader social life and a tendency to acquiesce is very dangerous. Over the years I have asked my students—what would you like to be termed as, rebels or conformists? I have found over the years that the number of people who want to be rebels is decreasing and the number of people who want to conform is increasing. And I have asked myself why is this so? Why is the element of thinking and criticality that is crucial to sustain the youthfulness of the young missing? Why is there no questioning of things going wrong? Why is there a blind acceptance of Rightist politics? There is a political vacuum in my campus and I think that would be the story of all small towns and their schools, colleges and universities. There is a vacuum and the only kind of politics which is filling this vacuum is the politics of the Right. In my understanding, it is not because of the problem of the youth. Young people are still in search of 'ideas', 'ideals' and 'ideology' but there are none available to appeal to them. There is no one to guide them, no one to give them an idea. There is a drought on that side.

When I consider this question I see that there is another issue, which Mridula Mukherjee has very nicely portrayed. I agree with her that there was a context of political mobilisation and a context of taking politics to the people because of which politics remained relevant to the people. What has happened now is that politics has lost its relevance among the young. It has become a dirty word and the young people do not want to relate to the kind of politics that is visible now because it actually doesn't represent anything. It does not have a meaningful and ideological content. Moreover, the lack of credibility in the politics that is generally operating now, is huge. So in that context I think it is important to relocate and redefine politics and bring it back to the people because the kind of questioning and interrogation we are looking for (and which is very important for our society to be healthy) will be possible through politics. We cannot afford a de-politicised society because that would mean an end to all criticality and normative context. Especially in the context of the youth it is very crucial for them to be brought back to politics so that we can regain the culture of dissent. If anything, it is politics that ingrains a quality of questioning and interrogation in the youth and gives them a sense of dignity. I think these two things are missing in our youth, both the tradition of questioning as well as self-respect.

Aijaz Ahmad

I want to go back to what Mridula Mukherjee was saying. The question is—what happened to the values of the national movement? As a value system I think much of it went deep into us. And it is a reference point for an astonishingly large number of people. Those who despair and those who hope are all within that world, that particular value system. Across the nation it went very deeply within us. But what went deep within us, found it increasingly more difficult to attach itself to things that are structurally a part of the world outside.

In the '50s and '60s, there was a structural continuity between the value system and the structures of the national movement and what was being sought to be put in their place. And even though the Nehruvian state in the '50s and '60s failed to live up to that, it was a complex and detailed reference point by which we could criticise it. Increasingly the reflection in the Indian state of the national movement became less and less, likewise in the way political parties function. So I go back to what Mridula was saying and I was wondering to myself what were the major elements of the national movement. One was the fight against external domination and the drain of wealth. What is very striking to me is that with the decline of the Non-aligned Movement, which was a declaration of independence on the part of India's foreign policy, and our non-aligned commitment by the 1980s, the issue of foreign domination disappeared. With the onset of neo-liberalism strategic partnerships became more important. When I hear India's views today, on foreign affairs issues like Palestine, I wonder what Panditji's views would have been? In his days there was a coherence between foreign policy, domestic policy, reform projects, and economics that gave us development and growth with collective responsibility and limits to personal greed while protecting our political liberty. Furthermore, the kind of political parties we had then had a sense of morality both collective and personal. We need a comprehensive coherent project of national reconstruction in which our major political parties and our government take active roles and call upon the people, both young and old in the millions, to do their bit.

Anita Rampal

I have been part of the same movement that Vinod Raina has just spoken about. Having trained as a physicist from Delhi University I have now come back after 20 years to try and see how we can re-look at education. Education for me is about transforming lives and society. However, problems arise when most concerns of society get imposed on the school. We have to move out of this didactic mode of viewing education and its transformative role. For instance, why do we think that just teaching 'comparative religions' (as suggested by Prem Shankar Jha) is going to solve the problem? We have to look at education more in terms of its engagement with science, culture and democracy, in areas of work within school and outside school. We have done this in our work with children in schools and also through melas, creative centres, libraries and camps. I want to give one example to show how education can help build critical and reflective abilities, without preaching or lecturing to children about human values or 'comparative religions'.

Having persuaded the Rajiv Gandhi Foundation to look at education and children more closely in Kashmir, we planned educational interventions through camps, which helped address the notion of identity and conflict in a creative manner. RGF had been helping children who had lost their parents in militant attacks through financial support to complete school. For the first time when we brought together children from the valley and children from Jammu camps, we saw the tremendous possibilities of their engagement in educational and collective activities that develop self-confidence and self-esteem. These were children who had been born and brought up during the last 15 years of violence, so they did not know what it meant to have friends or classmates from different religions. Their identity is so marked and polarised that a teacher in Kashmir University remarked that when her child heard her speaking warmly to a friend on the phone with a Hindu name she was utterly surprised. This is what it is like today. But these children were amazing when they came together in the camps, and vindicated our faith in the process of education. In a short span of time we covered a broad spectrum of activities—in science, creative writing, theatre, music, etc. We did science about the human body, about who I am. How many times does my heart beat in a minute, how does my memory work, what helps my brain concentrate, what is my height, etc.? Even children studying in classes X or XII knew very little about what had been taught in school. They could hold a metre scale in their hand but could not tell how many centimetres there are in one metre—they would say 91 centimetres, or a 105 centimetres! This is what our education system is all about. However, the same children—who were totally diffident, and wore caps and veils and wouldn't look at you straight in the eye on the first day—were transformed after a few days. I am not trying to romanticise or glamorise about what can happen in just 7 or 10 days. But I think when you look at education in this way, in a broad sense, of empowerment, of providing experiences to develop critical and creative abilities, this is what is possible and does happen.

These children taught us lessons about shared values and respect for 'religion'. We took the children to see Avantipura and the famous temple at Mattan. Those from Jammu had come for the first time to the Valley, and some of them saw their abandoned homes near Mattan. It was a traumatic and also a cathartic moment, especially for two of the mothers who were with them. Some local children happened to watch all this, those studying in schools near by, who had been brought up in the same culture of violence. I cannot forget Irfan, who was so moved by the sight of these women, distraught at seeing their abandoned homes, along with their children who had been brought up in refugee camps, that he insisted we all go to his house and at least have tea with his family, which unfortunately we could not. I cannot also forget how he took charge of all of us and proudly took us all to see the temple, after he heard that the Muslim children had been stopped by the priest from going in, on grounds that *'jo meat machhli khatein hain unko andar nahi aane de saktein hain'* (those who eat meat and fish cannot be allowed to enter). The children had looked really disappointed when they came to me, and my spontaneous reaction was that this is my home state

and I know that in Kashmir everyone eats meat and fish! At this Irfan, the local school boy, said, "this is our temple, we go regularly and I will take you in". With a tremendous sense of belonging he guided us all in. And I confess that I have never before been to a temple with such a deep sense of reverence. He told us *"yahan chappal uttaareeye"* (please take off your shoes here), do this, see this. The children seemed to know it all, as if they performed these rituals everyday; they rang the bell, stood with their eyes closed, drank the *'charnamrit'* and touched their hands to their heads, very confidently, with no awkwardness at all. These were mostly Muslim children, brought up in these trying times in different parts of Kashmir, in 15 years of debilitating violence. And here they were, showing us their understanding and respect for 'comparative religion', immensely better than what we could have done through school textbooks. We have been reading a lot about Kashmir, about conflict resolution through various solutions, but I believe very little is being thought or done about working with the youth and children, through education that is truly empowering. This is one thing we can no longer ignore.

33 | Concluding Remarks

(Section III — Society: Changing Values)

Amar Kanwar

I only want to say that it is necessary to understand what generates hope and despair. To confront despair we need to examine it from different dimensions, to analyse and see what is emerging from despair—that was my intention. The other thing that I would like to say is that I think we cannot create a new India without having an economic understanding of its future. What has been nice so far for me here has been that in spite of some fairly severe differences of opinion, especially on economic issues, there are thoughts and concerns expressed here which make it seem that we are all on the same side. And so I would like to implore that we should identify this. What is it that is actually pulling us together? We should take decisive steps to reconstruct our conception of our nation. Immediately, we need to address the law with reference to media and censorship and so on. But we also must evolve and support many informal and even unknown processes that actually create space for the

freedom of expression. It is absolutely critical and will probably help us all for many years to come.

Mridula Mukherjee

There is much truth in many apparently divergent statements. I do think Dipankar Gupta made a very important point which is very much a part of the Indian reality. But of course Chandra Bhan Prasad is also making a very relevant point. There are remnants of caste discrimination, but I think you would agree that the movement in India is in the positive direction, it is not in the direction of increase of caste-based discrimination, though one can find any number of instances and those remain part of our reality and have to be dealt with. And yet it is also important to look at the direction in which things are going. So I think it is extremely important to take into account in this whole discussion what Prem Shankar Jha was saying, and what Dipankar Gupta was saying.

In response to Vinod Raina's comment on the need to go the people as Gandhiji did, I do wish to say that Gandhiji didn't just go to the people. It was not just about personal contact, there were decades of deep thought behind Gandhiji going to the people. Behind him there was Dadabhai Naoroji who sat for decades in the British Museum (at the same time as Karl Marx), and worked out all those statistics about the drain of wealth from India to Britain. There were Gokhale and Ranade, and R.C. Dutt, and many others who spent their lives doing only intellectual work. There was Nehru who was an intellectual *par excellence*, and Gandhiji was a superb intellectual himself. He read very widely. He went to the people, therefore, with all that tradition of learning of the national movement and with all his own learning as well. You can't go to the people with just empathy. I am sure you didn't mean that, Vinod, but I am just clarifying my position.

There are just two more points that I want to make very briefly. One is that I am very worried about the use of the term Hindu nationalism for what is Hindu communalism and of Muslim nationalism for what is Muslim communalism. Our leadership of the national movement never made this mistake, Nehru never called communalism nationalism. He called it fascism, in fact he is the one who said communalism is the Indian form of fascism, if fascism ever comes to India it will come in the form of communalism. He said, "Definitely fascist ideas are spreading not only in the Muslim League but in the Hindu Mahasabha also," and "both the Muslim League and the Hindu Mahasabha talk in totalitarian language." In December 1947, he said, "We have a great deal of evidence to show that the RSS is an organisation which is in the nature of a private army and which is definitely proceeding on the strictest Nazi lines" (Jawaharlal Nehru, *Letters to Chief Ministers*, Vol. I, p. 33).

So please let us not call communalism as nationalism, because it is not nationalism, it is something quite different. I cannot understand how an ideology that doesn't even believe in national unity, which wants to split communities, can be termed as nationalist. For the sake of the convenience of some western scholars who don't understand the term communalism, let us not change our entire political discourse. I am sure we can find other suitable synonyms which can translate our realities to the West but let us not accept this kind of characterisation.

The second point with which I shall conclude is one of Gandhiji's most inspiring ideas which he put forward around the time of independence, that of the Lok Sevak Sangh. He said that one kind of struggle is over, but the Congress cannot just become a party of governance. He said that some people will go into government, but others will become the Lok Sewak Sangh. Otherwise, who will articulate the aspirations of the people, who will put pressure on the government? There was no opposition, there was no alternative, the Congress was everything. So it was a very creative leap, but it was very difficult, because how can you be both the government and the opposition? Nehru tried to be both, and often wrote under pseudonyms and criticised himself and told everybody how they should oppose him. But I think now the time has come for us to talk about a Lok Sewak Sangh or its equivalent, adapted to the needs of social transformation and the change of values.

When we talk about attacking such fundamental questions like communalism, and about deepening democracy, it is important to also look at strategies. Very often we know what to do but we don't quite know how to go about it. Discussing Gandhiji's strategy on the issue of caste, Nehru said, "He sought the weakest point in the armoury of the caste structure—that is, untouchability—and by undermining and dynamiting it, he shook the whole fabric without the people realising the earthquake he had unleashed. In this way, Gandhiji introduced new and revolutionary processes in the mass mind and brought about mighty social changes" (R.K. Karanjia, *The Mind of Mr. Nehru*, p. 22). There is another letter, which he wrote to Krishna Menon in 1936 and I think that is also very apposite right now. He said, "Try to imagine what the human material is in India—how they think, how they act, what moves them, what does not affect them. It is easy enough to take up a theoretically correct attitude, which has little effect on anybody. We have to do something much more important and difficult and that is to move large numbers of people to make them act" (*SW*, Vol. 7, p. 471). And that is what Gandhiji succeeded in doing and that is in a sense the very difficult task before India today.

Sudhir Kakar

A chairman is always condemned to self restraint, almost verbal celibacy. And so I won't try to summarise all of the session. I would have liked to talk more but our time is over. We talked of artistic expression and the need for removal of censorship on it. We started with India becoming increasingly a youthful society in the next 10 years. What the discussion conveyed to me is that there are reservoirs of what we should call 'immaterial goods' which will be available to us in the next 10 years. By immaterial resources I do not mean IT knowledge, etc. but reservoirs of youthful hope, youth's idealism and its capacity for self-sacrifice. We should not waste these resources but need to offer them direction. We need to tap these reservoirs, do something about them, otherwise they will easily turn into despair, for youth also has an easy capacity for bitterness and anger. And here I think equity or equality which we have been talking about becomes important. I think it is not only in economics where equity is important. The psychology of economics has shown in experiments that generosity and altruism are actually natural to human beings. People become extremely selfish and bitter, only when they feel some kind of injustice has been done to them. So equity is not only important for political and economic considerations but also for social reasons. It helps in mobilising what I have called immaterial resources in the service of the kind of country and society we all want.

Section IV

India and the World

BACKGROUND PAPERS, PRESENTATIONS AND DISCUSSION

CAN idealism be combined with efficacy in our external relations? What are the foreign policy implications of achieving a high rate of economic growth? How is globalisation shaping India's world view and sense of itself and how should India leverage its growing economic strength? How should India relate to the West and to the growing power of China? What importance should it attach to South-South cooperation? How does India see its role on global issues such as conflict prevention, terrorism, WMD proliferation and the future of the UN? How should India deal with the many sensitive issues in its immediate neighbourhood in South Asia? What importance should India give to 'soft' power? What role can Indian businesses, brands, cultural icons and the Indian diaspora as well as government institutions play? How can India's models of governance, and experience in religious, cultural and economic diversity, influence its role in the world? What values should India seek to project?

34 India and the World

SUNIL KHILNANI

THIS is a time for being brusque and direct—rather than subtle and well-styled.

We are, in the first decade of this 21st century, at a truly important moment in the future of the international order. It is a cliché to make such assertions; but in this case the cliché is true. In the 20th century, we've seen the unravelling of two systems of power that—for different durations—shaped the world: in mid-century, the imperial system unravelled, and less than 50 years later the global order of the Cold War came down. Britain and the Soviet Union, two once–great powers (with each of whom we have had intimate relations, not always on our own terms), are now spent as world powers.

Today, the global order is again in a state of turbulence. There is uncertainty over what the viable, durable currency of power will be. In debate today is whether we are moving from an era of multilateral institutions back to a classical balance of power system; whether multipolarity has been replaced by unipolarity; whether globalisation is imposing uniformity upon states and homogeneity upon cultures. And even as the importance of various forms of power—hard, soft—is apparent, we seem to be living through a moment when the priority of military power is being asserted. Yet all states, even those in possession of military power today feel a raised sense of danger and insecurity. State collapse and the rise of non-state actors have, among other things generated international turbulence, which disturbs even the most militarily secure states. There is a debate about role of security alliances and systems, about the legitimacy of pre-emption or preventative war, intervention, and about the extent to which the national security of any and all states are tied to a system of international security.

It is not yet clear what the new international settlement that emerges out of these very practical arguments will be. It should be clear, therefore, that this is not merely a routine moment at which we are asking about India's place in the world. Very briefly, the existing global patterns and settlements have been transformed from three directions.

a) The solidarities that held together the 'West' are loosening. The end of the Cold War was supposed to mark the triumph of the West; in fact it has prompted what has been called "a new age of geopolitical anxiety" (Calleo). Europe, trying to compose a new sense of itself in a new form, is also trying to figure out the terms of its relationship to its closest ally, the US. This will remain for some time a nervous relationship.

b) The dissolution and failure of Arab nationalism, and its replacement by varieties of Islamic extremisms—with no way out in sight.

c) Most significant, the rise of Asia, with China in the vanguard, and with India set to take its place.

Some aspects of the international order of course remain fixed features: for example, the conflict of interests between rich and poor. But these asymmetries of power are acquiring new forms. In the 20th century, poor states were usually weak, and their demands could be brushed aside by the more powerful. But in coming decades, certain states with large poor populations will become significant world powers: China, for instance, will be a relatively rich state, but with a still relatively poor population—it will have high national wealth, with low per capita income. This unevenness will apply to India too. The result will be internal tensions for each in face of their own people, and tensions in an international order which must accommodate them. These tensions will centre around struggles over the world economy and the environment, over control of high technology and of finance.

In these circumstances, every state with any international presence is today engaged in a warily strategic competition with each other, each trying to edge forward. All are playing hedging strategies—even as they assert one thing, they are searching out possibilities in other directions. It should be clear that for all our pressing, even overwhelming domestic concerns that have been discussed in the earlier sessions, India cannot afford not to give the highest priority to how it seeks to position itself in the world system. At this moment when international power is itself being redefined, it behoves us to instil and develop in our elites an instinct for power.

What can we take as axiomatic with regard to the world order over the next decade or so? First, it is axiomatic that the US will remain the single most decisive actor in the international field—whether it be in matters concerning the use of force, the global economy, or the operation of the international system and its institutions. The US, and its own insulated definition of its interests in these areas, will count for more that other states.

In this respect we have to recognise that to frame the issue in terms of a choice between a unipolar and a multipolar world order is misleading. It is certainly possible to imagine and important to work towards a world where power and decision making in each of these three areas is more evenly distributed. But we cannot fool ourselves. The ultimate test of multipolarity—if we are really referring to an effective system—is whether or not such a system can—collectively, or through any of its individual members—actually stop the actions of the most powerful when it comes to the use of force, the pursuit of economic interests, or the operations of the international system. The evidence is pretty clear that it has not been possible to stop the US if it decides to use force—and this fact is not likely to change markedly over the next decade. The US's continuing massive investment in the revolution in military affairs is well known, and will continue to keep it far ahead of any potential rival. Now, this is not to say either that such superiority can give it invincibility or even invulnerability; nor that the US can claim legitimacy for its actions in these fields. Indeed it's perfectly easy to show how the repeated use of force has expended and eroded much of its legitimacy: one might say that as Bush continues to 'spend political capital' he will leave the US with a legitimacy deficit as large as his economic one.

Going further, one could also say that not merely has the US run down its soft power, even when it comes to the use of hard power, it faces limits—the disaster of Iraq being a case in point. This is true. And yet, surely one lesson of Iraq for the rest of us is that the US will and can use force when it chooses to—as it did in Iraq, regardless of what any other state or a system of states thought—and that it can get it massively wrong, can bungle the whole operation—yet it can still absorb such bungling, without experiencing severe domestic

disruption. It is hard to imagine any other power (one of the potential poles, say, in a multipolar world) being able to survive such a major policy error without significant internal costs. The US can.

Internationally, there is today no state or group of states that can reliably restrict the scope of action of the US. Within the US too, the internal system of political checks and balances has been weakened: there are no domestic checks on the pursuit of an aggressive US international policy (the only constraints today are fiscal and logistical). The popular mandate for Bush in the US election earlier this month has created a second Bush presidency which now has utter control over the all branches of the American state—executive, legislative, and soon judicial—and is gripped by ideological zeal. Appointments in the new administration tighten this grip of the White House over the levers of the American state. This means that for at least the next four years (till 2009), whether one likes it or not, an aggressive, internationally hyperactive US is the state around which all other states must arrange their affairs. In many respects this is a cause for deep anxiety for the rest of us.

Given this unpalatable but undeniable reality, India will need to craft an appropriate international politics—a *realpolitik* that is also expressed through a vision and a set of values. Central to this will be how India manages its relationship with the US, what terms it works out. This will be the point of leverage of all our other relationships—whether it be Europe, China, Russia or

Pakistan, they will take us seriously to the extent that the US does.

What could be the basis for such a new vision/ideology? To Nehru, the architect of our sharpest vision of foreign policy, the intent was to create conditions for India to become an independent, great power, in the way it had that been as he saw it at earlier moments in its history. And he sought to do this within the frame of democratic and pluralist values—indeed to make India a beacon and vehicle for such values internationally. In the 1950s and 60s, it was right to see the principle of non-alignment as a basic organising concept—given both structure of the international order and India's domestic realities. But now a new organising vision is needed, more appropriate to today. In the 1950s and 60s, India managed from a relatively low power base to resist the pressures of, to refuse choice and alignment and maximise our space for manoeuvre and our legitimacy. We were able to join and help create groups of states that could further our interests—NAM, Commonwealth, and the UN. Today circumstances are different. The first is defunct, the second is a pale shadow, and the third is in crisis.

India's own position too is changed. In the mid-1950s, Nehru had said, "Asian strength exists in the negative sense of resisting", and this we turned into a fine art. But today we need to devise a more positive conception. Our economic growth is creating the basis for a greater international presence. Among our elites there is a rising sense of self-confidence, and we need

to direct that in useful and constructive ways—if not, this can mutate very easily into assertive and aggressive forms of nationalism that can lead to self-destruction. There are certainly political movements that would like to tap into this , to use it for their own ends.

On the other hand, the world too is coming forward to meet us. Delhi has not yet become the global destination that Beijing is—where all architects, businessmen must be seen, but it could be heading that way. And, while American understanding of India remains heavily restricted, there is a growing sense among policy elites in Washington, Beijing, Brussels and London, etc. that India is a crucial element in the rise of Asia.

What are India's interests today? We seek status, which we feel ought to be commensurate with our historical and emerging importance (e.g. UNSC); economic development; security—with regard to terrorism, nuclear non-proliferation, neighbours, energy etc; access to markets and to scientific technological resources and capacities. Yet as we pursue each of these, we very soon come up against the looming presence of the US (example of the nuclear non-proliferation regime—unless US agrees, there will be no change to this, in our favour; technology transfer, BPO).

In the first Bush administration, there was to some extent a division between what one might call universalists, those who held the view that the US should treat all other states in like manner, based on principles, (e.g. non-proliferation), and particularists—those who held that the US should operate a *quid pro quo* system, rewarding friends, punishing opponents. The debate has now been won by the particularists. Consider Bush's appointments to his second Cabinet—all based on rewarding loyalty. This will be extended to international relations. This is a White House that prefers decisions, not negotiations. It will be an administration that prefers to work with countries bi-laterally rather than through multi-lateral institutions, and one which will only accept multi-lateral institutions where it has a large voice (for example, East Asian security). The new Secretary of State Condoleezza Rice said explicitly in a speech in June 2003 that "Multipolarity has a throw back to an era of frequent wars and constant threats."

Further, we ought to expect serious hiccups in the US-India relationship in the near future—not least because of the way the US will conduct its policy towards Pakistan. For instance, the US will give Pakistan military assistance (F-16s, etc.) as a way of publicly rewarding Gen. Musharraf. Such assistance may even tip the military balance in Pakistan's favour. Given domestic sensitivities, this is bound to become an issue—how will we deal with it? Are we willing and able to absorb such blows, and still work to deepen the relationship?

Here we might look around for examples—China, for instance—of how to do this. In some respects the Chinese look to us for lessons—for example in how to operate multilateral institutions to our benefit. But we can learn too. Even when faced by direct US aggression, they have managed to find ways to deflect this, to pursue their own interests without alienating the US, and in fact

continuing to they draw the US into a relationship with deep economic interdependencies. Our governments of course face more vocal oppositions—but the point is that a way of dealing with this can and needs to be crafted.

India has now an opportunity to do something similar to what China has done, to develop a relationship which exists not simply at the level of security or strategic ends, but has a bedrock of interdependence. Bush II is rhetorically committed to open markets, and this can actually play to our advantage. US corporations see themselves as free to go wherever they can to find the cheapest services at the quality level they seek—India is now very much a destination, though of course we cannot rely on their interest remaining steady. We will have to work to keep that interest. The BPO backlash which we saw early in the US election campaign emphatically failed to gather stream, and Bush II, backed by corporate interests, prefers to keep it cooler still. By seizing the political opportunity this presents to India and escalating our economic interdependencies, we can actually protect ourselves against the more wayward aspects of US policy and administrations. We will need to take the initiative ourselves, not merely be dragged into situations.

As the example of China bears out, engaging more deeply with the US does not mean a supine stance. It means picking our fights more selectively, husbanding our resources, but also making our own pre-emptive moves.

Ultimately, our place in the world will be dependent on two things: a) our continued economic growth; and b) our ability to nurture our internal diversity and pluralism, through the structures of liberal constitutional democracy. From a) stems power; b) legitimacy. Today we live in a world where what has been called the "battle of ideas", and the battle of images, is a crucial terrain of action. At this moment when we are readying for a more active presence in the world, we have projected two quite opposing images of ourselves: to put it in shorthand, 'Bangalore and Gujarat'. On the one hand, a shrink-wrap, software package India, where 'brain arbitrage' is the new spice trade and where India is the world's electronic 'back office'; on the other hand India in terms of Hindutva, where—with mobile phone in one hand and *trishul* in the other, we see modern technology and medieval weapons joined in a lethal union. A choice between 'Brand Software' and 'Brand Saffron', the promise of Bangalore and the threat of Gujarat.

We should not make the mistake of thinking that economics, and economic development of itself, will do our political thinking for us, either in the short or long term—to guarantee our democracy. We are only at the beginning of a decades-long process of economic development, and the scale of the problems defy quick fixes. In the meantime, we will have to decide what we stand for, and what we wish others to see us as standing for. The case of Gujarat makes clear that economic growth is compatible with extremism—especially when such growth occurs within an already complex society. Instead of being homogenised as economic prosperity gives Indians more autonomy over their lives, we will likely see more conflict: more and more experiments in living, some incompatible with one another.

After all, economic development is simply a tool; it cannot of itself provide the rationale for a nation to hold together, nor endow it with a distinct identity. There is an independent realm of political values where we have to make choices. And these domestic political choices will seriously affect India's standing and influence in the world. We need to be able to define clearly what we stand for, to live this consistently, and to project it forcefully.

Fortunately, India does possess one vital and immediately available resource, which has imparted a distinct identity to it, and which is a true global currency of political legitimacy: it is a form of political capital that has been amassed over the past five and a half decades. This is represented by the steady operation of constitutional democracy, in a liberal and non-majoritarian form, over this period. We need both to preserve this democratic capital from erosion, to enhance it, and to make use of 'democracy dividend' which it yields—to be willing to play a role in the global 'battle of ideas'.

And even if dreams of multipolarity must be deferred for the duration, I think we have an opportunity now. Internationally, US legitimacy is more deeply in question than at least since the Vietnam War. Europe appears increasingly as a conservative force: protectionist, in relation to markets but also much else, hoping to keep what it has; it seems cornered by, on the one hand, a triumphant US, and on the other an emerging Asia. China may have a dynamic economy, but it remains a weakly legitimate actor in the global sphere. India, as the world's largest open society, is ideally poised to step into this opening.

The Prime Minister, in a recent speech in Delhi, made a powerful argument for how India can draw upon its rich democratic experience to help strengthen democracy in the world: "Just as many developed industrial economies assisted the so-called 'Economies in transition' to make the transition from centrally planned economies to open market economies, the experience of a democracy like ours can be of some help in enabling 'Societies in transition' to evolve into open, inclusive, plural, democratic societies'. I believe this is an extremely important statement of how India can find a role for itself in the world order—aiding other societies to emerge as democracies, without imposing this on them *via* interventionism. Given the rather botched efforts of the US to pursue such policies, India could offer an alternative. We should be alert to assisting democracy wherever it is taking root: in Afghanistan, by offering to train and educate, and in Iraq—we should offer to train civilian bureaucrats, to impart our knowledge of constitutional and judicial practices. And we should also be less timid in standing up for democracy in our immediate neighbourhood—in Nepal, in Burma, and in Pakistan. It's in our long-term interest, and it's right.

35 | Vision, Conviction, Strategy, and Will: The Four Deficits in India's Foreign-Military Policy

BHARAT KARNAD

JUDGING by great power standards, Indian foreign and military policy has got certain basics of international relations and the nature of the international system wrong. With the incorrect fundamentals in place, it is not surprising that the four policy characteristics of great power—Vision, Conviction, Strategy and Will, have been evidenced only sporadically.

Indian leaders after Jawaharlal Nehru have been unsure of, not what they want the country to be, but how to get from here to there and how India should behave *vis-à-vis* the outside world. Should it act as a proto-great power with a *status quo*-ist bent that is content with the international distribution of power as-is, or as an anti-*status quo* oriented country intent on reforming the world order by forcefully making space for itself at the high table, or as one geared to seeing the large mass of developing states get their due? (In this last, India's experience with the non-aligned movement is instructive. Because, at its most effective, the Movement was no more than a complaint-mongering shop, ignored by the two

superpowers except when it was expedient. Now that the Cold War has ended it is hard to see who it is to be non-aligned against?) Should its thrust be towards multilateral diplomacy pivoted on the United Nations as prototype 'World government', or should it rely mainly on itself and its own initiatives? Should it conduct itself as a powerful state and the natural counterpoise to China in Asia, or as a country, which having ceded the *numero uno* position to China, tries to cut a separate deal with Beijing? Should it act as a regional supremo that will not take lip from any of its neighbours (a stance India has affected thereby losing it goodwill in the neighbourhood and credibility worldwide as a leader of nations), or as the central country around which southern Asia can catalyse into a powerful bloc (requiring unilateral co-optative measures), which can then serve as a launch pad for India's grander ambitions?

Indian leaders have been ambivalent as well about what should guide and motivate India's actions—the national interest, ethical and moral values and/or considerations of universal good, or pragmatism. The lack of consensus in these areas has meant that national security policy (to use the short form for an all-encompassing foreign-military policy) has no fixed strategic vision for itself or a grand coordinated strategy and game-plan about how to realise it and the country lurches between disparate goals depending on the beliefs and attitude of the government of the day.

The problem has been compounded by the confusion about what makes a nation great. Is it military power or economic muscle? Or, does the secret to great power lie in the proper 'sequencing', i.e. in first becoming economically powerful before acquiring matching military clout? And, a more recent thought stream, does the road to great power not lie in maximising the cost and resource advantages to become the global provider of IT and services generally and the preferred source of quality but lower cost goods of all kinds for the world market?

So what's India to do? For a start, get the following realist fundamentals right:

1)   The international system in the 21st century is much as it has always been. It is a Hobbesian world rife with anarchy and featuring inter-state relations which, on important issues are reduced to, zero sum games (where if one state wins, another necessarily loses).

2)   In the prevailing system of nation-states, which has been around 1648 and the Peace of Westphalia, the highest value is attached to sovereignty and to ways of preserving and protecting it and extending the sovereign will of the nation to other countries and the world polity at large.

3)   National interest, expansively defined, is the only rationale or justification for any policy adopted by a country, which is to say, that all national policies are geared to only serving the national interest.

4)   Great powers think of national security in 'distant' terms, with their first line of defence invariably lying across the seas and on the landward ramparts at huge distances from the homeland; lesser states think only in terms of securing their territorial borders.

5)   Morality, regional and international organisations, universal causes like disarmament, etc. have to be seen as instruments of state and made primarily to advance the national interest (and, only secondarily, some collective good).

6)   Military and economic power together define great power. But, as history irrefutably shows, the military card trumps the economic card every time. (The Soviet Union, for instance, collapsed but only because of a series of wrong-headed political decisions by the President Mikhail Gorbachev-led regime.) Military power, moreover, can be leveraged to open markets for economic penetration and to create opportunities for increased trade and commerce.

7) The more unrestricted the strategic reach and clout and the capability to project power, the more unquestioned is a country's great power status.

8) There is a direct co-relation between size (territory, population, natural resources) and power. The reason why the US, Russia and China are unarguably great powers, but the UK and France (who got into the reckoning because of their vast colonial holdings in the immediate post-Second World War period) are slipping fast. And India and Brazil are talked of as 'naturals' to replace them.

9) Great powers are known by their equally great adversary/rival states. Conversely, big states lose credibility as great powers when they compete or fan rivalry with a small state in its vicinity. In this last situation, the small state gains at the expense of the bigger country.

10) Great powers are distinguished by the strength of their self-belief, self-image, and their conviction that they are right and what they do serves international interest and are prepared to exercise their will and expend their power in situations demanding their attention.

11) Great powers are completely autarchic in their defence, relying on no other country or international entity for any military requirements, including their armament needs. They protect themselves, but also extend their protection to other countries. The larger the number of states under its security umbrella, the more credible the nation's great power position.

12) Security dependencies of great powers do not themselves become great powers. Any compromising of national security for any reason is a sign of a pliable state, which then attracts big power machinations against it.

13) Risk-averse nations do not become great powers.

14) Great powers and would-be great powers always treat each other warily; their relations are marked by extreme suspicion and their military preparedness are based on blunting the threat posed by the military capabilities of other great powers.

15) The soft power of a state is derivative power depending on extraneous factors, like fickle external markets for its computer software and cultural products (Bollywood movies and music), and ultimately relies on the hard power and political leverage of the state to give it an edge. The proof of this may be found in the fact that the United States—the dominant military and economic power of today also sources the extant universal culture reflected in fast-food, fads and fashions and Hollywood films to social and political values and intellectual paradigms and problem-solving methods. There is not a part of the world that is not affected and influenced by

America. The US today is much like the United Kingdom in the 18th and 19th centuries, which had the Royal Navy as the globocop that kept the peace in the world and turned coercer and compeller (gunboat diplomacy) when British national interest required it do so. Such military power also forced open hitherto markets (China) and created trade opportunities. The *Pax Britannica* so established allowed English values, literature, social mores, art, systems of jurisprudence and government and ways of thinking to spread across the globe and constituted the universal culture of the day.

The confusion about these fundamentals, ironically, was absent in the early days of the Republic. (Ironic, because the official Indian historiography/hagiography of Nehru is blissfully ignorant of his record as an accomplished practitioner of *realpolitik*.) Whatever the nature of his vacillations, as a classical statesman Jawaharlal Nehru was mindful of the fact that national security was the first charge on government and that in the harsh world of inter-state relations 'might is right'.

Thus, the little-noticed but far reaching two-pronged policy of Nehru's to secure for India the military wherewithal of great power—nuclear weapons produced by, to use his phrase, the "Janus-faced" secretive nuclear programme to master the civilian as well as the military atom. He hoped to afford the country not just nuclear security and strategic independence but the greater benefits of international political leverage and a decisive

role in shaping the future world order. And, he established a comprehensive defence, scientific and industrial base to make India militarily self-sufficient. By these means, Nehru meant for India substantively to achieve the great power position. His successors in the prime ministerial chair, in varying degrees, not only lost the thread but replaced his clarity of purpose by their strategic compromises and political myopia.

Hence, Indira's assertiveness ended when the country was on the cusp of achieving genuine great power status. Under economic and other pressure from the United States, she did not go through with the additional two nuclear explosive tests she had approved, nor did she order open-ended nuclear weaponisation after the first test in October 1974. This loss of nerve resembled her predecessor Lal Bahadur Shastri's not ordering nuclear weaponisation in response to China's first nuclear test in October 1964 at a time when the country was clearly in a position to do so and had been provided with the perfect justification. And, in 1998 Atal Bihari Vajpayee's imposing an unwarranted moratorium on testing after just five tests, with a question mark hanging over the performance of the crucial thermonuclear design. And his government's cutting a deal with the United States to freeze the Indian nuclear deterrent at this unsatisfactory level and keeping such nuclear forces as are available in a half-cocked 'de-alerted, de-mated' mode that has rendered them vulnerable and robbed them of credibility. Thus, India has time and again been denied the strategic prowess that, along with the traditional elements of great power, like, size, location, human and material resources, a strong economy and versatile industry, and scientific and technological capability, would make it a power of consequence.

Why is the acquisition by India of unquestioned strategic might provided by high-yield, preferably megaton, thermonuclear weapons and intercontinental ballistic missiles (ICBMs), other than for the benefits already mentioned, so critical? Because, it fleshes out India's status as a great power, legitimates its expansive definition of its vital national interests and equally expansive sphere of influence. A meaningful Indian strategic arsenal (and not the minimal and ineffective 'minimum deterrent') coupled with geographically distant strategic stakes put down by the enunciation of an 'Indian Monroe Doctrine'—whose ambit should stretch from the East African littoral, West Asia, Central Asia, Tibet and Southeast Asia, inclusive of Vietnam on the South China Sea—will act as a force-multiplier for the 'soft power' of the country. (By the way, Jawaharlal Nehru first talked about, albeit, 'Asian' Monroe Doctrine. The geographic compass of the Indian Monroe Doctrine described above, incidentally, matches the regions covered by the concept of 'distant defence' of India that Governor General, Lord Minto, had delineated in the 1810s when British power was reaching its zenith.)

At a minimum, strategic military muscle establishes the great power bonafides of a country—the reason why notwithstanding the enormous progress China has made in the economic sectors and as a trading nation, Beijing is focused on securing the strategic military heft to neutralise the US.

If such strategic military power is yoked to moderate policies that seek peacefully to deal with countries starting with those in the immediate neighbourhood and moving outward, by offering them a slew of real economic and social benefits and gains from military and political cooperation, then very soon an ever-widening circle of well-disposed countries will, in slow stages, be co-opted into an Indian sphere of influence. Countries doing business and otherwise engaged with India will tend to be more reasonable and accommodating when it comes to resolving differences or even long-standing disputes. If, further, this close economic-political-military interactive order is laced with generous financial grants-in-aid and developmental, scientific and technological assistance to countries in desperate need of them, there will have been firmed up an architecture of genuine stability and peace in the extended region with India as the engine.

India's great power aspirations are no secret. But the path that New Delhi has chosen will only lead it to a dead-end. The problem is that Indian perceptions, policies and programmes are stuck in a deep rut that make nonsense of its stated goal. Three examples will suffice to illustrate the problem of a minor power-mindset and extremely shortsighted approach that have undermined India's great power objectives and interests:

(1) The Indian fixation with Pakistan. It has lost India goodwill in the proximal areas and

credibility as a would-be great power in international councils and strategically reduced it to Pakistan's size and the Indian military to a force incapable of decisive war fighting or even any kind of sustained operations much beyond the border. The difference in India's approach to its smaller neighbours, which is usually bellicose and *vis-à-vis* the big Western powers, which is obsequious, is stark and does not bode well. Because without having friendly and supportive states in the neighbourhood to bank on, India's search for great power will remain a chimera.

(2) With great foresight Jawaharlal Nehru set up an all aspect capability in defence science and industry only to have succeeding generations of politicians, bureaucrats and military officers prevent its development and growth by not off-taking its products, discouraging indigenous weapons development programmes, and distancing it from economic viability by negativing arms sales to the Third World, which last is something Nehru had hoped to see happen. Instead, the involvement of the private sector in weapons projects and the privatisation of huge loss-making Ordnance Factories, has been restricted in the first case and prevented in the other. The result is the Indian defence industry is stunted, its capacity not permitted to grow beyond schemes of licenced manufacture even as the Armed Services' brass complain about

shoddy locally produced goods and about time and cost over-runs, and in complicity with the politicians and the permanent secretariat, fill the order-books of Russian, Israeli, and French Companies (with the British and American firms standing in line eager to feed at the Indian trough). In short, the Indian government's policies are a lifeline to foreign defence industries while its own is gasping for life! The government may have belatedly realised the need to use arms purchases as leverage, but is yet to appreciate the far more powerful leverage provided by arms sales and the country becoming and an international arms supplier. As an arms manufacturer and marketeer, the requisite economies of scale will lead to the DR&DO and Ordnance factories producing competitive armaments of high quality, reducing the unit cost to the Indian military, amortising the defence debt and the investments in R&D, and making the local defence industry profitable.

(3) The double whammy the Indian nuclear complex has suffered owing to official policies. Its mastery of the civilian atom has been compromised by the same kind of short-sighted official outlook that has nearly killed off the Indian defence industry—the government prefers to pay foreign suppliers to put up power plants on turn-key basis rather than contract out the Indian nuclear industry with substantial

private sector involvement to build a host of heavy water-moderated, natural thorium fuelled INDU (a much improved version of the CANDU-type imported originally from Canada) reactor-run power stations to meet the country's growing energy needs. (A series of INDU reactor power stations will exploit India's reserves of thorium, which constitute some 70 per cent of the world's supply of this rare metal.) The INDU, incidentally, is so improved and with such novel features that the International Atomic Energy Agency in Vienna has classed it as an altogether new reactor type. Worse, its competence in the military atom is suffering attrition with the capping of the weapons programme at the 20 kilotonne fission level on the low, politically-useless, end of the weapons value spectrum.

Absent a grand strategic sense and integrated game-plan to realise India's great power potential and the government's unwillingness to properly mobilise the country's myriad resources or take the necessary steps to get its various departments to coordinate their policies and actions, India will continue to be a critical cog in the extant international system that is configured to serve the established great powers' interests. This is best seen in the nuclear non-proliferation arena. India is at once severely victimised by the 1968 Non-Proliferation Treaty (NPT) regime cobbled together by the P-5 (the five so-called NPT-recognised weapon states—the United States, Russia, China, France and the United Kingdom) and asked to uphold it! Rather than use the freedom provided by its NPT non-signatory status to show how grievously it can damage the non-proliferation order if it is not admitted into the club as a full member, New Delhi subsided under pressure and is apparently reconciled to this inequitable state of affairs! Can anything be more self-defeating? India's desire to be 'responsible' nuclear power is now turned against it.

The debilitating belief behind such policies, backed by quite incomprehensible levels of complacency, is that great power is some sort of an entitlement that will come to India because, well, of its size, etc. and because it deserves it! All that India has to do is to wait patiently and act 'responsibly' to please the US, in particular and the P-5 in general for such recognition to fall magically into its lap. To curry favour with the Americans, the Indian government has shown interest in buying into the American missile defence system and is mulling the possibility of joining the US-proposed Proliferation Security Initiative as well, notwithstanding the fact that both these measures strengthen the current non-proliferation order, will undercut India's sovereignty and turn it into a subsidiary ally of the United States. This may win it brownie points in Washington but not great powerhood for India.

India has been knocked around for over a millennia now, because Indians historically did not understand or appreciate the need to capture the vital strategic space by strategic means. The problem is the Indian people and their government in the present day and age still do not seem to have a clue about the nature of the international system, what matters in it, and what the vital national interests are and how to promote them.

India wishes to be a great power but does not want to earn it the old fashioned way—by expending blood, sweat and tears and riches and by taking risks—as other great powers have done throughout history. Moreover, it seeks to reach this goal on the cheap and without any of the necessary prerequisites—hefty strategic hardware, leadership of active alliances/cooperative security regimes, solid military presence on the fringes of an extensive defence perimeter at great distances from the mainland, and a system of extended deterrence ('nuclear umbrella') afforded distant states. Not convinced about its 'manifest destiny', India has not so far mustered the will to assert itself and the motive force to convert its great power pretensions, into reality.

36 India and the World

RADHA KUMAR

INDIA'S global position has changed dramatically over the past 20 years. Up until the 1970s India had a greater international reach than any other developing or post-colonial country. This position started to dwindle during the 1980s, when India was preoccupied with domestic tensions, though Rajiv Gandhi's attempt at peace making and peace enforcement in Sri Lanka was a notable departure which still provides valuable lessons to peace makers in post Cold War conflicts such as Bosnia.

The end of the Cold War saw India disengaging with the world; in fact India turned inwards after the USSR dissolved. This was an ironic reaction—at the height of the Cold War India had carved out a middle ground as a democracy that opposed superpower rivalry and great power *realpolitik* and we were disliked for our high moral ground; yet when the international milieu was finally receptive to the ideas India had developed during the Cold War, and would have welcomed a new global role for India, India withdrew. By doing so, we lost many friends in East Europe and Africa.

In the early 1990s it looked as if India had swung from high-minded if woolly idealism that discounted Indian interests, to a narrow and rather crude self-interest (sucking up to the US *via* Israel) that lost us friends in the Middle East without gaining us new allies in Europe and the US. By the end of the 1990s this trend had reversed—the fruits of Indian economic liberalisation, and in particular our software boom, focused international attention on India as a coming economic power that had the added advantage of being an established and open democracy. US President Bill Clinton put India back on the international radar, and President George Bush continued the process, but India seemed unsure of how to make the best use of this renewed interest.

It was only at the beginning of the 21st century that India swung cautiously back into action in the global arena. While our foreign policy is still in the making, there are several pluses that stand out, as well as gaps that need further attention.

On the plus side, India has put new energy into building global relationships through multilateral institutions. India has joined ASEAN, helped create BIMSTEC and is considering joining China's Shanghai cooperation initiative. We have a 'strategic partnership' with the US that is still largely limited to high technology cooperation; and an emerging strategic partnership with the EU that is potentially much broader. India has worked with Pakistan to re-energise SAARC, and has formed common cause with Japan, Germany and Brazil to expand the UN Security Council. The goodwill that India has today is reflected by the large number of votes she got at ECOSOC. We now have a centre for UN peacekeeping at the United Servicemen's Institute, and we might see a centre for UN policing at the Indo-Tibetan Border Police. And I hope India will join the G-8 in training African peace keepers.

On the minus side, India has not parlayed these new engagements into a comprehensive policy planning India's new global role in, say, 2025. Indian policy makers have yet to fully analyse the impact of 9/11 on existing as well as putative world orders, and are not yet, therefore, in a position to make the best use of the new opportunities that India has.

The Impact of 9/11

9/11 once again put national security at the forefront of US foreign policy, and the war on terrorism is going to remain the US' chief priority for the time being. This will constrain US-India relations, because the US will have to factor in Pakistan's rivalry *vis-à-vis* India. In other words, there will be a glass ceiling on US-India technological cooperation, especially in the military and security fields, as well as restrictions on India's regional peace and security role. India's capacity to aid Afghanistan in post-conflict stabilisation and economic recovery has already been severely restricted by Pakistani fears of encirclement (though this is clearly not India's intention). Equally important, India is prevented from opening a dialogue with NATO on Afghanistan, which is important both for India's role in the region and indeed for NATO's growing role outside Europe.

There are of course ways around this problem which India ought to be considering. One way is embassy to embassy cooperation in Afghanistan, which Germany has begun, and maybe other European countries will follow suit. But that is not a substitute for a dialogue with NATO—or cooperation on specific issues of security concern to India. India should explore the possibility of cooperation with NATO members in the area of peace and capacity building (training peace keepers, for example, or offering 'local culture' briefings (for example, in Afghanistan). India could also consider working with the new European security force as a stepping stone or alternative to NATO, both to improve inter-operability and in order to establish common peacemaking capabilities. The EU's suggestion of a joint European-Indian programme on conflict prevention, including jointly sponsoring a UN conference, is an offer that India should take up.

The other major issue of security concern to India is Iraq, and the Middle East in general. The enormous overreach of the war in Iraq, which might have entered the insurgency-counter-insurgency phase which is really difficult to get out of (as we know only too well), has made the Middle East more volatile than ever. The Indian government cannot send troops to Iraq now—and it would not be advisable anyway, given the way the war is being fought today—but it is in all our interests to help the US to withdraw, which will not be possible until some modicum of order has been restored. Because we cannot send troops we cannot really do much to help train a new Iraqi army (though we could offer limited training for batches of officers in India). But we can help train the Iraqi judiciary, who will be key to re-establish order in Iraq, especially because India's judiciary has such a fine record. We should also offer scholarships for Iraqis at our premier institutes, for example in medicine and information technology.

Finally, if India is to rebuild her relations in the Middle East, and help stabilise the region, it would make sense for her to take a more active role in the Israeli-Palestinian peace process. The UPA government had already moved in this direction by sending Minister Ahmad to meet President Arafat some weeks before he took ill. What would be helpful now will be to see if India can play a role, coordinated with the US, Russia and the EU, in pushing for the peace process to restart.

Soft *versus* Hard Power

One of the major ill-effects of India's inward gaze from the 1980s on was the loss of India's soft power, that had created such a reservoir of goodwill for India in Central Asia, the Caucasus and the Middle East. The Indian government should put revival of soft power high on their foreign policy agenda—Bollywood could be encouraged, for example, to plan movies shot in Central Asia, or joint ventures with Middle Eastern and Caucasus film companies. India could also consider encouraging its educational institutions to expand or create centres for pluralist Islam that could draw students from Asia and the Arab world.

The other big area of soft power is tourism. Given India's enormous tourist potential (both architectural and natural), it is a real shame that no Indian government has made the development of tourist infrastructure a priority. Yet this is an area in which India might find it easier to get investment, and it is also an area in which India would reap quick benefits. To take but one example—the Taj Mahal has brought India $ 500 million a year, which could easily be multiplied to a couple of billion if not more, if India were to develop Agra's infrastructure and make its people stakeholders (through building an international airport at Agra, letting local people run hotels, cafes and shops, keep the city clean and green, give local travel agencies first shot at travel planning, and ensure that a part of the proceeds go to the city authorities for further investment) in its development.

Finally, India's best resource for rebuilding its soft power is the Indian diaspora, which is a growing economic and cultural powerhouse, and which can help bridge the cultural divides that are an obstacle to India's expanding global position. The diaspora, by the way, would also be the most fruitful avenue to deepen and anchor our relations with the US. One lesson we have yet to take on board is that people to people, or business to business, works much better in the US than government to government (except in areas of common foreign policy interest).

India's Neighbours

I have left the regional issues to the last because they are the most complicated and entail the most difficult decisions. India has had a good neighbour policy since the mid-1990s, when she resolved to put neighbourhood relations first, and it has certainly paid dividends with Sri Lanka. Much depends, however, on whether India can turn the dawning peace process with Pakistan into a lasting peace. We cannot expect this to happen overnight, but we do have openings that we should build on quickly before they dissipate (as has so often happened with Kashmir). India needs to make up her mind to begin talks on Kashmir with Pakistan, but can only do so safely once the Indian government has begun a peace process within Kashmir. At the moment India has a window of opportunity to make peace with Pakistan. The international community backs India's peace initiative and has a common interest with India in stabilising and democratising Pakistan; Pakistan's people, including many within the army and policy community, are also coming to realise that peace with India is a better guarantee of Pakistan's stability than rivalry or covert war.

Windows of opportunity do not stay open for long. There is a reservoir of hostility towards India amongst Pakistan security establishment that will assume the dominant position as soon as the pressure for peace (i.e. as part of the war on terror) is over. If Bin Laden is captured and Afghanistan secured, our window will close.

Regrettably, Bangladeshi hostility towards India has mounted over the past couple of decades, and will continue to do so. Here the key is through Pakistan—if India's peace process with Pakistan progresses then it might be possible to work on improving relations with Bangladesh. If not, we can expect more trouble from our eastern neighbour.

To sum up, India is currently fortunately placed to expand economically, develop a new role in the international community, and push a South Asian growth path. But that will only happen if Indian policy planners work out a vision for India and then move step by step to reach the goal.

Section IV

[...continued...]

Presentations and Discussion

"INDIA AND THE WORLD"

This section corresponds to the proceedings of the Fourth Session of the Ninth Indira Gandhi Conference, November 19-21, 2004, New Delhi.

Chair:

- Shridath Ramphal

Lead Speakers:

- Sunil Khilnani
- Bharat Karnad

Discussants:

- Brahma Chellaney
- Sunita Narain
- Deepak Nayyar
- Shankar Bajpai
- Siddharth Varadarajan
- Radha Kumar
- Prem Shankar Jha

- Vivek Monteiro
- Naina Lal Kidwai
- C. Uday Bhaskar
- Kapila Vatsyayan
- Aruna Vasudeva
- Zoya Hasan
- K. Natwar Singh

37 | Opening Remarks

SHRIDATH RAMPHAL

I have literally been parachuted into this occasion and, as I am told by the professionals and have now discovered for myself, it is a wonderful experience—particularly to be parachuted into your company. I have heard of your proceedings so far, and I am sure they have been extremely enjoyable to all the participants. Indians, and I can say this as an Indian, like nothing better than spending time gazing at their own toenails...(laughter). I want to try to change that mould a little, and the organisers have given me the opportunity to do so by moderating this session which is devoted not just to India in the next decade but to India and the world in the next decade. I suspect that most of what you have discussed in the last few days will in some measure be relevant to the answers you provide to that question of India in the world.

I cannot start, however, without a note of personal reminiscence. Vigyan Bhawan, not this particular room but this building, is tied to my last memory of the late Prime Minister Indira Gandhi. In 1983, I sat with her at the closing press conference that she gave at the end of the Commonwealth Summit—a wonderful Summit, with its retreat in Goa. My memory is of her on that platform speaking to the assembled media of India and of a good part of the world as she expressed the high hopes with which the Conference of Heads of Government was closing.

So this place is very special to me; and it is very special to return here for this occasion. We were to lose the Prime Minister the next year. And now it is 20 years on. As we face a new decade, Indira Gandhi would have wanted us, I am quite sure, to be visionary, to be realistic and to be optimistic.

I suspect that in this decade India, like most of the rest of the world, will have to come to grips with the great paradox of our time—the paradox of rampant unilateralism in a globalised world. It is the enormous fundamental contradiction of human affairs, because as the world becomes palpably more in need of acting together, an American imperium threatens to destroy multilateralism, and any real prospect of global governance.

The argument between President Chirac and Prime Minister Blair is not just about trans-Atlantic relations between Europe and the United States, but about the very nature of the global neighbourhood. I venture to suggest to you at the outset that over the next decade, in the context I have described, India's mission must have at its centre two particular purposes. The first is to become an active player in global political affairs, including international security decision making. And the second is to share effectively in global economic management.

It is easy to say those things. The first means the reform of the United Nations; it means India as a permanent member of a reformed Security Council. This is a huge goal. And the second means the effective replacement of the G-8 as the economic directorate of the world by something like the G-20. That replacement is emerging, preferably within the framework of a revised United Nations system; but not necessarily so. The important thing is that India must be at the centre of that global change.

There is now in the world a qualitatively new level of respect for India. It is pervasive and real. It is a respect that arises out of the proven democratic credentials of this country. And it arises as well out of India's acquired economic strengths. A manifestation of it was in the columns of the *Financial Times* in the comments of the President of the World Bank in his appraisal, of how wonderful were the prospects that he foresaw for India. Praises of that kind don't come easily from the President of the World Bank. India is truly well poised at the start of the decade we are looking toward.

More than anything else, the world needs in that time to live by a new set of global values. India, to a larger degree than most countries in the world, can espouse those values with credibility. Many will espouse them, but few with as much credibility as India can bring.

If the next decade is going to do better for the world than the last has done, it has to be because India has been active in resolving our global paradox. This session of the conference gives us a chance to probe these and other issues of India in the world. The annotation of this session has identified a number of questions and issues to provoke your participation.

38 | India and the New World Order

SUNIL KHILNANI

WE are, in the first decade of this 21st century, at a truly important moment in the future of the international order. It is a cliché to make such assertions but in this case the cliché is really true. In the 20th century we saw the unravelling of two systems of power that for different durations shaped the world. In mid-century, the imperial system unravelled, and less than 50 years later the global order of the Cold War came down. Britain and the Soviet Union, two once–great powers with each of whom we have had intimate relations (not always on our own terms), are now spent as world powers. Today the global order is again in a state of turbulence and there is uncertainty over what will be the viable, durable currency of power. In debate today is whether we are moving from an era of multilateral institutions back to a classical balance of power system, whether multipolarity has been replaced by unipolarity, whether globalisation is imposing uniformity upon states and homogeneity upon cultures. And even as the importance of various forms of power—hard, soft, etc.—is apparent,

we seem to be living through a moment when the priority of military power is being asserted. Yet all states, even those in possession of military power, today feel a raised sense of danger and insecurity. State collapse and the rise of non-state actors have amongst other things generated this international turbulence which disturbs even the most militarily strong states. There is a debate today about the role of security alliances and systems, about the legitimacy of pre-emption or preventative war, about humanitarian intervention, and about the extent to which the national security of any and all states is tied to a system of international security. It isn't yet clear what the new international settlement that emerges out of these very practical arguments will be.

It should be clear, however, that this is not merely a routine moment at which we are asking about India's place in the world. Very briefly, I think the existing global patterns and settlements have been transformed from three directions. First of all, the solidarities that held together what has been called the West are loosening. The end of the Cold War was supposed to mark the triumph of the West. In fact it has prompted what has been called a "new age of geopolitical anxiety in the West". Europe, trying to compose a new sense of itself, a new form for itself, is also trying to figure out its relationship to its closest ally—the United States. And this will remain for sometime a nervous relationship. In this sense, the West is itself coming apart in some way. Secondly, the dissolution of Arab nationalism and its replacement by a variety of Islamic extremisms is a second direction from which change is coming and there is no clear way in sight of how it is going to get out of that predicament. And thirdly, and I think in some ways most significant for the next few decades, is the rise of Asia, with China in the vanguard, and with India set to take its place in that rise to.

Some aspects of the international order of course remain fixed features and have not really changed. For example the conflict of interests between rich and poor. But these asymmetries of power are acquiring new forms. In the 20th century poor states were usually weak and their demands could be brushed aside by the more powerful. But in coming decades certain states with large poor populations will become significant world powers. China for instance will be a relatively rich state but with a relatively poor population. It will have high national wealth but with relatively low per capita income. And this unevenness will apply to India as well. The result will be internal tensions for each of those states in the face of their own people and it will also result in tensions in an international order which must accommodate them and their demands. And these tensions will centre around struggles over the world economy and the environment, over the control of high technology and finance. In these circumstances every state with any international presence is today engaged in a warily strategic competition with each other. Each is trying to edge forward, and all are playing hedging strategies—even as they assert one thing one day they are searching out possibilities in other directions the next day or even the same day. It should be clear that for all our pressing, even overwhelming, domestic concerns—about which we have heard so much in the last three sessions—India cannot afford not to give the highest priority to how it seeks to position itself in this emerging world system. At this moment when international power is itself being redefined it behoves us to instill and develop in our elites an instinct for power.

What can we take as axiomatic with regard to the world order over the next decade or so? I think the first and probably the most reliable axiom for the next decade is that the United States will remain the single most decisive actor in the international field. Whether it be matters concerning the use of force, the global economy or the operation of the international system and its institutions, the US and its own insulated definition of its interests in these areas will count for more than any other state. In this respect we have to recognise that to frame the issue in terms of a choice between a unipolar and a multipolar world order is misleading. It is certainly possible to imagine and important to work towards a world order where power and decision making in each of these three areas I had mentioned is more evenly distributed. But we cannot fool ourselves. The ultimate test of multipolarity—if we are really referring to an effective system—is whether or not such a system can collectively or through any of its individual members actually stop the actions of the most powerful when it comes to the use of force or the pursuit of economic interests or the operations of the international system. The evidence is pretty clear that it has not been possible to stop the United States if it decides to use force. And this fact is not likely to change markedly over the next decade. The United States's continuing massive investment in the revolution in military affairs is well known and this will continue to keep it far ahead of any of its potential rivals. Now this is not to say either that such superiority can give it invincibility or even invulnerability, nor to say that the US can claim legitimacy for its actions in these fields. Indeed it is perfectly easy to show how the repeated use of force has expended and eroded much of its legitimacy. One might say that as President Bush continues to—as he put it—spend political capital, he will leave the US with a legitimacy deficit as large as the economic one. Going further one could also say that not merely has the US run down its soft power, even when it comes to the use of hard power it faces limits. The disaster of Iraq being a case in point. This is true, and yet surely one of the lessons of Iraq for the rest of us is

that the US will and can use force when it chooses to do so—as it did in Iraq, regardless of what any other states or a system of states thought—and that it can get it massively wrong, can bungle the whole operation, yet it can still absorb this bungling without experiencing severe domestic disruption. It is hard to imagine any other power—one of the potential poles say of a multipolar world—being able to survive such a major policy error without significant internal costs. The US can and I think that is another distinguishing mark that just sets it apart. Internationally there is today no state or group of states that can reliably restrict the scope of action of the United States. Within the United States too the internal systems of political checks and balances has been weakened. There are in fact no domestic checks on the pursuit of an aggressive US international policy. The only constraints today are fiscal and logistical. The popular mandate for President Bush in the US election in November 2004 has created a second Bush presidency which now has utter control over all the branches of the American state—the executive, the legislative and soon the judicial with new Supreme Court appointments. And it is gripped by ideological zeal. Appointments in the new administration tighten this grip of the White House over the levers of the American state. This means that for at least the next four years, till 2009, whether one likes it or not an aggressive, internationally hyperactive US will be the state around which all other states must arrange their affairs. In many respects this is a cause for anxiety for the rest of us. But given this unpalatable but undeniable reality, India will need to craft an appropriate international politics—a *realpolitik* that is also expressed through a vision and a set of values. Central to this will be how India manages its relationship with the United States, what terms it works out. And I think that this particular relationship will be the point of leverage of all our other relationships, whether with Europe, China, Russia or with our neighbour Pakistan. They will take us seriously to the extent that the United States does.

What could be the basis for such a new vision or ideology or conception of the world that India can stand for? To Nehru, the architect of our sharpest vision of foreign policy, the intent was to create conditions for India to become an independent great power in the way that—as he saw it—it had been at certain earlier moments in its history. He sought to do this within the frame of democratic and pluralist values—indeed to make India a beacon and a vehicle for such values internationally. In the 1950s and 60s it was right to see the principle of non-alignment as a basic organising concept, given both the structure of international order and India's domestic realities. But now a new organising vision is needed, one more appropriate to today. In the 1950s and 60s, India managed from a relatively low power base to resist the pressures of history—to refuse choice and alignment and maximise our space for manoeuvre and our legitimacy. We were able to join and help create groups of states that could further our interests, the Non-Aligned Movement, the Commonwealth and the United Nations. Today the circumstances are different—the first movement is defunct, the second is a pale shadow of itself and the third is in crisis. India's own position too has changed. In the mid-1950s Nehru had said and I quote, "Asian strength exists in the negative sense of resisting", and this we did turn to a fine art. But today we need to devise a more positive conception. Our economic growth is creating the basis for a greater international presence and amongst our elites there is a rising sense of self-confidence. And I think we need to direct this in useful and constructive ways. If not, that self-confidence can mutate very easily into an assertive and aggressive form of nationalism that will ultimately lead to self-destruction. And there are certainly political movements that would like to tap into that rising self-confidence and to use it for their own ends. On the other hand the world too is coming forward to meet us. Delhi hasn't yet become the global destination that, for example, Beijing is today, where all architects, businessmen, etc. must be seen. But it could be heading that way. And while American understanding of India remains heavily restricted, there is a growing sense amongst policy elites in Washington as well as in Beijing, Brussels and London and elsewhere that India is a crucial element in the rise of Asia.

What are India's interests today? We seek status which we feel ought to be commensurate with our historical and emerging importance (for example, the UN Security Council membership), we seek economic development, we seek security with regard to terrorism, to nuclear non-proliferation to our neighbours, to energy security, and we seek access to markets and to scientific and technological resources and capacities. Yet as we pursue each of these we very soon come up against the looming presence of the US. Take, for example, the nuclear non-proliferation regime—unless the United States agrees nothing will change there; another example will be technology transfer, third would be BPO and so on. In the first Bush administration there was to some extent a division between what one might call univeralists, those who held the view that the US should treat all other states in like manner based on principles, for example on non-proliferation issues and so on. And on the other hand particularists, those who held that the United States should operate a *quid pro quo* system, rewarding friends and punishing opponents. That debate has now been won by the particularists. Consider Bush's appointments to his second cabinet they are all based on rewarding loyalty, and this I think will be extended to US conduct of international relations. This is a White House that prefers decisions, not negotiations, and that will reward its friends and punish those that it sees as its enemies. It will be an administration that prefers to work with countries bilaterally rather than through multilateral institutions and one that will only accept multilateral institutions where it has a large say in those proceedings (for example, East Asian security). The new Secretary of State, Condoleezza Rice, said explicitly in a speech in June 2003 that multipolarity has a throwback to an era of frequent wars and constant threats and so on. Furthermore, we ought to expect serious hiccups in the US-India relationship in the near future. Not least

because of the way the United States will conduct its policy with Pakistan. For instance, the United States will give Pakistan military assistance, and most likely it will give the F-16s and so on as a way of publicly rewarding General Musharraf. And such military assistance may even tilt the balance in Pakistan's favour. Given our domestic sensitivities this is bound to become an issue. And the question really is how will we deal with it? Are we willing to absorb it, are we willing and able to absorb such blows and still work to deepen this relationship which as I had tried to suggest is going to be central to how we make our way in the world? And here I think we might look around for examples, China for instance, of how to do this. In some respects the Chinese actually today look to us for lessons, for example in how to operate multilateral institutions to our benefit. But we can also learn from them—even when faced by direct US aggression, they managed to find ways to deflect this, to pursue their own interests without alienating the US. And in fact they have continued to draw the US into a relationship with deep economic interdependencies. Our governments of course face a more vocal opposition than the Chinese. But the point is that a way of dealing with this can and needs to be crafted. I think India now has an opportunity to do something similar to what China has done in its relationship with the US. To develop a relationship which exists not simply at the level of security or strategic ends but on a bedrock of interdependence. Bush too is rhetorically committed to open markets and this can actually play to our advantage. US corporations see themselves as free to go wherever they can to find the cheapest services at the quality level they seek. India is now very much a destination for US corporations, though of course we can't rely on their interests remaining steady. We will have to work to keep that interest. The business processing, the BPO backlash which we saw early in the US election campaign emphatically failed to gather steam. And Bush too, backed by corporate interests, prefers to keep it cool. By seizing these political opportunities in order to escalate our economic interdependencies, we can actually protect ourselves paradoxically against the more wayward aspects of US policy and administrations. But I think here we will need to take the initiative and not merely be dragged into these situations. And again I think the example of China bears out that engaging more deeply with the United States does not mean a supine stance. It means picking our fights more selectively, it means husbanding our resources, but also making our own pre-emptive moves—in a sense moving forward the agenda and the argument on our part rather than always reacting to circumstances.

Ultimately, our place in the world will be dependent on two things. First of all our continued economic growth and secondly on our ability to nurture our internal diversity and pluralism through the structures of liberal constitutional democracy. From the first stems power, from the second stems legitimacy. Today, we live in a world where what has been called the battle of ideas and the battle of images is a crucial terrain of action. At this moment when we are readying for a more active presence in the world, we have projected two quite opposing images of ourselves. To put it in short—Bangalore and Gujarat. On the one hand, a shrink-wrap software package India where brain arbitrage is the new spice trade and where India is the world's electronic back office, on the other hand India in terms of *Hindutva* where, with mobile phone in one hand and *trishul* in the other, we see modern technology and medieval weapons joined in a lethal union. A choice between, if you like, brand software and brand saffron, the promise of Bangalore and the threat of Gujarat.

We should not make the mistake of thinking that economics and economic development of itself will do our political thinking for us, either in the short-term or in the long-term, or that it will guarantee our democracy. Mrs. Gandhi in her remarks mentioned that we should not take our democracy for granted. We are only at the beginning of a decades long process of economic development, and the scale of the problems we face defy quick fixes. In the meantime we will have to decide what we stand for and what we wish others to see us as standing for. The case of Gujarat I think makes clear that economic growth is compatible with extremism, especially when such growth is occurring within an already complex society. Instead of homogenising us, economic prosperity gives Indians more autonomy over their lives, and we will likely see more conflicts—more and more experiments in living, some incompatible with each other. After all, economic development is simply a tool—it cannot of itself provide a rationale to hold a nation together, nor can it endow it with a distinct identity. There is an independent realm of political values where we have to make choices. And these domestic political choices will affect our standing and influence in the world. We need to define clearly what we stand for, to live it consistently and to project it forcefully. Fortunately India does possess one vital and immediately available resource which has given us a distinct identity and which is a true global currency of political legitimacy. It is a form of political capital that has been amassed over the past 57 years. And that is of course represented by the steady operation of constitutional democracy in a liberal and non-majoritarian form. We need to preserve this democratic capital from erosion, indeed to enhance it and to make use of what might be called the democracy dividend which it yields—to be willing to play a role in the global battle of ideas. Even if dreams of multipolarity must be deferred for the duration, I think we have an opportunity now. Internationally, US legitimacy is more deeply in question than at least since the Vietnam War. Europe appears increasingly as a conservative force, protectionist in relation to markets, as well as much else, and demographically in decline. It seems cornered on the one hand by a triumphant United States, on the other hand by an emerging Asia. China may have a dynamic economy, but it remains a weakly legitimate actor in the global sphere. India as the world's largest open society, is ideally poised to step into this opening. The Prime Minister in his speech made a powerful argument for how India can draw upon its rich democratic experience to help strengthen democracy in the world. He said and I quote, "Just as many developed industrial economies assisted the so-called economies in transition to make the transition from centrally planned economies to open market economies, the experience of a democracy like ours can be of some help in enabling societies in transition to evolve into open, inclusive, plural democratic societies." I believe this is an extremely important statement of how India can find a role for itself in the world, by aiding other societies to emerge as democracies without imposing these values and practices on them by interventionism—given the rather botched efforts of the US to pursue this kind of policy India could offer an alternative way of promoting democracy in the world. I think we should be more alert to assisting democracy wherever it is taking root. In Afghanistan, by offering to train and educate, in Iraq we could offer to train civilian bureaucrats, and impart our knowledge of constitutional and judicial practices. And I think finally we should also be less timid in standing up for democracy in our immediate neighbourhood, in Nepal, in Burma and in Pakistan. It is in our long-term interests to do so—and it is right.

39 | Emerging Great Power?

BHARAT KARNAD

I accept everything that Prof. Khilnani has laid down by way of the emerging world order. He has talked about India's approach and I would call it soft *realpolitik*. I will provide the counterpoint by talking about hard *realpolitik*, because that is where I am coming from. I accept the state as sovereign. I accept the fact that the 1648 system of sovereign states, while a failure in many respects, still has much life in it. There is no world government. The United Nations, like most other international organisations, is in disrepute if not entirely inactive. If anything they have become handmaidens of the powerful. Now in this situation are we to consider ourselves as some kind of subsidiary allies of the major powers or should we or should we not think in terms of an independent role using the same means of national self-assertion as these powers have used to get to where they are now?

We can talk about morality, of ethics, we can talk of the fact that India represents democracy and the democratic instinct, and that India stands for something grand and amounts to something more, as Mrs. Gandhi said, than the sum of its parts. But that said, I cannot imagine India seeking to depart the reality and pursuing and advancing its national interest using—let me be blunt about it—ineffective means. Yesterday I brought up the subject of efficacious means to realise objectives.

The problem is, there is and there has been, for almost 40 years now, a great deal of confusion about what India stands for, and what India wants to become? If it does not want to be the usual kind of great power, then what kind of great power should it be and is the attainment of this other kind of great power, practicable? Are we to be the natural counterpoise to China in Asia? Or, is India to be a *status quo* power? We are by and large happy with the *status quo*, so perhaps we can just sort of tinker around at the margins of the present system, or are we anti *status quo*? Do we want to reform the world order, may be try to elbow out and make space for ourselves at the high table in a more forceful way than we have been doing? I am afraid there is no consensus about any of this. But there is, as I have said, a great deal of confusion. The confusion is there because of the same ends and means conundrum that has dogged other aspects of our national life and which we have not been able to resolve. What ultimately is the *raison d'être* for India trying to do whatever it wants to do?

Assuming there is a consensus about India becoming a great power, should the criterion for our policies be narrowly defined national interest? Should it be as a proponent of a democratic impulse and leader of a democratising movement, or should it be as a moral force, as an exemplar of ethical behaviour? We have tried many of these things, but discovered that they did not change the rank-ordering of states. When people say India has acquired a bit of heft and world standing, what they do not mention are the 1998 nuclear tests that got India to this position of reckoning. I do not want to simplify this, but the fact of the matter is that the possession of the 'absolute weapon', the military power generally to hurt, is not only a powerful deterrent, but a powerful means with which to edge into the strategic space that we are trying to carve out for the country. I am being very hard-headed about it. When we mention China and China's success in dealing with America, for instance, at the bottom are some 25 ICBMs that can take out the US West Coast. A standard 3.3 megatonne bomb over an American city on its Pacific coast is why America ultimately has not and will not fool around with China, and dare not do so with North Korea, which with its small nuclear arsenal has threatened, point blank, that if the

Americans embark on any kind of adventure against them they are going to atomic bomb Japan, and why the US has taken liberties with an Iraq that was short of nuclear weapons level. I don't mean to reduce international relations to threat mongering. But the fact of the matter is India can best prepare the ground for its acceptance by the world as a great power by speedily acquiring the thermonuclear wherewithal with an intercontinental ballistic missile reach.

For 50 years we have believed that we can become a great power on the cheap. We have believed that great power (and a seat in the Security Council) is some sort of an entitlement. Then again, does India deserve a seat in the Security Council, because it is a moral power? Or will India gain respect by acting its size and realising its legitimate ambition? What are the decisive factors? India has all the traditional attributes of great power—size, location, human and natural resources, etc. and yet not the recognition. The reasons for this that I have elaborated in my paper, are the four great deficits in Indian foreign military policy—Vision, Conviction, Strategy and Will, which have so far been evidenced only sporadically in Indian policy. But these factors have not converged, nor has any Indian government methodically pushed a policy with this convergence in mind. Time and again we have come to the edge of acquiring genuinely great power and drawn back. Indira Gandhi was a person of steel and yet in 1974 she did not permit the two additional tests that she had approved. Why? Because the Americans threatened, as they invariably do, economic sanctions and many other retributive actions. And incidentally, the fact that President Salvador Allende of Chile was assassinated by CIA in 1972 may have been transmitted to Indira. The point I am making is rather blunt. The US is a liberal society at home and a ruthless power abroad. That in a sense is its secret of great power. To deal with the USA, and with other great powers, including China, India has to meet the challenge on their terms.

This requires an understanding of the fundamental nature of the international system. In this era, as in the past, the system is Hobbesian. There is no order; there is mostly anarchy and the law of the jungle prevails in which might is right and anything goes. Thus, contrivances like the United Nations Organisations are instruments the great powers use to advance their national interests. Was it ever otherwise? If India sees the UN as some kind of a world government in embryo, it is a chimera that we have created to service our rhetoric, not further the national interest.

The blueprint to great power has to have a number of ingredients. Among them is the need to have enemies commensurate with India's great power pretensions. One of the things that has hurt India badly over the last 50 odd-years is our *idée fixe* with Pakistan. It has reduced this country strategically to Pakistan's size. We cannot let that happen. We have lost credibility in the world when we make Pakistan out to be the primary threat. Pakistan has never been a threat, can never be a serious military threat, even a thermonuclear weapon-armed Pakistan

cannot pose a credible threat to India. Talking about it in a purely military vein, if Pakistan is not a military threat, it can nevertheless be a nuisance, it can misbehave. The solution does not lie in India's marshalling its field armies but, more reasonably, by engaging in sustained punitive operations carried out by augmented special forces coupled with heightened intelligence activities and so on. But the fact is a country is known by the enemies it keeps. If Indians think of Pakistan as an enemy, make Bangladesh out to be a threat, then India is reduced to strategic insignificance. And no one, but no one can take India seriously. Pakistan has its own threat perceptions and security compulsions and if it wants to arm itself to the teeth, let it. That cannot hurt India.

The right course to follow is a policy of co-option of neighbours using preferential trade agreements, economic incentives, technological assistance, grants-in-aid packages, oil and gas pipelines, whatever, to tie the countries in an extended southern Asia into the Indian economic sphere. That is what great powers do, they co-opt lesser states and then utilise the ever-widening circle of co-opted/cooperative states to consolidate a growing sphere of influence and as a launch pad for their larger ambitions. This is what India's policies must be oriented to achieve on a priority basis.

Some of the building blocks of an expansive policy are already in place. The military and naval diplomacy involving officer training programmes, joint naval exercises, goodwill and flag-showing visits to littoral states and countries farther afield have generated considerable interest in these countries about possible security cooperation and partnership to maintain peace, order and stability. However, this should not be mistaken as an acceptance of India's role as a pusher of democracy on unwilling states. India cannot be the standard bearer of democracy in southern Asia or any other region, much as this may satisfy the national ego. If Pakistanis love democracy so much they should fight for it, if Myanmarese want to enjoy democratic rights they should agitate for it and not look to New Delhi to install a democratic regime in their respective states. And even less should the Indian government accommodate such pleas. No country in the world sacrifices its national interest for the sake of democracy in another country. It is the kind of intrusiveness that will create ill-will, as we saw happen in Myanmar when for long years we deigned not to do business with the military *junta* ruling in Yangon just because Aung San Suu Kyi was not getting her due.

India can be a great power but, ironically, many Indians (especially those constituting the intelligentsia and the so-called elite) are not persuaded that the country has adequate resources to achieve this aim. The reality, however, is that there is no dearth of resources. It is just that the deployable resources are consistently misused with wrong expenditure priorities. This is as true of the developmental sector as of the military arena.

Take, for instance, the case specifically of the military. There, too, vested interests have grown up around certain threat perceptions, combat arms and spending priorities. The Armed Services seem to have a stake in Pakistan as a threat because it is a convenient, easily manageable threat that poses no fatal challenge. Working up to meet the challenge of China is more difficult, because the Chinese believe in what they call "unrestricted warfare". This will require the Indian armed forces to be more proactive and intellectually and operationally agile. But really potent threats cannot be tackled by knee-jerk and predictable responses. Thus, the prospect of electronic warfare, electronic counter-measures, etc. *vis-à-vis* the US is more challenging than overcoming a weak Pakistan. Indeed, we have the capacity right now to do immense damage to even the most powerful economies in the world with our IT competencies and their penetration of the most advanced markets and societies in the world. Activation of 'logic bombs' inserted in computer software can, say, virtually turn off the lights on the US military. This is not an immediately realised capability but a potential that has to be translated into readily available military and policy options. We need to be hard headed.

We cannot think in terms of being always nice and good and hope that this will fetch us, say, a UN Security Council seat; the Security Council seat is not given to beggars. And the other things we talked about earlier, self respect, it is national self respect, that is at stake. Let there be no doubt about it. The reason why Washington takes India for granted is precisely because the Indian government seemingly acts without national self-respect in mind. By the same token, it is far more respectful of Pakistan. It is an elemental thing. They see a Pervez Musharraf, a tin-pot dictator of a relatively puny country on India's flank, standing up to India. Americans and international public opinion, whether you like it or not, appreciate and respect Pakistanis for not backing down from a confrontation with India. We on the other hand take incredibly perverse pleasure in doing down a small country and we think we are a great power in the region. Let us at least have a sense of perspective on what it is that can make India great.

Here I must recommend to all the Nehruvians to please look at what Jawaharlal Nehru did as Foreign Minister cum Prime Minister. Please do not go merely by what he wrote. Much of his writing was done before India gained independence. What he did in the prime ministerial chair is what is critical. What he did by way of priority programmes are two things. He was clear as to the great power requirements and how India would meet them. He said nuclear weapons are going to make India great. He said it in 1948 in the Constituent Assembly. In fact, the country's Atomic Energy Commission was set up a year before the United Sates set up its atomic energy commission. Here is a man who thought about what is going to make India great and he was not pusillanimous about it. He gave a *carte blanche* to Dr. Homi Baba and set up a nuclear decision loop keeping in mind the penetrability of the Indian governmental system. It consisted of just two people— Homi Baba and himself. It is a system, moreover, where

nothing is put down on paper and which every Prime Minister ever since has followed. There is no paper trail and that is one of the reasons why the CIA did not have a clue as to what was happening when we triggered the tests in 1974 and again in 1998. India has invested hugely in the nuclear establishment. It is amongst the most broad-based investments we have made, and a very fruitful, productive, one at that. We have the capacity not just to make fast breeder reactors but to design thermonuclear weapons of a very sophisticated kind with equal ease.

Concurrently, the other extraordinary thing Nehru did was set up an indigenous defence industry. As a classical historian, he rightly saw that national security was the first charge on government. To safeguard it he set up the DRDO complex and a string of defence ordnance factories. And he hoped that this whole complex would make India autarchic where military needs are concerned, which is one of the absolute prerequisites of a great power. If India has to depend on any other state for security and military supplies, it can never be a great power. He also said that the national defence industry has to be put on an economically sound basis, which can be accomplished by this industry selling its wares to third countries—a policy direction not followed by subsequent governments. Thus, the Ministry of External Affairs, aping the US State Department, has written up a 'munitions list' and routinely negates arms sales proposals put up by the Defence Ministry unmindful of the fact that such sales will amortise public investments in that sector, introduce economies of scale, reduce the unit cost for our own Armed Services, and, owing to the logic of the market forces, continuously improve the quality of the military goods they produce. These are the cascading benefits denied to the Indian defence industry which is in the doldrums even as the Indian military fills the order books of the Israeli, Russian, and French defence industries! In a similar vein, we signed with Russia to provide on a turn-key basis the Koodankulam 1000 megawatt VVER reactors, when the same monies could have been channelled to our own nuclear power corporation to set up a series of INDU Heavy Water-moderated, natural uranium-fuelled, reactors that the Department of Atomic Energy has developed over the years.

This is an extremely short-sighted, horrendously wasteful policy. The Indian government appears unwilling to bank on indigenous capabilities or to exploit the comparative advantages the country has developed in key sectors like atomic energy and defence industry, and yet it talks big of becoming a superpower, etc. Unless we are sure about what it is that is going to make India a great power, let us not even venture into the field because it is a very intolerant and unforgiving milieu. Nation states are made and they break down or they are broken. If we do not have the will to assert ourselves, the notion of India as a great power, which in any case is resting on a thin reed of pretension, simply cannot be sustained.

40 | Discussion

(Section IV — India and the World)

Brahma Chellaney

India needs to define its core interests and evolve a clear strategy to advance those interests. The inability to distinguish between strategy and tactics may lead to the pursuit of tactics in the belief that they constitute strategy. A point was made on whether we have the ambition to be great power and, if so, whether we have a political strategy to achieve that goal. Whether India will assume a global role commensurate with its size depends on a host of factors, including its leadership quality, strategic vision, pursuit of growth-boosting policies, control of corruption, spread of education, political stability and internal cohesion.

Sunil Khilnani raised the very practical issue facing our foreign policy—how does India adjust to a US-dominated international system. The United States will remain the dominant player in the foreseeable future. How should India deal with those realities and build a constructive, mutually beneficial relationship with the United States? That really is at the centre of our foreign-

policy challenge. How we build that relationship with the United States would influence our relationships with other players in the region and in the wider world.

When we look at India's place in the world, we have to start with the region in which India is located. What we find is a very troubled region around India. India faces important external-security challenges, given its regional security environment and the fact that this environment is becoming more difficult. We are wedged in an arc of autocratic states. We have Iran, Afghanistan and Pakistan to the west, we have China to the north, and we have Burma to our east. Several of the states around India are failing states, or problem states, or renegade states, whatever you wish to call them. These states pose important challenges to international and regional security. In fact, India is the only thriving democracy in a vast region stretching from West Asia to China. Democracy is India's biggest asset, but I am not sure whether India should promote freedom and democracy in its neighbourhood at the cost of its national interests. We should certainly help to the extent we can in the development of civil society in Pakistan, for example. And India also needs to help stabilise the situation in Nepal, especially given the fact that India has an open border with Nepal. The flawed democratic experiment in Nepal has contributed to the rise of political violence there and the spread of a Maoist insurrection. India can also aid democratic forces in Bangladesh, where the forces of radical Islam are in the ascendant. But we ought not to make the mistake that we made on Burma, allowing our desire to see democracy there to take precedence over our foreign-policy interests that helped push Burma into China's strategic lap. In recent years, we have pursued a better-balanced policy towards Burma.

India has come a long way since Independence by imbibing greater pragmatism and a sense of balance in foreign policy. Gone are the days when ideology drove foreign policy and when India sponsored UN resolutions to please others or marshal Third World solidarity. Like economic policy, foreign policy today places national interest above all other considerations. And just as economic-policy options have narrowed to within a short band, foreign policy does not materially change when political power changes hands.

One critical political factor in the projection of power is foreign policy. A foreign policy that is dynamic, goal-oriented and focused on an assertive promotion of national interests can go a long way to enhance India's international profile, role and influence. The strength of any nation's foreign policy depends on the health of its institutional processes of policymaking, on realistic goals, strategies and tactics, and on the timely exploitation of opportunities thrown up by external conditions.

Indian foreign policy, regrettably, has been characterised by too much *ad hocism*, risk aversion and *post facto* rationalisation. Institutional processes are operationally weak, and there is no tradition of strategy papers to aid political decision making. The building of greater professionalism, the strengthening of institutional processes and a broader, longer-term vision are necessary to inject dynamism and drive in Indian foreign policy. More broadly, if India is to be accepted as an important power in the world, it has to start behaving and acting like one. This entails a balance in foreign-policy priorities, a larger vision and a more extensive and active engagement with the world. If India behaves like a power confined to South Asia, it will be treated like one. It is only through an institutionalised, integrated, holistic approach to foreign policy that India can effectively utilise various military, economic, cultural and political levers to advance its vital interests.

Sunita Narain

I am going to change the concept of security a little bit and put on the table what I think are some of the new imperatives that are emerging in the world.

India needs to look at the world not just in terms of security in the old fashioned sense but also look at the new challenges. Over the last 10 years we all know of the processes of economic globalisation and the negotiations in the WTO. But there has been a parallel process of ecological globalisation that very few, working in foreign diplomacy, actually understand. It is not part of our jargon of foreign security and diplomacy. But there are negotiations and agreements on climate, biodiversity, forests, deserts, prior informal consent, (POP), hazardous waste, I could go on. These are not just agreements, they are negotiations about rules and regulations on how we are going to live together on earth. Essentially the forces of economic globalisation are pushing the world towards making rules for ecological globalisation. Rules in which we will share to, some extent, the resources of the world. These are not rules that concern our today but will determine our tomorrow.

One obviously big issue is multilateralism *versus* unilateralism. The United States has abdicated on each one of the conventions. Their strategy is simple—promote the agreement initially but then as multilateral rules begin to impinge on it, renege on commitment and start a parallel process, which defeats the multilateral process. In this it secures for itself the negotiating space, its own rules, and its own unilateral process. On the other side, the multilateral process is becoming weak with the lack of ability of the states who believe in multilateralism to really push it through. And that is really leading to a huge dilemma for us. I can give you a classic case based on an issue that I work on—climate change. The Kyoto Protocol is a critical agreement where

we really don't know which way to go. What the United States today promises us is a road to hell but it is a common hell. The US says that there should no commitments, join us because then we will not ask you for any commitments in the long term, only voluntary action. That is weak. What the multilateralists are asking for is to join them but they will make no promise when they will ask us for commitments. In this case we are not able to articulate what it is we want and therefore we end up supporting a weak and compromised position.

We don't see the climate change negotiations as being important negotiations. We do not see these as economic negotiations. But they are. Climate change is about sharing the world's resources and are intensely economic negotiations. We never expend the kind of energy that is needed both to understand the insecurity that global climate change will cause us, our vulnerability, and what is it that we should be arguing for, what is it that we should be demanding. I know Mr. Natwar Singh would have seen this a lot, but I am very clear that in global negotiations anyone who puts a paper in is the winner of the negotiations. It is your ability to be proactive in these debates, it is your ability to conceptualise what it is that you want which makes all the difference. And in this context I want to put on the table what I think is an opportunity that we are missing by getting lost in the traditional debate about security. And I am pitching myself somewhere between Bharat and Sunil in this—a space for political globalisation, a space for creating some amount of morality, though I agree there is no space for it any more in the global discourse, however much people like me may cry for it. I do agree that the role of the United States will determine everything that we do and it is sometimes easier for us to agree to join them rather than to fight them. But on the other hand I think if we could get ourselves together, here is an opportunity in which you could create a space for political globalisation which is globalisation of good politics, of good governance.

Let me give you three clear examples of a good compliance mechanism for the world. Many negotiations are discussing the need for a tool which would allow the world to discipline the rich and powerful corporate interests. Climate change gives you an opportunity to say it is the consumption of the rich which is making the poor more vulnerable. Here is a legal tool that could be developed. If we are proactive we can put together a tool which would demand the compliance of the rich and the powerful within the rule-making of the world. This is a new constitution in some ways for the world that has been charted out through all these negotiations. Similarly we need a liability mechanism, for instance the Bio Safety Protocol. Can we create a liability mechanism in which we hold the corporations of the world liable for the actions that they take across boundaries? The third issue concerns the preferential and differentiated basis of rule making which allows us to build principles of equity in each of these negotiations. The right to development is the fourth such issue. But these are issues which are not sexy, which are not very fancy when it comes to engaging global negotiators or diplomats,

but these are issues which concern the foundations of democracy that we are setting up in the world of global democracy.

Shridath Ramphal

You have made them sound very interesting.

Deepak Nayyar

I do not believe in binary worlds, but since you chose to divide us I should declare that I am a dove and not a hawk. I do not believe that we have come to the end of history. Nothing is forever. That is one thing we learn from history. I have two propositions and one question.

The first proposition is that the world has changed almost beyond recognition in the past two decades. For one, the distinction between East and West has vanished as communism collapsed, while the distinction between North and South has become much more diffused. Hence, the conflict and the rivalry that drove the international system have changed. So has the nature of the discourse. Europe, which began life as a political project, is still no more than an economic union. Therefore, whether we like it or not, we live in a unipolar world in the realm of politics. For another, globalisation has had a profound impact in terms of what it has done to the economic space available for nation-states, as there has been a distinct erosion of autonomy in the economic sphere. In the political sphere, however, nation states remain the main players. At the same time, we have an asymmetry in so far as economic space no longer coincides with geographical space which it did until 25 years ago. Rules and laws enacted by parliaments can be enforced within national boundaries. But there is no global governance, yet, which can provide rules and laws across borders. International public 'bads' now cross borders with so much ease that they are difficult to restrict, whether pollution, terrorism, corruption, or crime. There is a clear need for global governance, not in the sense of world government but in the sense of institutions, rules, practices, soft laws, or norms. But we live in a world characterised by huge democratic deficits. Developing countries account for 80 per cent of the world's population, 50 per cent of the world's output but have almost no voice in global governance. This is, in part, about incomplete and inadequate representation (G-8, P-5, Security Council) and in part about decision making which is undemocratic. Even the principle of one-country-one-vote in the WTO, or in the UN General Assembly, does not ensure that decision making is democratic.

The second proposition is that there is a role for India in this dramatically changed context. But India is going to have to decide. I think we need to recognise our strengths just as we need to recognise our weaknesses. Our real strengths are the resilience and depth of our political democracy, and the large size of our population, which is seen by the world as a market today but will be seen by the world as a resource tomorrow. There is also a new found confidence in the information technology world, which has given India and its first post-colonial generation a sense of confidence that they can compete in the world. But we have clear weaknesses. One-third of our population lives in poverty, illiteracy, and deprivation. And society is characterised by conflict—ethnic, communal and regional. What is more, we are not yet at peace with our neighbours. The advantage we have at this juncture is that perceptions about India in the world outside are changing rapidly, even though the realities of India are changing much less rapidly. People are taking more note of India now than they did of China 20 years ago.

In this context, I think we need to ask ourselves a question. China has clearly answered this question for itself. It wishes to be the next superpower that replaces the Soviet Union to rival the United States. Do we want to go that way, through military power, nuclear power or economic power? That is a game we will have to play by the existing rules of the game which are obviously unfair in a hegemonic world. Or, do we want to change the game we play? Do we wish to go for multilateralism? That is the only system which can protect poor countries and poor people in a world of unequal partners. I believe there are two good reasons for doing that. For one, a collective voice is much more likely to be heard than single voices, even if we are a large country because unequal rules or even fair rules for unequal partners can produce unequal outcomes. For another, a collective leadership may be the most effective strategy against hegemonic power in a unipolar world.

Shankar Bajpai

On Sunil's brilliant analysis, he would agree that our focus of concern and anxiety is not so much unilateralism as unipolarity. I think unilateralism has always been with us—great powers have always acted unilaterally. The French, who are so critical of the Americans today, didn't bother to consult anyone before they moved against Suez, or indeed on what they are doing today in the Ivory Coast. The Russians didn't worry about consulting anyone when they moved into Hungary. Great powers act like that. The question that of course now faces us is that the forces that were available internationally to act as conditioners of the great powers, are no longer available to us—whether it is the multilateral institutions, the non-aligned movement, the Commonwealth or UN, or the powers of the Warsaw Pact. None are available, so how do we deal with unilateralism? I don't have the answer, but in the interim we might consider the line that Sunil Khilnani indicated, of taking a leaf out of the Chinese book, of deflecting that element of American power that is adverse to us, while building up constituencies in the United States.

I would like to emphasise this second part, I don't think we deal enough with it. Deflection is not easy, but it helps if you have constituencies in the United States where intellectual centres count. Condi Rice, whom I knew as a Professor at Stanford, was sold on India as a possible counterpoise to China. Today you can't talk to her in those terms, China is the engageable power, whereas India doesn't figure any longer. The Chinese have built up their constituency by their international finesse and power. We have to try and develop that same kind of vested interest in America in good relations with India, as China has through the economic field. And I am not sure that we are intellectually ready to do so. We need to concentrate a great deal more on how we develop constituencies in the United States.

One last point, that is very important, is Bharat Karnad's. I am sure his analysis is as alarming to some as it is attractive to others. I would be delighted if India could behave the way he would like us to behave, but are we in a position in the foreseeable future even to attempt to think in those terms? We are not obsessed with Pakistan, but let us not underestimate the harm that Pakistan is doing us without our being able to develop counter-forces. You can develop any number of special forces but by themselves they will not be able to work. So it is a major threat to us, not in the conventional sense, but it is undermining our society very effectively. We have to develop means to deal with Pakistan. I don't think we can ignore it or underestimate it. But more than that, even the inability to deal with Pakistan is a reflection of the weakness of the machinery of the state in India. People say that foreign policy is a function of domestic policy, but even more than that, your ability to act abroad is a function of your ability to act at home. And the instruments of state through which you act are deficient today, whether it is our intelligence or planning ahead, across the spectrum. Somebody was suggesting we train the Afghans. We do have some good facilities, but we ourselves go abroad for training. Unless we can re-jig our domestic capabilities, which to me are a major area of concern, and make the instruments of state more effective, we won't be able to do any of the things that the speakers have referred to.

Siddharth Varadarajan

I am not very comfortable with the distinction between hard and soft because that sort of valorises the hard at the expense of the soft whereas it is not clear to me that hard is any more hard headed than the soft is. So I think let us leave that terminology aside. I found a lot that I agreed with in both Sunil's and Bharat's presentations even though they looked very different. I am not entirely sure that the position China enjoys with the United States is entirely because of 25 ICBMs. China tested for the first time in Lop Nor in 1965 and it took 8 or 9 years before they got to reclaim the Security Council seat. Their stake and problems in the world arose in the context of a very specific juncture in the bipolar division. And it is after the end of the bipolar division and the opening up of the Chinese economy that China really began to play a role on the world stage and I am not sure I would characterise it as hard *realpolitik*. I don't think the Chinese haven't militarised their economy. I would agree with Bharat completely that over the next 20-30 years, China and the United States are going to be military adversaries, perhaps not in the traditional sense. The Chinese approach is very incremental. They have research programmes and electronic warfare is a priority on the Chinese side. The Chinese are very worried about missile defence and are prime movers in the Conference on Disarmament for an attempt to block the militarisation of space. They want

to at least begin discussing it. But I think the Chinese have a very good mix of the military and economic approach to power and they combine that with long range vision, which we are completely devoid of in this country.

Sunil I am not sure I share your pessimism about the multipolar world. I don't think we should gauge the success of multipolarity by its ability to stop the use of force in a particular situation. Let us not forget that during the bipolar division, neither side was particularly successful in stopping the aggressions of the other. The bipolar division did not stop the invasion of Panama or Grenada or the harassment of Nicaragua. The Americans couldn't stop the invasion of Afghanistan. And if you look at the current situation, bleak though it does seem, I would argue that what is happening in Iraq today, at some level, reflects the limits of US military power. I think the inability to deal with Korea is partly because of, as Bharat said, the fact that the North Koreans have a deterrent and partly because of the involvement of other regional powers like China. These do impose effective constraints on the American ability to act and unilaterally use force. If there is an increased space today for the United States for what they did in Iraq, I would blame the multilateral Europeans for creating the ground with the attack on Yugoslavia. I would take heart from the fact that the attack on Iraq produced so much opposition worldwide as compared to the attack on Yugoslavia. The opposition to that was limited to two or three countries, India being one of them. And I think that limits the Americans. I know Bush II will be more unilateral and more aggressive. The US will seek to militarise different aspects of life and increase what they call full spectrum dominance. But I don't think that they will necessarily have it any easier.

My last point is on the role of India. I think if India is to play a role as a global power in the conventional sense, it has to have a policy for Asia. It has to be clear that it is an Asian country, part of the continent of Asia. In the early years of independence there was a consciousness about India as an Asian country which gradually went away. Today the salience of Asia within which cooperative security issues of energy security and the kind of role that India plays within this Asian context is very important. I think our relations with Asia are really the key. How you deal with Pakistan, and Bangladesh, holds the key. Sunil, I am not sure that the problem for Indian foreign policy is what the nature of its relationships would be with the US. I think the key problem is what is its relationship with South Asia.

For the past five years India has been dithering over the one billion dollar pipeline of LNG from Iran to India because of the so-called security implications of this pipeline traversing Pakistan. Even as we dither, the Chinese have signed a 20 year deal worth a 100 billion dollars for the supply of LNG. The pipeline is the only instance where Pakistan is willing to drop its Kashmir first policy. On every other issue it says first Kashmir then trade or anything else. Here is a concrete issue where Pakistan, for whatever reason, is willing to say let us have

the pipeline first and we are suspicious. Why are they saying this? Maybe they stand to gain more without realising that a pipeline gives Pakistan a stake, it opens up geographic and economic space as far as Iran and Central Asia. But this traditional mindset that perhaps Pakistan will gain more immediately is holding us back. We need to think of South Asia and Asia as the key determinants for Indian foreign policy. Of course the US is important, but what we do in our region will pay a much richer dividend for India as a world power.

Radha Kumar

I would like to begin by saying that I disagree fundamentally with both Sunil and Bharat. Both of you have started with the world rather than starting with India. And therefore I think that there are fundamental holes in what both of you were saying. Hole number one, yes the US is going to be the dominant world power, as it has been for quite sometime. However, that does not mean that India has to align its policies in relation to what the US does or does not do in exclusion to other relationships. The US is deeply overstretched at present, and therefore open to a number of different areas and levels of engagement. The end of the Cold War, the end of the bipolar world, has left a number of new spaces open for a range of different multilateral activities at different levels. We have seen that happening in the last 10 years. Europe is doing it, even the Middle East, which we tend to criticise so much for dependency, is trying to build a set of multilateral relations. We ourselves have quite skilfully expanded our multilateral institutional connection in the last few years, way beyond what we had before. We should look at these as potential sources of strength.

India is also exceptionally fortunate in relation to the US today. We are amongst the few countries that are exempt from the 'either you are with us or you are against us' paradigm. We don't yet begin to understand how to use this new warmth skilfully but we should consider it.

Secondly, a quick point on Nehru. I actually think that far from Nehru's vision having been overtaken by history, the end of the Cold War was a period in which Nehru's vision could have come into its own in a way which was not possible earlier because of the rise of the Cold War. We didn't understand this at the time, and the changes that the 9/11 attacks have made on the post-Cold War world limit the scope for optimism. Nevertheless there is a residue that remains in which some of the Nehruvian ideals can again find play internationally. We still have a lot of that space open today, and we would be incredibly foolish to neglect it.

Now turning to what I mean when I say why don't we begin with India. If I ask what are the two big things that have been Indian interests since Independence and continue to be today, the first is our relationship to the Middle East and North Africa, the Arab World and the Gulf States. Whether it is energy, diaspora, or labour pool, we have very strong interests in the region. And second, Southeast Asia, where we have begun to turn our gaze over the last 15 years and have begun to reap the benefits through a series of multilateral and bilateral engagements. On China, I don't know whether you are aware of the deep, deep envy that China felt for India's foreign policy successes during the '60s and the '70s. In the last 10 years China has moved systematically into the open spaces that India's retreat from the world has offered. China has taken oil fields in the Sudan, it has built new links with East and West Europe. Several Europeans have told me that Chinese policy analysts admit quite openly that they have learnt a very great deal from studying Indian diplomacy and how well India was able to develop a foreign policy, given how poor India's resource base was. We had an exceptional position in the world as a weak power with enormous great power moral capacity and international goodwill. I think we can avail of that goodwill today, and we are not thinking very clearly if we don't try and do it.

I completely agree that the US is an instrumental power. But the US will never tilt the military balance to Pakistan against India, that is not conceivable. Their problem is how to balance their short-term interests in Pakistan with their medium-to long-term interests in India. They don't know quite how to do it but we can help them, that is our job anyway. Our great asset, which I think Deepak Nayyar pointed to, is the strength of our diaspora. This again is something we don't look at sufficiently and we don't use sufficiently. The Indian diaspora is perhaps the most assertive diaspora in the US today, certainly the most successful of small diasporas, even if we compare them to the Chinese diaspora, which played a critical role in China's economic boom. We now have, I think, eight Indian American candidates who have won elections in the US at different levels of the political ladder, China, not one.

Europe too is starting to talk about closer and higher-level relationships with India. Some European countries are working with the Indian embassy in Afghanistan despite the US telling them to be wary of working with India and Afghanistan because of Pakistan. And if you look at the military now, Bharat, there are a whole series of joint venture proposals that are coming to India from companies abroad to produce armaments which would certainly upgrade the quality of our manufacturing, standards being so low, and our quality checking being so low. So again there is a whole new world opening over there, one you are not perhaps looking at closely enough.

Prem Shankar Jha

I have to start by agreeing with Bharat Karnad that in the world of today both power and influence come out of the barrel of a gun. But this is a relatively recent regression to a 'state of nature' brought about by the destruction of the Westphalian state system. The attack on it began immediately after the Cold War, but culminated with the invasion of Iraq. The Westphalian order has not been static during the 350 years of its existence. But three basic principles were always there. They were respect for sovereignty, non-interference in the internal affairs of other states, and the use of deterrence as a way of maintaining peace. All three are

essential parts of the UN Charter but were ignored by the US and UK and their 'coalition of the willing' when they invaded Iraq. So what has been very nearly destroyed in the past two years is the UN itself, and we are back in a Hobbesian world. The first imperative created by this change is to separate foreign from military policy. Military policy is based on other countries' capabilities, not necessarily on intentions, whereas diplomacy is based on intentions. In the highly uncertain world we have now entered, military policy must be designed to meet almost any conceivable threat to sovereignty and autonomy. We therefore need to look at our military policies with fresh eyes. But having said that, what is the purpose of having assured the military base of your sovereignty? That is where foreign policy also faces a major challenge. That challenge is to stem the drift that has now begun towards a unipolar world ruled by the US, and help to create a new world order based upon the principles of a kind of Commonwealth, whose collective will is reflected in a reformed UN Security Council.

We were going down that road, although increasingly in fits and starts, till 7 March 2003. Then, when the US and UK formally announced their intention to invade Iraq, we were derailed. To get back on track requires a well thought out, measured cooperation with Russia, China and the European Union in constructively engaging the USA. So far we have been rather reticent about doing this. The new government has a choice: either it keeps its head down, concentrates upon our region and creates as small a flutter as possible in the US. Or we decide that we are going to play a more positive role. I would much favour the latter.

Indeed we may soon be left with no other alternative. For the American bid for empire is failing. The reason is that empires are not built on military strength alone but rely for their stability upon the creation of hegemony. Hegemony is the legitimacy conferred on the hegemonic power by others' belief that what it is doing in its own interest is also to a large extent in consonance with their interest. America enjoyed that hegemony in much of the world between the Second World War and 7 March 2003 but has lost it today. American military power is already over-stretched and it does not have the capability to enforce its writ, other than by threatening wholesale destruction from the air, upon any other nation. Ruled neither by brute power nor by hegemony, a post–Westphalian world faces chaos. Therefore it is imperative for us to be a part of the process of multilateral reconstruction.

The reconstruction must start close to home. We cannot easily play the larger role I envision if we do not take Pakistan's present efforts to make peace with us seriously. If we can keep the peace process going it will become possible for India and Pakistan together to play a constructive role in our neighbourhood and elsewhere.

Vivek Monteiro

I will be speaking not as an expert but as a hard headed Indian citizen. Firstly I would like to question some of the presumptions made here, particularly the presumptions that Bharat Karnad made in his presentation. Security, nuclear weapons, deterrence are all areas where logic applies very strictly. So if your presumptions are not correct then your conclusions will also be wrong. I would like to point out that there may not be a consensus on the proposition that India should be a great power. India should be a great nation and being a great nation and a great power have to be distinguished from each other. I would like India to be a successful nation, a secure nation. Our military and security strategy can also be deduced from this presumption. In doing so, we might arrive at conclusions different from those based on India aiming to be a great power. I would like to recall here something that Nehru said. I don't remember the exact words but this is approximately what he had said, which I saw in a railway station somewhere in Karnataka. He said, "India will be what we are, our thoughts and actions will shape it. If we are big and broad minded so will India be. And if we grow mean and narrow minded, so also will India be." I thought this was a very profound, a very hard-headed assessment of what we need to do. Similarly on the issue of nuclear weapons I think that one of the statements made here—that Pokhran 1998 raised our status in the world—needs to be questioned. India's position was very high in the world at a time when we did not have nuclear weapons. All issues of weapons have to be looked at from the standpoint of our security. I think it is a highly questionable proposition that our security was improved by the tests which were done in

1998. Many things which were presumed turned out to be false. If you look at the statements that Advani made just after the nuclear tests about how this would put an end to the problem of cross border terrorism, etc. one sees that all those statements were entirely false, Kargil occurred after these tests. Perhaps the presumption was that only India would have nuclear weapons. That presumption changed when a few weeks later, Pakistan also acquired nuclear weapons. And if you look at the security balance when both India and Pakistan have nuclear weapons and compare it with the situation which existed before we exercised that option, I think there is very good reason to question whether or not India's security improved as a result of that particular action.

Naina Lal Kidwai

As a person of numbers, I struggle with how we as a country would spend scarce resources trying to be everything that we have tabled over the last hour. Do we spend our money in ruling by the barrel of the gun or do we spend it in industry, in infrastructure, in the social fabric of the nation? Unfortunately we do not have sufficient resources to do both well and so the decision as to which direction we go in is going to be paramount. The third leg, which I believe we should focus on, other than military and foreign policy strategy, is the economic leg. I think it is important to table here that no investor anywhere in the world right now can afford to ignore the huge potential of our country, a potential endorsed by the well thumbed BRIC report which has forecast that

India would under certain circumstances, become the third largest economy in the world by 2010, which is not very far away. This would only be returning India to her former glory. In 1820 Asia controlled 60 per cent of the world GDP in purchasing power parity terms, of which, India contributed 15 per cent as compared with a mere 5 per cent in 2001. So the reality is that we have been there before and we can get back there. As a nation we disengaged from the world but are now re-engaging with it.

We are, at a turning point where investors are truly engaged in terms of India's economic direction. We have not yet seen that flow of money come through and we can lose it very easily by giving the wrong signals or indeed by changing the direction which has been set. I am sure this direction has come as much by design as by the hard work of many who have positioned us there. We are riding a wave because of our successes in the IT sector, the BPO sector, all of which has profiled India. However, if we do not invest in infrastructure; if we continue to have creaking airports as arrival points; if we continue to have roads that don't exist; no amount of positioning and marketing will get us there. I don't know how many of you read a report by Stephen Roach recently on the Bombay Pune Highway—our showcase road—which talks about the mess of getting on and off it. It is a very poignant paper and his conclusion is that we haven't quite got it. We need to focus at this turning point for India and get back into the economic mainstream. Related to that would be the whole issue of engaging the world in terms of our own issues. If we can get global America and American corporates to engage with India, then when the day comes to protect India, those very corporates, who as we all know exercise significant influence on the policies of that nation, would also step up to support us, provided we get engaged. Otherwise we don't and won't matter.

C. Uday Bhaskar

A number of issues have been raised and I think they need some comment or reflection. Otherwise we might go back with some very black and white conclusions, which may not be accurate about the nature of the subject under discussion. The first proposition I want to make is apropos both Sunil's and Bharat's papers. My own take is that if you look at India and the world in the next decade in a strategic and in a security context, India has become more relevant and will become even more relevant in the coming years and decades. This is the first proposition. Extrapolating from Sunil's point, the challenge for India is that while the relationship with the United States will be very central, we will also have to bring China on board to ensure the right degree of calibration whereby neither of these countries is seen as stifling India's 'strategic' aspirations, or of stoking any of our security and strategic anxieties. This is the additional point I would like Sunil to consider.

The second observation which is slightly curious for me—I perhaps might be the only person in 'uniform' around this table, and for me to now make an

intervention and say that this kind of characterisation we heard from Bharat and Prem—that power comes only from the barrel of a gun—which is the standard *realpolitik* kind of reduction, needs to be more nuanced. This is a debatable assertion and we need to contextualise it apropos the current systemic reality and the attendant asymmetries. The United States might be an assertive military power, but that is because it has a certain strategic culture, a certain DNA about how it uses that military power. But to seek any kind of equivalence for India, I think, would be very misleading and hazardous. And it is in that sense that I am saying, recognise the gravitas. Yesterday, I drew attention to the internal security dimension of India. If you look at the figures, about 160 districts in India today are tainted by what we call LWE, Left Wing Extremism, the kind of problem which in military parlance translates into low intensity conflict and internal security.

Now, it is a case of motherhood and apple pie to say that in the next decade India must have a very vibrant and equitable democracy. We discussed it yesterday. We also noted the constraints as to why it is not a vibrant and equitable democracy. One would like India to be prosperous and have an equitable distribution of wealth, which again is a motherhood and apple pie formulation and nobody disputes it. But we must also recognise the systemic constraints in the domestic context. In like fashion, Bharat's formulation that we should be a strong and assertive power which is recognised in the global comity is well taken, but I think we also have to recognise our constraints. Here the one point that Bharat makes in his paper which needs to be reflected upon is the nature of India's own strategic culture in the long cycle of history—say the last 3,000 years. It is that of a diffident strategic culture; diffident in the sense it has not been characterised by the use of macro-military power in a manner that we have ascribed to others. I submit that you cannot change this DNA overnight, much as you wish to believe that you are now going to catch up with the rest of the pack and make yourself militarily proactive and assertive. So all I would say is that military power is no doubt relevant, but it has to be calibrated and perhaps the trans-border element needs to be acquired in a well-planned and focused way. Here I go back to my earlier point that we must still balance our relationship with the United States and China and at a remove, Russia. So that is one broad point.

The second is in terms of the relevances that we have spoken about, and I heard some references to this particular issue. Bharat and I have differed in other fora about the nature of the Indian nuclear posture. He has taken a maximalist position and he believes that that is the way out. I have repeatedly said, and there are others of my persuasion who have said, that India is a reluctant nuclear power—and that is an existential kind of reality. Now, there are many who would argue that the nuclear weapon itself is a dishonourable option. Yet, there is a certain inevitability about it and we have to focus on the credible part wherein you do not need equivalence with anyone but you need to acquire the right degrees of

mutuality. I thought I heard someone say that in this domain morality doesn't have any place and ethics do not need to be brought on board. But, I think, specific to the nuclear issue, we must be cognizant of these determinants. Here I would suggest the analogy of the story of Ulysses as he sails past the island of the Sirens. He wants to listen to their music, but at the same time is aware of the fact that this would mean he and his ship's crew would be impelled to jump overboard to reach the island and perish there as swine. Therefore, he orders his sailors to bind him to the ship's mast, while he ensures that they remain free to row but puts wax in their ears so that they cannot hear the seductive strains of the Sirens' music. He thus savours the Sirens' music while ensuring that he is safeguarded from its deleterious consequences. Now in that sense I believe India had brought a certain distinctive position to the global nuclear debate. I know it is fashionable to say that India's commitment to disarmament was really a kind of temporary posture till such time as we went nuclear. I believe otherwise. I think when we spoke about the public good yesterday in the Indian context, nuclear weapons and their existence degrade the universal good. Frankly, I have no sense of ambivalence about this, but accept that there is a certain inevitable element of *realpolitik* in the decisions taken. Yet, like Ulysses, we must remain lashed to the mast of nuclear sufficiency and the elusive goal of global nuclear disarmament. I do believe that the May 1998 decision has helped us to assuage our insecurities better. So, apropos the nuclear issue, by all means focus on credible deterrents but remain lashed to the mast of disarmament while taking the steps that we have to. These are issues that cannot be reduced to black and white, so we should recognise the complexity and gravitas embedded in them.

Kapila Vatsyayan

I have been listening intently for the last two days and was reminded of Kurosawa's film *Rashomon*. The story of India and the world has been presented from multiple points of view and in multiple dimensions, and yet it eludes coherence. The questions I raise are addressed to Sunil Khilnani, who is also the author of *The Idea of India*. The questions are on behalf of those who received the legacy of discovering India through Jawaharlal Nehru's book *The Discovery of India*. Also, equally relevant are Indira Gandhi's thoughts on India. Perhaps these perceptions on India have to be taken into account before addressing the question of 'India and the World'.

It appeared to me that the presentations overlooked both Jawaharlal Nehru's pointed reference to the continuity of Indian civilisation and how important it was to sustain this continuity in ethos and essence while engaging with contemporaneity/modernity, and Indira Gandhi's repeated emphasis on the immeasurable quality of the Indian experience. Time and again she referred to the need for India to be solidly grounded in the 'self'—the civilisational and cultural self—experienceable but not quantifiable, while participating and interacting with the world on equal terms.

Listening to the present discourse, it would appear that the emphasis has shifted from recognising this unique quality, however complex and indefinable but recognisable, to accepting the purely 'temporal' and so-called 'universal' categories of the international and global discourse. The critical question to be asked is, will our evaluative categories emerge from the vortex of the Indian 'ethos' and its unique civilisational value system of an avowed faith in interconnectivity, respecting differentiation and interdependence, or will we accept to conform only to have a dialogue on the basis of imposed uniformity and values? Also, do we have to participate in the future in a competitive race of 'power', power defined in Bharat Karnad's words, or economic power without perennial values or commitment to 'sustainable development', as referred to by Mridula Mukerjee and Vinod Raina? The polarities of stand-points are clear and hard choices have to be made at the level of maintaining ecological balance, fragile bio- and cultural diversity systems, etc. It is my belief that at this temporal moment, India is poised with the potential, the real potential and possibility of evolving a new and more appropriate paradigmatic model for a future 'World Order'. It is at this moment of India's confidence as an equal player that it can seize the opportunity to assert and affirm the conviction that fundamental paradigmatic shifts are necessary if planet earth and human kind have to be sustained in the future. To quote Gandhiji, "World order cannot be sustained on 'greed' and material power; all 'needs' must be met without entering the race of relentless power."

Aruna Vasudev

In all this talk on India and the world, the concentration has been on military strategy, security and economics. Don't you feel like I do, that democracy and development should be about the well-being of people? And if it is in the interest of the well-being of the people that you are talking of military strategies, security of the nation and economic development, it is as it should be. But in this scheme of things I feel the individual and how the individual feels and is he a better human being as a result of all these is an aspect that has not been taken into consideration with any degree of seriousness. And certainly not in terms of environment which Sunita Narain brought up and which a few others have touched upon.

I also think that the arts and culture must be treated as being a part of the process of development. India is one of the richest nations in the world, if not the richest, in terms of its art and culture. I know everyone say oh! arts and craft, forget it. It is not important. But it is important because the skills are so great and if those can be put to other uses, a whole range of people who have been marginalised and left out, will become a part of modern India and as a result, enrich it.

Unfortunately this is all dismissed as marginal, or mere entertainment. Whether it is dance or music, it is taken as 'just entertainment'. And cinema, as I said earlier this morning, with its enormous power, is also ignored. This cinema's power can be used in the development process within India, and to make friends and influence people outside India because our cinema is hugely popular wherever it is shown. If this can just be looked at in a systematic manner, it can win us an enormous amount of goodwill across the world. When you talk of India's position in the world and India's relationship with the world goodwill is a very important part.

In economic terms, cinema can be used to attract people to come to India as tourists, and to shoot their films here. Indian film-makers have been solicited by a number of countries across the world to come and shoot there because they realise that that brings in money. There are many aspects to this question and I would like to draw your attention to it.

Zoya Hasan

Doubtless the US is the superpower, perhaps even a planetary power, but we must not forget that today it is also an imperial power. For this reason, there is a great deal of opposition to the US in different parts of the world, most notably in Latin America, the Middle East, Europe, and in South Asia as well. Sunil Khilnani made the point that US legitimacy today is at its lowest since the end of the Vietnam War. I agree with that. Then the question is—should we be hitching our fortunes to the US when, one, it is an imperial power with a lot of opposition and resistance against it; and two, it lacks legitimacy? It does not make sense for us to be falling in line with America. This might be a moment for us to be independent rather than dependent on the US. We have heard two very forceful presentations this afternoon, but they seem one-dimensional in that they have reduced our foreign policy and India's relationship with the world to our relationship with the US and how we can further improve on that. Important as this may be, surely, we shouldn't be limiting ourselves to that.

This is a great moment for us to assert our independence. We can do this if we align our politics, economics and foreign policy. In the last two days there has been a great deal of convergence on certain issues which have to do with politics, democracy, inclusiveness and so on. But there are obvious divergences on other issues. We should really be building on the strengths of democracy and the great moral capital that we have built up from its success. There is considerable agreement on issues of politics, equity and inclusiveness in this conference and that the economy will have to be emphatically inclusive. We can play an important role in the world if we are socially responsible, economically inclusive, and socially tolerant. One of the common grounds that emerged from this conference is the understanding that there is a shift in political discourse from identity politics to equity, justice and inclusiveness. Why don't we just allow that discourse to determine both our foreign and economic policy?

41 | Concluding Remarks

(Section IV — India and the World)

Bharat Karnad

T. N. Ninan wondered whether we can afford to become a great power, meaning whether the country can afford the military wherewithal of a great power. I have costed a 400 plus weapons warheads-strong thermonuclear force; these numbers have not been refuted by anybody. In fact those who know, who have also done their own costing, have told me that I have exaggerated the numbers. They tell me that I am frightening the politicians. The acquisition costs are— and here some of you may blanch at the figure—but it has to be seen in perspective. The cost is some 90,000 odd crore of rupees over 30 years. Before you faint— listen to this. What the Indian army is going to spend between the years 2000 and 2020, on just the armoured forces, which this country is unlikely ever again to use in anger is projected at Rs. 100,000 crores plus. This is what I meant, when I earlier talked about mis-spending our money. If you talk to the army it matters a great deal to them that they have the armoured forces ready for use.

I don't know what sort of scenarios they have, many of them variants of the Second World War-type of actions in the Western Desert, at Tobruk and Benghazi! When the fact is the Indian armoured and mechanised forces cannot advance much beyond 10 miles in the defensively built-up sectors in Pakistani Punjab! This reaffirms the point I have made about buying the right sort of military hardware and paraphernalia for wars of the future (and not of the past).

The other thing is regarding the sequencing— should India become an economic power first before aspiring to military-wise great power status? Well, yes, that would be nice if that were possible. But in all history there has been no great power which has been an economic power first, excepting the United States. And the United States became an economic power first because they had the moats of the Pacific and the Atlantic to protect that country, and did not need to invest in military protection until after becoming a great economic power. India does not have the moats. The

Himalayas are eminently penetrable, as are the surrounding seas. What we haven't learnt from our own history is the need to occupy ever-enlarging strategic spaces with strategic means. We haven't done that through the ages and the country has suffered. And that is why anybody would come in through the seas on the pretext of trading with us. Anybody can now offer us technologies, when in fact the greatest advance in the most critical technologies was registered when sanctions were imposed by the United States after the '98 test. If you leave it to the Indian genius and the very broad based nuclear, space and defence science complexes to achieve goals, the record suggests that they invariably deliver. You can, however, take the easy way out. May be that is a peculiarly Indian trait, I don't know. Whatever it is or isn't, the fact is we take the easy way out by buying things instead of making them ourselves. The country should then be prepared to pay the cost of being reduced to a security dependency of great powers. Instead of worrying about sequencing, etc. India should act aggressively to attain a great power thermonuclear weapons threshold and use it as political leverage, as other great powers have done and continue to do, to open up markets and trade opportunities, which will eventuate in India's becoming an economic great power, as well. That is how Britain, for example, became a great power.

The level of ignorance about strategic matters and about the evolution of the country's strategic policy, is appalling. I wish that at least the people in the strategic community would read the latest literature on the subject and be aware of the latest revelations owing to substantive research in the field. India is the only major country in the world where the debate on strategic issues proceeds on the basis of newspaper columns, not serious research. Finally, the 'soft power' of the state, that is, India's IT power, India as a source of myriad services in the financial and other sectors, India as a manufacturing hub and as a producer of films propagating popular culture, etc. is derivative power predicated on the military power of the country. This is what the empirical record proves. Hollywood films, the American culture as the extant universal culture, is because of the US's military dominance and, secondarily, its economic pre-eminence. There is a direct correlation here. You can posit all kinds of other variables, but the fact of the matter is, if you have the military power as a back up, a country can sell anything including culture, values and even morality!

Sunil Khilnani

First of all I absolutely agree with Siddharth Varadarajan—I don't think the hard/soft distinction is actually serving us very well. Nehru interestingly in 1939 wrote an essay called "India looks at the World", and he used the phrase "intelligent self-interest". And I think that as a kind of precept of how we conduct our policy seems to be just right. It is a form of *realpolitik* but it is guided by what can make that legitimate as well. Pure self-interest would be self-destructive in the end. So I think we can get away from the hard/soft distinction.

The question that Kapilaji raises about values, in a sense connects with Aruna Vasudev's question as well. The point that the unit ultimately is the individual, we are talking about the individuals, and the state is there to further the rights and possibilities and options available to the individual. I think that is right. However, having said that, I think once we made the decision in 1947 to be an independent state, once the Gandhian alternative to be a decentralised series of village republics which did not have a centralised state was put aside, then we were in a system of states and we were in that game. I think Nehru saw that very clearly—that once we entered that competitive world where we exist as a state amongst other states, we do to some extent have to conform to the rules of that game, as well as the imperatives and injunctions that places on us, in order to serve the individuals in our state better. So I think that there is a sense in which we do have to conform once we decided to exist as a state within a system of other states.

I want to underline again this point that we are at a moment of opportunity. This isn't routine foreign policy like anytime else. And I think Brahma Chellany's point that we should not be risk averse is exactly right—we have to be willing to take a leap in whatever direction in the end we decide to, and it seems to me that for example in our conduct with the US we do need to be proactive, indeed even pre-emptive in how we deal with certain things.

A number of people were speaking of the possibility of the revival of multilateralism. Frankly I really don't see that as a real possibility, and in fact if we were to draw a list of what our primary or priority interests are, most of them will not be furthered through some notion of multilateralism. Some can be and I think the issue of the environment is a very important one in that respect. But I think on the issue of multilateralism today, we have to take a differentiated position—where it can serve our interests, we should pursue it and build that way. But in a lot of important areas it won't serve our interests best, and we have to craft a different kind of policy. It seems to me that it is just a fact of the way the world is at the moment.

I think Naina Lal Kidwai's point again speaks to the urgency of where we are today in terms of India and the world. There are investors who want to be involved with the India there, there are business corporations who want to be involved with us. Whether we like it or not most of those are in the US and that is whom we have to engage with, and really start developing those relationships, because again to come back to what I was saying earlier, if it is about furthering the possibilities of the individual, then it is about economic growth and the prospects that it brings to our citizens.

I think that the point about working more with China is absolutely right—I think that is a very crucial thing and I don't think we should get caught in a kind of US–India–China game which some in the Pentagon might want us to be involved in. I think that is absolutely right.

On the question of how we deal with our neighbours—yes, with Burma, national interest predominates. But I think we can do both, I think we can craft a policy whereby we engage with the Burmese state but also at the same time trying to help parliaments and civil society and democratic forces in Burma. The skill in crafting that would be part of the pursuit of intelligent self-interest.

I think that power today—and here I disagree with Bharat Karnad—power today is not primarily military, military power after all depends entirely on economic power. That ultimately is the lifeblood of any military power we might want to have. And that kind of power, economic power, which is the primary power, is based not on economic autarchy, not on taking ourselves out of the world market, not on protectionist measures—it is based on interdependencies. We have to build interdependencies to get our economic power up to where we want it. And there the most important interdependency again it seems to me is what we have to build with the United States, because that is the primary source and destination of capital and markets for us.

CLOSURE

K. Natwar Singh

I will be brief. When the discussion began on the subject we are debating, I thought, what a good time to be Foreign Minister of India. And when I heard it for three hours, I thought, my God, how awful to be Foreign Minister of India...(laughter...). So I am between two poles, it is both exciting and it is terrifying. And I have taken copious notes obviously because these discussions were at a high level.

As Foreign Minister I have to differentiate between what is desirable and what is possible. I know what is desirable but I also know what is possible because I sit in the highest body of the government which deals with nuclear issues. There are only four or five of us. Now this discussion has touched on a number of subjects, and you may take it for granted that I am aware of the various issues raised. There were two things we didn't devote enough time to. One is how does the Western world in particular deal with the Muslim world. I deliberately use the word 'Muslim' and not 'Islamic'. This is the mistake the West is making—that Islam is monolithic; it is not. There is Shia Islam, there is Sunni Islam, there are the Kurds, there are the Bohras, there are the Ismailis and what have you. And there is the Wahabi Islam of Saudi Arabia, the Islam of India, and the Islam of Indonesia. Unless the West comes to terms with the reality of the Muslim world, this is going to be an unsafe world. And this is where India can play a role. Islam came to India in the 8th century. Yes, we have had our own difficult times with Muslims in India, but still 140 million Muslims live in India. And the significant fact is that not a single Indian Muslim joined the Taliban or Al-Qaeda. This is not an ordinary fact; it is a great tribute to India.

Today there are 56 Islamic countries in the world from Mauritania to Medan in Indonesia. And if the Western world is unable to cope with this situation then we are in for a difficult time. We also need to be clear that all Muslims are not terrorists, and all terrorists are not Muslims. Yes, terrorism is a serious problem because of its increasing sophistication. It is an important issue on the international agenda.

The second issue concerns the disappearance of the Soviet Union. This has produced a situation with which the world is yet to come to terms. An alternative point of view has disappeared. Whether you agreed with that point of view or not is not the issue. At least, there was an alternative point and there is none now.

And finally, there is one superpower. How does the Foreign Minister of India structure India's foreign policy *vis-à-vis* the United States? There is no escaping this choice. It is in our national interest to have better relations with the US. At the same time, this idea that India and America should get together to take on a third country makes no sense. Our relations with the US are improving but so are our relations with China and Pakistan. In fact, we supported the Vajpayee government when it started the composite dialogue with Pakistan. For five years the NDA had five policies on Pakistan but on 6 January 2004, Shri Vajpayee took the courageous step of a statesman by extending a hand of friendship to Pakistan. And we are carrying this forward. It is in our interest to have better relations with Pakistan. And here again I think people in both countries want that solutions should be found to the problems between the two countries. So I do have an agenda but I do not have instant solutions, because foreign policy in democratic countries is evolutionary, not revolutionary.

Index